THE CANON LAW DIGEST

THE
CANON LAW DIGEST

Officially Published Documents
Affecting the Code of Canon Law
1942-1953

Volume III

By

T. LINCOLN BOUSCAREN, S.J.
S.T.D., LL.B.

THE BRUCE PUBLISHING COMPANY
MILWAUKEE

Imprimi potest: EDWARD GOULET, S.J.
Nihil obstat: JOHN A. SCHULIEN, S.T.D., Censor librorum
Imprimatur: ✠ ALBERTUS G. MEYER, Archiepiscopus Milwauchiensis
Die 13 Novembris, 1953

TO JOSEPH,
JUST MAN, HUSBAND OF
MARY

FOREWORD

Volume III of the CANON LAW DIGEST is here presented in final form, that is, as a closed volume, not to be changed to accommodate future documents. With Volumes I and II, it will constitute a repertory, intended to be as complete as possible, of the canonical documents issued officially since the promulgation of the Code of Canon Law.

This volume includes:

1. The documents which were officially published in the *Acta Apostolicae Sedis* from January 1, 1942, to December 31, 1952, that is, in Volumes 34 to 44;

2. Other documents belonging to the same period but which were not officially published;

3. A number of earlier documents which had hitherto evaded our search.

The plan of the book is the same as that of Volumes I and II; that is, the documents are arranged according to the numerical order of the canons of the Code which they principally concern. If, as frequently happens, a document refers to several canons, it is reported in full under one of them, and cross references to the full report are given under the other canons which may be affected. Besides these cross references there are quite a number of simple references indicating briefly the substance of certain other documents which were not considered of sufficient importance to merit being reported in full, or which could easily be found elsewhere. Both the cross references and simple references are inserted under the respective canons, after the full reports and in smaller print.

One slight change in arrangement should be mentioned to avoid confusion. The documents on Catholic Action, which in Volumes I and II were reported under canon 139, have been transferred in the present volume to canon 684 which properly concerns Associations of the Faithful.

The completion of several parts of the codification of the

Oriental Canon Law may create a problem for the future, as interpretations of that law become more frequent. For the present, the few documents which required notice have been reported either under the corresponding canons of the Latin Code, or under canon 1 of the Latin Code, which has a general provision concerning Orientals.

The present volume has *cumulative indices,* both chronological and general, of all three volumes, with page references throughout.

T. L. BOUSCAREN, S.J.

Rome
Feast of Pentecost
May 24, 1953

CONTENTS

PRELIMINARY SECTION

PRELIMINARY

Fundamentals of Jurisprudence: Address to Catholic Jurists (Pius XII, Allocution, 6 Nov., 1949) AAS 41-597.[1]

An Allocution of Pius XII to the Union of Catholic Jurists of Italy, assembled in Rome for their first national convention, is verbatim as follows:

It was a happy thought, beloved sons, which led you to choose the city of Rome, in preference to the other cities of Italy which might have given you a worthy welcome, for the site of the first national Congress of the "Union of the Catholic Jurists of Italy." You have during these days given it a definite form and internal constitution, discussing and approving its organic law and electing its President, whose duty it shall be, according to the fundamental norms which you have agreed upon, to promote its development and direct its activities. And so, while We congratulate you on the task you have accomplished, We cannot but observe how it has been your desire and solicitude, as true and genuine Catholic jurists, to adorn the cradle of your Association with a twofold aureola, the one reflecting the radiance of eternal Rome, the other corresponding to your distinguished profession.

For you are, to begin with, *jurists*, devotees of that noble science which studies, regulates, and applies the norms which form the basis of order and peace, of justice and security in the

---

[1] Since this document does not affect the Code of Canon Law directly, it obviously cannot be classified under any particular canon of the Code. Yet it seemed impossible to neglect so valuable a document, emanating from the Holy Father himself and dealing with the fundamental concepts of jurisprudence. We have accordingly created a Preliminary Section for documents of this class. This one is translated in full from the Italian.

civil relationships of individuals, societies, and nations; and Rome has the distinction of being the great mother of jurisprudence. If other peoples of antiquity were glorious for the splendor of their arts, for the loftiness of their philosophic speculation, for the refinement of their culture, the Roman people was second to none for its profound sense of law, for the erection of those marvelous juridical institutions through which it united the then known world and left a tradition which has resisted the gnawing tooth of time.

But, in addition to being jurists, you are and you profess yourselves to be *Catholic* jurists; and Rome is by divine disposition the ever resplendent beacon of the faith of Christ, the center of the visible unity of the Church, the seat of the supreme authority for the teaching of souls, where Catholicism manifests a peculiar force and greatness and becomes more tangible than in any other country of the world, by the confluence of all nations to the place of the chair and sepulcher of Peter. When the Empire of the Caesars crumbled before the onrush of the peoples surging against its boundaries, when the greatest and most august city of which history has record began to decline, two things survived: one was the *Corpus Iuris,* which became the law of all the countries of Europe and is in large measure still extant in the institutions of today, still the object of eager study, like a living trunk whose sap has not dried up with the passing of the years, still endowed with that power to unify which it had deployed in its slow process of formation; the other was the new faith which Peter and Paul brought here, the new throne of truth which the first visible Head of the Church, chosen directly by Christ and by Him invested with the supreme power of the Keys, established here when he chose Rome as his See. The centuries have passed, inclining before that block of granite without scarring it; the vicissitudes of history have pressed upon it to shake and shatter it, but in vain; you see it still firm and intact, raised amid the nations as a visible sign of the perennial durability of the work of Christ.

Thus it was that in Rome, and in the world which was already imbued with her civilization, these two vital realities — one the fruit of the juridical genius of a people, and hence of human origin, the other an irradiation upon the world of that revealed truth which had been announced by the Son of God made Man, and hence of transcendent and divine origin — met and were fused together in an intimate union, so that the Roman law, transfused with the new light emanating from the message of Christianity, was gradually transformed in its spirit, elevated in its concepts, perfected in many of its institutions, enriched in its dispositions, accumulating progressively the principles, the ideas, the higher exigencies of the new doctrine. The legislative work of the Christian Emperors was born of this fruitful union of human sagacity with divine wisdom, which has left indelible traces to prove to the modern world that true juridical science and the doctrine of Christianity, far from being in opposition, are in accord, since the Church cannot but place the seal of her approval upon the truth which the human mind discovers, considers, and organizes.

That is why We said that it was a wise counsel which led you to choose Rome for the place of your first Congress. But at the same time this choice reminds you how noble and exalted is your profession and what are the responsibilities which rest upon you in its practice, in view of the particular designation in which you glory.

The nobility of your profession was magnificently described by Ulpian, who defined jurisprudence as "the knowledge of the divine and human, the science of what is just and unjust."[2] What a noble object he assigns in this definition to the science of jurisprudence, and how far he exalts it above the other branches of human knowledge! The view of a jurist worthy of the name surveys an immense horizon, whose amplitude and variety are indicated by the things to which he must turn his attention and direct his study. He has to know, first of all, the divine, *divinarum rerum notitia*, not only because in the social life of man religion must have the first place and must guide the practical conduct of the believer, to which the law also will have to supply its own norms; not only because some of the principal institutions, such as marriage, have a sacred character which the law cannot ignore; but above all because, without this higher knowledge of things divine, the human panorama which is the second and more immediate object with which the mind of the jurist must

---

[2] *"Divinarum atque humanarum rerum notitia, iusti atque iniusti scientia."* — L. 10 D., 1, 1.

concern itself, *humanarum rerum notitia,* would be without that foundation which transcends all human vicissitudes in time and space and rests in the absolute, in God.

The jurist's profession indeed does not require him to apply himself to theological speculation in order to know the proper object of his study; but if he is unable to rise to the consideration of the supreme and transcendent reality upon whose will depends the order of the visible universe and of that small part of it which is the human race with its inherent and morally necessary laws, it will be impossible for him to see in all its marvelous unity and in its inner spiritual depths the network of social relationships which constitute the realm of law, with their regulative norms. If, as the great Roman jurist and orator said, *"natura iuris . . . ab hominis repetenda est natura,"*[3] the nature or essence of law can derive only from the nature of man himself; and since on the other hand the nature of man cannot be known even approximately, in its perfection, dignity, and elevation, and in the ends to which its actions are subject and subordinate, without the ontological connection which binds it to its transcendent cause, it is clear that the jurist cannot achieve a sound concept of law nor attain to a systematic organization of it, unless he ceases to look upon man and human affairs without that light which beams down from the divinity to illumine for him the laborious path of his studies.

The mistake of modern rationalism lay precisely in its attempt to construct the system of human rights and the general theory of law by considering the nature of man as a thing standing by itself without any necessary relationship to a superior Being upon whose creative and organizing will it depends in essence and in action. You know in what an inextricable maze of difficulties modern juridical theory has found itself entangled as a result of this initial deviation, and how the jurist who has followed the rule of so-called positivism has failed in his task, losing, together with the right knowledge of human nature, also the sound concept of law, thus shorn of that coactive influence on the human conscience which is its primary and principal effect. The divine and the human, which according to Ulpian's definition constitute the most general object of jurisprudence, are so intimately connected

---

[3] Cicero, *De legibus,* l. 1, cap. 5, § 17.

that one cannot ignore the former without losing the true evaluation of the latter.

This truth is still clearer from the fact that the more specific object of juridical science is the just and the unjust, *iusti et iniusti scientia*, that is to say justice in its exalted function of preserving a balance between the needs of the individual and the demands of society in the bosom of the human family. Justice is not only an abstract concept, an extrinsic ideal to which, as far as may be possible at any given period of history, human institutions must strive to conform; but it is above all something inherent in man, in society and its basic institutions, by reason of the sum of practical principles which it bestows and imposes, and of those more general norms of conduct which are part of the objective order of man and society as established by the supreme will of the Creator. The science of what is just and unjust supposes, therefore, a higher wisdom which consists in knowing the order of creation and consequently Him who made that order. Right, as Aquinas taught, is the object of justice;[4] it is the norm in which the great and fertile idea of justice becomes concrete and actual, and as such, just as it leads to God, who is eternal and immutable justice in His essence, so too it is from God that it receives light and clarity, vigor and force, meaning and content.

Hence the jurist in the practice of his profession moves between the infinite and the finite, between the divine and the human; and in this necessary movement lies the nobility of the science which he professes. His other titles to the respect of human society can be considered as consequences of this one. Though juridical norms are the object of his study, the subject for whom these norms are designed is man, the human person, which thus falls within the field of his competency. And, be it noted, it is not man in the lower and less noble part of his nature — that is the object of other sciences which are also useful and admirable — but man in the superior part of his nature, specifically in his character as a rational agent, who, in order to conform to the laws of his rational nature, must act under the guidance of certain norms of conduct which he receives either directly from his conscience, reflecting and announcing a higher law, or by the prescriptions of human authority regulating the life of men in

---

[4] St. Thomas, *Summa*, 2ᵃ 2ᵃᵉ, q. 57, a. 1.

society. It is true that to the eye of the jurist man does not always present himself under the higher aspects of his rational nature, but frequently presents the less desirable side, his evil inclinations, his disordered perversities, actions blameworthy or criminal; still, even under the clouds which dim the splendor of man's rational nature, the true jurist must always discern that basic humanity from which no fault or crime can utterly delete the seal set upon it by the hand of the Creator.

If you further consider man, the subject of law, through the eyes of Christian faith, you will see him wearing a crown of light. That is the crown with which he is adorned by the redemption of Christ and the blood which was shed for his ransom, the supernatural life to which Christ has restored him and in which He has given him a part, the ultimate destiny assigned to him as the goal of his earthly sojourn. In the new dispensation the subject of law is not man in the state of mere nature, but man elevated by the grace of the Saviour to the supernatural order, and by that very fact put in contact with the divinity through a new life which is a participation in the very life of God. His dignity thus grows to infinite proportions, and the jurist, who has Him as the object of his science, finds his own nobility enhanced in that same measure.

The irreconcilable conflict between the exalted conception of man and of law according to the Christian principles which We have tried briefly to set forth, and that of juridical positivism, can be the source of deep bitterness in professional life. We well know, beloved sons, how the Catholic jurist who wishes to remain faithful to the Christian concept of law, not infrequently finds himself at grips with conscientious difficulties, especially when he is in the position of having to apply a law which his own conscience condemns as unjust. Thanks be to God, your duty in this connection is already notably alleviated by the fact that in Italy divorce (the cause of so much mental anguish even for the judge who has to apply the law) has no legal standing. In truth, however, at the end of the eighteenth century, especially in those countries where persecution was raging against the Church, there were countless cases in which Catholic judges found themselves faced with the tormenting problem of the application of unjust laws. For this reason We take advantage of the opportunity afforded by your reunion in Our presence, to enlighten the conscience of Catholic jurists by the statement of some fundamental norms.

1) For every judgment the principle holds good that the judge cannot purely and simply disclaim all responsibility for his decision and let the responsibility rest entirely on the law and its authors. Certainly these latter are principally responsible for the effects of the law. But the judge, who by his decision applies it to a particular case, is a contributing cause and as such is concurrently responsible for those effects.

2) The judge can never by his decision oblige anyone to do an act which is intrinsically immoral, that is, by its nature contrary to the law of God or of the Church.

3) In no case can he expressly recognize and approve an unjust law (which, for that matter, can never constitute the basis for a judgment valid in conscience and before God). Hence he cannot pronounce a penal sentence which is equivalent to such approval. His responsibility would be still graver if his sentence were the occasion of public scandal.

4) However, not every application of an unjust law is equivalent to the recognition or approval of the same. In this case the judge can — perhaps in some cases he should — allow the unjust law to take its course, when that is a means of preventing still greater harm. He may inflict a penalty for the transgression of an unjust law, if the law is of such a nature that he who suffers the penalty is reasonably disposed to submit to it in order to avoid greater harm and to secure a good of far higher importance, and if the judge knows or can prudently suppose that the sanction will be willingly accepted by the accused for higher motives. In times of persecution, priests and laymen have often allowed themselves to be condemned, even by Catholic judges, without making any defense, to fines or to privation of personal liberty for the infraction of unjust laws, when by doing so it was possible to conserve for the people an honest judiciary and to avert from the Church and the faithful calamities of a still more dreadful nature.

Naturally, the graver are the consequences of the judicial sentence, the more important and general must be the good which is secured or the harm which is averted by such a procedure. There are cases where the idea of compensation through the attainment of higher goods or the prevention of greater evils has no application, as for example in the sentence of death. In particular the Catholic judge may not, except for reasons of great weight, pronounce a judgment of civil divorce (in countries where that is recognized by law) in the case of a marriage which is valid before God and the Church. He must not forget that in practice such a judgment has not only a bearing on the civil effects, but in reality rather leads to the false belief that the actual bond is dissolved and that the new one is consequently valid and binding.

And so, beloved sons, Our earnest wish for you is that divine Providence may grant you the happiness of ever practicing your profession in an atmosphere of legislation which is just and in accord with legitimate social exigencies. Make every effort to realize in yourselves the perfect ideal of the jurist, who by his competence, wisdom, conscientiousness, and rectitude, deserves and wins the esteem and confidence of everyone.

With this wish, and in pledge of the most abundant favors from God, We impart with paternal benevolence to you and to your newborn and already promising Association, Our Apostolic Blessing.

AAS 41–597; Pius XII, Allocution, 6 Nov., 1949. For a thorough study of these principles, with special application to a civil judgment of divorce, cf. *Periodica,* 39–5 (Abellán). Cf. *The Catholic Mind,* 1950, p. 53; 1952, p. 632.

The Ethical Basis of Law: Juridical Positivism and State Absolutism Destroy the True Concept of Law (Pius XII, Allocution, 13 Nov., 1949) AAS 41–604.

An Allocution of His Holiness Pius XII, delivered 13 Nov., 1949, to the Auditors and other Officials and Ministers of the Tribunal of the Sacred Roman Rota and to the Advocates and Procurators of the same, is as follows:

We are very happy to greet you, beloved sons, once more gathered here in Our presence, after We have just heard from your honored Dean the report of your activities during the juridical year 1948–1949, a report which, with the sober but luminous eloquence of facts, adds a new proof to the many others already given, of the high value and irreproachable rectitude of this your Tribunal.

The work of the Sacred Roman Rota, which We have been

able during the past ten years to follow more closely, has enabled Us to appreciate properly its unconditional respect for the truth of facts and for the precepts of the divine law, especially as regards the sanctity of marriage and the constitution of the family, and at the same time it inspires Us with the firm confidence that all your members will ever faithfully observe the norms which, in the fulfillment of Our Apostolic teaching office, We have already given, particularly in Our Allocutions of 3 October, 1941,[1] 1 October, 1942,[2] and 2 October, 1944.[3] This is all the more comforting to Our heart in the circumstances of the present time, which, in large measure though not everywhere, offer the spectacle of a crisis in the administration of justice, going beyond the usual deviations from the Christian moral conscience.

The immediate causes of this crisis will be found chiefly in juridical positivism and state absolutism; two manifestations which in turn usually support and depend upon each other. In truth, once you take from under the law its foundation, which consists in the divine natural and positive law and is for that very reason immutable, there is nothing left but to base it upon the law of the state as its supreme norm, and there you have the principle of state absolutism. Conversely, this state absolutism will inevitably seek to bring everything under its dominion, and especially to make the law itself subserve its own designs.

Juridical positivism and state absolutism have altered and marred the noble figure of justice, whose essential bases are law and conscience. This fact suggests a series of reflections which come down to two points: the objective norms of law and their subjective concepts. For today We shall confine Ourselves to speaking of the first point, deferring the consideration of the second to another occasion, if so it please the Lord.

In the science as in the practice of jurisprudence, there keeps coming up the question of what is true and just law. Is there, then, any other? Is there such a thing as false and illegitimate

---

[1] Canon Law Digest, 2, p. 454.

[2] Ibid., 3, under canon 1869.

[3] Ibid., 3, under canon 1960. For other Allocutions of Pius XII to the Rota, see Canon Law Digest, 3, canon 1553 (Allocutions of 1945 and 1947); and canon 2314 (Allocution of 1946).

law? Certainly the very conjunction of these two terms is shock-
ing and repugnant. Yet it is nonetheless true that the notion
which they express has always been alive in the juridical sense
even of the classic pagans. Among them no one perhaps has
expressed it more profoundly than Sophocles in his tragedy of
Antigone.[4] There he makes his heroine say that, thanks to the
services of Creon, Etheocles has been buried σύν δίκῃ δικαία.
Δίκαιος means one who fulfills his duties toward God and man,
who is just, pious, honest, righteous, humane; and so δίκη δίκαια
corresponds to what we call true and just law, whereas χεροιδίκης
or χειροδίκαιος, designating a violent person, one who uses the
right of the strong, indicates the man of false or unjust law.

The entire crisis to which We have referred is summed up in
the antagonism between true and false law. The interest with
which serious and penetrating juridical minds have applied themselves to the study of this subject seems to Us to augur well
for a solution of the crisis. But for this it will be necessary to
have the courage to wish to see clearly its root causes and to
acknowledge them in all sincerity.

Where then must we look for these causes if not in the field
of the philosophy of law?

It is impossible to observe attentively the material and spiritual,
the physical and moral world, without being struck with admiration at the spectacle of the order and harmony which reign in
all the degrees of the scale of being. In man, up to the dividing
line where his activity ceases to be merely unconscious, and where
conscious and free action begins, this order and harmony are
strictly realized according to the laws implanted by the Creator
in the existent being. Beyond that line, although the disposing
will of God is still valid, yet its realization and development are
left to the free determination of man, which can be either
conformed or opposed to the divine will.

In this sphere of conscious human action, of good and evil,
of precept, permission, and prohibition, the disposing will of the
Creator manifests itself through the moral commandment of God
inscribed in nature and in revelation, as well as through the
precept or law of legitimate human authority in the family, the
state, or the Church. If human activity governs and directs itself

---

[4] V. 23–24.

according to those norms, it remains of itself in harmony with the universal order willed by the Creator.

Here is the solution to the problem of true or false law. The mere fact of having been declared an obligatory norm by the legislative power in the state, taken alone and by itself, is not enough to create a true law. The "criterion of the simple fact" is valid only in the case of Him who is the Author and the sovereign standard of all law, that is, God. To apply it indiscriminately and definitively to the human lawgiver, as if his laws were the supreme norm of law, is the error of juridical positivism in the proper and technical sense of that term, an error which is at the root of state absolutism and which amounts to a deification of the state itself.

The nineteenth century is the great culprit as regards responsibility for juridical positivism. If its consequences have been late in making themselves felt in all their gravity in legislation, this is due to the fact that culture was still imbued with the Christian past, and that the representatives of Christian thought were still able practically everywhere to command a hearing in legislative assemblies. Still to come was the totalitarian state which, in principle or at least in fact, did away with all restraint imposed by a supreme law of God, and unveiled before the world the true face of juridical positivism.

Does one need to go far back in history to find a so-called "legal law," which strips man of all personal dignity; which denies him the fundamental right to life and physical integrity, putting both at the mercy of the party or the state; which does not recognize the right of the individual to his honor and good name; which contests the right of the parents over their children and their duty as regards their education; which above all considers that the recognition of God, the supreme Lord, and man's dependence on Him, are matters of no concern for the state and the human community? This "legal law" in the sense in which We have explained it, has overturned the order established by the Creator; it has called disorder order, tyranny authority, slavery liberty, crime patriotism.

Such was and such, We are bound to say, is still, in certain countries, "legal law." We have all been witnesses of the manner in which some who had acted according to this law, were later called to account for it before human courts of justice. The trials which thus developed not only brought real criminals to the fate they deserved; they also demonstrated the intolerable condition to which a state law which is completely dominated by juridical positivism can reduce a public official who otherwise, by nature and left free in his tendencies, would have remained an honorable man.

It has been observed that, according to the principles of juridical positivism, those trials should have resulted in just so many acquittals, even in the case of crimes which are repugnant to all sense of humanity and which strike the world with horror. The accused found themselves protected by the "extant law." What were they guilty of, other than doing the very thing which that law prescribed or permitted?

Certainly it is not Our intention to excuse those who are really guilty. But the heavier responsibility rests on the prophets and advocates and creators of a culture, of a state power and legislation, which refuses to recognize God and His sovereign rights. In all the countries where these prophets were and are still at work, there must be a resurgence and restoration of true juridical thinking.

The juridical order must once more be allied to the moral order and must not permit itself to go beyond the bounds that morality prescribes. Now the moral order is essentially founded in God, in His will, in His holiness, in His being. Not even the deepest and most subtle science of law could assign any other criterion to distinguish unjust laws from just ones, than the one already perceptible by the light of reason from the nature of things and of man himself, namely the law that is inscribed by the Creator in the heart of man,[5] and expressly confirmed by revelation. If law and juridical science do not wish to repudiate the only guide capable of keeping them on the right path, they must acknowledge the "ethical obligations" as objective norms valid also for the juridical order.

The juridical organization of the Catholic Church has never passed, and will never be in danger of passing through such a crisis. How could it be otherwise? Her alpha and omega is the word of the Psalmist: "Forever, O Lord, thy word standeth firm in heaven. . . . The beginning of thy words is truth: all the

---

[5] Cf. Rom. 2:14–15.

judgments of thy justice are forever."[6] This holds true for all of the divine law, including that which the God Man established as the foundation of His Church. In fact, from the beginning, in the first great promises,[7] He established His Church as a juridical society. Blind indeed is he who would shut his eyes to this reality.

The science and practice of Canon Law evidently do not recognize any "legal law" which is not also true law; their function is to direct the juridical system of the Church, within the limits fixed by divine law, constantly and entirely toward the end of the Church herself, which is the salvation and welfare of souls. The divine law serves this purpose perfectly; ecclesiastical law too must tend to the same end as perfectly as possible.

Happy in the knowledge that you, beloved sons, individually and collectively, are exercising your high juridical office in this spirit, We cordially impart to you, in pledge of the most abundant heavenly graces, Our Apostolic Benediction.

AAS 41–604; Pius XII, Allocution, 13 Nov., 1949.

Gratian's Decree: Eighth Centenary Celebration (Pius XII, Allocution, 29 April, 1952) **AAS 44–371.**

An Allocution of His Holiness Pius XII to the Delegates of the International Congress assembled in Rome to celebrate the eighth centenary of the publication of the *Decretum Gratiani,* is as follows:

Gentlemen: You wished to celebrate in an outstanding and solemn way the eighth centenary of the publication of Gratian's Decree. That was a wise undertaking and it has been successfully accomplished. Except for men of real learning and those who follow Canon Law and who practice in the courts, the majority even of educated men, though they are familiar with literature, the liberal arts, world history, and current events, yet rarely turn their attention and researches to subjects such as those which you have dealt with in this celebration.

It is therefore of the highest importance that, through you, they may fully understand or at least begin to suspect the greatness and importance of this work of Gratian.

---

[6] Ps. 118:89, 160.
[7] Matt. 16:16–20.

Hence, while We acknowledge with pleasure your homage and courtesy, We desire also to congratulate you on your work. It cannot fail to receive public recognition, whether one considers the magnitude of the long-continued labors of which Gratian's Decree is the happy outcome, or the use to which the work was put and the important results which followed from it, or the beauty, the sanctity and the maternal charity with which the Church went about her work of lawmaking and of judicial and executive functions, hidden though it all is in apparently severe and dry canonical formulas.

I. In order rightly to appreciate the magnitude of the task which Gratian undertook and accomplished very creditably, although with some unquestionable errors, one must enter the labyrinth of documents dating from the earliest ages of Christianity to the middle of the twelfth century which are brought together in it: it is a pile of writings from Sacred Scripture, from the Fathers of the Church, and from both canon and civil law.

One need but glance at the Tables in the *Prolegomena* of Friedberg's critical edition to see the ecclesiastical and juridical documents, almost like an endless network of arteries and veins through which, from the time of the Apostles through the first thousand years of Christianity, the life of the Church was diffused, conspicuous for the inexhaustible variety of forms both in the Orient and in the West, marked by struggles and triumphs, always dedicated to the earnest task of teaching all nations and forming them to Christian civilization, adding her own spiritual patrimony as a heritage to the ancient culture of the Orientals, the Romans, and the Germanic races.

What Justinian had done to systematize Roman Law, Gratian did in a similar way in Canon Law; and he took extraordinary pains to make the Decree a marvel of unity, orderly arrangement, and accord between the countless different parts which were collected and arranged in it.

First, unity. Certainly this is the principal merit and quality which the *Corpus Iuris* seeks to attain. But how difficult it was in Gratian's time to find a hinge which would bear all the weight of that unity, amid the mass and variety of laws from which ecclesiastical discipline had taken shape. The very title *Concordantia discordantium canonum*, which most probably the author himself, a Camaldolese monk, gave to his work, to the amazement of those who had the hardihood to set foot in the labyrinth of ecclesiastical law, casts a brilliant light on the magnitude of that plan, certainly born of genius, by which he hoped to cure the existing evil and at the same time avoid the difficulty which had proved an obstacle to so many before him.

This unity was far from being a more or less arbitrary and artificial heaping together of material. It is to the well-earned credit of the Master that he procured unity through the appropriateness and harmony of a methodical structure, for which the earlier Collections were far less esteemed. For this man stands out in the history of law like a leader who shows the way to a host of learners and teachers.

As everyone saw the great value of Gratian's work, they all abandoned the canonical handbooks of earlier times and set themselves to study and write commentaries on the *Concordia*. For here they found the matter of enacted legislation, not in a vast and undigested mass, but skillfully selected, arranged, coordinated, scrutinized, and weighed, so that the meaning and importance of the matter could be grasped. Thus there arose various schools of so-called Decretists: that of Bologna, the French, the Anglo-Norman, the Spanish, which vied with one another for the honor of showing the most sagacious and penetrating grasp of Gratian's text, or of giving the best explanation of the force and significance which he had assigned to his *Auctoritates* and to his famous *Dicta*. All these schools presented, like a magnificent exhibit, all sorts of documents of juridical and canonical learning; and these documents will arouse still greater admiration if, as may be hoped, they are edited in a *Corpus Decretistarum*.

It is no diminution of Gratian's glory to point out how much he owes to the canonists and theologians who preceded him and to men of his own time who were learned in the law, among whom the most eminent is Irnerius, *"lucerna iuris"* as he was called, easily first among the jurists of the school of Bologna.

To make something out of nothing is a singular and proper prerogative of God; and He shares it with no man. The works of men, exalted, sublime, and enduring though they be, and though they leave an imperishable imprint on human history, are yet always connected with some previous events which paved the way for them and made them possible. Future scholars may perhaps — we cannot altogether exclude the possibility — on the basis of new researches, contend that the *Decretum* should be attributed to a group of monks brought together at the one great Camaldolese monastery of Saints Nabor and Felix; but it will still be true and beyond doubt that the work of Gratian marks the beginning of a new era in the history of Canon Law, so that Sarti[1] could well say of its author that he "was thereafter considered as the father and author of Canon Law." Through him Canon Law reached such a degree of honor that it came to be considered quite necessary in legal doctrine, both for teaching it — as Gratian began to do successfully at Bologna — and for jurisprudence and legislation. As Gratian's Decree made its way into France, Spain, England, and Germany at the same time that the works of Irnerius and the jurists of Bologna were propagating and popularizing the knowledge of Roman Law in a new form, it immediately placed Canon Law on a par with it in dignity and gave rise to those *Summae, Glossae,* and *Apparatus* which, especially in the Universities of Bologna, Paris, and others, mark the beginning of the "golden or classical age" of Canon Law and made a capital contribution to the progress of Canon Law and of legal science in general.

II. Gratian's Decree, as is well known, never received the formal approval of the Holy See. Which is no wonder when one considers the purpose which the Camaldolese monk had in view in his work, the method and course which he followed in its composition and its final outcome. Undoubtedly there is a great difference between what Gratian accomplished by his own industry and labors, and what Tribonianus and his assistants did in making their Collection of the laws of Justinian at the Emperor's command.

The author of the *Concordia* himself said, as if chiseling his words in imperishable bronze: *"Negotiis definiendis non solum est necessaria scientia sed etiam potestas."*[2]

There is no indication that the Roman Curia commissioned the monk of Bologna to write his *Decretum.* Some have thought so, basing their opinion on a fragile conjecture from the title of the work, *Concordantia discordantium canonum.*

---

[1] *De claris Archigymnasii Bononiensis Professoribus a saec. XI usque ad saeculum XIV,* Bononiae, t. I, p. 344, n. XXVI.

[2] *Dictum Gratiani,* ante c. 1, D. XX.

Nevertheless the *Decretum* quickly gained the highest prestige, not only because it promptly won the favor of the Roman Pontiff Alexander III (Roland Bandinelli), who explained and abridged it, but also because the Curiae and the schools were eager to possess a handbook of the Sacred Canons in which contradictions and useless repetitions were eliminated. A further reason was that the authorities which he cited were usually a guarantee of the soundness of his doctrine.

The writing of the *Decretum* and the explanation of the canons which were apparently contradictory gave to Canon Law a place of equal dignity with that which Roman Law had attained after the remarkable advances made in it by the school of Irnerius. At the same time they put into the common discipline of the Church a vitality and vigor, the benefits of which became apparent in the centuries which followed. Theologians and students of the Sacred Canons, in a sort of mutual rivalry to cite and interpret, to untangle and reconcile excerpts and passages from this work, did a great deal to establish in the excellent subject of Canon Law a unity which was based on both theological and juridical foundations. There resulted a great benefit both to science and right conduct; for thereafter ecclesiastical judges could apply the law firmly and securely to the actual conduct of life.

We cannot, however, nor will We pass over in silence the mistakes which Gratian fell into: false or dubious passages which he included in his *Concordia;* ancient juridical documents of little value, often cited; not a few erroneous historical inscriptions presented. To say nothing of the fact that some of his opinions were not in agreement with the doctrine of later times, which contradicted or modified them.

Such mistakes are certainly excusable in so vast a work; nonetheless, they did call for the revision of the *Decretum,* which some of the Roman Pontiffs, notably Gregory XIII, entrusted to distinguished ecclesiastics and which other excellent scholars afterward continued.

It is evidently fitting that the work of the Roman Correctors, which was inserted into the first great Collection which is the *Corpus Iuris Canonici,* should remain there. But nothing prevents, in fact it is quite desirable, that a new critical edition should be prepared and published, as some have wisely suggested.

Thus the course of history in this matter will be made clear; a stronger light will be thrown upon the methods and ways in which the work was produced, the meaning of the explanations, the merits of the famous Camaldolese monk, and the progress of his work; a solution will be found for the knotty and intricate problems which sometimes confront those who follow the progress of the discipline of the Roman Church. This critical edition should be produced in the way demanded by the skill and science of the present day: for the Friedberg edition, of outstanding merit though it certainly is, no longer satisfies those who are foremost in the history of Canon Law.

III. Juridical science, civil as well as canonical, with its contents, laws, and codices, often enough has a false appearance of harshness and severity to those who have but an elementary knowledge of it: they find in it nothing but the constant repetition of the expressions *fas* and *nefas*. This is a clear sign that they do not understand it, and still more obviously that they have not penetrated to its inner depths. Any body of human laws reflects the mental culture of its author, whether he be an individual, a group, or a nation. The grandeur and dignity of ancient Rome enhanced with their own splendor the authority of the Laws of the Twelve Tables, which in the words of Livy[3] "with their immense mass of laws heaped one upon another" were "the source of all law, public and private."

Did not the law of God, even in the Old Testament, which is called the law of fear only by comparison with the New, show forth as in a magnificent radiance the supreme majesty and paternal clemency of the Creator and great Lord? Those who reverence it only through fear are far from seeing it in the same light as the Psalmist: "How sweet are thy words to my palate! more than honey to my mouth."[4]

Could the law of Christ, the law of charity, be wanting in those features which make it lovable? Never. Yet this mildness of spirit seemed to be restrained and repressed by the mass of particular laws which accumulated one upon another through the centuries. Recent studies of Gratian's work have shown that the special characteristic and merit of canonical legislation was its

---

[3] L. 3, n. 34.
[4] Ps. 118:103.

mildness, that is, the sense and spirit of the Christian truth and conscience which moves men toward "the unsearchable riches of Christ";[5] this it is which so exalts Canon Law that it quite surpasses the undeniable merits of the Roman Law.

In Gratian's Decree, because of the documents which it presents from various authors, theology and Canon Law appear as very closely united. Canon Law is there seen to throw its roots deep into the soil of Christian revelation, drawing from it the beneficent sap of *temperance, mildness,* the *renouncement of all asperity, charity.* Even from the beginning these virtues and alleviations gave to Canon Law a characteristic color and impressed upon it, as a seal upon wax, the mark of *Christian equity,* which soon developed into *canonical equity.* Some of the works which preceded Gratian's Decree, for instance, the *Liber de misericordia et iustitia* of Algerius Leodiensis (of Liége), the *Liber de vita christiana* of Bonitius, Bishop of Sutri, the *Panormia* of Ivo of Chartres, stir and nourish the inner life of the Church with the spirit of charity, which shines forth in these works with a new radiance.

In Gratian's work Catholic doctrine never loses this moderation by which the motherly charity of the Church, ever inclined to mercy, alleviates and mitigates the severity of the law, a moderation, let Us add, by which the Roman Pontiffs and the Fathers of the Church tempered the authority of ecclesiastical law. We might here adduce as examples the whole of Cause XXIII of the second part of the Decree, and the first Distinctions of Cause XXXIII (question III) which make up the celebrated treatise *de Poenitentia.*

How could the pastors of the Church of Christ be deaf to the constant call of charity urging the paternal heart to mercy? *"Cogunt enim multas invenire medicinas multorum experimenta morborum. Verum in huiusmodi causis, ubi per graves dissensionum scissuras non huius aut illius hominis periculum, sed populorum strages iacent, detrahendum est aliquid severitati, ut maioribus malis sanandis caritas sincera subveniat."*[6] Let this high warning ring in the ears of all who have some part in governing men; let legislators and judges heed it! Where could

---

[5] Eph. 3:8.
[6] C. XXV, D. L.

one find a more fitting or powerful description of those qualities which Saint Paul in his Pastoral Letters demands of those in power, than we have in the Distinctions of the first part of the *Decretum?*[7]

The defense of the Roman Pontiff, his activity in ruling and uniting the Church, ecclesiastical life purged of simony and lay usurpation, the regulation of property, the spiritual life of the faithful, especially their frequent use of the Sacraments, the duties of social life, the common life of the family, the sacred Liturgy, judicial procedure, ecclesiastical penalties; and all this illustrated by the ample citation of legal sources — this is something of a summary of the immense work composed by *"Magister Gratianus,* divinae paginae doctor egregius."[8]

It has been said of the Canonical Collections of the early Middle Ages that the fuller knowledge which we now have of them is progressively bringing to light their great value and importance for the history of opinions and doctrines even regarding the life, institutions, and government of the Church.[9] This is still more true of Gratian's Decree, for this work, presenting the facts as it were in vivid colors, shows clearly the spirit and tendency with which ecclesiastical discipline, the power of the Supreme Pontiffs, and the solicitude and care of the Bishops worked for the suppression of vices and disturbances and for the firm establishment of the moral law among individuals and in human society.

To the famous University of Bologna, which rightly takes pride in having Gratian among her distinguished sons and in celebrating, together with a great number of distinguished canonists and jurists from the entire world, the eighth centenary of his immortal *Decretum,* We extend today Our congratulations and best wishes: may she continue to give professional training to learned minds, to minds worthy to receive the heritage of past ages and thus to make an active contribution toward the preservation of the sacred patrimony of Christian culture. For Christian life and Christian civilization are the only forces which can prevent the human race from falling back into the fatal errors of

---

[7] D. XXV, ad D. L.

[8] *Cod. Mon. Lat. 16084 in Archiv für kath. Kirchenrecht,* Vol. 69, 1893, p. 382.

[9] Cf. De Ghellinck, S.J., *Le mouvement théologique du XII siècle,* p. 417.

barbarism and into moral decadence, and which can urge it on to higher and happier progress by keeping it fit to follow the paths of truth and virtue.

Finally, upon you who by your learning and industry have assured to this celebration a splendor commensurate with its importance, We invoke the plenitude of God's graces, and as a pledge of the same We heartily impart to you the Apostolic Benediction.

AAS 44–371; Pius XII, Allocution, 29 April, 1952. Annotations, with a good factual account of the Congress, *Monitor Ecclesiasticus,* 1952, p. 347 (Stickler).

————

Private Law and Its Coordination: Address of Pius XII to a group of 200 jurists and university professors from 30 nations, assembled at Rome for the First International Private Law Congress, 15 July, 1950. *The Catholic Mind,* 1950, p. 754.

BOOK I

GENERAL NORMS

Canons 1–86

BOOK I

GENERAL NORMS

Canons 1–86

CANON 1

**Form of Marriage and Disparity of Cult: Maronites Out-
side Patriarchal Territory** (Apostolic Delegate, U. S., reply
to consultation of 19 April, 1945) **Private.**

A petition addressed to the Holy See but evidently sent through
the Apostolic Delegation was as follows:

The undersigned Ordinary, prostrate at the feet of Your Holiness, humbly presents the following question: Whether the (diocesan) Tribunal is competent to declare the nullity of the marriage
in the following case:

John, born 21 May, 1911, was baptized in 1911 in the dissident
Oriental (Syrian) church of Saint George.

In February, 1935, John contracted marriage with Leah, an
infidel, before a civil magistrate. This marriage was later terminated by civil divorce.

On 14 June, 1936, in the dissident Oriental (Syrian) church
of Saint George, John contracted marriage with Mary, who had
been baptized in the Oriental (Syrian) church and had never
married before. This marriage was unhappy.

On 7 Sept., 1939, John attempted marriage before a civil magistrate with Martha, who had been baptized in the Oriental Catholic
(Syrian) church of the Sacred Heart. This marriage was later
terminated by civil divorce.

After the termination of the civil marriage between Martha

and John, Martha, now wishing to convalidate a marriage with Patrick, asks that her marriage with John be declared null and void.

Questions. The following questions were proposed:

1. Whether Martha is bound to the form of the Decree *Tametsi* (promulgated by the Maronite Provincial Synod which was celebrated on Mt. Lebanon in the year 1736)?

2. If the reply to 1 is in the affirmative, can the Ordinary declare the marriage of Martha, who was baptized in the Oriental Catholic (Syrian) Church, with John, null and void?

3. If the reply to 2 is in the negative, is the marriage between Martha and John invalid for want of form?

4. If the reply to 1 is in the negative, can the Ordinary declare the marriage of Martha, who was baptized in the Oriental Catholic Church, with John, null and void because of the impediment of *ligamen?*

5. If the reply to 4 is in the negative, is the marriage between Martha and John invalid because of the impediment of *ligamen?*

Reply. His Excellency the Apostolic Delegate replied as follows:

I wish to acknowledge your letter of April 19th with the enclosed letter regarding the MARTHA-JOHN marriage cause. Since this Apostolic Delegation possesses the information necessary for a response to your queries, I shall give them herewith, in the thought that you will thus be able to expedite the case at once.

The Tribunal of the diocese is competent in marriage causes of Catholics of Eastern Rites (excepting Ruthenians) according to the usual provisions of Canon Law for competence (canons 1556–1568).

In regard to your specific *dubia,* the answers are: *Negative ad primam.* Maronites living outside the patriarchal territory (having neither domicile nor quasi-domicile) are not bound by the provisions of the Synod of Lebanon of 1736. The second and third queries consequently do not apply in this case.

Ad quartum, affirmative. The first marriage contracted by John, a dissident Oriental, seems invalid because of the impediment of disparity of cult existing between him and Leah, who was not baptized. Disparity of cult invalidates the marriages of non-Catholics of Eastern rites. The second marriage of John, with

Mary, appears valid, and therefore his third marriage with Martha would be invalid *ratione impedimenti ligaminis.*

Trusting that this information will prove useful for a decision in the case, I remain . . .

(Private); Apostolic Delegate, U. S., reply to consultation of 19 April, 1945. Material kindly sent to us for the CANON LAW DIGEST by the Committee on Research of the Canon Law Society of America.

Confirmation: Administered by Latin Priests to Orientals
(S. C. Eccl. Or., Decree, 1 May, 1948) **AAS 40–422.**

A Decree, entitled *De Sacramento Confirmationis administrando etiam fidelibus Orientalium rituum a presbyteris Latini ritus, qui hoc indulto gaudeant pro fidelibus sui ritus,* is as follows:

Since, according to canon 782, § 4, of the Code of Canon Law, a priest of the Latin rite who has by indult the faculty to confer the Sacrament of Confirmation, can validly confer it only on the faithful of 'his own rite "unless the indult expressly provides otherwise"; and since, after the first and second terrible world wars, many of the faithful of Oriental rites remain dispersed in countries of the Latin rite, where they are cared for by priests of the Latin rite and grow up in the practice of that rite, so that often they think they belong to it or do not know to which rite they belong — the conferring of this Sacrament of Confirmation was not infrequently exposed to the danger of invalidity, especially in certain countries where the same local Ordinaries grant the above-mentioned indult to priests who have the care of souls.

And of course this danger was increased after the issuance of the Decree of the Sacred Congregation of the Sacraments, *De Confirmatione administranda iis qui, ex gravi morbo, in mortis periculo sunt constituti,* on the 14th of September, 1946.[1]

Wherefore, this Sacred Congregation for the Oriental Church, by agreement with the Sacred Congregation of the Sacraments, in order to provide for the spiritual welfare of the faithful of the Oriental rites who are living outside their own territory and under the jurisdiction of Ordinaries of the Latin rite, and also in order to provide for due reverence toward the Sacraments, deemed it necessary to petition His Holiness Pius XII that, whenever priests of the Latin rite in virtue of a lawful indult can validly and licitly

---

[1] See under canon 782; AAS 38–349.

administer the Sacrament of Confirmation to the faithful of their own rite, they can also administer it — provided it is clear that it was not already conferred, according to the usual practice, immediately after Baptism — to the faithful of the Oriental rites of whom they have the spiritual charge according to the Apostolic Constitution, *Orientalium dignitas,* of 30 November, 1894, art. 9, which provided: "every Oriental who is staying outside his patriarchal territory shall be under the administration of the Latin clergy."

As is evident, the same is true whenever the Sacrament of Confirmation can be administered as provided in the above-mentioned Decree of the Sacred Congregation of the Sacraments.

This petition was humbly presented to the Supreme Pontiff by the undersigned Cardinal Secretary of this Sacred Congregation for the Oriental Church in the Audience of 28 February, 1948; and His Holiness graciously deigned to approve it, and ordered that it be made public by this Decree.

Given at Rome, from the Sacred Congregation for the Oriental Church, 1 May, 1948.

AAS 40–422; S. C. Eccl. Or., Decree, 1 May, 1948.

Oriental Catholic Armenian Outside Patriarchate: Held to Form of Marriage Contracted With Non-Catholic in 1942 (Holy Office, 14 July, 1950) Private.

A Reply of the Holy Office:

In April, 1949, the Holy Office received a letter from your Most Reverend Episcopal Curia, asking whether a marriage contracted civilly in 1942 in the city of Hartford, between George, a Catholic of the Armenian rite, and Bonita, a non-Catholic, is valid as regards form. The question was put in these terms:

Whether a Catholic of the Armenian rite contracting marriage outside his patriarchate is bound to observe the form of marriage.

Reply. After having carefully considered the matter, this Sacred Congregation decided to reply: The marriage in question is invalid for want of form.

(**Private**); Holy Office, 14 July, 1950. Translation made from Latin text kindly sent us by the Committee on Research of the Canon Law Society of America.

Alienations and Debts Involving Ecclesiastical Property in the Oriental Churches: Amounts Which Require Papal Permission Defined (S. C. Eccl. Or., 10 May, 1952) AAS 44-632.

A Decree of the Sacred Congregation for the Oriental Church: Canons 66, 281, 282, 283, 291 from the *Motu proprio, Postquam Apostolicis Litteris*,[1] define the amount beyond which the permission of the Holy See is required in the alienation of precious property or other temporal property of the Church and in contracting debts and obligations.

But since those same canons do not declare that they refer to gold money values, this Sacred Congregation for the Oriental Church by the present Decree provides as follows:

While the present conditions continue, the *beneplacitum* of the Holy See will be necessary for the alienation of precious property or other temporal property of the Church and for contracting debts and obligations: in the Patriarchates, if the amount involved exceeds thirty thousand gold francs; and outside the Patriarchates, if it exceeds fifteen thousand gold francs.

Hierarchs who are subject to the jurisdiction of the Patriarch, as well as other religious Superiors in the Patriarchates, need the permission of the Patriarch, according to those same canons, if the value involved is between fifteen thousand and thirty thousand gold francs.

In the Audience of 10 May, 1952, His Holiness by Divine Providence Pope Pius XII deigned to approve all this upon receiving a report of the same from the undersigned Cardinal Secretary.

All things to the contrary notwithstanding.

Given at Rome, from the office of the Sacred Congregation for the Oriental Church, 10 May, 1952.

AAS 44-632; S. C. Eccl. Or., Decree, 10 May, 1952. Annotations, *Monitor Ecclesiasticus*, 1952, p. 583 (Herman).

---

[1] *Motu proprio,* Pius XII, 9 Feb., 1952; AAS 44-65; reported in this volume under canon 487. The canons referred to will be found in the AAS, Vol. 44, at pages 84, 139, 140, and 141 respectively.

Oriental Code: Extensive Interpretation of Canon 86 of the Marriage Code (Pontifical Commission for Drawing Up the Code of Oriental Canon Law, 8 July, 1952) AAS 44–552.

The Commission for the Oriental Code was asked:

I. Whether in virtue of canon 86, § 1, 2°,[1] the pastor and the local Hierarch within the confines of their territory licitly and validly assist at the marriage of the faithful of their rite even in places which are exclusively of another rite, provided there be the express consent of the Ordinary, or pastor, or rector of the aforesaid places.

Reply. In the affirmative.

II. Whether the interpretation given in the reply to I is declarative or extensive.

Reply. In the negative to the first part, in the affirmative to the second.

Given at Rome, 8 July, 1952. *De speciali mandato Sanctissimi.*

M. Card. Massimi, President

L S   A. Coussa, Basilian. Aleppen., Secretary

AAS 44–552; Commission for the Oriental Code, 8 July, 1952. Annotations, *Monitor Ecclesiasticus,* 1952, p. 421 (Herman).

Affinity: As affecting Maronites. See **c. 1077,** ref.

Books: Prohibition of, for Orientals. See **c. 1399;** AAS 36–25.

Brasil: Ordinariate for the faithful of the Oriental rites established. S. C. Eccl. Orient., 14 Nov., 1951 (AAS 44–382).

Communion, Paschal. See **c. 866;** private reply of 26 Jan., 1925.

Confirmation of Orientals in Danger of Death. See **c. 782;** AAS 38–349.

Consanguinity: As affecting Maronites. See **c. 1076,** ref.

Disparity of Cult: As affecting various Orientals. See **c. 1070,** ref.

Emigration of Orientals to non-Oriental countries. See **c. 248;** AAS 44–649, nn. 1, 2.

Encyclical of Pius XII on St. Cyril of Alexandria, *Orientalium decus,* 9 April, 1944 (AAS 36–129).

Faculties to Reduce Masses: Revoked in the Oriental Church. See **c. 828;** AAS 41–373.

---

[1] The text is: Can. 86. § 1. The pastor and the local Hierarch validly assist at marriages: . . . 2° Only within the confines of their territory whether the contracting parties are their subjects or not, provided they are of their rite (AAS 41–107).

Faculty of Latin Ordinary to Dispense Orientals. See c. 66; private; S. C. Eccl. Orient., 24 July, 1948.

Fast and Abstinence: Indult for Orientals modified. See c. 1252; AAS 41–31.

Five Scapulars: Formula for blessing and imposing the five scapulars in the Byzantine rite. See S. C. Eccl. Or., 7 Apr., 1943 (AAS 35–146).

Force and Fear: As affecting various Orientals. See c. 1087, ref.

Form of Marriage: Contracted before Oriental pastor. See c. 1097; AAS 40–386.

—— For Orientals. See c. 1099.

Gonyklisia: Place of, in Mass of Byzantine rite. See c. 818; AAS 43–217.

Greek-Ruthenians in Canada: New Organization of Hierarchy. Pius X, 15 July, 1912, established an Ordinariate or Exarchate for the Greek-Ruthenians in Canada, which was afterward further regulated by the Decrees, *Fidelibus Ruthenis,* 18 Aug., 1913, and *Graeci-Rutheni ritus,* 24 May, 1930 (CANON LAW DIGEST, 1, p. 29). Now further increases in the Greek-Ruthenian population of Canada require new provisions. Hence the one Exarchate is divided into three, as follows: (1) The Apostolic Exarchate of *Central Canada* (seat in Winnipeg; jurisdiction over Manitoba, Saskatchewan, and adjacent territories to the north; cathedral church, SS. Olga and Vladimir, Winnipeg); (2) The Apostolic Exarchate of *Eastern Canada* (seat in Toronto; jurisdiction over Ontario, Quebec, New Brunswick, Nova Scotia, Prince Edward Island, Newfoundland, Labrador; cathedral church, St. Josaphat, Toronto); (3) The Apostolic Exarchate of *Western Canada* (seat in Edmonton; jurisdiction over Alberta, British Columbia, Yukon and territories to the north toward Arctic Ocean; cathedral church, St. Josaphat, Edmonton). The three Exarchs are to be titular Bishops, immediately subject to the Holy See, with the same powers of order as other Bishops. Provision is also made for consultors, archives, division of property, *mensa exarchalis,* distribution of the clergy, etc. Until such time as a Greek-Ruthenian seminary can be established, the Exarchs are to seek admission for their candidates in Latin seminaries. See Pius XII, Apostolic Constitution, *Omnium cuiusvis ritus christifidelium,* 3 March, 1948 (AAS 40–287).

Hail Mary, as said by Orientals, good for indulgences. See c. 925; AAS 36–245.

Impediment of Force and Fear Among Oriental Dissidents. See c. 1087; Rota, 10 June, 1948.

Indulgences: Prayers and pious works for gaining of indulgences by Orientals, announced by S. C. Eccl. Or., 10 Aug., 1943, as having been granted by His Holiness in an audience to the Cardinal Major Penitentiary (AAS 36–47).

Judicial Procedure: New Code for Oriental Church. See c. 1552; AAS 42–5.

Marriage Law: New Code for Oriental Church. See c. 1012; AAS 41–89.

Oriental Catholics Married by Latin Pastor: What Delegation Required. See c. 1097; S. C. Eccl. Orient., 11 July, 1952.

Oriental Code: Canons on Religious, Ecclesiastical Property, Meaning of Terms. See c. 487; AAS 44–65.

Canons on Marriage. See c. 1012; AAS 41–65.

Canons on Judicial Procedure. See c. 1552; AAS 42–5.

Oriental Dissident: Marriage to Latin Catholic: Right to assist. See c. 1097; S. C. Eccl. Orient., 11 July, 1952 (two replies).

Children belong to Latin rite. See c. 1097; S. C. Eccl. Orient., 11 July, 1952 (second reply).

Public Propriety: As affecting Maronites. See c. 1078, ref.

Renewal of Consent, for Orientals to validate marriage, See c. 1133, ref.

Ruthenian Church: Encyclical of Pius XII on occasion of 350th anniversary of union with Holy See. Pius XII, 23 Dec., 1945 (AAS 38–33).

Ruthenian Ordinaries, U. S. and Canada: Faculties regarding marriage. See c. 66.

Studies, Oriental: To be promoted in seminaries. See Pius XI, Encyclical, *Rerum Orientalium,* 8 Sept., 1928 (AAS 20–277).

CANON 2

The Solemn Paschal Vigil Restored (S. C. Rit., 9 Feb., 1951) AAS 43–128.

A Decree of the Sacred Congregation of Rites:

The vigil of Easter Sunday, which Saint Augustine calls "the mother of all holy vigils" (*sermo* 219, PL, 38, 1088), was habitually celebrated in the Church from the earliest times with the greatest solemnity.

This vigil was celebrated during the nocturnal hours which precede the Resurrection of Our Lord. In the course of time it was for various reasons advanced, first to the evening hours, then to those of the afternoon, and finally to those of Holy Saturday morning, various changes being at the same time introduced, not without some detriment to the original symbolism.

But at the present time, with the growth of informed interest in the ancient liturgy has come a lively desire that especially the paschal vigil be restored to its primitive splendor by giving it its original place, that is, in the night hours which precede the Resurrection of the Saviour. There is also a special persuasive reason for this change from the pastoral standpoint, namely, to encourage the faithful to attend; for, as Holy Saturday is no longer considered as it formerly was, a holy day, very many of the faithful are unable to assist at the services in the morning.

Accordingly, supported by these reasons, many local Ordinaries, groups of the faithful, and religious have forwarded petitions to the Holy See asking that it permit the restoration of the paschal vigil to the night hours between Holy Saturday and Easter Sunday.

And the Supreme Pontiff Pius XII, graciously receiving these petitions, with the care and solicitude which so grave a matter demands, referred this question to a special Commission of liturgists so that they might carefully study and examine the whole matter.

Finally, upon receiving a report on the matter from the undersigned Cardinal Pro-Prefect of the Sacred Congregation of Rites, His Holiness deigned to approve the following Rubrics for the nocturnal celebration of the paschal vigil, to be established optionally for this year at the prudent discretion of the local Ordinaries and by way of experiment. The local Ordinaries, therefore, who shall make use of this faculty, are asked to inform the Sacred Congregation of Rites regarding the attendance and devotion of the faithful and the success of the restoration of the paschal vigil. Moreover, all publishers are forbidden to print this rite without the express permission of the Sacred Congregation of Rites.

All things to the contrary notwithstanding. February 9, 1951.

AAS 43–128; S. C. Rit., Decree, 9 Feb., 1951. Annotations, *Periodica,* 40–145 (Schmidt). The Rubrics were later considerably modified. See next document in this volume, under this same canon (AAS 44–48).

Optional Celebration of the Paschal Vigil Extended for Three Years, With New Ordinances and Changes in the Rubrics (S. C. Rit., 11 Jan., 1952) AAS 44–48.

A Decree of the S. C. of Rites entitled: "Concerning the extension for three years of the optional celebration of the restored paschal vigil, with additional ordinances and changes in the Rubrics," is as follows:

The restored paschal vigil which according to the Decree of the S. C. of Rites of 9 February, 1951,[1] was to be celebrated at the option of the local Ordinaries, and which was granted by way of experiment for one year, was celebrated, and with great success, notwithstanding the shortness of the time, in very many dioceses of the whole world.

Indeed very many local Ordinaries who made use of the

---

[1] AAS 43–128, reported above.

CANON 2 [AAS 44-48]

aforesaid faculty sent to this Sacred Congregation as requested their report on the celebration of the said paschal vigil, in which they generously praised the restored rite, told of the copious spiritual fruits derived from it, and asked that the permission to celebrate it be further extended.

Some local Ordinaries, however, upon the reports they received from pastors, also mentioned certain doubts and difficulties which occur in the celebration of the restored rite; having in view, of course, that the Holy See should by appropriate ordinances settle the difficulties and solve the doubts.

His Holiness Pius XII ordered that the same special Commission of expert liturgists which had prepared the rite of the paschal vigil should carefully examine the aforesaid reports. And this Commission, after having thoroughly discussed and considered the whole matter, decided that, if His Holiness approved, the permission to celebrate the restored paschal vigil should be confirmed and extended for three years; and that certain additional ordinances and changes in the Rubrics should be made.

Finally, on receiving a report on the matter from the undersigned Cardinal Pro-Prefect of the Sacred Congregation of Rites, His Holiness deigned to approve the following ordinances and rubrical changes for the optional celebration of the restored paschal vigil, according to the discretion of the local Ordinaries, for three years. The liturgical publication of the rite and Rubrics of this sacred vigil is reserved to the Holy See.

All things to the contrary notwithstanding. January 11, 1952.

AAS 44–48; S. C. Rit., Decree, 11 Jan., 1952. Annotations, *Monitor Ecclesiasticus,* 1952, p. 24 (Antonelli). The ordinances and revised Rubrics are contained in AAS, Vol. 44 at pages 50–63. They are also obtainable in a special booklet published by the Vatican Press.

Rubrics of Bishops' Ceremonial Revised as to Donning Sandals (S. C. Rit., Decree, 4 Dec., 1952) AAS 44-887.

A Decree of the Sacred Congregation of Rites:

According to the Bishops' Ceremonial (L. II, c. VIII, n. 2) and ancient ecclesiastical practice, there should be in all Cathedral Churches a room called a *secretarium,* separate from the church, where the Bishop, when he is to celebrate solemn Mass, puts on the sacred vestments. In case there is no such *secretarium,* it has become the practice for the Bishop to choose one of the chapels in the church. However, since it seems unbecoming to put on sandals and shoes in the church itself, the Sacred Congregation of Rites has decided to decree: that whenever, according to the Rubrics, the Bishop is to put on sandals and shoes in sacred ceremonies, he never do this in the church nor at the throne or faldstool, but either in the *secretarium* distinct from the church, or at home; and the Rubrics and decrees hitherto in effect are to be corrected in this sense. His Holiness by divine Providence Pope Pius XII ordered this decree to be published, all things to the contrary notwithstanding.

Given at Rome, from the Secretariate of the S. C. of Rites, 4 Dec., 1952.

AAS 44–887; S. C. Rit., Decree, 4 Dec., 1952.

Altar, Portable. See c. 1197; private reply of S. C. Rit., 21 Aug., 1950.

Antimensium Latinum: Faculty to use and formula for blessing. See c. 822; private, S. C. Prop. Fid., 8 March, 1950.

Archangel Gabriel: Heavenly patron of "tele-communications": telegraph, telephone, radio, television. Pius XII, Ap. Letter, 12 Jan., 1951 (AAS 44–216).

Candles: For Mass and Exposition of the Most Blessed Sacrament. See c. 1271; AAS 41–476.

Changes in Breviary and Missal, for Office and Mass of one or more Supreme Pontiffs. See S. C. Rit., 9 Jan., 1942 (AAS 34–105).

Forty Hours: Not permitted on Holy Thursday and Good Friday. See c. 1275; private reply of S. C. Rit., 15 March, 1950.

Good Friday: Translation of certain liturgical prayers. See c. 1399; AAS 40–342.

Liturgy: Encyclical of Pius XII, 20 Nov., 1947 (AAS 39–521). Annotations, *Periodica,* 37–59 (Hanssens) and 38–1 (Schmidt). Full English text, *The Catholic Mind.*

Martyrology: Additions to. See S. C. Rit., Decree, 27 Feb., 1948 (AAS 40–124).

Martyrology: New texts to be inserted. S. C. Rit., 9 May, 1952 (AAS 44–489).

Rite of Ordination. See c. 1002.

Saint Alphonsus Liguori: Patron of confessors and moralists. Pius XII, Ap. Letter, 26 April, 1950 (AAS 42–595).

Saint Barbara, Virgin and Martyr: Primary Patron of the artillery, navy, engineers, and fire-fighting departments of the Italian armed forces. Pius XII, Ap. Letter, 4 Dec., 1951 (AAS 44–616).

Saint John Baptist de la Salle: Patron of teachers of youth. Pius XII, Ap. Letter, 15 May, 1950 (AAS 42–631).

CANON 3

Portugal: Concordat in regard to the appointment of Bishops to certain dioceses of India, modifying in this respect the Concordat of 23 June, 1886, and the Accord of 15 April, 1928. Concluded and signed in Vatican City, 18 July, 1950 (AAS 42–811).

Spain: Concordat concerning religious assistance to the armed forces, 5 Aug., 13 Nov., 1950 (AAS 43–80).

Points of agreement between Spanish Government and Holy See. Pius XII, 7 June, 1941 (AAS 33–480).

CANON 6

Old Law Applied, in conferring of benefices. See c. 1435; AAS 35–399.

CANON 9

Immediately Effective: A reply of the Code Commission was so declared. See c. 2341; AAS 40–301.

CANON 12

Baptized Non-Catholics: Subject to canon 1088. See c. 1088; AAS 41–427.

CANON 17

Extensive Interpretation Declared. See c. 598; AAS 44–496.
Non-retroactive Reply of Code Commission. See c. 2341; AAS 40–301.
Oriental Code: Extensive interpretation. See c. 1; AAS 44–552.

CANON 20

Practice of Apostolic Datary: Applied as norm of law. See c. 1435; AAS 35–399.

CANON 33

Choosing Different Times for Formally Different Actions
(Code Com., 29 May, 1947) AAS 39–373.

The Code Commission was asked:

I. Whether, after one method of computing time has been chosen, this can be changed, in virtue of canon 33, § 1, in formally different actions.

Reply. In the affirmative.

II. Whether the three Masses celebrated on Christmas night are formally different actions.

Reply. In the negative.

AAS 39–373; Code Commission, 29 May, 1947.
Cf. *Periodica*, 36–334 (Aguirre); *Commentarium pro Religiosis*, 27–35 (Gutiérrez).

CANON 40

Dispensation of Matrimonial Impediment: Even when not mentioned in the petition. See c. 1052; AAS 40–386.

CANON 42

Failure to Mention Existing Impediment in petition for dispensation. See c. 1052; AAS 40–386.

CANON 66

Interpretation of Mission Faculties: Mass in Open or Without Server, Outside Proper Vicariate (S. C. Prop. Fid., 15 Dec., 1945) Private.

The Procurator General of the Oblates of Mary Immaculate asked the questions to which the following is the reply:

By letter of 10 April, 1945, Your Paternity presented the following questions to this Sacred Congregation:

1. Whether a missionary attached to a certain Vicariate Apostolic, in virtue of a permission granted him by his Vicar Apostolic according to article 4 of the Decennial Faculties, can licitly celebrate Mass in the open or without a server, while he is outside the territory of his own proper Vicariate Apostolic.

2. If the reply to the first question is in the affirmative: whether the said missionary in order to do this needs the permission, at least legitimately presumed, of the Ordinary of the place where he actually celebrates.

3. If the reply to the first question is in the negative: whether the said missionary can licitly do this even habitually, with the permission of the Ordinary of the place where he celebrates, granted however within the scope of canon 822, § 4 of the Code of Canon Law.

Reply. After hearing the opinions of the Reverend Consultors, I hasten to reply to the proposed questions as follows:

1. In the affirmative for the territories which are subject to this Sacred Congregation and in case of necessity, that is, when

there is no church or oratory in which the Mass can be celebrated.

2. In the affirmative.

3. Provided for in the reply to 1.

(Private); S. C. Prop. Fid., 15 Dec., 1945. Reported by Paventi in *Monitor Ecclesiasticus*, 1950, p. 379.

Quinquennial Faculties Extended to End of Year 1949: New Slightly Revised Formula of Faculties From the Holy Office (Apostolic Delegate, U. S., 19 May, and 29 June, 1946) Private.

The following are extracts from two letters of the Apostolic Delegate to the Ordinaries of the United States, together with the new formula of the Quinquennial Faculties from the Holy Office.

Letter of May 19, 1946

In the *Index Facultatum Quinquennalium* with which the Holy See grants the faculty to the Most Reverend Ordinaries of this country to dispense from the impediment of *disparitas cultus,* the cases in which there is question of marriage with a Jewish or Mohammedan person are excluded from the Most Reverend Ordinaries' faculty to dispense. This limited faculty may be found in the third paragraph of the faculties committed to the Most Reverend Ordinaries by the Supreme Sacred Congregation of the Holy Office.

Now I am instructed to inform the Most Reverend Ordinaries that, in an audience granted on April 12, 1945, the Holy Father, accepting the petition of the same Supreme Sacred Congregation, ordered that the restrictive clause in the aforesaid faculty be suppressed in regard to the marriages to be celebrated with a Jewish person, but that it remain in effect for marriages to be celebrated with Mohammedans.

This change will go into effect on July 1, 1946. From that date, therefore, you will be empowered to grant dispensations, in virtue of your quinquennial faculties, from the impediment *disparitatis cultus* when the non-Catholic party is Jewish, saving the special precautions which should be taken in all such cases.

Letter of June 29, 1946

The Supreme Sacred Congregation of the Holy Office has made certain modifications in the Quinquennial Faculties granted the

Most Reverend Ordinaries, particularly, as announced in my circular letter of May 19, 1946, in regard to dispensation from the impediment *disparitas cultus cum parte judaica.*

I now take pleasure in sending a sheet of revised pages for insertion in the *pagella* of the Index of Quinquennial Faculties. These new pages are to be substituted for pages 3, 4, 5, and half of page 6, i.e., down to "2. Ex S. C. de disciplina Sacramentorum" of the old *pagella.*

As stated in the circular cited, the above-mentioned faculty ("cum parte judaica") will go into effect on July 1, 1946. Furthermore, as already communicated in my circular of March 25, 1944, the Quinquennial Faculties for all the Most Reverend Ordinaries of the United States have been extended to the end of the year 1949.

REVISED FORMULA OF FACULTIES FROM THE HOLY OFFICE[1]

1. The faculty of granting for not more than three years permission to read or keep, with precautions, however, lest they fall into the hands of other persons, forbidden books and papers, excepting works which professedly advocate heresy or schism, or which attempt to undermine the very foundations of religion, or which are professedly obscene; the permission to be granted to their own subjects individually, and only with discrimination and for just and reasonable cause (cf. c. 1402, § 2); that is, to such persons only as really need to read the said books and papers, either in order to refute them, or in the exercise of their own lawful functions, or in the pursuit of a lawful course of studies.

(**Official Note.** *The above faculty is granted to Bishops to be exercised by them personally; hence not to be delegated to anyone; and moreover with a grave responsibility in conscience upon the Bishops as regards the real concurrence of all the above-named conditions.*)

2. To dispense, for just and grave reasons, their own subjects even outside their territory, and other persons within it, from the

---

[1] This formula entirely supplants the Faculties from the Holy Office as given in CANON LAW DIGEST, Vol. 2, pp. 30–33.

impediment of mixed religion, and if need be also from that of disparity of cult, *ad cautelam,* whenever there exists a prudent doubt of the reception of baptism by the non-Catholic party; when it has been found impossible before the marriage either to bring the non-Catholic party to the true faith or to deter the Catholic party from the marriage; provided that the promises have been regularly made in advance according to canon 1061, § 2, guaranteeing the fulfillment of the conditions required by the Church, and *provided the Ordinary himself be morally certain of their fulfillment;* to wit: on the part of the non-Catholic party, the promise to remove the danger of perversion from the Catholic, and on the part of both, the promise to baptize and educate all the children of both sexes in the holiness of the Catholic faith. Moreover the Catholic party must be informed of his or her obligation to use prudent measures to convert the other party to the Catholic faith.

The parties should be warned that according to canon 1063, § 1, they may not, either before or after their marriage before the Church, present themselves also before a non-Catholic minister in order to express or renew their matrimonial consent. This is forbidden to the Catholic party under pain of excommunication *latae sententiae* reserved to the Ordinary according to canon 2319, § 1, 1°. Moreover, the provisions of canon 1063, § 2, regarding the manner in which the pastor should act in such a case, are to be strictly observed.

If the parties are actually living in concubinage, appropriate measures must be taken to remove any scandal that may exist, and the Catholic party must be duly prepared to receive the grace of God, first receiving absolution from the excommunication which has been contracted if there has been an attempt to marry before a non-Catholic minister; and in this case also appropriate salutary penances are to be imposed. If a child has already been born of the illicit union, the parties must be warned of their grave obligation under the divine law to provide as well as they can for its Catholic education, and (in a proper case) for its conversion and baptism; an explicit promise should be required of the Catholic party to fulfill this obligation.

3. To dispense, for just and grave reasons, their own subjects even outside their territory, and other persons within it, from the impediment of disparity of cult (except for a marriage with

a Mohammedan), when this can be done without irreverence to the Creator, and when it has been found impossible before the marriage to bring the unbaptized party to the true religion or to deter the Catholic party from the marriage; provided that the promises have been regularly made in advance according to canon 1061, § 2, guaranteeing the fulfillment of the conditions required by the Church, and *provided the Ordinary himself be morally certain of their fulfillment;* to wit: on the part of the unbaptized party, the promise to remove the danger of perversion from the Catholic, and on the part of both, the promise to baptize and educate all the children of both sexes entirely in the holiness of the Catholic faith. Moreover, the Catholic party must be informed of his or her obligation to use prudent measures to convert the other party to the Catholic faith.

The parties should be warned that according to canon 1063, § 1, they may not, either before or after their marriage before the Church, present themselves also before a minister of a false religion in order to express or renew their matrimonial consent. Moreover the provisions of canon 1063, § 2, regarding the manner in which a pastor should act in such a case, are to be strictly observed. As regards the legitimation of the children, let canon 1051 be attended to.

If the parties are actually living in concubinage, appropriate measures must be taken to remove any scandal that may exist, and the Catholic party must be duly prepared to receive the grace of God; if a child has already been born of the illicit union, the warning must be given and the promise required as provided above in n. 2.

For the rest, whether the impediment be mixed religion or disparity of cult, let the provisions of canons 1026, 1102, and 1109 be observed as regards the publications, the questioning of the parties as to consent, and the sacred rites. After such a marriage has been celebrated, whether within or outside his own territory, let the Ordinary be watchful to see that the parties faithfully fulfill the promises they have made.

4. To grant a *sanatio in radice* for marriages that have been attempted before a civil officer or a non-Catholic minister, either in the case of their own subjects even outside their territory or of other persons within it, where there was the impediment of mixed religion or disparity of cult; provided that matrimonial

consent continues to exist in both parties, and that the same cannot be legitimately renewed, either because the non-Catholic party cannot be informed of the invalidity of the marriage without danger of grave damage or inconvenience to the Catholic party, or because the non-Catholic party can by no means be induced to renew consent before the Church or to give the promises as required by canon 1061, § 2; provided:

a) that it is morally certain that the non-Catholic party will not impede the baptism and Catholic education of all children who may thereafter be born;

b) that the Catholic party explicitly promise to provide, to the best of his or her ability, for the Catholic education of all children who may thereafter be born, and (in a proper case) also for the conversion, baptism and Catholic education of children already born;

c) that the parties did not, before their attempted marriage, bind themselves either privately or by a public act to educate the children as non-Catholics;

d) that neither party be actually insane;

e) that at least the Catholic party know of the sanation and ask for it;

f) that there be no other canonical diriment impediment for which the Ordinary himself has not the faculty to dispense or to grant a sanation.

But the Most Reverend Bishop himself must seriously admonish the Catholic party of the grave crime he or she has committed, must impose salutary penances, and if need be absolve the party from the excommunication incurred under canon 2319, § 1. He must at the same time declare that, as a result of the favor of the sanation which has been received, the marriage has been rendered valid, lawful, and indissoluble by divine law, and that the children who may have been born or may thereafter be born are legitimate. Moreover, he must remind the Catholic party of his or her grave obligation to take prudent measures for the conversion of the other party to the Catholic faith.

Since there must be proof in the external forum of the validity of the marriage and the legitimation of the children, the Most Reverend Bishop shall give orders that in each case the written document of sanation together with the attestation of its execution be carefully preserved in the local Curia. He must also see to it, unless in his prudent discretion he judge otherwise, that the notice of the validation of the marriage, with a notation of the day and year, be entered in the baptismal register of the parish where the Catholic party was baptized.

It is the mind of the Holy Office that the Bishop exercise this faculty of healing marriages in radice himself personally, that is, that he do not subdelegate it to anyone.

(**Official Note.** *1. In granting each of the above sanations or dispensations, the Bishop or Ordinary should mention expressly his delegation by the Holy See — c. 1057.*

2. At the end of each year the Ordinary shall report to the Sacred Congregation of the Holy Office the number and kind of dispensations which he has granted in virtue of this Indult.)

(**Private**); Apostolic Delegate, Letters, 19 May, and 29 June, 1946, with formula of faculties. These documents were kindly sent to us personally by the Most Reverend Apostolic Delegate.

Faculties of the Ruthenian Ordinaries in the United States and Canada in Questions Concerning Marriage (S. C. Or.) Private.[1]

CHAPTER II

Faculties Concerning the Sacrament of Matrimony

9. To dispense from the impediment of spiritual relationship, except that existing between *levantem et levatum,* and between the minister and the person baptized.

10. To dispense from the impediment of public propriety, arising from *iustis sponsalibus.*

11. To dispense from the impediment of crime, where there is no murder on the part of either party, both for marriages already contracted, in which case the parties are to renew their consent secretly, and in those to be contracted, a grave salutary penance to be imposed in both cases; also the faculty to restore the lost right of asking the *debitum.*

---

[1] These faculties were renewed by the Oriental Congregation on July 10, 1942, for another five-year period, for the Ruthenian Ordinaries in the United States. They were renewed for Bishop Ladyka in Canada on May 30, 1945. Faculties to grant dispensations from the impediments of mixed religion and disparity of cult come from special grants from the Holy Office.

12. To dispense in the third and fourth degree simple and mixed only, of consanguinity and affinity, and in the second, third, and fourth mixed, both for marriages already contracted and for those to be contracted; and also, for marriages already contracted, in the second degree only, provided it does not touch the first, for persons who are converted to the Catholic faith from heresy, schism, or infidelity, it being understood that if only one party is converted the guarantees prescribed by the Church must be given; and in the above cases to declare the children already born legitimate.

13. These matrimonial dispensations, namely, nn. 9, 10, 11, and 12, are given only with the clause: "provided the woman was not abducted, or if she was, that she is no longer in the power of the abductor," and in the dispensation, let the meaning of this faculty be stated, together with the time for which the dispensation was granted.

14. To dispense Catholics who are their subjects, both in marriages already contracted and in those to be contracted, from the impediment of affinity in the collateral line, in the simple first degree or in the first mixed with the second, when the affinity arises from licit copula, provided there is a just and legitimate cause for the dispensation.

15. To dispense, for just and legitimate cause, their Catholic subjects, both in marriages already contracted and in those to be contracted, from the impediment of affinity arising from illicit copula, either occult or public, in the first and second degree, simple or mixed, of either the collateral or the direct line, provided that, if there is question of the direct line, there be no possibility that the spouse is the offspring of the other party.

16. To dispense, only for the purpose of contracting marriage, from the simple vows of virginity, perfect chastity, not to marry, to receive sacred orders, and to embrace the religious state.

17. To cumulate dispensations from matrimonial impediments for which the same Ordinary has faculties, so that he can use the faculty to dispense in cases where two or more of the aforesaid impediments concur; and also in case the impediment of mixed religion also occurs, if he has already obtained the faculty to dispense from this impediment; but only for just and grave reasons, and in urgent cases in which there is not time to have recourse to the Holy See, and provided each of the faculties so

used, whether they were obtained by the Ordinary for the first time or have been renewed, are still in effect, and, if the faculties were given only for a certain number of cases, provided further that the cases do not exceed this number.

18. To heal and validate *in radice,* either personally or through some ecclesiastic expressly deputed, marriages which were contracted invalidly because of some impediment, provided both parties continue in present consent.

The one who dispenses must, in doing so, declare that he is acting in the name of the Holy See and as specially delegated by the Holy See; in case the marriage is criminally invalid, he must seriously admonish the party or parties of the grave crime that has been committed, impose salutary penances, and absolve them of censures and other ecclesiastical penalties which have in any way been incurred because of it; and he must at the same time declare that, because of the dispensation so granted and received, the marriage is made valid and legitimate, and becomes indissoluble by divine law, and consequently that the children already born or to be born are to be considered legitimate. Since there must be proof of the validity of the marriage in the external forum, the Ordinary shall order that the names, together with the other usual indications of the persons, be inscribed in the register of secret marriages; the autograph document of the grant, communication, acceptance, absolution, and declarations made as above provided, is to be kept in the Episcopal Curia, and an authentic copy is to be given to the party concerned, which the latter must carefully preserve.

In granting a convalidation or *sanatio in radice,* and as regards the legitimation of children, let the Ordinary have in mind the norms which are contained in the appendix, pages 21–22.[2]

19. To heal *in radice* marriages invalidly contracted between a Catholic and a non-Catholic, according to his prudent conscientious judgment, provided the consent of both parties continues and it is morally certain that the non-Catholic party will not impede the Catholic baptism and Catholic education of all the children (already born or)[3] to be born; either personally or

---

[2] On pp. 21 and 22 of these faculties are eight canons taken from the Latin Code, canons 1133–1140, which are quoted in full as norms to be followed in questions of convalidation and sanation.

[3] When these quinquennial faculties were renewed for Bishop Ladyka in

through another ecclesiastic specially deputed by the Ordinary himself, a previous dispensation being given from the impediments of ecclesiastical law which may have arisen.

The person who dispenses must himself seriously admonish the Catholic party of the very grave crime he or she has committed, impose on the party salutary penances, and absolve him or her from censures, if the marriage was contracted before a non-Catholic minister; and must at the same time declare to the party that, because of this dispensation which he or she has received, the marriage is made valid and legitimate, and becomes indissoluble by divine law, and that the children either already born or to be born in the future are to be considered legitimate.

He must moreover impose upon and declare to the Catholic party the obligation which always binds him or her, to fulfill the conditions prescribed by the Church: namely, to do what he or she can to obtain the conversion of the other party to the Catholic faith, and to have all the children of both sexes baptized and educated in the holiness of the Catholic religion, notwithstanding the opposition of civil laws if any there be.

And since there must be proof of the validity of the marriage in the external forum, the Ordinary shall order that the names, together with the usual indications of the persons, be inscribed in the register of secret marriages; the autograph document of the grant, communication, acceptance, absolution, and declarations made as above provided, must be kept in the Episcopal Curia, and an authentic copy is to be given to the party concerned, which the latter must carefully preserve.

The Ordinary, in using this faculty granted to him, must expressly mention his delegation by the Holy See.

20. In danger of death, Ordinaries of places, to provide for peace of conscience and in a proper case for the legitimation of children, can, both as to the form to be observed in the celebration of marriage and as to all and each of the impediments of

---

Canada on May 30, 1945, the following instruction was given: "In n. 19, the words *'tam natae quam'* must be suppressed, as the requirement of moral certitude that the non-Catholic party will not impede the baptism and the Catholic education of the offspring is limited to the offspring yet to be born. Instead, however, a serious promise must be obtained from the Catholic party to the effect that the latter will do whatever possible for the baptism and the Catholic education also of the children who have already been born."

ecclesiastical law, public or occult, even multiple, except the impediments arising from the sacred order of the priesthood and from affinity in the direct line when the marriage from which the affinity arose was consummated, dispense their own subjects anywhere, and all persons who are actually staying in their territory, provided that scandal be removed and that, if the dispensation is granted from disparity of cult or mixed religion, the usual promises be given.[4]

21. Ordinaries of places can also, subject to the clauses expressed in the preceding number, grant a dispensation from all the impediments mentioned in the preceding number, whenever the impediment is discovered when everything is already prepared for the marriage, and the marriage cannot, without probable danger of grave harm, be deferred until a dispensation is obtained from the Holy See.

This faculty is good also for the validation of a marriage already contracted, if there is the same danger in delay and there is not sufficient time for recourse to the Holy See.

Chapter V

Faculties for the Internal Forum
(From the Sacred Penitentiary)

49. To dispense from the occult impediment of crime, provided there is no question of any plotting of death, both in marriages already contracted, in which case the parties are to renew their consent secretly, and in marriages to be contracted, in both cases a grave salutary penance being enjoined; to restore the lost right of asking the *debitum*.

Chapter VII

Animadversiones

54. Faculties which do not require the episcopal character may

---

[4] The faculties add this footnote: "In the same circumstances, and only for cases in which even the Ordinary of the place cannot be reached, the same power of dispensing belongs to the pastor, to the priest who assists at the marriage, and to the confessor, but in this last case for the internal forum and in the act of sacramental confession only."

be subdelegated by the Ordinary to his priests, according to his prudent discretion.

55. The Ordinary can use all these faculties, either personally or through others, only within the limits of his jurisdiction.

56. He is to exercise them gratis, without any reward, and always making mention of his delegation by the Holy See.

57. If it should happen that the Ordinary should, through forgetfulness or inadvertence, make use of these faculties beyond the time for which they are granted, all the absolutions, dispensations, and concessions so given are to be considered approved and valid. Moreover, when the Ordinary has made out a petition for the renovation or prorogation of these faculties, they shall remain in effect until the reply of this Sacred Congregation has reached the said Ordinary.

(Private); S. C. for the Oriental Church. This formula of the faculties of the Ruthenian Ordinaries in the United States and in Canada, in questions concerning marriage, are translated from Marbach, *Marriage Legislation for the Catholics of the Oriental Rites in the United States and Canada,* pp. 257–261. The permission of the author is gratefully acknowledged.

Power of Latin Ordinary to Dispense Orientals by Virtue of Quinquennial Faculties in Territories Where They Have No Ordinary of Their Own (S. C. Eccl. Or., 24 July, 1948) Private.

A Latin Ordinary presented the following questions to the Sacred Congregation for the Oriental Church:

1. Whether the Latin Ordinary, in virtue of the Quinquennial Faculties from the Sacred Congregation of the Sacraments, without any explicit delegation from the S. C. for the Oriental Church, can validly grant a dispensation from a diriment impediment to Maronites (or other Orientals) who have here no Ordinary of their own?

Reply. In the affirmative (cf. Constitution, *Orientalium dignitas,* Leo XIII, 30 Nov., 1894, n. 9).

2. Whether the Latin Ordinary can validly grant such a dispensation to Orientals because of a presumption of the urgency of the case, or of danger of death, with consequent excessive difficulty of recourse to the S. C. for the Oriental Church, even though the petitioners said nothing in their petition about urgency or danger or difficulty?

Reply. In the affirmative.

3. If the Latin Ordinary can validly dispense, whether such a dispensation granted to Orientals is governed by the principle of canon 1052, so that the omission of another impediment of equal or minor grade does not render the dispensation invalid?

Reply. In the affirmative.

(**Private**); S. C. Eccl. Or., 24 July, 1948. Reported by Oesterle in *Monitor Ecclesiasticus,* 1952, pp. 106, 107.

Faculties and Indults for Latin America (S. Consistorial Congregation, 26 March, 1949) AAS 41–189.

A Decree entitled: "Concerning faculties and favors for Latin America" is as follows:

The conspicuous privileges which had been granted for thirty years by Pope Leo XIII of happy memory, to the Ordinaries, priests, and faithful of the dioceses of Latin America, were renewed for ten years by His Holiness Pius XI of happy memory in his Apostolic Letter of 30 April, 1929,[1] and, by Decree of the S. Consistorial Congregation of 18 April, 1939, were renewed until 30 April, 1949.[2]

Since at the expiration of the ten years above mentioned the Ordinaries of Latin America, seeing that the same circumstances continued to exist, earnestly petitioned that the privileges be continued, His Holiness Pius XII by divine Providence Pope, after having consulted the Sacred Congregations as to the matters within their respective competencies, graciously deigned to confirm and grant the requested faculties, with some modifications which seemed advisable, to all and each of the Ordinaries, priests, and faithful of the dioceses and ecclesiastical districts of Latin America, until the 31st day of December, 1959, in the manner hereinafter provided.

1. In regions or places where, because of the great distance or other difficulty, it is very difficult for pastors or missionaries to take from the baptismal fonts where it is kept and to carry with them the water which was blessed on Holy Saturday and Pentecost, Ordinaries of places can grant to pastors or missionaries the faculty of blessing baptismal water according to the

---

[1] AAS 21–554.

[2] AAS 31–224; DIGEST, 2, p. 42, ref.

shorter formula which was allowed for the missionaries in Peru by Our Predecessor of happy memory Paul III, and which is now in the Appendix to the Roman Ritual.

2. Pastors and missionaries, if for lack of time or great fatigue, or for other serious reasons, they cannot easily perform all the prescribed ceremonies for the baptism of adults, may licitly, with the previous consent, however, of the Ordinary, use only those rites which are specified in the Constitution of Pope Paul III of happy memory, *Altitudo,* of 1 June, 1537.

3. Likewise, local Ordinaries, excluding the Vicar General without the special mandate of his local Ordinary, can depute to administer the sacrament of confirmation, priests, if possible such as are invested with some ecclesiastical dignity or are acting as Vicars forane, but never simple priests staying in the places where the said sacrament is to be administered; observing the Instruction of the Sacred Congregation of the Sacraments for a simple priest who administers the sacrament of confirmation in virtue of delegation by the Holy See.[3]

4. The same Ordinaries can delegate to assist at marriages according to the form required by law, priests who go to places far from the seat of the parish on Missions to evangelize the faithful or to do any other pious work, as long as those same Missions continue, in the absence of the Ordinary, or pastor, or vicar assistant, and observing those things which, as far as the case permits and the conditions of place and time permit them to be observed, should be done before the marriage according to canon 1019 and the following canons of the Code of Canon Law; making express mention, however, of this apostolic indult in every case, and always observing the prescriptions of the sacred canons regarding the rights of pastors and the recording to be made in the parish registers.

5. The Ordinaries can likewise dispense from those matrimonial impediments of ecclesiastical law from which the Holy See has been accustomed to dispense, excepting therefore those which arise from sacred orders or from affinity in the direct line when the marriage was consummated; excepting also, because of its gravity, the impediment mentioned in canon 1075, 2° and 3°; and finally excepting the impediments of mixed religion and

[3] S. C. Sacr., 20 May, 1934; AAS 27–11; DIGEST, 2, p. 185.

disparity of cult, unless special faculties have been obtained from the Holy Office.

Likewise they are given permission to decree and declare legitimate the offspring of persons about to marry, provided such offspring be not conceived in adultery; making express mention, however, in every case, also in granting dispensations, of this apostolic indult.

6. To the faithful who contract marriage, it is granted that they may receive the nuptial blessing at any time of the year, provided they abstain from excessive festivities during those times when marriage is forbidden by the Church;[4] taking care, however, that if the nuptial blessing is given outside of Mass, the formula in the appendix *de Matrimonio* of the Roman Ritual be used.

7. It is also allowed to use old Sacred Oils, not more than two years old, provided they be incorrupt and it be impossible even with all diligence to obtain fresh or more recent Sacred Oils.

8. Ordinaries can permit to priests the use of a portable altar, provided, however, that this use be only for the benefit of the faithful and in places where there is no church or public oratory or where the parish church is too distant, but not at sea; provided the place of celebration be fitting and decent, that the Mass be said on a sacred altar stone, and that the pastors and other priests to whom this faculty is given instruct the faithful who are present with an explanation of the Gospel or a catechetical lesson.

9. Ordinaries can grant to priests the faculty of celebrating Mass on board ship only during the time of the voyage, provided the place where the Mass is to be said be in no way improper or unbecoming, that the sea or stream be so quiet that there is no danger of spilling the Precious Blood from the chalice; and that another priest, if one is available, stand by the celebrant vested in a surplice.

10. It is permitted to all the faithful of Latin America to fulfill the precept of annual confession and Communion from

---

[4] In view of canon 1108, § 1, the meaning of this last clause is undoubtedly "during the closed time," but we have translated the text as it stands. The Latin is "dummodo *illis temporibus, in quibus ab Ecclesia nuptiae prohibentur,* a nimia pompa abstineant."

Septuagesima Sunday to the Feast of the Holy Apostles Peter and Paul.

11. The same faithful, if they live in places where it is entirely impossible or at least very difficult to go to confession, are given the privilege of being able to gain indulgences and Jubilees which require confession, Communion, and fasting, provided that, having fulfilled the fast, they be at least interiorly contrite and make the firm resolution to go to confession as soon as they shall be able.

Given at Rome, from the S. Consistorial Congregation, 26 March, 1949.

AAS 41–189; S. C. Consist., Decree, 26 March, 1949. Annotations, *Monitor Ecclesiasticus,* 1949, p. 65 (Cappello).

Special Faculties From Propaganda to the Ordinaries of Latin America (S. C. Prop. Fid., 15 Sept., 1950) Private.

A Letter of the Sacred Congregation for the Propagation of the Faith renewing certain special faculties for the Ordinaries of Latin America subject to that Sacred Congregation:

Prot. N. 3394/50   Vatican City, 15 Sept., 1950

Your Excellency:

A number of privileges granted by the Supreme Pontiff Leo XIII in the Apostolic Letter, *Trans Oceanum,* of 18 April, 1897, for thirty years, to the dioceses and other ecclesiastical territories of Latin America, were renewed for ten years by Pius XI in the Apostolic Letter of 30 April, 1929. At the end of that time, as the Sacred Consistorial Congregation by decree of 28 April, 1939, extended these same privileges for another ten years for the dioceses subject to it, by authority granted to it by His Holiness Pius XII, so too this S. C. for the Propagation of the Faith granted favors of the same sort to the Ordinaries of the mission territories of Latin America which are under its jurisdiction, in as far as they are not contained in the new formula of general faculties, for ten years, beginning on January 1.[1]

And now this same S. C., in virtue of authority given to it by His Holiness Pius XII, does by these presents grant to you as

---

[1] For the various *Formulae* of these regular Decennial Faculties, with annotations, see *Monitor Ecclesiasticus,* 1950, pp. 353–383.

the Ordinary of that Mission and to the Mission itself, the following privileges, for ten years beginning on January 1, 1951, to-wit:

1. To use even old Sacred Oils, not, however, more than two years old, provided they be incorrupt and it is impossible even with all diligence to obtain fresh or more recent Sacred Oils.

2. The faithful can fulfill the precept of annual confession and Communion from Septuagesima Sunday to the Feast of the Holy Apostles Peter and Paul.

3. The same faithful, if they live in places where it is entirely impossible or at least very difficult to go to confession, are given the privilege of being able to gain Indulgences and Jubilees which require confession, Communion, and fasting, provided that, having fulfilled the fast, they be at least interiorly contrite and make the firm resolution to go to confession as soon as they shall be able.

4. As regards fast and abstinence:

a) Fast without abstinence is to be observed only on the Friday of the Ember Days in Advent, the Wednesdays of Lent, and Holy Thursday;

b) Fast and abstinence, on Ash Wednesday and the Fridays of Lent;

c) Abstinence without fasting, on the vigils of Christmas, Pentecost, the Assumption of Our Lady, the feasts of the Holy Apostles Peter and Paul and All Saints.

(**Private**) ; S. C. Prop. Fid., 15 Sept., 1950. Reported in *Monitor Ecclesiasticus*, 1950, p. 562, with annotations by Paventi.

———

Eucharistic Fast: New faculties. See c. 858.

Meaning of "Jew," in former restriction of faculties for disparity of cult. See c. 1070; two private replies of Holy Office, 7 July, 1943, and 11 Apr., 1945.

Mission Faculties: Decennial Faculties for Ordinaries of Missions subject to the S. C. Prop. Fid. (Formulae Maior et Minor: Prot. N. 449/41, 4200/47, 2416/50) valid from 1 Jan., 1951 to 31 Dec., 1960, are given in full in *Monitor Ecclesiasticus*, 1950, p. 353, with annotations by Paventi, p. 371.

Restrictive Clause as to Dispensation for Marriage With a Jew. See c. 1070; private reply of Holy Office, 4 July, 1952.

CANON 81

If Recourse to Holy See Through Apostolic Legate Is Easy, This Canon Cannot Be Applied (Code Commission, 26 June, 1947) AAS 39–374.

The Code Commission was asked:

Whether the clause of canon 81, "unless recourse to the Holy See is difficult," applies when Ordinaries can easily have recourse to the Legate of the Roman Pontiff in the country, who is in communication with the Holy See.

Reply: In the negative.

AAS 39–374; Code Commission, 26 June, 1947.

Cf. *Periodica,* 36–343 (Cappello); *Commentarium pro Religiosis,* 27–32 (Gutiérrez).

Dispensing Power Does Not Extend to Reserved Vows Nor to Obligation of Celibacy (Code Commission, 26 Jan., 1949) AAS 41–158.

The Code Commission was asked:

I. Whether the words of canon 81, *"a generalibus Ecclesiae legibus,"* include vows reserved to the Holy See.

II. Whether, in virtue of canon 81 and under the clauses there contained, Ordinaries can dispense subdeacons and deacons from the obligation of observing sacred celibacy.

Reply. In the negative to both.

AAS 41–158; Code Com., 26 Jan., 1949. Commentary by Goyeneche in *Commentarium pro Religiosis,* Vol. 29 (1949), p. 25.

Secular Institutes: Power of Bishop to dispense in certain matters during first ten years. See **c. 488**; AAS 40–293, n. 11, b.

BOOK II

PERSONS

Canons 87–725

BOOK II

PERSONS

Canons 87–725

CANON 87

Mystical Body of Christ: Encyclical of Pius XII, 29 June, 1943 (AAS 35–193).
Non-Catholics, If Baptized, Subject to Canon 1088. See c. 1088; AAS 41–427.
Outside the Church, No Salvation: Genuine meaning of this axiom. See c. 1324; private reply of Holy Office, 8 Aug., 1949.

CANON 91

Norms for Spiritual Care of Emigrants. See c. 248; AAS 44–649.

CANON 98

Rite of Child Wrongfully Baptized in Dissident Oriental Rite. See c. 756; private reply of S. C. Eccl. Orient., 11 July, 1952.

CANON 100

Knights of the Holy Sepulchre: Erected as moral person; new statutes approved. Pius XII, Ap. Letter, 14 Sept., 1949 (AAS 43–722).

CANON 109

Hierarchical Form of Judicial System in the Church. See c. 1553; AAS 37–256.

CANON 116

Decree on Clerics Going From the Dioceses of Europe to Australia or New Zealand (S. C. Prop. Fid., 21 Oct., 1948) **AAS 41-34.**

In order to safeguard ecclesiastical discipline in the territory of Australia and New Zealand, this Sacred Congregation for the Propagation of the Faith, because of the circumstances of the present time, has deemed it opportune to establish the following regulations:

Secular clerics or excloistered religious clerics during the period of exclaustration, and secularized religious, who for any reason wish to go from the diocese of Europe to the above-mentioned countries, even for a short time, are strictly bound to obtain permission in writing from this same Sacred Congregation for the Propagation of the Faith. If they go without observing this regulation they will be *ipso facto* suspended *a divinis*.

Ordinaries of places in Australia and New Zealand shall see to it that the above regulations are exactly observed.

In the case of clerics of the nations of Europe who use the English language, it is sufficient that the dismissing Bishop, before giving permission and discessorial letters, deal directly with the accepting Bishop according to the sacred canons, without having recourse to the Sacred Congregation of Propaganda.

When these provisions were reported to His Holiness Pius XII on 21 Oct., 1948, by the undersigned Cardinal Prefect of the S. C. for the Propagation of the Faith, His Holiness ratified and confirmed them and ordered the present Decree on the matter to be issued.

Given at Rome, from the S. C. for the Propagation of the Faith, the 21st of October, 1948.

AAS 41-34; Decree, S. C. Prop. Fid., 21 Oct., 1948.

CANON 117

Priests Emigrating Overseas From Europe: Incardination. See **c. 248**; AAS 44-649, n. 3.

CANON 120

Summoning Before Lay Tribunal: Crime defined. See **c. 2341**; AAS 40-301.

CANON 121

Military Service: Effect on solemn religious vows. See c. 574; two private replies of S. C. Rel., 14 Apr., 1939, and 23 Jan., 1940.

CANON 124

Priestly Virtue: Apostolic Exhortation of Pius XII, *Mentis Nostrae,* 23 Sept., 1950 (AAS 42–657). English text, *The Catholic Mind,* 1951, p. 37. Commentaries: *Monitor Ecclesiasticus,* 1951, p. 47 (Marchetti); *ibid.,* p. 281 (Urbani); *ibid.,* p. 286 (Jarlot); *ibid.,* p. 493 (de Angelis); *ibid.,* p. 643 (Landucci); *ibid.,* p. 656 (Romita).

CANON 129

Apostolic Training for Priests After Ordination: Institute of Saint Eugene in Rome (Pius XII, *Motu proprio,* 2 April, 1949) AAS 41–165.

The full text of this *Motu proprio* is as follows:

Whereas the church which is to be dedicated to Saint Eugene I and the house attached thereto will be ready, God willing, before very long — and We take this occasion to thank warmly all those whose generosity has made this project possible — it is Our wish and will that a parish be established there, to be governed by the same rules and to enjoy the same rights as the other parishes of Rome.

And moreover we intend to establish in those same buildings another institution which We trust will be extremely profitable to the clergy of Rome, always so dear to Us.

For some things are so necessary to the progress of the Christian religion that the condition and growth of the Church depend on them; and one of these certainly is the proper instruction and training of the younger clergy. It is for this reason that not only Our Predecessors but also Bishops in every part of the world have always made this a special object of their efforts. After the Council of Trent, this was accomplished chiefly by establishing in the various dioceses seminaries where chosen young men who had a divine call to the priestly life might be suitably educated.

However, when the newly ordained priests emerge from these houses of study to take up the duties of their calling, even though they be trained in sacred studies and fervently pious, when they feel the breath of the world and are drawn into the midst of the dangers and difficulties of these times, they often find themselves not sufficiently prepared to minister to the increasing needs of the people, and sometimes their spirit falters when they see that they themselves are exposed to the violent attacks of the foes of Christian truth and Christian living.

Young priests, therefore, fresh from ordination, must be trained in the doctrines and techniques which will enable them to exercise with readiness, skill, and alacrity also those new forms of apostolate which are current at the present time.

As everyone knows, the first years of the priesthood, when the sacred ministers emerge from the enclosure of the seminary into the world of men to put into practice what they have learned at school, are a time of special importance and sometimes of no little danger. Upon these years often enough depend the course of their future life and their progress in virtue and priestly work. Hence it is evident how desirable and necessary it is that at the beginning of their sacred service they have the best guides and teachers, who will give them a shining example, not only in doctrinal precepts but also in the exercise of the priestly ministry.

This is not something new in the history of the Church. It is well known what Saint Philip Neri did along this line in Rome, Saint Charles Borromeo in Milan, and what Saint Joseph Cafasso accomplished in Turin in the last century by his promotion of the "ecclesiastical common life"; and many other works and institutions of this sort could be mentioned, which have contributed very strongly to the excellent training of priests.

We have given long consideration to this matter, because it is Our ardent desire that the younger clergy of this Holy City, who are especially and rightly dear to Us, should not lack these advantages; and it is Our wish and will to establish in Rome a Pontifical Institute to which this most weighty charge shall be entrusted. Accordingly by this *Motu proprio* We decree that the buildings above mentioned shall be devoted not only to the new parish but also to the Pontifical Institute for the training of the younger Roman clergy along the lines which We have described.

We moreover establish and decree the following:

I. The Rector of this Pontifical Institute shall be chosen by Us or Our Successors, after hearing from the Cardinal Vicar of Rome.

II. Newly ordained priests of the Holy City shall live there for a certain time to be trained not only in virtue but also in the sacred ministry, and especially in those forms of apostolate which have become current in our time.

III. They are to learn what our times demand, what they need and lack, the dangers and difficulties which they present; and hence they are to be trained in all the appropriate methods by which they may more readily overcome these dangers and meet these needs in a way that is vigorous and suited to our times.

IV. They are to be exercised in sacred preaching and in the teaching of Christian doctrine; hence they are to go at stated times to the parish house, where their work will be properly and advantageously directed.

V. Likewise they are to be exercised under the guidance of the best masters in conducting and administering parochial offices.

VI. They are to live a common life, from which they will receive great spiritual profit.

As We pronounce these decrees We cherish the fondest hope that the priests of the Holy City will find in this Institute, under the influence of divine grace, the means of planning and providing more effectively and abundantly for themselves, for their sacred ministry, and for the people of Rome.

What has been decreed and established by the Letter given of Our own motion, We order to be kept firm and valid, all things to the contrary notwithstanding.

Given at Rome, from Saint Peter's, the second day of April in the year 1949, the eleventh of Our Pontificate.

AAS 41–165; Pius XII, *Motu proprio*, 2 April, 1949.

————

Clerics Studying in Civil Universities: Norms for Italy. See S. C. Sem., 20 Aug., 1942, in *Commentarium pro Religiosis*, 24–3, with annotations by Tabera.

CANON 132

Dispensation From Celibacy: Not authorized by canon 81. See c. 81; AAS 41–158.

CANON 135

Use of the New Latin Version of the Psalms in Reciting the Divine Office (Pius XII, *Motu proprio*, 24 March, 1945) AAS 37–65.

Among the daily prayers by which priests do honor to the majesty and goodness of the Most High God and take care of their own necessities as well as those of the whole Church and the entire world, surely a special place belongs to those exalted poems which the holy prophet David and other sacred writers composed under divine inspiration, and which the Church, following the example of the Divine Redeemer and His Apostles, has constantly used in divine services from the earliest times. The Latin Church received these Psalms from the faithful of the Greek tongue; that is, they were translated from Greek into Latin almost word for word, and in the course of time were industriously corrected and revised again and again, especially by Saint Jerome, the greatest of the Doctors in explaining the Sacred Scriptures. But those acknowledged mistakes of the Greek version itself, by which the sense and force of the primitive text are considerably obscured, have not been so completely removed by these corrections that the sacred Psalms can be easily understood by every one and in all their parts; it is well known that Saint Jerome himself did not consider it enough to have given to those of 'his own tongue that ancient Latin "translation most carefully revised," but that, at the cost of even greater effort, he made a translation of the Psalms into Latin from the very "truth of the Hebrew."[1] This new translation by the holy Doctor did not come into use in the Church; but gradually that revised edition of the old Latin translation, which is called the *Gallican Psalter,* gained such currency that Our Predecessor Saint Pius V deemed it proper to adopt it for the Roman Breviary and thus prescribe it for almost universal use.

The obscurities and mistakes of this Latin version, by no means corrected by Saint Jerome — since his sole purpose was to revise the Latin text according to the more correct Greek codices — have

---

[1] St. Jerome, *Praefatio in Librum Psalmorum iuxta hebraicam veritatem; PL*, XXVIII, col. 1125 (1185), *seq.*

in recent times become more and more conspicuous for a number of reasons: in the first place the knowledge of the ancient languages, especially of Hebrew, has made great progress; also the art of translating has been perfected; finally the rules of meter and rhythm in the Oriental languages have been more profoundly studied, and the laws of the so-called "textual criticism" are better understood. Moreover, the many translations of the Psalms from the primitive texts into modern languages, which have been made in various countries with the approval of the Church, have shown more and more clearly how wonderfully those poems, as they were in their native diction, excelled in crystal clearness, poetic beauty, and breadth of doctrine.

It is no wonder then that not a few priests, who wish to recite the prayers of the Canonical Hours not only with the greatest devotion but also with a fuller understanding of their meaning, have felt the need of having, for their daily reading of the Psalms, a Latin translation which would more clearly reveal the sense intended by the Holy Spirit who inspired them, which would express more perfectly the devout affections of the Psalmist, and would more clearly manifest the beauty of the language and the meaning of the words. This same desire and wish has not only been expressed repeatedly in books written by learned and approved authors and in the commentaries which are issued from time to time, but has also been signified to Us by not a few sacred ministers and Bishops, and even by some Cardinals of the Holy Roman Church. We, for Our part, in view of Our profound reverence for the Sacred Scriptures, judge that every effort should be made to the end that the sense of the Sacred Scriptures as given by the inspiration of the Holy Spirit and expressed by the pen of the sacred writer may be ever more fully opened to the faithful, as We not long ago explained in the Encyclical, *Divino Afflante Spiritu.* Accordingly, though We are far from underestimating the difficulties of the task, and are aware that the translation called the Vulgate is intimately connected with the writings of the holy Fathers and with the explanations of the Doctors of the Church, and that it has attained the highest authority in the Church through the usage of centuries, We have decided to favor these pious desires; and so have ordered that a new Latin translation of the Psalms be prepared, which shall on the one hand closely and faithfully follow the primitive texts, and on the other take account as well as possible of the ancient and venerable Vulgate and other old versions, and weigh their various expressions according to critical standards. For We know full well that not even the Hebrew text has come down to us without any mistakes or obscurities; and that it is therefore necessary to compare it with other texts which have come down to us from antiquity, in order to arrive at a more careful and genuine expression of the sense; nay, that it may sometimes happen that even after all the devices of the art of criticism and the science of languages have been employed, the sense of the words may not be altogether clearly exposed, and it may have to be left to future researches to study the matter as thoroughly as possible and thus throw further light on it. We have no doubt, however, that today, by the assiduous use of all the resources of modern scholarship, a translation can be made which shall express the sense and meaning of the Psalms with sufficient clearness that priests in performing the Divine Office may easily grasp what the Holy Spirit wished to express through the mouth of the Psalmist, and so be effectively stirred and moved by these divine words to a true and genuine devotion.

Now that the new translation which was desired has been made with due care and diligence by the professors of Our Pontifical Biblical Institute, We offer it with paternal affection to all those who are bound to the daily recitation of the Canonical Hours; and, upon full consideration, of Our own motion and with mature deliberation, We permit that, after it shall have been adapted to the Psalter of the Roman Breviary and published by the Vatican Press, they may, if they wish, use it in the public or private recitation of the Office.

In Our pastoral solicitude and paternal affection for the men and women who are devoted to God, We trust that henceforth all may derive from the performance of the Divine Office ever greater light, grace, and consolation, and that thus enlightened and encouraged they may, even in these most trying times of the Church, be more and more disposed to imitate the examples of sanctity which appear so resplendently in the Psalms, and may be moved to cultivate and cherish those sentiments of divine love, strenuous courage, and loving contrition to which, in the reading of the Psalms, the Holy Spirit invites us.

Let what We have decreed and established by these Letters,

given of Our own motion, be valid and firm, all things to the contrary, even such as are worthy of most special mention, notwithstanding.

Given at Rome, from Saint Peter's, the twenty-fourth day of March, in the year nineteen hundred and forty-five, the seventh of Our Pontificate.

AAS 37–65; Pius XII, *Motu proprio*, 24 March, 1945.

Cf. *Periodica*, 34–140 (Ogara).

Use of the New Latin Psalter Outside the Canonical Hours (Bibl. Com., 22 Oct., 1947) AAS 39–508.

The question was asked whether the new translation of the Psalms made from the primitive texts, which, according to the *Motu proprio* of 24 March, 1945,[1] can be used in the daily prayers or Canonical Hours, may be used in other liturgical prayers and ceremonies.

Reply. His Holiness Pius XII, in the audience graciously granted to the undersigned on 22 October, 1947, replied in the affirmative, extending the same faculty to all prayers, liturgical or extraliturgical, provided there is question of reciting or singing the *entire* Psalms outside the Mass.

Rome, 22 Oct., 1947.

AAS 39–508; Bibl. Com., 22 Oct., 1947.

Reading Breviary in English: Permission, asked by a priest for private reasons, to satisfy the obligation of the Breviary by reading it in English, was refused. S. C. Rit., 12 Sept., 1950 (N. I 10/50) (*Monitor Ecclesiasticus*, 1952, p. 448).

CANON 140

Clerics in Rome: Public Theaters, Cinemas, Athletic Exhibitions (Vic. Urb., 1 Feb., 1938) Private.

A Decree of the Cardinal Vicar of Rome, 1 Feb., 1938, approved by the Holy Father, repeats and extends the prohibitions of the

----

[1] Reported above in this volume, under this same canon 135.

earlier decree of 25 May, 1919.[1] The new Decree forbids clerics, seminarians, and students in ecclesiastical colleges from attending public theaters, cinemas, or any other public shows, such as riding and athletic exhibitions.

(Private) ; Vic. Urb., 1 Feb., 1938. See *Bolletino del Clero Romano,* 1938, p. 20.

———

Vacations of Religious. See c. 592; private reply of S. C. Rel., 15 July, 1926.

CANON 142

Business and Trading Forbidden to Clerics and Religious: New Penalty for Violation of This Canon (S. C. Conc., 22 March, 1950) AAS 42–330.

A Decree of the Sacred Congregation of the Council:

It is clear from many documents that secular businesses, especially business and trading, have at all times in the Church been forbidden under severe penalties and censures to clerics who are called to the inheritance of the Lord.

Indeed the Apostle himself in the Second Epistle to Timothy (Chapter II, verse 4) already sounded the warning: "No man, being a soldier to God, entangleth himself with secular businesses." It is no wonder then that the Council of Trent (Sess. XXII, Chapter I, *de reformatione*), treating of these crimes, did not hesitate to decree, "that the copious and useful provisions which have already been enacted by the Supreme Pontiffs and the Sacred Councils to the effect that clerics are to abstain from secular businesses, are in future to be observed under the same or greater penalties, to be imposed at the discretion of the Ordinary."

Accordingly the Code of Canon Law, adhering completely to this tradition, provided, in canon 142, regarding this matter: "Clerics are forbidden to conduct business or trade, either personally or through agents, either for their own benefit or that of other persons." And this prohibition applies also to religious

———
[1] See CANON LAW DIGEST, Vol. 1, p. 54.

according to canon 592. Moreover, the Code armed this pre-scription of law with special sanctions in canon 2380, where it is further provided: "Clerics or religious who, personally or through others, conduct commerce or trading in violation of the provision of canon 142, are to be visited with appropriate penalties by the Ordinary according to the gravity of the case."

To the end that a firmer and more uniform ecclesiastical disci-pline may be had in that matter and that abuses may be fore-stalled, His Holiness Pius XII has deigned to provide that all clerics and religious of the Latin rite mentioned in canons 487–681, not even excepting members of the recent secular Institutes, who conduct trade or business of any kind, even that which consists in exchange of currencies, either in person or through others, whether for their own benefit or that of others, in viola-tion of the provision of canon 142, shall incur, as being guilty of this crime, a *latae sententiae* excommunication specially re-served to the Holy See, and shall in a proper case be further punished by the penalty of degradation.

Superiors who shall have failed to prevent these same crimes according to their office and power, are to be deprived of their office and declared incapable of any office of government or administration.

Finally, for all persons to whose malice or negligence such crimes are attributable, there remains the obligation to make good the damages that have been caused.

All things to the contrary notwithstanding.

Given at Rome, 22 March, 1950.

AAS 42–330; S. C. Conc., Decree, 22 March, 1950. *Periodica*, 39–231 (Abellán); *Commentarium pro Religiosis*, 1950, p. 183; 1951, p. 151, etc. (Gutiérrez); *Monitor Ecclesiasticus*, 1950, p. 171 (***).

CANON 147

Appointment to Ecclesiastical Offices (S. C. Conc., 29 June, 1950) **AAS 42–601.**

A Decree of the S. C. of the Council "on canonical appoint-ments to or provision for ecclesiastical offices and benefices" is as follows:

The Catholic Church is, in virtue of its institution by Christ Himself, a perfect society hierarchically established, whose full and supreme power of government and jurisdiction rests with the Roman Pontiff, the successor of the Blessed Apostle Peter in the primacy. Hence no one can presume to intrude himself or others into ecclesiastical offices and benefices, without a legitimate canonical investiture or provision.

The true rule of canon law in this matter was stated in the first of the Rules of Law in VI° as follows: *"Beneficium ecclesiasticum non potest licite sine institutione canonica obtineri."* And the Council of Trent declared, "that those who undertake to exercise these offices merely at the behest of and upon appointment by the people or secular power and authority, and those who assume the same upon their own authority, are all to be regarded not as ministers of the Church but as thieves and robbers who have entered not by the door" (cap. IV, sess. XXIII, *de reform.*). More, the same Sacred Synod defined as follows: "If any one says . . . that those who are neither duly ordained nor sent by ecclesiastical and canonical authority, but who come from elsewhere, are legitimate ministers of the word and of the Sacraments, let him be anathema" (*ibid.*, can. VII; and cf. also Syllabus of Pius IX, n. 50).

Moreover, the Code of Canon Law has enacted these same principles and also established penalties against transgressors (cf. cc. 2331, § 2; 2334, 1° and 2°; 147, §§ 1 and 2; 332, § 1; 2394).

In order to preserve more inviolate these same sacred principles and at the same time forestall abuses in a matter of such great importance, His Holiness Pius XII has deigned to provide as follows:

An excommunication specially reserved to the Holy See is *ipso facto* incurred:

1) by those who contrive against legitimate ecclesiastical authorities or who attempt in any way to subvert their authority;

2) by anyone who, without a canonical investiture or provision made according to the sacred canons, occupies an ecclesiastical office or benefice or dignity, or allows anyone to be unlawfully intruded into the same, or who retains the same;

3) by those who have any part directly or indirectly in the crimes mentioned in nn. 1 and 2.

All things, even though worthy of special mention, to the contrary notwithstanding.

Given at Rome, 29 June, 1950.

AAS 42–601; S. C. Conc., Decree, 29 June, 1950.

Excommunication as *Vitandus* **Inflicted** for accepting office from lay authority. See **c. 2394**; AAS 42–195.

CANON 148

Privilege of Exercising Powers as Delegate Before Confirmation to Office (Code Com., 5 Aug., 1918) Private.

Among the Capuchins, an elected Provincial or Major Superior may exercise his office as soon as he is elected and before confirmation, as a delegate *a iure* of the General of the Order; but he acquires the title to the office after confirmation.

(**Private**); Code Commission, 5 Aug., 1918; reply to Procurator General. Cf. *Analecta Ordinis Minorum Capuccinorum,* Vol. 34, p. 163; *Constitutiones Fratrum Minorum Capuccinorum,* 1925, n. 149.

CANON 160

Election of Pope: New Apostolic Constitution supplanting the earlier one. See Pius XII, 8 Dec., 1945 (AAS 38–65). Principal change: majority of two thirds *plus one* required for election. For summary of entire document, see Bouscaren and Ellis, *Canon Law, a Text and Commentary,* can. 219.

CANON 175

Acceptance of Election After Confirmation: Right to Annul (Benedict XV, 11 Feb., 1920) Private.

The Order of Preachers addressed the following petition to the Holy Father:

The Superior General of the Order of Preachers, humbly prostrate at the feet of Your Holiness, considering that from the beginning of the Order the practice has been that the decree of election is communicated to the elect only after the confirmation of the election; considering further that canon 175 and the following canons on the notification of the election do not introduce a new law, since they are entirely in agreement with the provisions of the Council of Trent and with the Decretals themselves, earnestly petitions, with the consent of his Council, that Your Holiness, by your supreme authority, deign to approve and declare:

1. That in the Order of Preachers the original practice may be preserved, according to which even to this day, the intimation of the election is given to the elect by the one who confirms the election:

2. That in the Order of Preachers, according to the same original practice, the one who confirms the election has the right to annul it, even though it was conducted according to law, whenever, in his judgment, the annulment would be for the common good of the Order.

Reply. We grant the faculty requested, notwithstanding the provisions of the new law.

(**Private**); Benedict XV, 11 Feb., 1920; reported by Fanfani, *De Iure Religiosorum,* ed. 1920, p. 44, note 4.

CANON 177

Confirmation of Election: When It Can Be Refused
(Code Com., 4 Nov., 1919) **Private.**

The Code Commission was asked:

Whether the one who confirms an election is bound according to canon 177, § 2, to grant the confirmation, if he finds the elect fit and if the election was conducted according to law, or whether he can refuse the confirmation, not at his pleasure, but for the common good according to his judgment.

Reply. In the affirmative to the first part; but if there is a serious reason against the elect, that is a sign that he is not fit for the office, and therefore the Superior can refuse the confirmation.

(**Private**); Code Commission, 4 Nov., 1919. See Fanfani, *De Iure Religiosorum,* ed. 1925, n. 109, p. 126.

CANON 181

Postulation: to Whom to Be Addressed (Code Com., 4 Nov., 1919) **Private.**

The Code Commission was asked:
Whether the instrument of postulation is to be sent to the Provincial, or directly to another who has the faculty to dispense, that is, to the Superior General or to the Roman Pontiff.

Reply. The instrument of postulation, according to canon 181, § 1, can be sent to the Superior who has the right to confirm the election, etc., through the Provincial.

(Private); Code Commission, 4 Nov., 1919. Cf. Fanfani, *De Iure Religiosorum*, ed. 1925, n. 115, p. 132; *Analecta Ord. Praedic.*, 1924, p. 422.

CANON 196

Origin and Nature of Judicial Jurisdiction in the Church. See c. 1553; AAS 37–256.

CANON 197

Certain Canons on Jurisdiction May Apply to Dominative Power of Religious Superiors (Code Com., 26 March, 1952) **AAS 44–497.**

The Code Commission was asked:
Whether the prescriptions of canons 197, 199, 206–209, concerning the power of jurisdiction, are to be applied, unless the nature of the matter or the text or context of the law prevent it, to the dominative power which Superiors and Chapters have in religious Institutes and in Societies of men or women living in common without public vows.

Reply. In the affirmative.
Given at Rome, from Vatican City, 26 March, 1952.

AAS 44–497; Code Com., 26 March, 1952. Annotations, *Monitor Ecclesiasticus*, 1952, p. 418 (Bidagor).

CANON 198

Ecclesiastical Superior of Independent Mission Can Appoint Vicar Delegate (S. C. Prop. Fid., 7 Nov., 1929) **Private.**

Letter of the Cardinal Prefect of the Sacred Congregation of Propaganda:

On the 6th of November, 1919,[1] His Holiness Benedict XV, at the request of the undersigned Cardinal Prefect of the Sacred Congregation for the Propagation of the Faith, granted to Vicars and Prefects Apostolic of Missions the faculty to appoint a Vicar Delegate in the place of the Vicar General, whom in virtue of canon 198 they do not seem to have the power to appoint.

His Holiness granted to the Vicar Delegates named by the Vicars and Prefects Apostolic in practice the jurisdiction and faculties which according to canon law belong to the Vicars General.

Since the aforesaid faculty was explicitly granted only to Vicars and Prefects Apostolic, His Holiness is petitioned to extend it graciously also to the Ecclesiastical Superiors of independent Missions, that is, of those missions which are directly dependent on this Sacred Congregation; and, in order to avoid uncertainties and confusions, to declare at the same time that the canons of the Code of Canon Law which refer to Prefectures and Prefects Apostolic, may be applied, *servatis servandis,* in general also to independent missions and to their Superiors.

In the audience of this morning, His Holiness deigned to grant both requests.

(*Note by the Subsecretary.*) It is not intended to grant the privileges which concern prelatial vestments. The Delegate shall be called "Superior Delegate," as, in the case of a Prefecture Apostolic, he should be called "Prefect Delegate."

(**Private**); S. C. Prop. Fid., 7 Nov., 1929; *Sylloge,* n. 146.

Ecclesiastical Superior of Independent Mission Is an Ordinary, and Bound to Apply the Mass *pro Populo* (S. C. Prop. Fid., 31 Aug., 1934) **Private.**

Letter of the Sacred Congregation of Propaganda to His Excellency, Leo Peter Kierkels, Apostolic Delegate of the East Indies:

In your letter of the 2nd of this month (n. 4008–34), Your Excellency submitted to this Sacred Congregation the question proposed by the Superior of Bellary, whether the Ecclesiastical

---

[1] See CANON LAW DIGEST, Vol. 1, p. 144.

Superior of a Mission *sui iuris* is bound *in justice* to apply the Mass *pro populo* according to canon 339.

The reply of this Sacred Congregation is in the affirmative, for the reason that the Ecclesiastical Superior of a Mission *sui iuris* must be considered an Ordinary. It is true that the Code, as Your Excellency correctly observes, does not mention the "Superiors of Missions" among the Ordinaries; but it must be noted that, although a Mission *sui iuris* cannot be said to be, as a juridical type, a creation posterior to the Code, nevertheless, whereas even before the Code there were in existence some Missions *sui iuris,* it was only after the promulgation of the Code that the practice developed and was adopted by the Sacred Congregation, of erecting such Missions with a determined territory and with their own Ecclesiastical Superior.

(**Private**); S. C. Prop. Fid., 31 Aug., 1934 (Arch. Prop. n. 337–34 prot. rub. 12–6) ; *Sylloge,* n. 187.

The Jurisdiction of the Vicar Delegate Is Ordinary (S. C. Prop. Fid., 16 Nov., 1937) Private.

The Vicar Apostolic of the New Netherlands asked the Sacred Congregation for the Propagation of the Faith:

Whether the jurisdiction in spiritual and temporal matters which the letter of the Sacred Congregation says is practically granted to the Vicar Delegate is of its nature ordinary or delegated jurisdiction.

Reply. The Jurisdiction of the Vicar Delegate is ordinary.

(**Private**); S. C. Prop. Fid., 16 Nov., 1937. See Winslow, *A Commentary on the Apostolic Faculties,* p. 9, note 8.

CANON 199

Dominative Power of Religious Superiors: Application of this canon. See c. 197; AAS 44–497.

Episcopal Delegate *"ad universitatem negotiorum."* See c. 1096; AAS 35–58.

CANON 201

Faculty of Latin Ordinary to Dispense Orientals. See c. 66; private, S. C. Eccl. Orient., 24 July, 1948.

CANON 206

Dominative Power of Religious Superiors: Application of this canon. See
c. 197; AAS 44–497.

CANON 207

Dominative Power of Religious Superiors: Application of this canon. See
c. 197; AAS 44–497.

CANON 208

Dominative Power of Religious Superiors: Application of this canon. See
c. 197; AAS 44–497.

CANON 209

Assisting at Marriage Without Delegation: Prescription of Canon 209 Is to Be Applied (Code Com., 26 March, 1952) AAS 44–497.

The Code Commission was asked:

Whether the prescription of canon 209 is to be applied in
the case of a priest who, lacking delegation, assists at a marriage.

Reply. In the affirmative.

Given at Rome, from Vatican City, 26 March, 1952.

AAS 44–497; Code Com., 26 March, 1952. Annotations, *Monitor Ecclesiasticus,* 1952, p. 411 (Bidagor).

————

Dominative Power of Religious Superiors: Application of this canon. See
c. 197; AAS 44–497.

Doubt of Law Not Admitted as supplying jurisdiction to dispense from
disparity of cult for marriage with a Jew under former Quinquennial
Faculties. See c. 1070; private reply of Holy Office, 4 July, 1952.

CANON 211

Penal Reduction of Priest to Lay State: Association Dissolved (Holy Office, 30 May, 1951) AAS 43–477.

A Notification from the Holy Office:

The Supreme Sacred Congregation of the Holy Office, by
Decree of Wednesday the 17th of January, 1951, reduced to the
lay state the priest Michael Collin, who had already been
dismissed from the Congregation of Priests of the Sacred Heart

of Jesus and was wandering through several dioceses and had often and in various ways violated the Sacred Canons.

And as to the Association calling itself the "Institute of the Apostles of Infinite Love," which the aforesaid priest had dared to establish without the approval of competent ecclesiastical authority, the same Supreme Sacred Congregation has dissolved it and forbidden that it be again established.

Given at Rome, from the Holy Office, 30 May, 1951.

AAS 43–477; Holy Office, Notification, 30 May, 1951.

Equivalent Reduction to Lay State. See c. 955; AAS 42–489.

CANON 215

Establishment of New Prefectures and Vicariates Apostolic and Dioceses in Mission Lands (Instruction, S. C. Prop. Fid., 21 June, 1942) AAS 34–347.

An Instruction of the Sacred Congregation of Propaganda, 21 June, 1942, is as follows:

Before this Sacred Congregation for the Propagation of the Faith decides upon the establishment of new Missions, it is accustomed carefully to demand a report of all information which pertains to the matter. Lest these reports abound in superfluous matter or omit what is necessary, the following points should in future be borne in mind.

1. There should be a brief account of the history of Catholic Missions in the region in question, and the reasons in favor of a new erection should be briefly stated.

2. Give: the *name* of the proposed new Mission and its *grade* (Prefecture, Vicariate, or Diocese); the *surface character* of the area; the *boundaries* of the territory which the new Mission is to comprise, and the degrees of latitude and longitude within which it lies; a chorographic *chart* in colors, and if possible printed. As far as possible it should be arranged that the boundaries of the new Mission be the same as the civil boundaries of the State, Province, or District, etc., or, if convenient, that they be fixed according to tribes or languages. For, though it is clear that divine and human affairs are in different orders, and consequently that the Church, in establishing or changing the

boundaries of Missions, is not bound to follow the civil divisions of territory, yet there should be no hesitancy in conforming to them when the greater facility or convenience of the sacred ministry require it.

3. The forms of civil government should be stated; also the civil divisions of the territory, the number of important cities in the region; the number of inhabitants, of what races and languages; and moreover what is the prospect of success in the preaching of the Gospel among them.

4. The number of Catholics, and whether they practice the faith and the observance of their holy religion.

5. How many missionaries living in the country are available; what is their nationality, what languages they know, and how long they have been in the Missions.

6. Whether there are any native priests; how many; whether they are properly trained.

7. Whether there are any heretics or schismatics in the territory, and whether their errors are widely current.

8. Whether there are, and if so how many, schools or other institutions erected by non-Catholics.

9. Whether the Catholic religion can be freely preached and practiced in those places, and what are the obstacles which may hinder its progress, either on the part of the civil government or of heretics, schismatics, or pagans.

10. Whether the Catholics are grouped together in certain parts of the territory, or scattered throughout the territory and living among non-Catholics.

11. In what city or place it is proposed to establish the residence of the Ordinary; and whether there are in that place a church and residence in which the new ecclesiastical head can stay; if so, in what condition they are.

12. State the number and condition of the churches and chapels which are already erected in the territory; whether they are equipped with sacred furnishings, and whether the Most Blessed Sacrament of the Eucharist can be properly kept at least in the principal churches or chapels; whether they have a rectory attached to them or whether at least a suitable house for the priest can be secured in those places; finally, whether the aforesaid churches have any revenues, and what these are; how the revenues are administered.

13. What revenues can be assigned to the new Mission, and what provision can be made for the support of the Ordinary and the missionaries.

14. Whether the Catholic residents can contribute offerings for the support of the Mission.

15. Whether subsidies can be obtained from the civil government for the maintenance of churches, for the support of priests, and for the endowment of works, without prejudice to the liberty and independence of the Church.

16. Whether there are any catechists, and in sufficient numbers, to help the priests in taking care of the Christian population, and whether they have the necessary instruction.

17. Whether there are, and if so how many, religious Institutes of men or of women already working in the region; in what ministry and works the religious men and women respectively are engaged.

18. Whether there is a seminary for clerics, and whether the necessary means for supporting the young men, giving them a religious education and proper training in religious subjects, can be secured; and if not, whether there is any prospect of sending promising young men to some seminary outside the Mission for their ecclesiastical training.

19. Whether there are any Catholic schools or boarding schools either for boys or girls, especially natives, and whether they admit students of other religions; if there are no such schools, whether they could easily be opened.

20. Whether there are established in the territory any Confraternities, Hospitals, Orphanages, Catechumenates, or other pious places; whether they are properly conducted, how they are supported, and whether they depend exclusively on the authority of the Church.

21. If the new Mission is composed of territory taken away from another Mission, give the name and grade of the latter and also an account of the division of immovable and movable property according to canon 1500.

N.B. — These are the principal points on which, whenever the erection of a new Mission is proposed to this Sacred Congregation, the persons concerned, as well as others who are asked their opinion on the matter, must make a clear and distinct report. This Sacred Congregation will decide whether the circumstances are such as to make the erection advisable for the welfare of the Catholic population and the conversion of non-Catholics.

AAS 34–347; S. C. Prop. Fid., Instruction, 21 June, 1942.

Melbourne Archdiocese: Letter of congratulation on occasion of centenary. See Pius XII, Letter, 6 Apr., 1948 (AAS 40–177).

Organization of Hierarchy in China. See Pius XII, Apost. Const., 11 Apr., 1946 (AAS 38–301).

CANON 216

National Parishes: Competency of Sacred Consistorial Congregation. See c. 248; AAS 44–649, n. 4.

CANON 218

Encyclical, asking prayers for peace. See Pius XII, 18 Dec., 1947 (AAS 39–601).

CANON 230

Dress of Cardinals Modified (Pius XII, *Motu proprio*, 30 Nov., 1952) **AAS 44–849.**

This *Motu proprio* is as follows:

Very much concerned as We are over the peculiar conditions of our times, which laborious experiences and dangers are daily rendering more burdensome and difficult, and which merit the highest consideration and attention because of the aspirations toward which many persons to-day are tending with a certain noble eagerness, We have judged it appropriate and a part of Our duty to respond to the challenge which they present, to all, but in a special way to men belonging to a sacred order, that they accommodate themselves to a somewhat more sober, modest, and austere way of life.

For this reason, even as regards Ourselves, We have chosen to give an example in this matter: for We have modified the external rites which are connected with the fulfillment of Our Apostolic office, by reducing the sacred ceremonies to a simpler and shorter form; and We are very much pleased to observe that all men of judgment in both private and public life, including the clergy, are less interested in external pomp than in an earnest solicitude regarding the necessities of human life.

We are therefore minded to issue certain norms regarding the dress of the Cardinal Fathers, who are at the same time very dear to Us and of such great service to Us in the government of the universal Church. We know that they care little for the curious gaze of the admiring throng, but are interested rather in placing their exalted dignity and authority in the proper light. We know too that they not only abhor vain luxury but rather spend freely on works of charity whatever they have received from the patrimony of the Church or from the pious offerings of the faithful or perhaps from family resources. They know very well that it is according to the wise precepts of the Gospel that superfluous income, even from a rather modest way of life and dress, be used for the benefit of divine worship and works of charity and education.

Wherefore, even while We honor them with this deserved encomium, We believe that We shall facilitate the fulfillment of their laudable designs and Christian resolutions by these norms which by this *Motu proprio* We establish regarding the dress of the Cardinal Fathers:

I. The tail or train is to be removed from both the red and the violet cassock of the Cardinal Fathers.

II. The tail or train of their *cappa,* which is not to be let down either in the Chapels of the Supreme Pontiff or in the Sacred Consistories, is to be reduced to about half of the size which is now in use.

III. Their violet vestments (the cassock, mantelletta, and mozzetta) shall be of wool; however, Cardinals who were already provided with these violet vestments made of silk may continue to wear them at the appointed times.

IV. The rules governing ceremonies in the Roman Curia, relating to the dress of the Cardinals who are appointed to the Sacred College from among Canons Regular, Clerics Regular, or Religious Congregations, are to be restored.

V. These norms shall become effective on the first of January of next year, 1953.

Given at Rome, from Saint Peter's, the 30th of November, First Sunday of Advent, in the year 1952, the fourteenth of Our Pontificate.

AAS 44–849; Pius XII, *Motu proprio,* 30 Nov., 1952.

CANON 239

Apostolic Blessing, not given in Rome, even by Cardinals. See **c. 914;** AAS 36–221.

CANON 247

Special Index of Decisions of the Holy Office

Amplexus Reservatus: See **c. 1081;** AAS 44–546.

Apparitions at Heroldsbach declared not supernatural. See **c. 1261;** AAS 43–561.

Art, Sacred, Instruction on. See **c. 1261;** AAS 44–542.

Assistance at Marriage without guarantees, illicit. See **c. 1102;** private replies of 26 Nov., 1919, and 6 July, 1928.

Association Forbidden and Dissolved. See **c. 211;** AAS 43–477.

Banners of political parties not to be blessed. See **c. 1147;** AAS 29–130.

Baptism: Presumption as to validity in certain sects. See **c. 1070;** AAS 41–650.

Books: Summary of law on prohibition of. See **c. 1395;** AAS 35–144.
     Warning against lascivious and obscene books. See **c. 1395;** AAS 44–432.

"Catholic Action," Spurious, in Czechoslovakia. See **c. 2314;** AAS 41–333.

Catholic Schools: Subject to legitimate ecclesiastical authority. See **c. 1324;** private reply of 8 Aug., 1949.

Cautiones: Given equivalently. See **c. 1071;** private reply of 5 April, 1919; **c. 1067;** 21 Feb., 1949.

Communism: Associations for imbuing children with materialistic principles, condemned. See **c. 2316;** AAS 42–553.
     Doctrines, actions, and writings of Communist Party, condemned. See **c. 2314;** AAS 41–334.
     Marriages of Communists: assistance of priest. See **c. 1065;** AAS 41–428.
     Writings, *ipso iure* forbidden. See **c. 2314;** AAS 41–334.

Constitutions of Canon 1125: Interpreted. See **c. 1125;** private reply of 30 June, 1937.

Copula Dimidiata. See **c. 1081;** private reply of 30 Nov., 1921.

Devotions: Association called *"La Crociata Mariana"* forbidden. Holy Office, 8 March, 1941 (AAS 33–69 and *L'Osservatore Romano,* 31 July, 1937).
     Merciful Love. See **c. 1259;** private reply of 5 April, 1941.

Disparity of Cult: In China. See **c. 1067;** private replies of 27 Jan., 1949, and 21 Feb., 1949.
     Dispensation for marriage with a Jew. See **c. 1070;** private reply of 26 March, 1947.
     In marriage between Oriental dissident and infidel. See **c. 1070;** private replies of 18 May, 1949, and 17 April, 1950.

Dispensation for Marriage With a Jew: Former restrictive clause in Quinquennial Faculties, n. 3, applied to all Jews. See **c. 1070;** private reply of 4 July, 1952; but see also **c. 1070;** private reply of 26 March, 1947.

Documentum Libertatis: See **c. 1099;** private reply of 10 April, 1952; also **c. 1070;** private reply of 26 March, 1947.

Given by Holy Office in "Aut-Aut" case. See **c. 1119**; 27 Nov., 1943, and **c. 1127**; 16 June, 1945.

Ecumenical Movement: Instruction on. See **c. 1325**; AAS 12–142.

Ends of Marriage. See **c. 1013**; AAS 36–103.

Eucharistic Fast for Priests: Norms for dispensation. See **c. 808**; private, 1 July, 1931.

Special indults for France. See **c. 858**; private indult of 23 Oct., 1947, and **c. 867**; private indult of 23 Oct., 1947.

Excommunication Most Specially Reserved: New Penalty. See **c. 2245**; AAS 43–217.

Excommunicatus Vitandus. See **c. 2314**; private, 2 May, 1950.

Faculties: New Formula. See **c. 66**; letters of Ap. Del. U. S., 19 May and 29 June, 1946.

Form of Marriage: Armenian Catholic. See **c. 1**; private, 14 July, 1950.

Born of Catholic parents. See **c. 1099**; private, 3 Jan., 1950.

Born of non-Catholics: Question as to Catholic training. See **c. 1099**; private, 29 March, 1949.

Born of non-practicing Catholics. See **c. 1099**; private, 7 Jan., 1947.

Catholic Baptism in doubt. See **c. 1099**; private, 10 April, 1952.

In China. See **c. 1067**; private replies 27 Jan., 1949, and 21 Feb., 1949.

Maronite Catholic. See **c. 1**; private, 19 April, 1945.

Under *Ne temere.* See **c. 1099**; private, 14 Feb., 1947.

Fresno Case: Dissolution in favor of the faith, where marriage was with dispensation from disparity of cult. See **c. 1127**; private replies of 18 July, 1947, and 30 Jan., 1950.

Gonyklisia in Byzantine Mass. See **c. 818**; AAS 43–217.

Interpellations: Faculty to dispense from, delegated to Ordinaries. See **c. 1121**; 15 Nov., 1934.

Dispensing power of Apostolic Delegate. See **c. 1121**; 17 July, 1935.

Use by Ordinary, of delegated power to dispense. See **c. 1121**; 22 May, 1947.

Marriage: Dissolution of natural bond. See **c. 1125**; private, 25 May, 1933.

Dissolution of marriage contracted with dispensation from disparity of cult. See **c. 1127**; private replies of 18 July, 1947, and 30 Jan., 1950.

Of non-Catholics by proxy. See **c. 1088**; AAS 41–427. Procedure for declaration of nullity in these cases. See **c. 1088**; private reply of 16 Nov., 1949.

See also: **Assistance at Marriage;** *Cautiones;* Sanation; Constitutions of Canon 1125; *Documentum Libertatis;* Ends of Marriage; Interpellations.

Meaning of "Jew" in faculties for disparity of cult. See **c. 1070**; private replies of 7 July, 1943, and 11 April, 1945.

Mitigated Millenarianism, Unsafe. See **c. 1324**; AAS 36–212.

Non-Catholic Admitted as Plaintiff, to attack her non-Catholic marriage on ground of nonage. See **c. 1990**; private reply of 24 May, 1952.

Ordination With False Dimissorial Letters. See **c. 955**; AAS 42–489.

Reduction of Priest to Lay State. See **c. 211**; AAS 43–477, and **c. 955**; AAS 42–489.

Rotary Clubs. See **c. 684**; AAS 43–91.

Rumanian Schism: Leader declared excommunicated. See **c. 2314**; 2 May, 1950.

Sanation of Marriage After Wrong Use of Pauline Privilege. See **c. 1127**; private reply of 19 June, 1947.

Schismatics: Norms concerning sacraments and ecclesiastical burial. See **c. 731**; private, 15 Nov., 1941.

Sterilization Imposed by Unjust Law. See **c. 1068**; private reply of 16 Feb., 1935.

CANON 248

Norms for the Spiritual Care of Emigrants (Pius XII, Apostolic Constitution, 1 Aug., 1952) AAS 44–649.

This Apostolic Constitution of Pius XII occupies 56 pages in the *Acta Apostolicae Sedis*. It consists of two parts or Titles. The first Title, *"De Materna Ecclesiae in Emigrantes Sollicitudine"* is a magnificently documented historical summary of the Church's care of exiles and refugees from the earliest times to the present. Only the second Title, *"Normae pro Spirituali Emigrantium Cura Gerenda"* is reported here, with the last two paragraphs of the first Title by way of introduction.

The text:

We have ardently desired to find an opportunity to give to all local Ordinaries suitable norms, not differing from the laws of the Code but corresponding perfectly to their spirit and practice, and to give them the appropriate faculties, so that they may be able to give to foreigners, whether *advenae* or *peregrini*, in their necessities a spiritual assistance fully equal to that which the other faithful in their dioceses enjoy.

We thought also that it would greatly conduce to the salvation of souls and the improvement of ecclesiastical discipline if We should give a brief historical conspectus consisting of at least the more important things which our Holy Mother the Catholic Church has done, and of the norms still in effect which have been enacted for the care of emigrants from the end of the nineteenth century to our own time; and especially, if, partly abrogating or changing or improving the older norms, We should issue in one document the laws which are suited to present circumstances of place and time by which We intend more fully to provide for the spiritual care of emigrants and all newcomers — a care which We desire to remain especially entrusted to the Sacred Consistorial Congregation, in consideration of its competency over the faithful of the Latin rite. The first part of this plan, We have accomplished above; We now proceed to the second part.

Title II

NORMS FOR THE SPIRITUAL CARE OF EMIGRANTS

CHAPTER I

The Competency of the Sacred Consistorial Congregation Regarding Emigrants

Recognizing, approving, and confirming the regulations which Our Predecessors of happy memory and especially Blessed Pius X established in this matter, but at the same time modifying them somewhat as necessity seems to require, We will and decree that the following laws be observed in future.

1. § 1. It belongs to Our Sacred Consistorial Congregation and to its exclusive competency to examine and prepare whatever makes for the spiritual welfare of emigrants of the Latin rite, to whatever part of the world they may go, taking counsel of the Sacred Congregation for the Oriental Church or of the Sacred Congregation for the Propagation of the Faith, if there is question of emigration to territories which are under their respective jurisdictions.

§ 2. It pertains likewise to the Sacred Consistorial Congregation to examine and prepare the same matters in favor of emigrants of the Oriental rites, similarly consulting the S. C. for the Oriental Church, whenever emigrants of any Oriental rite go to places which are not subject to the Sacred Oriental Congregation and there is no priest of their own rite available.

2. § 1. The Sacred Consistorial Congregation alone will take care of priests of the Latin rite if they emigrate.

§ 2. Priests of the Latin rite who are subject to the S. C. for the Oriental Church or to the S. C. for the Propagation of the

Faith, desiring to emigrate to territories which are not subject to these Sacred Congregations, shall, without prejudice to the rights of these same Sacred Congregations, be bound to observe also the norms which the Sacred Consistorial Congregation has established or may establish in this matter.

§ 3. These same norms shall apply also to priests of the Oriental rites emigrating to territories which are not subject to the S. C. for the Oriental Church, without prejudice to the laws and the rites of this same Sacred Congregation.

3. § 1. 1° When priests desire to migrate from Europe or any Mediterranean country to foreign regions across the ocean, for any space of time, short, long or indefinite, or perpetually, it belongs exclusively to the Sacred Consistorial Congregation to give them permission to go and to remain there or to extend their stay.

2° Nuncios, Internuncios, and Apostolic Delegates can grant this same permission to priests of the nation to which they are permanently assigned, provided this faculty has been given them and been reserved to them.

§ 2. 1° The priests mentioned in § 1, 1° must obtain this same permission in order to be incardinated in a foreign diocese across the ocean, observing the other provisions of law.

2° Religious also need this same permission, except those who are sent by their Superiors to other houses of their Institute; so also do excloistered religious during the time of their exclaustration; as well as secularized religious who have been accepted by a benevolent Bishop either simply and definitely or by way of trial.

§ 3. This permission, however, without prejudice to the other laws established in this Decree, *Magni semper negotii*,[1] shall not be granted unless there is certainty regarding:

1° the testimonials of good conduct of the petitioner;

2° a just and reasonable cause for migrating;

3° the consent both of the Bishop *a quo* or, in the case of religious, of the religious Superior, and of the Bishop *ad quem;*

4° an indult obtained from the S. C. of the Council in the case of pastors, where the absence is to be for more than two months.

§ 4. Priests, whether secular or religious, who, having obtained

---

[1] S. C. Consist., 30 Dec., 1918; AAS 11–39; CANON LAW DIGEST, Vol. 1, p. 93.

permission to migrate to some country across the ocean, wish to go from one jurisdiction to another, even in the same country, need a new permission.

§ 5. Priests who, without observing these laws, rashly and arrogantly emigrate, incur the penalties which are declared in the said Decree, *Magni semper negotii.*[2]

4. Only the Sacred Consistorial Congregation will be able to grant an apostolic indult according to canon 216, § 4, so that parishes for different languages or nationalities may be established for the benefit of emigrants.

5. § 1. It belongs likewise to the Sacred Consistorial Congregation:

1° To approve, upon previous assurance regarding the petitioners' life, morals, and fitness, and with the consent of the Ordinary, priests, secular or regular, who wish to devote themselves to the spiritual care of emigrants of their own nationality or language, and of those who are making an ocean voyage or are on board ship for any purpose or attached to ships in any way; and to appoint, assign, or transfer them to be missionaries of emigrants or chaplains of ships; likewise to accept their resignation from such office and, in a proper case, to deprive them of it;

2° To choose and appoint, in any country, Chiefs or Directors of missionaries for emigrants of that nationality or language;

3° To choose and appoint Chiefs or Directors of ship chaplains;

4° To have the charge and supervision of all these, either through local Ordinaries or through a Delegate for Emigration or through other ecclesiastics to be applied to this office.

§ 2. 1° The grant of the rescript mentioned in § 1, 1° shall be communicated to both the Ordinaries, *a quo* and *ad quem;*

2° The Sacred Consistorial Congregation shall promptly make known the Chiefs or Directors whom it has appointed, to the Bishops of the country or district to which they are sent.

6. § 1. As We approve by Our authority the special Episcopal Boards or Commissions which have been set up in many jurisdictions of Europe and America for the spiritual care of emi-

---

[2] Such priests are *"ipso facto* suspended from sacred functions; if any (which God forbid) notwithstanding dare to perform such functions, they incur an irregularity; and they can be absolved from these penalties only by this Sacred Congregation." *Loc. cit.,* Chap. III, n. 16; AAS 11–43; CANON LAW DIGEST, Vol. 1, p. 97.

grants, and as We would wish that the same wise plan be instituted in other countries, We decree that the priests who are designated by the Bishops as Secretaries of these Boards can be promoted by the Sacred Consistorial Congregation to the office of Directors of the works of emigration in their respective countries.

§ 2. Where these Boards are not yet established, a Director can be appointed by the Sacred Consistorial Congregation from among the priests of the district who are presented by the Bishops.

7. § 1. In order that the work done for emigrants may be made easier, We by these presents erect and establish in the aforesaid Consistorial Congregation a Supreme Council of Emigration.

§ 2. In this Council the President shall be the Assessor of the Sacred Consistorial Congregation itself, and the Secretary shall be the Delegate for works of emigration.

§ 3. To this Council may be admitted:

1° Those priests who, in their country or district, either hold the office of Secretary of the said Episcopal Board for the spiritual assistance of newcomers, or are actually engaged in that spiritual assistance by command of the Bishop;

2° Priests living in Rome, secular or religious, who seem to excel in understanding of and zeal for such matters.

8. § 1. In the same Sacred Consistorial Congregation We wish to erect another board, that is, the General International Secretariate to regulate the Apostolate of the Sea, whose chief work is to advance the spiritual or moral welfare of maritime people, that is, those who board ships either to command or serve, and those who are assigned to ports to do the shore work in connection with ocean voyages.

§ 2. The Assessor of the Sacred Consistorial Congregation shall be in charge of this Secretariate as its President, and the Delegate for works of emigration shall be its Secretary.

§ 3. In this Secretariate the following may be members:

1° Those ecclesiastics who in their respective countries or districts are appointed by the Bishops as Directors of work of this kind;

2° Other priests who have served well in the promotion of this same work, and who are recommended by appropriate testimonials.

Chapter II

The Delegate for Works of Emigration

9. We constitute in the Sacred Consistorial Congregation the office of Delegate for Works of Emigration.

10. § 1. It is the proper function of the Delegate to attend to and promote by all appropriate means especially the spiritual welfare of Catholic emigrants of any language, race or nationality, and, *servatis servandis,* of any rite; for this purpose making arrangements where necessary with Our Secretariate of State or with civil magistrates and institutions.

§ 2. For this purpose the Delegate, in the name and by authority of the Sacred Consistorial Congregation, shall by his cooperation and counsel favor and assist all Catholic associations, institutions, and works, international, national, and — without prejudice to the rights of the Ordinary — diocesan and parochial, which are engaged in the same work.

11. § 1. The Delegate is in charge of the missionaries of emigrants and the chaplains of ships, whether these missionaries and chaplains be seculars or regulars, and of their Directors.

§ 2. He shall take charge of them by order of the Sacred Consistorial Congregation, watch over them and not fail to report on them.

12. The Delegate shall also seek and present to the Sacred Consistorial Congregation priests who wish to devote themselves to the spiritual care of emigrants or of those who have already emigrated, and also of those who are traveling by sea or are for any reason on board ships or attached to ships.

13. § 1. Priests who are approved for this work and who have been appointed by rescript of the Sacred Consistorial Congregation as missionaries of emigrants or chaplains of ships, shall be sent to their mission or ship by the Delegate.

§ 2. The Delegate shall diligently help them with whatever assistance they need, either directly and immediately in person or indirectly through the services of other ecclesiastics, especially of the Directors.

14. The Delegate shall notify Ordinaries of places and Directors regarding emigrants soon to arrive.

15. The Delegate shall seek to promote and regulate whatever

may seem to conduce to the better celebration of the annual day
for emigrants.

16. At the end of each year the Delegate shall draw up and
present to the Sacred Consistorial Congregation a report on the
material and spiritual state of the missions and on the observance
of ecclesiastical discipline on the part of the missionaries of
emigrants and chaplains of ships.

17. § 1. We therefore abolish and suppress and by this Apostolic Letter declare abolished and suppressed the office of Prelate
for Italian Emigrants.[3]

§ 2. Likewise We declare to be entirely withdrawn from their
office the Visitors or Delegates of whatsoever language or nationality, who have previously been appointed for the spiritual
welfare of the faithful who are emigrants or refugees in countries
of Europe or America.

CHAPTER III

Concerning Directors, Missionaries of Emigrants, and Ship Chaplains

18. § 1. Missionaries of emigrants and chaplains of ships, and
their Directors, shall perform their functions under the control
of the Sacred Consistorial Congregation and its Delegate for works
of emigration.

§ 2. The offices of missionary of emigrants and ship chaplain
and the office of Director do not produce excardination and do
not confer any exemption, either from one's own Ordinary or
religious Superior or from the Ordinary of the place where the
missionary or chaplain may happen to be.

19. Directors of missionaries of emigrants and ship chaplains
cannot, in virtue of their office, exercise any jurisdiction either
territorial or personal, except as mentioned below.

20. It is especially the right and duty of the Director:

1° To make arrangements with the Bishops of the country or
district in which the missionaries habitually stay, regarding all
matters which concern the spiritual welfare of emigrants of his
nationality or language;

---

[3] Cf. S. C. Consist., 23 Oct., 1920; AAS 21–534.

2° To have charge of the missionaries or chaplains, without prejudice to the rights of the Ordinaries.

21. § 1. Therefore the Director should inform himself:

1° Whether the missionaries or chaplains are conducting themselves according to the sacred canons and diligently performing their duties;

2° Whether they duly observe the decrees that are issued by the Sacred Consistorial Congregation and by the local Ordinary;

3° Whether proper care is taken for the elegance and neatness of the churches or chapels or oratories and of the sacred furnishings, especially in regard to the custody of the Most Blessed Sacrament and the celebration of Mass;

4° Whether sacred functions are celebrated according to the prescriptions of liturgical laws and the decrees of the S. C. of Rites; whether ecclesiastical property is diligently administered and whether the obligations attached thereto, especially those of Masses, are duly fulfilled; whether the parish books mentioned in nn. 25, § 3 and 35, § 2, are rightly inscribed and preserved.

§ 2. In order to inform himself on these matters the Director must frequently visit the missions or ships.

§ 3. It is also the Director's duty, as soon as he knows that some missionary or chaplain is seriously ill, to see that he does not lack spiritual and material assistance and a decent funeral in case he dies; and to see to it that during the illness or after the death, the books, documents, sacred furnishings, and other things belonging to the mission be not lost or carried off.

22. The Director, for just reasons which are to be approved by the Sacred Consistorial Congregation, may call together wherever he can all the missionaries and chaplains, especially so that they may all make the spiritual exercises together or assist at conferences regarding the better ways of performing their ministry.

23. At least once a year the Director shall faithfully report to the Sacred Consistorial Congregation on the missionaries and chaplains and the state of the missions; stating not only what has been well done during the year, but also what evils have crept in, the remedies that were applied to obviate them and whatever seems to be indicated for the improvement of the missions.

24. Missionaries of emigrants shall apply themselves to the spiritual care of the faithful of their language or nationality under the jurisdiction of the local Ordinary according to the norms which will be stated below in Chapter IV.

25. § 1. It is the proper work of ship chaplains during the voyage to exercise the care of souls, except as regards marriage, for those who are for any reason on board the ship.

§ 2. The chaplains, without prejudice to the provision of canon 883, shall receive special norms and faculties from the Sacred Consistorial Congregation.

§ 3. They are, moreover, bound to keep books of baptisms, confirmations, and deaths, of which they shall present a copy to their Director, together with their report of events, at the end of each voyage.

26. If the ship has a legitimate oratory, ship chaplains are equivalent, with due allowances, to rectors of churches.

27. § 1. Chaplains can perform divine offices, even solemn ones, in the ship's oratory, observing canonical and liturgical laws, and taking care that the services take place at hours which are convenient for the people on board.

§ 2. They shall also:

1° Announce feast days;

2° Give catechetical instructions, especially to the young people, and an explanation of the Gospel.

28. Ship chaplains shall see to it:

1° That in the oratory the divine services be properly performed according to the prescriptions of the sacred canons and that, when priests celebrate Mass, there be no danger of the spilling of the Precious Blood from the chalice, and that another priest, if there is one, assist vested in a surplice.

2° That care be taken for the conservation of the sacred furnishings and the neatness of the oratory;

3° That nothing be done which is in any way contrary to the holiness of the place and the reverence due to the house of God, and that neither the oratory nor the altar or sacred vestments be put at the service of non-Catholics.

29. § 1. Without at least the presumed permission of the chaplain, no one may celebrate Mass in the ship's oratory, nor administer the sacraments, preach, or perform other sacred functions there.

§ 2. Such permission should be given or refused in accordance with the common law.

30. The right to erect and bless an oratory in a ship belongs to the Ordinary of the place to which belongs the port where the ship habitually lies at anchor.

31. Missionaries and chaplains are permitted, with the consent of the Director, and moreover of the Superior, if there is question of a religious, to be away from the mission or ship for one month during the year, provided that the needs of the emigrants or ship's company be provided for through a suitable priest who has a rescript from the Sacred Consistorial Congregation; the same is allowed to Directors with the permission of the Sacred Consistorial Congregation and with the consent of the Superior in the case of religious, provided they leave in their place a substitute approved by the same Sacred Congregation.

CHAPTER IV

*The Care of Souls to Be Exercised by
Local Ordinaries for Foreigners*

32. As regards especially the care of souls to be exercised by local Ordinaries for foreigners of any class, whether *advenae* or *peregrini*, whenever for any reason it does not seem expedient to ask the Sacred Consistorial Congregation for an indult to erect a parish for the particular language or nationality, We decree that local Ordinaries shall hereafter carefully observe the following precepts.

33. Every local Ordinary should earnestly strive to entrust the spiritual care of foreigners or immigrants to priests, secular or religious, of the same language or nationality, namely to missionaries of emigrants who have the special mandate of the Sacred Consistorial Congregation as stated above.

34. Likewise every local Ordinary should try to grant to the said missionaries of emigrants the power of exercising the care of souls for the faithful *advenae* or *peregrini* of the same language or nationality, after having consulted the Sacred Consistorial Congregation and observing the other provisions of law.

35. § 1. A missionary of emigrants endowed with this power is equivalent in the care of souls to a pastor; and therefore he has the same faculties for the good of souls and is bound by the same duties, making due allowances, as pastors have and are bound by according to the common law.

§ 2. He shall therefore, above all, have the parish books mentioned in canon 470, of which at the end of each year he shall send a copy to the pastor of the place and to his Director.

36. § 1. This parochial power is personal, to be exercised only on the persons of the foreigners or immigrants.

§ 2. This same power is cumulative on even terms with that of the pastor of the place, even if it is exercised in a church or chapel or public or semi-public oratory entrusted to the missionary of emigrants.

37. § 1. Every missionary of emigrants, in as far as is possible, should have assigned to him some church or chapel or public or semi-public oratory for the exercise of the sacred ministry.

§ 2. If this is not done, the local Ordinary shall establish regulations according to which the said missionary of emigrants is allowed freely and fully to perform his functions in some other church, not excluding the parish church.

38. Missionaries of emigrants during their office are fully subject to the jurisdiction of the local Ordinary, both as to the exercise of their ministry and as to discipline, without any privilege of exemption.

39. Every foreigner, whether an *advena* or a *peregrinus,* has the full right to go for the sacraments, including marriage, to the missionary of emigrants of his own language or to the pastor of the place.

40. For the purpose under discussion, under the designation of *advenae* or *peregrini* are included:

1° All foreigners — not excepting those who came from the colonies — who are staying in foreign territory for any space of time and for any reason, including studies;

2° Their descendants in the first degree of the direct line, even though they have acquired the rights of nationality.

CHAPTER V

The Spiritual Assistance to Be Given to Emigrants by the Bishops of Italy

41. As this Apostolic See has usually been especially vigilant in the interest of Italians, among whom emigration is more fre-

quent than in other nations,[4] We by this Apostolic Letter confirm
and warmly recommend to the zeal of the Italian Bishops, which
We well know, those special norms which Our Predecessors
issued regarding Italians emigrating to foreign lands; and We
take this occasion earnestly to exhort the aforesaid local Ordinaries to do all they can to satisfy Our wishes.

42. Let them keep in mind as their rule in undertaking and
accomplishing this work, these words in which Blessed Pius X
recommended the formation of groups of associates and patrons
to help emigrants: "There were throughout Italy a goodly number of committees, as they are called, and associations of patrons,
for the benefit of emigrants, as well as other organizations of
the same sort established by Bishops and others of the clergy,
and also by lay people of great charity and well versed in
Christian wisdom."[5]

43. Let Ordinaries, therefore, see to it that committees and
sub-committees on emigration be established, especially in dioceses from which there are rather large numbers of emigrants;
these committees should be started by their authority and kept
under their control, but with the cooperation of the members of
Catholic Action and other Catholic groups for the religious,
moral, and social assistance of skilled and unskilled workers.

44. Let them likewise with due alacrity see to it that the committees on emigration so constituted rightly perform their allotted
task and that they strive to attain their purpose, that is, the
salvation of souls.

45. § 1. Local Ordinaries must not fail to instruct pastors to
attend to this part of their ministry with the usual diligence and
to take measures to protect the faithful against the spiritual
dangers which are wont to assail them from the first moment
of their departure from their home, family, and country.

§ 2. To this end, pastors must be zealous in giving suitable
catechetical instruction to the faithful who are about to emigrate.

46. Likewise Ordinaries must not fail to exhort pastors to
follow with their pastoral solicitude the faithful who have
emigrated.

47. The following precepts of the Sacred Consistorial Congregation should be religiously observed: "The Ordinaries of

---

[4] Cf. Pius X, *Motu proprio, Iam pridem,* 19 March, 1914; AAS 6–173.

[5] *Loc. cit.,* p. 174.

Italy, especially through the pastors or the associations which take care of emigrants, shall see to it that those who travel or emigrate be provided with an ecclesiastical card of identification before their departure."[6]

48. They must do their best, using the means that seem most effective, to bring to a happy and successful issue both the annual celebration of the day for Italian emigrants and the collection for the spiritual assistance of emigrants, which is then to be sent to the Sacred Consistorial Congregation.[7]

49. § 1. We congratulate those Ordinaries of dioceses outside Italy, whether in Europe or in countries overseas, who are striving through national or diocesan organizations, councils, or committees to provide spiritual and moral assistance to all the foreigners whom they have received as members of their own flock; and We ask that, in parishes where all or the majority of the faithful are of the Italian race, they have every year the celebration of the day for Italian emigrants as provided in n. 48 for the Ordinaries of Italy, and see that the money collected be sent to the Sacred Consistorial Congregation to promote the work for Italian emigrants.[8]

§ 2. The same thing with such adaptations as the case may require, may be done for emigrants of other nationalities or languages, so that the day for emigrants may be celebrated at one and the same time throughout the Catholic world, namely on the first Sunday of Advent.

50. Finally, the Italian Ordinaries will please urge the pastors in due time to apply one Mass a year for the intention of the Supreme Pontiff instead of *pro populo;* and exhort them to make this change faithfully and freely for the benefit of Italian emigrants.

---

[6] S. C. Consist., 26 Jan., 1923; AAS 15-112; CANON LAW DIGEST, 1, p. 499.

[7] Cf. S. C. Consist., Circular Letter to Ordinaries of Italy, 6 Dec., 1914; AAS 6-699.

[8] Cf. S. C. Consist., Letter to the Ordinaries of America, 22 Feb., 1915; AAS 7-145.

CHAPTER VI

The Pontifical College of Priests for Italian Emigrants

51. Our College of Priests which has been established for Italian emigrants[9] is hereby recognized and confirmed.

52. § 1. We desire this College to remain dependent upon the Sacred Consistorial Congregation — without, however, interfering with the jurisdiction of the Cardinal Vicar of Rome.

§ 2. It shall be the duty of the Sacred Consistorial Congregation:

1° To govern the College and watch over it both as regards the observance of discipline and its economic management and the administration of property;

2° To make laws for it;

3° To appoint the Rector and other officials.

53. Since the special purpose of the College, namely to prepare young Italian priests of the secular clergy to cultivate proper religious relations with and to help Italian emigrants,[10] is in perfect harmony with the purpose of the Pious Society of Missionaries of St. Charles for Italian Emigrants, We permit that the Rector and other governing officials and masters be chosen from among the priests of that Pious Society, and accordingly We freely entrust the College to that Society during Our good pleasure, without prejudice, however, to the provisions of the preceding number.

54. We enjoin moreover that in future no priest be given spiritual charge of Italian emigrants unless he has been suitably prepared for the work in the aforesaid College for a sufficient time, and has been found to possess the spiritual and mental qualities, the learning, skill in speaking, good health, and other qualities which are required for it.

55. Bishops, especially of those dioceses from which many emigrants depart, may be assured that they will do a thing very useful to the cause of religion and very pleasing to Us, if they send to this College some young priests who are outstanding in

---

[9] Cf. Pius X, *Motu proprio, Iam pridem,* 19 March, 1914; AAS 6–173; S. C. Consist., *Notificatio, Sacerdotum Collegium,* 26 March, 1921; AAS 13–309.

[10] Cf. S. C. Consist., 24 June, 1914; AAS 6–547.

virtue and zeal for souls and who desire to devote themselves entirely to work for emigrants.

56. Finally, in other places or nations outside Italy, from which there is emigration, and where perhaps there is not sufficient spiritual assistance for the Catholic emigrants from that nation, the Ordinaries would certainly act wisely if, taking into account the special circumstances of the country, they should earnestly adopt for their emigrants the procedures which have been mentioned in connection with emigrants from Italy, which are more fully publicized in the acts of the Roman Pontiffs and which We hereby approve.

Given from Castel Gandolfo near Rome, on the first day of August, Feast of Saint Peter in Chains, in the year 1952, the fourteenth of Our Pontificate.

AAS 44–649; Pius XII, Apostolic Constitution, 1 Aug., 1952. Annotations, *Periodica,* 41–318 (Fábregas) ; *Homiletic and Pastoral Review,* January, 1953 (Wycislo).

CANON 250

Vatican Institute for Charitable and Religious Works Incorporated as a Cardinalitial Commission Independent of the S. C. of the Council (Pius XII, 27 June, 1942) AAS 34–217.

Our Predecessor of venerated memory Leo XIII, for the purpose of preserving and administering the capital of pious foundations, after a careful study by a number of Cardinals whom he appointed to consider the matter, established a Commission of Cardinals which took the name of Commission *ad pias causas.* For the functioning of this Commission, he approved, on February 11, 1887, an Ordinance which remained in force until August 10, 1904, when Our Predecessor of holy memory Pius X, saw fit to approve a new Ordinance.

On 24 November of the same year 1904, the Commission *ad pias causas* took the name of the Cardinalitial Commission for the Works of Religion. This name it retained until 1908, when, according to the competency assigned to the Sacred Congregation of the Council by the Constitution *Sapienti consilio,* some of the charges theretofore exercised by the Commission passed to the said Sacred Congregation, and the Commission accordingly ceased to be Cardinalitial and became Prelatial.

Later, certain administrative considerations induced the S. C.

of the Council, with a special mandate of Our venerated Predecessor Pius XI, on 10 February, 1934, to approve by way of experiment a Statute for the Prelatial Commission Administering the Works of Religion.

Later still, on 17 March, 1941, the Cardinal Prefect of the same Sacred Congregation of the Council submitted to Us, and We approved, a Statute for the Administration of the Works of Religion — a new name for the same aforesaid Commission. Under this Statute the Administration was entrusted to a Commission of Cardinals.

A special meeting of Cardinals held on 18 January of the current year, 1942, has now expressed the wish that the aforesaid Administration of the Works of Religion should be constituted as a juridical person, for the purpose of giving it an organization more in accord with the needs of the times, and also in order to make it even more expressly clear that the responsibility of the aforesaid Administration is separate and distinct from that of the Offices of the Holy See, as the Holy See itself has always definitely desired.

Having decided after mature consideration that We can accede to this proposal, We now by Our Authority dispose as follows:

I. There is established and erected in Vatican City the Institute for the Works of Religion, which has a juridical personality and absorbs the Administration of the Works of Religion.

II. The purpose of the Institute is to provide for the custody and administration of capital (in securities or in money) and immovable property, which have been transferred or entrusted to the said Institute by physical or moral persons and are destined for works of religion or of Christian piety.

III. The dispositions of the Statute for the Administration of the Works of Religion, approved by Us on 17 March, 1941, remain in force and are to be applied to the Institute for the Works of Religion, in as far as they are not contrary to this Our present Chirograph and as long as it is not decided to amend them.

The Commission of Cardinals to which was entrusted the Administration of the Works of Religion assumes the supervision of the Institute. The Administrative Office of the Administration of the Works of Religion becomes the Administrative Office of the Institute.

IV. For all juridical purposes the Institute is represented

jointly by the Cardinal President of the Administrative Office and the Monsignor Secretary of the same Office.

V. The Institute shall continue to use, under lease, the offices hitherto occupied by the Administration of the Works of Religion, and shall for this purpose negotiate a contract with the Administration of the Property of the Holy See.

VI. Any disposition contrary to this Our present Chirograph is abrogated.

VII. This Chirograph shall be published in the *Acta Apostolicae Sedis*.

Given from the Apostolic Palace of the Vatican, the 27th of June, in the year 1942, the fourth of Our Pontificate.

AAS 34–217; Pius XII, Chirograph, 27 June, 1942.

Forbidden Writings: A Slovenian magazine was declared *ipso iure* forbidden under canon 1399 by the S. C. of the Council. S. C. Conc., 12 April, 1949 (AAS 41–221).

CANON 251

Sacred Congregation of Religious: Special Commission for Education of Aspirants, Novices, and Younger Religious (S. C. Rel., 24 Jan., 1944) **AAS 36–213.**

A Decree of the Sacred Congregation of Religious is as follows:

To the end that the S. C. of Religious may be able more effectively and fruitfully to perform the duty assigned to it by canon 251, His Holiness Pius XII, in the audience granted to the undersigned Secretary on 24 January, 1944, deigned to approve by his Apostolic authority the erection and establishment in this S. C. of a special Body or Commission of chosen men, which shall deal with all questions and matters pertaining in any way to the religious and clerical education and to the training in literature, science, and ministry, of aspirants, novices, and junior members of all religious institutes and societies living in common without vows.

The newly erected Commission shall have especially the following duties:

a) To define and outline the principal criteria and peculiar characteristics according to which the education and training of religious must always be conducted;

b) To watch over the ordinances which are enacted by Superiors and Chapters in matters which concern education and instruction; and to inspect and review the reports made on this matter by Superiors and Apostolic Visitors.

The Commission shall be convoked in ordinary or extraordinary sessions, plenary or partial, as the nature and importance of the business may require. The sessions shall be held under the presidency and direction of the Secretary of the Sacred Congregation. The discussions and decisions shall be duly entered in the record.

The Officials of the Sacred Congregation shall gather, arrange, and properly prepare all matters which are to be considered by the Commission and which are to be presented for study and examination to the individual members of the Commission or to experts; and they shall also preserve in the Archives the records and documents pertaining to the Commission, see to the execution of the decisions taken, under the direction of the President, and put into practice and expedite other matters pertaining to the work of the Commission.

All things to the contrary, even such as are worthy of special mention, notwithstanding.

Given at Rome, from the S. C. of Religious, January 24, 1944.

AAS 36–213; S. C. Rel., Decree, 24 Jan., 1944.

Periodica, 33–245 (Creusen).

NOTE: In order to implement this Decree, a Letter of the S. C. of Religious, 10 June, 1944 (N. 2090/44) was sent to a certain number of religious Major Superiors, together with a list of questions to be answered. These documents are published in *Periodica,* 33, p. 246.

Course of Practical Study: Established in S. C. of Religious. S. C. Rel., 23 Oct., 1951 (AAS 43–806).

Secular Institutes. See c. 488; AAS 39–114. Even in missions, are under exclusive jurisdiction of the Sacred Congregation of Religious. See c. 448; AAS 40–293, n. 2.

Sisters Caring for Men Patients. See Circular Letter of S. C. Rel., 12 Sept., 1940, reported by Sartori, *Enchiridion Canonicum,* ed. 1944, p. 56; cf. *Perfice Munus,* 1940, p. 117.

Sisters Caring for the Sick: Special office in S. C. Rel. See S. C. Rel., 25 July, 1932, reported by Sartori, *Enchiridion Canonicum,* ed. 1944, p. 55.

CANON 252

"The Apostolic Work Society": General Council for Ireland established in Dublin. See c. 721; AAS 40–423.

Collecting Money for the Missions: Instruction. See c. 622; AAS 44–549.

Religious Congregation Subject to Propaganda. A Congregation of pontifical right was declared to be proximately under the jurisdiction of this Sacred Congregation. See S. C. Prop. Fid., 2 Dec., 1942 (AAS 35–26).

CANON 256

North American College Re-established in Rome (Pius XII, Letter, 18 Feb., 1948) **AAS 40–108**.

This Letter addressed to the Cardinals, Archbishops, Bishops, and local Ordinaries of the United States, is as follows:

Beloved Sons and Venerable Brethren:

The approaching re-establishment here in Our dear Rome of the North American College, the knowledge of whose reopening has been communicated to Us by the Rector, affords Us the welcome opportunity of addressing Our paternal words to you, the Members of the Hierarchy of the United States. We rejoice not only in the fact that after a lapse of eight years you are once more sending your chosen young men to study in Our beloved City, to imbibe the sacred wisdom of Holy Mother the Church at its very source and to be nourished at the very heart of the Catholic world, but that you are also planning to erect in the very shadow of Our own dwelling a new and greater seminary to care for ever more young levites from America.

It was Our Predecessor of blessed memory, Pius IX, who nearly one hundred years ago first proposed to the American Bishops that they establish a national seminary in Rome, and it was the same Pontiff who purchased and graciously granted the use of the edifice that has housed the American students ever since that time.

Surely there is evident the hand of Divine Providence in the fact that the first steps were taken on the occasion of the definition of the dogma of the Immaculate Conception and that the College itself was opened for the first time on the very eve of the feast, on December 7th, 1859. And since that day Our Heavenly Mother, Queen of the Clergy, has never ceased to bless with every manifestation of divine favor a work that is of necessity so close to her maternal heart. The students nurtured in tender love of their Mother and Queen, developed in the image of her Divine Son, enlightened in the sacred sciences learned at the feet of Christ's Vicar, made strong and courageous by their close association with the places sanctified by the Prince of the Apostles and the martyrs, have returned to their own country to win ever greater triumphs for Christ and His Holy Spouse. As pastors and teachers, as administrators and also as

Bishops of the Church in America the men trained here have always been marked by a special loyalty to Us and to Our illustrious Predecessors, an inevitable consequence of their sojourn in this City, the See of Peter and of Peter's Successors.

Today as We look about the City of Rome We see on all sides the flower of the youth of the world, even from the most distant nations, drawn here by a common faith, sustained by common ideals, being trained in the same doctrine, sharing the same Divine Sacrifice, and all united by the same bonds of attachment to Us. Surely they are giving to the leaders and to the peoples of every land a magnificent example of unity and of the ability of mankind to live together in Christian peace and concord. The concurrence of so many thousands of men, later destined to play such an important part in the salvation of souls over the whole face of the earth, is a great consolation to Us; and it should be to you, Beloved Sons and Venerable Brethren, a reason especially appealing at this time, to be prompt in making every sacrifice necessary to maintain and even to enlarge the national seminary of your country.

So it is with particular joy that We have learned of your proposals to erect an even finer seminary and to plant your roots even closer to Us. Your wisdom and courage to look to the future and to plan for almost three hundred of your seminarians to study in Rome represent a most worthy initiative that can elicit only Our warmest commendation. At the same time you are keeping a close tie with your old and honored traditions in putting the former college building to use as a house of studies for priests wishing to train themselves in the higher branches of the sacred sciences. Both of these projects call forth Our heartiest approval and support; and the return in grace and wisdom that will accrue to the Church in America will amply reward the expenditures and sacrifices that are necessarily involved in their realization.

The united action taken in this matter by the American Hierarchy, always so ready and generous in their support of all measures for the extension of the Kingdom of Christ, once more demonstrates the flourishing condition of the Faith in your great nation. We are sure that the Bishops and priests and people will rally to the support of a cause which promises so much for the Church and which is so close to Our own heart. Already an abundant and fruitful harvest for God and for souls has been garnered from the past eighty-nine years of the existence of the North American College: and now your decisions for the future give abundant hope that succeeding generations will continue, in greater measure and with more ample facilities, to enjoy the richest blessings stemming from a priesthood nourished in the Eternal City.

With great joy then We give Our blessing to the plans that have been made known to Us by the Rector for the future of your seminary. We shall follow their unfolding and their realization with intimate pleasure and personal interest, and as a token of Our encouragement in the great task that lies ahead, We impart to you, Beloved Sons and Venerable Brethren, as also to the priests and the faithful of the United States, Our paternal Apostolic Benediction.

Given at the Vatican on the eighteenth day of February one thousand nine hundred and forty-eight, the ninth year of Our Pontificate.

AAS 40–108; Pius XII, Letter, 18 Feb., 1948.

Irish College in Rome: Declared "Pontifical." See S. C. Sem. et Univ., Decree, 25 Jan., 1948 (AAS 40–158).

Lithuanian College in Rome, erected. See S. C. Sem. et Univ., 1 May, 1948 (AAS 40–298).

Pontifical Work for Priestly Vocations: Statuta and Norms. See S. C. Sem. et Univ., 8 Sept., 1943 (AAS 35–369).

CANON 258

Validation of Marriage by Sacred Penitentiary. See c. 1040; private reply of 1927.

CANON 260

Vatican City: Institute for works of religion established. See Pius XII, 24 Jan., 1944 (AAS 36–45).

CANON 267

Letter of His Holiness Pius XII to President Truman
(Pius XII, 26 Aug., 1947) **AAS 39–380.**

Your Excellency:
We have just received from the hands of your personal

representative, Mr. Myron Taylor, Your Excellency's letter of August 6, and We hasten to express Our satisfaction and thanks for this latest testimony to the desire and determination of a great and free people to dedicate themselves, with their characteristic confidence and energy, to the noble task of strengthening the foundations of that peace for which all peoples of the earth are longing. As their chosen leader Your Excellency seeks to enlist and cement the co-operation of every force and power which can help to accomplish this task. No one more than We will hope for its success; and for the happy achievement of the goal We pledge Our resources and earnestly beg God's assistance.

What is proposed is to ensure the foundations of a lasting peace among nations. It were indeed futile to promise long life to any building erected on shifting sands or a cracked and crumbling base. The foundations, We know, of such a peace — the truth finds expression once again in the letter of Your Excellency — can be secure only if they rest on bed-rock faith in the one, true God, the Creator of all men. It was He who of necessity assigned man's purpose in life; it is from Him, with consequent necessity, that man derives personal, imprescriptible rights to pursue that purpose and to be unhindered in the attainment of it. Civil society is also of divine origin and indicated by nature itself; but it is subsequent to man and meant to be a means to defend him and to help him in the legitimate exercise of his God-given rights. Once the State, to the exclusion of God, makes itself the source of the rights of the human person, man is forthwith reduced to the condition of a slave, of a mere civic commodity to be exploited for the selfish aims of a group that happens to have power. The order of God is overturned; and history surely makes it clear to those who wish to read, that the inevitable result is the subversion of order between peoples, is war. The task, then, before the friends of peace is clear.

Is Your Excellency over-sanguine in hoping to find men throughout the world ready to co-operate for such a worthy enterprise? We think not. Truth has lost none of its power to rally to its cause the most enlightened minds and noblest spirits. Their ardor is fed by the flame of righteous freedom struggling to break through injustice and lying. But those who possess the truth must be conscientious to define it clearly when its foes cleverly distort it, bold to defend it and generous enough to set the course of their lives, both national and personal, by its dictates. This will require, moreover, correcting not a few aberrations. Social injustices, racial injustices, and religious animosities exist today among men and groups who boast of Christian civilization, and they are a very useful and often effective weapon in the hands of those who are bent on destroying all the good which that civilization has brought to man. It is for all sincere lovers of the great human family to unite in wresting those weapons from hostile hands. With that union will come hope that the enemies of God and free men will not prevail.

Certainly Your Excellency and all defenders of the rights of the human person will find whole-hearted co-operation from God's Church. Faithful custodian of eternal Truth and loving mother of all, from her foundation almost two thousand years ago, she has championed the individual against despotic rule, the laboring-man against oppression, Religion against persecution. Her divinely-given mission often brings her into conflict with the powers of evil, whose sole strength is in their physical force and brutalized spirit, and her leaders are sent into exile or cast into prison or die under torture. This is history of today. But the Church is unafraid. She cannot compromise with an avowed enemy of God. She must continue to teach the first and greatest commandment incumbent on every man: "thou shalt love the Lord thy God with thy whole heart, with thy whole soul, with all thy strength," and the second like unto the first: "thou shalt love thy neighbor as thyself." It is her changeless message, that man's first duty is to God, then to his fellow-man; that that man serves his country best who serves his God most faithfully; that the country that would shackle the word of God given to men through Jesus Christ helps not at all the lasting peace of the world. In striving with all the resources at her power to bring men and nations to a clear realization of their duty to God, the Church will go on, as she has always done, to offer the most effective contribution to the world's peace and man's eternal salvation.

We are pleased that the letter of Your Excellency has given Us the opportunity of saying a word of encouragement for all those who are gravely intent on buttressing the fragile structure of peace until its foundation can be more firmly and wisely established. The munificent charity shown by the American people to the suffering and oppressed in every part of the world, truly worthy of the finest Christian traditions, is a fair token of their sincere desire for universal peace and prosperity. The vast majority of the peoples of the world, We feel sure, share that desire, even in countries where free expression is smothered. God grant their forces may be united towards its realization. There is no room for discouragement or for relaxing of their efforts. Under the gracious and merciful providence of God, the Father of all, what is good and holy and just will in the end prevail.

Let Us assure Your Excellency of Our cordial welcome to Mr. Taylor, your personal representative, on his return to Rome; and We are happy to renew the expression of Our good wishes for the people of the United States, for the members of their government and in particular for its esteemed Chief Executive.

From Castel Gandolfo, August 26, 1947.

AAS 39–380; Pius XII, Letter to President Truman, 26 Aug., 1947.

Dispensation from Interpellations: Faculty of Ap. Del., U. S. See c. 1121; Holy Office, 1935, and Letter of Apostolic Delegate, 17 July, 1935.

    Questionnaire for application to Apostolic Delegate for this dispensation. See c. 1121; Ap. Del., U. S.

Recourse to Holy See through Apostolic Legate. See c. 81; AAS 39–374.

Religious: New Faculties of Apostolic Delegate regarding. See c. 858; Letter of Ap. Del., 3 Apr., 1947.

CANON 294

Apostolic Faculties: Interpretation. See c. 1165; private reply of S. C. Prop. Fid., 30 Jan., 1930.

Superior of Independent Mission: Can appoint Vicar Delegate. See c. 198; S. C. Prop. Fid., 7 Nov., 1929.

    Must apply Mass *pro populo*. See c. 198; S. C. Prop. Fid., 31 Aug., 1934.

CANON 305

Native Clergy. See Pius XII, Exhortation, 28 June, 1948 (AAS 40–374). This exhortation was delivered to the students resident at the College of St. Peter, on the Janiculum in Rome, which was founded as a residence for young priests coming from mission countries to Rome after their ordination, to take special studies and receive degrees, attending classes at the College of Propaganda. For further documents on the native clergy, see CANON LAW DIGEST, Vol. 1, pp. 462 and 656.

CANON 332

Occupying or Retaining Office Without Canonical Provision: Penalty. See c. 147; AAS 42–601.

CANON 335

Spiritual Care of Emigrants: Duty of Bishop. See c. 248; AAS 44–649.

CANON 339

Ecclesiastical Superior of Independent Mission: Must apply Mass *pro populo*. See c. 198; S. C. Prop. Fid., 31 Aug., 1934.

CANON 349

Episcopal Arms: Civil Titles of Nobility Excluded (S. C. Consist., 12 May, 1951) AAS 43–480.

A Decree of the Sacred Consistorial Congregation entitled "Concerning the prohibition against the use of civil titles of nobility in the inscriptions and coats of arms of Bishops":

In view of the dispositions which were long ago adopted concerning the use of titles and symbols of family nobility in the inscriptions and coats of arms of Bishops, namely, the Apostolic Constitution, *Militantis Ecclesiae*, of 19 Dec., 1644, and the Decree of the Sacred Consistorial Congregation of 15 Jan., 1915 (AAS 7–172), His Holiness by Divine Providence Pope Pius XII, deeply convinced that such secular titles or signs of nobility have lost their former juridical basis and are out of accord with the conditions of the world to-day, has deemed it altogether appropriate to modify the old regulations and to establish new ones.

Wherefore, by this present Consistorial Decree, His Holiness has deigned to ordain that all Ordinaries in their seals and insignia or coats of arms, as well as in the inscriptions of their letters and edicts, shall hereafter entirely abstain from the use of titles of nobility, coronets, or other secular symbols, even if such titles and the like are attached to the episcopal or archiepiscopal see.

All things, even such as are worthy of most special mention, to the contrary notwithstanding.

Given at Rome, from the Sacred Consistorial Congregation, 12 May, 1951.

AAS 43–480; S. C. Consist., 12 May, 1951. Annotations, *Monitor Ecclesiasticus*, 1951, p. 600 (Oesterle).

Dress of Bishops and Prelates Also Governed by *Motu Proprio* on Dress of Cardinals (S. C. Rit., Decree, 4 Dec., 1952) AAS 44–888.

A Decree of the Sacred Congregation of Rites:

After the appearance of the *Motu proprio, Valde solliciti*, of 30 Nov., 1952, on the dress of the Most Eminent Cardinals of the Holy Roman Church,[1] the following questions were presented for solution and declaration to the Sacred Congregation of Rites:

1. Are the provisions of the said *Motu proprio* regarding the cassock and the *cappa* of the Most Eminent Cardinals to be applied to the cassocks and *cappa* of Patriarchs, Archbishops, and Bishops of the Holy Roman Church and to Abbots, secular or regular, who have those privileges?

2. Should the cassocks of Prothonotaries, Prelates, and others who enjoy the privileges of Prelates, also be without a train or tail?

The Sacred Congregation of Rites, carefully considering that the same reasons which are mentioned in the *Motu proprio* are valid also in the case of Bishops and others, decided, upon the mandate of His Holiness to reply:

Reply. In the affirmative to both.

And so it replied, declared, and ordered to be done by all; all things to the contrary notwithstanding, even though worthy of special mention.

Given at Rome, from the Secretariate of the Sacred Congregation of Rites, 4 Dec., 1952.

AAS 44–888; S. C. Rit., Decree, 4 Dec., 1952.

CANON 396

Reservation of Dignities, Canonries, and Minor Benefices: Extinction of Right of Patronage (S. C. Conc., 29 Nov., 1944) AAS 37–118.

Facts. Pius VII, in the act of erection of the diocese of C,

---

[1] AAS 44–849, reported in this volume under canon 230.

granted to the municipality of the town of that name, which had endowed the cathedral Chapter, the right of patronage, including all dignities. The municipality formally and perpetually renounced this right of patronage in favor of the Bishop, in 1912. Since that time the Bishops of C, supposing that a lay right of patronage still existed, have been freely conferring not only canonries and minor benefices but dignities also, notwithstanding the reservations mentioned in canons 396, § 1, and 1435, § 1. They supposed that the nature of the lay right of patronage remained unchanged and that only its subject was changed (the Bishop being substituted for the municipality).

Remarks. 1. According to canon 1449, 2°, a right of patronage is lay or ecclesiastical according as the title by which the possessor has it is lay or ecclesiastical (citing Wernz-Vidal, *De Personis*). When a lay right of patronage is transferred to an ecclesiastical person, the title is changed, and, according to canonists and the practice of the Apostolic Datary, the right of patronage *eo ipso* becomes an ecclesiastical one (citing Viviani, *Praxis Iurispatronatus;* Pihring, *Ius Canonicum;* Barbosa, *Ius Ecclesiasticum Universum;* De Fargna, *Comm. in Singulos Canones de Iurepatronatus;* Riganti, *Comm. in Regulas Cancelleriae Apostolicae*).

2. In the present case, however, we have not a mere transfer of the right of patronage, but rather a formal and perpetual renunciation of it, as is expressly stated in the agreement between the municipality and the Bishop. Indeed there could be no transfer of the right of patronage in this case, since it is impossible that the same person (in this case the Bishop) should be at the same time the patron and the one who confers the benefice, for this would mean that he would present the candidate to himself and then confer the benefice on him. The extinction of the right of patronage is confirmed, in accordance with canon 18, by the parallel passages which are found in canons 1451, § 1, and 1470, § 1, 5°. If, for example, a patron renounces his right of patronage to the Bishop in order to receive spiritual suffrages according to canon 1451, § 1, no one would say that the right of patronage is transferred to the Bishop. And canon 1470, § 1, 5°, states expressly: "A right of patronage is extinguished . . . if with the consent of the patron the church or benefice is united to another one which is of free appointment, or if the church

becomes subject to the election of its incumbent, or becomes a church of regulars."

3. Hence, upon the renunciation of the right of patronage by the municipality in favor of the Bishop, the right of patronage was simply extinguished; the conferring of dignities, canonries, and other benefices in the cathedral church of C, which formerly was subject to the right of patronage, became from that time free according to the common law; and therefore the dignities are all reserved to the Holy See according to canon 396, § 1, the canonries and sextonships become subject to free appointment by the Bishop or by the Holy See according to canon 1435, § 1, 1°.

Question. Whether the dignities, canonries, and minor benefices of the cathedral church of C are reserved to the Holy See in this case.

Reply. In the affirmative.

Approved and confirmed by His Holiness, Pius XII, in the audience of 29 November, 1944.

AAS 37–118; S. C. Conc., *Dioecesis C, Reservationum Apostolicarum,* 29 Nov., 1944.

CANON 409

Violet Mantelletta Not Permitted to Canons: An Italian Bishop asked that the canon accompanying him according to canon 412, in violet vestments, be permitted to wear also a violet mantelletta as more becoming than a black cloak over the violet cassock. The reply, S. C. Rit., 29 March, 1950 (N. C. 71/50): *Non expedire (Monitor Ecclesiasticus,* 1952, p. 448).

CANON 420

Synodal Judges Absent From Choir on Official Duties, to Receive Distributions Even Though Their Official Services Were Compensated (S. C. Conc., 23 Feb., 1942) **AAS 34–299.**

Summary. Although canon 420, § 1, 14° states without qualification that synodal judges, when absent from choir because of official duties, are to receive both the income of the prebends and the daily distributions, the Chapter in this case raised a question regarding the daily distributions for the synodal judges.

For regarding the right of the synodal judges to the distributions as doubtful, the Chapter adduced two reasons: first, canon 421, § 1, 3° lays down a different rule for certain other officials, namely, the Vicar General, Vicar Capitular, officialis, and chancellor; secondly, the synodal judges in this case received compensation for their services, and a pre-Code case (S. C. Conc., 20 Feb., 1915; AAS 7–262) had held that no capitular should receive the daily distributions when absent on official business if he received compensation for those services.

Remarks. 1. Since canon 420, § 1, 14° is perfectly clear and makes no distinction, no distinction should be introduced. *Ubi lex non distinguit, nec nostrum est distinguere.*

2. The Code Commission has declared that the words of canon 421, § 1, 1°: "those who with the permission of the Ordinary of the place teach sacred theology or canon law," etc., apply even to those who receive compensation for such teaching.[1] Hence, by analogy, the circumstance of compensation should make no difference in the present case.

3. The probable reason why the Code (c. 420, § 1, 14°) allows the daily distributions to synodal judges absent on official business, while at the same time (c. 421, § 1, 3°) it refuses the distributions to the Vicar General and other officials similarly absent, is that the Vicar General, etc., have a permanent and stable compensation for the exercise of their office, whereas synodal judges have not so stable an office, nor is their compensation certain.

Question. Should a capitular who is absent from choir while performing the office of synodal judge, receive the daily distributions, even though he receives special compensation for his services as judge.

Reply. In the affirmative.

His Holiness Pius XII, in the audience granted to the Secretary on the 23rd of February, 1942, deigned to approve and confirm the above reply.

AAS 34–299; S. C. Conc., 23 Feb., 1942.

---

[1] Code Com., 24 Nov., 1920; AAS 12–573; CANON LAW DIGEST, Vol. 1, p. 240.

CANON 422

Jubilarians Entitled to Distributions *Inter Praesentes*
(S. C. Conc., 22 Feb., 1942) **AAS 35–182.**

Facts. Two capitulars, both jubilarians in the sense of canon 422, § 1, claimed the right to receive the distributions *inter praesentes,* although absent from the functions to which these distributions were attached. The capitulars based this claim on the provision of canon 422, § 2. The Chapter resisted it on the ground, first that custom was against it, and secondly that it was excluded by the Statutes of the Chapter, based on an earlier diocesan Synod.

Discussion. 1. There is no proof of a custom contrary to the provisions of canon 422, § 2.

2. As to a contrary law, the S. C. pointed out that the Statutes of the Chapter showed a misunderstanding of the distinction which exists under the Code between ordinary or daily distributions and distributions *inter praesentes;* and also that the Statutes were based on a misunderstanding of the earlier provisions of the diocesan Synod, which they had attempted to follow. Consequently, the Statutes could not be sustained as a norm of law, and could not, therefore, be accepted as creating an exception to the general rule under canon 422, § 2.

Question. Whether jubilarians are entitled to the distributions *inter praesentes* in this case.

Reply. In the affirmative, unless there is an express will of the founders or offerers to the contrary; and it is moreover ordered that the Chapter revise its Statutes to conform to the Code of Canon Law.

His Holiness Pius XII, in the audience of 22 Feb., 1942, deigned to approve and confirm this resolution.

AAS 35–182; S. C. Conc., 22 Feb., 1942. *Periodica,* 33–149 (Aguirre).

CANON 451

Instruction on Military Ordinariates (S. C. Consist., 23 April, 1951) **AAS 43–562.**

An Instruction of the Sacred Consistorial Congregation "on Military Vicars" is as follows:

This Apostolic See has always been solicitous that, as far as is possible, the general laws of the Church be piously and conscientiously observed by all her members everywhere; yet it is necessary at times because of special circumstances to enact new norms to provide for new needs of the faithful. Accordingly, this Sacred Consistorial Congregation, derogating from the common law as far as may be necessary, decrees as follows:

1. One who has the office of Military Vicar has ordinary but special jurisdiction, to be exercised for the spiritual good of the faithful committed to his charge.

2. The jurisdiction which the Military Vicar enjoys is personal, that is, it extends only to those subjects who are mentioned in the Decree of the Sacred Consistorial Congregation erecting his Military Vicariate, even if those same subjects should reside in military posts and in various places especially allocated to the soldiers.

The jurisdiction of the Military Vicar is not exclusive; hence it does not withdraw the persons, the posts, and places reserved for soldiers (i.e., military barracks, naval armories, airfields, military hospitals, etc.) from the power of the local Ordinary: and this jurisdiction does not produce any exemption, nor does the position of chaplain effect any excardination from the diocese.

However, in these places the local Ordinaries and pastors should exercise their power over the subjects of the Military Vicariate in only a secondary manner. Hence it is necessary that their work be mutually coordinated by some sort of agreement and that their actions and functions be performed concordantly, especially outside the limits of the military posts.

3. No canonical domicile is recognized except a diocesan or parochial one.

For judicial causes affecting the subjects of the Military Vicariate, whether they be contentious cases among themselves or criminal cases, the Military Vicar designates once for all some diocesan or metropolitan tribunal, to be approved by the Holy See.

4. Whenever new buildings are to be especially allocated to soldiers, or when ships or aeroplanes are to be blessed, and in other similar cases, the following rule is to be observed:

If the ceremony is ordered by the military commanders, the Military Vicar imparts the blessing: if he is unable to do it, the Ordinary of the place in which the ceremony is arranged, after the Military Vicar advises him of his inability to come, gives the blessing by his own authority.

If the ceremony is ordered by the civil authorities, only the local Ordinary is competent.

5. The Military Vicar should inform the local Ordinaries about the chaplains who are sent into their dioceses or who depart from the same.

6. The registers of baptisms, confirmations, marriages, and deaths, inscribed according to the usage approved by the Church in the Roman Ritual (Tit. XII, I–IV), the Military Vicar should order to be kept either in the general archives of the Military Vicariate or in the central archives of the chaplains, if there is one; but in this case there is an obligation to send to the Curia of the Military Vicariate an authentic copy of these same books at the end of every year, as provided in canon 470, § 3 of the Code of Canon Law.

7. The Military Vicar has authority to produce the *Ordo* of the divine Office and Mass for the use of military chaplains, when circumstances make it advisable for him to do so, observing in all details the common laws of the Church, especially the rules laid down in the Constitution, *Divino afflatu* of 1 Nov., 1911 (AAS 3–633), the *Motu proprio, Abhinc duos annos,* of 23 Oct., 1913 (AAS 5–449), and in the Instructions which have been or may be issued by the Sacred Congregation of Rites. This *Ordo* may be used by the military chaplains everywhere when they celebrate Mass for the benefit of the soldiers, and by priests who celebrate in churches or oratories reserved for the soldiers.

8. The Military Vicar can obtain Quinquennial Faculties just as other local Ordinaries do, and Decennial Faculties in places where these are usually given.

9. The Military Vicar is bound to send to this Sacred Congregation every three years a report on the activities and conditions of the Vicariate.

10. Every chaplain in exercising the care of those souls who have been entrusted to him by the Military Vicar must remember that he is bound by the duties and obligations of pastors, in as far as these are applicable in his position.

11. The chaplains as well as the Military Vicar are entirely free from the obligation of applying the Mass *pro populo;* however, if they receive a salary or any notable compensation from their office, the Military Vicar can oblige them to apply the Sacrifice of the Mass at least on the days specified in canon 306; and this same rule applies to the Vicar himself.

12. Priests who are assigned as chaplains "should be resplendent examples of high sanctity, worthy ministers of Christ, faithful dispensers of the mysteries of God, effective helpers of God, ready for every good work" (Pius XII, Exhortation, *Menti Nostrae;* AAS, 42–658), so that, borne on by the inspiration of their calling, they may perform their almost parochial office with energy, and what is most important, that they may do battle for souls so that their apostolate may glow with life after the example of Christ.

In this connection let the Military Vicar consider well the exhortation of our Holy Father:

"We exhort you, Venerable Brethren, that, as far as it is possible to avoid it, you should not plunge priests who are as yet inexperienced into the midst of active service, nor assign them to places remote from the principal city and other large cities of the diocese. For if they live in such conditions, isolated, inexperienced, exposed to dangers and with no one to give them prudent guidance, they and their fitness for their work might certainly suffer harm" (Exhortation, *Menti Nostrae, l. c.,* p. 692).

13. Also excellent and well tried religious priests should be chosen for the office of chaplain, observing however the special norms laid down for them by the Sacred Congregation of Religious; and these men if possible should be assigned to places where there is a house of their Institute.

14. Chaplains must wear the ecclesiastical dress, according to the legitimate customs of the countries, and should not wear the uniform unless their duties require it or the civil laws prescribe it, always however using some special symbol of their ecclesiastical office.

So too, if such is the custom, they should always wear the clerical tonsure or *corona* according to the Sacred Canons.

15. In order that the chaplains may be motivated by the desire of doing God's will, it is necessary that the spirit of prayer be alive and alert in them. They must constantly draw strength from the devout celebration of the Eucharistic Sacrifice and from those practices approved by long use in the Church, which especially enable men to avoid sin and to practice the solid virtues: among these, all agree that spiritual exercises hold the first place.

16. The various forms and methods of apostolate which to-

day, because of the special needs of the Christian people, are so important and serious, should be carried on by chaplains who are well instructed and well trained.

17. The chaplains should try to be present at the meetings or conferences which in accordance with canon 131 of the Code of Canon Law are held in the diocese in which they are staying.

18. The Military Vicar gives testimonial letters to those who, after they have finished their military service, wish to enter religion or to go on for Sacred Orders, in all cases where such testimonials according to the Sacred Canons are required from the local Ordinary.

His Holiness by divine Providence Pope Pius XII, upon receiving the report of the undersigned Cardinal Secretary of the Sacred Consistorial Congregation, deigned to approve this Instruction and ordered that it be published. All things, even though worthy of special mention, to the contrary notwithstanding.

Given at Rome, from the Sacred Consistorial Congregation, on the 23rd day of April, 1951, Feast of Saint George, Martyr.

AAS 43–562; S. C. Consist., 23 April, 1951. Annotations, *The Jurist,* 1952, Vol. 12, p. 141 (Marbach); *Monitor Ecclesiasticus,* 1951, p. 581 (Pugliese).

Brazil: Decree erecting military Ordinariate, S. C. Consist., 6 Nov., 1950 (AAS 43–91).

Canada: Decree establishing military Ordinariate. S. C. Consist., 17 Feb., 1951 (AAS 43–477). Annotations, *Monitor Ecclesiasticus,* 1952, p. 193 (Pugliese).

Chaplains, Military: Qualifications: "It is necessary that the priests who are deputed as military chaplains, conspicuous for their learning, piety and zeal for souls and earnest in seeking the glory of God, be qualified to present to the soldiers the norm of Christian living and to give them apostolic services such as are suited to the needs of the present time." S. C. Consist. to the Ordinaries of Spain, 2 June, 1951 (AAS 43–565).

Chaplains of Ships: Appointment and Duties. See c. 248; AAS 44–649.

Confirmation in Danger of Death: By pastor of territory. See c. 782; AAS 38–349.

By military chaplain. See c. 782; private reply of S. C. Sacr., 2 Jan., 1947.

France: Decree erecting military Ordinariate. S. C. Consist., 26 July, 1952 (AAS 44–744).

Military Chaplain: General delegation for marriage. See c. 1096; private reply of S. C. Sacr., 21 July, 1919.

Missionary of Emigrants: Appointment, faculties, duties. See c. 248; AAS 44–649, nn. 32–40.

Philippines: Decree erecting military Ordinariate. S. C. Consist., 8 Dec., 1950 (AAS 44–743).

CANON 458

Reasons for Deferring Appointment to Parish (Code Commission, 3 May, 1945) AAS 37–149.

The Code Commission was asked:

Whether the words of canon 458: *peculiar circumstances of places and persons,* include also the economic needs of the diocese.

Reply. In the negative.

AAS 37–149; Code Com., 3 May, 1945.
Periodica, 34–280 (Aguirre).

CANON 464

Chaplains of Exempted Places: As regards confirmation in danger of death. See c. 782; private reply of S. C. Sacr., 30 Dec., 1946.

CANON 466

Vicar of Parish, which is fully united to the *mensa episcopalis,* is bound to apply the Mass *pro populo.* See c. 471; AAS 37–297.

CANON 470

Chaplains, Military: To send copies of baptismal register, etc., to Military Vicariate at end of year. See c. 451; AAS 43–562.

Chaplains of Ships: To keep parish books. See c. 248; AAS 44–649, n. 25.

Missionary of Emigrants: To keep parish books. See c. 248; AAS 44–649, n. 35.

CANON 471

Vicar of Parish Which Is United *Pleno Iure* to the *Mensa Episcopalis* Is Bound to Apply the *Missa pro Populo* (S. C. Conc., 20 July, 1938) AAS 37–297.

Facts. The Bishop of the diocese of R has a parish which is united *pleno iure* to his own *mensa episcopalis.* The vicar who is in charge according to canon 471, § 1 believes that since the Code he is free from the obligation of the *Missa pro populo.*

Remarks. According to the Code, the vicar has all the obligations of a pastor (c. 471, § 4), among which is the obligation of applying the *Missa pro populo* (c. 466, § 1). The Bishop has the obligation of applying the *Missa pro populo*, according to canon 339, § 1, for "the people committed to his care." The question involved here is whether the Bishop, in applying the Mass for all the people committed to his care, satisfies at the same time the obligation of the vicar to apply the Mass for the people of the parish. The obligation of the Bishop is distinct from that of individual pastors. The people of a parish have a right to the benefit of two Masses *pro populo* on any designated day, that of the Bishop, in which they share as part of the people committed to the care of the Bishop, and that of the pastor or vicar, as the people committed to the care of the pastor or vicar. Canons 466, § 2, and 339, § 5, cannot be applied by any analogy to effect a merger of these two distinct obligations.

Question. Whether the *vicarius curatus* of a parish which is fully united to the *mensa episcopalis* is bound to apply the Mass *pro populo* in this case.

Reply. In the affirmative.

Approved and confirmed by His Holiness, Pius XI, in the audience of 20 July, 1938.

*AAS 37–297; S. C. Conc., 20 July, 1938.

Vicar: Confirmation in danger of death. See c. 782; AAS 38–349.
    Mass *pro populo*. See c. 466; AAS 37–297.

CANON 479

Chaplains of Ships: When equivalent to Rectors of Churches. See c. 248; AAS 44–649, n. 26.

CANON 485

Sacred Art: Instruction on. See c. 1261; AAS 44–542.

CANON 487

The Religious Life (Pius XII, Allocution, 8 Dec., 1950) **AAS 43–26.**

An Address of Pius XII to the assembled delegates of all religious Orders and Congregations, Societies and Secular Institutes, after their first general Congress held in Rome near the close of the Holy Year, 1950, is as follows:

1. The Holy Year through no merit of Ours but through the favor of God's mercy has proved more bountiful in blessings

than the foresight of men had anticipated. In the eventful cycle of its notable achievements, it has manifested the strong faith and richly abundant life of the Church of Christ, our Mother. Your Congress rightly takes its place among the more significantly important events and over them your fraternal gathering reflects its own characteristic luster. To you now We wish to address Our words of affectionate greeting.

2. The annals of Church History record no meeting similar to this. Here for the first time, religious organizations whose members have selected as the goal of their lives the attainment of consummate evangelical perfection have assembled in large numbers over a period of several days to discuss and weigh the problems of their common interest.

3. It was Our judgment that the circumstances of the times made it altogether necessary to do so. For the changed conditions of the world which the Church must encounter, certain points of doctrine touching upon the status and condition of moral perfection, not to mention the pressing needs of the apostolic work which you have so widely and so generously undertaken, all these have called you to devote yourselves to this systematic study and discussion.

4. Your work is at its close. It was energized by careful discussions, it has been prolific in proposals, and it will be no less fruitful, We hope, in perfecting the virtues which will realize your projects. With the resolute cooperation of your wills, the grace of God will enkindle those virtues, the grace, that is, which your prayers and religious acts of self-denial, more especially, because of their burning devotion, those of your Sisters in Christ, have already invoked upon this present undertaking.

5. You have requested the fatherly blessing of the Vicar of Christ as a pledge of divine guidance and assistance so that your Congress might be fittingly completed and terminated. But before imparting that blessing to you, We think it proper to present to you orally certain thoughts on the religious life which call for an explanation and which, once explained, may serve hereafter as a norm to direct your thoughts and actions.

I

6. First of all, it will be useful for Us to indicate briefly the place held in the Church by the religious Orders and Congrega-

tions. You are, of course, aware that Our Redeemer founded a Church endowed with an hierarchical organization. For between the Apostles and their successors, with whom must also be grouped their assistants in the ministry, and the ordinary faithful He drew a definite line of demarcation, and by the union of these two elements the structure of the Kingdom of God on earth stands firm. Consequently the distinction between the clergy and the laity is fixed by divine law (cfr. can. 107). Interposed between these two grades is the religious state which deriving its origin from the Church has its existence and strength from its intimate connection with the end of the Church herself, which is to lead men to the attainment of holiness. Though every Christian should scale these sacred heights under the guidance of the Church, nevertheless the religious moves toward them along a path that is peculiarly his own and by means that are of a more exalted nature.

7. Moreover, the religious state is not restricted to either of the two groups which exist in the Church by divine right, since both clerics and lay persons alike can become religious, and on the other hand, the clerical dignity lies open to religious and those who are not religious. One would therefore be mistaken in appraising the value of the foundations which Christ laid in building His Church, if he should judge that the peculiar form of the secular clerical life as such was established and sanctioned by our Divine Redeemer, and that the peculiar form of the regular clerical life, though it is to be considered good and worthy of approbation in itself, is still secondary and auxiliary in nature, since it is not derived from Christ. Wherefore, if we keep before our eyes the order established by Christ, neither of the two special forms of clerical life holds a prerogative of divine right, since that law singles out neither form, nor gives to either precedence over the other. What, then, the difference is between these two forms, what their mutual relations are, what special task in working out the salvation of mankind has been assigned to each, all these details Christ left to be decided according to the needs and conditions of succeeding ages; or rather, to express Our mind more exactly, He left them to the definitive decisions of the Church herself.

8. Undoubtedly it is according to the divine law that every priest, be he secular or regular, should fulfill his ministry in

such a way as to be a subordinate assistant to his Bishop. This has always been the customary practice in the Church, and the prescriptions in the Code of Canon Law which deal with the members of religious societies as pastors and local Ordinaries make this clear (can. 626–631; 454; par. 5). And it often happens in missionary territories that all the clergy, even including the Bishop, belong to the regular militia of the Church. Let no one think this is an extraordinary or abnormal state of affairs to be regarded as only a temporary arrangement, and that the administration should be handed over to the secular clergy as soon as possible.

9. Again, the exemption of religious Orders is not contrary to the principles of the constitution given to the Church by God, nor does it in any way contradict the law that a priest owes obedience to his Bishop. For according to Canon Law, exempt religious are subject to the authority of the local Bishop so far as the administration of the episcopal office and the well regulated care of souls require. But even putting aside this consideration, in the discussions of the past few decades concerning the question of exemption perhaps too little attention has been paid to the fact that exempt religious even by the prescriptions of Canon Law are always and everywhere subject to the authority of the Roman Pontiff as their supreme moderator, and that they owe obedience to him precisely in virtue of their religious vow of obedience (can. 499, par. 1). Indeed the Supreme Pontiff possesses ordinary and immediate jurisdiction over each and every diocese and over the individual faithful just as he does over the universal Church. It is therefore clear that the primary law of God whereby the clergy and the laity are subject to the rule of the Bishop is more than sufficiently observed as regards exempt religious, as it is no less clear that both branches of the clergy by reason of their parallel services conform to the will and precept of Christ.

II

10. There is another question connected with what has so far been said which We wish to explain and clarify. It concerns the way in which the cleric and the religious should strive for their due moral perfection.

11. It is a distortion of the truth to say that the clerical state

as such and as divinely established demands either by its very nature or by some postulate of that nature that the evangelical counsels be observed by its members, and that for this very reason it must be called a state of achieving evangelical perfection. A cleric therefore is not bound by the divine law to observe the evangelical counsels of poverty, chastity, and obedience; above all he is not bound in the same way or for the same reason as the one for whom such obligation arises from vows publicly pronounced upon entering the religious life. This does not, however, prevent the cleric from assuming these bonds privately and of his own accord. So too, the fact that the priests of the Latin rite are bound to observe holy celibacy does not remove or lessen the distinction between the clerical and the religious states. Moreover a member of the regular clergy professes the state and condition of evangelical perfection not inasmuch as he is a cleric, but inasmuch as he is a religious.

12. And although we have declared in Our Apostolic Constitution *Provida Mater Ecclesia* that the form of life followed by the Secular Institutes is to be considered as a state of evangelical perfection and recognized as such by the common law of the Church, since their members are in some way bound to the observance of the evangelical counsels, still this in no way contradicts what We have just affirmed. Assuredly there is no reason preventing clerics from joining together in Secular Institutes so that by their choice of this manner of life they may strive for the attainment of religious perfection; but in that case they are in a state of acquiring perfection not inasmuch as they are clerics, but inasmuch as they are members of a Secular Institute. After all such an Institute adopts, in the way of life it proposes to follow, the evangelical counsels which are proper to the religious state and are there realized in their highest perfection; but the Institute so achieves that end that it is not dependent on the traditional pattern of the religious state but stands by itself in an external form of life which bears no necessary relation to the perfection just mentioned.

III

13. We think it timely now to touch upon some of the reasons which the religious state holds out to men as motives for embracing it.

14. It is asserted by some that the religious state by its very nature and purpose, even though meriting approval, is nothing but a safe refuge offered to the fearful and timid who have not the strength to stand up to the dangers of life's storms, and lacking the knowledge, or perhaps the will, to face difficulties, are led by their indolence to bid farewell to the world and fly to the haven of cloistered peace. Wherefore we must inspire self-confidence and reliance on God's grace in those who seek such idle tranquillity, so that they may overcome these traits of character and attain the courage to face the struggles of common life. Is this indeed true?

15. It is not Our purpose here to evaluate the various motives inducing individuals to betake themselves to the religious life. We do wish, however, to indicate the principal and indeed the valid reason that should induce one to enter the protected enclosure of the cloister. And it is certainly different from that distorted opinion stated above, which if taken as a whole, is both untrue and unjust. For not otherwise than the resolution to enter the priesthood, the resolve to embrace the religious state, together with a firm constancy in executing it, demands greatness of soul and an ardent zeal for self-consecration. The history of the Church in its record of the glorious achievements of the saints in heaven and of the religious Institutes on earth, in its account of successful missionary enterprises, in its sketching of the Church's ascetical teaching, no less than experience itself, indicates more clearly than the light of day that men and women of indomitable and whole-souled courage have flourished in the religious state as well as in the world. Again, do those religious men and women who so strenuously exert themselves to spread the Kingdom of the Gospel, who tend the sick, train the young, and toil in the classrooms, shun the society of their fellow men and shut them out from their love? Are not very many of them, no less than the secular priesthood and their lay helpers, fighting in the very front ranks of the battle for the Church's cause?

16. Here We cannot refrain from directing Our attention to another matter which completely denies the false assertion mentioned previously. If the number of candidates wishing to enter the enclosed garden of the religious life is diminishing, especially among young women, the reason very frequently is that they find it too difficult to divest themselves of their own judgment

and surrender their freedom of action, as the very nature of the vow of obedience demands. Indeed some praise as the real peak of moral perfection, not the surrender of liberty for the love of Christ, but the curbing of such surrender. The norm therefore to be preferred in the formation of a just and holy person would seem to be this: restrict liberty only where necessary; otherwise, give liberty free rein as far as possible.

17. We transmit the question whether this new foundation on which some are trying to erect the edifice of sanctity will be as effective and as solid in supporting and augmenting the apostolic work of the Church as was the one which through fifteen hundred years has been provided by that ancient rule of obedience undertaken for the love of Christ. What is now of supreme importance is to examine this proposal thoroughly, to disclose what lies concealed beneath the surface. This opinion, if carefully considered, not only fails to appreciate the nature of the evangelical counsel, but it somehow twists it to a meaning in accord with its theory. No one is obliged to choose for himself the counsel of perfect obedience, which essentially is a rule of life whereby one surrenders the control of his own will; no one, We repeat, be it an individual or a group. They can if they wish conform their conduct to this new rule. But words must be understood and accepted according to their obvious meaning, and if this norm is compared with the vow of obedience, it surely does not possess the same supreme value, nor is it an adequate expression of the wonderful example recorded in Holy Scripture: "He humbled Himself becoming obedient unto death" (Phil. 2:8).

18. He therefore is himself deceived and deceives others who forgetting the propensities of the soul and the inspiration of divine grace, offers as a guide to one seeking advice about entering the religious state only that new norm. Hence if it is clear that the voice of God is calling someone to the heights of evangelical perfection, without any hesitation he should be invited for the attainment of this lofty purpose to offer freely the sacrifice of his liberty as the vow of obedience demands, that vow, We proclaim, which the Church through so many centuries has weighed, has put to the test, has properly delineated, and has approved. Let no one against his will be compelled to this self-consecration; but if he does will it, let no one counsel him against it; above all, let no one hold him back.

IV

19. But enough on this point. At the moment, We wish to speak on external works and the interior life. Hardly any question of grave importance for the life of regulars, or for the religious life in general, has been treated at greater length. Nevertheless We wish to present Our own judgment on this matter.

20. It was not mere chance that brought about, in our day, the rise and elaboration of the philosophy known as "Existentialism." The men of our time, when confronted by events which bring up difficult metaphysical and religious problems to be solved, gladly, without a thought of higher principles, persuade themselves that it is enough to act as the exigencies of the moment demand. But the man who professes our holy faith refuses to follow such principles and to make each passing moment of time his whole concern, hurling himself headlong into the stream of life. He knows that the "things that appear not" (Heb. 11:1) are to be considered of supreme worth, are preeminently true, and so enduring in the future as to last forever. Yet — be it said with sorrow — though warnings and exhortations have not been lacking, even some ecclesiastics, not excepting religious, have been deeply infected by this contagion, and while not denying a reality that transcends the senses and the whole natural order, they esteem it of little importance.

21. Has this grave and dangerous crisis been overcome? Thanks be to God, We may hope that it has. Certain things which We have Ourselves witnessed, and which events have made known to Us, offer this assurance.

22. The most active zeal can be closely allied with the quest for the riches of the interior life. Two stars that shine in the firmament of the religious life, St. Francis Xavier and St. Teresa of Jesus, are brilliant proofs of this.

23. An eager external activity and the cultivation of the interior life demand more than a bond of fellowship; as far at least as evaluation and willed effort are concerned, they demand that they should march along together step by step. With the growth of devotion to exterior works therefore, let there shine forth a corresponding increase in faith, in the life of prayer, in zealous consecration of self and talents to God, in spotless purity of

conscience, in obedience, in patient endurance of hardship, and in active charity tirelessly expended for God and one's neighbor.

24. This is true not only of the individual religious, who really is such in heart as well as in habit, but it is also the reason why communities as a whole are solidly founded in the sight of God and men, and are deserving of the most generous praise. The Church insistently demands of you that your external works correspond to your interior life, and that these two maintain a constant balance. Do you not, both clerical and lay religious, profess that you have embraced the state of evangelical perfection? If so, bring forth the fruits proper to your state, so that the Mystical Body of Christ, which is the Church, may draw ever-increasing vitality from your strength and fervor. This is the very reason why religious Orders totally dedicated to the contemplative life are in their own way necessary to the Church, since they are for her a perpetual ornament and a copious source of heavenly graces.

25. You know, of course, that it has often been remarked that charity to the neighbor is gradually losing its religious character and is becoming secularized. But an honorable and kind treatment of others that has no foundation in faith, and springs from some other source, is not charity nor may it be called Catholic. Charity possesses a dignity, an inspiration, and a strength that is lacking in mere philanthropy however endowed with wealth and other resources. Thus if We compare our Catholic Sisters who nurse the sick with some others who perform this same task out of mere humanitarianism or for pay, We discover in them something entirely different and of higher value. They may at times be inferior to others in technical advantages, and We take this occasion to urge them not only to keep abreast of others in this matter but even to surpass them. But where our religious women, deeply imbued with the vital spirit of their Institutes and daily prepared for the love of Christ to lay down their lives for the sick, perform their labors, a different atmosphere prevails, in which virtue works wonders which technical aids and medical skill alone are powerless to accomplish.

26. Therefore let those religious Orders and Congregations that devote themselves to the active life keep ever before their

eyes and inwardly cherish all that stamps their souls with the lineaments of holiness and nourishes the fire of the Holy Spirit in the depth of their pure souls.

V

27. Dearly Beloved, We wish also to refer briefly to the efforts of religious Institutes to adapt themselves to our changed times, and to join the new and the old in harmonious union.

28. When young people hear the statements: "We must keep up to date" and "Our efforts must be commensurate with the times," they are fired with an extraordinary ardor of soul, and if they are serving under the standard of the religious militia, they keenly desire to direct the efforts of their future religious undertakings according to this principle. And to a certain extent, this is proper. For it often has happened that the founding fathers of religious Institutes conceived new projects in order to meet the challenge which newly emerging needs were urgently presenting to the Church and her works; and in this way they harmonized their enterprises with their age. Hence if you wish to walk in the footsteps of your predecessors, act as they acted. Examine thoroughly the beliefs, convictions, and conduct of your own contemporaries, and if you discover in them elements that are good and proper, make these worth while features your own; otherwise you will never be able to enlighten, assist, sustain and guide the men of your own time.

29. However the Church possesses a patrimony preserved intact from her earliest origin, which is unchanged in the course of ages, and which is in perfect accord with the needs and the aspirations of the human race. The Catholic faith is the most important part of this patrimony, and in the Encyclical Letter *Humani Generis* We recently defended it from new errors. Preserve most diligently this faith undefiled by any blemish; hold firmly to the conviction that it contains within itself exceedingly powerful forces that can mold any age.

30. A part of this patrimony is the good pursued in the state of perfection and this you must seek with the utmost zeal, so that by the use of its methods and resources you may become holy yourselves, and either directly or indirectly make your neighbors also holy. In this manner they, sharing ever more richly in divine grace, may live a holy life and die a holy death.

Another factor in this patrimony is the lofty and sublime truth that self-denial for the love of Christ must be considered the only path to perfection. This truth the changing times can never change.

31. There are however circumstances, and not a few, when you can and ought to accommodate yourselves to the temper and the needs of men and the age. Indeed to a great extent this has actually been done, and now the task is being completely and perfectly accomplished by your combined counsels and plans. As may be seen from the variety of your undertakings both as individuals and as Institutes, you have already initiated many adjustments in schools, in the training of youth, in the alleviation of human misery, and in the cultivation and promotion of learning. Hence it must be admitted, and Our affirmation admits of no denial, that a vast amount of energy is even now being expended to meet the altered conditions of our era with new and effective resources.

32. Nevertheless in striving to adapt yourselves to the exigencies of the present, it is, in Our judgment, of paramount concern that you shrewdly investigate what spiritual forces lie latent in your contemporaries, by what secret desires they are motivated, and what the true picture is of their souls. We do not, of course, mean the picture that manifests their detestable and censurable qualities and expresses the tumult of passion and the corruption of vice. But in men as men, and most of all as Christians, though entangled in error and sin, there is not a little good and even a desire for greater good. You must encourage these good impulses and foster these aspirations, being always careful, however, not to accept from the world what keeps it wretched and evil, but rather to infuse into the world what is good and holy in yourselves, and in harmony with these salutary longings. Being solicitous, therefore, for that feeble good in the hearts of others, furbish and develop it, molding from its grains of gold precious vessels and gathering its rivulets into mighty streams.

33. Some think, and perhaps rightly, that three marks are characteristic of our age: amplitude in thought and discussion, unification of plan and organization, and speed in execution. Are not these three notes also distinctive marks of the Gospel? Are they not characteristic of those who profess the Catholic faith and live according to its principles? What greater amplitude of

vision can be opened to our minds than that offered in the words of the Apostle: "All things are yours and you are Christ's and Christ is God's" (1 Cor. 3:25)? What closer unity in understanding and love than the simplicity and the unity declared to you in the Sacred Scripture: "God, all in all" (1 Cor. 15:26) and "Thou shalt love the Lord thy God with thy whole heart and with thy whole soul and with thy whole mind and with thy whole strength. . . . Thou shalt love thy neighbor as thyself" (Mark 12:28–34)?

34. To enable us to be swift and spirited and unhampered by the recollection of perishable things, we are admonished: "No man putting his hand to the plow and looking back is fit for the Kingdom of God" (Luke 9:62). And if you wish to behold models of virtue in whom these three laudable qualities shine forth, recall to your minds the Apostle Paul and all those who have been engaged in wondrous exploits worthy of an immortal remembrance.

35. Moreover the ideals which light your way to contemplation and action, as well as the goal of the Church's other children, both priests and laity, are the achievement of Christian perfection and the salvation of the human race. For your part, you have at hand the most effective aids, namely the evangelical counsels through the profession of your vows of religion, and through these by unremitting warfare you can overcome the concupiscence of the flesh, the concupiscence of the eyes, and the pride of life (cfr. 1 John 2:16), and thus become ever holier and efficient servants of God for the salvation of mankind. Direct your thoughts and your actions to reach these lofty heights, "so that being rooted and grounded in love" (Eph. 3:17), steadfast in the power of faith and rich in humility, you may lose no opportunity to lead men, your brothers, to their Creator and Redeemer, as stray sheep returning to their Shepherd.

36. Faithful and true to your duty of good example, see to it that your conduct harmonizes with the name you bear, and that your whole manner of life conforms to your profession. According to the words of the Apostle of the Gentiles: "Careful to preserve the unity of the Spirit in the bond of peace" (Eph. 4:3), let peace reign within you and among you, among members of the same Institute and among members of the same community, and with those of other Institutes; between you

and all who labor with you and with whom you labor to win men for Christ. Put far from you discords and disagreements which weaken and cripple undertakings begun with the highest hopes. The Church, as a field for apostolic endeavor, is spread out all over the world, and an opportunity for toil and sweat is open to all.

37. If the faith of religious is strengthened by the example of a life whose pattern is unyielding observance of the vows, if the priest regards nothing as hard or irksome in his quest for the salvation of souls, then the expression of the Apostle when referring to the word of God will also be true of them today, "living . . . and efficient and keener than any two-edged sword" (Heb. 4:13). We recently warned the faithful that in these calamitous days, when the misfortune and grievous want of many is in sharp contrast to the immoderate luxury of others, they should be willing to live temperately and to be generous to their neighbors oppressed by poverty. Come then, excel all others by your example in this insistent work of Christian perfection, justice, and charity, and thus lead them to imitate Christ.

38. Finally, with a great hope that the efficacious grace of Our Lord Jesus Christ may bring forth from your Congress benefits of enduring value, and as a pledge of our abiding love, We affectionately bestow upon all here present and upon religious communities everywhere in the world the Apostolic Benediction.

AAS 43–26; Pius XII, Allocution, 8 Dec., 1950.

NOTE: The above translation, made by the Reverend S. F. McNamee, S.J., and others of the Maryland Province of the Society of Jesus, and reproduced in the CANON LAW DIGEST with due permission, is also obtainable separately (with Latin and English parallel texts) from the Maryland Province of the Society of Jesus, 720 North Calvert Street, Baltimore 2, Maryland.

Oriental Code: Canons on Religious, Church Property, and Meaning of Terms Promulgated (Pius XII, *Motu Proprio*, 9 Feb., 1952) AAS 44–65.

The *Motu proprio, Postquam Apostolicis,* of Pius XII:

By the Apostolic Letters given of Our own motion under date of 22 February, 1949, and 6 January, 1950, respectively, We provided for regulating the discipline of marriage[1] and the con-

---

[1] *Motu proprio,* 22 Feb., 1949; AAS 41–89, reported in this volume under canon 1012.

duct of ecclesiastical trials[2] in the Oriental Churches. We now turn Our attention and Our thoughts to two other questions, the first concerning religious Institutes, and the second concerning ecclesiastical property.

Everyone knows with what virtues and merits monasticism has flourished through the centuries. From the earliest times of Christianity, monks, like buds bursting into flower in the garden of the Church, shone with evangelical splendor. Responsive to the call of divine grace, dominating the concupiscence of the flesh, the concupiscence of the eyes, and the pride of life, and so freed from earthly impediments, aflame with love of God and men, they devoted themselves to attaining the perfection of evangelical morality. Anchorets, cenobites, and sacred virgins, by prayers, heavenly contemplations, voluntary corporal penances, and the practice of the other virtues, scaled the mountain of God with eager steps. The active life also in all its forms was not neglected by the monks of the Oriental Churches. They regarded it as a sacred and inviolable duty to practice and defend the Catholic faith, to teach it more thoroughly to the Christian people, and to propagate it among the nations who were deprived of that highest good. History bears brilliant witness to the ardor and success with which the followers of Anthony, Pachomius, Aphraates, Ephraem, Hilarion, and Basil the Great cultivated both sacred and civil studies and the theory and practice of the liberal arts. It is true that this splendor of supernatural life and this readiness and zeal in active works gradually waned among them and in some places, owing to the well known ills which long afflicted the Oriental Churches, disappeared entirely.

Nevertheless the provident and wise labors of certain restorers of religious discipline, such as Theodore of Studion, Josaphat Kuntsevyc, and Mekhitar, and the maternal care of the Holy See brought it about that in those districts of the Oriental Churches which followed the teaching of the Chair of Peter, the ancient vigor was born anew.

But experience soon showed that the norms of the ancient law had to be perfected and adapted to the needs of the present time, so as to be made more concordant and helpful to the life and progress both of the monks and of those who have embraced

[2] *Motu proprio,* 6 Jan., 1950; AAS 42–5, reported in this volume under canon 1552.

other later forms of evangelical perfection: We refer to the Orders, Congregations, and Societies of men who, although they have not publicly professed the three customary religious vows, are yet bound by the ties of religious community life. These defects will easily be discerned by anyone who reads either the laws which are still in effect regarding the form of religious Institutes, or the prescriptions which have been enacted by recent Synods. For this reason, among other measures which the Sacred Congregation for the Oriental Church proposed to undertake, the principal one was this: to revise, amend, and improve the said statutes and decrees. The obstacle to the fulfillment of this most urgent and well conceived plan is that there is as yet no common primary legal norm which may serve as a guide for the other changes and amendments which ought to be made. For this reason We judged it most opportune that these canons on religious should be promulgated.

Equally clear and evident is the reason which induces Us to present the canons on ecclesiastical property: Since in certain countries the effort is being made to take away or impair the inherent right of the Church to possess property, We judged it to be part of Our Apostolic duty to assert and defend all these rights and each of them. And we take this occasion to warn those persons who are in any way in control of such property, that they are bound by the strictest obligation to administer it completely, faithfully, and diligently as is required by its purpose; and that purpose is to provide for the elegance of divine worship, the decent support of sacred ministers, and the relief of the poor. Wherefore, all who are charged with the administration of such property must see to it that they clear themselves of all evil suspicion and incur not even the slightest blame for the manner in which they fulfill their offices. But it is also necessary that wise and absolute laws, by prohibitive, preceptive, and precautionary norms, stand as a potent authority to govern and control the administrators of ecclesiastical property, so that they may care for and administer it "as it were under the eyes of God"[3] and "with all solicitude and in good conscience before God who knoweth all things."[4]

Now the Commission for preparing a Code of Canon Law for

---

[3] *Canones SS. Apostolorum,* 38.

[4] *Syn. antiochena,* can. 24.

the Oriental Churches has attentively considered laws concerning both of these questions, and after hearing from the Bishops of the Oriental Churches and others whose opinions it was useful to know, has proposed the canons on the aforesaid juridical institutions for Our approval, at the same time asking Us to promulgate also a chapter *on the meaning of terms,* since this is quite necessary for the right understanding of these canons on religious.

After carefully considering all this in the presence of God with earnest prayers to the Divine Majesty, We have decided to grant without delay the petition made to Us, and to promulgate at once, if not the entire Code of Laws for the Oriental Churches, at least those canons which concern religious Institutes, ecclesiastical property, and the meaning of certain terms; and, for the reasons given, We have decided of Our own motion, from certain knowledge and in the fullness of Our authority, by this Letter presently to promulgate those canons which concern the discipline of religious Institutes, the temporal property of the Church, and the significance of certain words, which canons were prepared by the Commission for preparing the Code of Laws for the Oriental Churches.

The canons, which We approve with Our Apostolic authority, are the following:

Canons 1–231: on Religious
Canons 232–301: on Ecclesiastical Property
Canons 302–325: on the Meaning of Terms[5]

By this Apostolic Letter given of Our own motion We promulgate the above canons and endow them with the force of law for the faithful of the Oriental Churches, wherever on earth they may be and even though they be subject to a Prelate of another rite. As soon as these canons become effective by this Apostolic Letter, every statute, general, particular, or special, even though enacted by Synods which were approved in the special form, and every prescription and custom still in effect, general or particular, shall lose all force; so that the discipline of religious and of ecclesiastical property and likewise the significance of certain words will be governed exclusively by these same canons, and

---

[5] For the text of the canons, cf. AAS 44, pp. 67–150.

particular laws which are contrary to them will no longer have any effect except when and in as far as they are admitted in them.

But in order that this Our will may have time to come to the notice of all concerned, We will and ordain that this Apostolic Letter given of Our own motion shall go into effect from the twenty-first day of November, the Feast of the Presentation of the Blessed Virgin Mary, all things to the contrary, even those worthy of the most special mention, notwithstanding.

Given at Rome, from Saint Peter's, the ninth of February, Feast of Saint Cyril of Alexandria, Pontiff and Doctor, in the year 1952, the thirteenth of Our Pontificate.

AAS 44–65; Pius XII, *Motu proprio,* 9 Feb., 1952. Annotations, *Monitor Ecclesiasticus,* 1952, p. 233 (Herman).

Monastic Nuns: Apostolic Constitution, *Sponsa Christi.* See c. 600; AAS 43–5.

CANON 488

Apostolic Constitution on Secular Institutes (Pius XII, 2 Feb., 1947) AAS 39–114.

An Apostolic Constitution of 2 February, 1947, entitled: *On the Canonical States and on Secular Institutes for Acquiring Christian Perfection,* is as follows:

The care and maternal affection with which Holy Mother Church has ever solicitously striven on behalf of the children of her predilection, who have given their whole lives to Christ in order to follow Him freely on the arduous path of the counsels, that she might constantly render them worthy of their heavenly resolve and angelic vocation, and at the same time make wise provisions governing their way of life, is witnessed by a host of documents and memorials of Popes, Councils, and Fathers, and is clearly proved by the whole course of church history and by all the canonical legislation on the subject up to our own time.[1]

Certainly from the very beginnings of Christianity, the Church in her *magisterium* earnestly developed the doctrine of Christ

----

[1] The original text contains a wealth of footnote references to Sacred Scripture and the Fathers, invaluable for historical study of the religious life. We reproduce only the few footnotes which refer to recent canonical sources.

and the Apostles and their example inviting souls to perfection, by securely teaching how a life devoted to perfection was to be lived and properly ordered. At the same time, by her work and ministry, she so earnestly favored and propagated an entire dedication and consecration to Christ that in the early ages the Christian communities, by practicing the evangelical counsels, freely offered good ground prepared for the seed and giving secure promise of a rich harvest; and shortly afterward, as can easily be proved from the Apostolic Fathers and the older ecclesiastical writers, the profession of the life of perfection was so flourishing in the various churches that its followers were beginning to constitute in the bosom of the Church, as it were a distinct order and social class, which was clearly recognized under various names — ascetics, continents, virgins, among others — and which was approved and held in honor by many.

In the course of the centuries, the Church, ever faithful to Christ her Spouse, and true to herself, under the guidance of the Holy Spirit, with continuous and unhesitating progress up to the establishment of the present Code of Canon Law, gradually developed the discipline of the state of perfection. With a peculiar motherly affection for those who freely, under various forms, made external and public profession of a life of perfection, she constantly gave them every encouragement in their pursuit of so holy a purpose, and that under two distinct heads. In the first place, the individual profession of the life of perfection, always, however, to be made publicly and before the Church — such as the ancient and venerable liturgical blessing and consecration of virgins — was not only admitted and recognized, but the Church herself wisely sanctioned and strongly defended it, and attached to it a number of canonical effects. But the principal favor and more diligent care of the Church, from the earliest times after the peace of Constantine, were rightly and properly directed toward and exercised in favor of that complete and more strictly public profession of the life of perfection, which was made in societies and organized groups erected with her permission or approval or by her positive authority.

It is common knowledge that the history of the holiness of the Church and of the Catholic apostolate is most closely and intimately connected with the history and records of the canonical religious life, as, under the constant vivifying grace of the Holy

Spirit, it continued from day to day to exhibit a wonderful variety and at the same time to grow into a new and ever deeper and stronger unity. It is not to be wondered at that the Church, even in the field of law, faithfully following the direction which the provident Wisdom of God clearly indicated, purposely cultivated and regulated the canonical state of perfection in such wise that she rightly and properly designed to build the edifice of ecclesiastical discipline upon this as upon one of its cornerstones. Hence, in the first place, the public state of perfection was counted as one of the three principal ecclesiastical states, and in it alone the Church found the second order and grade of canonical persons (c. 107). Here is something surely worthy of attentive consideration: while the other two orders of canonical persons, namely clerics and the laity, are found in the Church by divine law, to which the ecclesiastical institution is superadded (cc. 107, 108, § 3), in as much as the Church is established and organized as a hierarchical society, this class, namely that of religious, intermediate between clerics and the laity and capable of being participated in by both clerics and the laity (c. 107), is entirely derived from the close and very special relationship which it has to the end of the Church, that is, to the efficacious pursuit of perfection by adequate means.

Nor was this all. Lest the public and solemn profession of holiness should be frustrated and come to nothing, the Church with ever increasing strictness was willing to recognize this canonical state of perfection only in societies which were erected and governed by herself, that is, in religious Institutes (c. 488, 1°), whose general form and purpose she had approved by her *magisterium* after a slow and careful examination, and whose institute and rules she had in every case not only scrutinized more than once doctrinally and in the abstract, but had also tested by actual trial. These requirements are laid down so strictly and absolutely in the Code of Canon Law, that in no case, not even by way of exception, is the canonical state of perfection recognized, unless its profession is made in a religious Institute approved by the Church. Finally, the canonical discipline of the state of perfection as a public state was so wisely regulated by the Church that, in the case of clerical religious Institutes, in all those matters in general which concern the clerical life of the religious, the Institutes took the place of dioceses, and membership in a religious society was equivalent to the incardination of a cleric in a diocese (cc. 111, § 1; 115; 585).

After the Code of Pius and Benedict, in the second Part of Book II, which is devoted to religious, had diligently collected, revised, and carefully improved the legislation regarding religious, and had thus in many ways confirmed the canonical state of perfection also in its public aspect, and, wisely perfecting the work begun by Leo XIII of happy memory in his immortal Constitution, *Conditae a Christo*, had admitted Congregations of simple vows among religious Institutes in the strict sense, it seemed that nothing remained to be added in the discipline of the canonical state of perfection. Yet the Church, with her great breadth of mind and vision and with true maternal solicitude, decided to add to the legislation on religious, a brief title as an appropriate supplement. In this title (Title XVII of Book II), the Church declares as in a fairly complete sense equivalent to the canonical state of perfection, certain societies, of great value to herself and frequently also to the State, which, though they lacked some of the requirements which are necessary for the complete state of perfection, such as public vows (cc. 488, 1° and 7°; 487), yet in other respects which are regarded as essentials of the life of perfection, bear a close similarity to religious Institutes and are almost necessarily connected with them.

When all this had been wisely, prudently, and lovingly ordained, ample provision had been made for the great number of souls who wish to leave the world and to embrace a new canonical state strictly so called, exclusively and completely dedicated to the attainment of perfection. But the good Lord, who without respect of persons again and again invited all the faithful to seek and to practice perfection everywhere, in the admirable designs of His divine Providence, so disposed that even in the world, depraved by so many vices especially in our own time, there have been and are now great numbers of chosen souls who not only burn with the desire of individual perfection, but who, while by a special vocation from God they remain in the world, are able to find excellent new forms of Consociation, beautifully corresponding to the needs of the times, in which they can lead a life very well adapted to the acquirement of Christian perfection.

While We heartily commend to the prudence and zeal of spiritual directors the noble strivings of individuals toward perfection in the internal forum, We turn Our attention at this time to the Associations which, before the Church, in the so-called external forum, work and strive to lead their own subjects as it were by the hand to a life of solid perfection. Yet We are not dealing here with all Consociations which sincerely seek Christian perfection in the world, but with those only which, in their internal constitution, in the hierarchical order of their government, in the full dedication, unlimited by any other ties, which they require of their members strictly so called, in their profession of the evangelical counsels, and finally in their manner of exercising the ministry and apostolate, bear a closer essential resemblance to the canonical states of perfection, and especially to the Societies without public vows (Tit. XVII), even though they do not practice the religious life in common, but make use of other external forms.

These Consociations, which shall hereafter be called "secular Institutes," began to be founded, not without the inspiration of divine Providence, in the first half of the last century, in order faithfully "to follow the evangelical counsels in the world and to devote themselves more freely to works of charity, which, owing to the iniquity of the times, were almost or entirely forbidden to religious."[2] Since the older Institutes of this class have given a good account of themselves and have sufficiently and increasingly demonstrated, by the severe and prudent selection of their members, by their careful and sufficiently protracted training, and by an appropriate blending of firmness and flexibility in their way of life, that even in the world, with a special vocation from God and with the help of divine grace, it is certainly possible to attain a rather strict and effective self-consecration to God, which is not merely internal but also external and almost religious, and that thus a very appropriate instrument of penetration and apostolate is provided — for all these reasons, "these Societies of the faithful have more than once been commended by the Holy See in the same way as have true religious Congregations."[3]

The prosperous growth of these Institutes has shown with increasing clarity in how many ways they can be turned to the effective service of the Church and of souls. For living seriously

---

[2] S. C. Ep. et Reg., 11 Aug., 1889; ASS 23–634.
[3] *Ibid.*

the life of perfection at all times and in all places; for embracing such a life in many cases where the canonical religious life was either impossible or not appropriate; for the thorough Christian renovation of families, professions, and civil society through an intimate and daily contact with a life perfectly and entirely dedicated to holiness; for exercising a varied apostolate and ministry in places, times, and circumstances forbidden or inaccessible to priests and religious — for all these purposes, these Institutes can easily be used and adapted. On the other hand, experience has shown that this free and independent living of the life of perfection — without the protection of an external religious habit, without the support of a common life, without supervision on the part of Ordinaries, who could easily remain unaware of its existence, or of Superiors, who frequently were far away — was at times, nay rather easily, attended by certain difficulties and dangers. There had also arisen some discussion about the juridical nature of these Institutes, and about the mind of the Holy See in approving them. Here We think it useful to mention the Decree, *Ecclesia Catholica,* which the Sacred Congregation of Bishops and Regulars issued, and which was confirmed on the 11th of August 1889[4] by Our Predecessor of immortal memory, Leo XIII. In this Decree the commendation and approval of such Institutes was not forbidden, but it was stated that the Sacred Congregation, when it did give commendation or approval to these Institutes, had wished to commend and approve them, not as religious Institutes of solemn vows, nor as true religious Congregations of simple vows, but only as pious sodalities, in which, not to speak of the other things which are wanting according to the present discipline of the Church, no religious profession in the proper sense is pronounced, but the vows, if there are any, are considered private, and not public in the sense of being accepted by the legitimate Superior in the name of the Church. These sodalities, moreover — said the same Sacred Congregation — are commended or approved under this essential condition, that they become fully and perfectly known to their respective Ordinaries and be entirely subject to their jurisdiction. These prescriptions and declarations of the Sacred Congregation of Bishops and Regulars made a timely contribution toward

---

⁴ *Ibid.*

defining the nature of these Institutes, and guided without impeding their development and progress.

In this present century secular Institutes have quietly multiplied, and have taken on a considerable variety of forms, some autonomous and some united in various ways to religious Institutes or Societies. The Apostolic Constitution, *Conditae a Christo*, makes no provision for them, as it was exclusively concerned with religious Congregations. The Code of Canon Law also was intentionally silent as regards these Institutes, and, since they did not seem to be yet mature, it left it to future legislation to determine what provision should be made for them.

Having more than once considered all this in view of Our conscientious duty and Our paternal affection for the souls who so generously seek holiness in the world; and to the end that a wise and searching discrimination may be exercised in regard to these Societies, and that those only which authentically profess the full life of perfection be acknowledged as true Institutes; in order to avoid the dangers of the continual erection of new Institutes — which are sometimes founded without prudent consideration; and at the same time that those Institutes which do merit approval may have the special juridical regulation which corresponds suitably and fully to their purposes and conditions, We have considered and decided upon doing for secular Institutes what Our Predecessor of immortal memory, Leo XIII, so prudently and wisely provided for Congregations of simple vows by the Apostolic Constitution, *Conditae a Christo*. Accordingly, the general statute of secular Institutes, which had been carefully examined by the Supreme Sacred Congregation of the Holy Office in matters relating to its competency, and had been, by Our will and direction, carefully drawn up and revised by the Sacred Congregation of Religious, We now approve by this present Letter; and do by Our Apostolic authority declare, decree, and establish the following.

And for putting into execution the provisions as above established, We depute the Sacred Congregation of Religious, investing it with all necessary and appropriate faculties.

Special Law of Secular Institutes

Art. I

Societies, whether clerical or lay, whose members, in order to

attain Christian perfection and to exercise a full apostolate, profess
the evangelical counsels in the world, that they may be properly
distinguished from other common Associations of the faithful
(Part Three, Book II of the Code of Canon Law) are rightly
called Institutes, or secular Institutes, and are subject to the
norms of this Apostolic Constitution.

Art. II

§ 1. Secular Institutes, since they neither admit the three
public vows of religion (cc. 1308, § 1, and 488, 1°), nor oblige
their members to live the common life, that is, to dwell together
under the same roof, according to the canons (cc. 487 sqq.,
and 673 sqq.):

1° By law, according to their rule, neither are nor can properly
be called religious Institutes (cc. 487 and 488, 1°) nor Societies
of the common life (c. 673, § 1);

2° They are not bound by the proper and special law of religious Institutes or of Societies of the common life, nor can they
use the same, except in as far as some provision thereof, especially
of the law governing Societies without public vows, may by way
of exception have been legitimately adapted and applied to them.

§ 2. These Institutes, without prejudice to the common norms
of canon law which concern them, are governed by the following
prescriptions as their proper law, more closely corresponding to
their peculiar nature and condition:

1° By the general norms of this Apostolic Constitution, which
constitute as it were the peculiar statute of all secular Institutes;

2° By the norms which the Sacred Congregation of Religious,
according as necessity shall demand and experience shall suggest,
may decide to issue, either by way of interpreting this Apostolic
Constitution or of perfecting and applying it for all or some
of these Institutes;

3° By the particular Constitutions, approved according to
the Articles which follow (Art. V-VIII), which may prudently
adapt the general rules of law and the special norms set forth
above (nn. 1° and 2°) to the quite different purposes, needs, and
circumstances of the various Institutes.

Art. III

§ 1. In order that any pious Consociation of the faithful may be erected as a secular Institute according to the Articles which follow, it must satisfy, in addition to those of the common law, the following requisites (§§ 2–4):

§ 2. As regards the consecration of life and the profession of Christian perfection:

Persons who desire to be ascribed to the Institutes as members in the strict sense, in addition to practicing those exercises of piety and self-denial which all must practice who aspire to the perfection of Christian life, must effectively tend toward that same perfection also in the special ways which are here enumerated:

1° By making profession before God of celibacy and perfect chastity, which shall be confirmed by vow, oath, or consecration binding in conscience, according to the Constitutions;

2° By a vow or promise of obedience, so that they dedicate themselves entirely to God and to works of charity or apostleship by a stable bond, and are always in all respects morally in the hands and under the guidance of their Superiors, according to the Constitutions;

3° By a vow or promise of poverty, in virtue of which they have not the free use of temporal property, but a restricted and limited use, according to the Constitutions.

§ 3. As regards the incorporation of the members in their own Institute and the bond arising therefrom:

The bond by which the secular Institute and its members in the strict sense are to be united must be:

1° Stable, according to the Constitutions, either perpetual or temporary but to be renewed at its expiration (c. 488, 1°);

2° Mutual and complete, so that, according to the Constitutions, the member gives himself wholly to the Institute, and the Institute takes care of and is responsible for the member.

§ 4. As regards the establishments and houses of secular Institutes:

Secular Institutes, though they do not impose upon their members the common life and cohabitation under the same roof according to the common law (Art. II, § 1), yet should have one or more common houses, according to need or utility, in which:

1° Those may live who have the government of the Institute, especially the supreme or regional government;

2° Where the members may live, or to which they may come,

to receive and complete their training, to make spiritual exercises, and for other such purposes;

3° Where members may be received when, because of ill health or other circumstances, they cannot provide for themselves, or when it is not advisable that they live privately, either by themselves or with others.

Art. IV

§ 1. Secular Institutes (Art. I) are under the Sacred Congregation of Religious, without prejudice to the rights of the Sacred Congregation for the Propagation of the Faith according to canon 252, § 3, as regards Societies and Seminaries destined for the Missions.

§ 2. Consociations which have not the character or do not fully profess the purpose described in Article I, and those also which lack any of the elements mentioned in Articles I and III of this Apostolic Constitution, are governed by the law of Associations of the faithful as in canons 684 and the following canons, and are under the Sacred Congregation of the Council, except as provided in canon 252, § 3 for the territory of the Missions.

Art. V

§ 1. Secular Institutes can be established and erected as moral persons according to canon 100, §§ 1 and 2, by Bishops, but not by Vicars Capitular or Vicars General.

§ 2. Bishops should not, however, establish them nor allow them to be established without consulting the Sacred Congregation of Religious, according to canon 492, § 1, and the following Article.

Art. VI

§ 1. In order that the Sacred Congregation of Religious may give Bishops the permission to erect Institutes, when they consult it on the matter in advance according to Article V, § 2, the said Sacred Congregation must be informed, making due allowances according to its own judgment for the differences between the respective cases, of all those matters which are specified in the Norms issued by the same Sacred Congregation for the erection of a Congregation or Society of the common life (nn. 3–5),[5] and

---

[5] S. C. Rel., 6 March, 1921; AAS 13–312. Not contained in CANON LAW DIGEST because the publication of translations was forbidden by the Holy See.

also of other matters which have been or shall in future be required by the practice and procedure of the same Sacred Congregation.

§ 2. When Bishops have obtained the permission of the Sacred Congregation of Religious, there will be nothing to prevent their freely using their right and erecting the Institute. They should not fail to send official notice of the erection to the same Sacred Congregation.

Art. VII

§ 1. Secular Institutes which shall have obtained approval or a decree of praise from the Holy See, become Institutes of pontifical right (cc. 488, 3°; 673, § 2).

§ 2. In order that secular Institutes of diocesan right may be able to obtain a decree of praise or of approbation, in general, making due allowances according to the judgment of the Sacred Congregation of Religious for the differences between the respective cases, the same conditions are required which according to the Norms (nn. 6 sqq.) and according to the practice and procedure of the same Sacred Congregation, have been, or may in future be prescribed and defined for Congregations and Societies of the common life.

§ 3. The procedure in granting the first, any further provisional, and finally the definitive approval of these Institutes and their Constitutions, shall be as follows:

1° A first discussion of the case, after it has been prepared according to the usual practice and illustrated by the opinion and explanation of at least one Consultor, shall take place in the Commission of Consultors, under the leadership of the Most Excellent Secretary of the same Sacred Congregation, or of some one taking his place.

2° Then the entire matter is to be submitted to the examination and decision of the full *Congressus* of the Sacred Congregation, with the Eminent Cardinal Prefect of the Sacred Congregation presiding, and in the presence of learned or more learned Consultors who have been invited in order to scrutinize the case more carefully as necessity or utility may suggest.

3° The decision of the *Congressus* shall be reported by the Eminent Cardinal Prefect or the Most Excellent Secretary to His Holiness in an audience, and be thus submitted to his supreme judgment.

Art. VIII

Secular Institutes, besides being subject to their own laws if they have any or if any be established in the future, are subject to the Ordinaries of places, according to the law which is in effect for nonexempt Congregations and Societies of common life.

Art. IX

The internal government of secular Institutes may be arranged hierarchically after the manner of the government of religious Institutes and Societies of common life, due allowances being made in the judgment of the same Sacred Congregation for the respective differences, and taking into account the nature, ends and circumstances of the Institutes themselves.

Art. X

As to the rights and obligations of Institutes which are already established and were approved either by the Bishops after consulting the Holy See or by the Holy See itself, this Apostolic Constitution makes no change.

Thus We decree, declare, and provide, decreeing moreover that this Apostolic Constitution is and shall always be firm, valid, and effective, and shall have its full and entire effects, all things to the contrary, even such as are worthy of most special mention, notwithstanding. Let no one therefore infringe this Constitution promulgated by Us, nor rashly dare to contravene the same.

Given at Rome, at Saint Peter's, the second day of February, Feast of the Purification of the Blessed Virgin Mary, in the year nineteen hundred and forty-seven, the eighth of Our Pontificate.

AAS 39–114; Pius XII, Apostolic Constitution, 2 Feb., 1947.

Cf. *Commentarium pro Religiosis,* 26–12 (Goyeneche) ; *Periodica,* 36–118 (Creusen).

Commission for Secular Institutes Appointed (S. C. Rel., 25 March, 1947) AAS 39–131.

A Decree of the Sacred Congregation of Religious:

Now that the Apostolic Constitution, *Provida Mater Ecclesia,*[1] has been made public, whatever seems necessary or opportune for its interpretation, application, or complement should be carefully

---

[1] The Apostolic Constitution on secular Institutes, 2 Feb., 1947, reported above in this same volume, under this same canon 488.

prepared. Accordingly, by authority of His Holiness in an audience granted to the undersigned Cardinal Prefect of this Sacred Congregation on the 24th of the present month of March, a special Commission of jurists is established, which shall assist the Sacred Congregation in all matters which concern legislation in any way affecting secular Institutes and the approval and development of such Institutes.

As members of this Commission, to which other members will be added as necessity or utility may suggest, the following reverend Fathers have been appointed:

The Very Reverend Emmanuel Suarez, Master General of the Order of Preachers;

The Very Reverend Joseph Grendel, Superior General of the Congregation of the Divine Word;

The Very Reverend Agatangelus a Langasco, Procurator General of the Order of Friars Minor Capuchin;

The Very Reverend Joseph Creusen, of the Society of Jesus, Professor of Canon Law in the Pontifical Gregorian University;

The Very Reverend Servus Goyeneche, of the Congregation of the Sons of the Immaculate Heart of Mary, Professor of Canon Law in the Pontifical Lateran Athenaeum *Utriusque Iuris*;

The Very Reverend Alvarus del Portillo, Procurator General of the secular Institute *"Opus Dei,"* Secretary.

Given at Rome, from the Sacred Congregation of Religious, March 25, 1947.

AAS 39–131; S. C. Rel., 25 March, 1947.

Secular Institutes Commended and Confirmed (Pius XII, *Motu proprio*, 12 March, 1948) AAS 40–283.

This *Motu proprio,* entitled *"De Institutorum Saecularium Laude atque Confirmatione,"* is as follows:

Now that the first year has passed since the promulgation of Our Apostolic Constitution *Provida Mater Ecclesia,*[1] having in mind the great number of souls "hidden with Christ in God,"[2] who aspire to sanctity in the world and joyfully consecrate their whole life to God "with a great heart and a willing mind"[3] in the

---

[1] Pius XII, 2 Feb., 1947; AAS 39–114. Cf. this Volume, p. 151.

[2] Col. 3:3.

[3] Mach. 1:3.

new Secular Institutes, We cannot but give thanks to the Divine Goodness for this new division which has come to swell the army of those who profess the evangelical counsels in the world, and also for the strong arm which has come to reinforce the Catholic apostolate in these troubled and sorrowful times.

The Holy Spirit, Who ceaselessly re-creates and renews the face of the earth,[4] constantly desolated and defiled as it is with so many and such great evils, has called to Himself by a great and special grace many beloved sons and daughters, whom We lovingly bless in the Lord, to the end that, being united and organized in Secular Institutes, they may be the salt of the earth — of that world of which they are not,[5] yet in which by the will of God they must remain — the unfailing salt which, ever renewed by the grace of vocation, does not lose its savor;[6] the light of the world which shines in the darkness and is not extinguished;[7] the small but potent leaven which, always and everywhere active, mingling with every class of persons from the lowest to the highest, strives by example and in every way to reach and to transfuse them individually and collectively until the whole mass is so permeated that it is all leavened in Christ.[8]

In order that, through this consoling outpouring of the Spirit of Christ,[9] the many Institutes which have arisen everywhere may be effectively governed according to the Apostolic Constitution *Provida Mater Ecclesia,* and may bring forth in abundance those excellent fruits of sanctity which We hope for; also that, drawn up in solid and well-ordered battle array,[10] they may be able to fight valiantly the battles of the Lord in the special and common works of the apostolate, We now very joyfully confirm the aforesaid Apostolic Constitution, and with mature deliberation, of Our own motion, from certain knowledge and out of the fulness of Apostolic power, We declare, decree and establish the following:

I. Societies, whether of clerics or of lay persons, which profess Christian perfection in the world, and which seem certainly and

---

[4] Cf. Psalms 103:30.
[5] Cf. John 15:19.
[6] Cf. Matt. 5:13; Mark 9:49; Luke 14:34.
[7] Cf. John 9:5; 1:5; 8:12; Eph. 5:8.
[8] Cf. Matt. 13:33; 1 Cor. 5:6; Gal. 5:9.
[9] Cf. Rom. 8:9.   [10] Cf. Cant. 6:3.

fully to possess the elements and requisites prescribed in the Apostolic Constitution *Provida Mater Ecclesia,* should not and may not arbitrarily on any pretext be left among the common Associations of the faithful (cc. 684–725), but must necessarily be brought up and advanced to the proper nature and form of Secular Institutes which aptly correspond to their character and needs.

II. In this elevation of Societies of the faithful to the higher form of Secular Institutes (cf. n. I), and in working out the general as well as the particular organization of all these Institutes, this must always be kept in mind, that in all of them their special and peculiar character as *secular* Institutes, which is the whole reason for their existence, be clearly expressed. Nothing is to be subtracted from the full profession of Christian perfection, solidly based on the evangelical counsels, and in substance truly religious; but this perfection is to be exercised and professed *in the world,* and therefore in all things which are licit and which can be brought into conformity with the duties and works of that same perfection, it must be adapted to the secular life.

The whole life of members of Secular Institutes, sacred to God through the profession of perfection, must be turned toward the apostolate, which ought to be so constantly and virtuously practiced through purity of intention, interior union with God, generous forgetfulness of self, strong self-denial and love of souls, that it shall bear the mark of the interior spirit which informs it and at the same time shall constantly nourish and renew that spirit. This apostolate embracing the whole of life is usually felt so constantly, deeply and sincerely in these Institutes that, by the aid and according to the plan of Divine Providence, an ardent thirst for souls seems not only to have furnished the happy occasion for a life of consecration but to have impressed upon it largely its peculiar nature and form, and in a marvelous way to have demanded and brought forth the so-called specific end of the Institute as well as its generic end. This apostolate of Secular Institutes is to be faithfully practiced not only *in the world,* but as *of the world,* and therefore with avowed aims, practices, forms, and in places and circumstances corresponding to this secular condition.

III. According to the Apostolic Constitution *Provida Mater Ecclesia*, things which pertain to the canonical discipline of the religious state do not concern Secular Institutes, and in general religious legislation neither should nor can be applied to them (Art. II, § 1). On the other hand, those elements in the various Institutes which are found to be in friendly accord with their secular character, provided they in no way detract from a full and entire self-consecration and are consistent with the Constitution *Provida Mater Ecclesia*, may be retained.

IV. An interdiocesan and universal hierarchical organization can be applied to Secular Institutes (Art. IX), and such application should without doubt give them internal vitality, a wider and more powerful influence and greater stability. In this organization however, which should be adapted to each Institute, the nature of the end which the Institute professes, the greater or lesser expansion which it may expect, its degree of development and maturity, its circumstances and other such matters must all be considered. Nor should those forms of Institutes be rejected or despised which exist as federations and wish to retain and moderately to favor a local character in various nations, regions, or dioceses, provided such character be right and in due accord with the catholicity of the Church.

V. Secular Institutes, even though their members live in the world, still by reason of the full dedication to God and to souls which they profess with the approval of the Church, and by reason of the internal interdiocesan and universal hierarchical organization which they can have in varying degrees, are according to the Apostolic Constitution *Provida Mater Ecclesia* rightly and properly numbered among the states of perfection which are juridically constituted and recognized by the Church. It was therefore of set purpose that these Institutes were assigned and entrusted to the competency and care of that Sacred Congregation which has the control and charge of *public states of perfection*. Hence, always without prejudice, according to the canons and the express provision of the Apostolic Constitution *Provida Mater Ecclesia* (Art. IV, §§ 1 and 2), to the rights of the Sacred Congregation of the Council regarding common pious sodalities and pious unions of the faithful (c. 250, § 2) and of the Sacred Congregation for the Propagation of the Faith regarding societies of ecclesiastics and[11] seminaries for the foreign missions (c. 252, § 3), all societies anywhere in the world — though they have the approval of the Ordinary or even of the Holy See — as soon as they are known to have the elements and requisites proper to Secular Institutes, must immediately be conformed to this new standard according to the norms above set forth (cf. n. I), and in order that unity of direction be preserved, We have decreed that they are rightly assigned and entrusted exclusively to the Sacred Congregation of Religious, in which a special Office for Secular Institutes has been established.

VI. To the moderators and assistants of Catholic Action and of other Associations of the faithful, in whose maternal bosom are being trained to full Christian living and introduced to the exercise of the apostolate so many chosen young people who are called by divine vocation to a higher life either in Religious Institutes and Societies of common life or in Secular Institutes, We recommend with fatherly affection that they generously promote such holy vocations, and that they lend a helping hand not only to Religious Institutes and Societies but also to these truly providential Institutes, and as far as their own internal government permits, freely make use of their services.

The faithful execution of all these provisions which We have made of Our own motion, We in virtue of Our Apostolic Authority entrust to the Sacred Congregation of Religious and the other Sacred Congregations above mentioned, to the Ordinaries of places and to the Directors of the Societies concerned.

And We order that what We have established by this Letter given of Our own motion shall be forever valid and firm, all things to the contrary notwithstanding.

Given at Rome, from Saint Peter's, the 12th of March in the year nineteen hundred and forty-eight, at the commencement of the tenth year of Our Pontificate.

AAS 40–283; Pius XII, *Motu proprio*, 12 March, 1948.
Periodica, 37–266 (Creusen).

Instruction on Secular Institutes (S. C. Rel., 19 March, 1948) AAS 40–293.

---

[11] It seems evident from the canon cited and from the context that the word *ad* of the original is a misprint for *ac*.

This Instruction, entitled *"De Institutis Saecularibus,"* is as follows:

When His Holiness Pius XII promulgated the Apostolic Constitution, *Provida Mater Ecclesia*,[1] he deigned to depute for the more effective execution of all its wise provisions the Sacred Congregation of Religious, within whose competency the Secular Institutes were placed (*Lex Peculiaris,* Art. IV, §§ 1 and 2), and for this purpose he granted to the said Sacred Congregation all necessary and appropriate faculties.

Among the functions and duties which rest upon this Sacred Congregation according to this pontifical deputation and the express provision of the Constitution itself, is this, that the Sacred Congregation can issue norms "according as necessity shall demand and experience shall suggest, either by way of interpreting this Apostolic Constitution or of perfecting and applying it," which may be deemed necessary or useful for Secular Institutes in general or for some of them in particular (Art. II, § 2, 2°).

Now, although complete and definitive norms regarding Secular Institutes had best be postponed to a more opportune time lest the present-day development of the said Institutes be dangerously restricted, yet it is expedient that some of the provisions of the Apostolic Constitution, *Provida Mater Ecclesia,* which were not clearly understood and rightly interpreted by all persons, be immediately made clearer and placed beyond danger of misunderstanding, keeping carefully the prescriptions which are laid down in the Letter, *Primo feliciter,* given by His Holiness of his own motion on the 12th of this month.[2] Hence the Sacred Congregation has decided to put together in clear arrangement and so to issue by way of an Instruction the supreme norms which may rightly be regarded as fundamental for the solid initial establishment and regulation of Secular Institutes.

1. In order that an Association, even though it be ardently dedicated to the profession of Christian perfection and to the exercise of the apostolate in the world, may have the full right to assume the name and title of a Secular Institute, not only must

---

[1] Apostolic Constitution, 2 Feb., 1947; AAS 39–114; CANON LAW DIGEST, Vol. 3, under canon 488.

[2] *Motu proprio,* 12 March, 1948; AAS 40–283; See this volume under canon 488, p. 147.

it possess all and each of the elements which are mentioned and explained in the Apostolic Constitution, *Provida Mater Ecclesia*, as necessary and integral in Secular Institutes (Art. I and III), but it is moreover quite necessary that the Institute be approved and erected by some Bishop after having previously consulted this Sacred Congregation (Art. V, § 2; Art. VI).

2. All Associations of the faithful in any part of the world, whether in territories subject to the common law or in those of the Missions, if they have the character and features described in the Apostolic Constitution, are according to the Constitution itself dependent on this Sacred Congregation of Religious (Art. IV, §§ 1 and 2) and are governed by the *Lex Peculiaris* or Special Law of the said Constitution; nor may they on any ground or pretext, according to the *Motu proprio, Primo feliciter* (n. V), remain among common Associations of the faithful (Book II, Part III of the Code of Canon Law), without prejudice to n. 5 of this Instruction.

3. To obtain permission to erect a new Secular Institute, the Bishop of the place and none other must apply to this Sacred Congregation, informing it clearly of all the matters which are explained in the Norms for the erection and approval of Congregations, issued by this same Sacred Congregation of Religious (*Normae*, 6 March, 1921, nn. 3–8; AAS 13–312),[3] with appropriate adjustments to fit the case (Art. VII). Copies of the Constitutions must also be sent (at least six) in Latin or in one of the other languages accepted in the Roman Curia, as well as the Directory and other documents which can be of service in showing the nature and spirit of the Association. The Constitutions should contain everything which concerns the nature of the Institute, classes of members, government, form of consecration (Art. III, § 2), the bond arising from the incorporation of the members in the Institute (Art. III, § 3), common houses (Art. III, § 4), the training of the members and exercises of piety.

4. Associations which, prior to the Constitution, *Provida Mater Ecclesia*, and legitimately according to the then existing law, had been erected or approved by Bishops or had obtained some sort of pontifical approval as Associations of lay persons, in order to obtain recognition from this Sacred Congregation as Secular Institutes whether of diocesan or pontifical right, must send to this

---

[3] See CANON LAW DIGEST, Vol. 1, p. 272.

Sacred Congregation their documents of erection or approval, the Constitutions under which they have hitherto been governed, a brief account of their history, discipline and apostolate, and, especially if they be only of diocesan right, also testimonials from the Ordinaries in whose dioceses they have houses. After all this has been considered and carefully examined according to Articles VI and VII of the Constitution, *Provida Mater Ecclesia,* the permission to erect, or the Decree of praise as the case may be, can be granted.

5. Associations which have only recently been founded or are not sufficiently developed, as well as those which spring up from time to time, even though they give good ground for the hope that if things go well they may develop into solid and genuine Secular Institutes, had best not be presented immediately to this Sacred Congregation to obtain from it the permission to erect them. As a general rule, which should admit of exceptions only for grave reasons strictly proved, these new Consociations, until they shall have proved themselves sufficiently, should be retained and exercised under the paternal hand and guardianship of diocesan Authority, first as mere Associations existing in fact rather than *de iure,* and then, not in one leap but gradually and by degrees, should be developed under some of the forms of Associations of the faithful, such as Pious Unions, Sodalities, Confraternities, as may seem appropriate according to the case.

6. While these preliminary developments (n. 5) are going on to prove clearly that the Associations in question really aim at an entire consecration of life to perfection and the apostolate, and that they have all the other features which are required in a true Secular Institute, vigilant care must be exercised to see that nothing be permitted either internally or externally to these Associations, which is beyond their present condition and seems to belong specifically to Secular Institutes. Those things especially should be avoided which, in case the permission to erect the Assotion as a Secular Institute is later refused, could not easily be taken away or undone and would seem to exert a sort of pressure on Superiors to make them grant approval outright or too easily.

7. In order to form a safe practical judgment whether an Association has the true character of a Secular Institute, that is, whether it effectively leads its members in the secular state and condition to that full consecration and dedication which repro-

duces even in the external forum the figure of a complete state of perfection in substance truly religious, the following questions must be carefully considered:

a) whether the persons who are members of the Association in the strict sense, "in addition to practicing those exercises of piety and self-denial" without which the life of perfection must be judged illusory, profess in a practical and substantial way the three general evangelical counsels in one of the various forms admitted by the Apostolic Constitution (Art. III, § 2). It is permitted, however, to admit as members in the broad sense, ascribed to the body of the Association by a more or less firm bond or intention, persons who aspire to evangelical perfection and strive to practice it in their condition of life, even though they do not or cannot embrace all the evangelical counsels in the highest degree;

b) whether the bond by which the members in the strict sense are attached to the Association is stable, mutual and complete, so that, according to the Constitution, the member gives himself wholly to the Association, and the Association is already, or it is seriously foreseen that it will be, such as will and can take care of and be responsible for the member (Art. III, § 3, 2°);

c) whether, and how or under what aspect, the Association has or is striving to acquire the common houses which are prescribed in the Apostolic Constitution (Art. III, § 4) for the attainment of the ends for which these houses are destined;

d) are those things being avoided which would not be in accord with the nature and character of Secular Institutes, as for example: a habit which is inappropriate for life in the world, a common life externally ordered (Art. II, § 1; Art. III, § 4) after the manner of religious common life or in a manner equivalent to that (Book II, Title XVII of the Code of Canon Law).

8. According to Art. II, § 1, 2°, of the Apostolic Constitution, *Provida Mater Ecclesia,* and without prejudice to Art. X and Art. II, § 1, 1°, of the same Constitution, Secular Institutes are not bound by the special and peculiar law of religious Institutes or Societies of common life, nor may they live by such law. Yet the Sacred Congregation may by way of exception, according to the tenor of the Constitution (Art. II, § 1, 2°), adapt and apply to them some particular provisions of the law of religious which may be suitable also to Secular Institutes, and may even prudently

borrow from the aforesaid law certain more or less general criteria which are approved by experience and are in accord with the inner nature of things.

9. In particular: *a*) Although the provisions of canon 500, § 3 do not strictly concern Secular Institutes and need not be applied to them as they stand, yet a solid criterion and clear guidance may be purposely drawn from them for the approval and ordering of Secular Institutes.

b) Although according to law (c. 492, § 1) there is no objection to Secular Institutes being aggregated by special concession to religious Orders and even to other religious Institutes, and to their being helped in various ways by the latter, and even in a sense morally guided by them, yet other forms of closer dependence, which would seem to detract from the autonomy of government of Secular Institutes, or to subject that autonomy to a more or less strict tutelage, even though such relations may be desired and asked for by the Institutes themselves, especially if these be Institutes of women, can be granted only with difficulty, upon careful consideration of the good of the Institutes, after pondering their spirit and the nature and character of the apostolate to which they are dedicated, and only with appropriate precautions.

10. Secular Institutes: (*a*) by reason of the state of full perfection which they profess and of the entire dedication to the apostolate which they impose, are, within that same kind of perfection and of apostolate, evidently called to higher things than those which would seem sufficient for the faithful, even the best of them, working in merely lay Associations or in Catholic Action and other pious works; (*b*) must however take up the peculiar apostolic exercises and ministries which constitute their special ends, in such a way that their members — carefully avoiding all confusion — may be able to do their best in giving to the other faithful who see and observe them an outstanding example of self-denying, humble, and constant collaboration with the Hierarchy, always without prejudice to their own internal government (cf. *Motu proprio, Primo feliciter,* n. VI).

11. *a*) The Ordinary, when after obtaining permission from the Holy See he erects a Secular Institute which formerly existed as an Association either *de facto* or in the form of a Pious Union or Sodality, may determine whether it is advisable, in connection

with fixing the condition of persons and computing the requisites laid down in the Constitutions of the Institute, to take account of things that were done antecedently, for example probation, consecration, and the like.

b) During the first ten years of a Secular Institute, counting from the time of its erection, the Bishop of the place has the power to dispense from requirements of age, time of probation, years of consecration, and other such matters which may be prescribed for all Institutes in general or for some one in particular, as regards offices, occupations, grades and other juridical effects.

c) Houses or centers founded before the canonical erection of the Institute, if they were established with the permission of both Bishops as required by canon 495, § 1, *ipso facto,* become parts of the Institute upon its erection.

Given at Rome, from the Sacred Congregation of Religious, on the 19th of March, Feast of Saint Joseph, Spouse of the Blessed Virgin Mary, in the year 1948.

AAS 40–293; S. C. Rel., Instruction, 19 March, 1948.
Periodica, 37–266 (Creusen); *Review for Religious,* 10–296 (Korth).

Benedictines: Order of St. Benedict: Confederation of Monastic Congregations: Among recent papal documents the following may be consulted:

1) Pius XII, Encyclical, *Fulgens radiatur,* on the fourteenth centenary of the death of Saint Benedict, 21 March, 1947 (AAS 39–137).

2) Pius XII, Homily delivered at St. Paul's outside the walls on the occasion of the election of an Abbot Primate, 17 Sept., 1947 (AAS 39–452).

3) Pius XII, Ap. Letter formally approving the *Lex propria* or revised Constitutions of the Confederation of Monastic Congregations of the Order of Saint Benedict, 21 March, 1952 (AAS 44–520). Annotations, *Monitor Ecclesiasticus,* 1952, p. 549 (Oesterle).

Carmelites: Letter of Pius XII to Cardinal Piazza commemorating the fifth centenary of the founding of the Second and Third Orders, 25 July, 1952 (AAS 44–811).

Franciscan Order: Letter of Pius XII to General of Franciscans, O.F.M. Conventuals, O.F.M.Cap. and Third Order Regular, 15 Aug., 1952 (AAS 44–814).

Junior Religious, Novices, and Aspirants: Special Commission of S. C. Rel., for. See **c. 251**; AAS 36–213.

Quinquennial Report. See **c. 510**; AAS 40–378.

Solemn Vows: Permission for. See **c. 600**; private reply of S. C. Rel., 12 Nov., 1951.

Teaching Sisters: Apostolic Exhortation of Pius XII to the International Convention of Teaching Sisters, 13 Sept., 1951 (AAS 43–738). English text, *The Catholic Mind,* 1952, p. 376.

CANON 489

Custom Books of Religious, where contrary to Statutes of S. C. Rel., on Externe Sisters, 16 July, 1931 (*Digest,* II, p. 170), are abrogated. See c. 600; private reply of S. C. Rel., 1936.

CANON 492

Secular Institutes: Approval of, by Bishop. See c. 488; AAS 40–293.
   Attached to Order or Congregation. See c. 488; AAS 40–293, n. 9, b.

CANON 495

Secular Institutes: Houses in different dioceses established before erection of Institute. See c. 488; AAS 40–293, n. 11, c.

CANON 499

Obedience to Roman Pontiff on part of exempt religious priests. See c. 487; AAS 43–26.

Religious Congregation Subject to Propaganda. A Congregation of pontifical right was declared to be proximately under the jurisdiction of the S. C. Prop. Fid. See S. C. Prop. Fid., 2 Dec., 1942 (AAS 35–26).

CANON 500

Secular Institutes of Women: Direction of, by Institutes of men. See c. 488; AAS 40–293, n. 9, a.

CANON 501

Dominative Power of Religious Superiors: Subject to certain canons on jurisdiction. See c. 197; AAS 44–497.

Privilege of Elected Major Superior to Act Before Confirmation. See c. 148; Code Com., 5 Aug., 1918.

Superiors of Religious Women: Allocution of Pius XII, 13 Sept., 1952 (AAS 44–823). English text, *Review for Religious,* 11–305.

CANON 510

Decree on the Quinquennial Report of Religious and Others, and on the Annual Prospectus (S. C. Relig., 9 July, 1947) AAS 40–378.

A Decree entitled: "Concerning the quinquennial report which is to be made by religious Institutes, Societies of common life and secular Institutes," is as follows:

As more than twenty-five years have passed since the publica-

tion of the Decree, *Sancitum est,* of 8 March, 1922,[1] regulating
the quinquennial report which is to be sent to the Holy See by
the General Superiors of religious Institutes (c. 510), and as
experience has clearly shown which of its provisions seem to
merit definitive confirmation, what should be added to them,
and which ones should be revoked or amended, as that Decree
itself intimated, the Sacred Congregation of Religious, in the
plenary session of the Eminent Fathers of 4 July, 1947, decided
to provide as follows:

I. According to the Code (c. 510), the Abbot Primate, the
Abbot Superior of a monastic Congregation (c. 488, 8°), the
Superior General of every religious Institute, Society of common
life without public vows (c. 675), and secular Institute, of
pontifical right, and the President of any Federation of houses
of religious, Institutes, Societies of common life, or secular Institutes, and, in default of the above-named persons or if they
are prevented from acting, their Vicars (c. 488, 8°), must send
to the Holy See, that is to this Sacred Congregation of Religious,
a report on the state of their religious Institute, Society, secular
Institute or Federation, every five years, even if the year assigned
for sending the report falls wholly or partly within the first two
years from the time when they entered upon the office.

II. The five-year periods shall be fixed and common to all those
mentioned above in n. I; and they shall continue to be computed
from the first day of January, 1923.

III. In making the reports, the following order shall be
observed:

1° From among the religious Institutes, Societies of common
life, secular Institutes and Federations of pontifical right, whose
members are men, the report is to be sent:

in the first year of the five-year period: by the Canons
Regular, Monks, and Military Orders;

in the second year: by the Mendicants, Clerics Regular, and
other Regulars;

in the third year: by the Clerical Congregations;

in the fourth year: by the lay Congregations;

in the fifth year: by the Societies of common life, secular
Institutes, and Federations.

2° From among the religious Institutes, Societies of common

---
[1] AAS 14–161; DIGEST, 1, p. 282.

life, secular Institutes, and Federations of pontifical right, whose members are women, the report is to be sent, according to the region in which the principal house is juridically established:

in the first year of the five-year period: by the Superioresses of religious Institutes in Italy, Spain, and Portugal;

in the second year: by the Superioresses of religious Institutes in France, Belgium, Holland, England, and Ireland;

in the third year: by the Superioresses of religious Institutes in other parts of Europe;

in the fourth year: by the Superioresses of religious Institutes in the countries of America;

in the fifth year: by the Superioresses of religious Institutes in other parts of the world, and moreover by the Superioresses of Societies of common life, secular Institutes and Federations throughout the world.

IV. In order that the Sacred Congregation may be able to obtain certain and authentic information regarding all those monasteries and independent houses of pontifical right, of both men and women, which are not bound by canon 510 to send the quinquennial report, and also regarding Congregations, Societies of common life and secular Institutes, of diocesan right, the following are to be observed:

1° Major Superiors of monasteries or independent houses of men which, although they are of pontifical right, neither belong to any monastic Congregation nor are federated with others, shall send to the Ordinary of the place, at the time and in the order mentioned above (n. III, 1°), a summary report of the five-year period, signed by themselves and by their proper Councillors. The Ordinary in turn shall send a copy of this report, signed by himself, with any remarks he may see fit to add, to this Sacred Congregation within the year in which the report was made.

2° Major Superioresses of monasteries of nuns, with their proper Council, according to the order above prescribed (n. III, 2°) for General Superioresses, shall send a brief and concise report of the five-year period, signed by all of them, to the Ordinary of the place if the nuns are subject to him, otherwise to the Regular Superior. The Ordinary of the place or the Regular Superior shall carefully transmit a copy of the report, signed by himself and adding any remarks he may see fit to make, to this

Sacred Congregation within the year in which the report was made.

3° The General Superiors of Congregations, Societies of common life, and secular Institutes, of diocesan right, shall send a quinquennial report, signed by themselves and by their proper Council, to the Ordinary of the place where the principal house is, at the time and in the order above prescribed (n. III, 1° and 2°). The Ordinary of the place shall not fail to communicate this report to the Ordinaries of the other houses, and he shall within the year send to this Sacred Congregation a copy signed by himself and adding his own judgment and that of the other Ordinaries regarding the Congregation, Society, or secular Institute in question.

4° Independent and autonomous religious houses and houses of a Society without vows or of a secular Institute, which are not united in a Federation, whether they be of diocesan or of pontifical right, shall send a summary report of the five-year period to the Ordinary of the place, in the order above prescribed (n. III, 1° and 2°). The Ordinary in turn shall send a copy of the said report, signed by himself, with any remarks he may see fit to make, to this Sacred Congregation, likewise within the year.

V. In making out their reports, all religious Institutes, monastic Congregations, Societies of common life, secular Institutes and Federations, of pontifical right, even though they be exempt, must follow exactly the schedule of questions which will be made out by the Sacred Congregation and sent to them directly.

Monasteries of nuns, autonomous houses of religious Institutes and of Societies and secular Institutes of pontifical right, and Congregations, Societies, and secular Institutes of diocesan right, shall use shorter formulas which will be approved for them.

VI. The replies given to the questions proposed must always be sincere and as far as possible complete and based on careful inquiry; and this is an obligation in conscience according to the gravity of the matter. If the replies are deficient in necessary matters, or if they seem uncertain or not sufficiently reliable, the Sacred Congregation will *ex officio* see to it that they are completed, and if need be will even itself directly conduct the investigations.

VII. Before the report is officially signed by the Superior and by the individual Councillors or Assistants, it is to be carefully examined personally and collectively.

The General Superioress of religious Institutes of women, and of Societies of common life, secular Institutes and Federations, of pontifical right, shall send the report, signed by herself and by her Council, to the Ordinary of the place of the Generalate house, so that he, according to law (c. 510), may sign the report; she shall then in due time see that the report signed by the Ordinary of the place is sent to this Sacred Congregation.

VIII. If any of the Superiors or Councillors who have to sign the report has any objection of any consequence to make to it, which he was not able to express in giving his vote, or if he judges that anything concerning the report should in any way be communicated to the Sacred Congregation, he may do this by a private letter, and may even be in conscience bound to do so according to the case. However, let him be mindful of his own condition and remember that he will gravely burden his conscience if he dares to state in such a secret letter anything which is not true.

IX. At the end of each year, all religious Institutes, Societies of common life, secular Institutes and Federations, whether of diocesan or pontifical right, shall send directly to the Sacred Congregation of Religious the annual prospectuses according to the schedules contained in the formulas which will be made out and distributed by the Sacred Congregation, stating the principal matters which concern the state of person, works, or other things which should be of interest either to the Sacred Congregation or to Superiors.

His Holiness Pius XII, in the Audience given to the undersigned Secretary of the Sacred Congregation of Religious on 9 July, 1947, approved the text of this Decree and ordered that it be observed by all and that it be published, all things to the contrary notwithstanding.

AAS 40–378; S. C. Rel., Decree, 9 July, 1947.

For practical directives on the Quinquennial Report, cf. *Review for Religious,* Vol. 8 (1949), p. 234 (Ellis); Vol. 10 (1951), p. 20 (Ellis); Vol. 11 (1952), pp. 12, 69, 151 (Gallen); *Monitor Ecclesiasticus,* 1950, p. 188 (Pugliese).

List of Questions for the Quinquennial Report of Papal Institutes (S. C. Rel., 9 Dec., 1948) Private.

The following is the English version of the "List of Questions" or Questionnaire, officially published by the Sacred Congregation of Religious for the Quinquennial Report of papal Institutes. It is entitled: "The List of Questions Which Are to Be Answered by Religious Institutes and Societies in the Report to Be Sent to the Holy See Every Five Years According to the Decree, *Cum Transactis.*"

Points to Be Noted

A) *Regarding the drawing up and writing of the quinquennial report.*

a) Before the reply to each question, there should be a clear indication of the number and letter by which that question is designated in this list.

b) Whenever a pontifical document is brought in, its date and Protocol number should be faithfully and uniformly given.

c) The reply is to be developed as each case may require, and is not to be dismissed with a simple affirmation or denial.

d) Clerical religious Institutes and Societies are to make out the Report in Latin; others may do it either in Latin or in one of the following modern languages: English, French, German, Spanish, or Italian.

e) The Report should be typed and in clear characters. If for some just cause the Report is written by hand, the handwriting must be clear.

f) The paper to be used must not be translucent nor too thick, but durable.

g) The questions marked with an asterisk are to be answered only by religious Institutes of men; those marked with a cross, only by Institutes of women.

B) *Regarding things which are to be sent to the Sacred Congregation with the Report.*

1. In the first Report following the issuance of this formula, the following things are to be sent:

a) Two well bound copies of the Constitutions or Statutes, revised to conform to the Code.

b) Two copies of existing privileges, printed or at least typed, of which one at least should be bound.

c) Two copies of the books in which special laws, practices, and customs are contained.

d) Two copies of the liturgical books and prayer books.

e) Two copies of the Statutes for houses of religious and clerical training, and also of the systems of piety, education, and studies.

f) Special Statutes for affiliated tertiaries, oblates, or other such persons.

g) The formularies which are in use either for appointments to offices or for making reports and visitations, and other formularies if there be any.

h) A historico-juridical report of the religious Institute, Society, or other Institute, in which are to be indicated: the founder, the year of foundation and of the temporary and definitive approval of the Institute and of the Constitutions, and in an accurate summary the principal events in the history of the Institute or Society. All these are to be sent neatly and stoutly bound.

i) If the Institute has according to law (c. 596) a distinctive habit for the professed and novices, a picture faithfully representing the same either photographically or otherwise is to be sent in duplicate; two pictures of the same size as those just mentioned should also be sent, showing the habit in colors.

l) As far as possible, let there be sent also the principal works, even though they be old, which show the spirit, way of life, history, and works of the Institute or Society; and collections of the documents of the Holy See which concern the Institute or Society.

2. As soon as they appear, or at least with the Report at the end of the five-year period, the General Superior shall send to the Sacred Congregation:

a) The official commentaries of the religious Institute or Society.

b) The minutes of the General Chapters.

c) The instructions, ordinances, and other important documents of the Superior General.

3. Religious Institutes, Societies, and other Institutes which may in the future obtain a decree of praise shall faithfully send the things which have been mentioned at least on the occasion of their first quinquennial Report to the Sacred Congregation.

The Following Things Must Appear on the First Page of the Report

The name of the religious institute or society:
(the official title in Latin, and the common name)

Its symbols; that is, the initials or letters commonly used to designate it:

The seat of the generalate house:

(complete information: post office address, telephone number, telegraphic address)

The years which are covered by the report:

THE LIST OF QUESTIONS

Concerning the Preceding Report

1. *a*) When was the last Report sent to the Holy See.

b) Whether and when a reply was received from the Sacred Congregation.

c) Whether the observations which may have been made by the Sacred Congregation upon the Report were faithfully carried out in practice.

2. Whether the matters of information contained in the last Report can be conscientiously considered reliable and complete, or whether anything concerning them would seem to require modification.

CHAPTER I

The Institute and Its Government

ARTICLE I

Concerning the Institute in general and its parts

§ 1. CONCERNING THE INSTITUTE IN GENERAL

3. What is the juridical nature of the Institute or Society (c. 491, § 1).

Concerning the special end

4. What is the special end of the Institute.

5. Was the special end authoritatively changed during the five-year period, and by what authority.

6. In practice is this end faithfully retained, or is it in part

abandoned; or are any works undertaken which do not pertain
to it.

7. What are the principal works through which the special end
is pursued.

*Concerning Second Orders, Congregations, Societies, Institutes of
women, which are subject to the Institute or Society*

8.*[1] Whether the Institute has an Order of women (a Second
Order) subject to it by law or by privilege.

9.* How many Monasteries of this Second Order are subject
to the Institute, and what are they; how many are subject to the
local Ordinaries, and what are they.

10.* Whether the Institute or Society has subject to it or
specially entrusted to it any, and if so what, Congregations or
Societies of women, and what are the apostolic indults upon
which this subjection or direction is based (c. 500, § 3).

11.* Whether the Institute has affiliated to it any, and if so
how many, religious Congregations of Tertiaries of simple vows.

12.* How many sodalities of secular Tertiaries depend on the
Order, and how many individual secular Tertiaries are there.

13.* Whether the Institute has as peculiar to itself any, and
if so what, Associations of the faithful (c. 886, § 3), and what are
the indults upon which these relationships are based.

§ 2. CONCERNING THE INTERNAL ORGANIZATION AND

DIVISION OF THE INSTITUTE

Concerning Assistancies and Congregations, etc.

14. *a*) Whether, and if so according to what criterion (geo-
graphical, ethnological, historical, etc.), the Provinces are grouped
into Parts or Assistancies, from which the general Definitors, or
Consultors, Socii, etc., are chosen.

b) Whether any complaints or appeals have been made against
the fairness of the arrangement.

15. Whether there is in the Institute any recognized internal
division of the members into various Families or Congregations.

---

[1] Questions marked with an asterisk * concern only religious Institutes
of men.

Concerning Provinces, Vice-Provinces, and other equivalent units

16. Is the Institute legitimately divided into Provinces (c. 494, § 1); if not, does it seem that it should be so divided.

17. Has any new Province been established since the last Report, or have any of the then existing Provinces been suppressed or modified.

18. In case of the division, new establishment, or suppression of Provinces (c. 494, § 2), by whom and how were the division and distribution of property made.

19. Are there in the Institute any other forms of union between houses: Vice-Provinces, Commissariats, regional Delegations, etc.

Concerning the houses

20. Which houses were modified either externally or internally during the five-year period (c. 497, §§ 1 and 4).

21. In the erection and suppression of houses, were the rules of law (cc. 497, 498) and the standards of prudence observed, among which must be numbered a written contract, clear, complete, and drawn up in accordance with Canon Law and the Constitutions, with due regard to the civil law.

22. Are all the houses provided with those things which are necessary for the common life, especially:

a) A separate cell for each person; or, if the dormitories are common, at least a separate bed for each person, properly set apart from the others.

b) A separate place fully suitable for the care and assistance of the sick.

23. Are the rooms for receiving guests sufficiently separate from the part of the house which is reserved to the community.

ARTICLE II

Concerning the juridical government of the Institute

Concerning the general government

24. *a*) Is the general Council at present up to its full membership.

b) Do all the general Councillors reside in the Curia.

c) If any are elsewhere, why is this, and where do they live (the place, Province, Diocese).

25. What other general offices are there (Procurator [can. 517, § 1]; Bursar, Secretary, Prefect of studies, etc.).

Concerning the general Chapter; its convocation and session

26. Within the period covered by the Report, has there been a session of the General Chapter.

27. Were the norms of the common law and of the particular law (the Constitutions, etc.) which concern the General Chapter faithfully observed; i.e.:

a) The time of the session, the designation of the place, the letter of convocation.

b) The elections of delegates to the Chapter, and of Tellers and a Secretary of the Chapter.

c) The elections of the Superior General, Consultors or Assistants and General Officials who are elected by the Chapter (e.g., Procurator, Secretary, General Treasurer).

28. In all these matters, even in seeking information about the candidates, did all avoid procuring votes either directly or indirectly, for themselves or for others (c. 507, § 2).

29. Who presided at the Chapter:

a) In the election of the Superior General.

b) In the other elections and in the business meetings.

30. Did each of the Provinces and other equivalent units submit their own report to the Chapter.

31. Did the aforesaid reports of the Provinces faithfully represent the true state of affairs, so that they constitute authentic documents upon which general reports may safely be based.

32. Were the following reports presented to the General Chapter in due time, so that they could be conveniently examined by each of the Capitulars and by a Commission elected in the Chapter if that is prescribed:

a) The report on the state of persons, discipline, and works since the last General Chapter, drawn up by the Superior or Vicar General and approved by the General Council.

b) The report on the true and complete financial condition of the Institute, drawn up by the Bursar General and approved by the Superior General with his Council.

33. Was the decision on these reports read in Chapter and seriously weighed and discussed before the general elections.

34. Were the minutes of the General Chapter which was held within the five-year period sent to the Sacred Congregation.

Concerning promulgation and execution

35. When and how did the Superior General promulgate those decrees and decisions of the General Chapter which were to be communicated.

36. In the promulgation, were any of the provisions omitted or not faithfully reported; if so, why, and by what authority.

37. What measures were taken by the Superior General with his Council and by the other Superiors and Councils to see that the prescriptions of the General Chapter be faithfully reduced to practice.

Concerning appointments to offices

38. Were the norms of the common law and of the Constitutions observed:

a) Regarding the requisites and qualifications of Superiors and Officials (cc. 504, 516).

b) Regarding the manner of appointment (cc. 506, 507).

c) Regarding the duration of offices (c. 505).

39. How many and what dispensations from the provisions of the common or particular law were granted by the Holy See or by Major Superiors:

a) For appointments to positions or offices.

b) For the renewal of the same.

c) Were the conditions attached to these dispensations faithfully observed.

40. Did the Superiors of clerical Institutes duly fulfill, according to c. 1406, § 1, 9° and § 2, their obligation of making the profession of faith before the Chapter or Superior who appointed them, or before their delegate.

Concerning the duties of Superiors: Residence — Making known and observing the Decrees of the Holy See — the canonical visitation — Freedom of epistolary correspondence

41. Did the Superior General, the General Councillors, Procurator and the other Superiors, observe the law of residence according to the common law (cc. 508, 517) and the Constitutions.

42. How do Superiors see to it that the decrees of the Holy See which concern religious be known and observed by their own subjects (c. 509, § 1).

43. Is perfect freedom left to subjects, without any inspection of letters by Superiors, in their epistolary correspondence with those persons who, according to the common (c. 611) and particular law, have this right.

44. Were there any cases of secret and clandestine epistolary correspondence, either between religious or between these and secular persons, and what was done to correct these abuses.

45. *a*) Did the Superior General and other Major Superiors make at the proper time, in person, their prescribed visitations of Provinces, Missions, and houses.

b) Did the above-named Superiors make these visitations through delegates.

46. Were the visitations which were made according to the common law (cc. 513, 2413) and the particular law, complete so as to include:

a) All persons, as regards discipline, religious perfection, priestly life, religious and clerical training, and the ministries and works of the Institute.

b) Things and property; their conservation and administration.

c) Places, especially sacred places, divine worship, pious foundations, etc.

47. Were any duly appointed extraordinary delegated visitors sent at any time; what were the reasons and what were the results.

48. What was done to see that the decrees of the visitation be carried out in practice.

Concerning Council meetings

49. Are Council meetings held at the prescribed times and in the required cases:

a) By the Superior General.

b) By Major Superiors.

c) By local Superiors.

50. *a*) Was the opinion of all the Councillors always asked.

b) Do absent Councillors give their opinion, and if so how.

c) Were any of the Councillors neglected; if so, what was the reason.

51. How often each year during the five-year period did the

Superior General and Major Superiors convoke their Councils.

52. Are the matters in which, according to the common and particular law, Councillors have a deliberative or consultative vote, faithfully submitted to a meeting of the Council.

53. Is the proper liberty of all and each of the Councillors duly recognized in the Council meetings; and in the decisions, appointments, and votes of whatever kind, were the norms of the common law (cc. 101; 105, 1°, 2°, 3°) and of the particular law always observed.

54. Are the minutes of the meetings duly drawn up and signed.

55. Are the Archives of the Institute, Provinces, and individual houses properly equipped and carefully arranged.

56. Are all the offices of the general provincial and local officials actually filled, or are any of them vacant.

Concerning corrections and the abuse of power

57. Do Superiors exercise their function of vigilance and correction either privately or publicly; by what means and in what manner do they do this.

58. Have any abuses arisen or taken root, without being corrected and without efficacious remedies being applied to prevent and remove them.

59. How often and for what reasons were canonical admonitions and penalties imposed.

60. In applying these remedies, were the sacred canons and the Constitutions of the Institute observed.

61. Were there any cases of abuse of power by Superiors, or at least were any appeals or complaints on this matter received from subjects.

62. Were Superiors guilty of any grave infringements of Canon Law or of the Constitutions, either as regards the common obligations of religious or the obligations which concern their particular office.

63. In these cases, were the penalties either common or special, which are provided for by the common law (e.g., cc. 2389, 2411, 2413, etc.) or by the Constitutions, applied.

Concerning the exercise of authority

64. What means are taken in order that the Superior General and his Curia be constantly, fully, and sincerely informed as to the state of the Institute.

65. Are periodical reports to be made to Major Superiors, and how often.

66. Is a faithful observance of the prescriptions in this matter insisted upon.

67. Are there in the Institute any established means by way of internal bonds which unite the members among themselves, as for example: reports on work done, published bulletins of houses, Provinces, and the whole Institute.

68. Are any other means used as necessity may require, to promote union among the Provinces and houses of the Institute; if so, what are they.

69. Is there also for each house a chronicle in which the principal events are carefully recorded.

Concerning relations with the Ordinaries of places

70. *a*) Are the provisions of the Code regarding the subjection of religious to the local Ordinaries faithfully observed.

b)* Are good and friendly relations with the Ordinaries fostered, and do the religious, without prejudice to religious discipline, exercise priestly ministrations in favor of the diocese.

c) Have there been in any Province or house litigation, disputes, or difficulties with the local Ordinaries; if so what were they.

71. What remedies have been or can be applied to restore harmony.

ARTICLE III

Concerning the spiritual government of the Institute

Concerning confessors

72.* Are several confessors appointed for each house according to c. 518, § 1.

73.* Without prejudice to the Constitutions which may prescribe or recommend that confessions be made at stated times to fixed confessors, are the religious left free to go, in accordance with canon 519, without prejudice however to religious discipline, to a confessor approved by the local Ordinary, even though he be not among the fixed confessors.

74.†[2] Are the norms of the common law and of the Constitutions faithfully observed regarding the appointment and reappointment of the ordinary, extraordinary, special, and supplementary confessors (cc. 520, §§ 1–2; 521; 524; 526; 527).

75.† Did Superioresses faithfully observe the prescriptions made for them regarding supplementary confessors (c. 521, § 3), occasional confessors (c. 522), and confessors in case of grave illness (c. 523).

76. Do Superiors take means and exercise a prudent vigilance to see that all the religious, according to law (c. 595, § 1, 3°) and the Constitutions (c. 519), approach the sacrament of penance at least once a week.

77. Have Superiors been guilty of any abuses, and if so what were they, by which the liberty of conscience of their subjects has been restricted (cc. 518, § 3; 519, 520, § 2; 521, § 3; 522; 2414).

78. Did Major Superiors and Visitors correct these abuses.

79. Has there been, under pretext of liberty of conscience, any detriment to religious discipline on the part of subjects; did any other abuses arise; were the abuses corrected by Superiors and Visitors without prejudice to liberty.

Concerning spiritual direction

80.* How do Superiors provide for the solid training of spiritual Directors.

81.* Whether care is taken to see that in Novitiates (c. 566, § 2) and also in all clerical and religious residence-halls, the prescribed confessors and spiritual Directors be provided and chosen, and, in the case of clerical Institutes, that they reside there (c. 566, § 2, 2°).

82. Whether Superiors, in accordance with Canon Law (c. 530, §§ 1, 2) leave their subjects free in regard to making a strict manifestation of conscience to themselves.

83. In what ways do Superiors strive to promote spiritual direction.

Concerning the reception of the Most Blessed Eucharist

84. Whether Superiors, in accordance with c. 595, §§ 2–3, pro-

---

[2] Questions marked with a cross † concern only Institutes of women.

mote among their subjects frequent and even daily reception of
the Most Sacred Body of Christ, always without prejudice to full
liberty of conscience according to law (c. 595, § 4) and the
Instructions of the Holy See.

85. Do Superiors diligently see to it that confessors be easily
available before Communion, and do they allow their religious
subjects a suitable time for preparation and thanksgiving.

86. Do Superiors see to it that, according to the Constitutions
and the common law, there be spiritual and catechetical instructions for the entire house (c. 509, § 2, 2°), for the novices (c.
565, § 2), for the scholastics (c. 588, § 1), for the *conversi*, for
the domestics and servants (c. 509, § 2, 2°).

ARTICLE IV

Concerning the financial government of the Institute

§ 1. CONCERNING THE ACQUISITION AND LOSS
OF PROPERTY

Concerning the acquisition and registration of property

87. *a*) What if any immovable property or precious movable
property was acquired by the Institute, Provinces, and houses;
what was the value of these acquisitions.

b) Was the aforesaid property acquired by gift or other
gratuitous title, or by purchase, and in this latter case was it with
the funds of the Institute, Province, or house, or with borrowed
money.

88. Has the Institute, the Province, and each house an inven-
tory of its movable property, especially of that which is classed
as precious (by reason of workmanship, history, or material) (c.
1522, 2°), and of its immovable property.

89. When must these inventories be revised, and are they in
fact revised.

90. In cases where works which are not the property of the
house, such as clerical or religious residence-halls, hospitals,
churches, etc., are entrusted to the religious houses, are these

properties kept clearly distinct from those which belong to the religious house itself.

91. By what method or in whose name before the civil law is the religious property registered; and can this registration be regarded as safe in civil law.

92. What forms of registration have been adopted as the more secure in various localities.

93. If societies have been established for this purpose, was everything done in accordance with the civil law and is everything actually being kept in good order.

94. As regards the aforesaid societies:

a) Were all persons to whom the administration or management of property is entrusted, chosen with due care, after making all the previous investigations which were necessary or useful.

b) Were the members of the Institute itself given the preference over outsiders for offices of administration, whenever this could prudently be done without loss.

c) What safeguards were used against dangers arising from abuses of administration.

d) Is a constant vigilance conscientiously exercised according to law, through the checking of accounts and through ordinary and other extraordinary and timely inspections of safety deposits and other properties.

Concerning expenses

95. Were extraordinary expenses paid from ordinary or extraordinary income proper, or on the contrary with borrowed funds.

96. Did the individual houses and other units subject to the Provinces contribute toward meeting the expenses of the Provinces.

97. Did the Provinces and equivalent units and the houses which are immediately under the Superior General contribute to the common necessities of the Institute.

98. By what authority (Chapter, Council, General or Provincial Superior), on what principles and in what proportion are the contributions to the general and provincial funds determined.

99. Were these contributions paid willingly or more or less under pressure.

100. Are the Provinces and houses allowed to retain whatever is prudently foreseen to be necessary or very appropriate for

their own life and growth, in view of the good of souls and the welfare of the Institute.

Concerning the alienation and diminution of property

101. What capital property, whether immovable, or stable (i.e., consisting of capital funds), or precious was alienated, and by what authority.

102. In the alienation of property, were the provisions of law (cc. 534, 1531), especially regarding the previous appraisal by experts, and the norms of the Constitutions, observed.

103. Did the Institute, Provinces, and houses consume any stable or founded property or capital funds; for what reasons and by what authority.

104. Are the general, provincial, and local Superiors and Bursars making serious efforts to recover this property.

105. What properties of the Institute, Provinces, and houses have suffered loss; and what were the reasons.

Concerning debts and obligations

106. *a*) What debts were contracted, and by whom.

b) What debts are actually outstanding.

107. In contracting debts and obligations, were the following faithfully observed:

a) The provisions of c. 534.

b) The precautions mentioned in c. 536, § 5.

c) The norms of the Constitutions regarding permissions, the consent of the Council, etc.

108. Was the interest on debts and obligations faithfully paid, and is diligent care taken toward the gradual payment of a debt or the amortization of the capital (c. 536, § 5).

§ 2. Concerning the Conservation and Administration of Property

109. Is the administration of property conducted, not arbitrarily, but according to the common law and the Constitutions, under the direction and vigilance of Superiors and their Councils (cc. 516, §2; 532, § 1).

110. Are there designated Bursars (c. 516, §§ 2, 3, 4) according to the common law and the Constitutions:

a) For the entire Institute.

b) For the different Provinces and other similar units.

c) For the individual houses and works.

111. Does the Superior in any case act also as Bursar (c. 516, § 3).

112. Do the Councils have their part in the administration and exercise vigilance in regard to it, even when the Superiors are acting also as Bursars (c. 516, § 1); how do they do this.

Concerning the rendering of accounts

113. How many times a year and to what Superiors and Councils must the Bursars and other Administrators render an account of their administration.

114. Was a clear and complete rendering of account demanded of all and each of the Bursars and Administrators during the five-year period.

115. Were there presented together with the accounts the documents showing the expenditures and receipts.

116. Was there regularly an inspection and checking of the safe.

117. Are the necessary directions given to the Bursars and Administrators; if so how is this done, and what sanctions are imposed in case of necessity.

118. Have Superiors, Bursars, or Administrators, or any other religious, any money or property which they can freely use without giving a regular account of it, even though it belongs to the Institute, Province, or house.

Concerning the investment of money and changes of investment

119. Did Superiors, Councils, and Administrators lawfully, safely, and profitably invest (c. 533) the money which was to be invested according to law and the will of benefactors, observing the rules of law and the Constitutions.

120. Did Superiors, Bursars, and Administrators make temporary investments of surplus funds which were not required for ordinary expenses, so that they should not lie idle but might draw a reasonable interest.

Concerning the conservation of property

121. Are money, securities, contracts, precious articles care-

fully conserved, observing exactly the common norms and the provisions of the Constitutions.

122. On what terms, if ever:

a) Were money or precious articles received from outsiders on deposit.

b) Or conversely were such deposits made with outsiders by Superiors, Bursars, Administrators, or private religious.

123. Do Superiors, Bursars, Administrators conscientiously strive that all the property of the Institute, Province, and house be religiously conserved and providently administered (c. 532, § 1).

Concerning foundations, pious causes, etc.

124. What legacies and pious foundations were accepted.

125. In accepting pious foundations and legacies, were the rules of law (c. 1544, ss.) and of the Constitutions observed.

126. Was the money of foundations and pious causes, according to law and with the consent of the local Ordinary when that was required, invested (cc. 533, §§ 1, 2; 1547) and separately and faithfully administered (cc. 535, § 3, 2°; 1546, 1549).

127. Were the obligations attached to foundations faithfully and conscientiously fulfilled (cc. 1514; 1549, § 2).

128. Did Visitors demand documentary proof of their fulfillment and an account of the administration of the property.

Concerning business and trade, etc.

129. Did any religious, Superiors or subjects, personally or through others, engage in illicit business, that is, business not permitted to religious, in violation of cc. 142, 592.

130. In cases where for just reasons the permission of the Holy See was obtained for engaging in business (give the date and Protocol number), was every semblance, not alone of fraud but also of avarice, diligently avoided.

131. What precautions were taken that religious who are occupied in business dealings may not suffer spiritual harm.

132. Whether Superiors and Councils were attentively watchful that, according to c. 1539, § 2, in the administrative exchange of securities payable to bearer, all appearance of commerce or trading be avoided.

*Concerning actions or affairs which involve
financial responsibility*

133. How did Superiors exercise vigilance over the actions and dealings of their subjects from which there might arise according to law a financial responsibility on the part of the Institute or of the Province or house (c. 536, § 2) or of the individual religious (c. 536, § 3).

134. Did Superiors clearly and effectively, according as the circumstances required, take prompt action to clear the Institute, Province, and house of all responsibility for actions and dealings done by individual religious without observing the norms of the common or particular law.

135. Do Superiors see to it that, in all matters which concern finances, or in those generally which could give occasion to litigation in the canonical or civil courts, everything be done exactly according to law, on the basis of previous written contracts and with the guarantee of perfectly valid signed agreements, etc. (c. 1529).

136. Have any lawsuits or losses resulted from failure to observe the prescribed formalities of civil law according to n. 135.

137. Have Superiors and Bursars diligently seen to it that extern workmen and all persons who work for the Institute, Province, or house receive at the agreed time a just and fair compensation according to law (c. 1524), and that the provisions of law regarding the contract of hire and other matters be faithfully observed.

138. What provision is made for the spiritual welfare of those who work in the house, especially if they also reside there.

CHAPTER II

Concerning the Religious and the Religious Life and Discipline

*Concerning the diversity of classes — The vows
of each class*

139. What are the different classes, if any, among the members of the Institute; does harmony exist among the different classes and is fraternal charity observed among them.

140. Besides the persons who belong to the Institute or Society as members, by religious profession or lawful incorporation, are there others who are dedicated or given to it, or the like, without being members.

141. Is provision made in fairness and charity for the spiritual life of these persons and also for their material security.

142. Are there any legitimately approved statutes for them.

ARTICLE I

Concerning the admission, formation, and profession or incorporation of members

Concerning the postulantship in the wide sense
(Apostolic Schools)

143. Are there in the Institute any aspirantships or postulantships in the wide sense: apostolic schools, etc.

144. For how long a time does the instruction and education in these places last.

145. In these apostolic schools and similar houses and in the residence halls, are the students of tender age habitually kept separate from the older ones.

Concerning the postulantship in the canonical or strict sense

146. Are the postulantships properly conducted according to law in the houses of noviceship (c. 540, § 1), or in houses where perfect religious observance exists (c. 540).

147. Was the time assigned by the common law (c. 539) or by the Constitutions for the postulantship abbreviated or prolonged; if so, for how long a time and by what authority.

Concerning the admission of aspirants

148. What means are used to arouse and attract vocations.

149. Are there also advertisements inserted in public bulletins and papers. If so, in what bulletins or papers did they appear.

150. Taking into account the different circumstances of various localities, what causes are regarded as having an influence on the increase or diminution of vocations.

151. What are the obstacles which aspirants most frequently have to overcome in order to follow their vocation.

Concerning documents, testimonials, and informations

152. Were the documents required by the common law (c. 544) and by the Constitutions demanded before admission in the case of each aspirant.

153. At least before entrance into the novitiate, were the following testimonial letters demanded and obtained:

a)* The common testimonial letters which are to be given by the local Ordinaries and are prescribed for all (c. 544, § 2).

b) The special testimonial letters which are to be given under oath by the Rector or Major Superior for those who have been in a Seminary or a residence-hall which is equivalent to an ecclesiastical one, or in a postulantship or novitiate of a religious Institute (c. 544, § 3).

c) Likewise the testimonial letters which are required in the case of clerics and professed religious (c. 544, §§ 4, 5).

154. Besides the documents and testimonials which are specially prescribed by law or by the Constitutions, were further informations, which it seemed necessary or useful to know in order to judge with certainty of the vocation and fitness of the aspirants, diligently sought (c. 544, § 6).

Concerning impediments and admission

155. From what impediments or defects, if any, which are imposed by the common or particular law, was a dispensation granted; how often and by what authority was this done.

156. Were the admissions of aspirants always done by the competent Superiors, observing the rules of law (c. 543).

Concerning the noviceship — The house

157. Was every novitiate house erected or transferred after obtaining in advance the permission of the Holy See (c. 554, §§ 1, 2).

158. Does perfect religious observance flourish in the novitiate houses.

159. Did Superiors assign to them or permit to remain in them religious who are not exemplary in their zeal for religious observance (c. 554, § 3).

Concerning the beginning of the noviceship

160. Did all fulfill the prescribed days of spiritual exercises before entering the noviceship (c. 541).

161. Were the rite and the rules prescribed for admission to the noviceship faithfully observed (c. 553).

Concerning board and expenses for the postulantship and noviceship

162. Is the right of the Institute to demand payment for the expenses of the religious habit and board during the postulantship and noviceship, given in the Constitutions or customarily recognized by express agreement.

163. Who determines the amount to be paid.

164. Was there any instance of the grave abuse of delaying the profession because the expenses of the postulantship or noviceship had not been paid.

Concerning the discipline of the noviceship

165. Did all the novices and each of them from the beginning of the noviceship have a complete copy of the Constitutions.

166. Are the novices, according to law and the Constitutions, kept separate from the professed, and is any undue communication between them tolerated (c. 564, §§ 1, 2).

167. Did all and each of the novices before their profession perform the canonical year of noviceship complete and continuous, without counting the first day, in a house of noviceship lawfully erected, under the care and direction of a Master (cc. 555, § 1; 556; 557).

168. Was the noviceship extended or shortened beyond the limits fixed by law (c. 571, § 2) and the Constitutions; if so, for how long a time and by what authority was this done.

Concerning the government of the noviceship

169. Was there always in every novitiate a Master of novices duly appointed or elected (c. 560).

170. Have the novice Master and his Socius all the qualifications and all the requisites prescribed by the common law (c. 559, §§ 1, 2) and the Constitutions, or did dispensations have to be asked for and obtained.

171. Are the Master and Socius free from all offices and minis-

tries in or out of the house, which might interfere with their care and government of the novices (c. 559, § 3).

172. Do the Masters of novices, according to law (c. 561) and the Constitutions, under the vigilance and direction of Superiors and Visitors, have full possession of their proper authority and use it for the government and training of the novices.

173. Do all the Masters fulfill their office properly (c. 562) and remain constantly in the novitiate house.

174. Do the Master of novices and his Socius abstain from hearing sacramental confessions unless the penitents of their own accord ask them to do so according to c. 891.

Concerning the spiritual training of the novices

175. Were the novices, under the guidance of the Master, during the first or canonical year of the noviceship, engaged exclusively according to law (c. 565, §§ 1, 2) in exercises of piety and other exercises proper to novices; or on the contrary were they assigned to hearing confessions, preaching, and external works or ministries; or did they apply themselves expressly to the study of literature, science, or humanities (c. 565, § 3) beyond the limited measure in which this has been approved by the Sacred Congregation.

176. During the second year of noviceship or during the time which is over and above the canonical year, were the norms which were given in the Instruction of the Sacred Congregation of Religious (2 Nov., 1921) observed:

a) Regarding the manner of exercising the external ministries of the Institute (nn. I, II).

b) Regarding the conditions under which alone the novices may be sent outside the novitiate house (III).

c) Regarding the two months' preparation for the profession (IV).

Concerning the documents to be drawn up before the profession

177. Did all the novices, according to c. 569, § 1, before the first profession of simple vows, freely cede the administration and either cede or dispose of the use and usufruct of their property.

178. In case the aforesaid cession and disposition was not duly made before the profession, or in case new property was acquired

thereafter, was it made or completed after the profession (c. 569, § 2).

179. Were any changes of the aforesaid cession and disposition after the profession, made always in accordance with c. 580, § 3.

180. *a*) Did the novices of the Congregation, before their first profession of temporary vows, freely make a will in due form, valid according to the civil law, regarding their present or future property (c. 569, § 3).

b) Did they afterward render this will valid according to the civil law (c. 569, § 3).

181. Were any changes which may have been made in this will after profession, made according to c. 583, 2°.

182. Are the aforesaid documents *a*), *b*) faithfully kept in the Archives.

Concerning admission to profession and the act of profession

183. Do the General Superior and General Council carefully and constantly keep a severe watchfulness as regards admissions; have they issued any special norms in this matter.

184. Does there seem to be in any Province too great facility regarding admissions, and have the prescribed norms and sound criteria been faithfully observed.

185. Has the first profession, after eight full days of spiritual exercises, always been made validly and licitly according to law and the Constitutions (cc. 572, 573, 575) in the novitiate house itself (c. 574, § 1).

186. Was the prescribed rite observed in making the profession, and was the document attesting it duly drawn up (c. 576).

Concerning the canonical examination

187.† Did the Major Superioresses, or others acting in their name, two months before admission to the noviceship, to the first temporary profession, and to perpetual profession, give timely notice to the local Ordinary (c. 552, § 1), so that he or his Delegate might gratuitously conduct the canonical examination regarding the free and conscious will of the postulant or candidate (c. 552, § 2).

188.† Was the prescribed examination always made.

Concerning the dowry — The obligation and delivery of the dowry

189.† According to the Constitutions, is the dowry obligatory in the Congregation, or is it left entirely or partly optional (c. 547, § 3).

190.† Was the delivery of the dowry made according to law (c. 547, § 2) and the Constitutions.

Concerning the investment, conservation, administration, and return of the dowry

191.† Were the dowries, immediately after the first profession, always invested by the Major Superioress, with the deliberative vote of her Council and the consent of the Ordinary of the place where the capital of the dowries is kept (c. 549).

192.† Were the dowries spent or encumbered in any way before the death of the religious concerned; if so, by what authority was this done. Were the dowries so spent or encumbered, even though it were done after obtaining lawful permission, afterward restored or cleared of the encumbrance; what is their condition at the present time (c. 549).

193.† Where and how are the dowries administered. Are the rules of law faithfully observed regarding their administration (cc. 550; 535, § 2).

194.† Is all property which is brought in as dowry, even though it be in excess of the sum required for a dowry in the Constitutions, or even though there be in the Congregation no obligation to bring in a dowry, accepted, invested, administered, etc., with the observance of the norms which govern dowries.

195.† In case of the departure of a professed religious, for whatever cause it occurred, and in case of transfer, were the dowry and likewise the personal belongings which the novice brought with her at her entrance, in the condition in which they were when she left, restored to the religious departing or transferring, without the income which had already accrued (cc. 551; 570, § 2).

196.† Is this done also with property freely contributed for increasing the dowry even beyond the sum required by the Constitutions.

197.† In case of the departure of a professed religious who had been received without a dowry or with an insufficient one, if she was unable to provide for herself out of her own property, did the Institute out of charity, according to law (c. 643, § 2), give her whatever was needed that she might safely and decently return home and be decently supported for a time.

Concerning the profession and the renewal of profession

198. What if any dispensations were necessary for the pronouncement of the vows.

199. How many and what sanations were afterward necessary.

200. Were the temporary vows which are prescribed by law and by the Constitutions (c. 574, § 1), when the time for which they were taken had elapsed (c. 577, § 1), always renewed according to law (c. 577, § 2), so that no one ever remained without vows.

201. How often was the temporary profession extended beyond the six-year period allowed by law, and by what authority was this done (c. 574, § 2).

202. Conversely, how often was the time of the temporary vows, which is prescribed by law (c. 574, § 1) or by the Constitutions, shortened.

Concerning the solemn profession

203. Did all the professed of simple vows in Orders, within sixty days before their profession of solemn vows, duly make the prescribed renunciation of the property which they actually possessed, in the form of a true cession but not in the form of a will, to whomever they chose, on condition of their future profession (c. 581, § 1).

204. After the profession was made, were all things immediately done which were necessary in order that the renunciation be effective in civil law (c. 581, § 2).

205. Did the Superior who received the solemn profession give notice of it to the Pastor of baptism in accordance with cc. 470, § 2; 576, § 2.

Concerning the religious life and discipline

Concerning the vows — Poverty and the common life

206. Is a perfect common life according to c. 594, the Rule and the Constitutions, observed everywhere, but especially in novitiates and houses of studies (cc. 554, § 3; 587, § 2).

207. What has been done and is being done positively to safeguard and promote the virtue and spirit of poverty.

208. Do Superiors and officials, out of religious charity and in order to ward off for the religious occasions of sinning against poverty, provide, within the limits of poverty, what is necessary and appropriate in the way of food, clothes, and other things.

209. Do they allow the religious to ask for or receive these things from externs.

210. Are there complaints about these things; are these complaints seriously considered, and are abuses on the part of Superiors and subjects alike corrected with equal severity.

211. Are the sick and the aged religious attended to with special care and helped in both body and soul with paternal charity, so that, within the limits of religious poverty, they lack nothing which seems necessary for the recovery of their health and for their spiritual consolation.

212. Are all the above cared for in the house; and if in a case of peculiar necessity they have to be cared for out of the house, are they frequently visited.

213. Is there a suitable house for sick and aged members.

Concerning chastity and its safeguards

214. Did all Superiors make it a matter of conscientious duty to be attentively vigilant regarding those things, both in and out of the house, which may easily contain dangers against religious chastity, i.e., regarding:

a) Familiarities, either in the parlors or elsewhere, with persons of the other sex, young people, and children.

b) Epistolary correspondence.

c) The reading of books and papers which are unbecoming to religious.

d) Abuses of the telephone and uncensored listening to radio programs, etc.

215. Were any rules and regulations issued by Superiors and Chapters regarding the public and private use of the radio. (Cite the documents.)

216. If, which God forbid, religious committed any offense against the Sixth Commandment with younger students entrusted to their care, did Superiors immediately remove the culprits from the occasion and punish them, and thereafter carefully watch over their life. In the more serious cases did Superiors have recourse to the Holy See.

217. Are the provisions of the law and the Constitutions regarding cloister (cc. 598–599, 604) faithfully observed. Did any abuses creep in.

218. Did Superiors, in violation of the norms of the Constitutions, allow visits without a companion, frequent and too protracted visits and conversations with externs, especially those which are evidently useless or can become dangerous, which disturb silence, especially that which is more strictly to be observed, which interfere with exercises of piety or other community exercises, and which are in general opposed to the religious spirit.

219. *a*) Are the parlors so arranged that what goes on in them can be seen from the outside.

b) Is the frequency of parlor visits regulated according to the Constitutions and religious prudence.

220. Do Superiors themselves diligently observe and cause others to observe the prescriptions of the Constitutions concerning religious going out of the house and receiving visits from and making visits to externs.

221.† Except in cases of prudent necessity, do Superiors assign a companion to religious when they go out of the house, especially for the purpose of making a visit (c. 607).

222.† Do the rooms which are reserved for Chaplains and Confessors or Preachers have a separate entrance and no internal communication with the habitations of the religious.

Concerning obedience

223. Is religious discipline observed, and is the government of Superiors made easy by the docility of the subjects.

224. Was it often necessary to impose formal precepts in virtue of the vow of obedience.

225. Were such precepts given in due form according to the Constitutions, and never without grave reason.

Concerning the Rule and the Constitutions

226. Are the Rule and the Constitutions faithfully observed (c. 593).

227. Are the Rule and the Constitutions read publicly at the prescribed times (c. 509, § 2, 1°).

228. Is the private reading of the Rules and the Constitutions favored.

229. *a*) Are there any customs in effect which are contrary to the Rule and the Constitutions.

b) Do Superiors allow new ones to spring up, or on the contrary do they strive to prevent this and to eradicate the old ones.

230. In what places, if at all, since the last Report, did abuses spring up or become rooted.

Concerning the religious habit

231. Has the Institute a habit of its own (c. 596).

232. Was the habit modified or abandoned without due permission; if so, by what authority.

233. Does the habit everywhere correspond to the prescriptions of the Rule and the Constitutions, and is it uniform for all, with due allowance for the differences which may be lawfully recognized for each different class of religious.

234. Is the religious habit faithfully worn according to law (c. 596).

235. Do the excloistered religious continue to wear the habit.

Concerning exercises of piety

236. Do Superiors see to it that in all the houses the exercises of piety which are prescribed for every day, every week, every month, every year, or for other fixed times, be faithfully and worthily performed according to the Constitutions.

237. Do Superiors see to it that all the religious:

a) Make a retreat every year.

b) Be present at Mass every day if not legitimately prevented.

c) Give themselves to mental prayer every day.

d) Attend earnestly to the other offices of piety which are prescribed by the Rules and Constitutions (c. 595, § 1, 1° and 2°).

238. Do Superiors see to it that all the members be able to be present at community exercises.

239. Do they give to those religious who, either because of their particular duties or for other just cause, or by way of abuse, are not present at community exercises, time in which they can conveniently and worthily make up the obligatory exercises.

240. Do they see to it that all these exercises be actually made up.

Concerning choir service and the divine Office

241. If choir service is prescribed by the Constitutions, is it held exactly and worthily in each of the houses according to their Constitutions and the common law (c. 610, § 1), the religious who are bound to choir and not actually lawfully impeded being present.

242. Do Superiors see to it that priests, clerics in major orders, and the solemnly professed, who were absent from choir, recite the divine Office privately with attention and devotion (c. 610, § 3).

Concerning religious charity

243. Are the relations between the different members of the Institute, between Superiors and subjects, etc., characterized by a true spirit of charity.

244. Are defects against charity severely corrected.

245. Do contentions and rivalries between Assistancies, Provinces, and various localities in the Institute exist, and are they tolerated. Is there any special cause which is an obstacle to fraternal charity.

Concerning the reading of books

246. Are Superiors watchful that no books be used, whether in manuscript or published form, if they are not entirely safe.

247. Are the spiritual books which the religious use privately, according to law approved by the Church, conformed to the religious state and suitable for the welfare of the individual religious to whom they are permitted.

Concerning those who have departed or been dismissed, and others who leave the Institute

Concerning those who have gone out from the Institute

248. *a*) How many in the Institute and in each Province, at the expiration of their vows did not renew them, either because they chose not to do so or because they were not allowed to do so.

b) How many of the professed of temporary vows were dispensed during their vows, and how many of the professed of perpetual vows were dispensed.

249. Were those who were dispensed from their vows at their own request or with their consent, forced, or without serious and grave reasons and precautions permitted, to leave the religious house before the rescript was duly executed.

250. How many transfers, if any, were there to another Institute.

Concerning apostates and fugitives

251. *a*) How many apostates and fugitives, if any, were there during the five-year period.

b) Did the Society or Institute observe the provisions of law concerning apostates and fugitives, by seeking them (c. 645, § 2), and if this proved fruitless, by proceeding against them according to law, so that their juridical condition should be clearly defined. Were the provisions of law regarding those who came back observed (cc. 2385, 2386), and is watchful provision made for their spiritual good.

Concerning those dismissed by Superiors and those not admitted to profession

252. *a*) Since the last Report, how many of the professed of temporary vows and how many of the professed of perpetual vows have been dismissed, according to Provinces.

b) In the dismissal of religious, whether of temporary or of perpetual vows, were the norms of the common law (cc. 647, § 2; 649–672) as well as those of the Constitutions observed.

c) Was the same done in regard to not admitting the professed of temporary vows to the renewal of their vows or to perpetual profession (c. 637).

253. Were the dismissed of temporary vows, while the recourse duly made within ten days was pending (c. 647, § 2; S. C. of Religious, 20 July, 1923, AAS 15, 1923, p. 457), and the dismissed of perpetual vows, before the decree or judgment of dismissal had been confirmed by the Sacred Congregation (cc. 652, 666), forced to leave the Institute.

254. Are the dismissed who are not in sacred orders released from their vows by the dismissal (c. 669, § 1); and if the vows remain, does the Institute show solicitude regarding their condition (c. 672, § 1).

Concerning those dismissed by the law itself and those sent back to the world

255. What were the cases, and the causes which led to them, for both the professed of temporary and those of perpetual vows, where they were either sent back to the world on account of grave scandal or very grave harm (cc. 653, 668) or dismissed by the law itself (c. 646).

256. Were steps immediately taken according to the Code (cc. 646, § 2; 653; 668) to determine the condition of those dismissed by the law itself and of those sent back to the world.

257. Is there any such person whose condition still remains undetermined.

258. What cases if any have occurred of the reduction to the lay state of religious who had received sacred orders; how many were voluntary and how many penal.

Concerning those who were excloistered

259. How many cases of exclaustration were there, if any; are the causes carefully and conscientiously pondered in the presence of God before the petition is recommended and the rescript executed.

260. Does the Institute take care:

a) That if it seems necessary to ask for an extension of the indults, they be renewed in due time.

b) That the persons who are excloistered lead a worthy religious life and return as soon as possible to some house of the Institute.

261.* Likewise does the Institute take care regarding those who have been secularized on trial, and regarding their return to religion if at the expiration of the three-year period the indult is not renewed or they are not accepted by the Ordinary.

Concerning absences from the house

262. Do Superiors see to it that subjects remain out of the house only for a just and grave reason and for the shortest possible time, according to the Constitutions (c. 606, § 2).

263. For absences which exceed six months, except for studies or ministries according to law and the Constitutions, was the permission of the Holy See always obtained (c. 606, § 2).

264. Is it allowed by reason or under color of a vacation, that time be spent with one's parents or outside a house of the Institute.

Concerning the deceased

265. Were the prescribed suffrages faithfully and promptly performed for all the deceased.

ARTICLE IV

Concerning the various classes and conditions of religious

§ 1. CONCERNING CLERICS

(This is dealt with in the Report on formation and studies.)

§ 2. CONCERNING *Conversi* OR COADJUTORS

Concerning their education and training

266. Do Superiors, in accordance with c. 509, § 2, 2° give to those religious who belong to the class of *conversi,* instruction in Christian doctrine; and do Superiors, both before and after their profession but especially during the earlier years, carefully attend to their spiritual, intellectual, civil, and technical education according to the functions which they have to fulfill.

267. Are the religious allowed to engage in works which do not seem to be suitable to the religious state.

268. Do Superiors with paternal charity diligently provide also for the bodily health of the *conversi* or coadjutors.

§ 3. Concerning Those Who Are Applied to Military Service

Concerning the profession of those who are to be called for the first time to active military service

269.* Did Superiors regulate according to the decrees of the Holy See the temporary professions of those who are to be called for the first time to active military service or its equivalent.

270.* Were perpetual professions permitted before the first active military service or its equivalent, to which the young men are liable to be called.

Concerning the religious during their military service

271.* *a*) Did Superiors take care of their members in the service, watch over their life, communicate frequently with them, requiring a periodical account of their conduct, their actions and exercises of piety, etc.

b) What special means were used to secure their perseverance.

272.* In cases of dismissal for just and reasonable causes, or of voluntary separation from the Institute, did the Major Superior follow the prescribed procedure and faithfully conserve all the documents in the Archives.

Concerning the renewal of temporary profession after military service and the making of perpetual profession

273.* For admission to the renewal of temporary profession, was everything done which is prescribed by the common law and in the decrees regarding this matter.

274.* Was the prescribed time of the temporary profession completed after military service, and also the time of the temporary vows which is prescribed by law and by the Constitutions before the making of the perpetual profession.

CHAPTER III

Concerning the Works and Ministries of the Institute

ARTICLE I

Concerning ministries in general

Concerning the special end and the works of the Institute in general

275. Were the ministries proper to the Institute abandoned or neglected.

276. Were any works engaged in which are not contained in the special end of the Institute; if so, with what permission was this done.

Concerning abuses in the exercise of ministries

277. Were any abuses in the exercise of ministries introduced during this time; if so, what were they.

278. Is all appearance of avarice carefully avoided on the occasion of ministries.

279. Was begging from door to door, according to law (cc. 621, 622) and the Constitutions, done with the required permissions.

280. Moreover, in begging, were the rules of law (c. 623), the instructions of the Holy See (c. 624), and the norms of the Constitutions observed.

281. By reason of or under pretext of ministries, are an excessive or too worldly communication with seculars and frequent and prolonged absences from the religious house permitted.

282. What precautions are taken in this communication in order to avoid harm to the religious and scandal to seculars.

Concerning difficulties with the secular clergy or with other Institutes, etc., because of the ministries

283. On the occasion of the ministries did any friction occur with ecclesiastical Superiors, with pastors and the secular clergy, with other Institutes or with Chaplains. What were the chief

instances of such difficulties and where did they occur.

284. What probable reasons can be assigned for these difficulties, and what remedies can be suggested for their avoidance.

ARTICLE II

Concerning special ministries

Concerning Missions among infidels and heretics

285. In the Missions, or in any one of them, did the religious life suffer any harm, and if so, what were the reasons for this.

286. What safeguards were used or should have been used so that in the apostolate the faithful observance of religious discipline and the care of one's own sanctification be better secured.

287.* In the Missions, is the internal religious Superior distinct from the ecclesiastical Superior.

288.* Did this union of offices in the same person result in advantages or rather in disadvantages.

Concerning Parishes, Churches, and Sanctuaries

289.* For the incorporation or union of parishes, was an indult of the Holy See obtained, according to cc. 452, § 1; 1423, § 2, so that there should be a union or incorporation properly effected.

290.* In what form were Parishes united to the Institute: *pleno iure* (absolutely, at the will of the Holy See), *in temporalibus*, etc., and from what date. (A copy of the document should be sent if there is one.)

291.* Was an agreement made with the Ordinary of the place to accept any parish. (Send copies of the agreements made during the five-year period.)

292.* How do Superiors watch over and assist those of their subjects who are pastors (c. 631, §§ 1–2), and in case of need admonish and correct them.

293.* Was the office of local Superior ever united with that of pastor, observing c. 505; did this union give rise to difficulties, or was it on the contrary attended with good results.

294.* Did the Institute obtain from local Ordinaries that Churches or Sanctuaries should be entrusted to it; if so, with what permission and on what terms and conditions was this done.

295.* How do all Superiors see to it that religious discipline suffer no harm from the ministries engaged in by the religious in parishes or in public churches which are entrusted to them.

Concerning Colleges, Schools, and Seminaries

296.* Has the Institute entrusted to it any Seminaries of clerics, and if so, on what terms. (Documents and agreements entered into regarding this matter during the five-year period should be attached.)

297.* In these Seminaries, are there any difficulties with the Ordinaries, concerning either the religious life and discipline or the government of the Seminary.

298.* What measures and efforts are employed toward the sound and thorough training and religious education of the students.

299. Are there houses for the residence of young people who are attending public schools.

300. In these cases is very special care taken to see that the schools are safe from the standpoint of both instruction and education; especially is a careful supervision maintained over the instruction and religious education; and if there are any deficiencies are they carefully remedied.

301.† Are there schools which are attended by both sexes; as regards fixing the age beyond which boys may not be admitted or retained, have the prescriptions made by the Ordinaries been observed.

302. Do Superiors strictly see to it that Rectors, Prefects, Teachers, and Professors receive adequate preparation for their work:

a) Scientifically, by acquiring knowledge which corresponds adequately to the grade of the class, and by obtaining degrees and certificates, even such as are recognized outside ecclesiastical circles.

b) Pedagogically, by the study and practice of the art of teaching.

c) Spiritually, so that they may exercise the office of teaching with a genuine zeal for souls and make it a means of sanctification for themselves and others.

303. Do Superiors carefully see to it that the work of teaching be properly harmonized with religious discipline.

304. Did they promptly remove from the office of teaching those who in practicing it make light of the religious life and are not a good example to the students.

Concerning the practice of the corporal works of mercy

305. Does the Institute practice the corporal works of mercy toward the sick, orphans, the aged, etc.

306: Are there:

a) Guest-houses and hospitals for persons indiscriminately, even for those of the other sex.

b) In this case, by what authority were these institutions accepted and what precautions are used to avoid dangers and suspicions.

307. What, if any, difficulties have arisen.

308. Do superiors diligently see to it that all persons who are to be engaged in various capacities in these institutions be competently prepared:

a) Scientifically, by obtaining even State certificates and other equivalent credentials.

b) Practically, by a suitable period of trial.

309. In the assistance and care of the sick and in the exercise of corporal charity, are the provisions of the Constitutions and the norms which have been given in this matter by the Holy See and by the Ordinaries observed.

310.† Do the religious women who attend the sick in private houses faithfully observe the special provisions of the Constitutions; do they carefully take appropriate precautions to avoid dangers.

311. Do Superiors see to it that the bodily health of the religious who are engaged in these ministries be preserved by suitable food and sleep; that moral dangers be avoided; that the religious life and the exercise of charity be properly harmonized; that zeal be kept, both in fact and in appearance, free from any form of avarice or admixture of other human affection.

Concerning the apostolate of the press

312. Does the Institute exercise the apostolate by writing, publishing, or editing and distributing books and papers.

313. Were the publications submitted according to law to the

previous censorship of the Major Superiors and Ordinaries of places (c. 1385, § 2).

314. Was the necessary permission of Superiors and Ordinaries of places obtained for publishing books treating of profane matters, and for cooperating in the production of papers, magazines, or reviews or editing them (c. 1386, § 1).

315. In the distribution and sale of books, is the appearance of excessive profit avoided, and are proper precautions used to avoid dangers.

Concerning Catholic Action

316. Do the religious strive to promote Catholic Action and to collaborate in it.

317. Have any difficulties arisen in this matter, either with the directors or with the secular clergy.

318. What remedies have been used to remove these difficulties, and what further remedies can be recommended.

Concerning priestly ministrations — The celebration of the Holy Sacrifice, and Mass stipends and obligations

319.* Do Superiors diligently see to it that the religious priests do not fail to prepare themselves by pious prayers for the Sacrifice of the Eucharist, that they celebrate worthily and devoutly, observing the rubrics faithfully and giving the proper amount of time to it; and that after the Mass they give thanks to God for so great a gift.

320. Whether each house has, according to cc. 843, § 1; 844, a book in which are marked in due order the number of Masses received, the intention, the stipend, and who has said the Mass and when.

321. How often and by what Superiors are the books of Masses of each house examined and signed.

322. Whether all the houses as regards the manual stipend of Masses observed the decrees of the local Ordinaries and the customs of the dioceses according to cc. 831, §§ 2–3, 832.

323. Whether in each of the houses the obligations of Masses, both perpetual and manual, were faithfully satisfied in due time according to cc. 834, 1517.

324. Were any special concessions made in this matter, either as regards the reduction of the stipends or intentions, or as to deferring the celebration of the Masses; if so, what were they.

325. In accepting the obligations of Masses, in collecting and in giving up or transmitting the intentions, and in fulfilling them, did Superiors conscientiously observe the provisions of law (cc. 835–840, 842), those of the Constitutions or Statutes, and the terms of the Foundations.

Concerning domestic services

326.† Do the religious women perform any services in Seminaries, ecclesiastical residence-halls, Communities of clerics or of religious men, or in other Colleges or institutions destined for male students, or in parishes. How many such Seminaries, Colleges, etc., have they, and by what permission did they accept them?

327.† Were the prescribed precautions for avoiding all danger and difficulty faithfully observed.

328.† Was there any such difficulty to be deplored during this time, and what was done about it.

CONCLUSION

A summary comparative judgment regarding the state of the Institute

Concerning striving toward perfection

329. What is to be said about the desire for and the actual striving toward evangelical perfection on the part of the members (cc. 487; 488, 1°).

330. In this respect is there in the Institute progress or retrogression as compared with the preceding five-year period, and how is this manifested or proved; what are the reasons for the progress or retrogression.

331. What has been done by Superiors during the five-year period to promote the tendency toward perfection and to prevent relaxation.

Concerning the state of discipline

332. What is to be said summarily about the observance of the vows and of the provisions of Canon Law, the Rule, and the Constitutions, both absolutely and in comparison with the preceding five-year period.

333. What are the points of religious discipline which are more easily and frequently violated.

334. What causes may be assigned for the progress in religious observance or for its decline.

335. What difference, if any, is there between the various Provinces or localities in regard to religious observance.

336. What has been done by Superiors to secure faithful and complete regular observance in every locality, Province, and house.

337. What are the difficulties and the chief obstacles which obstruct the work of Superiors and impede its effectiveness.

Concerning the economic condition

338. What, in itself and in comparison with the preceding five-year period, is the condition of the Institute and of its Provinces if there are any, with regard to capital and finances.

339. To what causes is the growth or diminution of capital and income to be attributed.

340. What are the plans of Superiors and what provisions are needed for the good of the Institute and its members.

Concerning the special end and works

341. In comparison with the preceding five-year period, was there an increase or diminution in the activity of the Institute in regard to its specific end. What are the reasons for the increase or diminution.

342. Were there any new means or works looking toward the attainment of the specific end introduced during the five-year period, and what concrete plans are entertained for the future.

Given at Rome, from the Sacred Congregation of Religious, the 9th day of December, 1948.

Private; S. C. Rel., 9 Dec., 1948.

NOTE: This document is immediately followed by a "Conspectus of the Condition of the Houses," also published by the S. C. Rel. and to be filled out with the Quinquennial Report, and by a "Concordance of the Three Questionnaires," which we reproduce with due permission from the *Review for Religious*.

Name of the Institute (Society) ....

Diocese:[2] ....

Five-year Period:[3] ....   **CONSPECTUS OF THE**

I	II	III
PROVINCE[4]	DIOCESE	HOUSE

[1] The annex is to be made out exactly like this model.

[2] In which the generalate house is located.

[3] The years are to be indicated so as to include in the five-year period both the first and the last years, e.g., 1949–53.

[4] The individual houses are to be listed according to Provinces or similar units (Vice-Provinces, etc.), and if there are no Provinces, then according to nations; in the Province or nation, the houses are to be listed according to the Diocese in which they are located, e.g., Province of the Holy Name of Jesus, or of Italy (col. I), Diocese of Bergamo (col. II), and then let the individual houses of this Diocese be listed (col. III).

[5] If the Institute has only one class of members, all are to be listed in the first column under each title.

[6] How many priests, whether of perpetual or temporary vows, even though they are included in the foregoing classifications.

[7] The various works are to be listed as briefly as possible.

ANNEX TO THE QUINQUENNIAL REPORT[1]

CONDITION OF THE HOUSES

IV MEMBERS[5]							V
Nov.		Temp. vows		Perp. vows			WORKS WHICH ARE PRACTICED[7]
1 class	2 class	1 class	2 class	1 class	2 class	Priests[6]	

TOTALS
{
Provinces ....
Vice-Provinces ....
Houses ....
Members ....
}
{
Priests ....
Perp. vows ....
Temp. vows ....
Novices ....
}

A CONCORDANCE OF THE THREE QUESTIONNAIRES (from the Review for Religious)

There are three editions of the *Elenchus Quaestionum*: 1. (P) for pontifical institutes — 342 questions; 2. (D) for diocesan institutes — 322 questions; 3. (M) for independent monasteries and houses — 171 questions. However, only one English translation has been made — that for pontifical institutes. Hence, it seems advisable to publish the following correlation of numbers so that those using questionnaire 2 or 3 may be co-ordinated with the one and only translation.

D	P	M	D	P	M	D	P	M	D	P	M	D	P	M	D	P	M	D	P	M
1	1	1	36	48		88	101	41	137	150	77	187	201	113	231	251	144	281	301	158
2	2	2	37	49		89	102	42	138	151	78	188	202		232	252	145	282	302	159
3	3		38	50		90	103	43	139	152	79		203	114	233	253	146	283	303	160
		3	39	51		91	104	44	140	153	80		204	115	234	254		284	304	
4	4		40	52	19	92	105		141	154	81	189	205	116	235	255	147	285	305	
5	5		41	53	20	93	106	45	142	155	82	190	206	117	236	256		286	306	
6	6		42	54	21	94	107	46	143	156		191	207	118	237	257		287	307	
7	7		43	55	22	95	108	47	144	157		192	208	119	238	258	148	288	308	
8	8		44	56			109	48	145	158	83	193	209	120	239	259	149	289	309	
	9		45	57		96	110	49	146	159	84	194	210		240	260		290	310	
	10		46	58		97	111		147	160		195	211	121	241	261	150	291	311	
	11		47	59		98	112		148	161		196	212		242	262		292	312	
	12		48	60		99	113		149	162		197	213		243	263		293	313	
	13		49	61		100	114	50	150	163		198	214	122	244	264		294	314	
	14		50	62		101	115	51	151	164	85	199	215		245	265	151	295	315	
	15		51	63		102	116	52	152	165	86		216		246	266	152	296	316	
	16		52	64		103	117		153	166	87	200	217	123	247	267		297	317	
	17		53	65		104	118	53	154	167	88	201	218	124	248	268	153	298	318	
	18		54	66		105	119		155	168	89	202	219	125	249	269		299	319	
9	19		55	67		106	120		156	169	90	203	220	126	250	270		300	320	
10	20		56	68		107	121		157	170	91				251	271		301	321	
			57	69	23	108	122	54	158	171	92				252	272		302	322	
			58	70		109												303	323	

Special Questions Not Included in the Questionnaire for Papal Institutes

For Diocesan Institutes

4. Supposing all the requisite conditions, has a petition been sent to the Holy See, or is it intended to send one, to obtain the status of a Papal Congregation? Are any difficulties foreseen, or were there any actually? Enumerate them.

9. Is the Congregation perchance divided into provinces: how long ago, how many, and by what authority?

233. Same as 253 for Papal, except at the end which reads: ". . . before the decree or judgment had been *confirmed by the local Ordinary*" (c. 650, § 2, 1°; 652, § 1).

For Independent Monasteries and Houses (Sui Iuris)

3. What is the juridical nature of the monastery or house:

a) To which Order does it belong, if any, and which Rule is followed?

b) Are the vows solemn or simple; or simple, though solemn normally (c. 488, 7°)?

5. Are there any filial houses subject to the independent monastery or house? How many?

6. Does the monastery depend on the local Ordinary or on the Regular Superior?

17. Has the canonical visitation of the local Ordinary taken place, as well as that of the Regular Superior, if the monastery is subject to him?

32. Is there an appointed chaplain, or have other provisions been made sufficient for the spiritual good by sacred functions? Are there any difficulties with regard to the spiritual good?

48. Are there any difficulties of an economic nature, and what are they?

65. How are the economic needs of the monastery provided for: by the labor of the community or by alms?

66. What, if any, activity does the community engage in for its own support?

72. Is the condition of the extern Sisters regulated according to the statutes promulgated by the S. Congregation on July 16, 1931?

85. How many novices are there at present?

123. What kind of cloister is observed? Are the places subject to cloister clearly marked and sufficiently guarded? Are the prescriptions of the law and of the constitutions regarding cloister faithfully observed (cc. 598–604)?

124. Were the cases of dispensation from the law of cloister frequent, either for going out, or for going in? Which were the principal ones?

125. Are difficulties experienced in the observance of cloister, especially when nuns are engaged in the works of the apostolate, of education, etc.?

154. What works are carried on in the house (apostolate, education, manual labor for pay)?

162. Is the independent monastery or house fully self-sufficient: with regard to the personnel to fill the various offices of government and of personal activity? And with regard to the religious formation, as well as with regard to economic means, so that regular observance can flourish fully?

How to Fill in the Annual Report (S. C. Rel., Circular Letter, 9 Feb., 1950) Private.

To the Reverend Superiors General:

On the 9th of July, 1947, the Holy Father deigned to approve the Decree *Cum Transactis* of the S. C. Rel. concerning the new formula of the Questionnaire to which all the Religious of pontifical or diocesan right must answer in the *Quinquennial Report*.

This decree was published in the *Acta Apostolicae Sedis*, Vol. 50 (1948), pp. 378–381, and was annexed to the new formulary, now ready for distribution at the Archives of the Sacred Congregation.[1]

In the same decree (n. IX) an *Annual Report* for statistical purposes was also required to be filled according to the questions which the Sacred Congregation was to send later. These questions have been printed and will be sent to every Religious Order, although those who have houses or representatives in Rome may secure them directly by applying to the Archives of the Sacred Congregation.

In order to help in preparing the answers to these questions,

---

[1] The decree is reported in this volume under canon 510.

this Sacred Congregation thinks it opportune to give the following directions:

I. In filling the Quinquennial Report, according to the instructions prefixed to the Questionnaire, it is not necessary to include the question in the answer, but it is sufficient to put before the answer the number of the question.

The time when the Quinquennial Report must be sent back is substantially the same as that established since 1922 and reproduced in the Decree annexed at the foot of the Questionnaire.

II. The Annual Report is especially required for statistical purposes, and therefore it must be of the greatest possible precision and up to date as of the 31st of December of the year preceding the one in which the report is sent.

According to the Decree, the Annual Report is independent of the Quinquennial Report, and of the questions which it contains. It has its own questions and inquiries.

Contrary to what is done for the answers to the questions of the Quinquennial Report, the Annual Report must be made on the very forms received, and these must be returned directly to the Sacred Congregation by the Superior General of every Religious Order.

The questions do not apply to all Religious in the same way; every Religious Order must answer according to its own activities, filling in the pages which refer directly to its own scope of action.

The languages to be used may be those of the Quinquennial Report, e.g., Latin for clerical Religious; French, English, Italian, Portuguese, Spanish, and German for lay Religious.

The period of time to be included in the Annual Report must extend from the 1st of January to the 31st of December; at the top, on the right of the forms, where the year is required, the year to which the data of the Report refer must be inserted, not the year in which the Report is sent.

The partial totals of the various divisions of the statistical data, houses, personnel, works, must be added up and forwarded, showing clearly by means of a line the grand total.

The Annual Report must be sent within the first three months of the year following the one to which the data refer: for example, the data of the year 1950 must be sent during the first three months, January–March, 1951.

The obligation of sending in the reports begins in 1951 during the first three months of which year must be sent the information relating to the year 1950 brought to date as of December 31st of the said year.

In order to insure uniformity of presentation, it would be advisable to mind the following directions in filling the respective forms:

Cover: At the word *Dioecesis* should be written the name of the present Diocese and also that of the former if the Curia Generalizia or Mother House has been transferred of late.

Inside Cover: All the required information must be entered in the synoptical form.

Question I: At the word *fondatore* (founder), must be written in parentheses the dates of the birth and death of the founder.

Question II: At the words *Status domorum I,* all Religious must answer, those who are divided into provinces as well as the others. It must be noticed that it is not necessary to give the complete list of all the houses of every nation, but only the total number. This is the reason that there is only one line for each nation, and the four blanks are always filled with regard to the total number of houses of the nation.

The order of nations should be the alphabetical order of the language used in the report. Then all the nations should be arranged according to the five parts of the world in alphabetical order as follows: Africa, America, Asia, Europe, Oceania.

The word *Domus* is understood as a house canonically erected, whether it be "formed" (at least six professed members) or not; but, if in the same building there are several sections or communities, as for example the Curia, the Novitiate, and so on, such building should be considered as only one house or one *"domus."*

Question III: At the words *Status domorum II* should answer only the Religious Orders which are divided into provinces, meaning by provinces those parts regularly divided by the Order or Institute according to the norms of Canon Law, even if those parts bear other names such as Inspectorate, etc., provided the Major Superiors be truly Major Superiors. The provinces should include also the quasi-provinces regularly established. The divisions which constitute a separate unit, but which have been made only by the immediate Major Superiors, are not to be included with the provinces.

Here again, in the compiling of this form, only the grand total is required.

The order of the provinces follows the alphabetical order of their denomination in the Congregation, arranging them according to the nations where are the greater number of provinces, and always in the alphabetical order of the nations and of the parts of the world.

Under the words *ambitus territorialis* must be indicated briefly the nation or part of nations or countries, etc., where every province extends.

Questions IV and V: In these forms also, only the aggregate number of persons in the province or nation is required. The words *primae classis* indicate a division of the community in the sense that in the clerical religious Orders, the first class is that of priests, the second that of the lay brothers or members; in the lay religious congregations, the first class is that of Religious known as such, the second that of the serving religious.

The Religious who have only one class of members fill in only the space under *primae classis*.

For the registration of the members according to the various nations or provinces or houses, the norms of the Institute must be followed. The nationality does not matter if no account of it is taken in the official registration of the Institute.

The word *novices* applies only to those religious who according to the Constitutions of the Institute or Order may so be called canonically.

Question VI: This form is compulsory only for the Religious who are divided into provinces; it is enough for the others to have filled the foregoing papers.

Question VII: In this form again, only the aggregate numbers are required. The form is divided into two parts:

First part: *cura infirmorum* with four horizontal divisions: the word *quot* requires the total number of the works indicated by the horizontal divisions, while the words *religiosi addicti* require the total number of the Religious employed in such works.

Second part: *Asyla,* with three spaces, in which, under the word *quot* is asked the number of works, and under the word *degentes,* the total number of sick or assisted, while *quaenam* requires the kind of persons assisted, giving also other informations that might be useful.

In this enumeration, the alphabetical number of nations must be followed as aforesaid.

Question VIII: This form is only for clerical Religious. It requires the aggregate number by nations and provinces.

Question IX: This form deals only with Religious who have schools for outsiders, that is, those who are not aspirants to the Order itself. The word *domus* in this form means college, school, etc., and it is required to state how many colleges are owned by the Religious, and how many are not, but which are either used, directed, or employed by the members of the Order; moreover, all kinds of colleges or schools, etc., are to be counted, even though they may not be recognized by the State.

If in one building there are different types of teaching, primary, intermediate, superior, and professional, these are considered as different and as many colleges, schools, etc. Therefore in the report must enter the total number of schools or colleges of the different types, primary, intermediate, superior, or professional, of every nation, arranged in alphabetical order as said before.

The title *scholae professionales* carries under two different blanks; if there are more than two classes of schools, they must be reduced to two common divisions or classes, one being *"Arti e mestieri:* technical," and the other "Commercial, Normal, etc."

If it is difficult to classify any particular school, it must be entered into one of the above classes and after the number an explanation may be given in parentheses.

The word *media* refers to types of schools such as ginnasio liceo, baccalaureato, mittelschule Gymnasium, High School, Humanités anciennes et modernes, etc.

The word *elementaria* refers to lower studies, and *superiora* to superior studies of the university type.

Question X: The words *gradus interni* may refer to all the degrees of the Order itself; it is sufficient to mention them in the vertical spaces.

In the space *gradus facult. et Institut. civilium* must be inserted all the degrees obtained, even if there are degrees which are not of the university type, such as diplomas, certificates, etc.

In the mention of the members who have academic degrees, the total number of the members who obtained degrees before the 31st of December of the year for which the report is made should also be specified. The total number of the members of the Order who have obtained degrees or diplomas at any time before must be inserted in parentheses under the number during the year being reported.

(**Private**); S. C. Rel., Circular Letter, 9 Feb., 1950. English translation made by the Sacred Congregation of Religious and officially printed and published.

For an explanation of the Annual Report, cf. *Review for Religious*, Vol. 9 (1950), p. 309 (Ellis).

CANON 534

Alienation: Amount for Which Permission of Holy See Required (S. C. Consist., 13 July, 1951) AAS 43-602.

A Decree of the Sacred Consistorial Congregation:

Since the changed value of money and the wavering of the currency has occasioned in certain places special difficulties in applying the prescriptions of canons 534, § 1 and 1532, § 1, 2° of the Code of Canon Law, the Holy See has been asked to issue appropriate regulations.

Wherefore, His Holiness by divine Providence Pope Pius XII, after having carefully considered the matter, has graciously deigned to provide by the present Decree of the Sacred Consistorial Congregation that, while the present conditions continue and at the good pleasure of the Holy See, recourse is to be had to the same Apostolic See whenever the sum of money involved exceeds ten thousand gold francs or lire.

Given at Rome, from the Sacred Consistorial Congregation, 13 July, 1951.

AAS 43-602; S. C. Consist., 13 July, 1951. Annotations: *Commentarium pro Religiosis*, 30–255 (Gutiérrez); *Periodica*, 41–150 (Jarlot); *Review for Religious*, 11–301 (Ellis).

In the Oriental Churches: Amount for which papal permission is required in alienations and debts. See **c. 1**; AAS 44–632.

New Faculty of Apostolic Delegate to permit loans and alienation by a religious Institute up to half a million gold dollars. See **c. 858**; Letter of Apostolic Delegate, 3 Apr., 1947.

CANON 539

New Faculty of Apostolic Delegate to shorten or prolong postulancy. See c. 858; Letter of Apostolic Delegate, 3 Apr., 1947.

CANON 554

Special Commission of Sacred Congregation of Religious in charge of care and education of novices. See c. 251; AAS 36–213.

CANON 569

Will to Be Made by Novice in Congregation Even Though Invalid in Civil Law (Code Commission) Private.

The Code Commission gave the following reply to the question proposed by the Superior General of the Redemptorists:

The will mentioned in canon 569, § 3, is to be made, even though it is invalid by civil law, and also if the novice has no present property but only may acquire it in future. . . . But care should be taken that as soon as it can be done the will be made valid according to civil law, without however changing any of its dispositions except in accordance with canon 583, § 2.

(Private); Code Commission. Quoted by Hannan, *The Canon Law of Wills*, p. 218. Many authors cite the document, but none whom we have found give its date, nor is the date given in *Theologisch-praktische Quartalschrift*, Vol. 73, 1920, p. 343, the source usually cited. Vermeersch (*Epit. I. C.*, ed. 6, Vol. II, n. 716, p. 514, note 1) states that there have been several private replies of the Holy See to this effect.

CANON 574

Exclaustration of Religious Clerics of Solemn Vows During Military Service (S. C. Rel., 14 April, 1939) Private.

The Minister General of the Friars Minor asked the Sacred Congregation for Religious:

Question. Whether also in the case of clerics professed of solemn vows, who are called upon for military service, the solemn vows are suspended during their military service, as the temporary vows are suspended under these circumstances, according to the decree *Inter reliquas* and later declarations about it.

Reply. Major Superiors, especially in the places in question, are given the faculty to provide in individual cases of this kind, while the necessity of military service continues and during such service, by granting an indult of exclaustration, as far as possible according to canon 639.

(Private) ; S. C. Rel., 14 April, 1939. See *Acta Ordinis Fratrum Minorum,* 1939, p. 158. Cf. *Commentarium pro Religiosis,* 1939, p. 213.

Effect of Second Call to Military Service or of General Mobilization on Religious Vows (S. C. Rel., 23 Jan., 1940) Private.

A letter of the Sacred Congregation of Religious, 23 Jan., 1940, to the Sacred Congregation of Propaganda, communicated the following norms:

1. The decree *Inter reliquas* of 27 Aug., 1910,[1] concerns religious who are called for the first time to military service. The replies to questions which arose concerning the decree, published in the *Acta Apostolicae Sedis* on 1 February, 1912, are always applied to the religious who is called for the first time.

2. As regards those called a second time and general mobilization, this Sacred Congregation of Religious, from the audience granted by the Holy Father to the Cardinal Prefect on 2 January, 1940, holds to the following norms:

a) If there is question of religious who have already pronounced perpetual vows (simple or solemn), it considers those who are recalled or mobilized during extraordinary military service as "excloistered according to law."

b) If on the other hand there is question of religious who have temporary vows, these are bound by the said vows until their expiration; but they are not admitted during their military service to perpetual vows; they may be permitted by their Superiors to renew their temporary vows for a year.

c) If there is question of those whose status is still undetermined — that is, those who have never fulfilled their military service but have not been definitely declared exempt from it — these cannot, during this period of uncertainty, pronounce the perpetual vows (simple or solemn), "because the civil law does not grant them exemption from military service but merely a deferment of it, and consequently they remain subject to service," and any such who might be taken for military service would

[1] See CANON LAW DIGEST, Vol. 1, p. 106.

evidently be included among those called for the first time, and, if they had during the period of deferment pronounced their perpetual vows (simple or solemn) without the necessary indult from the Holy See, such vows would be invalid.

(Private); S. C. Rel., 23 Jan., 1940. See Schaefer, *De Religiosis*, ed. 1940, n. 671, p. 1124.

NOTE: Later the S. C. of Religious declared that in view of the difficulties of existing conditions religious under temporary vows who are recalled to military service may be admitted by their Superiors to perpetual profession at the expiration of the temporary vows, provided the other conditions required for perpetual profession are verified. S. C. Rel., 30 March, 1943. *Documentation Catholique*, 1945, col. 331.

Pre-military Service: The decree *Inter reliquas* of 1 Jan., 1911 (*Digest*, Vol. I, p. 106) is applicable to young men who, in Germany, are obliged to engage in pre-military service called *Arbeitdienst*. See S. C. Rel., 10 Apr., 1937, reply to Bishop of Limburgh; *Commentarium pro Religiosis*, Vol. 18, pp. 78 and 141.

Religious of the Sacred Heart: Temporary vows not required. See private reply of Code Commission mentioned by Vermeersch, *Epitome*, I, ed. 1937, p. 522, and Schaefer, *De Religiosis*, ed. 1940, p. 585. The date of this declaration is not given.

Society of Jesus: Temporary vows not required. See Code Com., 29 June, 1918; reported by Schaefer, *De Religiosis*, ed. 1940, p. 585, note 96, from Biederlack-Führich, *De Religiosis*, 1919, n. 94, note 4.

CANON 576

Profession or Renewal of Vows in Mass: The Superioress General of a Congregation of Sisters asked the S. C. of Rites for permission to have the ceremony of profession or renewal of vows at the Offertory of the Mass, instead of before Mass as prescribed in the Ceremonial approved for the Institute. Reply, 8 July, 1950 (N. C. 112/50): *Negative* (*Monitor Ecclesiasticus*, 1952, p. 450). The proper procedure would seem to have been to apply to the S. C. of Religious for permission to amend the Ceremonial.

CANON 583

Making a Valid Will to Replace an Invalid One is not a change of the will. See c. 569; private reply of Code Commission, undated.

CANON 589

Studies of Religious: In Italy. See joint letter of S. C. Rel. and S. C. Sem. et Univ., 2 Feb., 1941, addressed to the Superiors General of Religious Orders and Congregations in Italy; *Il Monitore Ecclesiastico*, Vol. 53, 1941, p. 34.

CANON 592

Religious: Permission Rarely to Be Given to Go to Bathing Resorts: Precautions to Be Taken (S. C. Rel., 15 July, 1926) **Private.**

A letter of the Sacred Congregation of Religious to all General Superiors of religious Orders and Congregations, after calling attention to the fact that dangers and scandals can arise from the attendance of clerics and religious at bathing resorts (*stationes balneares*) and mineral springs, gives the following prescriptive norms:

a) Superiors are to see to it that the religious of their Institute do not easily get permission to attend such places.

b) When there is sufficient and reasonable cause for such permission from the standpoint of health, they are to see to it that their religious live in some religious house or at least in some respectable house suitable to their state.

c) The religious are to be absolutely forbidden to lay aside their religious habit for any reason, and to attend theaters, plays, cinemas, and other shows of the kind; and they are to avoid all companionship of the sort that is unbecoming to religious men.

d) Superiors are to exercise due supervision to see that these prescriptions are observed, and in case of violation the subjects are to be severely punished.

Attention is called to the fact that the Sacred Congregation of the Council (in the letter of 1 July, 1926; CANON LAW DIGEST, Vol. 1, p. 138) enjoined upon Ordinaries of places to be watchful in this matter even as regards religious.

(**Private**); S. C. Rel., 15 July, 1926. Cf. Schaefer, *De Religiosis*, 3 ed., 1940, n. 312, p. 667, note 25; *Analecta Ord. Min. Cap.*, Vol. 42, p. 244.

Catholic Action in the Training and Activities of Religious of Both Sexes. See letter of Cardinal Pacelli as Secretary of State to the Superiors General of all religious Institutes of either sex, on the promotion of Catholic Action; 15 March, 1936; Italian and Latin texts, *Periodica*, Vol. 25, 1936, p. 209; English translation in *The Religious and Catholic Action* by Father Anderl and Sister Ruth (St. Rose Convent, La Crosse, Wisconsin), p. 91.

Ipso Facto Excommunication for Negotiatio. See c. 142; AAS 42–330.

Public Cinemas, Theaters, Etc., in Rome. See c. 140; Vic. Urb., 1 Feb., 1938.

CANON 593

The Use of Tobacco in the States of Perfection (S. C. Rel., 10 Jan., 1951) **Private.**

A Circular Letter sent by the Sacred Congregation of Religious to the Superiors General is as follows:

Prot. N. 2511/51 S. R.

Very Reverend Father:

During the past few years following the last war not a few consultations, complaints, declarations, and formal accusations have come from General Superiors and Chapters, from individuals zealous for religious observance, and even from local Ordinaries, regarding the use of tobacco by members of the states of perfection.

In those religious Institutes and Societies in which the use of tobacco is forbidden by the Constitutions or by legitimate and accepted traditions and prescriptions of Chapters or Superiors, the intervention of the Sacred Congregation, invoked in various ways, has been effectively to repress and extirpate the illicit use which had crept in here and there chiefly as a result of the war.

In religious Institutes and Societies in which the use of tobacco is not generally forbidden, it has been noted that it often gives occasion to rather grave abuses. These abuses regularly harm and impair in many ways religious poverty, the spirit of mortification, and external modesty.

On the occasion of the recent Congress on the States of Perfection the question of the use and abuse of tobacco might have been dealt with. It was not done at that time for various reasons, but the Sacred Congregation considers it a duty to take the matter up immediately in a clear and straightforward way with the Very Reverend Superiors General, in order to communicate to them the proper criteria to be observed in regard to the use of tobacco, and to stimulate their zeal in repressing the abuses of tobacco, if any such exist in their Institutes and Societies. For members of the states of perfection ought to be in this respect an example of fidelity and Christian and religious poverty, temperance, and modesty to everyone.

These then are the general norms which the Sacred Congregation considers as expressing the criteria to be observed regarding the use of tobacco.

I. In religious Institutes, Societies, and Institutes in which according to approved Constitutions or by legitimate and accepted prescriptions of Chapters and Superiors the use of tobacco is either forbidden or held within very narrow limits or subject to strict conditions, these lawful prescriptions are to be sacredly observed and enforced. The Sacred Congregation confirms and defends those provisions as rightly and for good reason forming a part of the mortification and regular religious observance in those religious Institutes, Societies, and Institutes.

II. In religious Institutes, Societies, and other Institutes in which a moderate use of tobacco is allowed and legitimate, this use is so to be regulated that religious poverty be unimpaired both as regards expense and dependence on Superiors, that the spirit of asceticism and religious mortification, which is one of the prime foundations of the states of perfection, suffer no harm, and finally that the use of tobacco as regards place, manner, and time, neither harm nor threaten in any way the good example and edification which should be given to the faithful or externs.

III. In order to avoid these dangers (n. II) and to strengthen the effectiveness of legitimate existing prescriptions of Constitutions or Chapters (n. I), Superiors with their proper Consultors may and should, if necessary, issue special norms to regulate the use of tobacco as to manner, quantity, time, and place.

IV. In general the Sacred Congregation is opposed to the introduction of tobacco, to departure from the regulations regarding its use, and to the relaxation of discipline in this matter, whether in religious Institutes, Societies, or other Institutes. For we must sincerely confess that according to actual experience these relaxations, deviations, permissions are in general not helpful and in fact can easily become seriously harmful to the religious spirit.

V. If the Ordinaries of places have made any regulations for clerics in their dioceses regarding the use of tobacco, especially in public, Superiors should strive in every way that religious and others who follow evangelical perfection shall observe them exactly, as befits their public profession of sanctity. If Ordinaries of places notify Superiors of any infraction of such regulations or of any abuses of tobacco by their religious subjects, the Superiors should deal with the matter effectively and diligently.

While I communicate these matters to Your Paternity, I beg you to present to this Sacred Congregation whatever regulations are already established in your Institute, or those which Your Paternity with your Council may have decided to establish at this time.

His Holiness by divine Providence Pope Pius XII, in the audience graciously granted to the undersigned Cardinal Prefect on the 8th of January, deigned to give his approval to this Circular Letter.

Rome, 10 January, 1951.

(**Private**); S. C. Rel., Circular Letter, 10 Jan., 1951. *Monitor Ecclesiasticus,* 1951, p. 441; annotations, *ibid.,* p. 443 (Gutiérrez).

NOTE: In the annotations, Gutiérrez reports a private reply of the S. C. to questions proposed by a Superior General of an Institute in which the use of tobacco is forbidden (Prot. N. 10272/50):

1. Whether, everything considered, a general precept binding in conscience can be imposed or confirmed in this Congregation: (*a*) which obliges all members, Superiors and subjects, not to use tobacco for smoking either in public or in private; (*b*) which binds all Superiors not to spend any part of the money of the Congregation, even the slightest, for smoking tobacco for the use of members of the Congregation; (*c*) which forbids all, Superiors and subjects, from spending for smoking tobacco any personal money or value, no matter how it may have come to the religious in question.

Reply. In the affirmative to *a, b,* and *c*.

2. Whether the general precept mentioned in question 1 can, in particular cases: (*a*) be imposed *sub gravi;* (*b*) and be confirmed also under the vow of obedience.

Reply. To *a:* in the affirmative, provided the matter in the individual case can certainly be said to be grave *in itself* (by reason of the quantity which is illicitly used or to be used, the frequency, the habit, etc.) or *by reason of the circumstances* (the form in which it is used, scandal, etc.); to *b:* in the affirmative according to common and right doctrine.

3. Whether, in case of the certain violation of a grave particular precept which is binding also under the vow of obedience, measures may be taken against the transgressors according to law, using also admonitions and canonical sanctions.

Reply. In the affirmative, observing the norms of Canon Law.

(**Private**); S. C. Rel., N. 10272/50; date not specified.

CANON 598

Wives of State Governors in U. S. Can Enter Cloister of Men (Code Com., 26 March, 1952) **AAS 44-496.**

The Code Commission was asked:

I. Whether according to canon 598, § 2, the wives of Governors of individual States in the United States with their retinue may be admitted within the cloister of men regulars.

Reply. In the affirmative.

II. Whether the interpretation given in the above reply to question I is declarative or extensive.

Reply. In the negative to the first part, in the affirmative to the second.

Given at Rome, from Vatican City, 26 March, 1952.

AAS 44-496; Code Com., 26 March, 1952. Annotations, *Monitor Ecclesiasticus,* 1952, p. 407 (Bidagor), *Commentarium pro Religiosis,* 1952, p. 225 (Gutiérrez).

CANON 600

Externe Sisters Not to Reside in Cloister (S. C. Rel., 1936) **Private.**

The Cardinal Archbishop of Genoa received the following rescript from the Sacred Congregation of Religious:

This Sacred Congregation in the meeting held on the 28th of this month considered the petition received from Your Eminence, in which you asked the following:

1. The faculty to permit monastic nuns from Italy or from foreign countries who pass through Genoa, to be received as guests in the cloister of the monastery of the same Order, during their temporary or provisional stay.

This Sacred Congregation, after carefully considering the whole matter, grants to Your Eminence the requested faculty for three years, *adhibitis cautelis ne quod oriatur inconveniens.*

2. Whether approval could be given to the *immemorial* custom or to the provisions of the *Consuetudinarium* or ancient books of a monastery of solemn vows permitting externe Sisters to reside in the cloister, notwithstanding the prescriptions of this S. C. of 16 July, 1931,[1] that they should reside in external places annexed to the monastery.

---

[1] See CANON LAW DIGEST, Vol. 2, p. 170.

In this matter the decision of this S. C. is that all customs or provisions of ancient books or directories are abrogated by the statutes which were issued on 16 July, 1931.

Consequently, monasteries which have suitable places are obliged to observe the aforesaid statutes. To those who have no such external places, this Sacred Congregation grants the permission for five years to follow the same practice as heretofore, *provided that in the meantime they make provisions* conformable to the said statutes.

(**Private**); S. C. Rel., 1936. See *Periodica*, Vol. 26, p. 81, with annotations by Ellis; and *Commentarium pro Religiosis*, Vol. 17, p. 209, with annotations by Larraona.

Monastic Nuns (Pius XII, Apostolic Constitution, *Sponsa Christi*, and General Statutes, 21 Nov., 1950) **AAS 43-5.**

The Church, the Spouse of Christ, has from the very beginning of her history not only repeatedly manifested by action and inference but also clearly expressed in her authentic teaching the esteem and tender maternal affection which she bears toward Virgins consecrated to God.

And no wonder, for Christian Virgins, "the choice portion of the flock of Christ,"[1] impelled by charity, disdaining all the distracting preoccupations of the world and conquering the easy but perilous temptation to divide their affections, not only consecrated themselves entirely to Christ as the true Spouse of their souls, but dedicated their whole lives, resplendent with the jewels of all Christian virtues, to the Lord Jesus Christ and to His Church forever.

This mystical attachment of Virgins to the service of Christ and their dedication to the Church was, in the earliest Christian times, done spontaneously and by acts rather than words. Afterward, however, when Virgins came to constitute not merely a certain class of persons but a definite state and order recognized by the Church, the profession of virginity began to be made

---

[1] St. Cyprian, *De habitu virginum*, 3 (*PL*, 4, 455). In the official text of the Constitution, this is the third of forty-five abundant and most valuable footnotes referring to the Fathers, theologians, and ecclesiastical documents. The immediate practical purpose of this DIGEST compels us to omit these footnotes almost entirely. Anyone making so thorough a study of the subject will surely have access to the *Acta Apostolicae Sedis* and the original text.

publicly, and to become more and more strictly binding. Later still the Church, in accepting the holy vow or resolution of virginity, inviolably consecrated the Virgin to God and to the Church by a solemn rite which is rightly counted among the more beautiful records of the ancient liturgy, and thus clearly set her apart from others who bound themselves to God by a merely private bond.

The profession of the life of virginity was protected by a watchful and severe discipline and was at the same time nourished and promoted by all the practices of piety and virtue. The early teaching of the Fathers, of the Greeks and other Orientals as well as of the Latins, gives us a faithful and very beautiful picture of the Christian Virgin. With the greatest care and affection the Fathers illustrated and vividly described in their writings all the elements, whether internal or external, which could have any connection with virginal sanctity and perfection.

How well the angelic life of Christian Virgins in that first stage of its history corresponded to the exhortations and descriptions of the Fathers, and how lofty were the heroic virtues which adorned it, we know in part from the direct and certain testimony of historical documents and records, and in part we can conjecture and even deduce beyond any doubt from other reliable sources.

Especially after peace was granted to the Church, it became the more and more frequent practice, after the example of the Hermits and Cenobites, that the state of virginity consecrated to God should be completed and confirmed by an express and explicit profession of the counsels of poverty and strict obedience.

Women making profession of virginity, who, through love of solitude and for protection against the very grave dangers which threatened them on all sides in the corrupt Roman society, had already come together in a community life segregated as much as possible from ordinary human contacts, later, when circumstances became favorable, rather quickly followed the example of the great number of Cenobites, and, leaving the eremetical life mostly to men, imitated the cenobitical life, and nearly all of them entered into it.

The Church recommended to Virgins in general the common life understood in a rather wide sense, but for a long time did not wish strictly to impose the monastic life even on consecrated Virgins, but rather left them free in the world, though honored as befitted their state. It came about, however, that Virgins liturgically consecrated and living in their own homes or in a common life of a freer sort became more and more rare, until they were in many places no longer recognized in the law of the Church and were as a matter of fact extinct everywhere; they were never generally restored as a legal institution, and later still were even prohibited.

*   *   *

Consequently the Church turned her maternal solicitude chiefly upon those Virgins who, choosing the better part, abandoned the world entirely and embraced a life of complete Christian perfection in monasteries, professing strict poverty and full obedience as well as virginity. The Church provided an external safeguard for their profession of the common life by increasingly rigorous laws of cloister. At the same time she so regulated the internal order of their life that in her laws and religious discipline there gradually emerged as a clearly defined type the figure of the Monastic Sister or Nun entirely devoted to the contemplative life under a strict and regular regime.

About the beginning of the middle ages, when consecrated Virgins living in the world had entirely disappeared, these Monastic Nuns, who had grown tremendously in number, in fervor, and in variety, were regarded as the sole heirs and legitimate successors of the Virgins of earlier times; yet not only as their heirs and successors, but also as the faithful representatives and industrious managers of the continuing heritage, who after having received five talents had gained other five over and above. This origin and dignity of Monastic Nuns, together with their merit and holiness, are proved and vindicated by liturgical records, canonical documents, and historical testimonies of every kind, in writing, sculpture, and painting.

For several centuries up to the close of the middle ages, as clearly appears from the Decretals and from the entire *Corpus Iuris Canonici,* the state of perfection, which had already been so solemnly approved and so fully recognized that its public nature was more and more evident, had as its sole representatives among women the Monastic Nuns, side by side with the Monks and Canons Regular.

After that, though many grave difficulties had to be overcome, first all the Brothers, who were called Mendicants, or Hospitalers, or for the Redemption of Captives, or by some other name, and then about three centuries later also the Clerics who were called Regulars, were included among true religious and regulars along with the Monks and the Canons Regular; while all the Nuns, both those who clung to the old monasticism or to the life of canonesses and those who were received into second Orders of the Mendicant Brothers, canonically belonged to one and the same noble and ancient institute and followed the same way of religious life.

Hence, up to the time of the first Congregations of women, which arose either in the sixteenth or in the seventeenth century, they only were considered Nuns who in fact and in law professed an acknowledged form of the religious life. And even after the Congregations were tolerated, and in the course of time recognized first in fact and then as a sort of working arrangement by the law, up to the promulgation of the Code of Canon Law, Nuns alone were strictly recognized as true religious and regulars.

And if we turn our attention to the inner elements of the monastic life, who can number and weigh the treasures of religious perfection which lay hid in monasteries? How many flowers and fruits of sanctity these enclosed gardens presented to Christ and to the Church! What efficacious prayers, what treasures of devotedness, what benefits of every sort did not the Nuns strive to bring to their Mother the Church for her embellishment, support, and strengthening!

*   *   *

The strict and well defined figure of the Nun, as it was engraved on the pages of Canon Law and of religious practice, was accepted readily, and in its main outlines faithfully too, by the numberless Orders, Monasteries, Convents which constantly existed in the Church, and was tenaciously retained for several centuries. From this general fidelity and constancy the sacred institution of Nuns acquired a solid consistency which always enabled it to resist innovations of any kind more vigorously than institutes of any other regulars or religious of either sex. Within certain proper limits this is certainly to its credit.

This essential unity among Nuns, which We have commended, does not mean that there were not, even from very early times, both as regards practice and interior discipline, various figures and varieties, with which God, who is wonderful in His Saints, endowed and adorned the Church of His Spouse. These variations among Nuns seem to have sprung from variations of the same sort in Orders and religious Institutes of men, to which the Orders of Nuns were in a sense accessory. In fact nearly all the Monks, Canons Regular, and especially Mendicants, sought to establish second Orders which, keeping the general character of institutes of Nuns, yet differed among themselves in much the same way as did the first Orders. Similarly in more recent times some Orders of Clerics Regular and some Congregations of men have established Nuns of their own Institutes.

These variations among Nuns are worthy of attentive consideration, both from the standpoint of the history of the institution and from that of the interior changes which were common to all its forms. They won for this ancient institution as it were a resurgence of sanctity, without changing the general character of the contemplative life or the chief norms and principles of the established discipline.

In still more recent times, especially toward the close of the sixteenth century, some new forms of Orders of Nuns were introduced and were gradually approved by the Church; as for example the Institute of Saint Ursula, of the Angelics, the Congregation of the Sisters of Notre Dame, the Order of the Visitation, the Society of Our Lady, the Sisters of Notre Dame de Charité, and many others. These new foundations, while they were, either from the start or later, induced or morally compelled to accept the common law as currently applied to Nuns — since they wished to profess a truly religious life and this was then the only form of it admissible for women — were yet in various ways paving the way for a renovation of the law itself.

These new forms of institutes of Nuns, though they professed a life which was canonically classed as contemplative, and though in deference to the opinions of that time they finally accepted sincerely if reluctantly the strict papal cloister, yet sometimes did not engage to recite the divine Office. On the other hand, they did with commendable zeal accept as their part and perform many apostolic and charitable works which were suited to their sex and to their canonical state.

*   *   *

As time went on, either through the example given by the new Orders or because of the growth of Congregations and Societies, which sought to combine with the life of perfection a fruitful apostolate of charity, assistance, and education, or finally because of the general trend of events and ideas, not a few monasteries of many of the Orders which according to their Institute followed a purely contemplative life, accepted apostolic works in many places with the approval and under the prudent guidance of the Holy See.

From that time on, it gradually came about that the general institution of Nuns not only began to include divers Orders with their own Rules and Constitutions, but also began to admit a deeper line of demarcation between those Orders and Monasteries which followed a purely contemplative life, and those others in which, either because of their particular Constitutions or by subsequent permission of the Holy See, certain canonically approved works of the apostolate were appropriately added to the life of contemplation.

In our day the entire institution of Nuns both in those Orders and Monasteries which hitherto had practiced faithfully the pure contemplative life, and also especially in those which under the direction of the Church combined the works of the apostolate with the life of contemplation, has been not a little affected by the variations and changes of times and circumstances. Naturally, as these Orders now engage in education and other similar charitable works, which, owing either to the habit of the people or to public regulations, are now practiced in such a way that they are almost or quite incompatible with some of the classical norms of the papal cloister, these norms have had to be judiciously modified, without prejudice to the common notion of cloister, so as to be compatible with these works. This was, of course, for the good of the Church and of souls, for had it not been done the works could not have been undertaken at all or at least not in the same way. And not only the apostolic Orders but also the purely contemplative ones have been at times induced or compelled by circumstances and the grave need in which they find themselves, to modify these same norms or to interpret them more broadly.

For example, public opinion to-day will scarcely tolerate too rigorous an interpretation of canon 601, even in the case of contemplative Nuns. Hence the Holy See with maternal solicitude provides ever more liberally for many necessities and useful purposes, which according to ancient standards were not considered so serious as to justify the infraction of papal cloister or exemption from it. For that matter, the security and sanctity of residences, which, though not the sole reason for papal cloister, was one among other reasons which in various ways and at various times contributed to its establishment and regulation, is to-day better protected than it used to be.

*   *   *

Having briefly sketched the origin and development of the sacred institution of Nuns, We now propose to designate clearly its proper and necessary elements, those which directly concern the canonical contemplative life of Nuns, which is the first and principal end of their Institute. To these innate and principal features by which the canonical figure of Nuns is clearly defined as a matter of law, must be added certain other important ones which, though not strictly essential, are yet complementary, because they serve rather well and help to secure the public purpose for which Nuns exist. On the other hand there are some elements in the institution of Nuns which are neither necessary nor complementary, but merely external and historical, since they certainly owe their existence to the circumstances of former times which are now very much changed. These, if they are found to be no longer of any use or liable to hinder greater good, seem to have no special reason for being preserved.

Accordingly, without the least prejudice to any of the native and principal elements of the venerable institution of Nuns, as to the rest, which are found to be external and adventitious, We have decided to make with caution and prudence certain adaptations to present times, which may not only do honor to the venerable institution but at the same time enlarge its effectiveness.

We are induced or even impelled to make these moderate adjustments in the institution of Nuns, by the full information which We have on the subject from various parts of the world and the certain knowledge drawn therefrom regarding the extreme need in which Nuns often, not to say always, find themselves. Actually there are not a few Monasteries which, alas, are on the verge of extinction from hunger, misery, and want; there are many which, because of domestic difficulties, are leading a hard and almost intolerable life. Besides there are some Monasteries which, though not indigent, are so cut off and separated from any other Monasteries that they lack vitality. Frequently also the strict law of cloister easily gives rise to serious difficulties. Finally, with the ever growing necessities of the Church and of souls and the urgent need for a variety of helping hands from all classes of persons to meet them, the time seems to have come for combining the monastic life, generally even in the case of Nuns, who are given to contemplation, with some moderate apostolic work.

And this judgment of Ours on this matter has been repeatedly confirmed by the testimony which has come to Us almost unanimously from local Ordinaries and religious Superiors in certain countries.

*   *   *

It will be useful at this point to consider some of the measures enacted below in the General Statutes of Nuns, and to draw from them some rules and conclusions which will help toward an easy, safe, and correct understanding of all the provisions.

First, as regards the contemplative life of Nuns, one thing has always been true according to the mind of the Church, and it must be kept firm and inviolate: all Monasteries of Nuns must always and everywhere canonically profess the contemplative life as their first and primary end. Therefore, the works and ministries in which Nuns may and should engage must be of such a character and must be so regulated and arranged as to place, time, manner, and method, that a truly and solidly contemplative life, both for the Community as a whole and for the individual Nuns, shall be not only preserved but constantly nourished and strengthened.

The dispositions and concessions which were formerly made under stress of circumstances for certain countries, by which the solemn vows were changed to simple ones, certainly implied an odious dispensation (canon 19); the more so as this immunity is contrary to the principal characteristic of Nuns; for the solemn vows, which imply a stricter and fuller consecration to God than other public vows, contain the principal and canonically essential characteristic of religious Orders. Consequently, since long experience in various places has clearly shown that the solemn vows both of men Regulars and of Nuns, even though the civil law makes no account of them, can easily and without difficulty be observed, and that the security of the other common goods can likewise be properly provided for by other means, even though in some places juridical personality is denied to religious Institutes and Monasteries, the legislation and practice of the Holy See for many years now have rightly tended to restrict these odious exceptions and as far as possible to remove them altogether. And surely it is not right to deprive Nuns of the honor, merit, and joy of pronouncing the solemn vows which are their proper heritage.

For the safer custody of the solemn vow of chastity and the contemplative life, and that the enclosed garden of Monasteries might be protected from the intrusion of the world, from all crafty and insidious violation, and from all disturbance through secular and profane contacts, and so become a true cloister of souls where Nuns might serve the Lord with greater freedom, the Church with wise and vigilant solicitude established strict cloister as a distinctive feature of the life of Nuns, regulated it with care, and always safeguarded it with grave pontifical sanctions. This venerable cloister of Nuns, which is called "papal" because of the supreme authority from which it emanates and the sanctions by which it is protected within and without, is, by this Constitution of Ours, not only purposely and solemnly confirmed, for the various sorts of Monasteries which have hitherto been obliged to it, but is cautiously extended also to those Monasteries which until now have not been bound to it on account of dispensations lawfully obtained.

Monasteries which profess a purely contemplative life and which do not admit within the confines of the religious house any regular works of education, charity, recollection, and so on, shall retain or accept that papal cloister which is dealt with in the Code of Canon Law (canons 600–602) and which shall be called *"major."*

As for those Monasteries which, either by their Constitutions or by lawful provision of the Holy See, harmoniously combine with the contemplative life, in the Monastery itself, certain works which are consistent with it, the papal cloister, while retaining its essential and innate elements, is modified in some points which can scarcely or not at all be observed; as to other points which are not regarded as so essential to the papal cloister as described in the Code (canons 599, 604, § 2), it is appropriately supplemented by new provisions. This papal cloister modified and adapted to present needs, which shall be called *"minor"* to distinguish it from the stricter ancient cloister, may be allowed also to those Monasteries which, while retaining the purely contemplative life, either have not solemn vows or lack some of the conditions which are required for the major papal cloister according to the jurisprudence and practice of the Roman Curia. All these elements of the minor papal cloister will be accurately defined below in the General Statutes and in the Instructions which shall be issued by Our Authority and in Our name by the Sacred Congregation of Religious.

As to the autonomy or mutual liberty of Monasteries of Nuns, We think it appropriate to repeat here and to apply to Nuns what We said of Monks in the homily which We pronounced in the patriarchal Basilica of Saint Paul's outside the walls on the eighteenth of September, 1947, on the occasion of the fourth centenary of the death of Saint Benedict of Nursia. In view of changed circumstances there are now many considerations which make it advisable and sometimes even necessary to confederate Monasteries of Nuns. Such are, for example, an easier and better distribution of offices, the temporary transfer of individual religious from one monastery to another for a number of reasons of necessity or usefulness, mutual economic assistance, the coordination of works, the protection of common observance, and so on. That all this can be done and attained without impairing essential autonomy nor in any way weakening the observance of cloister or harming recollection and the strict discipline of monastic life, is abundantly clear not only from the ample experience of the Monastic Congregations of men, but also from the example of not a few Unions and Federations which have already been approved for Nuns. Besides, the establishment of Federations and the approval of the Statutes by which they are to be governed, will remain reserved to the Holy See.

Work, whether of the hands or of the spirit, is for all humanity, including men and women who lead a contemplative life, not only an obligation of the law of nature, but also a duty of penance and reparation. Moreover, work is a general means through which the soul is preserved from dangers and led to higher things; through which we cooperate with divine Providence in the natural and in the supernatural order; through which we practice works of charity. Finally, work is the norm and primary law of the religious life, and that from its very origin, according to the maxim, *"ora et labora."* Surely a large part of the discipline of the religious life has always consisted in the assignment, the management, and the performance of work.

The work of Nuns, from the point of view of eternity, should be such that she who undertakes it do so first of all with a holy purpose, that she often think of God as present, that she accept the work through obedience and find in it a means of voluntary mortification. If work is done in this spirit, it will be a powerful and constant exercise of all the virtues and a pledge of the suave and effective union of the contemplative and the active life after the example of the Holy Family of Nazareth.

If monastic labor is considered from the standpoint of nature or of discipline, it must, according to the Rules, Constitutions, and traditional customs of the various Orders, not only be proportionate to the strength of the Nuns, but also be so managed and performed that, in the long run and according to the circumstances, it will not only produce the necessary sustenance for the Nuns themselves but also redound to the benefit of the poor, of human society in general and of the Church.

Since the perfection of Christian life consists especially in charity, and since it is really one and the same charity with which we must love God alone above all and all men in Him, Holy Mother Church demands of all Nuns who canonically profess a life of contemplation, together with a perfect love of God, also a perfect love of the neighbor; and for the sake of this charity and their state of life, religious men and women must devote themselves wholly to the needs of the Church and of all those who are in want.

Let all Nuns therefore be thoroughly convinced that theirs is a fully and totally apostolic vocation, hemmed in by no limitations of space, matter, or time, but always and everywhere extending to whatever in any way concerns the honor of the heavenly Spouse or the salvation of souls. And this universal apostolic vocation of Nuns makes it perfectly appropriate that Monasteries should consider as recommended to their prayers the needs of the Church as a whole and of all individuals and groups.

The apostolate which is common to all Nuns and by which they should work zealously for the honor of the divine Spouse and promote the good of the universal Church and of all the faithful, disposes principally of the following means:

1. The example of Christian perfection; for their life, though without words, yet speaks strongly, ever drawing the faithful to Christ and to Christian perfection, and like a standard rallies the good soldiers of Christ for battle and invites them to the crown of glory.

2. Prayer, both that which is offered publicly in the name of the Church by the solemn recital to God of the canonical hours seven times each day, and that which is offered privately to God, continuously and in every form.

3. The generous offering of themselves, so that the hardships which come from the common life and from faithful regular observance, may be supplemented by other exercises of self-denial either prescribed by the Rules and Constitutions or undertaken entirely of their own accord, so as generously to "fill up those things that are wanting of the sufferings of Christ, for His body, which is the Church."[2]

Now that We have given a historical summary of the institution of Nuns and have accurately described the ways in which it can be adapted to the needs of present-day life, We proceed to state the general norms by which that adaptation can be made to achieve its purpose. The Sacred Congregation of Religious will attend to the administration of this entire Constitution and of the General Statutes as applied to all Federations of Monasteries already formed or to be formed in the future and to individual Monasteries; the same Sacred Congregation is empowered to do by Our Authority, through instructions, declarations, responses, and other documents of the kind, everything which concerns putting the Constitution carefully and effectively into practice and securing the faithful and prompt observance of the General Statutes.

---

[2] Col. 1:24.

GENERAL STATUTES OF NUNS

Art. I

§ 1. The name *Nuns* in this Constitution, according to law (c. 488, 7°), means, besides religious women of solemn vows, those also who have pronounced simple vows, perpetual or temporary, in Monasteries in which solemn vows are either actually taken or should be taken according to their institute; unless the contrary is certain from the context or from the nature of the case.

§ 2. The lawful use of the name of Nuns (c. 488, 7°) and the application of the law of Nuns, are in no way hindered by: 1) *simple profession* lawfully made in Monasteries (§ 1); 2) *minor papal cloister* if that is prescribed for or has been duly granted to the Monasteries in question; 3) *the exercise of works of the apostolate* in conjunction with the contemplative life, either by reason of Constitutions approved and confirmed by the Holy See for certain Orders, or by reason of lawful prescription or concession of the Holy See for certain Monasteries.

§ 3. This Apostolic Constitution does not legally apply to: 1) religious Congregations (c. 488, 2°) and the Sisters who are members thereof (c. 488, 7°), who by their institute take only simple vows; 2) Societies of women living in common after the manner of religious, and their members (c. 673).

Art. II

§ 1. The special mode of monastic religious life, which Nuns must faithfully practice under a strict regular discipline, and for which they are destined by the Church, is the canonical contemplative life.

§ 2. By the term *canonical contemplative* life is meant, not that interior and theological life to which all souls living in religion and even in the world are called, and which each one for himself can live no matter where, but rather the external profession of religious discipline which, through the observance of cloister, through practices of piety, prayer, and penance, and finally through the work to which the Nuns must devote themselves, exists for the sake of interior contemplation, so that the pursuit of this latter easily can and should effectively pervade their life as a whole and all its activity.

§ 3. If the canonical contemplative life under strict regular discipline cannot be habitually observed, the monastic character is not to be conferred, nor, if it is already conferred, to be retained.

Art. III

§ 1. The solemn religious vows, pronounced by all the members of a Monastery or at least by one class of them, constitute the principal note by reason of which Monasteries of women are classed, not among religious Congregations, but among regular Orders (c. 488, 2°). But in these Monasteries all the professed religious come within the appellation of Regulars in law, according to canon 490, and are properly called, not Sisters, but Nuns (c. 488, 7°).

§ 2. All Monasteries in which only simple vows are taken shall be entitled to ask for the instauration of solemn vows. In fact, unless there are grave reasons to the contrary, they shall take steps to return to the solemn vows.

§ 3. The ancient solemn formulae for the consecration of Virgins, which are in the Roman Pontifical, are reserved to Nuns.

Art. IV

§ 1. The strict cloister of Nuns which is called papal, saving always and for all Monasteries those characteristics which belong, so to speak, to its very nature, shall be hereafter of two classes: *major* and *minor*.

§ 2. 1° The *major* papal cloister, that is, the one which is described in the Code (cc. 600–602), is fully confirmed by this Our Apostolic Constitution. The Sacred Congregation of Religious, by Our Authority, shall declare for what reasons dispensation from major cloister may be granted, so that, without prejudice to its nature, the cloister may be better adapted to the conditions of our time.

2° Except as hereinafter provided in § 3, 3°, the major papal cloister must be in effect as a matter of law in all Monasteries which profess the purely contemplative life.

§ 3. 1° The *minor* papal cloister shall retain from the ancient cloister of Nuns those elements and shall be protected by those sanctions, which are expressly declared in the Instructions of the Holy See to be necessary to preserve and vindicate its natural character.

2° Subject to this minor papal cloister are Monasteries of Nuns of solemn vows which, either by their institute or by lawful permission, undertake works with externs to such an extent that many of the religious and a notable part of the house are habitually occupied in them.

3° Likewise all Monasteries, even though purely contemplative, in which only simple vows are taken, shall be subject at least to the provisions of this cloister.

§ 4. 1° Papal cloister either major or minor is to be regarded as a necessary condition, not only in order that solemn vows may be taken (§ 2), but also in order that those Monasteries in which simple vows are taken (§ 3) may hereafter be considered true Monasteries of Nuns according to canon 488, 7°.

2° If the rules of at least the minor papal cloister cannot for the most part be observed, the solemn vows which are in use shall be taken away.

§ 5. 1° The minor papal cloister, especially as regards those notes in which it differs from the cloister of Congregations or of Orders of men, is to be observed in places where Nuns do not take solemn vows.

2° If however it appears with certainty that in some Monastery even the minor cloister cannot regularly be observed, that Monastery is to be converted to a house of either a Congregation or a Society.

Art. V

§ 1. The Church deputes Nuns alone among the women consecrated to God, for the public prayer which is offered to God in her name either in choir (c. 610, § 1) or privately (c. 610, § 3); and these she binds under grave obligation, by law according to their Constitutions, to perform this prayer by daily reciting the canonical hours.

§ 2. All Monasteries of Nuns and all individual Nuns professed of the solemn or simple vows, everywhere, are bound to recite the divine Office in choir according to canon 610, § 1 and their Constitutions.

§ 3. According to canon 610, § 3, Nuns who were absent from choir, if they have not taken solemn vows, are not strictly bound to recite the hours privately, unless the Constitutions expressly provide otherwise (c. 578, 2°); however, it is the mind of the Church, not only, as We stated above (art. IV), that solemn vows for Nuns be put in effect everywhere, but also, if this is temporarily impossible, that Nuns who in place of the solemn vows have taken perpetual simple vows, faithfully perform the divine Office.

§ 4. The conventual Mass corresponding to the Office of the day according to the Rubrics should be celebrated in all Monasteries every day if possible (c. 610, § 2).

Art. VI

§ 1. 1° Monasteries of Nuns, unlike other houses of religious women, are, by reason of and according to the Code, *sui iuris* (c. 488, 8°).

2° The Superioresses of the individual Monasteries of Nuns are according to law Major Superiors, and have all the faculties which belong to Major Superiors (c. 488, 8°), unless as to some of them it is clear from the context or from the nature of the case that they pertain only to men (c. 490).

§ 2. 1° The extent of the condition of being *sui iuris,* or the so-called autonomy of Monasteries of Nuns, is defined by both the common and the particular law.

2° Neither this Constitution nor the Federations of Monasteries which are permitted by it (art. VII) and established by its authority, derogate in any way from the juridical supervision which the law gives either to local Ordinaries or to regular Superiors in regard to individual Monasteries.

3° The juridical relations between individual Monasteries and local Ordinaries or regular Superiors, continue to be governed by the common and particular law.

§ 3. This Constitution does not in any way determine whether individual Monasteries are under the power of the local Ordinary or are, within the limits defined by law, exempt from it and subject to the regular Superior.

Art. VII

§ 1. Monasteries of Nuns are not only *sui iuris* (c. 488, 8°) but also juridically distinct from and independent of each other, and are not united and bound together by any other than spiritual and moral bonds, even though they be legally subject to the same first Order or religious Institute.

§ 2. 1° The mutual liberty of Monasteries, which is rather

accepted as a fact than imposed by law, is in no way impaired by the formation of a Federation; neither are such Federations to be considered as forbidden by law nor as in any way inconsistent with the nature and purposes of the religious life of Nuns.

2° Federations of Monasteries, although they are not prescribed by any general rule, are nevertheless highly recommended by the Holy See, not only as a safeguard against the evils and inconveniences which can arise from complete separation, but also as a means of promoting regular observance and the life of contemplation.

§ 3. The establishment of any form of Federation of Monasteries of Nuns, or of Confederations made up of such Federations, is reserved to the Holy See.

§ 4. Every Federation or Confederation must necessarily be organized and governed according to its laws approved by the Holy See.

§ 5. 1° Without prejudice to art. VI, §§ 2, 3 or to the essential notion of autonomy as above defined (§ 1), nothing forbids that, in forming a Federation of Monasteries, after the example of certain Monastic Congregations and Orders of Canons or of Monks, certain equitable conditions and suspensions of this autonomy, which are considered necessary or advantageous, be adopted.

2° However, forms of Federation which seem contrary to the autonomy of which We have spoken (§ 1) and which approach the idea of a central government, are especially reserved to the Holy See, and cannot be set up without Its express permission.

§ 6. Federations of Monasteries, in view of their source and of the Authority on which they directly depend and by which they are governed, are of pontifical right according to Canon Law.

§ 7. The Holy See may, according to need, exercise immediate vigilance and authority over a Federation through some religious Assistant, whose office it shall be not only to represent the Holy See but to see to the preservation of the genuine spirit of the Order and to give aid and counsel to the Superioress in the right and prudent government of the Federation.

§ 8. 1° The Statutes of a Federation must be conformed not only to the prescribed norms which shall be worked out with Our Authority by the Sacred Congregation of Religious, but also

to the nature, laws, spirit, and traditions, ascetical, disciplinary
or juridical, and apostolic, of the Order in question.

2° The principal purpose of a Federation of Monasteries is to
give each other fraternal aid, not only in promoting the religious
spirit and regular monastic discipline, but also in managing
economic matters.

3° In approving Statutes, special norms may in a proper case
be given to regulate the faculty and moral obligation of mutually
asking for and granting to each other such Nuns as may be
thought necessary for the government of the Monasteries, for
the training of novices in a common novitiate to be established
for all or several Monasteries, or finally for supplying other moral
or material needs of the Monasteries or of the Nuns.

Art. VIII

§ 1. Monastic work, to which even Nuns of the contemplative
life must apply themselves, should be as far as possible in
accord with the Rule, the Constitutions, and traditions of the
Order in question.

§ 2. The work should be so managed that, together with the
other means approved by the Church (cc. 547–551, 582), and
the aid which Divine Providence will supply, it may assure the
proper support of the Nuns.

§ 3. 1° The Ordinaries of places, regular Superiors, and the
Superioresses of Monasteries and Federations, are bound to use
all diligence to see to it that the Nuns may never lack necessary,
adequate, and productive work.

2° The Nuns, on the other hand, are bound in conscience, not
only to earn by the sweat of their brow the bread by which
they live, as the Apostle warns (2 Thess. 3:10), but also to
render themselves daily more fit for various works according to
the needs of the time.

Art. IX

All Nuns, in order to be faithful to their divine apostolic
vocation, must not only use the general means of the monastic
apostolate, but must moreover observe the following:

§ 1. Nuns who in their own Constitutions or lawful prescriptions have definite works of some special form of apostolate, are
bound to give and consecrate themselves faithfully to those works

according to their Constitutions or Statutes and prescriptions.

§ 2. Nuns who profess a purely contemplative life:

1° If they have or have had in their own traditions some accepted special form of external apostolate, shall faithfully retain the same, adapting it to the needs of the present day, always without prejudice to their life of contemplation, and if they have lost it, they shall diligently see that it is restored. As regards adaptation, if any doubt arises let them consult the Holy See.

2° On the other hand, if their life of pure contemplation has hitherto not been coupled in any permanent and constant way with the external apostolate either by the approved Constitutions of the Order or by tradition, in that case they may, and at least out of charity they should be employed, only in cases of necessity and for a limited time, especially in those individual or personal forms of the apostolate which, according to criteria to be fixed by the Holy See, seem compatible with the contemplative life as it is observed in the Order in question.

Whatever has been decreed by this Letter shall, according to Our will and command, be firmly established and valid, all things to the contrary notwithstanding, even though they be worthy of most particular mention.

And it is Our will that copies or excerpts of this Letter, even in print, provided they are subscribed by some public notary and adorned with the seal of some ecclesiastical dignitary, shall receive the same faith and credit as would be shown to the Letter itself if it were presented and shown.

Let no one, therefore, infringe or rashly impugn this page of Our declaration and will; if anyone presume to attempt it, let him know that he will incur the wrath of Almighty God and of the holy Apostles Peter and Paul.

Given at Rome, from Saint Peter's the twenty-first day of November, Feast of the Presentation of the Blessed Virgin Mary, in the Year of Jubilee, Nineteen Hundred and Fifty, the twelfth of Our Pontificate.

AAS 43–5; Pius XII, Apostolic Constitution and General Statutes of Nuns, 21 Nov., 1950.

Cf. *Commentarium pro Religiosis,* Vol. 31 (1952), p. 27 (Escudero) ; p. 37 (Tabera). *Monitor Ecclesiasticus,* 1951, p. 226 (Pugliese) ; *Periodica,* 40–78 (Abellán).

Instruction on the Apostolic Constitution *Sponsa Christi* (S. C. Rel., 23 Nov., 1950) **AAS 43–37.**

An instruction of the Sacred Congregation of Religious "for putting into practice the Constitution *Sponsa Christi,*" is as follows:

I. Among the remarkable documents by which our Holy Father, Pius XII, by Divine Providence Pope, has willed to adorn and crown the Holy Year as with so many precious jewels, assuredly not the least is the Apostolic Constitution, *Sponsa Christi,* which deals with the renewal and advancement within God's Church of the holy and venerable institution of nuns. This Sacred Congregation, which as its appointed task, promptly and faithfully assists the Holy Father in all things pertaining to the state of perfection, has reverently and joyfully received from him the commission of putting into execution this Constitution, truly remarkable from so many points of view, and of making its application assured and easy.

II. To fulfill this honorable duty, the Sacred Congregation has assembled in this Instruction some practical norms for those points which offer greater difficulty.

III. Now, the points in the Apostolic Constitution which offer difficulty and hence require special clarification are: (1) those which refer to the major or minor cloister of nuns; (2) those which deal with the establishment of federations and the limitation of autonomy; (3) finally those which have to do with obtaining and co-ordinating productive labor for the monasteries.

I. MAJOR AND MINOR CLOISTER FOR NUNS

IV. The Apostolic Constitution, *Sponsa Christi* (art. IV), prescribes a special cloister for monasteries of all nuns which differs from the episcopal cloister of congregations (c. 604), and which, according to the general norm of the law, is papal, as is the cloister of orders of men (c. 597, § 1). In fact, regarding a number of prescriptions dealing with both the entrance of externs into the limits of the cloister and the going out of the nuns from the same, the regulations are stricter than those which control the papal cloister of men.

V. Hereafter there will be two types of papal cloister for nuns: the one *major*, which is reserved for monasteries in which solemn vows are taken and a purely contemplative life is led, even though the number of the nuns may have decreased; the other *minor*, which, as a rule, is applied to monasteries in which a life is led which is not exclusively contemplative, or the nuns take simple vows only.

A. Major Papal Cloister

VI. *Major* papal cloister is that which is described in the Code (cc. 600, 602) and accurately defined by the Sacred Congregation in its Instruction, *Nuper edito,* approved by the late Pope Pius XI on February 6, 1924. This cloister is fully confirmed in the Constitution, *Sponsa Christi,* safeguarding the following declarations which the Constitution empowers the Sacred Congregation to make (art. IV, § 2, 1°) so that its observance may be prudently adapted to the needs of the times and to local circumstances.

VII. Nuns bound by major papal cloister, after their profession, by reason of the profession itself and by the prescription of ecclesiastical law, contract a grave obligation:

1° of remaining always within the precincts of the monastery which have been put within the definite limits of the cloister, so that they may not leave the cloister even for a moment under any pretext or condition without a special indult of the Holy See, except in those cases only which are provided for in the canons and instructions of the Holy See, or which are envisioned in the constitutions or statutes approved by the Holy See itself.

2° of not admitting to the parts of the monastery subject to the law of cloister any person whatsoever no matter of what class, condition, sex, or age, even for a moment, without a special indult of the Holy See. Certain exceptions, however, of persons and cases are expressly made in the canons and in instructions of the Holy See, as well as in the constitutions or statutes approved by it.

VIII. 1° Indults and dispensations to leave the major cloister after profession (VII, 1°) or to enter it or to admit others (VII, 2°) are reserved exclusively to the Holy See, and can be granted by it alone or in its name and by its delegation.

2° Reasons for obtaining dispensations should be proportionately grave, due consideration being given to the circumstances of cases, times, and places, keeping in mind the practice and style of the Roman Curia.

IX. 1° The faculty to dispense may be given *ab homine,* either for a definite period of time for all cases occurring during it, or for a certain number of cases. There is nothing, however, to hinder the granting of certain permissions habitually in particular law having legitimate approval, for instance, in the constitutions, in the statutes of federations, and in similar documents.

2° Whether granted *ab homine* or by general or particular law, indults and dispensations must determine, according to the instructions of the Holy See and the practice and style of the Roman Curia, the conditions and precautions to which the dispensation is subject.

X. The penalties against those who violate the laws of cloister remain as stated in the Code (c. 2342, 1°, 3°).

B. Minor Papal Cloister

XI. *Minor* papal cloister:

1° retains intact the fundamental rules of the cloister of nuns, inasmuch as it differs greatly from the cloister of congregations (c. 604) as well as from that of orders of men (cc. 598–599);

2° must safeguard and facilitate for all the observance and care of solemn chastity;

3° it must protect and efficaciously foster the contemplative life of the monastery;

4° The employments which the Church has designedly entrusted to these monasteries must be so harmonized with the contemplative life within the confines of the minor papal enclosure that the latter may by all means be preserved while these works are properly and advantageously performed.

5° In monasteries which engage in approved works, the prescription of canon 599, § 1 for the cloister of orders of men, which is likewise applied by canon 604, § 2 to the cloister of congregations, is to be strictly and faithfully observed, in such a way that a clear and complete separation be ever maintained between buildings or sections thereof set apart for the living quarters of the nuns and for the exercises of the monastic life, and those parts made over to necessary works.

XII: Minor papal cloister includes:

1° a grave prohibition against admitting into the parts of the house set aside for the community of nuns and subject to the law of cloister (c. 597) any persons whatsoever who are not members of the community, regardless of class, condition, sex, or age, according to canon 600;

2° another grave prohibition forbidding the nuns after profession to leave the precincts of the monastery, in the same way as nuns subject to major cloister (nn. VII–IX).

XIII. 1° The passage of the nuns from the parts reserved to the community to the other places within the precincts of the monastery destined for the works of the apostolate is allowed for this purpose alone, with the permission of the superior, and under proper safeguards, to those who, according to the norms of the constitutions and the prescriptions of the Holy See, are destined for the exercise of the apostolate in any way.

2° If by reason of the apostolate, dispensations from the prescriptions of n. XII, 2° become necessary, they may be given only to nuns and other religious who are lawfully assigned to the employments, under grave obligation in conscience for superioresses, for ordinaries, and for superiors regular, to whom the custody of the cloister is entrusted (c. 603).

XIV. Admittance of externs to the parts of the monastery devoted to employments of whatever kind is governed by these norms:

1° Habitual admittance is allowed to pupils, boys or girls, or to other persons in whose favor ministries are performed, and to such women only with whom necessary contact is demanded by reason and on the occasion of such ministries.

2° The local ordinary should, by a general or habitual declaration, define as such those exceptions which must be made of necessity, for instance, those ordinarily required by the civil law for the purpose of inspections, examinations, or for other reasons.

3° Other exceptions, should such at times seem truly necessary in individual cases, are reserved to the express grant of the ordinary, who is in conscience bound to impose prudent precautions.

XV. 1° Nuns who unlawfully leave the precincts of the monastery *ipso facto* incur excommunication reserved simply to the Holy See according to canon 2342, 3°, or, by express grant reserved to the local ordinary.

2° Nuns who illicitly leave the parts of the monastery reserved to the community and go to other places within the precincts of the monastery, are to be punished by the superior or by the local ordinary, according to the gravity of their fault.

3° Those who illicitly enter the parts of the monastery reserved to the community and those who bring them in or allow them to enter, incur excommunication reserved simply to the Holy See.

4° Those who illegitimately enter the parts of the monastery not reserved to the community, as well as those who bring them in or permit them to enter, are to be severely punished according to the gravity of their fault by the ordinary of the place in which the monastery is located.

XVI. Dispensations from minor papal cloister, except those admitted by law, are, as a rule, reserved to the Holy See.

Faculties more or less broad, as circumstances seem to require, can be granted to ordinaries either *ab homine* or in the constitutions and statutes.

II. FEDERATIONS OF MONASTERIES OF NUNS

XVII. Federations of monasteries of nuns, according to the norm of the Constitution, *Sponsa Christi* (art. VII, § 2, 2°) are earnestly recommended, both to avoid the harmful effects which both more grievously and more readily befall entirely independent monasteries, and which by union can to a great extent be avoided more effectively, as well as to foster both their spiritual and temporal interests.

Although, as a rule, federations of monasteries are not imposed (art. VIII, § 2, 2°), nevertheless, the reasons which would recommend them in general, could, in particular cases be so strong that, everything considered, they would be deemed necessary by the Sacred Congregation.

XVIII. Federations of monasteries are not to be impeded by the fact that the individual monasteries which intend to form them are subject to superiors regular. Provision will have to be made for this common subjection in the *Statutes of the Federation.*

XIX. When, because of the intention of the founder or for any other reason that may occur, there already exists some kind of beginning of a union or federation of monasteries of the same order or institute, anything already done or outlined must be taken into account in the development of the federation itself.

XX. A federation of monasteries in no way directly affects the relation, already in existence according to the common or to the particular law, of the individual monasteries to the local ordinaries or to the superiors regular. Hence, unless an express and lawful derogation is made to this rule, the powers of ordinaries and superiors are neither increased nor diminished nor changed in any way.

XXI. The statutes of a federation may grant certain rights over the federation to ordinaries and to superiors which as a rule do not belong to them, leaving intact generally the right over each individual monastery as such.

XXII. The general and principal purposes and advantages of unions and federations are the following:

1° the legally recognized faculty and the canonically sanctioned duty of a mutual fraternal assistance, both in the conservation, defense, and increase of regular observance, and of domestic economy, as well as in all other things;

2° the establishment of novitiates common to all or to a group of monasteries for cases in which, either because of a lack of personnel necessary for the directive offices, or because of other circumstances moral, economic, local, and the like, a solid and practical spiritual, disciplinary, technical, and cultural training cannot be given in the individual monasteries;

3° the faculty and the moral obligation, defined by certain norms and accepted by federated monasteries, of asking for and of mutually interchanging nuns who may be necessary for government and training;

4° the possibility of and freedom for a mutual temporary exchange or ceding of subjects, and also of a permanent assignment, because of health or other moral or material need.

XXIII. The characteristic notes of federations which are to be considered essential when taken together are enumerated as follows:

1° *From the source* from which they spring and *from the authority* from which as such they depend and which governs them directly, federations of nuns are of *pontifical right* according to the Code (c. 488, 3°). Hence not only their establishment, but also the approval of their statutes, and the enrollment of monasteries in, or their separation from, a federation, belongs to the Holy See exclusively.

Provided all the rights over individual monasteries granted by the Code to ordinaries are safeguarded, federations are subject to the Holy See in all those matters in which pontifical institutes of women are directly subject to it, unless a lawful exception has been expressly provided for. The Holy See may commit certain items of its prerogatives, either habitually or in single instances, to its immediate assistants or delegates for federations.

2° *By reason of territory or of extension,* federations of monasteries are to be established preferably along regional lines, for easier government, unless the small number of monasteries or other just or proportionate causes demand otherwise.

3° *By reason of the moral persons* which constitute them, inasmuch as they are collegiate persons (c. 100, § 2), federations are composed of monasteries of the same order and of the same internal observance, though they need not necessarily depend on the same local ordinary or superior regular, nor have the same kind of vows or form of cloister.

4° Confederations of regional federations can be allowed if need, or great advantage, or the traditions of the order recommend them.

5° From the standpoint of the independence of the monasteries, the bond which holds the federated monasteries together should be such that it does not interfere with their autonomy, at least in essentials (c. 488, 2°, 8°). Although derogations from autonomy are not to be presumed, they can be granted with the previous consent of each monastery, provided that grave reasons seem to recommend or demand them.

XXIV. All federations of monasteries of nuns must have their own statutes subject to the approval of the Holy See before they can be established. The statutes must accurately determine the following:

1° the aims which each federation proposes to itself;

2° the manner in which the government of the federation is to be regulated, either with regard to constitutive elements, as for example, president, visitators, council, and the like; or as to the manner of appointment to these offices; or, finally, the power of this government and the manner of conducting it;

3° the means which the federation should use that it may be able to carry out its aims pleasantly and vigorously;

4° the conditions and means to be used in putting into execution the prescriptions regarding the mutual interchange of persons laid down in art. VII, § 3, 2° of the Constitution, *Sponsa Christi;*

5° the juridical standing of nuns transferred to another monastery, whether in the monastery from which the transfer takes place, or in that to which it is made;

6° the economic help to be given by each monastery for the common enterprises of the entire federation;

7° the administration of the common novitiate or of other works common to the federation, if there be such.

XXV. 1° In order that the Holy See may be able to exercise a direct and efficacious vigilance and authority over federations, each federation can be given a religious assistant, as need or usefulness may suggest.

2° The religious assistant will be appointed by the Sacred Congregation according to the statutes, after all interested parties have been heard.

3° In each case his duties will be accurately defined in the decree of appointment. The principal ones are as follows: to take care that the genuine spirit of a profoundly contemplative life as well as the spirit proper to the order and institute be securely preserved and increased; likewise, to see that a prudent and exact government be established and preserved in the federation; to have regard for the solid religious training of the novices and of the religious themselves; to help the council in temporal matters of greater moment.

4° The Holy See will delegate or commit to the assistant such powers as may seem opportune in individual cases.

III. MONASTIC LABOR

XXVI. 1° Since, by the disposition of Divine Providence, the temporal necessities of life are at times so pressing that nuns seem morally compelled to seek and accept labors beyond their accustomed ones, and even perhaps to extend the time given to labor, all should as true religious submit themselves promptly and humbly to the dispositions of Divine Providence, as the Christian faithful do in like circumstances.

2° They should do this, however, not anxiously or capriciously or arbitrarily, but prudently as far as may seem truly necessary or suitable, seeking with simple hearts a balance between their understanding of fidelity to the letter and to tradition, and a filial subjection to the permissive and positive dispositions of Divine Providence.

3° Keeping these directives in mind, let them submit to ecclesiastical or to religious superiors, as the case may require, whatever arrangements seem advisable.

XXVII. Ecclesiastical and religious superiors must:

1° by all means seek and obtain profitable labor for the nuns who need it, and, should the case require it, also employ committees of pious men or women, and, with due caution and prudence, even secular agencies established for such purposes;

2° maintain a careful supervision of the quality and orderly arrangement of the work, and require a just price for it;

3° to superintend diligently the coordination of the activities and the labor of individual monasteries so that they may help, supply, and complement one another, and see to it that every vestige of competition is entirely avoided.

AAS 43–37; S. C. Rel., Instruction, 23 Nov., 1950.

NOTE: The above translation is reproduced with the kind permission of the Editors, from the *Review for Religious,* Vol. 10, p. 205.

For annotations on this Instruction, cf. *Periodica,* Vol. 40 (1951), p. 78 (Abellán).

Apostolic Constitution and General Statutes to Be Explained to Monasteries of Nuns (S. C. Rel., Letter, 7 March, 1951) Private.

A Letter of the Sacred Congregation of Religious:

Your Excellency:

His Holiness has entrusted to the Sacred Congregation of Religious the task of putting into effect the Apostolic Constitution *Sponsa Christi* of 23 Nov., 1950, and the General Statutes therein contained, which are designed to promote the greater good of monasteries of Nuns (*Moniales*).

For the exact fulfillment of the mandate of His Holiness, the Sacred Congregation now appeals to Your Excellency, with entire confidence that Your Excellency will fully supply whatever cooperation is demanded by the interests of the monasteries in the country in which Your Excellency so worthily represents the Holy Father.

Above all the Sacred Congregation considers it very important that the Apostolic Constitution *Sponsa Christi* and the Instruction of the same Sacred Congregation, which appeared in the *Acta Apostolicae Sedis*, Vol. 43, p. 5 sq., be made known to all monasteries of Nuns, so that they may appreciate the love which the Church bears toward them and her solicitude for them, that those timely improvements which experience and the present state of religious life suggest, may serve for the defense and advancement of their state of life.

I. Hence the Sacred Congregation asks Your Excellency to entrust to the Most Excellent Bishops the task of presenting and explaining the aforesaid pontifical documents to the monasteries of Nuns which are under their jurisdiction.

So that the explanation may be made in the manner best suited to the spirit of each Monastery, Your Excellency will kindly ask the Most Excellent Ordinaries to designate: *a*) for Monasteries of a Second Order, preferably Religious of the corresponding First Order who are qualified for this important work, whether they reside in the diocese or out of it; *b*) for the other monasteries, let the Most Excellent Ordinaries select qualified persons among the Religious or diocesan or extra-diocesan priests.

The names of the persons chosen for each Monastery should in every case be reported to Your Excellency, who will according to your prudent judgment definitely confirm the appointment.

Finally, for monasteries of Nuns which are actually under Apostolic Visitation, and for those which are subject to Regulars, this Sacred Congregation will assign the task of explaining the two pontifical documents, to the Apostolic Visitors and to the Regular Superiors respectively.

II. Your Excellency will please recommend that the persons appointed explain to the Nuns the following points especially:

1) These new documents are a new concrete proof of the solicitude of the Church for the true welfare of Monasteries of Nuns, in line with her practice throughout the centuries according to the exigencies of various times and places. It is due to this action of the Church that the monastic life of Nuns, while remaining in substance unchanged, has been enriched with new elements, profiting from the improvements and wise adaptations which the religious life has manifested in various centuries (cf. *Sponsa Christi*, AAS, Vol. 43, pp. 6–11).

2) Far from wishing to encroach upon the contemplative life of those who, "choosing the better part" (*Sponsa Christi, loc. cit.,*

p. 6), have retired to Monasteries, the Apostolic Constitution, after having explained the nature of the contemplative life (Statutes, Art. II), desires that, both for the Community as a whole and for the individual Nuns, "a truly and solidly contemplative life shall be not only preserved but constantly nourished and strengthened" (*Sponsa Christi, l. c.,* p. 11). To this end the Constitution emphasizes the obligation according to the Constitutions, and the public character of Choir in Monasteries of Nuns.

For the same reason, papal cloister remains substantially unchanged; however, in monasteries which have apostolic works, cloister is regulated and adapted so that the contemplative life may suffer no harm and that at the same time the works, nourished by the contemplative life, may be able to develop as need may require (Statutes, Art. IV; Instruction, nn. XI–XV).

3) So that the religious life of Nuns may correspond more perfectly to their desire of complete consecration to God, the Holy See earnestly exhorts those Monasteries where — in the past — the profession of solemn vows had to be abandoned because of special circumstances, to resume them, unless there still exist grave reasons to the contrary (Statutes, Art. III).

4) The two documents also bring out the fact that the vocation of Nuns, though it be a vocation to a purely contemplative life, is in the fullest sense an apostolic vocation, seeing that the love of God cannot be separated from the love of the neighbor. It is for this reason that these documents recommend to all the apostolate of good example, prayer, and sacrifice (*Sponsa Christi, l. c.,* p. 14). The Apostolic Constitution recalls the rise of Institutes of Nuns which harmoniously combined the contemplative life with apostolic works, and recommends to these Institutes and to the monasteries which have a tradition to that effect, to dedicate themselves wholeheartedly to it (Statutes, Art. IX). For Monasteries of the purely contemplative life, on the other hand, it provides that only by reason of special necessity may or shall the external apostolate be practiced; and this must always be of such a character that the contemplative life shall suffer no harm therefrom (Statutes, Art. IX).

5) The introduction of Federations of monasteries of Nuns appears as the source of numberless advantages, spiritual, disciplinary, and even economic (*Sponsa Christi, l. c.,* p. 13).

In exhorting Monasteries to unite in Federations, the Holy Father repeats in the Apostolic Constitution what he had already said in 1947, in his Homily to the Benedictines in the Basilica of St. Paul's.

Coming out of the complete isolation in which monasteries professing the same Rule and the same norms of life and spirituality existed for centuries, will mean: *a*) a mutual fraternal collaboration for the attainment of their proper end; *b*) the possibility of making better provision for young vocations and of finding a way out of difficult situations in which the Monasteries may be implicated; *c*) a guarantee of fidelity to the proper spirit and tradition of the Order (Instruction, nn. XVII–XXII).

All these benefits will be furthered by the presence and activity of a religious Assistant for such Federations, appointed by the Holy See (Instruction, n. XXV).

Naturally, in order that the Federations may actually produce the benefits mentioned, it will be necessary that they be carefully prepared and wisely organized. This Sacred Congregation will not be backward in offering its own assistance and in giving all the instructions which the various cases may require.

6) Federations will also facilitate the organization of that productive monastic labor, which is presented to Nuns as a duty of penance, a way of mortification, and a means of support (Statutes, Art. VIII, Instruction, nn. XXVI–XXVII). To promote their development, ecclesiastical authorities and pious lay persons will not fail to offer their benevolent cooperation. Among other benefits, this will help to extricate the Monasteries from the serious economic difficulties in which not a few of them are entangled.

Your Excellency will kindly require of the Most Excellent Ordinaries and then transmit to this Sacred Congregation a report covering especially the following points: *a*) how the two pontifical documents have been explained to the different Monasteries; *b*) how the said explanation was received; *c*) what benefits are expected from it in the various Monasteries; *d*) what difficulties may arise from the explanation and application of the documents.

This Sacred Congregation expresses in advance its gratitude to Your Excellency and to the Most Reverend Ordinaries who will be good enough to furnish the required information and thus

enable the Sacred Congregation to fulfill the task assigned to it
by the Holy Father.

Thanking Your Excellency in advance . . . etc.

(Private); S. C. Rel., Letter, 7 March, 1951. Translation made from the
Italian text which was printed officially by the Sacred Congregation. Annotations, *Periodica,* 40–298 (Abellán).

NOTE: The above Letter was sent to the Apostolic Nuncios, Internuncios, and Delegates in the various countries. Another Letter almost
identical with this and bearing the same date, was sent to the Superiors
General of the various Orders of Regulars which have Monasteries of
Nuns dependent on them, asking them to see that the Regular
Superiors explain the Apostolic Constitution and the General Statutes
to the Monasteries subject to them, following the same order of points
as outlined above.

Permission to Take Solemn Vows and Observe Papal Cloister (S. C. Rel., 12 Nov., 1951) Private.

Inasmuch as the nuns of the Monastery of the Discalced
Carmelites of N.N. have petitioned from the Holy See the faculty
of taking solemn vows and of observing the major papal cloister,
the S. C. for the affairs of Religious, having heard the wish of
the Ordinary of N.N., and having given the matter careful
attention, has decreed that for the future, in the aforesaid
Monastery, the nuns, having first made temporary vows according to the norm of canon 574 of the Code of Canon Law, may
take solemn vows; and that the papal cloister, as prescribed by
the Code of Canon Law and by the Apostolic Constitution, *Sponsa
Christi* and the Instruction of the S. C. of Religious, *Inter prae-
clara,* of Nov. 23, 1950,[1] should be observed. All this should be
done prudently, however, in such a manner that the nuns will realize the obligations of their solemn vows and with provision made
for their proper sustenance.

When all these circumstances have been provided for, the
Ordinary of N.N., either personally or through a delegate, can
in the name of the Holy See receive the solemn vows of the
Superior of the Monastery; she in turn can receive the solemn
profession of the other nuns, provided they have been professed
for at least three years.

If any of the present members of the community wish not to

---

[1] Both documents reported above in this same volume under canon 600.

oblige themselves by solemn vows, they are free to remain in simple vows, but they must realize that they are nevertheless bound to a strict observance of all the laws of the major papal cloister. Extern sisters, having completed their period of temporary vows, are to be admitted only to simple perpetual vows.

Finally it is committed to the Ordinary of N.N. to publish this Decree in the Monastery of the Carmelite nuns at N.N., once he is certain that the required conditions have been fulfilled. A document attesting to the publication and execution of this Decree is to be preserved in the archives of the Monastery, and a copy of that Document is to be sent to this Sacred Congregation. All things to the contrary notwithstanding.

(Private); S. C. Rel., 12 Nov., 1951. This Rescript (N. 11646/51) was given to an Archbishop in the United States for a Monastery of Discalced Carmelites. We reproduce it with the kind permission of the Archbishop and through the kindness of the Reverend Adam Ellis, S.J.

CANON 610

Divine Office in Choir: Permission to recite it in Italian refused. The nuns of a certain monastery, for the benefit of those of the community who did not know Latin, asked for permission to say the Divine Office in Italian. The reply, S. C. Rit., 29 March, 1950 (N.A 28/50): *Negative* (*Monitor Ecclesiasticus*, 1952, p. 448).

Monastic Nuns: Obligation of Choir. See c. 600; AAS 43-5, Art. V.

CANON 611

Correspondence of Exempt Religious With Bishop (Code Com., 27 Nov., 1947) AAS 40-301.

The Code Commission was asked:

Whether exempt religious, in the cases in which they are subject to the Ordinary, can, according to canon 611, freely send to the said Ordinary and receive from him letters subject to no inspection.

Reply. In the affirmative.

AAS 40-301; Code Com., 27 Nov., 1947.
Periodica, 37-286 (Cappello).

CANON 615

Freedom of Correspondence: Of exempt religious with Bishop. See c. 611; AAS 40-301.

CANON 622

Collecting Money for the Missions (S. C. Prop. Fid., 29 June, 1952) **AAS 44-549.**

An Instruction of the Sacred Congregation for the Propagation of the Faith on the proper way of collecting money for the missions is as follows:

For many years now the Christian people are increasingly zealous in promoting the propagation of the Catholic faith among infidels, by supplying not only preachers of the Gospel but also financial support.

According to norms laid down by the Roman Pontiffs, all the funds which are offered for the progress of the Missions are brought together both through the two Pontifical Works for the Propagation of the Faith, namely that of Saint Peter the Apostle for the Native Clergy and that of the Holy Childhood, and through the Collection which is to be taken up at the time of Epiphany for the African Negroes.

Those norms, in the words of Pius XI of happy memory in his *Motu proprio, Romanorum Pontificum,* provide for "all Catholic Missions, through collections taken up in a certain way and method, from the whole Catholic world, so that even small sums collected in all nations from all the children of the Church, are put together in one fund destined to take care of the Missions in general, and all this money, which is entirely under Our control and disposal and that of the Sacred Congregation for the Propagation of the Faith, is distributed among all the Missions according to each one's needs, by men chosen by Ourselves."[1]

In order diligently to develop for the benefit of the Missions the cooperation of all the resources of the faithful in their respective countries according to the prescriptions of the sacred canons (cf. cc. 622, §§ 1 and 2; 691, §§ 3-5; 1341, § 1; 1503) and of the *Motu proprio* documents, *Romanum Pontificum* of 3 May, 1922, *Vix ad Summi* of 24 June, 1929,[2] *Decessor Noster* of 24 June, 1929,[3] and others, this Sacred Congregation for the Propagation of the Faith felt that certain norms ought to be recalled to the minds of all Directors, national or diocesan, who

[1] Cf. *Motu proprio* of Pius XI, 3 May, 1922; AAS 14-321; CANON LAW DIGEST, 1, p. 163. This language is quoted from AAS 14-323.
[2] AAS 21-345.   [3] *Ibid.,* 21-342.

are in charge of Pontifical Mission Works, and also of the religious Orders and Congregations and the Societies without vows, all of which for brevity's sake will be referred to in this Instruction as Missionary Institutes; and it has accordingly decreed that the said norms be exactly observed by all the persons and organizations above mentioned.

1. Missionary Institutes are allowed to make known to the faithful through sermons and publications the needs of their schools for the training of missionaries and of the Missions entrusted to them, and to urge the faithful to generosity. They should not forget, however, to inform their hearers and readers of the particular purpose of the Pontifical works, and should persuade them to give their support to those works, especially when Mission Day comes round.

2. Missionary Institutes, in promoting any kind of missionary cooperation in their respective countries, shall obtain the permission of the Diocesan Mission Board and shall avoid using names and appearances which might create in the minds of the faithful false notions about the purpose of the Missionary Institutes and of the Pontifical works, or which might seriously interfere with the progress of those same Works.

3. Missionary Institutes shall take care to cooperate willingly in the preparation and celebration of Mission Day. They shall send to the proper Diocesan Board all the money which is collected on that day, even in parishes and churches which are entrusted to the care of religious; and in order to avoid interfering in any way with the successful celebration of that day, they shall, at least for a reasonable time before the annual recurrence of Mission Day, abstain from all profit-seeking or appearance of securing any advantage for their Missions.

4. The National Directors shall be watchful that no one, abusing the purpose of the Pontifical Mission Works, take up collections for the Missions in general in order to meet necessities existing in territories which are not dependent on this Sacred Congregation for the Propagation of the Faith.

5. The National and Diocesan Directors shall so manage the activities which they are to promote among the faithful for the benefit of the Missions, as to avoid all unnecessary expenses and all projects which do not conduce directly to consolidate the work for the Missions.

6. Mission Day shall be celebrated in accordance with the norms established by authoritative documents and with the regulations which the various National Boards shall see fit to adopt in view of special circumstances.

7. In schools, academies, and all such institutions which are controlled by religious and sisters, the persons in charge shall consider it their duty to favor enrollment of the young people as members of the Pontifical Missionary Works and to celebrate Mission Day with special solicitude, sending to the proper Diocesan Board all the money that is collected both from the enrollments and by contributions.

Given at Rome, from the office of the Sacred Congregation for the Propagation of the Faith, the 29th day of June, Feast of the Holy Apostles Peter and Paul, in the year 1952.

AAS 44–549; S. C. Prop. Fid., 29 June, 1952. Annotations, *Monitor Ecclesiasticus,* 1952, p. 399 (Paventi).

Norms for Religious Institutes in Italy, Collecting for Their Foreign Missions: S. C. Prop. Fid., Letter, 21 March, 1951 (*Monitor Ecclesiasticus,* 1951, p. 252). Annotations, *ibid.,* p. 255 (Paventi).

CANON 627

Religious Appointed Prefect Apostolic, is subject to this canon during his office. See private reply *ex audientia Sanctissimi,* 2 Dec., 1920, reported by Vermeersch in *Epitome,* I, ed. 1937, n. 787, p. 581.

CANON 632

Religious Women of Simple Vows Transferring From One Independent House of Their Institute to Another, Are Subject to This Canon (S. C. Rel., 19 Nov., 1931) Private.

The following question was asked by the Bishop of Brooklyn:

Question. Having in mind the provisions of canon 632 and the replies of the S. C. of Religious of 9 Nov., 1926,[1] we ask whether religious women who according to their Constitutions pronounce only simple vows, are bound by the prescription of canon 632, if each of their houses is entirely independent of the other houses of the same Institute.

---

[1] Canon Law Digest, 1, p. 324.

For such religious women acknowledge no Superioress other than the local one, and hence their houses seem to be as it were independent. In the Constitutions their houses are generally called monasteries. On the other hand, they can in no sense be called monastic nuns, and so they cannot be included in the terms of the above mentioned replies.

Since the canonists whom we have consulted are not of one mind on the question, it would seem that appropriate instructions in the matter would be very useful.

On 19 Nov., 1931 (N. 26/31), the Secretary of the S. C. sent the following reply:

Reply. After having carefully considered the question presented by Your Excellency: whether the Sisters Adorers of the Most Precious Blood, who according to their Constitutions pronounce only simple vows, are bound by the prescription of canon 632, if each of their houses is entirely independent of the other houses of the same Institute, this S. C. considering all aspects of the question, has decided to and does reply as follows: The provision of canon 632 (633, § 3) is to be observed also in the transfer of Sisters of the Most Precious Blood to another monastery of their Institute.

(**Private**); Secretary of the S. C. Rel., 19 Nov., 1931. Published in Konrad, *The Transfer of Religious to Another Community,* pp. 102, 103.

CANON 638

Excloistered Religious Going From Europe to Australia or New Zealand. See c. 116; AAS 41–34.

CANON 639

Exclaustration of Religious of Solemn Vows During Military Service. See c. 574; S. C. Rel., 14 Apr., 1939.

CANON 640

Religious Secularized Before the Code, If Readmitted Need Not Repeat Noviceship or Profession (S. C. Rel., 25 Jan., 1923) **Private.**

A rescript of the S. C. of Religious to the Procurator General of the Capuchins is as follows:

I am happy to inform Your Paternity that religious who were secularized before the Code came into effect, if they are allowed to reenter religion, are not bound to a new noviceship nor to a new profession, because by the terms of the indult of secularization which was usually granted before May 19, 1918, they were not released from their vows but were merely dispensed from such obligations as could not be reconciled with their new state, and so they remained religious, bound to the substantial observance of their vows.

(**Private**); S. C. Rel., 25 Jan., 1923; *Analecta Ord. Min. Capuccin.*, 1925, p. 36; *Periodica*, 14–78.

CANON 654

Dismissal After Perpetual Vows in Society of Jesus (Code Com., 29 June, 1918) **Private.**

The dismissal of religious professed of perpetual vows in the Society of Jesus is regulated, as before, by the law of the Society itself, with the following reservations:

a) The provision of canon 647, § 2 as to the causes for dismissal must be observed.

b) The one to be dismissed must be given a full opportunity to reply to the charges against him (c. 650, § 3) and his replies must be faithfully reported to the Father General.

c) There is a recourse with suspensive effect to the Holy See.

(**Private**); Code Commission, 29 June, 1918. Reported by Vermeersch-Creusen, *Epitome,* Vol. I, ed. 1937, n. 820, p. 606, from Biederlack-Führich, *De Religiosis,* n. 175, note. As regards dismissal of the professed of *solemn* vows, the Society of Jesus is governed by the common law.

CANON 659

Fugitive From Religion: Impossibility of Warnings and Citation for Trial (Code Com.) **Private.**

Reply. If a fugitive from religion cannot be reached by way of warning or citation, the case is sufficiently provided for in the canons which treat of the penalties against apostates and fugitives from religion.

(**Private**); This reply is reported, without indication of the date or source, in Vermeersch-Creusen, *Epitome,* Vol. I, ed. 1937, n. 815, p. 603. Cf. also *Antonianum,* 1942, p. 223.

CANON 684

Catholic Action in India (Pius XII, Letter, 30 Jan., 1948)
AAS 40–328.

A Letter addressed to the Archbishops, Bishops, and other local Ordinaries of India, and published officially *in English*, is as follows:

During recent years We have been following with special interest the outcome of the efforts which you, Venerable Brethren, have been making to promote and foster Catholic Action in your respective dioceses in India. That these efforts have achieved a large measure of success is abundantly evident from the fact that in 1945 you deemed it opportune to found, under your authoritative direction, the Committee of Catholic Action, whereby Catholic Action was formally established on a national basis in India. We welcomed therefore with particular gratification the letter which, as National Director, the Archbishop of Madras, mindful of Our Apostolic office and of Our paternal interest in such matters, recently communicated to Us; and gladly acceding to the filial request therein contained, We have deemed it good to share your joy and prosper your undertaking by addressing you on the subject of Catholic Action.

Your beloved country has reached a turning point in its history; a new era has dawned; the flaming torch of liberty with justice has warmed the hearts and fired the minds of your beloved people, and in the burning fervor of newly won national independence, the destiny of your great nation is being shaped. At this juncture in your history, when problems of national importance have to be faced and solved, it is of great consequence that the faithful committed to your care should be in a position to make a worth-while contribution to the future of your nation, by sharing with their brothers in blood that heritage of sound doctrine which as Catholics they possess and cherish.

Catholic Action, wherein the first and essential duty of personal sanctification is combined with an intense apostolic activity under the mandate and encouragement of the Hierarchy, provides an excellent means whereby the faithful, intensifying their own spiritual life and deepening their religious convictions, may confer on the nation those blessings which accrue to civil society from the due observance of the divine law and the zealous fulfillment of Christian duties. This high purpose 'has been aptly stated in these words of Our Predecessor of blessed memory: "It is the function of this type of Action to form, as it were, a great army of good citizens, men and women, and especially young people of both sexes, whose first and dearest desire is to take some part in the sacred ministry of the Church and to strive valiantly under her leadership and guidance to spread the Kingdom of Christ in private and public life,"[1] the promotion of which is the acquisition for human society of the highest of all goods.

Wherefore We rejoice with you, Venerable Brethren, that under your pastoral direction and encouragement, this active and militant form of Catholic life is being firmly established in your dioceses; and it is Our fervent prayer that all those who enroll in its apostolate, so necessary in these days, "may walk worthy of God, in all things pleasing: being fruitful in every good work and increasing in the knowledge of God."[2]

Having as its aim and purpose the promotion of the Kingdom of Christ, it is obvious that Catholic Action transcends the aims of political parties and provides an apostolate whereby Catholics, without distinction of age, or sex, or class, or party, may promote whatever pertains to religion and morality. In so far as such activity is a direct collaboration of the laity in the spiritual and pastoral work of the Church, clearly it must be subordinated to the authority of the Bishops whom, under the jurisdiction of the Vicar of Christ, "the Holy Ghost hath placed to rule the Church of God,"[3] in their respective dioceses. In its social aspects also, where it may exert an impact on civil society, this sharing of the laity in the apostolic work of the Church must likewise be guided and directed by the Hierarchy, which is for Catholics the competent authority regarding the moral implications of questions arising in the social-economic order. For these reasons, Venerable Brethren, it is most opportune that one of the sections of the Catholic Bishops' Conference of India should be charged with the direction of the All-India Catholic Action Organization. This "Committee of Catholic Action," under its episcopal director, will be an effective means to co-ordinate the various Catholic Action

---

[1] Pius XI, Letter to the Cardinal Archbishop of Toledo, 6 Nov., 1929; AAS 21–664. See CANON LAW DIGEST, Vol. 1, p. 132.

[2] Col. 1:10.

[3] Acts 20:28.

groups, to acquaint them with the mind of the Church and ensure that, in serried ranks, they act in close co-operation with you in the matters of national interest requiring definite Catholic leadership and a precise statement of Catholic thought and teaching. Moreover it will be in a position to facilitate and encourage a cordial collaboration between Catholic Action groups and the existing associations, whose labors, whether in the field of personal sanctification or social service, deserve so well of the whole Church, so that, though retaining their autonomy, all may yet rejoice in the blessed bond of fraternal solidarity which, according to the mind of Our Predecessor of happy memory, should unite all who dedicate themselves, each in his own measure, to the upbuilding of the Body of Christ.[4]

The guiding principle therefore of all those who collaborate in this apostolate should be *"sentire cum Ecclesia,"* to have the mind of the Church, to be intimately acquainted with the doctrine of the Church, which is "the pillar and the ground of truth."[5] Wherefore We commend to you, Venerable Brethren, in a special manner, the necessity of the sound religious training and moral formation of all who undertake this apostolate. They must be "nourished up in the words of faith and of good doctrine" and "exercise themselves unto godliness."[6] In a word, they must undergo a training which embraces the whole man, and which brings mind and heart and will into subjection to Christ, so that each apostle of Catholic Action may show himself "an example of good works in doctrine, in integrity."[7] It is this integrity of Christian life, solidly grounded in doctrine, nourished by the frequent reception of the Sacraments, supported by prayer and the practice of Christian virtue, that characterizes the Catholic Actionist and makes him a faithful soldier of Christ in his home, in his work or profession, and in every phase of his social life. This task of training falls primarily on the clergy and religious who, by the zealous fulfillment of this sacred duty, will provide an ever increasing number of fervent men and women and of youth, who, obedient to the voice of the Supreme Pastor and to the directions of their Bishops, will become devoted and earnest co-workers in leading others to God and to His Holy Church. Here then is the special field for your zealous collaborators, for those generous souls consecrated to Catholic Action,

---

[4] Eph. 4:12.   [5] 1 Tim. 3:15.   [6] 1 Tim. 4:6–7.   [7] Tit. 2:7.

whose one great desire is to devote themselves to the spreading of the Kingdom of Christ. As apostles of their brothers in blood they may win countless souls to Christ, and, enlarging His Kingdom in India, may effect an ever wider extension of the inestimable blessings of that Kingdom of truth and life, of holiness, of justice, of love, and of peace. What greater blessings could We wish your nation, what nobler ambition could inspire the Catholics of all India than the realization of such a divine plan?

With all Our heart therefore We commend to the clergy and faithful committed to your care this admirable apostolate, which corresponds so effectively to the needs of the Church in these days. And as an earnest of Our paternal interest, as an incentive to still greater effort, as a pledge of abundant celestial favors, We cordially impart to you, Venerable Brethren, and to all those who under your guidance may collaborate with you in the noble work of spreading the Kingdom of God, the fullness of Our Apostolic Benediction.

Given at the Vatican on the thirtieth of January, nineteen hundred and forty-eight, the ninth year of Our Pontificate.

AAS 40–328; Pius XII, Letter, 30 Jan., 1948.

Sodality of Our Lady: New Apostolic Constitution (Pius XII, 27 Sept., 1948) AAS 40–393.

Pius Bishop

Servant of the Servants of God as a Lasting Memorial

On the happy occasion of the second centenary of the date when Benedict XIV in the Golden Bull *"Gloriosae Dominae"* confirmed with new privileges the Sodalities of Our Lady which had been erected and perpetually constituted[1] by Gregory XIII, We consider it part of Our Apostolic office not merely to congratulate paternally the directors and members of these Sodalities, but also, on account of their numerous and great services to the Church, to declare ratified and solemnly confirmed the privileges and great favors which in the course of almost four centuries many of Our Predecessors,[2] and We Ourselves, have bestowed.

---

[1] Bull *Omnipotentis Dei,* 5 Dec., 1584.

[2] Xystus V, Bull *Superna dispositione,* 5 Jan., 1587; Bull *Romanum decet,*

We fully realize, to use the words of Benedict XIV in the aforesaid Golden Bull, not only "what utility has in the past been derived from this praiseworthy and pious organization for men in every walk of life";[3] but also with what zeal and energy these serried ranks of Our Lady, following closely in the footsteps of their predecessors and exactly observing their rules, are seeking, under the leadership and guidance of the ecclesiastical Hierarchy, the first place for themselves in undertaking and ever promoting works for the greater glory of God and for the good of souls. Indeed in propagating, spreading, and defending Catholic doctrine they must be considered among the most powerful spiritual forces;[4] and that for several reasons.

When we look at the history of the Sodality of Our Lady we must admit that although it has always flourished in perfectly disciplined ranks, its members cannot compare in numbers with those of the present, although they do compare with them in the fervor of their apostolate. In former centuries in fact the increase of Sodalities affiliated to the *Prima Primaria* never exceeded ten in a year, but from the beginning of the twentieth century these yearly affiliations are counted by the thousands.

But it is of the greatest importance that the observance of the rules and constitutions of the Sodalities should be considered of much more import than the numbers of Sodalists, for through them the members are gently led to that perfection of spiritual life[5] from which they can scale the heights of sanctity[6] and especially by means of those steps which are most useful in form-

---

29 Sept., 1587. — Clement VIII, Brief *Cum sicut Nobis,* 30 Aug., 1602. — Gregory XV, Bull *Alias pro parte,* 15 Apr., 1621. — Benedict XIV, Brief *Praeclaris Romanorum Pontificum,* 24 Apr., 1748; "Bulla Aurea" *Gloriosae Dominae,* 27 Sept., 1748; Brief *Quemadmodum Presbyteri,* 15 July, 1740; Brief *Quo Tibi,* 8 Sept., 1751; Brief *Laudabile Romanorum,* 15 Feb., 1758. — Clement XIII, Bull *Apostolicum,* 7 Jan., 1765. — Pius VI, Decrees, 2 May, 1775; 9 Dec., 1775, 20 March, 1776. — Leo XII, Brief *Cum multa,* 17 May, 1824. — Pius IX, Decree, 8 July, 1848; Brief *Exponendum,* 10 Feb., 1863. — Leo XIII, Brief *Frugiferas,* 27 May, 1884; Brief *Nihil adeo,* 8 Jan., 1886. — Pius X, Decrees, 10 May, 1910; 21 July, 1910. — Benedict XV, Allocution 19 Dec., 1915 on the fortieth anniversary of his own reception into the Sodality. — Pius XI, Allocutions, 30 March, 1930; 29 Aug., 1935.

[3] Benedict XIV, "Bulla Aurea" *Gloriosae Dominae,* 27 Sept., 1748.

[4] Pius XII, Letter to Cardinal Leme, 21 Jan., 1942.

[5] Cf. *Reg. Comm.,* 1, 33.

[6] Cf. *ibid.,* 12.

ing perfect and wholehearted followers of Christ. These helps are the Spiritual Exercises[7] and the practice of daily meditation on things divine; examination of conscience;[8] the frequentation of the Sacraments;[9] child-like docility in their relations with a definite spiritual director;[10] the total and continual dedication of self as a client of the Virgin Mother of God;[11] and the firm determination to devote oneself to the promoting of one's own perfection and that of others.[12]

All these helps naturally tend to fan those flames of divine love in the Sodalists of Our Lady and to nourish and strengthen that interior life which is so necessary in our times when — as with sorrow We have given warning elsewhere — such vast numbers of men are afflicted "with barrenness of soul and grave spiritual need."[13]

That these things are not only contained in its most wise rules but are admirably brought into the daily life of the Sodality of Our Lady, is evidently proved from the fact that wherever Sodalities are in a flourishing condition — provided that the way of life and rules are faithfully observed — holiness of life and solid attachment to religion readily grow and flourish. Besides, under divine guidance, there spring forth numerous groups of Sodalists sincerely seeking Christian perfection for themselves and others either in the ecclesiastical state or within the cloister, and there are not a few who with sure flight reach the arduous heights of sanctity.[14] From this fervent zeal of the interior life results an apostolic training which almost spontaneously flourishes and which is adapted to the new and ever varied human needs and circumstances, so that We do not hesitate to assert that the perfect Catholic, such as the Sodality of Our Lady has been accustomed to envisage from the very beginning, is no less in keeping with the needs of former times than of our own, since there is perhaps greater need now than before of men solidly formed in the Christian life.[15]

---

[7] Cf. *ibid.*, 9.   [9] Cf. *ibid.*, 37, 38, 39.
[8] Cf. *ibid.*, 34.   [10] Cf. *ibid.*, 36.
[11] Cf. *ibid.*, 27, 1, 40, 43.
[12] Cf. *ibid.*, 1.
[13] Pius XII, Encyclical *Summi Pontificatus*, 20 Oct., 1939; AAS 31-415.
[14] Pius XII, Allocution to the Sodalists of Our Lady, 21 Jan., 1945.
[15] *Ibid.*

Hence, beholding from the See of Peter, as if from a lofty watch-tower of the entire world, the wonderful zeal of the faithful everywhere in protecting, defending, and promoting the faith, We consider as deserving special praise the worthy members of the Sodalities of Our Lady, who from the very beginning have looked upon it as their own and as a thing completely in accord with their rules[16] to undertake individually or collectively any apostolic work approved by the Church[17] and under the leadership of their Pastors.[18] The repeated and lucid pronouncements of the Roman Pontiffs have eloquently proved how well they have fulfilled this task and with what happy results for the advancement of religion.[19] In this present age disturbed by so many upheavals, it is a great consolation for Us to contemplate the Sodalities of Our Lady all over the world working strenuously and effectively in every field of the apostolate, either stirring up people of every social rank, youths especially and workers, by means of the Spiritual Exercises to the practice of virtue and the desire of a deeper Christian life, or coming to the help of those in grave corporal or spiritual need; this they do not merely in their private capacity and from a kindly disposition but also by promoting in national assemblies and as heads of states, laws that are in keeping with the Gospel principles and social justice.[20]

Nor must We pass over in silence associations promoted or helped by the Sodalities of Our Lady that aim to put a stop to bad plays and films and to protect morals from the flood of evil literature, nor the many free schools for the young and for adults of the poorer classes, technical institutes to give workers fuller training in their trades,[21] and especially a more expert knowledge

---

[16] Pius XI, Allocution to the Sodalists of Our Lady, 30 March, 1930.

[17] Cf. Pius XII, Letter to Father Daniel Lord, 24 Jan., 1948.

[18] Cf. Pius XII, Letter to Cardinal Leme, 21 Jan., 1942.

[19] Cf. *Reg. Comm.*, 1, 12, 43. — Benedict XIV, "Bulla Aurea" *Gloriosae Dominae,* 27 Sept., 1748. — Benedict XV, Allocution to the Sodalists of Our Lady, 19 Dec., 1915. — Pius XI, Letter to the Administrator Apostolic, Bishop Sigismund Waitz, at Innsbruck in Austria, 2 Aug., 1927; Letter to the Sodalists of Germany, 8 Sept., 1928. — Pius XII, Apostolic Letter *Nostri profecto,* 6 July, 1940; Allocution to Catholic Actionists of Italy, 4 Sept., 1940; Letter to Cardinal Leme, 21 Jan., 1942; Letter to Father S. Ilundain, 26 Aug., 1946; Radio address to the Congress of Barcelona, 7 Dec., 1947.

[20] Cf. Pius XII, Letter to Father Daniel Lord, 24 Jan., 1948; Allocution to the Sodalists from the *"Conférence Olivaint,"* 27 March, 1948.

[21] Cf. Pius XII, Letter to Father Daniel Lord, 24 Jan., 1948.

of the different arts and professions.[22] These forms of the apostolate so necessary in present day conditions are adopted by many Sodalities, especially inter-parish Sodalities, for the benefit of groups of similar work or employment.[23]

Many of these activities are of the greatest benefit to the Catholic cause. The Sodalities of Our Lady are to be praised in this matter because they have always desired, particularly in recent times, to co-operate harmoniously with other Catholic associations and thus, with united forces and under the authority and guidance of the Hierarchy, they gain greater results for the kingdom of Christ by their united efforts; moreover, as We have noted elsewhere in speaking of Italian Catholic Action,[24] the first groups of this kind in some countries were started by Sodalists, others afterwards followed in their footsteps and gave their earnest support to Catholic Action, thus showing that in reality Sodalists are rightly to be considered among the chief promoters of Catholic Action.

Besides, since the entire force of Catholics united into one army in battle-array consists in obedience to the authority of their Pastors, who does not see how opportune as instruments of apostolate the Sodalities of Our Lady should be considered on account of their unflinching and fervent devotion in a spirit of humble submission and docile obedience not only to this Apostolic See, which is the source and foundation of all ecclesiastical jurisdiction,[25] but also, in keeping with their character and scope, to the decrees and counsels of the Bishops?[26]

Anyone who has thoroughly examined the internal constitution of the Sodality can easily see that some are governed by Bishops and Parish Priests, others, through special privilege, by Us, and in virtue of Our delegated power, by the General of the Society of Jesus: but all, in undertaking and continuing apostolic works, are subject to the authority of the local Bishops or even sometimes of the Parish Priest. Hence, since they are accepted by the Ecclesiastical Hierarchy among the forces of the militant apostolate, they fully depend on the Hierarchy in undertaking and carrying out their work, and by every right and title, as We have noted

---

[22] Cf. Pius XII, Allocution to the Sodalists of Our Lady, 21 Jan., 1945.
[23] Ibid.   [24] Ibid.
[25] Cf. Conc. Vat., Sess. IV, Const. I "De Ecclesia Christi."
[26] Cf. Pius XII, Letter to Cardinal Leme, 21 Jan., 1942.

elsewhere,[27] should be called co-operators in the hierarchical apostolate. This almost natural "reverence and deference of Sodalists of Our Lady towards their holy Pastors" is of necessity to be drawn from their very rules, according to which it is a sacred duty to make profession in their life and morals of whatever the Catholic Church teaches, "praising what she praises, abhorring what she abhors, agreeing with her in everything, and never being ashamed to act in public or in private as becomes a faithful and most dutiful son of such a Mother."[28]

It is not contrary to the close and almost military unity of Catholics that this type of sodality was first started by the Ignatian family and seems to be as it were an offshoot and branch of it especially since a number of them, though not very large, are directed by priests of the Society of Jesus with Our delegation, as We have explained. Rather, from its very beginning the Sodalities of Our Lady proposed to themselves as a headline the rules "for thinking with the Church," and seem to have developed an almost natural tendency of obeying the words of those whom "the Holy Spirit placed as Bishops to rule the Church of God" (Act 20:28); hence they have been and shall be in the future a most powerful help to the Bishops in spreading the kingdom of Christ. The fact that they ever had the common good of the Church at heart and not some private interest, is proved by the unimpeachable witness of that most brilliant series of Sodalists to whom Mother Church has decreed the supreme honors of the Altars; their glory throws luster not merely on the Society of Jesus but on the secular clergy and on not a few religious families, since ten members of the Sodalities of Our Lady became founders of new Religious Orders and Congregations.

All this goes to show clearly that the Sodalities of Our Lady, as their rules approved by the Church openly profess, are associations imbued with an apostolic spirit,[29] which not only urge their members, who are sometimes led to the very heights of sanctity,[30] to strive to obtain, under the guidance of their Pastors,[31] the christian perfection and eternal salvation of others, and to safeguard the rights of the Church,[32] but also provide

---

[27] Pius XII, Allocution to Catholic Actionists of Italy, 4 Sept., 1940; AAS 32-369.

[28] Cf. *Reg. Comm.*, 33.   [30] *Ibid.*, 12.   [32] *Ibid.*, 1.

[29] Cf. *ibid.*, 1, 43.   [31] *Ibid.*, 33.

tireless heralds of the Virgin Mother of God and fully trained propagators of the kingdom of Christ.[33]

Hence, whether one considers the rules and purpose of the Sodalities of Our Lady or what they have achieved, there is no characteristic lacking which belongs to Catholic Action since this is correctly defined, as Our Predecessor of happy memory Pius XI so often declared: "the apostolate of the faithful who assist the Church and to a certain extent complete its pastoral work."[34]

The structure and peculiar character of the Sodalities of Our Lady are no obstacle whatever to their being called with the fullest right "Catholic Action under the auspices and inspiration of the Blessed Virgin Mary";[35] for as they have been in the past, "they are and will continue to be a means of safeguarding and protecting the formation of outstanding Catholics."[36] As has often been declared by this Apostolic See, "Catholic Action is not confined within a closed circle,"[37] hemmed in, as it were, by certain rigidly determined limits that must not be transgressed, nor is it such that "it pursues its object according to a special method and system,"[38] so as to abolish or absorb the other active Catholic organizations. Rather it should consider as its duty "to join them together, to unite them in a friendly manner, making the progress of one serve toward the advantage of the others, in all concord, union, and charity."[39] For, as We have pointed out quite recently, "in this excellent zeal for the apostolate, which meets with Our highest approval, there must be avoided the error made by a certain number who desire to reduce all that is done in the interest of souls, to a single pattern."[40] Since this attitude must be considered completely alien to the mind of the Church,[41]

---

[33] *Ibid.*, 43.

[34] Pius XI, Letter to Cardinal van Roey, 15 Aug., 1928; AAS 20-296; Letter to Cardinal Segura, 6 Nov., 1929; AAS 21-665.

[35] Cardinal Pacelli, Allocution to Sodalists of Our Lady in Menzingen (Switzerland), 22 Oct., 1938.

[36] Pius XI, Allocution to the Sodalists of Our Lady, 30 March, 1930.

[37] Pius XI, Encyclical *Firmissimam constantiam*, to the Bishops of Mexico, 28 March, 1937; AAS 29-210.

[38] Pius XI, Letter *Quae Nobis* to Cardinal Bertram, 13 Nov., 1928; AAS 20-386; CANON LAW DIGEST, Vol. 1, p. 128.

[39] Pius XI, Allocution to Catholic Actionists of France, 20 May, 1931.

[40] Pius XII, Radio address to Congress of Barcelona, 7 Dec., 1947; AAS 39-364.

[41] Pius XI, Allocution to Catholic Actionists of Italy, 28 June, 1930.

which is so far from approving[42] such "restriction on the growth
and flowering of life" whereby any apostolic work is entrusted to
one single organization or to a single parish, that it actually favors
a multiform unity[43] in carrying out such works, by means of a
brotherly co-operation, under the guidance of the Bishops, and
with their efforts united and directed to one end.[44] Such organizations will more easily obtain this "harmonious agreement,
ordered collaboration and mutual understanding, which We have
recommended time and again,"[45] when having put aside all controversy regarding priority,[46] "they love one another with
brotherly affection, with honor preventing one another,"[47] and
have solely God's glory in view; then they can rest assured that
they will prevail more than others, when they have learned to
give to them the first places.[48]

As a result of these considerations and Our ardent desire that
these schools of piety and Christian apostolate should daily increase in life and vigor,[49] with Our Apostolic Authority We
briefly indicate some points that are common to Sodalists throughout the world and should be observed with religious exactitude
by all interested.

I. Sodalities of Our Lady, duly affiliated to the *Prima Primaria*
of the Roman College, are religious societies erected and established by the Church[50] and have been enriched with the fullest
privileges[51] by her for the better fulfillment of the work entrusted
to them.

II. That only is to be considered a lawful Sodality, which has
been set up by the Ordinary who has power to do so; that is to
say, in places belonging to the Society of Jesus or entrusted to
its care, by the Father General,[52] in all other places by the Bishop

---

[42] Pius XI, Letter *Quamvis Nostra* to the Bishops of Brazil, 27 Oct., 1935;
AAS 28–160.
[43] Pius XI, Allocution to the Sodalists of Our Lady, 30 March, 1930.
[44] Cf. Pius XII, Letter to Father S. Ilundain, 26 Aug., 1946.
[45] Pius XI, Letter *Quamvis Nostra* to the Bishops of Brazil, 27 Oct., 1935;
AAS 28–163.
[46] Cf. Mark 9:33.
[47] Rom. 12:10.
[48] Cf. Matt. 20:26–27.
[49] Pius XII, Letter to Cardinal Leme, 21 Jan., 1942.
[50] Cf. Gregory XIII, Bull *Omnipotentis Dei*, 5 Dec., 1584.
[51] Cf. documents cited in notes 1 and 2 above.
[52] Sixtus V, Bull *Romanum decet*, 29 Sept., 1587.

of the place, or with his formal consent, by the aforesaid Father General.[53] In order that a Sodality thus erected should enjoy all the privileges and indulgences granted to the *Prima Primaria,* it must be duly affiliated to it.[54] This affiliation, however, which may only be sought with the consent of the Ordinary of the place and which it is in the power only of the General of the Society of Jesus to grant,[55] gives neither to the *Prima Primaria* nor to the Society of Jesus any rights over such a Sodality.[56]

III. Sodalities, since they answer fully to the present-day needs of the Church[57] must, in accordance with the will of Sovereign Pontiffs, keep intact their laws, their character, and constitution.[58]

IV. The Common Rules, whose observance, in substance at least, is required for affiliation,[59] are earnestly recommended to all Sodalists as a summary and pattern of the way of life followed by the first Sodalists and established by constant practice.[60]

V. All Sodalities, with a dependence that may differ in minor matters though substantially the same, are subject to the Ecclesiastical Hierarchy not less than other organizations consecrated to apostolic works.[61]

---

[53] Sacred Congregation of Indulgences, Decree, 23 June, 1885.

[54] Cf. canon 686, Code of Canon Law; "Bulla Aurea" *Gloriosae Dominae,* Sept., 1748; Leo XII, Decree, 17 May, 1824; S. C. of Indulgences, 23 June, 1885.

[55] Cf. S. C. Indulg., Rescript 17 Sept., 1887; canon 723 Code of Canon Law; *Reg. Comm.,* 2.

[56] Cf. canon 722, § 2, Code of Canon Law; Declaration of Very Reverend Father Louis Martin, General of the Society of Jesus, 13 April, 1904.

[57] Cf. especially: Pius XII, Allocution to the Sodalists of Our Lady, 21 Jan., 1945; Letter to Father S. Ilundain, 26 Aug., 1946; Letter to Father Daniel Lord, 24 Jan., 1948.

[58] Cf. especially: Pius XI, Allocution to the Sodalists of Our Lady, 30 March, 1930; Allocution to the Sodalists of the *Prima Primaria,* 24 March, 1935. — Pius XII, Telegram to the Convention of Sodalists of Italy, 12 Sept., 1947; Radio Address to the Congress of Barcelona, 7 Dec., 1947; Letter to Father Daniel Lord, 24 Jan., 1948.

[59] Cf. S. C. Indulg., Decree, 7 March, 1825; Decree, 23 June, 1885; Rescript, 17 Sept., 1887.

[60] Cf. Pius XII, Allocution to the Sodalists of Our Lady, 21 Jan., 1945; Letter to Father Daniel Lord, 24 Jan., 1948.

[61] Cf. *Conc. Vat.,* Sess. IV, Const. *"De Ecclesia Christi,"* cap. 3; Code of Canon Law, canon 218, § 2; Pius XII, Allocution to Catholic Actionists of Italy, 4 Sept., 1940; AAS 32-369; Letter to Cardinal Leme, 21 Jan., 1942; Allocution to Congress of Barcelona, 7 Dec., 1947; AAS 39-634.

VI. While following faithfully in the footsteps of those who preceded them and keeping abreast of the times, lest, in propagating the kingdom of God and defending the rights of the Christian warfare, their own ranks be thrown into disorder and their forces weakened, Sodalists should be mindful of the following points:

a) The local Ordinary

1. has power, as laid down in the Sacred Canons, saving always the prescripts and documents of the Apostolic See, over all Sodalities within his jurisdiction with regard to the external exercise of the Apostolate;

2. he has power over Sodalities that are erected outside the houses of the Society of Jesus and can accordingly give them rules provided the substance of the Common Rules remains intact.[62]

b) The Parish Priest

1. is the normal president of parish Sodalities, which he accordingly governs as the other societies of his parish;

2. he possesses over all the Sodalities engaged in apostolic work in his parish that power which has been given him by Canon Law and by legitimate diocesan statutes for the right ordering of the external apostolate.[63]

VII. Any legitimately appointed director of a Sodality, who of course must always be a priest, although he is altogether subject to his ecclesiastical Superiors, enjoys however, according to the Common Rules, complete power in the internal life of the Sodality. It is fitting that he should generally exercise this power by means of sodalists, chosen to help him in his office.[64]

VIII. These Sodalities are to be called "Sodalities of *Our Lady*" not only because they take their name from the Blessed Virgin Mary,[65] but especially because each Sodalist makes profession of special devotion to the Mother of God[66] and is dedicated to

---

[62] Cf. Code of Canon Law, canons 334, § 1, 335, § 1; *Statuta Generalia CC. MM.*, 31 Aug., 1885, II, 5.

[63] Cf. Code of Canon Law, canon 464, § 1; Declaration of Very Reverend Louis Martin, 13 April, 1904.

[64] Cf. Benedict XIV, "Bulla Aurea" *Gloriosae Dominae*, 27 Sept., 1748; Brief *Laudabile Romanorum*, 15 Feb., 1758; *Statuta Generalia*, 31 Aug., 1885; *Reg. Comm.*, 16, 18, 50.

[65] Cf. *Reg. Comm.*, 3; "Bulla Aurea" *Gloriosae Dominae*.

[66] Cf. *Reg. Comm.*, 1, 40.

her by a complete consecration,[67] undertaking, though not under pain of sin,[68] to strive by every means and under the standard of the Blessed Virgin for his own perfection and eternal salvation as well as for that of others.[69] By this consecration the Sodalist binds himself forever to the Blessed Virgin Mary, unless he is dismissed from the Sodality as unworthy, or himself through fickleness of purpose relinquishes the same.[70]

IX. In the enrollment of Sodalists care should be taken to choose[71] those who are by no means satisfied with an ordinary and common kind of life,[72] but who strive "to place the most lofty sentiments in their hearts," (cfr. Ps. 83:6)[73] according to the ascetic norms and exercises of piety proposed in the Rules.[74]

X. It is the duty, then, of Sodalities of Our Lady to train their members according to the condition of each, so that they can be proposed as models to their companions of Christian life and apostolic endeavor.[75]

XI. Among the primary ends of Sodalities[76] is to be reckoned every kind of apostolate, especially the social apostolate for the

---

[67] Cf. *ibid.*, 27.

[68] Cf. Pius XII, Allocution to the Sodalists of Our Lady, 21 Jan., 1945; *Reg. Comm.*, 32.

[69] Cf. Pius XII, Allocution to the Sodalists of Our Lady, 21 Jan., 1945; Letter to Father Daniel Lord, 24 Jan., 1948.

[70] Cf. *Reg. Comm.*, 1, 27, 30.

[71] Cf. *Reg. Comm.*, 23, 24, 26; Benedict XV, Allocution to the Sodalists of Our Lady, 19 Dec., 1915. — Pius XI, Encyclical *Ubi arcano*, 23 Dec., 1922; AAS 14–693. — Pius XII, Letter to Cardinal Leme, 21 Jan., 1942; Allocution to the Sodalists of Our Lady, 21 Jan., 1945; Letter to Father S. Ilundain, 26 Aug., 1946; Telegram to the Convention of Sodalists of Italy, 12 Sept., 1947; Radio Address to the Congress of Barcelona, 7 Dec., 1947; AAS 39–634.

[72] Cf. *Reg. Comm.*, 1, 35.

[73] *Ibid.*, 12.

[74] Cf. *ibid.*, 9, 33–45.

[75] Cf. *Reg. Comm.*, 14, 1, 33, 43; Pius XII, Allocution to the Sodalists of Our Lady, 21 Jan., 1945; Telegram to the Convention of Sodalists of Italy, 12 Sept., 1947; Letter to Father Daniel Lord, 24 Jan., 1948; Allocution to the Sodalists of the *"Conference Olivaint,"* 27 March, 1948.

[76] Benedict XIV, "Bulla Aurea" *Gloriosae Dominae*, 27 Sept., 1748. — Benedict XV, Allocution to the Sodalists of Our Lady, 19 Dec., 1915. — Pius XI, Letter to the Administrator Apostolic, Bishop Sigismund Waitz, at Innsbruck in Austria, 2 Aug., 1927. — Pius XII, Letter to Cardinal Leme, 21 Jan., 1942; Letter to Father S. Ilundain, 26 Aug., 1946; Radio Address to the Congress of Barcelona, 7 Dec., 1947; AAS 39–633.

propagation of the kingdom of Christ and the defence of ecclesiastical rights,[77] entrusted to them by the Ecclesiastical Hierarchy.[78] To further this true and complete co-operation with the hierarchical apostolate[79] the norms proper to the Sodalities, determining the means of this co-operation, are in no way to be changed or modified.[80]

XII. Finally, the Sodalities of Our Lady are to be considered on the same level as the other organizations dedicated to the apostolate,[81] whether they are allied to these, or to the central organization of Catholic Action. Moreover, since it is the duty of Sodalities, under the guidance and authority of their Pastors,[82] to lend their aid to every other organization,[83] it is not required that each Sodalist should also become a member of some other association.[84]

Thus We announce and proclaim, decreeing that this letter is and remains fully valid and efficacious and has full and complete effect now and for the future, and that it should abundantly favor those whom it concerns, and it is in this sense that it must be judged and defined; and if anything contrary to this, whether

---

[77] *Reg. Comm.*, 1; Pius XII, Allocution to the Sodalists of Our Lady, 21 Jan., 1945.

[78] Cf. Letter of Cardinal Pacelli to Cardinal Faulhaber, 3 Sept., 1934; Pius XII, Apostolic Letter *Nostri profecto,* 6 July, 1940; Allocution to the Sodalists of Our Lady, 21 Jan., 1945; Letter to Father S. Ilundain, 26 Aug., 1946; Letter to Father Daniel Lord, 24 Jan., 1948.

[79] Pius XII, Allocution to Catholic Actionists of Italy, 4 Sept., 1940; AAS 32-369; Letter to Cardinal Leme, 21 Jan., 1942; Cardinal Pacelli, Allocution to the Sodalists of Our Lady at Menzingen (Switzerland), 22 Oct., 1938.

[80] Cf. Pius XII, Radio Address to the Congress of Barcelona, 7 Dec., 1947; AAS 39-634.

[81] Cf. Pius XII, Allocution to the Catholic Actionists of Italy, 4 Sept., 1940; AAS 32-368; Telegram to the Convention of Sodalists of Italy, 12 Sept., 1947; Radio Address to the Congress of Barcelona, 7 Dec., 1947; AAS 39-634.

[82] Cf. among others: Pius XII, Telegram to the Convention of Sodalists of Italy, 12 Sept., 1947; Letter to Father Daniel Lord, 24 Jan., 1948; Letter to the Bishops of India on Catholic Action, *"During recent years,"* 30 Jan., 1948; AAS 40-328, reported in this volume of Canon Law Digest under canon 684.

[83] Cf. especially: Pius XI, Letter to the Bishops of Brazil, 27 Oct., 1935; AAS 28-161; Canon Law Digest, 2, p. 57; Allocution to the Sodalists of Our Lady, 30 March, 1930. — Pius XII, Allocution to the Catholic Actionists of Italy, 4 Sept., 1940; AAS 32-369.

[84] Cf. Pius XII, Letter to Father S. Ilundain, 26 Aug., 1946.

knowingly or unknowingly, shall be attempted by anyone whomsoever and by whatever authority, it shall henceforth be null and void. Anything to the contrary notwithstanding.

Given at Castel Gandolfo, near Rome, 27th September, on the occasion of the second centenary of the Golden Bull *"Gloriosae Dominae,"* in the year 1948, the tenth of Our Pontificate.

AAS 40–393; Pius XII, Apostolic Constitution, 27 Sept., 1948. *Periodica,* 37–358 (Aguirre).

Apostleship of Prayer and League of the Sacred Heart
(Pius XII, Letter, 19 Sept., 1948) **AAS 40–500.**

A Letter of His Holiness Pius XII, addressed to the Very Reverend John Baptist Janssens, General of the Society of Jesus and Director General of the "Apostleship of Prayer," is as follows:

Beloved Son, health and Apostolic Benediction.

We heartily rejoice that the Directors of the "Apostleship of Prayer," which you worthily govern, have come to Rome in such numbers, "of all nations, and peoples, and tongues,"[1] to mobilize powerful forces in aid of the needs of our time, by common counsel among themselves deriving force and security from long experience. We are well aware with what zeal you bend your energies to spread devotion to the divine Heart of Jesus, by this sodality of yours which grants free admission to all men. For, not only by the "Messengers of the Sacred Heart" published in nearly forty languages, and numerous other writings as well, but also by the most up-to-date inventions of the age, the cinema and the radio, you strive to impart to the faithful the spirit of the apostolate, as befits members of that Church to which Our Lord Himself said: "Going, teach ye all nations."[2]

This Apostolate is not truly fulfilled by the mere recitation of certain prayers. Rather it tends of its very nature to present to its members the Christian life in its perfection, and enables them to achieve it. No one who deserves the name of Christian, who has been incorporated by Baptism into the Mystical Body of Christ, can be content to take care of his own sanctification while neglecting the eternal salvation of others, forgetting that the Lord "gave to every one commandment concerning his neighbor."[3] Now by devotion to the Most Sacred Heart of Jesus the faithful are most effectively made one and built up into a corporate whole

---

[1] Apoc. 7:9.   [2] Matt. 28:19.   [3] Eccli. 17:12.

with each other and with Christ. So true is this that the Apostleship of Prayer can rightly and properly be called a perfect form of devotion to the divine Heart of Jesus, and in turn devotion to the Sacred Heart of Jesus cannot be separated from the Apostleship of Prayer. For it is characteristic of this devotion to cultivate love of God and the neighbor to the point of complete dedication of oneself. Hence your sodality has taken as its motto the words of the Our Father, "Thy Kingdom come." For through the daily Morning Offering, which if duly weighed must be acknowledged to be a true consecration to the divine Heart of Jesus, and which seems to require as its complement the consecration not only of families and private groups but also of States; through the devotion to the Immaculate Heart of Mary, which shows a wonderful growth from day to day; through the practice of more frequent Communion among the faithful; through an ardent loyalty to the Vicar of Christ; and finally through the special intentions which are proposed to the members every month and the practice of the so-called "Around-the-clock Masses for the Pope" — through all these means the "Apostleship of Prayer" molds to religion and piety and enkindles to apostolic fervor not only the faithful in general but also select groups; and that, not only among peoples who have long been enlightened by the Gospel, but even in lands only recently brought under the sweet yoke of Christ.

In consideration of all this, just as did Our Predecessor of happy memory, Pius XI, so We too have declared and gladly declare once more that We would be most happy to see every one of the faithful enlist in this sacred militia, so as to surpass by far the number of its present membership, which easily reaches thirty-five million.

This could not arouse in any one the suspicion that the "Apostleship of Prayer" was trespassing as it were upon the harvest fields of others; for those who were led by divine Providence to found this Apostleship stated in the plainest terms that they intended to make no innovations where pious associations were already flourishing, but would seek only to radiate the fire of divine love and apostolic zeal upon other associations without in any way disturbing their organization. Accordingly, long before that happy outburst of energy in spreading the Kingdom of Christ which We are happily witnessing today in the organization of the laity, these men had already prepared that solid body of doctrine with which to nourish the interior life and sustain the endeavors of those who are filled with the apostolic spirit. Moreover, as if foreseeing the dangers of the life of action to which We have drawn attention in speaking of the "heresy of action," while commending and encouraging zeal in spreading the Kingdom of Christ, they desired to give the first place to the interior life, well knowing that this is of immensely greater value than any human activities whatsoever in winning souls to God.

Consequently, as We called to mind when commemorating the centenary of the founding of the "Apostleship of Prayer," all associations of the faithful, and especially those which go by the name of "Catholic Action," will necessarily be united the more closely to Christ and among themselves by that charity "which is the bond of perfection," the more abundantly they draw from this copious fountain "of water springing unto eternal life." Through this union of spirits and harmony of activities, not only will they reap a richer harvest from their labors, but above all they will enthrone in the hearts of men the triumphant peace of Christ, in which all are called in one body.[4]

In the course of time, owing to special circumstances, certain other societies have either grown out of the "Apostleship of Prayer" or become associated with it, adopting its devotional practices while at the same time having their own peculiar methods and aims. Such are, for example, the "Eucharistic Crusade" and the "League of the Sacred Heart." The former, which has had a great development among youth the world over, has drawn amazing numbers of children — the delight of the Sacred Heart — to the practice of frequent and even daily Communion, has inspired them with genuine love of God and a steadfast zeal for the winning of souls, and has even enkindled in very many the desire to give themselves entirely to God; so that Our Predecessor Pius XI declared that the "Eucharistic Crusade" should be called as it were the training ground and apprenticeship of "Catholic Action." Hence We are very happy to learn that this organization, duly adapted to more advanced age-groups, has enrolled under various names great numbers of young people who are receiving a more exact and complete training in the school of Christ.

Worthy of special mention is the association called the "League

---

[4] Col. 3:14.

of the Sacred Heart" or "League of Perseverance," which brings together either men of mature age or young men who have already often made the Spiritual Exercises, especially for the purpose of meeting at least once a month to attend Mass and receive Holy Communion in a body. How many of the faithful in town and country, impressed by these outstanding examples of Christian life, have been gently constrained to return to a better way of living! How many, by freely enrolling in these armies of peace, either for the "re-education of the moral sense" or for the promotion of temperance or for other enterprises of the same sort, have by their example highly proved of what value for restoring Catholic life are these associations of men fighting for religion and for hearth and home under the standard of the Most Sacred Heart of Jesus. Small wonder then that, in view of so many great benefits already accrued to the Catholic cause, sure pledges of even greater harvests in the years to come, the Bishops in a number of places have declared that the Leagues of the Sacred Heart are the picked troops of "Catholic Action," because they are admirably organized and trained to do that work.

In this connection We would not pass over in silence those radio transmissions which, only recently begun, are now broadcast in various languages from more than six hundred stations, reaching fifteen million people. These radio programs, kindling as it were sparks of virtue and love of God in the hearts of the listeners, are well designed not only to nourish but also to stimulate to fresh activity the desire of a fervent Christian life, in the home, in the business and professional world and in the conduct of government. While heartily congratulating each and every member for all these benefits to the Church and praying that God may prosper your undertakings with ever more abundant fruit, We impart with deep affection to you, beloved Son, and to all your colleagues in this work, as well as to all the members of the "Apostleship of Prayer" and to all the associations which are linked with it either in origin or by the bonds of charity, Our Apostolic Benediction, as a pledge of the divine munificence and a testimony of Our own good will.

Given at Castel Gandolfo near Rome, the nineteenth day of September, in the year nineteen hundred and forty-eight, the tenth of Our Pontificate.

AAS 40-500; Pius XII, Letter, 19 Sept., 1948.

The J.O.C.: Letter of Pius XII on Twenty-Fifth Anniversary (Pius XII, 21 March, 1949) AAS 41-324.

A Letter of Pius XII to Canon Joseph Cardijn on the twenty-fifth anniversary of the founding of the *Jeunesse Ouvrière Chrétienne:*

Among the joys which divine Providence seems to have in store for Us on the occasion of the coming Holy Year, one which will be particularly consoling to Our heart, burdened as it is with all sorts of sorrows and anxieties, is the coincidence of this great Jubilee of all christendom with the one whereby Our sons and daughters of the *Jeunesse Ouvrière Chrétienne* will celebrate the twenty-five years of their dear and glorious movement. A quarter of a century ago, when in the midst of countless difficulties and contradictions you were laying on the soil of Belgium the first foundations of this edifice, who could have dreamed that within a few years it would grow to such vast proportions and would soon extend not only to Belgium and to many countries of Europe, but even to far-off America and nearly to the whole world?

It has been so because this movement came at its appointed hour in the design of Providence to help in the solution of a problem which is not peculiar to one region or to one continent, the problem presented to-day to the Christian conscience by the lot of so many workers menaced with the loss of their most precious good — faith in God, the supernatural life, the eternal salvation of their souls. To give them or give them back, beginning with the young people, to Christ and to the Church, that was from the beginning the ideal which inspired you, and with which you have been able to inspire thousands of straightforward and generous hearts. The results we have before our eyes: they are those admirable ranks of militants of both sexes, of whom the Church is rightly proud because she sees in them a promise and pledge of the rechristianization of the world of labor.

It was well that the fruits of the intense and often unheralded devotedness of these disciples of Christ should be manifested openly, as they will be on the occasion of this Jubilee Convention.

But far more than its territorial extent — which was so strikingly shown by the recent *Semaine d'Études* of Montreal, with its delegates from 42 nations — what the J.O.C. will manifest to the world on this memorable occasion, and what constitutes its real greatness, is the deep Christian formation, the apostolic and conquering ardor, which it has been able to give its adherents, sending forth, like leaven in the dough, these young heralds of the good cause, who fearlessly confess their faith before those who have lost the faith and who despise or oppose it. We appreciate too well the merits of these young workers, both men and women, who paying no attention to mockeries and taunts steadfastly pursue their work of conquest, to refrain from giving them here the praise which is their due. Let them continue their work, never slackening their drive! The conditions of the hour in this turning point of history demand their apostolate more urgently than ever before.

It is surely evident that, if every social condition has its important part to play in a transformation of the world such as is going on today, the working class for its part is called upon to assume today responsibilities which were unknown to it in the past. And it is equally clear that many of its members, seduced by a false ideal of human redemption, claim to find in the false theories of atheistic materialism the only adequate solution to the distressing problems of the working class. Now, it is not by assuming in the face of the false leaders a negative and merely defensive attitude, that one can hope to solve these problems. It is by the active presence in the midst of the factories and yards, of pioneers fully conscious of their double vocation — as Christians and as workers — determined to shoulder their responsibilities to the full and to acknowledge neither compromise nor halt until they have transformed their environment according to the demands of the Gospel. It is by such positive, constructive work that the Church will be able to extend her life-giving action to the millions of souls whom she embraces with such ardent maternal solicitude; and it is also to this sublime task that the young Christian leaders of labor formed by the J.O.C. are called to lend a hand.

For this work which might seem superhuman, they will find strength in the daily living of a sacramental and eucharistic life ever more intense, in a never-ceasing union with the Master of all purity, of all love, of all apostolate, the Saviour Jesus, in filial recourse to His Mother, the Most Holy Virgin Mary. They will find it also in loyal and generous adherence to the directives of the Hierarchy, and especially to the social doctrine of the Church, and in a fraternal and joyous cooperation with the other movements of Catholic Action, with a view to establishing the Kingdom of God throughout human society.

To this goal, We are sure, have been directed the personal efforts of all those — militants, jocists, chaplains — who are now methodically preparing for the celebration of the twenty-fifth anniversary of their movement. We are deeply convinced that this is also the pledge of effective and durable action on the part of this Jubilee Convention, which, far from aiming solely at an external and passing success, wishes to be the occasion for a deepening and renewal of spirit and of the apostolic methods and influence of the J.O.C. in the world.

Even now We invoke the most abundant graces of God upon this preparation, upon those who inaugurated it and those who will carry it through. And in order to give you a new token of the benevolence with which We have followed, with Our good wishes and Our prayers, the development of the J.O.C. and the imposing task which the coming celebrations are to consecrate, We send to you, dear Son, to yourself personally and to all the Jocists of the world, and in particular to those who, in the name of their distant brethren, will during these days form a magnificent crown around their founder and father, Our affectionate paternal Apostolic Blessing.

The Vatican, 21 March, 1949.

AAS 41-324; Pius XII, Letter, 21 March, 1949.

Sodality of Our Lady: How to Be Propagated (Pius XII, Letter, 15 April, 1950) AAS 42-437.

An Apostolic Letter of Pius XII to the Very Reverend John Baptist Janssens, General of the Society of Jesus:

Beloved Son, health and Apostolic Benediction.

When We learned that the so-called "Promoters" of the Marian Congregations which depend upon the Society of Jesus were meeting in Rome in order to confer together on the promotion and advancement of these Congregations according to Our wishes, which had already been frequently expressed especially in the Apostolic Constitution, *Bis. saeculari,*[1] We were unwilling to let

---

[1] Ap. Const., Pius XII, 27 Sept., 1948; AAS 40-393; reported in this same Volume 3 of CANON LAW DIGEST, under this same canon 684.

the occasion pass without communicating to these, Our very dear children, by this Letter, Our paternal assent and approval.

We know very well that the Consociations of this kind which are governed by you are very few in number compared with all the Sodalities to-day existing in the world; but We know too that not infrequently the Congregations which you have are such as may be an example to others. And this certainly must be a stimulus to you to strive that all your Sodalities may be truly worthy, and may daily grow more worthy, to be looked up to as models. For, although the Sodalities which are affiliated to the *Prima Primaria* of the Roman College are a thing not peculiar to the Society of Jesus alone but common to the universal Church, yet it cannot be denied, as We have said elsewhere (AAS 40, p. 397), that, from their beginning and thereafter in the course of time, they absorbed from the Society of Jesus their spirit of more excellent sanctity and of more ardent apostleship; and that even to-day they can expect from the sacred militia of Ignatius the most perfect example and the most effective inspiration.

For this reason We were thinking also of you, sons of the Society of Jesus, when We expressed Our ardent desire that these spiritual forces should be propagated as widely as possible and should flourish vigorously throughout the world (AAS 40, p. 399), and when We further declared that now, of all times, they are especially necessary (*ibid.*, p. 395); when We said that they "lack no characteristic which belongs to Catholic Action" (*ibid.*, p. 398), since the Church rather favors "a multiform unity in carrying out apostolic works, which, by brotherly cooperation under the guidance of the Bishops, should be directed through united efforts to one goal" (*ibid.*, pp. 398, 399). For We had this in mind when We encouraged the Sodalities of Our Lady to regard it as their peculiar task to form and lead into action most select bands of apostles, who should prove themselves the salt of the earth and as it were a heavenly leaven of virtue among men (*ibid.*, 40, pp. 395, 401; 39, p. 632). We do not doubt that these Our wishes are entirely known to you, and that, with your traditional will to obey, you ardently desire to put them into practice to the best of your ability. But We are pleased here once more to declare that, in this magnificent progress and expansion of the lay apostolate which is characteristic of our times, it is for the Vicar of Christ a source of intense joy and consolation to see the Marian Sodalities occupying as it were a conspicuous place; and that he expects the sons of your Society according to the spirit of their Institute to work vigorously in developing and promoting these Sodalities. The Church expects much of you; she wishes that the Marian Sodalities shall hold their place everywhere; in other words that they may be fit to be called with full right, Catholic Action under the patronage of the Blessed Virgin, and that they may have the same rank as other Consociations which further the work of the apostolate under the one authority of the Ecclesiastical Hierarchy (*ibid.*, 40, p. 402).

Now We wish to say to you what We said once before of the Sodalities which are affiliated to the *Prima Primaria*, and which therefore must have the peculiar qualities which We described in the Apostolic Constitution, *Bis saeculari*. We declared that these special characteristics "are no obstacle whatever to calling the Marian Congregations with the fullest right, Catholic Action under the auspices and inspiration of the Blessed Virgin Mary" (*ibid.*, p. 398); and that these very qualities give them surely a notable place in the ranks of Catholic Action, and one which is most useful and almost absolutely necessary. For the Marian Congregations, such is their history and nature, are peculiarly designed to develop these very beautiful qualities: first, the quality of sanctity which is a true and solid sanctity and which may be said to be the best according to the state of life of each Sodalist (*ibid.*, pp. 394, 395); then the quality of the Christian formation of the Sodalities so that really every one of them is an example to his associates in family and social life (*ibid.*, p. 407); finally, the quality of complete and unfailing obedience and reverent service to Christ and His Church, under the guidance and leadership as it were of the Blessed Virgin Mary; and this is surely a most favorable sign for this century of ours, which will be distinguished by the name of Mary and has the happiness of experiencing more intimately the protection and powerful patronage of the Mother of God.

In view of all this, We urge you to go forward fearlessly in this way which you have chosen, even though you will find in it at times various obstacles to be encountered. Relying on the help of God and His Mother, remembering the wishes and commands of the Vicar of Jesus Christ, lay aside all hesitation and delay, and advance the work of the Marian Congregations with energy, according to their spirit and laws: first of all, see to it that there be a severe screening of candidates, and that only those be chosen who really aspire to higher things and have a desire for the apostolic spirit; also, let interior spiritual training have the principal place in your Sodalities, for without this you should regard all merely exterior activity as empty or suspect. But this solid spiritual training and the apostolic activity which flows from it must have an altogether Marian character; for indeed the pious propensity to honor and love the Blessed Virgin, which your Sodalities have always professed, should everywhere and always be regarded as the talisman and distinguishing mark of true faith and sound doctrine.

And do not be too solicitous to win the approval of the crowd: for after the example of Christ the Lord you have come, not to flatter the ears of the worldly, but to give testimony to the truth. Finally, do not hesitate to use this most effective instrument of sanctity and apostleship especially among those classes of people who most need to be imbued with this spirit of Christ, or who are best able to infuse it into the veins of human society; first among working people, and also among those who are engaged in higher studies. We well know that work of this kind is not easy, that it offers many difficulties; but we know too that it is not your habit to devote yourselves to the easier tasks, but rather to those which are more fruitful for the greater glory of God. Besides, since God has entrusted you with a great gift such as the Marian Congregations, you must regard as addressed to you that warning of Jesus Christ: "unto whomsoever much is given, of him much will be required" (Luke 12:48).

We do not think it necessary to dwell at great length on this Our exhortation, since We well know your consideration for the Bishops and Ordinaries of places and your due obedience to them; We are also quite aware that it is your sincere desire to cooperate in fraternal concord with other apostolic groups according to the norms which We laid down in the Apostolic Constitution, *Bis saeculari*.

Meanwhile, as a token of heavenly blessings and a mark of Our paternal benevolence, We affectionately impart to you, beloved Son, to all the members of the Society of Jesus, and especially to those who are engaged in promoting and directing

Marian Congregations, and to their students, Our Apostolic Blessing.

Given at Rome, from St. Peter's, the 15th of April, in the year 1950, the twelfth of Our Pontificate.

AAS 42–437; Pius XII, Apostolic Letter, 15 April, 1950. Cf. *Periodica*, 39–299 (Fábregas).

Rotary Clubs: Clerics Not to Join or Attend Meetings (Holy Office, 11 Jan., 1951) AAS 43–91.

A Decree of the Holy Office:

This Supreme Sacred Congregation has been asked whether it is allowed to Catholics to join the Association commonly called "Rotary Club."

The Eminent and Most Reverend Cardinals who are in charge of the protection of faith and morals, after having heard the opinion of the Reverend Consultors, in the plenary session of Wednesday the 20th of December, 1950, decided to reply:

Reply. Clerics are not allowed to join the Association "Rotary Club," nor to be present at its meetings; the laity should be urged to observe the prescription of canon 684 of the Code of Canon Law.

And on the 26th day of the same month and year, His Holiness by divine Providence Pope Pius XII, in the audience granted to His Excellency the Most Reverend Assessor of the Holy Office, upon receiving a report of the resolution of the Eminent Fathers, approved it and ordered it to be published.

Given at Rome, from the Holy Office, 11 January, 1951.

AAS 43–91; Holy Office, Decree, 11 Jan., 1951. Annotations: *Periodica*, 40–111 (Hürth); *Monitor Ecclesiasticus*, 1951, p. 213 (Pellegrini).

The Apostleship of Prayer: Efficacious Means of Apostolate (Pius XII, Letter, 28 Oct., 1951) AAS 44–365.

A Letter of His Holiness Pius XII to John Baptist Janssens, General of the Society of Jesus and World Director of the Apostleship of Prayer, approves the new Statutes and recommends the Association to Prelates and pastors.

Text of the Letter:

Beloved Son, health and Apostolic Benediction:

Religious organizations best serve the needs of the times when, on occasion, without giving up their peculiar spirit, they adapt themselves to changing conditions. The Apostleship of Prayer often has recognized this in the past. In one hundred years this association has grown from humble origins into a vast undertaking, and from time to time, as in 1896, it has revised its Statutes without surrendering those elements essential to its peculiar spirit.

Through the past fifty years the Holy See has issued many letters and exhortations having to do with various phases of the apostolate. These letters have praised the Apostleship of Prayer as being most suited to our times. With wise judgment the Directors thought to make the Apostleship even more effective by incorporating into it the strengthening ideas of these Apostolic letters. Accordingly they have reconsidered the Statutes of the Association and have submitted them in new form to this Holy See.

We ourselves are very familiar with the fruitful work of the Apostleship of Prayer. Out of zeal for souls and for the extension of Christ's Kingdom, We have recommended it many times to all. So We had these revised Statutes examined and have found them to be most worthy of Our full approbation.

The Statutes set forth clearly the weighty importance of the Association. They show the Apostleship to be a very efficacious instrument of modern apostolic ministry both for the salvation of individuals and for the general pastoral good of souls. From those features in the new Statutes which assist most in the pastoral care of souls We pick out three as being worthy of special recommendation.

First, the Association encourages the faithful to help in the conversion of souls by the offering to God of their prayers, works, and sufferings. This labor for the extension of Christ's Kingdom not only kindles a zeal for souls, a concern for the eternal salvation of the neighbor, but it promotes and puts to work those supernatural means upon which the real success of all apostolic labor depends. Hence the Association makes the work of the apostolate most effective. Its energy is not dissipated in externals, but made to produce solid and lasting fruit.

Secondly, attention should be called to the perfect way in which the members of the Apostleship of Prayer are urged to pray for and to dedicate themselves to apostolic endeavors. They are not asked merely to recite certain prayers. Their whole lives

must be offered to God as a prayer and a sacrifice for the cause
of the apostolate. The daily offering of self is the essence of the
Apostleship of Prayer. This is perfected by other acts of piety,
especially by devotion to the Sacred Heart of Jesus. The daily
life of each member is thus converted into a sacrifice of praise,
reparation, and impetration. In this way the forces implanted in
Baptism are activated and the Christian offers his life as a sacrifice in and with Christ for the honor of God the Father and for
the salvation of souls.

All the sacred practices of which the Apostleship of Prayer
makes use to round out and to perfect this oblation, taken
together, contain the sum total of Christian perfection. Through
this sacrifice demanded by the apostolate, they put into the
hands of all men the means by which Christians sanctify their
lives. Personal holiness renders their apostolate most fruitful.

Finally, in as much as the Apostleship of Prayer offers "the
most perfect form of Christian life" (Letter of Pius XII to the
General of the Society of Jesus, 19 Sept., 1948; AAS 40–500)[1]
and contains within itself a rule and compendium for the pastoral care of souls, pastors will find the Apostleship of great use
in all the ramifications of their ministry.

If the reverend pastors will introduce the flocks committed to
their care to the spiritual practices of the Apostleship of Prayer,
they will satisfy no small part of their pastoral obligations. For
when they persuade the faithful to make the daily Morning
Offering, they are teaching them that one's whole life should be
offered, together with the offering of Christ, to God the Father.
They are teaching them that they should aspire daily to the
perfection of Christian life, in which each one tries to make
himself a worthy offering to God. When they prompt the faithful
to unite this self-offering with the Eucharistic Sacrifice and to
approach the Holy Table as often as possible in a spirit of
reparation, these reverend pastors are teaching their people to
consider the unbloody Sacrifice of the Altar as the very center
of their lives.

Moreover, when a pastor urges his people, as devoted children
of Mary, to make their daily offering through her, when he
persuades them to say the Rosary in honor of her merciful and

---

[1] Reported above in this volume under this same canon 684.

loving heart, he is instilling in them an active and solid devotion to the Virgin Mother of God. Likewise, when the associates are taught to offer daily their prayers, sufferings, and works for the needs of the Church according to the wishes of the Vicar of Christ, or as it is usually put, for his intentions, they not only foster in themselves love for the Church and full conformity with her, but they also promote an intense love for the Supreme Pontiff, without which there can be no true union between the members and the Head of the Mystical Body of Christ. Finally, through a most ardent devotion to the Sacred Heart of Jesus, which is as it were the soul of this Pious Association, the faithful are led to an intimate union with Christ; for then brotherly love becomes more fervent, their prayers, works, and sufferings acquire the utmost efficacy, then in fine is enkindled the desire to consecrate themselves to the Divine Heart and to offer Him assiduous acts of atonement, for which, as He promised, we know that He will and actually does pour out upon the human race involved in so many miseries, torrents of mercy and of grace.

Nor should we overlook the fact that the Apostleship of Prayer, which We have termed as it were a compendium of the pastoral ministries, can, by means of the special "sections" organized by it, such as the "Leagues or Federations of the Most Sacred Heart" for men, the "Eucharistic Crusade" for children, both of which this Apostolic See has more than once highly praised, adapt itself to different classes of people and thus more fully satisfy the temperament, aspirations, and requirements of each individual.

Therefore by virtue of Our authority We most willingly approve of the new Statutes of the Pious Association of the Apostleship of Prayer; and again We recommend it to the Bishops in the full confidence that they on their part will do their best to promote it with all diligence and care. We also cherish the certain hope that this Pious Association, far from obstructing or supplanting the functions of other apostolic works, will rather raise them to a higher degree of sanctity, infusing into them that spirit of holiness and love for God and men which is perpetually burning in the Most Sacred Heart of Jesus and kindles all with its own fire.

As a pledge of heavenly favors and as a sign of Our paternal benevolence, We lovingly in Our Lord impart to you, Beloved

Son, to the Directors and to all the members of the Association, the Apostolic Benediction.

Given at Rome, from Saint Peter's, the twenty-eighth day of October, the Feast of Our Lord Jesus Christ the King, in the year 1951, the thirteenth of Our Pontificate.

AAS 44-365; Pius XII, Letter, 28 Oct., 1951. Annotations, *Monitor Ecclesiasticus,* 1952, p. 370 (Schwendimann).

Society for Old Testament Study (Pius XII, Allocution, 10 April, 1952) **AAS 44-411.**

To the Delegates from the British "Society for Old Testament Study," His Holiness Pius XII spoke as follows:

When We come to expressing a word of welcome and encouragement to such an elect group of Scripture scholars, Our memory goes back at once to what Our saintly Predecessor, Damasus, well on to sixteen centuries ago, wrote to the learned St. Jerome: "I do not believe there can be a subject more worthy of conversation between us than the Scriptures."[1] Nothing could be truer, when one reflects that from the *in principio* of Genesis to the *veni, Domine Jesu* of the Apocalypse the Holy Scriptures contain the word of God. What a precious vein of untold riches is opened up by almost any one of its sentences. But We must be brief. "Pleasant is a meadow," wrote Chrysostom, "a garden is fair; but still more pleasant is the study of Holy Scripture. In the meadow we find flowers, but they quickly fade; in Holy Scripture we hear words that have the power of immortal life. In the meadow the zephyrs blow; in the Scripture the Holy Spirit breathes. . . . In the meadow there is the passing pleasure of the senses; the reading of Scripture procures advantages of lasting value to the soul."[2]

But those spiritual advantages will be genuine and solid in proportion to one's certain and accurate knowledge of what the sacred author has said. Hence the ever present need of devoted scholars, who in their tireless research to unfold the exact meaning of the divine word will be equipped to make wise and judicious use of that vast apparatus of biblical philology, geography, history, archaeology, textual criticism, and the natural sciences,

---

[1] Ep. XXXV — Migne, *PL,* Vol. 22, col. 451.
[2] Migne, *PG,* Vol. 52, col. 395-396.

so that Eternal Truth in all its splendor may shine forth to enlighten and warm the minds and hearts of men.

It is gratifying to note from a perusal of your program that such scholars are not lacking today in the various parts of the world, and We fondly hope that many others, who have been blessed by God with large measure of natural talent, of piety and learning, will follow you in the same praiseworthy apostolate.

You are closing your study-week on a day hallowed by the memory of the glorious triumph of Him, whose sacred person hovers over all the pages of the Bible. Its different parts, like so many converging rays, focus their light on His radiant figure, the promised, the long-expected One, who at the appointed time came to fulfill the hopes and aspirations of all mankind for eternal life. His proffered gift was peace — peace with God, the Father of all. This too is the burden of Our daily prayer, the aim of all the toil and sufferings of the Church. When all men have sought and found peace with God, they will have come a long way to enjoying the blessings of a true peace between nations.

May the peace and joy of the risen Christ fill your own hearts and the hearts of those who are near and dear to you.

AAS 44-411; Pius XII, Allocution, 10 April, 1952.

NOTE: We report this address as an example of the sort of gracious and cordial courtesy which the Holy Father is happy to show toward a scholarly association which is *not distinctively Catholic*. Another notable example: the Allocution of 7 Sept., 1952 (AAS 44-732) to the World Congress of Astronomy. This latter is not to be confused with the longer discourse delivered on 22 Nov., 1951, to the members of the Pontifical Academy of Science (AAS 44-31; *The Catholic Mind*, 1952, p. 182).

Association Dissolved and Forbidden by Holy Office. See c. 211; AAS 43-477.

Belgian Christian Workers' Movement (Mouvement Ouvrier Chrétien de Belgique): Allocution to the Federated Societies. Pius XII, 11 Sept., 1949 (AAS 41-547).

Boy Scouts: Pius XII, Address to First International Congress of Catholic Boy Scouts, Rome, 6 June, 1952 (AAS 44-578).

Catholic Action: Beginning with the present Volume 3, documents on Catholic Action are reported under canon 684 instead of under canon 139 as in Volumes 1 and 2.

In Italy: Allocution of Pius XII to young women of Catholic Action in Italy, 5 Sept., 1948 (AAS 40–405); Allocution of Pius XII to young men of Catholic Action in Italy, 12 Sept., 1948 (AAS 40–409); Exhortation of Pius XII, 25 Jan., 1950 (AAS 42–247).

Catholic Press: Allocution of Pius XII to International Congress of Catholic Journalists, Rome, 17 Feb., 1950 (AAS 42–251).

Clerics and Rotary Clubs. See c. 684; AAS 43–91.

Communist Associations Condemned. See c. 2316; AAS 42–553.

Discussions With Non-Catholics. See c. 1325; AAS 40–257.

Federation of Catholic Universities: Established by Ap. Letter, Pius XII, 27 July, 1949 (AAS 42–385).

Growth of Association Into Secular Institute. See c. 488; AAS 40–293, nn. 4–7.

International Catechetical Congress. Allocution, Pius XII, 14 Oct., 1950 (AAS 42–816).

International Thomistic Congress. Allocution, Pius XII, 17 Sept., 1950 (AAS 42–734).

International Union of Societies for the Protection of the Rights of the Family: Allocution, Pius XII, 20 Sept., 1949 (AAS 41–551).

J.O.C.: Radio Address, Pius XII to the J.O.C. at their twenty-fifth anniversary reunion in Brussels, 3 Sept., 1950 (AAS 42–639).

Lay Apostolate: Allocution of Pius XII to the World Congress of the Apostolate of the Laity, 14 Oct., 1951 (AAS 43–784). English text, *The Catholic Mind,* 1952, p. 115.

Scapular of Mt. Carmel: Letter of Pius XII to the Most Rev. Kilian Lynch, O.Carm. Prior General, on the occasion of the seventh centenary of the institution of the Scapular of Our Lady of Mt. Carmel, 30 June, 1951 (AAS 43–589).

Letter of Pius XII on celebration of same centenary in Brazil, 6 July, 1951 (AAS 43–592).

Social Doctrine: Catholic Labor Unions. Allocution, Pius XII, 11 March, 1945 (AAS 37–68). Annotations, *Periodica,* 34–270 (Gundlach).

Pax Romana: Letter, Pius XII to the World Congress of Pax Romana at Amsterdam, 6 Aug., 1950 (AAS 42–635).

Public Ownership and Labor-Management Relations: These two aspects of the Church's social doctrine are touched upon in the Allocution of Pius XII to *"L'Union Internationale des Associations Patronales Catholiques,"* 7 May, 1949 (AAS 41–283).

Rural Life and Agrarian Reform. Allocution of Pius XII to farm workers of Italy, 15 Nov., 1946 (AAS 38–426). Annotations, *Periodica,* 36–83 (Gundlach).

Unemployment: the Salary Contract. Allocution of Pius XII to members of the International Congress of Social Studies, 3 June, 1950 (AAS 42–485).

Society of St. Vincent de Paul: Address of Pius XII to the assembled delegates on their apostolate of charity, 27 April, 1952 (AAS 44–468). English text, *The Catholic Mind,* 1952, p. 693.

Sodality of Our Lady and Catholic Action: Allocution, Pius XII, 5 May, 1951. English text, *The Catholic Mind,* 1951, p. 524.

Sodality of Saint Jerome (devoted to the printing and diffusion of the Gospels): Letter of Pius XII to Cardinal Tedeschini, 7 June, 1950 (AAS 42–552).

Spurious "Catholic Action" in Czechoslovakia Condemned. See c. 2314; AAS 41–333.

CANON 691

Collecting Money for the Missions: Norms. See c. 622; AAS 44–549.

CANON 692

No General Faculty to Substitute Medal for Scapular in Third Orders (S. C. Rel., 25 March, 1922) AAS 14–353.

A Reply of the Sacred Congregation of Religious:

Whereas the petition had often been made that, in view especially of the needs of certain countries, for the benefit of the faithful who might desire to join the secular Third Order of Saint Francis or other secular Third Orders, the faculty be granted to commute the little habit or scapular of the said Third Orders to a brass medal bearing some pious image, with all the rights, indulgences, and privileges which are attached to the little habit, this Sacred Congregation of Religious, after having thoroughly studied the matter, thought it appropriate to ask our Holy Father by divine Providence Pope Pius XI to determine by his Apostolic Authority what should be done in this regard.

Now His Holiness, in the audience granted on the 20th of March, 1922, to the Most Reverend Secretary of this Sacred Congregation, decided that, everything considered, the request for the said faculty ought not to be granted.

Yet, considering what Leo XIII of happy memory provided in Chapter III, § 6 of the Rule of the secular Third Order of Saint Francis, namely: "If a grave and just cause prevents someone from observing certain points of this Rule, it is allowed to dispense him in part from the Rule, or prudently to commute those points. And this faculty and power is given to the Prefects Ordinaries of the First and Third Orders of the Franciscans, and to the Visitors," His Holiness willed that the Superiors of the secular Third Order of Saint Francis should make use of the aforesaid faculty to grant the commutation above mentioned, in favor of their Tertiaries, when there is a grave and just cause for it.

Moreover he revoked, and does by the present declaration revoke, any faculty to commute the habit of any secular Third Order to a medal, which may heretofore have been granted either by rescript or in person by the Supreme Pontiffs, in writing or verbally.

All things to the contrary notwithstanding.

Given at Rome, from the Secretariate of the S. C. of Religious, 25 March, 1922.

AAS 14–353; S. C. Rel., 25 March, 1922. *Periodica*, 11–82 (Vermeersch).

Pious Works Also Required (Code Com., 4 Jan., 1946) AAS 38-162.

The Code Commission was asked:

Whether canon 692 is to be understood in the sense that, in order to enjoy the rights, privileges, indulgences, and other spiritual favors of an association of the faithful, the pious works which are legitimately prescribed for this are also necessary.

Reply. In the affirmative.

AAS 38–162; Code Com., 4 Jan., 1946.

Cf. *Periodica*, 35–188 (Schönegger) ; *Commentarium pro Religiosis*, 27–23 (Gutiérrez).

CANON 694

Adscription to a Confraternity, Even in Danger of Death, Is Invalid If the Norms of the Statutes Were Not Observed (S. C. Conc., 18 March, 1941) Private.

In a letter to the Archbishop of Taranto the Sacred Congregation of the Council declared that the adscription of the faithful in confraternities, made in danger of death, without observing the norms prescribed in the *Statuta* of the confraternities, are to be considered invalid; and that there is no occasion to revise the statutes to provide for such cases.

(**Private**) ; S. C. Conc., 18 March, 1941. Reported by Sartori, *Enchiridion Canonicum*, ed. 1944, c. 694, p. 190, from *Perfice Munus*, 1941, p. 558.

CANON 701

Precedence of Franciscan Tertiaries in Processions (S. C. Rel., 30 March, 1925) Private.

The Procurator General of the Friars Minor proposed the following questions:

1. Do the insignia which the Tertiaries of Saint Francis must wear in order to have the right of precedence according to canon 701, § 3, consist only in the sack (that is, the large outer garment of the Order, which cannot be worn publicly without the special permission of the Ordinary), or do they consist also in the chaplet which Tertiaries usually wear over their ordinary garments?

Reply. According to decrees given at other times, the Tertiaries of Saint Francis have no right of precedence in processions in which other pious lay Associations wear the sack, unless they too march in their full habit, with the sack.

2. Likewise, for the enjoyment of the aforesaid right of precedence, can the standard, which many Congregations of the Third Order use, take the place of the cross?

Reply. In the affirmative, without prejudice to legitimate custom.

(Private); S. C. Rel., 30 March, 1925. Reported by Sartori, *Enchiridion Canonicum*, ed. 1944, c. 701, pp. 191, 192, from *Il Terz' Ordine Francescano*, of Vicenza, 1926, p. 88.

CANON 706

Substitution of Standard of Tertiaries for Cross, in Processions. See c. 701; S. C. Rel., 30 March, 1925.

CANON 721

"The Apostolic Work Society": General Council for Ireland Established (S. C. Prop. Fid., Decree, 18 Nov., 1947) **AAS 40–423.**

A Decree, entitled *"De Concilio Generali Operis Apostolici in Hibernia Constituendo,"* is as follows:

The Apostolic Work under the patronage of the Holy Women of the Gospel, which, after having been started in France in the year 1838 by a pious woman named Marie Zoë Du Chesne, spread to other countries, was approved by the Supreme Pontiffs, and was several times enriched with indulgences and spiritual privileges, has lately grown to such an extent in Ireland that it has nine *diocesan centers* there, namely, in the Archdioceses of

Armagh and Dublin and in the Dioceses of Clogher, Dromore, Down and Connor, Kilmore, Limerick, Meath, and Raphoe.

The Diocesan Directors of this Apostolic Work, after their Convention held in Dublin on 24 September, 1947, asked the Sacred Congregation for the Propagation of the Faith to establish in that city a center duly acknowledged and approved for the entire Apostolic Work for Ireland, to which the diocesan centers already established or hereafter to be established might be aggregated. Accordingly, this Sacred Congregation, receiving favorably the petition so presented by the aforesaid Directors, now by this present Decree provides as follows:

1° The Pious Union of the faithful under the name of the Apostolic Work under the Patronage of the Holy Women of the Gospel, commonly called "The Apostolic Work Society," which already exists in the above-named dioceses of Ireland, or which may be established in others with the consent and by authority of the Ordinaries, shall depend entirely on the Sacred Congregation for the Propagation of the Faith.

2° The purpose of this Apostolic Work is to provide for the Catholic foreign Missions, through the industry of the pious women who are associated together, priestly vestments and other sacred furnishings necessary for divine worship and Holy Mass, and also to pray often for the growth of the Missions, especially on the occasions of the meetings of the Association and on its religious feasts.

3° The General Council, which, as requested in the aforesaid petition shall have its proper headquarters in the city of Dublin, shall consist of the diocesan Directors named by the respective local Ordinaries.

4° The General Director, who must be an ecclesiastic, shall be elected by the General Council and approved by the Sacred Congregation for the Propagation of the Faith.

5° The General Director shall never be chosen from the religious Orders, Congregations, or pious Societies whose members in virtue of their foundation are devoted to the foreign missions.

6° It shall be in the power of the General Council to choose a woman of commendable piety and moral character, who has deserved well of the foreign Missions, to take part in the meetings and deliberations of the Council as a representative of the associated pious women.

7° The various diocesan centers which have heretofore been canonically erected in Ireland as well as those which may hereafter be established with the consent and by authority of the Ordinaries, shall be fully aggregated according to the Code of Canon Law to the General Council in Dublin.

8° Every year an account is to be rendered by the General Director to the Sacred Congregation for the Propagation of the Faith, of the state of the Apostolic Work, the administration of temporal affairs, and the things which have been supplied to the foreign Missions.

9° General Statutes of the Apostolic Work shall as soon as possible be drawn up by the General Council and submitted for examination and approval to the same Sacred Congregation.

Finally, the members of the aforesaid Consociation will be entitled to all the indulgences and spiritual privileges which the Supreme Pontiff Pius XI of happy memory, by his Apostolic Letter in the form of a Brief, of 29 June, 1926, already granted to the Apostolic Work, "to the end that the Apostolic Work may continue to grow from day to day, not only in the dioceses of France and Italy but also in other parts of the Christian world." An index of these indulgences and spiritual privileges is annexed to this Decree.[1]

Given at Rome, from the Sacred Congregation for the Propagation of the Faith, on the 18th of November, Feast of the Dedication of the Basilicas of the Holy Apostles Peter and Paul, in the year 1947.

AAS 40–423; S. C. Prop. Fid., Decree, 18 Nov., 1947.

---

[1] It is omitted from this translation; see AAS 40–425.

BOOK III

THINGS

Canons 726–1551

BOOK III

THINGS

Canons 726–1551

CANON 731

Norms Concerning Sacraments and Ecclesiastical Burial for Schismatics (Holy Office, 15 Nov., 1941) **Private.**

The Apostolic Visitor for the Ukrainians in Germany addressed the following questions to the Holy Office:

Questions: 1. As cases frequently arise in which "Orthodox" Christians, who are not united to the Church, when they cannot have an Orthodox minister, call for the services of a Catholic priest, especially in dangerous illness, is it allowed to assist an Orthodox person who is ill, by prayers, by moving him to an act of contrition, and to confer the sacraments on him if he explicitly asks for them?

2. It goes against the inclination of a Catholic priest to leave an Orthodox brother in Christ without any ecclesiastical burial. On the other hand, to turn a deceased Orthodox person over to a Protestant minister for ecclesiastical funeral services is contrary to Catholic sentiment. What should be done in such a case?

3. Orthodox parents present their children for baptism. No Orthodox priest is available. Is it allowed to baptize the child (not in the church) in the sacristy, and to inscribe his name in the baptismal register, not in the ordinary series of names, but separately?

Reply. After having thoroughly considered these questions,

299

this Supreme Sacred Congregation, in the plenary session of Wednesday 29 Oct., 1941, decided to reply:

Let the Catholic priest, with generous charity, endeavor to bring back to the Church those schismatics whom Ordinaries and pastors are bidden to regard as *especially commended to them in the Lord* (c. 1350, § 1). He should paternally visit the sick and, especially if they are in danger of death, exhort them to prayer, to contrition for their sins and submission to the will of God (c. 1350, § 1).

However, it is forbidden to administer the sacraments of the Church to schismatics, even if they are in good faith and ask for them, unless they have previously rejected their errors and been reconciled to the Church (c. 731, § 2). Even when they are in danger of death, it is required that, at least implicitly, they reject their errors as far as this can be done (considering the circumstances and persons), and make a profession of faith.

To those who are in good faith and already deprived of consciousness, the sacraments may be administered conditionally, especially if there is reasonable ground to conjecture that they have at least implicitly rejected their errors.

Care must always be taken, however, that scandal and even the suspicion of interconfessionalism be avoided. And the less danger there is in delay, the more should an explicit retractation of errors and a profession of the Catholic faith be required.

As to burial, the *Roman Ritual*, Tit. VI, c. 2, concerning those who are to be refused burial, is to be observed (c. 1240). But the priest may, without any sacred vestments or sacred rites, recite prayers privately at the house where the body is laid out, accompany the funeral for the sake of civil courtesy, and also recite prayers privately at the grave in the cemetery, avoiding all occasion of scandal.

Children who are presented by schismatical parents for baptism, except in danger of death, should generally not be baptized by a Catholic priest unless there is probable hope of their Catholic education (c. 751).

(**Private**); Holy Office, 15 Nov., 1941. *Il Monitore Ecclesiastico*, Vol. 54, 1942, p. 114. Cf. *Periodica*, 37–97 (Umberg).

Communists: Marriage of, as to assistance of priest. See **c. 1065**; AAS 41–427. To be refused the Sacraments. See **c. 2314**; AAS 41–334.
Discussions With Non-Catholics. See **c. 1325**; AAS 40–257.

CANON 733

Use of the Vernacular in Administration of Sacraments Not Granted (S. C. Rit., 29 July, 1950) **Private.**

A certain Bishop asked for his priests the faculty of using the vernacular in a particular ritual for administering Baptism and Extreme Unction, and for himself the faculty of using the same in administering Confirmation.

Reply. The S. C. of Rites, 29 July, 1950 (Prot. N. P. 45/50) replied: *Non solere concedi.*

(Private); S. C. Rit., 29 July, 1950. *Monitor Ecclesiasticus,* 1952, p. 449. The annotator in *Monitor Ecclesiasticus* (Indelicato) states, however, that in 1947 the Sacred Congregation approved for the dioceses of France a ritual with a predominantly Latin text, in which certain variations in French were permitted. More recently a Swiss Ordinary, because of the proximity of his diocese to France, asked for the same privilege, which was granted by the S. C. Rit., 19 May, 1952 (Prot. N. L. 31/52).

CANON 734

One-Year Indult to Use Last Year's Sacred Oils (S. C. Rit., Decree, 28 Jan., 1944) **AAS 36–60.**

A Decree of the Sacred Congregation of Rites, entitled, *Sacred Oils Prepared in the Year 1943,* is as follows:

Since for various reasons, in the disturbed conditions of the present time, it is in many places scarcely possible to obtain olive oil in suitable quantities for making the sacred chrism, oil of catechumens, and oil for the sick, the Sacred Congregation of Rites, wishing to meet this difficulty as best it can, declares that, in dioceses where new olive oil cannot be obtained in sufficient quantity, after the Bishop shall have as usual prepared the holy oils during the Mass on Holy Thursday according to the *Roman Pontifical,* the old chrism, oil of catechumens, and oil for the sick shall not be burned, but the sacred ministers shall continue to use it until it is exhausted, and then shall use the new holy oils. The present indult is to be good only for this year.

All things to the contrary notwithstanding. January 28, 1944.

AAS 36–60; Decree, S. C. Rit., 28 Jan., 1944.

CANON 750

Observance of This Canon: Urged by Pius XII. See c. 1099; AAS 40–305.

CANON 751

Infants of Schismatical Parents: Baptism. See c. 731; Holy Office, 15 Nov., 1941.

Observance of This Canon: Urged by Pius XII. See c. 1099; AAS 40–305.

CANON 756

Child Born of Dissident Oriental Father and Latin Catholic Mother and Wrongfully Baptized in Dissident Oriental Church, Belongs to the Latin Rite (S. C. Eccl. Or., 11 July, 1952) **Private.**

The S. C. for the Oriental Church was asked:

Titius was born in 1932 of a dissident Oriental father and a Latin mother. But in 1930 his father and mother, after giving the usual *cautiones,* contracted marriage before the Latin pastor of the mother. Notwithstanding these *cautiones,* the father had Titius baptized in the dissident Oriental church. Later the father died and the mother saw to it that Titius attended the Latin church, so that he never appeared in any Oriental church. Now Titius wants to contract marriage with a Latin Catholic; and the question is whether Titius is to be regarded as belonging to the Oriental rite, so that the marriage should be contracted before an Oriental pastor.

Reply. Titius certainly belongs to the Latin rite (c. 756). (Private); S. C. Eccl. Or., 11 July, 1952. *The Jurist,* 12–475, 476, 477.

Children of Oriental Dissident-Latin Catholic Marriage belong to Latin rite. See c. 1097; private reply of S. C. Eccl. Orient., 11 July, 1952.

CANON 759

The Use of Saliva in the Administration of Baptism (S. C. Rit., 14 Jan., 1944) **AAS 36–28.**

Decree of the Sacred Congregation of Rites:

The care and vigilance with which the Catholic Church strives to observe the rites and ceremonies which are established by apostolic tradition and the decrees of the holy Fathers in the Holy Sacrifice of the Mass and in the administration of the sacraments, is clear from her constant solicitude in publishing liturgical books and requiring them to be faithfully used everywhere. Moreover the Council of Trent (Sess. VII, cap. 13) issued a decree regarding these rites as follows: "If any one says that the accepted and approved rites of the Catholic Church, which are customarily used in the solemn administration of the sacraments, can be contemned, or omitted at will by the ministers without sin, or changed into other new rites by any pastor of churches, let him be anathema." Nevertheless, this constitutes no objection against the change of the rites and ceremonies by competent ecclesiastical authority, when a grave reason makes it advisable, lest the faithful become alienated from the reception of the sacraments. Now, since many Bishops, priests and missionaries have made it known that sometimes in the administration of baptism both to children and to adults, there is danger of contagion in touching the ears and nostrils of the person being baptized, with saliva from one's own mouth, the Sacred Congregation of Rites, by command of His Holiness Pius XII, decreed that the rubric of the *Roman Ritual,* Tit. II, cap. II, n. 13, be revised as follows: *"Postea sacerdos pollice accipit de saliva oris sui (quod omittitur quotiescumque rationabilis adest causa munditiei tuendae aut periculum morbi contrahendo vel propaganda) et tangit aures et nares infantis. . . . "*; and ordered that it be inserted in future editions of the *Roman Ritual.* All things to the contrary notwithstanding. January 14, 1944.

AAS 36–28; S. C. Rit., Decree, 14 Jan., 1944.
Periodica, 33–252 (Hanssens).

CANON 782

Confirmation in Danger of Death (S. C. Sacr., 14 Sept., 1946) **AAS 38–349.**

This important document consists of three sections, of which we present a complete translation of the first two.

I

DECREE

ON THE ADMINISTRATION OF CONFIRMATION TO PERSONS WHO ARE IN DANGER OF DEATH FROM GRAVE ILLNESS

Catholic doctrine proclaims that the gifts of the Holy Spirit are conferred by the sacrament of Confirmation. Hence it is the earnest desire of the Church that children, after they have been cleansed in the waters of baptism, shall receive this sacrament, through which the gifts of the heavenly Paraclete are imparted to strengthen the faith conferred in baptism, so that, suffused with the fulness of grace and marked with the character of soldiers of Christ, they may be equipped in fact and by profession for every good work.

Though it is beyond dispute that Confirmation is not required as a necessary means to salvation (canon 787), yet because of its high excellence and the abundance of precious gifts which it bestows, pastors and other shepherds of souls should make every effort that no one who has the opportunity to receive so great a sacrament of the Redemption should fail to do so; for it is a wonderful help to fight valiantly against the wiles of the devil and the allurements of the world and the flesh, and to obtain on earth an increase of grace and of all virtues, and in heaven an added crown of glory.[1]

It is true, the watchful shepherds of souls do their utmost to see that all baptized persons be duly fortified with this sacrament, and that this be done as soon as they attain the age of reason, that is, at about the age of seven years: and it is of course quite licit to anticipate this age, as is expressly provided in canon 788, "if an infant is in danger of death or if the minister of the sacrament for just and grave reasons thinks it expedient." Yet it is a fact proved from the records available in this matter, that very many children, being more exposed to mortal perils even long before they reach the age of reason, die without being confirmed, especially in these times following the dreadful scourge of war; and daily experience shows that the same is true of not a few adults who for various reasons were unable to receive Confirmation in their youth.

There is a provision against this evil in the Oriental Church, where it is the practice to confirm infants immediately after they have received baptism. Indeed this same discipline was in use also among the Latins in the first centuries of the Church, and in some countries it is still followed through legitimate custom: but the common law of the Latin Church, adopted in canon 788

---

[1] St. Thomas, *Summa*, III, q. 72, a. 8, ad 4.

just cited, provides that the administration of this sacrament is to be put off until about the age of seven, when the children, after receiving suitable catechetical instruction, can share more fully in the effects of the sacrament.[2]

Now the chief reason why so many Christians die without receiving the sacrament is that when they are in danger of death they have no opportunity to receive it because of the absence of the Bishop.

It is defined doctrine that only a Bishop is the *ordinary* minister of Confirmation[3] (canon 782, § 1): accordingly the Holy See has always earnestly sought that, as far as possible, the administration of this sacrament should be reserved to the Bishop as a right and duty which pertain to him. And this Sacred Congregation has always been conscientiously on guard that the reverence due to this sacrament be not diminished nor the pious expectations of the people be disappointed through being deprived of the presence of the Bishop; and that the conspicuous splendor of its administration be not allowed to wane, nor its solemn and becoming ceremonial be slighted.

Yet, when necessity and the good of the faithful have demanded it, the Holy See has more than once been obliged to permit that, when the Bishop owing to peculiar circumstances could not be had, he might be replaced by a simple priest who has some ecclesiastical dignity, as the *extraordinary* minister of this sacrament (canon 782, § 2); who should do it with becoming ceremony, always informing the people that the Bishop is the exclusive ordinary minister of this sacrament, and that it is being conferred by the priest by favor of the Holy See,[4] as clearly appears from a great number of papal indults.[5]

Hence, in order to provide for the spiritual welfare of so many infants, children, and adults, who are in danger of death because of grave illness, and who would most certainly die without Confirmation if the provisions of the common law regarding the

---

[2] Cf. S. C. Sacr., 20 May, 1934, AAS 27–11, CANON LAW DIGEST, Vol. 2, p. 185; S. C. Prop. Fid., 4 May, 1774, *Fontes,* n. 4565, Vol. VII, p. 95; Holy Office, Instruction, July, 1888.

[3] Conc. Trid., sess. VII, *De confirmatione,* can. 3.

[4] Cf. Instruction of S. C. Sacr., 20 May, 1934, Section III.

[5] Cf. the same Instruction, Section I, n. 2 (DIGEST, Vol. 2, p. 185); the Instructions of the S. C. of Propaganda and of the Holy Office cited in note 2; the Formulae of Faculties of the S. C. of Propaganda.

ordinary minister were strictly insisted on; it has appeared
necessary to this Sacred Congregation to find and apply some
remedy, to the extremely important end that so many of the
faithful may be given an opportunity of receiving Confirmation.

Reflecting on the importance of this matter, His Holiness
Pope Pius XII, desiring to provide more amply for the good of
souls, in accordance with his great solicitude for the entire Church,
deigned to commission this Sacred Congregation, empowered as
it is to solve this question, to consider the matter carefully and
thoroughly in its plenary sessions, and to report to him the
resolution which it would consider appropriate.

This Sacred Congregation then, after hearing the opinions of
a number of consultors noted for their learning and prudence,
and after having moreover carefully reviewed all the previous
documents and records which are available on the discipline of
Confirmation, carefully submitted the entire matter to the consideration of the Cardinals in several plenary sessions.

After maturely considering the opinion which was the result
of these deliberations, the same Supreme Pontiff, in the audience
granted to the Secretary of this Sacred Congregation on May 6,
1946, ordered this Sacred Congregation to issue a decree which
would set forth the discipline regarding the administration of
Confirmation in the peculiar circumstances above stated, according to the norms which he himself, of certain knowledge and
after mature deliberation, had approved and graciously declared.

Accordingly, this Sacred Congregation, in faithful obedience to
the Apostolic mandate, by the present decree decided to establish
the following provisions:

1. By general indult of the Holy See, the faculty to confer the
sacrament of Confirmation as extraordinary ministers (canon
782, § 2), only in the cases and under the conditions mentioned
below, is given to the following priests and to them only:

a) To pastors who have a territory of their own, exclusive
therefore of personal and family pastors unless these also have
their own proper, even though cumulative, territory;

b) To the vicars mentioned in canon 471 and to vicar administrators (*vicariis oeconomis*);

c) To priests to whom the full care of souls with all the rights
and duties of pastors has been entrusted in an exclusive and stable
manner in a definite territory with a determinate church.

2. The aforesaid ministers can validly and licitly confer Confirmation themselves personally, only upon the faithful who are staying in their territory, including the persons who are staying in places which have been withdrawn from the parochial jurisdiction; including, therefore, seminaries, guest-houses, sanitaria and other institutions of every sort, and religious Institutes howsoever exempt (c. 792); *provided these faithful by reason of grave illness are in genuine danger of death from which it is foreseen that they will die.*

If these ministers overstep the limits of this mandate, they must fully realize that they act invalidly and confer no sacrament, and that moreover the provision of canon 2365 remains in full operation.

3. They can use this faculty either in the episcopal city itself or outside it, whether the See is occupied or vacant, provided the Bishop of the diocese cannot be had or is lawfully impeded from conferring Confirmation in person, and there is at hand no other Bishop who is in communion with the Apostolic See, even a merely titular one, who might take his place without grave inconvenience.

4. Confirmation is to be conferred observing the discipline introduced by the Code of Canon Law as adapted to this matter, and using the rite taken from the Roman Ritual, both of which are transcribed at length and in full below: *and it is to be conferred without charge on any ground.*

5. If the persons to be confirmed have attained the use of reason, there is required in addition to the state of grace some disposition and instruction, that they may be able to receive this sacrament with profit. It is therefore the part of the minister to teach these sick persons, in a way suited to their condition, the truths which they must know, and to arouse in them some intention to receive this sacrament which will strengthen their souls. If they should afterward recover, those whose business it is should see to it that, through appropriate instructions on the mysteries of the faith, they be carefully taught the nature and effect of this sacrament.[6] (Cf. canon 786.)

6. According to canon 798, the extraordinary minister shall make a notation of the fact that the sacrament has been conferred, in the parish confirmation register, by inscribing in it his own

---

[6] Cf. Holy Office, 10 April, 1861, in *Collectanea S. C. de Prop. Fid.*, ed. 1907, Vol. 1, p. 663, n. 1213; *Catechismus Romanus, De Confirmatione.*

name and the names of the person confirmed (and in case the latter is not his own subject, also the diocese and parish to which he belongs), and of the parents and sponsor, the date and the place, finally adding the words: *"Confirmation conferred by Apostolic indult, the person being in danger of death from grave illness."* An annotation should also be made in the baptismal register according to canon 470, § 2.

If the person confirmed belongs to another parish, the minister shall as soon as possible personally give notice of the administration of the sacrament to the proper pastor by an authentic document which shall contain all the information above mentioned.

7. Extraordinary ministers are also obliged to send immediately each time to the proper diocesan Ordinary an authentic notice of the Confirmation which they have conferred, with all the circumstances which affect the case.

8. It is the part of the Ordinary of the place to inform the extraordinary ministers above mentioned, in the manner which he deems best, of the provisions of this decree, and to explain the same to them in detail, so that they may be entirely prepared to perform this important work.

9. It is also the duty of the same local Ordinary to send to this Sacred Congregation at the beginning of each year a *report* giving the number of persons so confirmed in the year just preceding, and the manner in which the extraordinary ministers in his territory have proceeded in performing this important function.

His Holiness by Divine Providence Pope Pius XII, in the audience granted to the Secretary of this Sacred Congregation on 20 August, 1946, deigned to approve the above decree and to give it his Apostolic Authority, all things to the contrary, even those worthy of special mention, notwithstanding; and he ordered that the decree be published in the *official commentary, Acta Apostolicae Sedis,* and that it have the force of law from the 1st day of January, 1947.

Given at Rome, from the office of the Sacred Congregation of the Sacraments, 14 September, 1946.

II

1. The priest to whom this faculty has been given must clearly understand that the sacrament of Confirmation must be conferred by the imposition of the hand and anointing with chrism on the forehead and by the words which are prescribed in the pontifical books approved by the Church (canon 780).

2. This sacrament, which imprints a character, cannot be repeated; but if there is a prudent doubt as to whether it was really conferred at all, or as to whether it was conferred validly, let it be conferred again conditionally (canon 732).

3. The chrism which is used in the administration of this sacrament, even by a simple priest, must be consecrated by a Bishop who is in communion with the Holy See, on the last preceding Holy Thursday; nor should old chrism be used except in case of necessity. When the blessed oil is about to give out, other olive oil which is not blessed should be added to it, even repeatedly, but in lesser quantity (canons 734, 781). It is never allowed to administer Confirmation without chrism, or to receive the chrism from heretical or schismatical Bishops. The anointing should not be done with any instrument, but with the very hand of the minister duly imposed on the head of the person to be confirmed (canon 781, § 2).

4. A priest of the Latin rite who has this faculty by indult, confers Confirmation validly on the faithful of his own rite only, unless the indult expressly provides otherwise. Priests of the Oriental rite who have the faculty or privilege of conferring Confirmation together with baptism on infants of their own rite, may not administer Confirmation to infants of the Latin rite (canon 782, §§ 4 and 5).

5. A priest who has an Apostolic privilege is bound to confer this sacrament on the persons in whose favor the faculty was granted, when they duly and reasonably ask for it (canon 785, §§ 1 and 2).

6. Although this sacrament is not necessary as a means of salvation, yet it is not right for any one to neglect it when the opportunity to receive it is presented; and pastors must see to

it that the faithful receive it in due time (canon 787).

7. According to a very ancient custom in the Church, just as in baptism, so too in Confirmation, a sponsor should be used if one can be had (canon 793).

8. The sponsor shall present only one or two persons to be confirmed, unless for just cause the minister shall judge otherwise; also there should be one sponsor for each person to be confirmed (canon 794).

9. For a person to act as sponsor, the following conditions are necessary:

1° He too must be confirmed, must have attained the use of reason and have the intention of acting as sponsor;

2° He must not belong to any heretical or schismatical sect, nor be excommunicated by a condemnatory or declaratory sentence, nor infamous by law, nor excluded from legitimate acts, nor be a deposed or degraded cleric;

3° He must not be the father, mother, or spouse of the person to be confirmed;

4° He must be designated as sponsor by the person to be confirmed, or by the latter's parents or guardians, or, in case there are none or they fail to do it, by the minister or the pastor;

5° He must, in the very act of Confirmation, physically touch the person to be confirmed, either himself or through a proxy (canon 795).

10. In order that one may be licitly admitted as sponsor, the following conditions are necessary:

1° He must be a different person from the sponsor of baptism, unless in the judgment of the minister there is a reasonable cause to the contrary, or unless Confirmation is legitimately conferred immediately after baptism;

2° He must be of the same sex as the person to be confirmed, unless in particular cases the minister for reasonable cause judges otherwise;

3° He must have attained his fourteenth year, unless the minister for just cause judges otherwise;

4° He must not be, because of any notorious crime, either excommunicated or excluded from legitimate acts or infamous by law, even though there have been no sentence, nor must he be under interdict or otherwise publicly criminal or infamous in fact;

5° He must know the rudiments of the faith;

6° He must not be a novice or professed religious in any institute, unless it is a case of necessity and the express permission of at least the local Superior has been obtained;

7° He must not be in sacred orders, unless the express permission of his proper Ordinary has been obtained (canons 796 and 766).

11. From valid Confirmation there arises between the person confirmed and the sponsor a spiritual relationship, by reason of which the sponsor has the obligation to regard the person confirmed as perpetually recommended to him, and to see to his Christian education (canon 797). But this spiritual relationship is no longer an impediment to marriage (canon 1079).

12. To prove the fact of Confirmation, as long as it is not prejudicial to any one, a single unexceptionable witness is sufficient, as is also the oath of the confirmed person himself unless he was confirmed in infancy (canon 800).

13. A priest who has dared to administer Confirmation without having the faculty to do so either by law or by grant of the Roman Pontiff, is to be suspended; if he has presumed to overstep the limits of the faculty given him, he is *ipso facto* deprived of the faculty (canon 2365).

AAS 38–349; S. C. Sacr., 14 Sept., 1946.

Commentarium pro Religiosis, 26–54 (Gutiérrez); *Nouvelle Revue Théologique,* 69–82 (Bergh).

NOTE: Section III, which consists of the Latin text of the rite to be used when Confirmation is conferred under this decree, has for obvious reasons been omitted from the translation. It is to be found in new editions of the Roman Ritual. A full and authoritative commentary on this decree, by the sub-Secretary of the Sacred Congregation, is Zerba, *Commentarius in Decretum Spiritus Sancti Munera* (Vatican Press). Cf. also: *Periodica,* 35–380 (Cappello); *Ecclesiastical Review,* 1947–256 (Connell); *Clergy Review,* 1947–80 (Mahoney); *Irish Ecclesiastical Record,* 1947–432 (Conway); *The Jurist,* 1947–226 (Hannan); *Theological Studies,* 1947–118 (Ellis).

Chaplains of Institutions Exempted From Parochial Jurisdiction Have Not the Faculty to Confirm in Danger of Death (S. C. Sacr., 30 Dec., 1946) **Private.**

The Sacred Congregation of the Sacraments was asked by a certain Ordinary:

Question. Here we have four institutions which are exempted from all parochial jurisdiction — the large city hospital, the home for the aged poor, the provincial hospital for the insane, and a sanitarium for consumptives — which are commonly called internal parishes or chaplaincies with the care of souls.

The priests or religious who are assigned to the care of the inmates have the complete care of souls, so that they can baptize, assist at marriages, perform funeral services, and are bound to keep parish registers, etc.; they lack only the obligation of applying the Mass *pro populo* or according to the intention of the Ordinary.

The diocesan Synod has the following provision in this connection: "The pastoral authority and charge of every chaplain with the care of souls is confined to the buildings which are directly used for the purpose of the pious institution, and includes only those faithful who stay there day and night as patients or servants or in the performance of some other office. Consequently, whenever the seat of some pious institution is transferred to another locality, or when the building is enlarged or diminished, without of course changing the purpose of the institution, the privilege of exemption also undergoes the same changes as do the seat or buildings themselves."

Such therefore being their juridical position, it is asked whether these chaplains can be counted among the priests mentioned in the Decree, section I, n. 1, c: "to whom the full care of souls with all the rights and duties of pastors has been entrusted in an exclusive and stable manner in a definite territory with a determinate church."

The reason for doubting is that they have not all the parochial obligations, as for example, that of applying the Mass *pro populo*. Nevertheless they are immediately subject to the Bishop and are removable at his will.

Reply. The reply of the S. C. of the Sacraments, 30 Dec., 1946, n. 8263, was: The chaplains of the four institutions mentioned, since they do not fulfill the conditions expressly and exclusively laid down in the decree of this Sacred Congregation, *Spiritus Sancti munera,* 14 Sept., 1946, section I, n. 1, c, have not the power to confirm.

(Private); S. C. Sacr., 30 Dec., 1946. Translated, with the permission of the author, from Zerba, *Commentarius in Decretum "Spiritus Sancti munera,"* p. 54. Monsignor Zerba adds the comment that an exempt territory such as this is not *territorium proprium.*

Military Chaplains Not Included in Decree on Confirmation in Danger of Death (S. C. Sacr., 2 Jan., 1947) Private.

The Sacred Congregation of the Sacraments was asked by a certain military Ordinary:

Petition. The decree, *Spiritus Sancti munera,* issued on the 14th of September, 1946,[1] seems to call for certain clarifications regarding the faculties which it may perhaps grant to military chaplains.

As is evident, these chaplains fulfill the office of pastors in all respects toward the soldiers to whose service they are assigned: therefore, within the bounds of the camp hospitals, barracks, etc., they perform all parochial functions.

The aforesaid decree gives the extraordinary faculty of administering Confirmation in the cases and under the conditions therein defined: "to pastors who have a territory of their own, exclusive therefore of personal and family pastors unless these also have their own proper, even though cumulative, territory."

The question is whether a military chaplain, who fulfills the office of pastor toward the soldiers of whom he has charge, can be considered a *personal pastor* who has his own proper territory, although cumulative; and *if not,* the same Ordinary petitions the Sacred Congregation to ask of the Holy Father the faculty of confirming for military chaplains.

Reply. The same Sacred Congregation, on the 2nd of January, 1947, n. 7687, decided to reply: *Non expedire.*

(Private); S. C. Sacr., 2 Jan., 1947. Translated, with the permission of the author, from Zerba, *Commentarius in Decretum "Spiritus Sancti munera,"* p. 46. Monsignor Zerba comments that we may implicitly infer from this reply that the Decree does not give the faculty to military chaplains.

---

[1] Reported above in this same volume under canon 782.

Confirmation in Danger of Death (S. C. Prop. Fid., Decree, 18 Dec., 1947) **AAS 40–41.**

This Decree, entitled *"De confirmatione administranda iis, qui ex gravi morbo in periculo mortis sunt constituti,"* is as follows:

Since the enactment by the Sacred Congregation of the Sacraments of the Decree *"Spiritus Sancti munera,"* of 14 September, 1946 (AAS 38–349), this Sacred Congregation for the Propagation of the Faith has received many petitions from Ordinaries of missions asking for the same or still wider faculties.

His Holiness by Divine Providence Pope Pius XII, in the audience of the 18th of this month, at the instance of the undersigned Cardinal Prefect, deigned to receive these petitions favorably.

Accordingly His Holiness granted to all local Ordinaries who depend on this Sacred Congregation for the Propagation of the Faith, without prejudice to other indults which they already have in this matter, the power by Apostolic indult (can. 782, § 2) to give to all priests who are subject to them and have the care of souls, the faculty to administer Sacred Confirmation validly to the faithful, whether adults or infants, who are within the territorial boundaries of the mission and are in danger of death; and to administer it licitly in the place of residence of the Bishop, provided there is no Bishop present in that place who is not lawfully prevented from attending; always observing the formula prescribed by the Roman Ritual.

His Holiness ordered that the present decree be prepared and published.

Given at Rome, from the Sacred Congregation for the Propagation of the Faith, the 18th day of December, 1947.

AAS 40–41; S. C. Prop. Fid., Decree, 18 Dec., 1947.

Cf. *Il Monitore Ecclesiastico,* 1948, p. 92. The anonymous commentator calls attention to the fact that the *text,* in contrast to the *title,* does not require that the danger of death be occasioned by illness.

***

Orientals: Confirmation by priest of Latin rite. See **c. 1**; AAS 40–422.

CANON 788

Ordinary Cannot Forbid That Confirmation Be Administered to Children Under Ten (Code Com., 26 March, 1952) **AAS 44–496.**

The Code Commission was asked:

Whether, considering canon 788, a mandate of the local Ordinary forbidding that the Sacrament of Confirmation be administered to children who have not reached the age of ten years, should be sustained.

Reply. In the negative.

Given at Rome, from Vatican City, 26 March, 1952.

AAS 44–496; Code Com., 26 March, 1952. Annotations, *Monitor Ecclesiasticus*, 1952, p. 408 (Bidagor).

CANON 804

Priests Celebrating Mass in Churches of Rome Must Have Written Permission From the Vicariate (Vicariate of Rome, 20 May, 1951) **Private.**

The following is the text of a Notification sent to Rectors of Churches in Rome in the name of Cardinal Micara, Vicar of Rome:

Our Predecessors frequently issued regulations regarding the admission of priests to celebrate Mass in the churches and oratories of this Holy City. Experience has shown how necessary these regulations were for maintaining discipline and preserving the respect due to the priestly character, and We consider it a duty to insist that they be continued in full force and that their observance be required.

Hence in the name and by the authority of the Holy Father, and derogating as far as may be necessary from the general dispositions of Canon Law in the matter, We ordain as follows:

1. Every priest in Rome, whether domiciled here or coming from outside, in order to be admitted to celebrate Holy Mass, must present to the rector of the church a written document from Us, granting permission to celebrate, which must be duly renewed when it expires. This document must be asked for by the rectors, even of priests who are personally known to them.

2. Priests who are not resident in Rome may be permitted to celebrate without the aforesaid document, only on the day following their arrival and on days on which it is impossible for them to obtain the document because the offices of the Vicariate are closed. But in these cases they must present authentic and valid letters of their own Ordinary, on which the rector must

attest to the consequent celebration of Mass, affixing the seal of the church.

3. These same dispositions must be observed by all who have the privilege of a private oratory, both for choosing a chaplain and for admitting other priests to celebrate Mass there.

4. In the churches and chapels of communities of women, the sister in charge of the sacristy shall receive from priests who ask to celebrate Mass, the aforesaid document in order to have it examined by the rector of the church or the chaplain of the community, who may not be appointed without Our explicit consent.

5. In the sacristy of every church, public oratory, or community chapel, a book shall be kept in which are noted the names of the priests who celebrate there either regularly or exceptionally. From this book a record of the said notations shall be taken every month, to be sent to the Vicariate; these forms must be withdrawn from the Vicariate by the rectors at the beginning of each year.

6. Both the book of priests who celebrate and the register of Masses must be immediately presented upon request to the person authorized by Us to request them.

7. Whoever contravenes the above regulations shall be subject to a fine, and in case the offense is repeated, to other penalties at Our discretion, including suspension *a divinis* in the case of priests.

8. All the above dispositions, by the express will of the Holy Father, apply also to rectors of the churches of regulars or to those which are for any reason exempt (can. 804, § 3).

9. This notice must be kept posted in a prominent place in the sacristy, so that no one can claim to be ignorant of it.

From the Vicariate, 20 May, 1951.

(**Private**); Vicariate of Rome, Notification, 20 May, 1951.

CANON 808

Norms for Dispensation From Eucharistic Fast for Priests Celebrating Mass (Holy Office, 1 July, 1931) **Private.**

This important document, not officially published, is entitled: "Norms to Be Observed by Local Ordinaries in Asking Dispensations From the Law of Eucharistic Fast for Priests Before the Celebration of Mass."

1. A dispensation from the law of Eucharistic fast can be granted so that something may be taken either in the way of drink to restore or sustain physical strength, or in the way of true medicine to obviate the effects of illness.

2. Since the reason for a dispensation to take drink is the public good of the faithful, such a dispensation can be obtained only by priests who are employed in the care of souls; a dispensation to take true medicine, since it is allowed also for private convenience, can be granted also to other priests. The former is granted only for feast days or ferial days on which Mass is to be celebrated by reason of the ministry at a late hour (after ten o'clock); the latter can be granted for any day.

3. A dispensation of this sort, since it is a grave relaxation of the law of the Church, evidently requires a *grave cause*, which must be proved in each case; hence the dispensation is never given indiscriminately to indeterminate priests, but always only to determinate individual priests, with due consideration of their personal circumstances.

4. In the petition to be addressed to the Sacred Congregation, the following must be indicated:

a) The age of the petitioner;

b) His office or charge, that is, whether he is engaged in the care of souls as a pastor or at least as a parochial vicar (canons 451–478);

c) The state of his health evidenced by the testimonial of a physician, showing what his ailment is and whether it is necessary for him to take something by way of drink or medicine, and in either case, specifically what drink or medicine is required;

d) Whether he celebrates one or two Masses on Sundays and feast days; at what hour, and in case he celebrates twice, where he does so, namely, whether in the same church or in different churches, with an indication in this latter case of their distance from each other, especially if the journey has to be made on foot;

e) Whether his place can be taken by another priest who is in better health.

All the above must be indicated the first time the dispensation is asked, but they are not required for the prorogation of the favor after it has been once obtained, if the same circumstances of the petitioner, which were explained before, continue to exist.

5. The petition of secular priests must be signed by the Bishop

himself, with an annotation of his recommendation; the petition of religious priests who are engaged in the care of souls must be signed both by the Bishop of the place where their religious house is established and by the Superior General himself; the petition of religious priests who are not engaged in the care of souls must be signed only and exclusively by their Superior General.

6. In asking for a prorogation, the earlier rescript must be presented or at least its number must be indicated.

Rome, from the Holy Office, 1 July, 1931.

(Private); Holy Office, 1 July, 1931; published in *Periodica*, Vol. 21, p. 105, with annotations by Vermeersch. See also Anglin, *The Eucharistic Fast*, p. 149.

CANON 813

An Instruction on Asking Indults for: Private Oratories: Portable Altar: Mass Without a Server: Keeping the Blessed Sacrament in Private Chapels (S. C. Sacr., 1 Oct., 1949) AAS 41–493.

An Instruction entitled: "To local Ordinaries for petitioning for apostolic indults for (I) a domestic oratory, with the extensions of such an indult; (II) a portable altar; (III) celebrating Mass without a server; and (IV) keeping the Most Blessed Sacrament in private chapels" is as follows:

1. That the respectability and beauty of the place where the unbloody Sacrifice of the New Law is celebrated is of the highest importance in view of the holiness of that same Sacrifice, is shown by the utmost care which the Catholic Church has always exercised in the choice of such a place. It is true that during the first three centuries of our era, while the persecutions were raging, the sacred Mysteries were celebrated even in private houses. But after the liberty of the Church was established and the first Christian basilicas were built, although even then Mass continued to be celebrated often enough through necessity outside the churches, yet in the course of time churches and public oratories which had been withdrawn from profane use and reserved exclusively to divine worship by a consecration or blessing, were designated as the proper place for the celebration of Mass.

And this later discipline has been received into the Code of Canon Law in canons 820–823 and 1188–1196.

2. This practice having once become firmly established, the indults which were granted by the Holy See in the course of time allowing the celebration of Mass *in private chapels* or *on a portable altar*, with the faculty of thus fulfilling the precept of hearing Mass, are to be considered as exceptions to the aforesaid law, allowed indeed for just cause, but subject to strict interpretation.

3. By a similar discipline the Church has safeguarded the *keeping of the Most Blessed Eucharist*. For, although in the first ages and even later after the restoration of peace, the Most Blessed Eucharist was kept in private houses and carried on journeys for the convenience of the faithful, yet in the course of the centuries the law became established that It too should be kept exclusively in churches and public oratories. Only by way of special privilege in favor of certain persons among the faithful who were held in high esteem because of very special services to the Church, the Holy See began in the course of time to permit that the Sacred Species be preserved also in their private chapels, under prescribed conditions and regulations suited to the holiness of this Sacrament; and this is also the law of the Code (cc. 1265–1275).

4. From an ancient practice introduced in the course of many centuries it is the accepted rule that, when Mass is to be celebrated even privately, someone should assist as minister, to serve the priest at the altar and make the responses (cf. c. 813).

Except only in certain extraordinary cases (as will be seen later in III, 2), a priest, in order to be able to say Mass without a server, needs an apostolic indult. And the sole judge of the sufficiency of the reason alleged in asking for such an indult is the Holy See itself, which must therefore be approached with a statement of the circumstances of each case.

5. Now it is known that in asking for and in using all the aforesaid faculties, no slight excesses and abuses have at times occurred. This Sacred Congregation, therefore, to which the entire discipline of the control of these indults is entrusted (c. 249), in order to remove the difficulties and inconveniences and to forestall them for the future (as stated below in I, 4), has decided to subject to a special scrutiny the entire discipline of the afore-

said indults and to supply the appropriate remedies, which are enumerated below, so that everything be put in proper order.

An effective stimulus to the performance of this task was also supplied by the Encyclical of the now gloriously reigning Pontiff, Pius XII, *Mediator Dei*, of 20 Nov., 1947,[1] on the Sacred Liturgy. This Encyclical teaches that *"the Mystery of the Most Blessed Eucharist, head and center as it were of the Christian religion,"*[2] is to be treated with due worship and appropriate religious devotion; and at the same time it earnestly recalls the liturgical and canonical prescriptions on the subject.

I. ON ASKING FOR THE INDULT OF A PRIVATE ORATORY AND EXTENSIONS OF THE SAME

1. As we have said, according to the law of the Code the proper place for the celebration of Mass is a church or a public or semi-public oratory. And except for the private chapels in cemeteries, which are mentioned in canon 1190, in order that the divine Sacrifice may be offered and that those present be able to satisfy the precept of hearing Mass in domestic oratories, there is need of a privilege or indult, which is granted only as a favor by the Holy See. The only exception is some extraordinary case, in which *by way of act,* for a just and reasonable cause, the local Ordinary, or in a house of an exempt religious Institute the Major Superior, can give permission to celebrate outside a church or oratory on a sacred stone in a fitting place, but never in a bedroom (cf. cc. 822, 1249).[3]

2. Before the Council of Trent, Bishops allowed the celebration of Mass in private oratories for the convenience of both clerics and the laity: and some regular orders had the same faculty for their subjects. But as the exercise of this right had resulted in too many indults and grave abuses were frequent, the same Sacred Synod (Sess. XXII, *de observandis et evitandis in celebratione Missae*) took this faculty away from Bishops and

---

[1] AAS 39, p. 521 seq.

[2] Cf. in the original text, AAS 39, p. 547.

[3] This faculty is to be strictly interpreted, according to the reply of the Code Commission of 16 Oct., 1919; AAS 11-478; CANON LAW DIGEST, 1, p. 384.

N.B. Except for the references to the DIGEST, all the footnotes to this Instruction are in the official text.

regular orders, with very few exceptions, and reserved it exclusively to the Roman Pontiff.

But this was not enough to prevent entirely the return of the evils which had been banished, and which usually had arisen especially from an immoderate indulgence in granting this privilege for the benefit of lay persons,[4] since Benedict XIV, who was Secretary to the S. C. of the Council which then had charge of this matter, did not hesitate to write: "it can scarcely be stated what great care and diligence were used for the right administration of this law."[5]

3. Hence various formulae of this indult were issued to suit the circumstances of the times, by which better provision might be made for the due honor of the divine Mysteries; *safeguards* were prescribed, some concerning the *decency and respectability of the place* destined for the erection of the chapel, some *determining the reasons* for which the Roman Pontiff would grant the favor, some *fixing the term* for which the indult should be valid, some finally concerning *other conditions* to which the granting of a private chapel should properly be subject; taking care especially that this indult be not granted too freely, lest, owing to the scarcity of priests, public spiritual harm to the faithful might result as regards their fulfillment of the precept of hearing Mass.

4. Even in our own times, not a few grave evils have occurred rather commonly in certain countries as a result of having too many private chapels and of neglecting the conditions attached to the apostolic indults; and these paved the way for other intolerable abuses.

These abuses, *in the matter of private oratories of lay persons,* usually flow from the following sources:

a) the *great number of these private oratories;* and in some places, because of the rivalry which the granting of the indult arouses among the faithful, this number threatens to keep on growing and to exceed all bounds;

b) the *excessive ease* with which such an indult is obtained in these days, owing to the frequent petitions of the faithful, which local Ordinaries sponsor and recommend without hesitation;

---

[4] Cf. Benedict XIV, Encycl., *Magno cum,* 2 June, 1571; *Fontes,* n. 413, Vol. II, p. 318.

[5] *Ibid.,* § 12.

c) the *lack of priests* for saying Mass in churches and public oratories on Sundays and feast days of obligation, to the spiritual harm of the faithful, if priests are drawn off to say Mass in private oratories;

d) the *place assigned to the private chapel*, which at times fails to meet canonical and liturgical requirements, is not equipped with proper furnishings, and is below the required standard of neatness and dignity, whereas often enough the other rooms of the private house are resplendent with luxury and magnificence;

e) the *excessive number of divine offices and sacred functions* which people presume to perform in such chapels, so as almost to suppress the difference between churches or public oratories and private chapels;

f) the *excessive breadth of such indults*, which often includes in addition to the persons who obtained the indult also their children, relatives by blood and marriage without limit, servants, boarders and guests, and sometimes even all persons present; extending moreover to all the days of the year without exception, and even including other faculties;

g) the *long term* of the indult, which is generally asked for the entire lifetime of the petitioner and his children, so that it sometimes happens that the privilege passes to persons who prove to be less worthy or entirely unworthy of it.

5. In order, therefore, to repress these evils and to prevent their recurrence in the future, this Sacred Congregation has decided to give to local Ordinaries the following *norms* to be carefully observed, governing *petitions* for the indult of a private oratory and the *proper use* of the indult, *especially as regards the laity*.

6. Local Bishops are to remind the faithful who ask for the indult of a domestic chapel, that the public church is the natural or certain place for divine services, and hence that it is there that the Catholic people must convene to give public social worship to God especially by assisting at Mass.

Nevertheless special circumstances may exist, together with sufficient reasons (cf. 8 below), in which it may be prudently decided that it would be very advisable that certain persons among the faithful, *who excel in moral character and in their open profession of the faith*, should for their spiritual solace be honored with the indult of a private chapel, even though they may be legally dispensed from the obligation of hearing Mass on Sundays and feast days of obligation, for example by infirmity or distance from the church. Then the Ordinaries, *after hearing, if they think proper to do so, from the local pastor,* are not forbidden to sponsor and recommend the petitions of such persons and send them to the Holy See.

The recommendation is to be made personally by the Bishop, or in case the See is vacant, by the Prelate who is his successor in the administration.

Great care should be taken that the faithful who are outstanding in authority, wealth, and position in the state, if they merit the distinction of having a domestic chapel, should go to the churches, at least on the more solemn feasts of obligation, to give good example to the people.

Greater indulgence may be shown in the case of *priests suffering from illness or weak health owing to disease or old age,* when they ask for an indult to say Mass in the house.

7. However, before receiving a petition, the Bishop should *first of all consider whether a priest is available* who can say Mass in the private oratory on Sundays and feast days of obligation without harm to the public good of the faithful.

In this connection let them wisely take note of the fact that a priest is forbidden to celebrate in such an oratory *if he has already celebrated or is to celebrate another Mass somewhere else;* and if in the place (village or city) where the private chapel is established, the pastor, or if there are several at least one of them, or another priest stopping in the same place, has to binate on the days mentioned for the public good of the faithful, a priest must be found elsewhere to say the Mass in the domestic chapel.

Similarly, domestic oratories already canonically erected with the faculty of having more than one Mass in virtue of a temporary indult, when this expires will find this Sacred Congregation rather disinclined to renew it.

8. Next, the Bishop must attentively consider the *reasons* which are adduced for the indult.

a) The *principal* one should be the *truly singular merits of the petitioner toward the Church and religion;* and this should be duly set forth in the petition. For example, if he made a conspicuous donation of lands or buildings; if he built at his own

expense a church, seminary, Catholic school, or some pious establishment for the sick, the aged, children, and so on; if he founded
or endowed an ecclesiastical benefice, or the like; if he rendered
very special and notable services for the good of the Church or
of the Holy See, for instance if some public official had the
principal part in causing laws to be enacted for the progress of
religion.

b) Other reasons which are commonly adduced, such as *physical infirmity, the distance from the church and the consequent
grave inconvenience of going there on foot,* especially *in the
country,* and the like, in order to be considered sufficient for
obtaining this indult, will usually have to be supplemented by
some outstanding service or liberality in favor of some pious work
to be designated by the Ordinary in proportion to the resources
of the petitioner.

c) Any of the following reasons, *standing alone,* is insufficient
to obtain the indult and hence should be rejected: that the parents or ancestors of the petitioner had the same indult; that the
petitioners bought the house or villa already provided with an
oratory, even though the latter, as sometimes happens, be well
built and properly equipped; that the petitioners are recommended
for their honorable Christian life.

9. Bishops may show themselves more lenient if the petition
is for a private oratory to be erected *in the country,* in places
which are quite far from any church, especially if it appears that
this will not only benefit the petitioners but will also redound
to the spiritual good of the people who work on the farms and
of the faithful living in the neighborhood, who otherwise, because
of the difficulty of going to the church to fulfill the precept, would
find it morally impossible to be present at Mass and catechetical
instructions.

But before receiving a petition for the erection of a private
oratory in the country, Bishops should urge the petitioners to
build on their lands or property, not a private but a *public oratory*
according to law, so that all should have the right to enter it and
there to assist at divine services (canon 1191).

10. Bishops should refrain from *asking for too many extensions;* it will be better to name as recipients of the indult, only
the father and mother of the family, but not their children; let

these latter be satisfied with the faculty of fulfilling the precept in the same oratory.

This faculty should be restricted to *relatives by blood and marriage* within the line and degree in which consanguinity and affinity are a diriment impediment to marriage (cc. 1076, §§ 1–2; 1077, § 1), and *persons living in the same house;* its extension to persons not living in the same house should not be asked without a sound and valid reason. As regards *servants,* the extension of the indult may be asked for all those who are attached to the house, whether the oratory be in the country or not. Petitions for the extension of the indult to *all persons present* should especially be avoided; this should be quite extraordinary and granted only for the gravest reasons. Care should also be taken that the private oratory be not made to look like a church.

11. In a private oratory, according to canon 1195, § 1, *other divine services and sacred functions are excluded, and only one Mass and that a low Mass may be celebrated,* at which it is permitted to distribute Holy Communion, unless the indult expressly provides otherwise. For any other function, it will be more easily tolerated that permission be given by the Ordinaries (cc. 776, § 1, 2°; 908–910; 1109, § 2) sparingly and prudently each time *per modum actus* and for just cause (not to be renewed on the recurrence of certain days), than that such permission be granted by indult of the Holy See.

12. Ordinaries must also be *cautious about asking for extensions to the more solemn days, and most cautious about asking extensions to the most solemn days, Easter being always excepted.*[6]

13. If in the prudent judgment of the Bishop the secular or religious priest who is celebrating in a private oratory is *needed* on Sundays or feast days of obligation to celebrate in a church or in a public or semi-public oratory, lest a notable part of the faithful be deprived of Mass, the Bishop should *forbid him to*

---

[6] According to the present law, the *more solemn* days are: Christmas, Epiphany, Easter, the Ascension, Pentecost, St. Joseph (19 March), the Assumption, the Immaculate Conception, Peter and Paul, All Saints.

For France, the four more solemn days are: Christmas, Easter, Pentecost, the Assumption.

The *most solemn* are: Christmas, Easter, the Assumption.

say Mass in the private chapel, and no one can take exception to such a ruling (cf. 7, above). It is well that the Ordinary bring this case of necessity to the attention of the recipient of the indult at the time of its execution, in order to forestall any complaints that might later be made because Mass in his oratory is forbidden for this reason.

14. It pertains to the Bishop alone to designate the priest for a Mass to be celebrated in a domestic oratory, whether he be a secular, even from another diocese but approved by his own Ordinary, or a religious with the regular permission of his own Superior; but when a priest, either secular or religious, who is approved as above stated, is presented by the person who has the indult, the Bishop should not reject him, unless in his prudent judgment he considers him unfit. The holder of the indult must acquiesce in the judgment of the Bishop, and has no recourse.

15. As regards the *place* where the oratory is to be set up, the Ordinary must execute exactly the clauses of the apostolic indult: but in every case he must either personally or through some other ecclesiastic inspect the place before giving permission to celebrate Mass there, to see *whether it be suitable and respectable,* as this great Mystery requires, and whether it be equipped with proper furnishings according to liturgical requirements.

Ordinaries should note that it is forbidden to use a *bureau* with an altar enclosed in it, which for the celebration of Mass is placed on a chest of drawers, table or desk, book-case, or the like, that is, in places which serve indiscriminately for domestic and profane uses. Such a practice on the other hand is not objectionable, provided the conditions regarding the decency and respectability of the place where such a bureau is set up are fulfilled, if there is question of a *Mass to be said in the house* for priests who are infirm with age or suffering from illness, and in the case of an *indult of a portable altar,* which is dealt with below (II, 9).

16. *As to the time* for which the indult of an oratory should be valid, this Sacred Congregation will fix it according to the nature of the reasons for which the privilege is granted.

17. Local Ordinaries must not fail to exhort persons who receive the privilege of a private chapel, to strive to gather into the oratory every day, at least in the afternoon or evening, the whole household, including the servants who may belong to it, to recite

a third part of the holy Rosary in honor of the Blessed Virgin Mary and to offer other pious prayers to God: for this would be a fine example to all members of the family and would contribute greatly to promote genuine piety toward God and the establishment of Christian living, so that the real faith and fine moral qualities of the parents be propagated and continued in the children and grandchildren.

18. The Ordinaries should make a complete *list* in writing and carefully keep it in the archives of the Curia with the necessary annotations and remarks, showing all the private oratories which have been erected in their diocese; and they should carefully secure copies of the documents of their erection. If they find any oratories which cannot show any canonical authorization, they must suppress them as having been introduced contrary to law, and revoke the permission to say Mass there, in the meantime referring the matter to this Sacred Congregation.

Those that have been legitimately erected, they must duly inspect on the occasion of the visitation of the diocese, to see if all their equipment is in accord with liturgical laws, and if they find anything unworthy or unbecoming which detracts from the sanctity of the divine Mysteries and the reverence due to them, they should remove it immediately. Still more are they to investigate whether any evils or abuses have crept in; if so, they must see that these are entirely eradicated; and in the meantime they should in either case suspend the permission to say Mass there, and not grant it again until the evils have been removed and proper precautions taken that they shall not recur, referring the matter meanwhile to this Sacred Congregation. Any recourse which may be taken to the Holy See against such a decree of the Ordinary is only *in devolutivo*. The right which he has to visit these oratories as often as he prudently judges necessary, the Ordinary must unflinchingly maintain in relation to the person who has the privilege.

19. At the end of the year 1950 the Ordinaries are to send to this Sacred Congregation a complete *list* of the private Oratories existing in their diocese, mentioning their canonical titles of erection.

II. ON ASKING FOR THE PRIVILEGE OF
A PORTABLE ALTAR

1. Somewhat akin to the indult of a private chapel is that of a *portable altar* (*ara portatilis*, or *ara viatica, gestatoria,* or *itineraria*); this is broader in scope, as it *"imports the faculty of celebrating anywhere, in a respectable and suitable place, not however at sea"* (c. 822, § 3): hence in this case the celebration of Mass is not limited to a place exclusively reserved for divine worship, and the place needs no inspection or approval of the Bishop.

In view of the greater amplitude of this favor, all the greater are the dangers of abuse and of impairing the honor due to the august Sacrifice of the Mass, which are to be feared; and this can happen in two ways: *because of the place,* if the one chosen is unworthy of this great Mystery (for example, a bedroom); and *on the part of the holder of the privilege,* if he abuses it by immoderate use.

Certainly every effort must be made to avoid these dangers, and the privilege is to be granted sparingly and prudently, in view of the history of the privilege itself, and especially in view of the strict discipline introduced by the Council of Trent, which took away also the faculty of granting this indult from the Bishops and certain regular orders who had it. Afterward, receding from the earlier severity, the Holy See granted the privilege only to certain Bishops for their honor and according to their needs, and to mission countries.[7]

2. Two sources of the privilege of a portable altar are mentioned in the aforesaid canon 822, § 2, namely, *the law* and *an indult of the Holy See.*

According to the *law* of the Code, this privilege is enjoyed only by: Cardinals of the Holy Roman Church (c. 239, § 1, 7°); residential and titular Bishops (c. 349, § 1, 1°); Vicars and Prefects Apostolic (cc. 294, § 1; 308); Abbots and Prelates *nullius* (c. 323, § 1) and Apostolic Administrators (c. 315).

However, in virtue of the Constitution, *Ad incrementum,* of

---

[7] Cf. S. C. Prop. Fid., 13 Aug., 1669, *Collectanea,* I, p. 60, n. 184; S. C. Rit., *Congr. Missionum Provinciae Lituaniae,* 11 Iul., 1699 (*Decr. Auth.,* n. 2032).

Pius XI, 15 Aug., 1934,[8] the same privilege is enjoyed by a very limited number of persons holding ecclesiastical dignities, who have important duties in the Roman Curia, namely: the Most Excellent Prelates who hold the office of Assessor or Secretary in the Roman Congregations; the Master or Prefect of the Secret Chamber of the Supreme Pontiff; the Secretary of the Tribunal of the Apostolic Signatura; the Dean of the Sacred Roman Rota; the Substitute of the Secretariate of State; the Most Reverend Prothonotaries Apostolic *de numero participantium;* the Prelates who are Auditors of the Sacred Roman Rota; the Clerics of the Reverend Apostolic Camera; the *Praelati Votantes* and *Referendarii* of the Apostolic Signatura.

All these have also the privilege of a domestic oratory and can say Mass there every day excepting only the days which are excluded by the priest's own rite (c. 820). And all the faithful who assist at their Mass always satisfy the precept of hearing Mass.

In these two cases, in view of the distinguished position and rather limited number of the persons who enjoy this privilege, it does not seem likely that evils will arise; for moderation in the use of the privilege seems to be assured by the dignity of the persons.

3. *Indults* of the Holy See can be a far more prolific source of this privilege, unless their concession is held within certain limits and protected by cautious circumspection: hence, in asking for an indult of such importance, Bishops must use special care and deliberation.

4. This Sacred Congregation usually grants this privilege for reasons of *real necessity or evident utility,* and exclusively or principally for the benefit of religious worship, *to priests only,* since they give greater assurance of its proper use.

The principal cases and those which most frequently occur, concern priests having the care of souls, either among the faithful living in remote localities where churches are lacking or very far off, or in countries of heretics or schismatics (*diaspora*). The former case is likely to be verified in the vast regions especially of Asia and America, where the faithful are few and scattered, and are unable to assist at Mass unless it is said outside of

---

[8] AAS 26–497.

sacred places or in the open air, for example during harvest time.

Sometimes the need for the indult may arise from some religious or even civil festivity which is to be celebrated by a great throng of people for whom there would not be room in the church.

The Holy See does not refuse to grant the indult of a portable altar in the case of youths of Catholic Action or of similar institutions, who under the guidance and with the assistance of their chaplains take trips through the open country or mountains, where there are no sacred places, and go from one place to another for recreation: indeed the concession of the privilege in this case does much to preserve and promote in them devotion to the Most Holy Eucharist.

At times the privilege is also granted in Eucharistic Congresses, in order to give to the priests who attend them the opportunity of saying Mass, when because of their great number the church cannot accommodate them all.

5. For the *personal* benefit of the priest alone, this privilege is granted only *because of illness*, if this is such as to seem to require such an indult. In this case this Sacred Congregation makes the indult subject to special precautions so that the privilege be not the occasion of abuses and vain display, which was not the least among the reasons which led to the suppression of the privilege by the Council of Trent. The privilege itself may be revoked if some disorder regarding its exercise becomes known to the Sacred Congregation; and to this end the Ordinaries are obliged to watch and to report on the improper use of the privilege.

6. It is indeed a source of anxiety that in these days, especially since the last war, the very dangerous and detestable practice has somehow found its way among the faithful, of celebrating the ceremonies of divine worship and even the most holy Mysteries of our faith without necessity outside their proper place, which is the church or a place set apart for that purpose by a consecration or blessing. This practice must be opposed most vigorously as an abuse and a really illegal attempt to convert to profane use the august sacraments of the Church and her venerable functions and rites.

The Ordinary should seriously reflect on this when priests apply to him for the indult of a portable altar.

7. The place where a portable altar is set up must be appropriate and decent, or fitting and honorable, lest because of its unworthy and unbecoming character grave injury and irreverence redound to the divine Mysteries.

An *appropriate place* demands security and space, so that the Mass can be offered safely and conveniently without any danger of profanation or of the spilling of the Precious Blood from the chalice; a *decent place* refers to the quality of the place, that is, it demands that the Mass be not celebrated in a bedroom where someone usually sleeps, nor in any other place unbefitting the dignity of so great a Sacrifice.

Decency also concerns the immediate place, that is, the table on which the portable altar is laid, that it be not unclean nor devoted to profane uses. This table must be of sufficient length and breadth to afford safe control of the stone, support for the Missal, and proper and becoming celebration of the Mass.

8. A considerable mass of disorders springs from a false notion of this indult. For it should be noted that this privilege, as regards the celebration of Mass, is strictly *personal* and is available only to the person who has the privilege, unless the indult expressly provides otherwise. Therefore the priest who has the indult and he alone can say Mass on that altar, and no other priest is allowed to do so unless that is clearly stated in the indult.

To prevent other abuses the Holy See usually adds certain clauses to the indult and states whether it is valid also for the fulfillment of the precept on the part of persons who are present at the Mass. But, if this is not expressly provided for in the indult, it will be well to remember what Gatticus says (*De usu altaris portatilis opusculum,* cap. XV, n. 14): "As regards other persons (besides the holder or holders of the indult) who may be present (at the Mass which is celebrated at the portable altar), it is evident that *they by no means satisfy the obligation of hearing Mass, unless the benefit of the privilege is expressly extended to them.*"

Nevertheless, if in virtue of this indult Mass is celebrated in the open (*sub dio*), then by canon 1249 any of the faithful who assist at it fulfill the obligation of hearing Mass.

9. In view of the above, Bishops of places must bear in mind the following points in asking for this privilege:

a) When this privilege is asked by priests *because of illness,* let the Bishop first consider whether the need can be met *by an indult to say Mass in the house,* or *in an honorable and decent place,* always excluding however, a bedroom in which someone usually sleeps, and hence in some enclosure which, though ordinarily used for profane purposes, yet has nothing in its appointments which is indecorous or unworthy and thus repugnant to the sanctity of the Eucharistic Sacrifice. In this case there is no objection to the use of the *bureau* mentioned above in I, 15.

If so, the Bishop should refrain from asking for the indult of a portable altar, but may, as has been said, apply for *the faculty of saying Mass at home in an honorable and decent place.*

In case the necessity of celebrating Mass exists for several places outside the diocese of the petitioner, places for example to which he has to go *for reasons of health,* it is allowed to extend this faculty to several dioceses.

b) In every case, however, whether the source of the faculty be an indult to say Mass at home in an honorable and decent place, or the privilege of a portable altar, *it must always be carefully provided that the priest is not to celebrate it in a bedroom;* hence if he can say Mass, let him do so in some suitable room of the house, properly equipped.

c) Bishops should proceed cautiously in accepting petitions asking for this truly conspicuous privilege which is properly called that of a *portable altar.* It should be in the service only of the public good of the faithful: hence the Bishop himself in his pastoral solicitude should carefully investigate whether in each case there exists the legitimate reason of *true necessity* or *evident utility,* as stated in n. 4.

He should act with equal caution when this favor is asked for the private benefit of priests adducing the reason of *ill health:* he should then strictly inquire into the existence of that reason, and into the gravity and nature of the illness; for it must be such that it necessarily calls for the concession of this indult. In making this investigation he should not easily rest satisfied with the affirmation of the petitioners, but should explore the truth of the matter also through a competent physician, to be appointed if need be *ex officio.*

Moreover, before accepting the petition, he should make sure that the priests who are asking for this privilege, either for their private benefit because of illness or for the public good of the faithful, will make a temperate and proper use of so singular a privilege and will avoid all disorder and irreverence toward the divine Mysteries.

These circumstances are to be described with entire accuracy in the petition sent to this Sacred Congregation, to which in any event is always reserved *ex Audientia Sanctissimi* the decision as to the sufficiency of the reasons for the concession.

The recommendation of the petition is to be made personally by the Bishop himself or by the Prelate who is his successor in office.

d) The Sacred Congregation usually adds to the indult of a portable altar one or the other of the clauses: *"de consensu Ordinariorum"* or *"praemonito loci Ordinario,"* according as the holder of the indult, who is going to various dioceses, will find it easy or difficult to approach the local Ordinary for the legitimate exercise of his privilege.

Either clause therefore commits to the Ordinaries the duty of vigilance to prevent abuses in the use of the privilege. If they learn of anything done by the holder of the indult contrary to the reverence due to the divine Mysteries, let them understand that they have the power to revoke the exercise of the privilege immediately, putting aside all human respect. If such an abuse is detected outside the diocese to which the holder of the indult belongs, the Ordinary of the place where it has occurred shall forbid the use of the privilege in his diocese, and is bound in the meantime to notify the proper Ordinary of the person concerned, and the latter shall suspend the use of the privilege and apply to the Sacred Congregation for further instructions. Any recourse which the holder of the privilege may take is to be considered only *in devolutivo.*

e) If it happens that after the expiration of the indult it is to be renewed because the same reasons for which the indult was originally granted continue to exist, or for some other grave reason, Bishops are bound to report on how the holder of the indult has exercised his privilege.

f) Finally, care must be taken that the portable altar be treated with honor and reverence, for the consecration of the stone demands it. Hence in journeys it is to be transported with care and carefully guarded: and it should be placed in a clean box, so as to be protected from all danger of profanation. Nothing need be said of the necessity of the other things which according to the sacred rites are required in every offering of the Sacrifice, such as the vestments, the sacred vessels, the three clean altar cloths and all the rest, from which no one is dispensed by the grant of a portable altar.[9]

III. ON ASKING FOR THE FACULTY TO CELEBRATE MASS WITHOUT A SERVER

1. "Because of the dignity of this most august Mystery, We wish and urge — what Holy Mother Church has, for that matter, always prescribed — that no priest go to the altar unless there be a minister to serve him and make the responses, according to canon 813."[10] In fact canon 813 of the Code of Canon Law forbids a priest to say Mass without having a server to wait upon him and make the responses.

The server represents the assembly of the faithful, according to Saint Thomas (*Summa,* III, q. 83, a. 5, ad 12): "(the server) takes the place of the whole Catholic people": the same is shown from the most ancient practice of the Church, according to which the priest performed the sacred Mysteries with the assistance of deacons and other ministers, and the whole people responded. The celebration of Mass by the priest alone with one server belongs to a later period. It is clear also from the universal and concordant teaching of liturgists and moralists.

Moreover, some parts of the Mass (the Orations, *Confiteor, Orate fratres* with its response *Suscipiat,* and not a few versicles, etc.) contain expressions in the plural number so as to show the presence of some minister assisting the priest. Besides it is most appropriate that the priest in celebrating have the cooperation or support of one server to assist him in performing some of the rites, and in case of some sudden physical disability to come to his aid and do whatever may be necessary.

The practice of celebrating Mass without a server, or even *with no one present at all,* seems to have arisen in the monasteries.

---

[9] Cf. *Missale Romanum,* tit. *Rubricae Generales Missalis,* c. XX, *de praeparatione altaris, et ornamentorum eius.*
[10] From the Encyclical, *Mediator Dei* (AAS 39–557).

2. The law of having a server at Mass allows very few exceptions, and authors learned in liturgy and moral theology agree in limiting them to the following cases:

a) if Holy Viaticum has to be given to a sick person and there is no server at hand;

b) to enable the people to satisfy the precept of hearing Mass;

c) in time of pestilence, when it is not easy to find someone to serve, and the priest would otherwise be obliged to abstain from celebrating for a notable time;

d) if the server leaves the altar during the Mass, even outside the time of the consecration and offertory; in which case the reverence due to the Holy Sacrifice requires that it be continued even in his absence.

Outside of these cases which are allowed by the unanimous consent of the authors, this law is modified only by apostolic indult, which is given especially in mission lands.

3. This, however, must be remembered: as between the absence of a server and the use of one who is not entirely fitting, the latter alternative is to be preferred, provided the server in question is able at least to perform the principal ceremonies, such as to present the cruets, to move the missal, to ring the bell.[11]

4. Except for the cases of necessity mentioned in n. 2, the presence of a server at the celebration of Mass is required in virtue of canon 813; the rubric of the Missal prefers, when a choice is possible, a cleric to a lay person; the latter should be used if no cleric is available, and should also be of the male sex: all the authors teach unanimously that it is forbidden under pain of mortal sin for women, even nuns, to serve *at the altar*.

In the early ages, therefore, the Church wisely provided that the person chosen as server at a private Mass should be a cleric who had received the first tonsure (S. C. Rit., *Decr. Auth.*, n. 113, ad VI); only in the course of time, when clerics available for this service had become scarce, the Church through necessity allowed that lay persons be used, especially boys (*ibid.*, n. 3647, ad VII): and this practice is very widespread at the present time.

As regards boy servers, they should be carefully instructed so as to become really fit for the performance of this noble function.

---

[11] Cf. *Missale Romanum*, tit. *de defectibus in celebratione Missarum occurrentibus*, c. X, n. 1.

5. In case of necessity, when no male, either cleric or lay, is available, canon 813 allows that a woman may serve the Mass, on condition however that *"she make the responses from a distance, and on no account come to the altar."* The same was true under the law of the Decretals,[12] hence the service of a woman is limited to *making the responses* to the celebrant:[13] consequently it is necessary that everything that is needed for the divine Sacrifice be conveniently set out for the priest before the Mass, as is usually done in the chapels of nuns when there is no server.

In order that a woman be employed instead of a male server, according to the prescription of the aforesaid canon, a just cause is required.

In the indults which are granted by this Sacred Congregation to celebrate Mass without a server, a clause is always added requiring that care be taken: *"ut ad mentem canonis 813, nedum pueri edoceantur de modo inserviendi S. Missae sed etiam fideles ipsaeque mulieres addiscant quomodo possint Missae inservire, legendo responsiones sacerdoti celebranti reddendas."*

Recently His Holiness ordered that another clause be inserted in the indult to say Mass without a server, namely: *"dummodo aliquis fidelis Sacro assistat,"* and to this it is not advisable to make any modification.

IV. ON ASKING FOR THE INDULT TO KEEP THE MOST BLESSED EUCHARIST IN PRIVATE CHAPELS

1. The petitions which are presented to this Sacred Congregation to obtain this indult are shown by experience to be almost equal in number to those for a private oratory: frequently both indults are asked for at the same time, or, as soon as the oratory is granted, the permission to keep the Most Blessed Eucharist there is requested. And the petitioners do not subside after one or two refusals, but continue urgently, and at times most insistently, to pursue the object of their desire.

---

[12] C. 1, *de cohabitatione clericorum et mulierum*, III, 2.
[13] S. C. Rit., *Veronen.*, 27 Aug., 1836, ad VIII; *Alatrina*, 18 Mart., 1899, ad VI; *Decr. Auth.*, n. 2745, ad VIII, and 4015, ad VI.

Now, on the one hand, frequently no guarantees are given that due reverence and honor and continued adoration be given to the Sacred Species; and sometimes the required certainty is lacking regarding the safe custody of the Most Blessed Sacrament according to the Instruction of this Sacred Congregation of 26 May, 1938.[14]

On the other hand, the reasons which the petitioners give in support of their petitions are for the most part found to be insufficient for the concession of this most distinguished privilege. They are almost always reduced to the following:

a) to satisfy and foster the devotion of the petitioners toward the Most Blessed Eucharist;

b) some merits on their part toward the Church, usually expressed only in general terms;

c) the distance of their residence from the church where the Most Blessed Eucharist is kept, and sometimes the fact that they are prevented from making daily visits to It by old age or infirmity; and other reasons of this sort, or of even less consequence.

2. The faculty of keeping the Most Blessed Eucharist is sometimes sought for oratories situated *in the country* (in camps), far removed from any church, where the petitioner's family either lives habitually or sojourns for a notable part of the year, for example in the summer or autumn: in such places as a rule there are wide stretches of countryside and permanent homes of farm workers, sometimes quite numerous, who when they are seriously ill are regularly assisted also by receiving the Most Blessed Eucharist as Viaticum.

But by far the greater number of the petitions for this indult concern the keeping of the Most Blessed Sacrament in private oratories which are erected in a city or town, for the private benefit of the petitioners and of the persons who live with them, frequently very few in number.

3. Now, in the first case, this Sacred Congregation is more easily persuaded to grant the favor, provided the other required conditions exist together with guarantees both as to the safe custody and reverence which are due to the Blessed Sacrament and as to continued adoration on the part of the faithful living in

---

[14] AAS 30–198; CANON LAW DIGEST, 2, p. 377.

the neighborhood, for which it provides in the indult by requiring that at least during some hours of the day the doors of the oratory be open to those persons who wish to visit the Most Blessed Eucharist.

In the second case, this Sacred Congregation is disinclined to grant the indult, and will reject even urgent petitions which are directed to it. It is appropriate to recall that the primary and original purpose for which the Sacred Species are reserved in churches outside of Mass is to administer Holy Viaticum; and that the secondary purposes are to give Holy Communion in the churches outside of Mass and to provide for the adoration of Our Lord Jesus Christ under the Sacred Species.

The keeping of the Most Blessed Eucharist in domestic chapels, therefore, seems inopportune for the following reasons:

a) the absence of the primary and principal reason for which the Most Blessed Sacrament is reserved;

b) the lack of necessity to distribute Holy Communion frequently outside of Mass in that place;

c) the danger of profanation, irreverence, or insufficient adoration.

4. In order that the Most Blessed Eucharist may be kept in private chapels, an apostolic indult is required; the local Ordinary cannot give this permission even by way of act, and even though there be a just cause (c. 1265, § 2). No one is permitted to keep the Most Blessed Eucharist in his possession or to carry It with him on a journey (*ibid.*, § 3).

According to an ancient and constant practice the Holy See does not usually grant permission to keep the Most Blessed Eucharist in the domestic chapels of private houses *"except in extraordinary cases, for grave reasons, upon the previous recommendation of the Bishop and with appropriate safeguards."*

Let the Most Excellent residential Bishops, therefore, thoroughly understand that *all the conditions enumerated below must exist together* before they allow themselves to ask for the faculty of reserving the Most Blessed Eucharist.

This indult is granted only:

a) *in really extraordinary cases:* and such cases are to be held to a minimum in proportion to the size of the diocese;

b) *for grave reasons:* the petitioners must be altogether outstanding, highly deserving of the Church and religion, either because of personal services rendered or of some distinguished benefit or liberality conferred upon pious uses; persons who, because of their open profession of the faith, the uprightness of their private and public life and the Catholic education of their children, are really outstanding examples to the rest of the faithful;

c) if the petition is recommended personally by the Bishop or the Prelate who is his successor in office;

d) if in the petition distinct guarantees are given: as to the safe custody of the Blessed Sacrament; frequent adoration on the part of the petitioner and his household or also of others of the faithful; the frequent renewal of the Sacred Species according to the rubrics; the presence of a lamp burning day and night in the oratory before the tabernacle; and the observance of the other liturgical prescriptions regarding due honor and reverence toward the Most Blessed Eucharist (c. 1265, § 1).

5. Ordinaries of places have the duty frequently to inspect, either in person or through some other ecclesiastic, a domestic chapel which has the indult for keeping the Most Blessed Eucharist, and to see whether all the liturgical and canonical regulations and the special clauses which are incorporated in the indult are being exactly observed; and if they find anything which is contrary to security or to the required honor and reverence, let them take notice that they have the power to use the remedies that may be necessary to remove all abuses, even to the deprivation of the right to keep the Blessed Sacrament, and of the oratory itself, if the gravity of the case requires it, without prejudice to a recourse *in devolutivo* to the Holy See.

When the Eminent and Most Reverend Cardinals who are in charge of this Sacred Congregation had carefully examined the foregoing Instruction at the Plenary Session of 26 March, 1949, they approved it and recommended that it be made public if His Holiness should so decide.

His Holiness Pius XII, in the Audience granted to the under-signed Secretary of the S. C. on 6 Sept., 1949, deigned, of certain knowledge and with mature deliberation, to approve the above Instruction and to give it Apostolic Authority, all things, even those worthy of special mention, to the contrary notwithstanding; and ordered that the same Instruction be published in the official commentary, *Acta Apostolicae Sedis,* to be carefully and religiously observed by all priests and faithful of the Latin rite.

Given at Rome, from the S. C. of the Sacraments, 1 Oct., 1949.

AAS 41–493; S. C. Sacr., Instruction, 1 Oct., 1949. *Periodica*, 38–416 (Cappello). *Monitor Ecclesiasticus*, 1949, p. 90; 1950, p. 30 (Zerba).

In Missions: Faculty for Mass without server interpreted. See **c. 66**; private, S. C. Prop. Fid., 15 Dec., 1945.

CANON 818

Priest Lacking Right Arm: Rites of Mass (S. C. Rit., 28 Jan., 1920) Private.

The Sacred Congregation of Rites, 28 Jan., 1920, gave an Instruction for the celebration of Mass, with an apostolic indult, by priests lacking the right arm.

I. Before Mass: General Rules:

1. Besides the chalice on the corporal, the open Missal is to be placed on the altar beforehand; and, on the Epistle side, a vessel with water for purifying the fingers of the assistant priest.

2. If it is necessary to put on the vestments at the altar, this is to be done at the Gospel side, the priest who is to celebrate standing on the platform, from which, after putting on the vestments, he shall descend in the usual way to begin the Mass.

3. It will be well to compress the host slightly with some suitable instrument along the line of division, so that at the proper time it may more easily be divided.

4. The kissing of the amice should not be omitted; the placing of the amice on the head, etc., should be done with the aid of assistants.

5. The right sleeve of the alb (unless the priest has an artificial right arm) is to be tucked under the cincture.

6. The maniple should be attached to the left arm near the elbow, so that it may be not at all in the way during the sacred action.

II. During Mass:

a. General Rules:

1. Another priest should always assist the Celebrant, besides the customary server when the latter can be had.

2. The assistant priest shall stand at the *left* of the Celebrant:
   a) At the *Confiteor,* unless there is a server;
   b) At the Gospel, etc.;
   c) At the Secrets, etc.;
   d) To wipe and arrange the chalice;
   e) At the last Gospel.

He shall stand at the *right* of the Celebrant:
   a) At the Introit, etc.;
   b) At the Offertory, etc.;
   c) At *Qui pridie,* etc.;
   d) At the "Communion," etc.;
   e) At the prayers after Mass.

3. The Celebrant shall make the sign of the cross with his left hand, both upon himself and over or toward things or persons, in the manner in use among the Latins, that is, making the transverse stroke always from left to right.

4. The Celebrant shall hold his hand extended upon his breast (but without disjoining the index and thumb after the consecration), whenever he should otherwise hold his hands joined before his breast, or at the edge of the altar, unless by the use of an artificial right hand he can becomingly observe the rubric.

5. Whenever the rubric prescribes the extension of the hands after they have been joined, the Celebrant shall make the gesture with his left hand from his breast and back to his breast, elevating it also when this is prescribed. At the Orations, Preface, etc., he shall hold his hand as indicated by the rubric.

6. The turning of the pages of the Missal shall generally be done by the assistant priest; but if there is a server vested in a surplice, the latter shall, after the elevation, stand by the Missal to turn the pages, at least in case it should be necessary, namely if the Celebrant can not easily do it himself; otherwise, unless the Celebrant can do it himself, the assistant shall do it, or help the Celebrant to do it.

7. The assistant shall wear the stole from the beginning of the Canon to the Communion inclusive.

8. Whenever the Celebrant uncovers and covers the chalice, the assistant, by way of precaution, will place the fingers of his right hand on the base of the chalice: likewise at the sign of the cross at the words, *Per Ipsum,* etc.

   b. Particular Rules:

1. When the Celebrant kisses the text of the Holy Gospel, he shall place his left hand on the Missal, which the assistant shall lift up.

2. At the Offertory, the assistant shall uncover the chalice, and do the other things which are done by the assistants when a Bishop is celebrating, and by the ministers in solemn Masses: but he shall not kiss the hand of the Celebrant when he hands him the paten and the chalice: afterward he shall place the paten under the corporal.

3. The Celebrant, at the words, *Qui pridie quam pateretur* (the assistant helping him with his right hand, as also always in the actions which follow), shall take up the host saying: *Accepit panem in sanctas ac venerabiles manus suas,* and immediately (in accordance with the rubric as regards the chalice) put it down, or leave it in the hand of the assistant, so that he may make the sign of the cross over it, saying *benedixit,* and then take it up again to go on with the Sacrifice.

4. The pall shall be taken off and replaced on the chalice always by the assistant: the Celebrant meanwhile placing the fingers of his left hand on the base of the chalice.

5. Before the words, *Per Ipsum,* etc., the assistant shall help the Celebrant to pick up the Host, and shall afterward purify and wipe his fingers.

6. At the words: *omnis honor et gloria,* the assistant shall elevate the chalice, while the Celebrant according to the rubric still holds the Host in the fingers of his left hand.

7. After the *Pater noster,* etc., the assistant shall handle the paten as the assistant does for a Bishop who is celebrating, and as the deacon does in a solemn Mass; except as to kissing the hand.

8. The Celebrant places the paten under the Host with the help of the assistant.

9. Likewise, the breaking of the Sacred Host upon the paten is to be done with the help of the assistant: the separation of the Particle to be put into the chalice can be done by the Celebrant, the assistant in this case inclining the upper part of the half of the Host.

10. At the words: *Panem caelestem accipiam,* the Celebrant does not take the Host in his hand, since he must presently strike his breast.

11. At the words, *Domine, non sum dignus,* etc., the Host is to remain on the paten; and when the Celebrant receives the Sacred Host, the assistant shall help him by placing one part over the other, and then with his right hand holding the paten up to the face of the Celebrant: afterward he shall purify and wipe his fingers.

12. After gathering up the fragments, the Celebrant shall collect them with his finger at the edge of the paten on the corporal, and then, while the assistant lifts the paten over the chalice with his right hand and holds the base of the chalice with his left, the Celebrant shall put the fragments into the chalice.

13. The assistant, at the Communion and at the taking of the purification of the chalice, shall with his right hand hold the paten to the face of the Celebrant.

14. In order to receive the ablution of the fingers, the Celebrant shall place the chalice on the altar at the Epistle corner.

15. Finally the assistant shall wipe the chalice and place it in the usual manner in the middle of the altar.

(Private); S. C. Rit., Instruction, 28 Jan., 1920. See Moretti, *Caeremoniale Iuxta Ritum Romanum,* Vol. II, p. 491.

Priest Lacking Left Arm: Rites of Mass (S. C. Rit., 28 Jan., 1920) Private.

The Sacred Congregation of Rites, 28 Jan., 1920, gave an Instruction for the celebration of Mass, with an apostolic indult, by priests lacking the left arm.

I. Before Mass: General Rules:

1. Besides the chalice on the corporal, the open Missal is to be placed on the altar beforehand; and, on the Gospel side, a vessel with water for purifying the fingers of the assistant priest.

2. If it is necessary to put on the vestments at the altar, this is to be done at the Gospel side, the priest who is to celebrate standing on the platform, from which, after putting on the vestments, he shall descend in the usual way to begin the Mass.

3. It will be well to compress the host slightly with some suitable instrument along the lines of division, so that at the proper time it may more easily be divided.

4. The kissing of the amice should not be omitted; the placing of the amice on the head, etc., should be done with the aid of assistants.

5. The left sleeve of the alb (unless the priest has an artificial left arm) is to be tucked under the cincture.

6. The maniple should be attached to the right arm near the elbow, so that it may be not at all in the way during the sacred action.

II. During the Mass:

a. General Rules:

1. Another priest should always assist the Celebrant, besides the customary server when the latter can be had.

2. The assistant priest shall stand at the *left* of the celebrant:

    a) At the *Confiteor,* unless there is a server;

    b) At the Gospel, etc.;

    c) At the Secrets, etc.;

    d) At: *Da propitius pacem,* etc.;

    e) At the last Gospel.

He shall stand at the *right* of the Celebrant:

    a) At the Introit, etc.

    b) At the Offertory, etc.

    c) At: *Libera nos,* etc.;

    d) At the "Communion," etc.;

    e) At the prayers after Mass.

3. The Celebrant shall hold his hand extended upon his breast (but without disjoining the index and thumb after the consecration) whenever he should otherwise hold his hands joined before his breast or at the edge of the altar, unless by the use of an artificial left hand he can becomingly observe the rubric.

4. Whenever the rubric prescribes the extension of the hands after they have been joined, the Celebrant shall make the gesture with his right hand from his breast and back to his breast, elevating it also when this is prescribed. At the Orations, Preface, etc., he shall hold his hand as indicated by the rubric.

5. The turning of the pages of the Missal at the Gospel corner shall be done by the assistant; at other times the latter shall at least assist in the action.

6. The assistant shall wear the stole from the beginning of the Canon to the Communion inclusive.

7. Whenever the Celebrant uncovers and covers the chalice, the assistant, by way of precaution, will place the fingers of his left

hand on the base of the chalice; likewise at the signs of the cross at the words: *Per Ipsum,* etc.

b. Particular Rules:

1. When the Celebrant kisses the text of the Holy Gospel, he shall place his hand on the Missal, which the assistant shall lift up.

2. At the Offertory, the assistant shall uncover the chalice, and do the other things which are done by the assistants when a Bishop is celebrating, and by the ministers in solemn Masses.

3. The Celebrant, at the words: *Qui pridie* (the assistant helping with his left hand), shall take up the host, saying: *Accepit panem in sanctas ac venerabiles manus suas,* and immediately (in accordance with the rubric as regards the chalice) put it down or leave it in the hand of the assistant, so that he may make the sign of the cross over it, saying *benedixit,* and then take it up again to go on with the Sacrifice.

4. Before the words: *Per Ipsum,* etc., the assistant shall help the Celebrant to pick up the Host, and shall afterward purify and wipe his fingers.

5. At the words: *Omnis honor et gloria,* the assistant shall elevate the chalice, while the Celebrant according to the rubric still holds the Host in the fingers of his right hand.

6. After the *Pater Noster,* etc., the assistant shall handle the paten as the assistant does for a Bishop who is celebrating, and as the deacon does in a solemn Mass, and shall again return to the left.

7. The assistant shall help the Celebrant when the latter puts the paten under the Host.

8. Likewise, the breaking of the Host upon the paten is to be done with the help of the assistant.

9. At the words: *Panem caelestem accipiam,* the Celebrant does not take the Host in his hand, since he must presently strike his breast.

10. At the words: *Domine, non sum dignus,* etc., the Host is to remain on the paten; and when the Celebrant receives the Sacred Host, the assistant shall help him by placing one part over the other, and then holding the paten up to the face of the Celebrant; afterward he shall purify and wipe his fingers.

11. After gathering up the fragments, the Celebrant shall collect them with his finger at the edge of the paten on the corporal; and then, while the assistant lifts the paten over the chalice with his

left hand and holds the base of the chalice with his right, the Celebrant shall put the fragments into the chalice.

12. The assistant, at the Communion and at the taking of the purification of the chalice, shall with his left hand hold the paten to the face of the Celebrant.

13. In order to receive the ablution of the fingers, the Celebrant shall place the chalice on the altar at the Epistle corner.

14. Finally the assistant shall wipe the chalice and place it in the usual manner in the middle of the altar.

(Private); S. C. Rit., Instruction, 28 Jan., 1920. See Moretti, *Caeremoniale Iuxta Ritum Romanum,* Vol. II, p. 494.

Calendar of Tertiary Sisters to Be Used by Priest Celebrating in Their Churches and Oratories (S. C. Rit., 4 June, 1920) Private.

The Procurator General of the Order of Preachers proposed the following question to the Sacred Congregation of Rites:

Whether, by reason of the Decree of the S. C. Rit. of 28 Feb., 1914, priests who celebrate in the churches and oratories of Tertiary Sisters, are bound, when they celebrate Mass, to conform to the calendar which the Sisters use.

Reply. In the affirmative.

(Private); S. C. Rit., 4 June, 1920. Reported in *Periodica,* Vol. 26, 1937, p. 38.

NOTE: The Decree of 28 Feb., 1914, referred to in the question, was as follows: "Regular Orders must absolutely have their own calendar, which is likewise to be used by the nuns and Sisters of the same Orders" (*Decr. Auth.,* n. 4312). The "calendar which the Sisters use" is therefore the calendar of the Order to which they belong as Tertiaries. Hecht, in his annotations to this reply in *Periodica,* points out that such Sisters have a right to use the calendar of the Order even though they recite only the Little Office of the Blessed Virgin, and not the Divine Office (*contra, Commentarium pro Religiosis,* Vol. 16, p. 160).

Calendar for Mass in Churches and Chapels of Vicariates and Prefectures Which Are Entrusted to Religious Who Have a Calendar of Their Own (Three replies: S. C. Rit., 23 March, 1929; S. C. Prop. Fid., 18 May, 1932; S. C. Prop. Fid., 7 Nov., 1932) Private.

These three private replies on a rather complicated matter are grouped together for better understanding.

I. S. C. Rit., 23 March, 1929, Prot. N. C. 41/929.
Cf. Periodica, *21–34.*

Joseph Rutten, Superior General of the Congregation of the
Immaculate Heart of Mary (Scheut), humbly asks the S. C. of
Rites to give a solution to the following questions:
1. According to the Decree of 22 Apr., 1910 (N. 4252),
Secovien., if a parish is united to a monastery or religious house,
or if it is entrusted perpetually or for an indefinite time to the
care of such a monastery or house, the religious calendar is
always used in Masses; otherwise, the diocesan calendar is used,
as in the case where the church is entrusted, not to the religious
family but only to some private person belonging to it, according
to the Decree, *Urbis,* of 15 Dec., 1899.

But in territories of Missions which are entrusted to a particular missionary Institute, the churches which are built are
quasi-parochial or belong to a mission station not yet erected as
a quasi-parish, and a missionary from the same religious Institute
has charge of them as rector.

The question is whether churches of quasi-parishes or of a
mission station which is not yet erected as a quasi-parish, are
considered as entrusted to the Congregation, or only to a private
person; hence, whether in these churches the calendar of the
Congregation or of the Vicariate Apostolic is to be followed.

2. On 14 Dec., 1927, Saint Thérèse of the Child Jesus was
declared the special Patroness of all Missionaries of both sexes
and of Missions all over the world, on a par with Saint Francis
Xavier, "with all the liturgical rights and privileges which belong
to this title."

The question is whether it follows from this that in territories
of Missions and in Congregations of Missionaries the feast of
Saint Thérèse of the Child Jesus should be celebrated as a duplex
of the first class, with a common octave and the *Credo* in
the Mass.

The S. C. of Rites, having heard the opinion of the special
commission and duly considered everything, decided to reply:
Replies. 1. Let the calendar of the religious Congregation be
used until the ecclesiastical hierarchy has been established in
the place in question.
2. In the affirmative, in all respects for the secular clergy, but

without the octave for the regular clergy. And it was so decreed and replied, March 23, 1929.

II. S. C. Prop. Fid., 18 May, 1932, Prot. N. 1672/32.
Cf. Periodica, *21–248.*

Some questions have been proposed to this Apostolic Delegation (Pekin) regarding the calendar to be used in the Missions and regarding the celebration of feasts in honor of Blessed Odoric of Pordenone, the Blessed Chinese Martyrs, and the principal Patrons of the Missions. It has therefore been thought advisable to refer the matter to the Holy See for a reply which may settle all the discussions which have arisen on the subject.

The S. C. for the Propagation of the Faith, by Rescript N. 1672/32 of 18 May, 1932, replied as follows to the following questions:

1. Whether, in Missions which are entrusted to a certain religious Order or Congregation, the (religious) Ordinary can adopt, for the secular clergy subject to him, the calendar proper to the Institute, or whether he must on the contrary conform to the Decree of the S. C. of Rites of 28 Oct., 1913 (AAS, 5–463, sect. V, 2, e) and establish a proper calendar, for example the calendar of the universal Church, in which are to be added the special feasts of the place, the feasts in honor of Blessed Odoric of Pordenone, of the Blessed Chinese Martyrs, and of those principal Patrons of the Missions, Saint Francis Xavier and Saint Thérèse of the Child Jesus.

Reply. In the negative to the first part, in the affirmative to the second.

2. Whether religious missionaries who for the recitation of the Office follow their own calendar, can celebrate the Mass which is assigned in the calendar of their Institute, also in churches (of the Vicariate or Prefecture), which do not *de iure* belong to their Order or Congregation; or whether on the contrary they too must, in these churches, celebrate the Mass which is assigned in the proper calendar of the Mission in which they are staying.

Reply. In the negative to the first part, in the affirmative to the second.

3. Whether the religious missionaries, although they have a calendar of their own, are obliged everywhere in China to celebrate the Mass and recite the Office in honor of the Blessed

Chinese Martyrs and Blessed Odoric of Pordenone according to the provisions of the Decrees of the S. C. Rit. (namely, the Decrees of 13 Nov., 1925, 13 March, 1930, 8 July, 1931, 16 Feb., 1932, etc.); and whether moreover these same religious missionaries must celebrate the feasts of the principal Patrons of the Missions, Saint Francis Xavier and Saint Thérèse of the Child Jesus, as duplexes of the first class.

Reply. In the affirmative to all, *et ad mentem:* the mind is that religious who are endowed with the title of missionaries to pagan nations should for this very reason feel the appropriateness of celebrating the feasts in honor either of the Patrons of the Missions or of the Blessed of the people among whom they are "Ambassadors of Christ." Hence the various Orders are to be warned that they should add as a supplement to the Office of their Missions the proper feasts of the Church in China.

While I am sending these replies to Your Excellency, let me at the same time recommend that the above prescriptions of the Holy See regarding the feasts above mentioned be put into effect in your territory, in order to obtain the desired uniformity in the Missions and especially in order to implore the aid of the heavenly Patrons.

III. S. C. Prop. Fid., 7 Nov., 1932, Prot. N. 3984/32
Cf. Periodica, 22–194.

The Regular Superior, S.J., in the Vicariate Apostolic of Anking (Anhwei) humbly asks the Sacred Congregation to provide an answer to the following question:

Question. Whether there is a contradiction between the replies to the second question of the Apostolic Delegate, of 18 May, 1932, and to the first question proposed by Father Rutten, 23 March, 1929 (quoting both questions and replies as given above). In other words, there could be a doubt whether the churches of the Vicariate should be considered as belonging *de iure* to the Order, since they are entrusted to it, or as not belonging, although entrusted to the Order. We have hitherto used the calendar proper to the religious Institute, since the ecclesiastical hierarchy is not yet established and the Mission of Anking is entrusted to the Society of Jesus. I therefore ask how these churches are to be considered and which calendar is to be followed.

Reply. In the celebration of Masses you are to follow the calendar of the Order in churches which are adjacent to a real convent in the sense that all the functions are celebrated by the Fathers of the Convent and by the Community itself; in other churches, however, you are to follow the calendar of the Vicariate. This Sacred Congregation recently gave an answer in this same sense to the Vicar Apostolic of Bac-Ninh.

(Private); S. C. Rit., 23 March, 1929; S. C. Prop. Fid., 18 May, 1932; S. C. Prop. Fid., 7 Nov., 1932.

NOTE: As Vermeersch had correctly conjectured in his commentary on the two apparently conflicting replies (*Periodica*, 22–30*), the conflict is reconciled by considering the earlier reply of the S. C. Rit. as a particular favor rather than as a norm of law. This is confirmed by the S. C. Prop. Fid. in those parts of its latest reply (7 Nov., 1932) which are omitted from our report.

Some Abuses of the Liturgical Movement (Bishop of Linz, 1937) **Private.**

The Bishop of Linz issued for his diocese the following *Monitum* on "avoiding exaggerations in the Liturgy":

The Liturgical Movement is daily producing new and lamentable errors. They turn the altar around so as to celebrate Mass facing the people; they remove the tabernacle from the middle of the altar and put it in some wall; lay people receive Holy Communion standing; the *"Missa cantata et recitata"* is cheapened by daily mechanical repetition; they omit the *Ave Maria* after the *Pater Noster;* they forbid the recitation of the Rosary during Mass.

Tendencies of this sort merit public and severe condemnation. We therefore strictly provide as follows for both religious and secular clergy:

1. All without exception are strictly forbidden to turn the altar and celebrate facing the people. Let no one at his own whim introduce practices which may have been in use in the primitive Church; this conduces neither to the edification of the people nor to the genuine Liturgical Movement, but introduces disturbing novelties contrary to the existing practice of the Church.

2. To remove the tabernacle from the center of the altar and place it in some part of the wall is expressly forbidden by the Code and by the Roman Ritual. Canon 1269, § 1: "The Most

Blessed Sacrament must be kept in an immovable tabernacle set in the middle of the altar." The Roman Ritual (tit. IV, c. 1, n. 6): "The tabernacle is to be placed in the main altar or in another altar."

3. To receive Holy Communion standing is expressly forbidden by the Roman Ritual (tit. IV, c. 1, n. 3): "They are to receive the Sacrament kneeling on both knees"; and (*ibid.*, n. 4): "If Holy Communion is to be given, let it be given to those who are kneeling at the altar step."

4. In the public recitation of the divine Office the *Ave Maria* is by no means to be omitted after the *Pater Noster*. The distorted and one-sided idea which calls itself "christocentric" must not be allowed to diminish devotion to Mary — least of all in our land of Upper Austria which is most devoted to her.

5. The holy Rosary is not to be prohibited during Mass on the pretext that it is a "nonliturgical prayer"; on the contrary, scarcely any other devotion presents the nature and meaning of the Sacrifice of the Mass so neatly, so graphically, and in a way so well suited to the people, as does the recitation of the holy Rosary. The Sacrifice of the Mass mystically represents and renews, not only the Passion but the whole life of the Saviour: "*Memores nos servi tui, sed et plebs tua sancta, eiusdem Christi Filii tui Domini nostri tam beatae passionis, necnon et ab inferis resurrectionis, sed et in caelos gloriosae ascensionis.*" These mysteries are commemorated in the three cycles of the Rosary. Seeing that Leo XIII explicitly ordered for the month of October the recitation of the Rosary during Mass, no liturgical movement can exclude it from the Mass.

6. Let not the Liturgical Movement degenerate into a subjectivist and separatist game, a liturgical trifling and sport for certain individuals; but let it be directed toward the general care of souls as its supreme and unchanging principle. Feeding the whole flock through preaching and the Sacraments, through social works and organizations, through a live Catholic Action and lay apostolate, is of more worth than the specialized liturgical training of chosen groups. The exterior, mechanical, or violent inculcation of the liturgical idea and practice will do little good; in fact it turns people away and alienates the faithful from the sound and true liturgical life of the Church, and creates the danger of separations, to say nothing of schisms.

And the same is true of the Mass which is called *cantata et recitata*. The endless repetition of an identical prayer, with at most a merely verbal variation, reduces the hearing of Mass to a schedule, a thing which is very annoying to many, and which they have begun to regard as a sort of religious regimentation. At times even the *Missa cantata et recitata* can be used to advantage; but to have it every Sunday or even every day is excessive, wearisome, and destructive of all personal devotion. "Community Liturgy" should not consist in having certain individuals impose their liturgical ideas on the community. What happens to please certain so-called liturgical groups is not to be forcibly imposed as a duty on the faithful as a whole. In this way the Liturgical Movement is not promoted but rather weakened.

7. Especially we again admonish the junior clergy that in cultivating the Liturgical Movement they follow strictly and without exception the orders, wishes, and counsels of their pastors; let them make no innovation along these lines without the pastor's express approval and permission; let them make more account of the sound and long-tried judgment of their own pastor and of all the senior pastors than of these unsettled novelties and the articles of a certain popular liturgical literature. Not everything which is allowed is to be recommended. Brethren, be sober. Many are deceived by the appearance of good.

(**Private**); Bishop of Linz, 1937; *Linzer Diözesenblatt*, 83–114; *Periodica*, 27–167 (Hertling).

Priest With Failing Sight: Instruction on Use of Apostolic Indult for Votive Masses (S. C. Rit., 3 Sept., 1942) Private.

An Instruction of the Sacred Congregation of Rites "for a priest with failing sight, concerning the celebration of Masses allowed him by apostolic indult" is as follows:

1. PRELIMINARY REMARKS

1. A priest who is growing blind or whose eyesight is transiently or habitually so weak that he can read only very heavy type, can obtain from the Sacred Congregation of Rites a dispensation to celebrate, according to the norms hereinafter to be explained, either the votive Mass of the Blessed Virgin or the daily Mass of the deceased.

2. The conditions of this privilege must be exactly observed.

3. If, while the privilege is in effect, the petitioner becomes entirely blind, he must abstain from saying Mass until he obtains a new indult from the Sacred Congregation of the Sacraments; and after he has obtained it he is under a grave obligation to make use of the assistance of another priest.

2. RULES REGARDING THE VOTIVE MASS OF THE BLESSED VIRGIN

I. *Which one of the votive Masses of the Blessed Virgin is to be said?*

1. A priest who has this dispensation should say the *fifth* of the votive Masses of the Blessed Virgin at all times of the year, always in white vestments.

2. If he still has enough eyesight to read also the other four votive Masses of the Blessed Virgin according to the different times of the year, he may say those Masses.

II. *When the votive Mass of the Blessed Virgin is to be said*

1. The votive Mass of the Blessed Virgin *may* be said at any time of the year; it *must* be said on all days when, according to the calendar of the church where such a priest is celebrating, daily votive Masses for the deceased are not permitted; without prejudice, however, to the further privileges regarding Masses for the deceased, which are explained below in section 3 of this Instruction.

2. During the sacred triduum of Holy Week the priest must abstain entirely from celebrating Mass.

3. On the Feast of the Nativity he can say three Masses.

III. *The rite of the Mass*

1. If a votive Mass of the Blessed Virgin is celebrated both for a grave reason and for a public cause, the priest with failing sight always says: one Oration, the *Gloria,* the *Credo,* the Preface in the solemn tone, the *Ite Missa est* and the Last Gospel of Saint John, *In principio,* even though priests who have not this privilege should on that day make some commemoration, or say

an *Imperata* ordered by the Ordinary, or say at the end the Gospel of a commemorated feast, according to the Rubrics.

2. In all other cases:

a) The *Gloria in excelsis* is said:

I. Whenever it is to be said in the Mass of the day, according to the calendar of the church where the Mass is celebrated;

II. In the jubilee of the priest's own priestly ordination;

III. Within octaves, even simple ones, of the Blessed Virgin Mary, according to the calendar of the church where the Mass is celebrated;

IV. On Saturday.

b) As to Orations, the following rules are to be observed:

I. A second and third Oration are not added when these are excluded by the rite of the Mass of the day, according to the calendar of the church in which the Mass is celebrated;

II. Otherwise three Orations are said, namely the second of the Holy Spirit and the third *contra persecutores Ecclesiae* or *pro Papa*.

c) The *Credo* is said:

I. Whenever it is to be said in the Mass of the day, according to the calendar of the church where the Mass is celebrated;

II. On the jubilee of the priest's own priestly ordination.

d) In the Preface, *et te in veneratione* is said, except on feasts and during octaves, even simple ones, of the Blessed Virgin Mary, in which cases the Preface is said just as if the Mass of the feast or of the octave were being celebrated.

e) The Last Gospel is always that of Saint John, *In principio*.

f) In private oratories the priest celebrating follows his own calendar.

3. RUBRICS FOR THE MASS OF THE DECEASED

1. On days when the daily Mass for the deceased is allowed according to the calendar of the church in which the Mass is celebrated, or according to the priest's own calendar in a private oratory, the priest with failing sight can celebrate this Mass. either singing or reading it.

2. He celebrates this same Mass (and three times if he wishes) also on the day of the Commemoration of all the Faithful Departed, in which however he shall say only one Oration, namely, *Fidelium*. If he celebrates two or three Masses on this

day, he shall observe the Constitution of Benedict XV, *Incruen-tum Altaris Sacrificium,* in virtue of which he can apply only one Mass for anyone he chooses, and can receive a stipend for that, but must apply the other Masses, without stipend, for all the faithful departed and according to the intention of the Supreme Pontiff, just as other priests.

3. In this Mass one single Oration is said, whenever this daily Mass takes the place of one in which, according to the Rubrics, only one Oration should be said. Otherwise at least three Orations should be said, but the first and second may vary according to the special intention and application of the Mass, according to the Rubrics.

4. The priest with failing sight is never bound to say the Sequence, *Dies irae.* However, in case he sings the Mass, even though he does not read the Sequence, the choir should not fail to sing it.

ROMANA

This Instruction regarding the celebration of the Holy Sacrifice of the Mass by priests with failing eyesight who have obtained an apostolic indult, already approved by His Holiness Benedict XV and now revised, is published by order of the undersigned Cardinal Prefect of the Sacred Congregation of Rites. All things to the contrary notwithstanding.

Sept. 3, 1942   C. Cardinal Salotti, *Prefect* of the S.C.R.
                       A. Carinci, *Secretary.*

(Private); S. C. of Rites, Instruction, 3 Sept., 1942. Translation made from the text officially published by the S. C. of Rites.

Versions of Scripture in Vernacular: Private and Public Reading: Former Reply Explained (Bibl. Comm., 22 Aug., 1943) AAS 35-270.

Reply of the Biblical Commission, entitled: *Responsum De Versionibus Sacrae Scripturae in Linguas Vernaculas:*

The Pontifical Biblical Commission, in order to answer a question proposed to it about the use and authority of translations of the Bible, especially from primitive texts, into vernacular languages, and in order to explain more fully its decree *De usu versionum Sacrae Scripturae in ecclesiis,* of 30 April, 1934,[1] deems

---

[1] CANON LAW DIGEST, Vol. 2, p. 196; AAS 26-315.

it appropriate to publish and recommend the following norms:

Whereas Leo XIII, in his Encyclical *Providentissimus Deus* (*Acta Leonis XIII*, Vol. 13, p. 342; *Enchiridion Biblicum*, p. 91) recommended that the primitive texts of the Bible be used for the deeper knowledge and fuller explanation of the word of God; and whereas that commendation, which surely was not made exclusively in the interest of exegetes and theologians, seems to have envisaged also the translation of those same primitive texts into commonly known or vernacular languages, such work to be done, of course, under the vigilant care of competent ecclesiastical authority and according to approved norms of both sacred and profane science;

And whereas the collections of biblical passages which are to be publicly read in the liturgical books of the Latin Church at the Holy Sacrifice of the Mass and in the divine Office, are for the most part taken from the Vulgate, the one and only Latin version among those current at that time which the Ecumenical Council of Trent declared to be authentic (*Conc. Trid.*, sess. IV, decr. *De editione et usu Ss. Librorum; Ench. Bibl.*, n. 46):

Now therefore, *servatis servandis:*

1. Translations of the Sacred Scripture into vernacular languages, whether made from the Vulgate or from primitive texts, provided they are published with the permission of competent ecclesiastical authority in accordance with canon 1391, may be properly used and read by the faithful according to their private devotion; and moreover, if, after a diligent examination of both the text and the annotations has been made by men who are highly competent in biblical and theological science, any particular translation has been found to be more faithful and appropriate, the Bishops, either singly or united in councils of their province or nation, may if they wish especially recommend it to the faithful under their care.

2. The translation of biblical passages into the vernacular, which priests celebrating Mass may perhaps wish to read to the people according to custom and convenience after reading the liturgical text itself, must, according to the reply of the Pontifical Biblical Commission,[2] be conformed to the Latin, that is the liturgical, text, with full liberty, however, of appropriately ex-

---

[2] *Ibid.*

plaining the said translation, if desired, by means of the original text or of some other clearer translation.

His Holiness Pius XII, in the audience graciously granted to the undersigned *Consultor ab Actis* on the 22nd of August, 1943, approved this reply and ordered that it be published.

Rome, 22 August, 1943.

AAS 35–270; Bibl. Comm., 22 Aug., 1943.

Ablutions Without Wine (Decree, S. C. Rit., 12 May, 1944) AAS 36–154.

Decree of the Sacred Congregation of Rites:

A number of Ordinaries of places have informed our Holy Father Pius XII that the priests of their dioceses, because of increasing difficulties due to the war, will suffer also from a shortage of wine for the Holy Sacrifice of the Mass; and they have accordingly petitioned him to deign to make such provision as may be made for the conservation of the supply of wine. And in the audience granted to the undersigned Cardinal Prefect of the Sacred Congregation of Rites on the 12th of May, 1944, His Holiness, in view of the peculiar circumstances of the present time, and for as long as these circumstances continue, graciously permits that the purifications and ablutions of the chalice, which are to be made in the Mass according to the rubrics, first with wine and afterward with wine and water, may be made with water only, in those places where, according to the prudent judgment of the Ordinary, a scarcity of wine is already felt or is foreseen in the future. All things to the contrary notwithstanding. May 12, 1944.

AAS 36–154; S. C. Rit., Decree, 12 May, 1944.

Extravagant Rites Not to Be Introduced in the Mass (S. C. Rit., 20 Jan., 1945) Private.

The following authentic reply of the Sacred Congregation of Rites, N. S 62/44, was sent to us by the Most Reverend Apostolic Delegate to the United States.

Question. Whether certain practices recently introduced in some churches can be sustained, namely:

1. At the time of the Offertory in the Sacrifice of the Mass, two servers standing at the sides of the altar lift up the money

offerings of the collection in the baskets and offer them while the celebrant is offering the host.

2. In a certain religious house, at the time of the Offertory in the Mass, Sisters approach the altar in procession and offer a host and wine to the priest, and while the priest offers the *oblata,* the Sisters recite the Offertory prayer with the celebrant in Latin.

Reply. The above practices can absolutely not be tolerated. (**Private**) ; S. C. Rit., 20 Jan., 1945.

NOTE: The Archbishop of Chicago, in transmitting a copy of this document to his priests on March 12, 1945, accompanied it with the following letter:

"I am sending you with this letter a copy of a recent important decision of the Sacred Congregation of Rites. Although I am sure that the practices condemned do not obtain in this Archdiocese, the fact that on one occasion some few years ago I had to forbid the introduction of them prompts me to inform the clergy of this decision. While it answers two specific questions proposed, the underlying principle in it is that novelties may not be introduced into the liturgy. We have seen how easy it is for such things as linen ciborium covers, silk or rayon surplices, etc., to creep in. Our duty is to see that liturgical laws be observed and that there be permitted no novelties.

"I wish to take this occasion also to call attention to the decision which I made some years ago on the question of the *Missa Recitata.* This practice must not be taken to be more than a piety permitted, if the public recitation of the prayers is limited to the liturgical prayers indicated in my decision. The prayers which according to the rubrics the priest says secretly must not be said aloud.

"We are very much interested in developing a greater appreciation of the liturgy, but our devotion to the liturgy demands that we do not introduce any novelties. I have even heard it said that the recitation of the rosary, as commanded by Pope Pius XII during October during Low Mass is not a devout assistance at Mass. Such an assertion is foolish and runs counter to theology. We shall always do well if we keep ourselves in the mind of the Church."

Gonyklisia, Where in Use in Byzantine Rite, to Be Made After Words of Consecration, Not After *Epiclesis* (Holy Office, 12 Feb., 1951) **AAS 43-217.**

This Supreme Sacred Congregation has been asked the following question:

Whether the great prostration (*gonyklisia*), in those places where it is in use in the celebration of the Mass of the Byzantine rite, is to be made after the words of Christ, pronounced in the consecration of the bread and wine, or after the *Epiclesis* has been said.

The Eminent and Most Reverend Cardinals in charge of the protection of faith and morals, in the plenary meeting held on Wednesday, Dec. 20, 1950, after hearing the opinion of the Reverend Consultors, decided to reply:

Reply. In the affirmative to the first part; in the negative to the second.

And on the following Thursday His Holiness by divine Providence Pope Pius XII, in the audience granted to His Excellency the Most Reverend Assessor of the Holy Office, approved the resolution of the Eminent Fathers when it was reported to him, and ordered that it be published.

Given at Rome, from the Holy Office, 12 February, 1951.

AAS 43–217; Holy Office, Decree, 12 Feb., 1951. Annotations; *Periodica,* 40–434 (Hanssens); *Monitor Ecclesiasticus,* 1950, p. 219 (Crovini).

Ambrosian Rite Outside Archdiocese of Milan: A priest of the Archdiocese of Milan asked for the faculty of using the Ambrosian rite outside the Archdiocese, for reasons of private devotion. The reply, 2 May, 1950 (N. 44/50): *Negative* (*Monitor Ecclesiasticus,* 1952, p. 449).

Antimensium: Use of, instead of altar stone. See **c. 822**; private replies of S. C. Prop. Fid., 8 March, 1950, and S. C. Rit., 26 June, 1950, and note.

Assumption: Text of New Mass. S. C. Rit., 31 Oct., 1950 (AAS 42–793).

Candles for Mass: Indult allowing electric light modified. See **c. 1271**; AAS 41–476.

Christmas: Three Masses are not formally different actions as regards computing time. See **c. 33**; AAS 39–373.

Common of One or More Supreme Pontiffs. See S. C. Rit., 9 Jan., 1942 (AAS 34–105).

Easter: New Liturgy of. See **c. 2**; AAS 44–48.

Encyclical of Pius XII, on the Liturgy. See Pius XII, 20 Nov., 1947 (AAS 39–521). English text, *The Catholic Mind,* 1948, p. 321. Annotations, *Periodica,* 37–59 (Hanssens) and 38–1 (Schmidt).

Holy Saturday: Restoration of Solemn Paschal Vigil. See **c. 2**; AAS 43–128 and AAS 44–48.

Indults for: Domestic Chapel; Portable Altar; Mass Without Server; Keeping Blessed Sacrament in Private Oratories. See **c. 813**; AAS 41–493.

Indult to Say Mass in the House. See **c. 813**; AAS 41–493.

Liturgy: Encyclical on. Pius XII, 20 Nov., 1947 (AAS 39–521).

Mass: After midnight. Rescript allowing it to Priest Adorers of the Blessed Sacrament on occasion of missions preached by them, on the following conditions: with permission of Bishop; Mass to begin a half hour after midnight; services to last about three hours including time of Mass; celebrant to have satisfied all the obligations of the Pious Union. S. C. Sacr., 11 July, 1949 (*Monitor Ecclesiasticus,* 1950, p. 32).

At altar where Blessed Sacrament is solemnly exposed. See **c. 1274**; private reply of S. C. Rit., 26 June, 1950.

On board ship: Faculty to permit this during Holy Year, given to Ap. Del. U. S., S. C. Sacr., 2 Feb., 1950 (*Monitor Ecclesiasticus,* 1950, p. 33).

On train reserved to pilgrims during Holy Year. See **c. 822**, ref.

Missions: Faculty for Mass in open air interpreted. See **c. 66**; private, S. C. Prop. Fid., 15 Dec., 1945.

Religious Profession During Mass: If not according to Constitutions, not permitted. See **c. 576**; private, S. C. Rit., 8 July, 1950.

Transfers and Variations in Celebration of Feasts: 1) A Congregation of priests asked that the feast of St. Joseph be permitted to be celebrated in their churches on the 19th of March in spite of the concurrence of any other celebration except Passion Sunday or Holy Week. The reply, 26 Jan., 1950, S. C. Rit. (N. 16/50): *Non expedire (Monitor Ecclesiasticus,* 1952, p. 454).

2) A certain Chapter in Mexico asked permission to celebrate every year as a double of the first class the Feast of the Maternity of the Blessed Virgin on the anniversary of the solemn coronation of a particular image of the Blessed Virgin. The reply, S. C. Rit., 1 June, 1950 (N. M. 52/50): *Non expedire (Monitor Ecclesiasticus,* 1952, p. 454).

3) The Superioress General of a Congregation of Sisters asked that the Feast of their holy founders be granted an octave of the first class. The reply, S. C. Rit., 12 June, 1950 (N. C. 105/50): *Non expedire (Monitor Ecclesiasticus,* 1952, p. 454).

4) A pastor (outside the diocese of Padua where the feast in question has special privileges) asked that in his parish it be allowed to celebrate the Feast of the Tongue of St. Anthony of Padua, Confessor, with the Mass and Office which are approved for the diocese of Padua. The reply, S. C. Rit., 15 Sept., 1950 (N. C. 108/50): *Non expedire (Monitor Ecclesiasticus,* 1952, p. 454).

Votive and Requiem Masses: Various Replies: 1) The Provincial of a Congregation of priests asked that it be permitted in his Province to celebrate the votive Mass of the Holy Ghost on the first Thursday of each month in the same rite as the Mass of the Sacred Heart is permitted on the first Friday. The reply, S. C. Rit., 29 March, 1950 (N. C. 44/50): *Non expedire (Monitor Ecclesiasticus,* 1952, p. 451).

2) An Ordinary asked that the votive Mass of the Blessed Virgin be permitted on the occasion of a Marian pilgrimage during Lent. The reply, S. C. Rit., 18 Feb., 1950 (N. V. 18/50): *Non solere concedi (Monitor Ecclesiasticus,* 1952, p. 452).

3) The Ordinary of a certain diocese in Spain asked permission to have solemn Requiem Mass for the souls of the priests who were killed out

of hatred of the faith during the Spanish civil war, the celebration to be held *during the octave of Easter,* which is a privileged octave of the first class. The reply, S. C. Rit., 2 March, 1950 (N. V. 4/50): *Non expedire* (*Monitor Ecclesiasticus,* 1952, p. 452).

4) The Ordinary of a certain diocese in England, to satisfy the faithful who ask for a solemn Requiem Mass of "month's mind," i.e., on the thirtieth day after the death, asked for an indult to celebrate such Masses during privileged octaves of the second and third orders. The reply, S. C. Rit., 12 April, 1951 (N. A. 29/51): *Tantum in octavis tertii ordinis, ad quinquennium* (*Monitor Ecclesiasticus,* 1952, p. 453).

CANON 822

Antimensium Latinum: **Rescript Permitting It Instead of Altar Stone: Formula for Consecration** (S. C. Prop. Fid., 8 March, 1950, and S. C. Rit.) **Private.**

Prot. N. 982/50

Ordinarius Archidioecesis Calcuttensis, ad pedes Sanctitatis Vestrae provolutus, humiliter petit facultatem permittendi sacerdotibus missionariis sibi subditis ut loco altaris portatilis seu petrae sacrae in Sacrosancto Missae Sacrificio celebrando substituatur aliquod linteum ex lino vel cannabe confectum.

Et Deus . . .

Sacra Congregatio de Propaganda Fide, vigore facultatum a Sanctissimo Domino Nostro Pio Divina Providentia Pp. XII sibi specialiter tributarum, benigne indulget ut Ordinarius Calcuttensis Orator, in iis regionibus ubi viarum et curruum deest copia, sacerdotibus missionariis sibi subditis facultatem concedere valeat substituendi loco altaris portatilis seu petrae sacrae aliquod linteum ex lino vel cannabe confectum et ab Episcopo benedictum, in quo reconditae sint Sanctorum Reliquiae ab eodem Episcopo recognitae, super quo iidem sacerdotes missionarii Sacrosanctum Missae Sacrificium celebrare queant, iis tantum in casibus, et onerata eorum conscientia, in quibus aut nulla ecclesia vel oratorium sive publicum sive privatum exstet, et valde incommodum sit lapideum altare secum in itinere transferre aut in promptu habere. Servatis de cetero servandis iuxta Rubricas, praesertim quoad tobaleas et corporale.

Contrariis non obstantibus quibuscumque etiam speciali mentione dignis.

Praesentibus valituris usque ad exspirationem facultatum generalium, die 31 Decembris 1960.

Datum Romae, ex Aedibus S. Congregationis de Propaganda Fide, die 8 mensis Martii A.D. 1950.

(Private); S. C. Prop. Fid., 8 March, 1950. This particular rescript is identical with the general formula reported by Paventi in *Monitor Ecclesiasticus,* 1950, p. 378.

NOTE: The formula for the blessing is as follows:

BENEDICTIO LINTEI

loco altaris portatilis a missionalibus dumtaxat
adhibendi pro celebratione Missae

Pontifex, postquam aliquas authenticas Reliquias sanctorum Martyrum recognoverit, eas in parvo quodam lineo sacculo includit, qui in angulo dextero lintei benedicendi assuatur, deinde linteum benedicit, dicens:

V. Adjutorium nostrum in nomine Domini.

R. Qui fecit caelum et terram.

V. Dominus vobiscum.

R. Et cum spiritu tuo.

Oremus

Majestatem tuam, Domine, humiliter imploramus ut linteum hoc ad suscipienda populi tui munera praeparatum per nostrae humilitatis servitium bene ✠ dicere, sancti ✠ ficare et conse ✠ crare digneris: ut super eo sanctum sacrificium Tibi offerre valeamus, ad honorem Beatissimae Virginis Mariae et Sanctorum N.N., quorum reliquias in eo reposuimus, et omnium Sanctorum; et praesta, ut per haec sacrosancta mysteria vincula peccatorum nostrorum absolvantur, maculae deleantur, veniae impetrentur, gratiae acquirantur, quatenus una cum Sanctis et Electis tuis vitam percipere mereamur aeternam. Per eundem Christum Dominum Nostrum.

R. Amen.

Et aspergit illud aqua benedicta.

(Private); S. C. Rit., formula for blessing the *"antimensium Latinum";* reported by Paventi in *Monitor Ecclesiasticus,* 1950, p. 379.

Permission to Use *Antimensium* Not Granted by the S. C. of Rites (S. C. Rit., 26 June, 1950) Private.

Several Ordinaries, in view of the difficulties of communication experienced by priests of the territory when obliged to say Mass in remote places for the needs of the faithful, asked the Sacred Congregation of Rites for the faculty whereby the priests, instead of the altar stone which was difficult to carry under the circumstances, might use for the celebration of Mass a linen cloth specially blessed and containing the relics, like the *antimensium* which is permitted to priests of the Oriental rite.

Reply. *Non expedire.*

(Private) ; S. C. Rit., 26 June, 1950 Prot. N. C. 7/50. *Monitor Ecclesiasticus,* 1952, p. 450.

NOTE: Although the S. C. of Rites does not grant this faculty, it has approved a formula for the blessing of the Latin *antimensium.* (Cf. private reply of S. C. Prop. Fid., 8 March, 1950, and note, reported above in this volume under canon 822.) The faculty is regularly granted by the S. C. Prop. Fid. for territories subject to it. The S. C. for the Oriental Church grants the faculty of using the Greek *antimensium* in the territories over which it has jurisdiction. The Sacred Consistorial Congregation does not grant it regularly, but has delegated at least one Ordinary (of Diamantina in Brazil) the general faculty to grant permission to use the Latin *antimensium* to priests who have to make difficult journeys where it would be most inconvenient to carry the altar stone.

Mass on Train Reserved to Pilgrims during Holy Year: Faculty to permit this was granted to Archbishop Valeri, President of the Commission for the Holy Year, under certain conditions, especially that the train be stopping in the station for forty-five minutes. S. C. Sacr., 24 Dec., 1949 (*Monitor Ecclesiasticus,* 1950, p. 33).

Precept of Hearing Mass is satisfied by hearing it in places mentioned in canon 822, § 4. See c. **1249**; AAS 44–497.

CANON 825

Masses Celebrated by Chapter by Order of the Bishop on Anniversaries of His Election and Consecration, Must Also Be Applied for His Intention (S. C. Conc., 11 Nov., 1950) **AAS 43–177.**

A Resolution of the S. C. of the Council, *Lucerina et Aliarum, Missae pro Episcopo,* is as follows:

Question. This Sacred Congregation has received for solution the following question: Whether at the command of the Bishop, on the anniversary days of his election or transfer and of his consecration, the Chapter is bound only to celebrate the solemn Mass or also to apply it for the Bishop.

Remarks. The *Caeremoniale Episcoporum* (lib. II, cap. 35,

n. 1) provides: "Every year on the anniversary days of the election and consecration of the Bishop, it is proper that a solemn Mass be celebrated by the Bishop himself, or by some dignitary or canon in his presence."

And upon a command by the Bishop, this propriety becomes an obligation. For, the S. C. of Rites, to the question: "Whether the solemn Mass on the anniversary days of the election and consecration of the Bishop has the force of a *precept* in the Cathedral and Collegiate Churches of the diocese, although the *Caeremoniale Episcoporum* (lib. II, cap. 35, n. 1) says merely: *celebrari convenit,*" replied on 14 Aug., 1858, in *Granaten.*, N. 3078: "In the affirmative if there is moreover a command from the Bishop." The obligatory character of this Mass is confirmed in the very Rubrics which are to be observed according to the Apostolic Constitution, *Divino afflatu* of Pius X, of 1 Nov., 1911 (AAS, 3–649).

That the celebration of the Mass in question carries with it also the obligation of applying it for the Bishop, is deduced from canon 825, n. 4 of the Code of Canon Law: "It is never allowed . . . to receive one stipend for the mere celebration and another for the application of the same Mass, unless it is certain that one of the stipends is offered for the celebration without the application." This exception certainly does not occur in the present case: therefore the obligation to apply the Mass for the Bishop is logically contained in the obligation of celebrating the Mass.

Moreover it cannot even be presumed that the Bishop, in ordering that the Mass be celebrated, intends merely the external rite and wants to exclude the spiritual fruit of the Mass.

And this is confirmed by the *Caeremoniale Episcoporum* itself, which provides regarding the Mass for the deceased former Bishop: "The actual Bishop must remember his deceased immediate predecessor, and every year on the anniversary of his death must, for the repose of his soul, celebrate a Mass or at least have a Mass celebrated by some dignitary or canon, and assist at it himself and give the absolution at the end" (lib. II, cap. 36, n. 1).

Here there is no doubt that the celebration of the Mass for the soul of the deceased Bishop implies also its application.

Resolution. Therefore, to the question as stated above, the Eminent Fathers of this S. C., in the plenary meeting held on

11 Nov., 1950, replied: In the negative to the first part, in the affirmative to the second.

And in the audience of the 22nd of the same month and year, His Holiness Pius XII deigned to approve and confirm this resolution.

AAS 43–177; S. C. Conc., 11 Nov., 1950.

CANON 828

Faculties to Reduce Masses: Revoked (S. C. Conc., 30 June, 1949) AAS 41–374.

A Decree of the S. C. of the Council:

Since the extraordinary circumstances on account of which the prescriptions of the Code of Canon Law were sometimes suspended have ceased, the Sacred Congregation of the Council, after conferring with the S. C. of Religious and the S. C. of Propaganda, in pursuance of a special mandate of His Holiness by divine Providence Pope Pius XII, confirms the Decree of 1 Aug., 1941 (N. 3165/41), and at the same time declares that all faculties to reduce Masses — except the so-called "quinquennial" faculties given to Ordinaries — by whatsoever authority, in whatever way they may have been granted, even by word of mouth, and for whatever length of time, either to Ordinaries of whatever class, or to religious Superiors, or to any other physical or moral persons, are to be considered from the end of the year 1949 as revoked and of no effect.

Hence hereafter according to the Code of Canon Law (cf. cc. 1517, § 1 and 1551, § 1) recourse must be had to the Holy See in each case.

All things to the contrary notwithstanding.

Given at Rome the 30th of June, 1949.

AAS 41–374; S. C. Conc., 30 June, 1949.

Faculties to Reduce Masses: Revoked Also in Oriental Church (S. C. Eccl. Orient., 30 June, 1949) AAS 41–373.

A Decree of the S. C. for the Oriental Church:

Since the extraordinary circumstances on account of which the prescriptions of law regarding the reduction of Masses were sometimes suspended have ceased, the Sacred Congregation for the Oriental Church, in pursuance of a special mandate of His

Holiness by divine Providence Pope Pius XII, declares to all who are subject to its jurisdiction that all faculties to reduce Masses, by whatsoever authority, in whatsoever way they may have been granted, even by word of mouth, and for whatever length of time, either to Ordinaries of whatever class, or to religious Superiors, or to any other physical or moral persons, are to be considered from the end of the year 1949 as revoked and of no effect.

Hence hereafter recourse must be had to the Holy See in every case.

All things to the contrary notwithstanding.

Given at Rome, from the Sacred Congregation for the Oriental Church, the 30th of June, 1949.

AAS 41–373; S. C. Eccl. Orient., 30 June, 1949.

CANON 858

Eucharistic Fast: Faculty to Dispense Persons Hospitalized, So That They May Take Drink or Medicine (S. C. Sacr., 25 March, 1946, and Letter of Ap. Del. U. S., 17 May, 1946) **Private.**

This faculty was announced by the Most Reverend Apostolic Delegate as follows:

His Eminence the Cardinal Prefect of the Sacred Congregation on the Discipline of the Sacraments writes me that he submitted to the consideration of the Holy Father the petition of the Episcopate of this country for the faculty to dispense from the Eucharistic fast *ad modum potus et medicinae* the faithful who are hospitalized during their illness.

His Holiness, in the audience of 25 March, 1946, graciously deigned to grant *ad triennium* to all the Most Reverend Ordinaries of the United States the faculty to grant dispensations from the Eucharistic fast *per modum potus et medicinae pro infirmis in nosocomiis degentibus, durante tantum male affecta valetudine, remota quavis scandali vel fidelium admirationis occasione.* This faculty, as I need not add, may not be invoked in favor of priests for the celebration of holy Mass, but only for the reception of holy Communion.

(**Private**); S. C. Sacr., 25 March, 1946. The Most Reverend Apostolic Delegate kindly sent us the letter in which this indult was announced.

NOTE: *Priests* may be dispensed as above if they are confined by illness to their rectory or to a religious or private house. See letter of Apostolic Delegate of 3 April, 1947, reported below under this same canon 858.

Religious: Apostolic Delegate of U. S. has faculty to dispense religious from Eucharistic fast so that they may take something *per modum potus et medicinae* when their physician considers the keeping of the fast injurious to their health. See letter of Apostolic Delegate of 3 April, 1947, reported below under this same canon 858.

Eucharistic Fast: Indult for Night Workers (S. C. Sacr., 27 May, 1946) Private.

On behalf of the Ordinaries of the United States, the Apostolic Delegate sent the following petition to the Sacred Congregation of the Sacraments:

The Metropolitans, Bishops, and other local Ordinaries of the United States of North America humbly ask as a favor the faculty to dispense from the Eucharistic fast the faithful who habitually work after midnight, so that they may be able to receive Holy Communion through devotion, in the absence of all scandal and amazement, when they have abstained from solid foods for four hours and from drink for one hour, provided that any drink taken after midnight be non-alcoholic.

The Most Reverend Apostolic Delegate, in a letter of 26 July, 1946, announced that His Holiness, in an audience of 27 May, 1946, had granted this faculty *for a period of three years,* under the following conditions:

1. The Most Reverend Ordinaries, in granting dispensations under this faculty, must proceed in a way that is certain and determinate, not leaving the use of this privilege to the judgment of the faithful.

2. The dispensation may be given for Sundays and feasts of precept and for one other day during the week as the devotion of the individual communicant may dictate; furthermore, in the case of nursing Sisters dispensation may be granted for *daily* Communion whenever the previous night has been spent in the service of the sick.

3. At the expiration of the faculty, a report is to be made to the said Sacred Congregation on the use of the faculty and on its advantages and possible disadvantages.

(**Private**); S. C. Sacr., 27 May, 1946. The Most Reverend Apostolic Delegate kindly sent us the letter in which this indult was announced.

NOTE: *Nursing Brothers* may be dispensed from the Eucharistic fast on the same conditions as above provided for nursing Sisters. See letter of Apostolic Delegate of 3 April, 1947, reported below under this same canon 858.

Extensions of Indult on Eucharistic Fast: New Faculties of Apostolic Delegate (Apostolic Delegate, U. S., 3 April, 1947) Private.

Your Excellency:

In connection with the faculties announced in my letters of May 27 and July 26, 1946, I am pleased to inform Your Excellency that His Holiness has graciously acceded to the petitions of the Most Reverend Ordinaries of the United States and extended the faculty of dispensing from the Eucharistic fast those who are hospitalized. By this extension the Most Reverend Ordinaries can now dispense for the reception of holy Communion, according to the terms of that faculty, priests confined by illness to their rectory or to a religious or private house.

The Holy Father, likewise, extended in favor of religious brothers who act as nurses or infirmarians the other faculty conceded to the Most Reverend Ordinaries in favor of nursing Sisters. In virtue of the extension these religious brothers may be granted an indult to receive holy Communion, even daily, if they are fasting for four hours from solid food and for one hour from liquids and if they have spent the preceding night in the continuous service of the sick.

The foregoing grants will remain in force until the expiration of the original concessions.

The relative tax due from each diocese to the Sacred Congregation for these grants is five dollars, which may be made payable to this office, whence it will be duly reported to the Sacred Congregation in your name.

I am also pleased to inform Your Excellency that the Sacred Congregation for Religious has granted faculties to this Apostolic Delegation:

a) To permit the contraction of loans, sales, and alienations of property belonging to a religious institute, when the sum involved does not exceed a half a million gold dollars, provided that there

is observance of the norms which were made known to the Most
Reverend Ordinaries and to the religious Superiors by this Apostolic Delegation on November 13, 1936;[1]

b) To dispense religious for the reception of holy Communion
from the obligation of the Eucharistic fast so that they may take
something *per modum potus aut medicinae,* when their physician
considers the keeping of the fast injurious to their health;

c) To shorten or prolong the postulancy prescribed by the
Code of Canon Law.

Will Your Excellency kindly call these faculties to the attention
of the religious Superiors of your diocese in the manner you deem
opportune.

(Private); Apostolic Delegate, 3 April, 1947. The Most Reverend Apostolic
Delegate kindly sent us the letter in which these faculties are announced.

Eucharistic Fast: Modified in France by Indult for Cele-brant and People (Holy Office, 23 Oct., 1947) Private.

I. His Holiness Pius XII, by Divine Providence Pope, acceding
to the wishes of the Eminent Fathers of the Holy Office, and after
having heard from the Cardinal Prefect of the Sacred Congregation of the Sacraments, in view of the altogether extraordinary
circumstances prevailing at the present time in France, particularly the poor physical condition of priests and people resulting
from the hardships of the recent terrible war and being constantly further weakened by the difficulty of procuring food, in
view also of the lack of priests to attend adequately to the care
of souls, desiring to satisfy the desire of many of the faithful to
receive Holy Communion frequently, has deigned, derogating for
France from the prescriptions of canons 808 and 858, § 1, to grant
to priests who celebrate Mass and to the faithful who receive Holy
Communion in France after nine o'clock, the permission to take
non-alcoholic drink until one hour before Mass or Communion.

The same permission is given to priests who celebrate Mass
and to the faithful who receive Holy Communion before nine
o'clock, when they have to make a long trip to reach the nearest
church, or if they have to do heavy work for a considerable time
before Mass or Communion.

These grants are good for one year, at the end of which the

---

[1] See CANON LAW DIGEST, Vol. 2, pp. 161–166.

Bishops Ordinaries in France, after having grouped their observations, shall report to the Holy Office with the greatest care and in detail, the use that has been made of this permission.

(**Private**); Holy Office, 23 Oct., 1947.

NOTE: We translate this indult from *La Semaine Catholique de Toulouse*, 16 Nov., 1947, p. 549, which gives also the following summary: In virtue of the first indult, priests who celebrate Mass and the faithful who receive Holy Communion in France after nine o'clock have permission to take non-alcoholic drink until one hour before Mass or Holy Communion. The same permission under the same conditions for priests and faithful before nine o'clock, when they have to make a long trip or do heavy work for a considerable time.

A second indult given at the same time will be found under canon 867.

Eucharistic Fast: Various Indults for the United States
(Reported in Letter of Archbishop of New Orleans, 16 August, 1949) **Private.**

The following letter was sent to the clergy of the Archdiocese of New Orleans:

Reverend Dear Fathers:

His Excellency, the Most Reverend Archbishop, recently received through the Apostolic Delegation in Washington a communication from the Sacred Congregation of the Sacraments respecting the renewal of the faculty of the Most Reverend Metropolitans, Bishops, and Ordinaries of Places in the United States to dispense from the eucharistic fast. Briefly, the documents contain the following:

Sacred Congregation of the Sacraments

In an audience with the Holy Father on 25 Apr., 1949, His Holiness granted the renewal of Rescripts N. 1975/46 of April 4, 1946, N. 1975/46 of February 8, 1947, N. 1975/46 of May 27, 1946, regarding the faculties:

1) To dispense from the law of the eucharistic fast by way of drink or medicine:

a) the *faithful sick in hospitals,* for the duration of their ailment;

b) *priests who are sick in their rectories or in a religious or private house,* in order to receive Holy Communion *more laicorum.*

2) To dispense from the law of the eucharistic fast, observing, however, the fast of four hours from the taking of solid food and one hour from liquids, provided the liquids taken after midnight be non-alcoholic;

a) on Sundays and Holy Days of Obligation or another day in the week, the *faithful who work habitually after midnight;*

b) even on successive days (daily) in the case of *Religious Sisters or Brothers* dedicated to the care of the sick on all-night duty.

3) Over and above, the Holy Father extended the indult granted for the benefit of the faithful sick in hospitals to *all the sick faithful who reside outside a hospital,* whether in a Rest Home, Sanatorium, or even in private homes.

All of the above faculties are granted for three years from the date mentioned above, i.e., April 25, 1949. The only conditions placed are these: that the occasion of any scandal or "admiration" of the faithful be removed, and *"servatis de iure servandis."*

The Sacred Congregation for Religious

In an audience with the Holy Father on 25 Oct., 1948, His Holiness benignly granted the extension of the Rescript N. 1975/46 of April 4, 1946, regarding the dispensation from the eucharistic fast of hospitalized and sick priests *to all religious communities of men and women* in the United States, even to those who live after the manner of common life. This faculty is granted to Ordinaries of places, Bishops, and Metropolitans for three years from the date mentioned above, i.e., October 25, 1948.

In virtue of the above extension of faculties to dispense from the eucharistic fast, I am pleased herewith to subdelegate you in the exercise of these faculties according to the terms specified and for the duration indicated. I recommend careful study and faithful observance of the privileges granted.

Expressing the hope that many graces may flow from their application in the ministry of souls, I am,

Faithfully yours in the Lord,

Lucien Joseph Caillouet, Vicar General,

Archdiocese of New Orleans

(Private); Archbishop of New Orleans, 16 Aug., 1949. Text kindly supplied for the DIGEST by the Reverend Eugene J. O'Connor, S.J., with the consent of the Most Reverend Archbishop.

Eucharistic Indult for Mariners (S. C. Sacr., 24 March, 1952) Private.

The petition and rescript are as follows:

The Apostolic Delegate at Washington, prostrate at the feet of Your Holiness, humbly petitions on behalf of the Ordinaries of the United States of America the faculty to dispense from the eucharistic fast the mariners of the American merchant marine and the mariners of other nationalities who are serving on ships in American ports, so that they may take something before going to Holy Communion.

Reply. N. 9734/51 *Ex Audientia SS.mi* 24 March, 1952

His Holiness Pope Pius XII, having received the report from the undersigned Cardinal Pro-Prefect of the Sacred Congregation of the Sacraments, considering the representations made in the petition, deigned to grant to the Most Excellent petitioner the favor as asked, but only by way of drink, observing a fast of one hour from drink, and all occasion of scandal or wonderment being removed.

All things to the contrary notwithstanding.

The present indult to be good for three years.

Under the name of drink are included drinks consisting of coffee, tea, milk, juice, and other substances even having nutritive value, provided they are in a liquid form.

(**Private**); S. C. Sacr., 24 March, 1952. *The Jurist,* 12–474.

NOTE: Although this and all similar indults are revoked by the Apostolic Constitution, *Christus Dominus* of 6 Jan., 1953 (effective 16 Jan., 1953), AAS 45–15, we retain these reports for their possible historical value.

Eucharistic Fast: Faculty to Dispense Faithful Sick Even at Home: Conditions: Extension of Other Indults (S. C. Sacr., 5 May, 1952) Private.

His Excellency, the Most Reverend Joseph Francis Rummel, Archbishop of New Orleans, on May 23, 1952, communicated to "the Right Reverend, Very Reverend and Reverend Fathers, Archdiocese of New Orleans" the faculties granted to the local Ordinaries of the United States by a Rescript of the Sacred

Congregation of the Sacraments of 5 May, 1952 (N. 3090/52), which is verbatim as follows:

The Metropolitans, Bishops, and other local Ordinaries of the United States of America, prostrate at the feet of Your Holiness, humbly ask for an extension of the Rescript N. 1596/49, given on April 25, 1949, in an audience with Your Holiness, respecting the following faculties:

1. To dispense, for the duration of their illness, from the law of the eucharistic fast by way of drink or medicine, the faithful who are sick in hospitals; priests who are sick in their rectories, in religious houses, or in private houses, in order to receive Holy Communion after the manner of a lay person; the faithful who are sick, and cared for outside hospitals, in convalescent homes, or even in private homes;

2. To dispense the faithful who work habitually after midnight, on Sundays and Holy Days of Obligation, and on one other day of the week, and even daily if there is question of religious sisters or brothers who are occupied with the care of the sick for continuous night duty; as long as these conditions last, these will observe the fast for four hours from solid food and one hour from liquid, provided the liquid taken after midnight be not alcoholic.

The Reply. *Ex Audientia SS.mi,* April 28, 1952.

Our Most Holy Father, Pius XII, having heard the report of the undersigned Cardinal Pro-prefect of the Sacred Congregation of the Sacraments, having considered the contents of the above petition, has deigned to grant the favor of the extension; however, the breaking of the eucharistic fast is *limited to the taking of liquid or medicine only,* even as regards the second part of the above petition, observing the fast for one hour from drink, removing any occasion of scandal or surprise on the part of the faithful, and observing all other things required under the law.

All things to the contrary notwithstanding.

These faculties are to be valid for three years.

Under the term *potus* (liquid or drink) are included coffee, tea, milk, and other substances, even those that have nutritive value, allowed by law, provided the form of liquid predominates.

(**Private**) ; S. C. Sacr., 5 May, 1952. This translation was kindly sent to us by the Reverend Eugene J. O'Connor, S.J., with the consent of the Most Reverend Archbishop.

CANON 866

Orientals Satisfy Paschal Precept by Receiving Communion in Another Rite (S. C. Eccl. Or., 26 Jan., 1925) **Private.**

The Sacred Congregation for the Oriental Church declared that the favors of this canon 866 extend also to Oriental Catholics, so that they as well as Latin Catholics satisfy the precept of paschal Communion by receiving in a rite other than their own.

(**Private**); S. C. Eccl. Or., 26 Jan., 1925. Reported in Cicognani-Staffa, *Ius Canonicum*, Vol. I, p. 35; also in Wernz-Vidal, *Ius Canonicum*, ed. 1938, Vol. I, p. 115.

CANON 867

Afternoon or Evening Mass With Modified Eucharistic Fast, in France, on Sundays and Days of Obligation Only (Holy Office, 23 Oct., 1947) **Private.**

II. His Holiness Pius XII, by Divine Providence Pope, acceding to the wishes of the Eminent Fathers of the Holy Office and after having heard from the Cardinal Prefect of the S. C. of the Sacraments, in view of the altogether extraordinary circumstances of the present time, has graciously deigned to grant to the Bishops Ordinaries in France, with an obligation in conscience to verify that a true necessity exists, the faculty to grant to priests who are subject to them the permission to celebrate, on feast days and days of obligation only, a second or third Mass in the course of the afternoon, whenever too great fatigue from their sacred ministry or the distance make it impossible to celebrate this second or third Mass before one o'clock in the afternoon. They will then be obliged to fast before Mass for three hours as to solid food, and for one hour as to non-alcoholic drink or medicine.

Moreover, the Sovereign Pontiff grants to the Bishops Ordinaries in France the faculty to permit the celebration of Mass in the course of the afternoon on days of obligation only, whenever a sufficient proportion of laborers who have to work in the morning or of public employees who are detained by their duties in the morning, have to attend such a Mass in order to satisfy their obligation. In this case also, the celebrant observes the fast before the celebration of Mass, for three hours as to solid food and for one hour as to drink or medicine, excluding all alcohol.

As regards the faithful who assist at these Masses, the Sovereign Pontiff grants them permission to receive Holy Communion at such Masses whenever, in the judgment of their confessor, they could not without grave inconvenience satisfy the provisions of canons 867, § 4 and 821, § 1.[1] Then they shall likewise observe the fast before Holy Communion for three hours as to solid food and for one hour as to drink or medicine, excluding all alcohol.

These grants are good for one year if the above mentioned exceptional circumstances continue. At the end of the year, the Most Reverend Bishops Ordinary in France shall send to the Holy Office a circumstantial report on the dispensations which they shall have granted.

All things to the contrary notwithstanding.

(**Private**); Holy Office, 23 Oct., 1947.

NOTE: Translated from *La Semaine Catholique de Toulouse*, 16 Nov., 1947, pp. 549–550, which gives also the following summary: In virtue of the second indult the Bishop can allow priests to celebrate, on days of feasts of obligation only (Sundays and the four feasts) a second or third Mass in the course of the afternoon (fast for three hours as to solid food, one hour as to non-alcoholic drink or medicine), by reason of fatigue or distance, or in order to make it possible for those who cannot assist in the morning to be present at Mass. The faithful may, under the same conditions as to fasting, receive Communion at the Mass said in the afternoon, according to the judgment of their confessor.

A first indult given at the same time is reported under canon 858.

CANON 872

Jurisdiction for Confessions Granted in Extraordinary Manner to Dispersed Religious Behind Iron Curtain (Vatican Radio, Broadcast, 17 Sept., 1952) **Private.**

The Vatican Radio on 17 Sept., 1952, and for some days following, by order of the Holy See broadcast the following notice in various languages:

To religious priests who, because of the deplorable circumstances under which the Church is to-day oppressed in certain countries, are obliged to live outside the houses of their Institute, the Supreme Pontiff grants jurisdiction for hearing the confessions

---

[1] The copy we have gives canon 861, § 1, obviously an error for 821, § 1.

of the faithful of both sexes in any territory where the aforesaid conditions exist, without regard to the boundaries of the various dioceses, provided the said priests:

1. Had the faculty to hear confessions in some place at the time when they were deported or expelled from their religious house, and were not thereafter deprived of the same faculty according to the sacred canons because of their own fault;

2. And are unable, because of the aforesaid circumstances, to obtain the said faculty from the legitimate local Ordinary.

Only for the duration of the circumstances above mentioned.

(**Private**); Vatican Radio by order of the Holy Father Pius XII, 17 Sept., 1952.

CANON 874

Faculties of Ship Chaplains. See c. 248; AAS 44–649, n. 25.

CANON 883

Priests Traveling by Air: Faculties for Confessions (Pius XII, *Motu proprio*, 16 Dec., 1947) **AAS 40–17.**

A *Motu proprio,* entitled *"De facultate audiendi confessiones sacerdotibus aërium iter arripientibus concedenda,"* is as follows:

As some Ordinaries of places have indicated to this Apostolic See that it would be opportune that the provisions of canon 883 of the Code of Canon Law, giving to priests who undertake an ocean journey the faculty to hear confessions, be extended to journeys by air, We in our zeal for souls, realizing that these journeys are to-day daily growing in frequency, and desiring that the faithful have the benefit which would accrue for the sanctification of their souls from granting the said wish of the Ordinaries, receive their petition with great satisfaction to Our own heart, and do of our own motion, from certain knowledge and with mature deliberation, out of the fulness of Apostolic power, establish and decree that the provisions of canon 883 of the Code of Canon Law regarding the faculty of hearing confessions on the part of priests taking an ocean journey, shall apply and be extended, with the appropriate adjustment of the clauses to fit the case, to priests who make a voyage by air.

What We have decreed by this Our Apostolic Letter given of

Our own motion, We desire to remain firm and valid forever, all things to the contrary notwithstanding; and moreover We order that these provisions shall go into effect at the same time that this Our Apostolic Letter is placed in the Official Commentary called the *Acta Apostolicae Sedis*.

Given at Rome, from Saint Peter's, the 16th day of December, in the year nineteen hundred and forty-seven, the ninth of Our Pontificate.

AAS 40–17; Pius XII, *Motu proprio*, 16 Dec., 1947.

Cf. *Periodica*, 37–166 (Bertrams); *Commentarium pro Religiosis*, 1948, p. 12 (Pujolras).

Faculties of Ship Chaplains. See c. 248; AAS 44–649, n. 25.

CANON 886

Sacramental Absolution Given in General to a Number of Persons (Instruction, S. Paen., 25 March, 1944) **AAS 36–155.**

An Instruction of the Sacred Penitentiary is as follows:

In order to remove doubts and difficulties in interpreting and using the faculty of granting sacramental absolution under certain circumstances by a general formula or common absolution, without a previous confession of sins being made by each of the faithful, the Sacred Penitentiary deems it opportune to declare and decree the following:

I. Priests, even though not approved for receiving sacramental confessions, have the faculty of absolving in a general manner and all together:

a) Soldiers when a battle is imminent or in progress, as being in danger of death, when, either because of the great number of soldiers, or for lack of time, their individual confessions cannot be heard.

But if the circumstances are such that it seems morally impossible or very difficult to absolve the soldiers when the battle is imminent or in progress, then it is licit to absolve them as soon as it is judged necessary (cf. the reply of this Sacred Penitentiary of 10 Dec., 1940; AAS 32–571).[1]

---

[1] CANON LAW DIGEST, Vol. 2, p. 146.

b) Civilians and soldiers in danger of death during hostile incursions.

II. Outside of cases in which there is danger of death, it is not licit to give sacramental absolution to many at the same time, nor to individuals who make only a partial confession, merely because of a great concourse of penitents, such as might occur for example on a day of some great feast or indulgence (cf. Prop. 59 of those condemned by Innocent XI, 2 March, 1679):[2] but it is allowed if some other altogether grave and urgent necessity arises, which is proportionate to the gravity of the divine precept to make an integral confession, for example if the penitents otherwise without any fault of their own would be deprived for a long time of sacramental grace and of Holy Communion.

The decision as to whether the crowd of soldiers or prisoners or civilians are actually in such necessity is reserved to the Ordinaries of places, to whom priests must apply in advance, whenever this is possible, in order that they may licitly give absolution in this way.

III. The giving of sacramental absolution to many persons together by priests on their own authority, outside the cases mentioned in I, or without obtaining the previous permission of the Ordinary, when the latter could be reached, according to what was said in II, is to be regarded as an abuse.

IV. Before giving sacramental absolution, priests must, in as far as circumstances permit, inform the faithful:

a) That it is necessary that each one be sorry for his sins and resolve to abstain from sinning in future. It is appropriate also that priests duly admonish the penitents to give some external sign of their act of contrition if possible, for example by striking their breast.

b) Moreover, that it is altogether necessary that those who receive absolution in a crowd shall, the first time thereafter when they receive the Sacrament of Penance, duly confess all their mortal sins which they have not already confessed.

V. Priests must plainly tell the faithful that, if they are conscious of a mortal sin which has not yet been properly mentioned and forgiven in confession, and if the obligation to confess

---

[2] Cf. Denzinger-Umberg, *Enchiridion Symbolorum*, n. 1209.

completely their mortal sins applies to them by divine or ecclesiastical law, they are gravely forbidden from purposely evading the fulfillment of this obligation by waiting for an occasion when absolution may be given to them in a crowd.

VI. Ordinaries of places must remember to inform priests of these norms and of their very grave duty, when they permit them, in special circumstances, to give sacramental absolution to many together by a general formula.

VII. When there is time, this absolution is to be given with the usual and complete formula, in the plural number; otherwise, the following shorter formula may be used: *"Ego vos absolvo ab omnibus censuris et peccatis in nomine Patris et Filii et Spiritus Sancti."*

The above having been reported to His Holiness Pius XII by the undersigned Cardinal Major Penitentiary, His Holiness, in the audience of the 18th of this month, graciously approved and confirmed the Instruction of the Sacred Penitentiary, and ordered that it be published.

Given at Rome, from the Sacred Penitentiary, 25 March, 1944.

AAS 36–155; Instruction, S. Paen., 25 March, 1944.
Periodica, 33–276 (Restrepo).

CANON 888

Norms for Confessors in Matters Pertaining to the Sixth Commandment (Holy Office, 16 May, 1943) Private.

The following Instruction was issued by the Holy Office to Ordinaries under the title: Some Norms on the Conduct of Confessors in Dealing with the Sixth Commandment.

The Church has constantly exercised all care and solicitude lest the Sacrament of Penance "given by divine bounty as a refuge after the loss of baptismal innocence, through the wiles of the devil and the malice by which men abuse the gifts of God, become for miserable and shipwrecked sinners an occasion of eternal ruin,"[1] and lest what was established for the salvation of souls be in any way turned to their harm and to the detriment of priestly holiness and dignity through human inattention and levity.

---

[1] Const. of Benedict XIV, *Sacramentum Poenitentiae*, 1 June, 1741.

Especially there is in this matter no slight danger if in questioning and instructing penitents on the sixth commandment —
a thing which is to be done with consideration and circumspection as required by the difficulty of the matter and the dignity
which is due to the Sacrament — the confessor fails to restrain
himself and goes too far afield, beyond what is called for by his
duty of seeing to the integrity of the confession and the welfare
of the penitent; or if his whole conduct, especially in dealing
with women, lacks the sanctity and gravity which it should have.
For these faults easily do harm to the souls of the faithful, give
occasion to suspicions, and can be the first step in the profanation
of the Sacrament.

In order to provide with all its resources and energy against
such a danger, this Supreme Sacred Congregation has thought it
well to recall to mind those norms, to which confessors must
earnestly apply their minds and hearts, and to which the attention
of future confessors in seminaries and schools of theology must
be drawn in good time.

I. The Code of Canon Law very appropriately warns confessors
not to detain anyone with curious and useless questions, and especially not to ply young persons imprudently with questions about
matters of which they are ignorant (canon 888, § 2). Useless
questions are those which are clearly altogether unnecessary to
supplement the penitent's self-accusation and to enlighten the
confessor as to his interior dispositions. For the penitent is by
divine law obliged to confess only all and each of the grave sins
which, after a careful self-examination, he is conscious of having
committed since his Baptism and which have not yet been directly
forgiven through the power of the keys entrusted to the Church,
and to explain in confession the circumstances which change the
species of the sin;[2] provided, however, that when he committed
the sin he knew the specific malice contained in it and was
therefore guilty of the same. It is, therefore, only these matters
on which the confessor is usually obliged to question the penitent,
if he has reason to suspect that they have been omitted from the
confession either in good or in bad faith; and if it occasionally
happens that he has to make the entire examination of conscience
for some individual penitent, he must not go beyond the bounds

[2] Council of Trent, Sess. XIV, cap. 5; Code of Canon Law, c. 901.

of reasonable conjecture, taking the circumstances of the penitent into account.

He must, therefore, omit as useless, troublesome, and in this matter very dangerous, all questions about sins of which there is no positive and firm reason to suppose the penitent to be guilty; also about kinds of sin which he is not likely to have committed; about material sins, unless the good of the penitent himself or danger to the common good make it necessary or advisable to warn the penitent about them; finally, about circumstances which are morally indifferent, and especially about the manner in which the sin was committed. Even if the penitent of his own accord, through ignorance or on account of scruples or with evil intent, should exceed the bounds of moderation or offend modesty in explaining sins or temptations of impurity, the confessor should prudently, but promptly and firmly, stop him.

Moreover the confessor must remember that the divine precept regarding the integrity of confession is not binding where it would involve a grave harm to the penitent or to the confessor, which is extrinsic to the confession; and therefore that questioning should be omitted whenever there is prudent ground to fear that it may cause scandal to the penitent or ruin to the confessor. And in doubt, let him constantly bear in mind the common warning of moralists that in this matter it is better to err on the side of caution than to expose oneself or another to ruin by going too far.

Finally, the confessor, in asking questions, should always proceed with the greatest caution, asking first rather general questions and later, if the case requires it, more definite ones; and these latter should always be brief, discreet, decent, avoiding absolutely any expressions which might excite the imagination or the senses or give offense to a pious soul.

II. The confessor needs no less prudence and gravity when in the fulfillment of his function as physician and teacher he comes to the task of warning and instructing penitents. Let him first of all be deeply conscious of the fact that it is the healing, not of bodies but of souls, which is entrusted to him. Consequently it is usually not his business to advise penitents in regard to medicine and hygiene, and he must entirely avoid whatever would cause astonishment or scandal. If any advice of this sort is regarded as necessary, even for reasons of conscience, it should be given by an expert who is upright, prudent, and acquainted with moral doctrine; to such a one therefore the penitent should be referred.

Likewise the confessor should not dare, either on his own initiative or at the request of anyone, to instruct penitents on the nature and manner of the act by which life is transmitted; and under no pretext should he ever be induced to do this.

He should, however, give his penitents moral instruction and appropriate direction according to the doctrine of approved authors, and should do this prudently, decently, and moderately, without going beyond the real needs of the penitent; and it is to be observed that a confessor who in his questions and admonitions seems to be almost exclusively concerned with sins of this kind, is acting inconsiderately and is not rightly performing his office.

III. Finally it must never be forgotten that the world is seated in wickedness,[3] and that "the priest is by daily association like one in the midst of a depraved people, so that often in the very ministering of pastoral charity, he has to be on his guard against the hidden wiles of the infernal serpent."[4]

Hence he must always conduct himself with the greatest caution, especially in dealing with women penitents, watchfully avoiding anything which might savor of familiarity or encourage dangerous affection. Let him not, therefore, be curious to learn who they are, nor dare to ask their names directly or indirectly. In speaking to them, he should never use the pronoun "*tu*" in places where that denotes a familiar relationship; he should not allow their confessions to last longer than is necessary; he should not in confession speak of things which are not matters of conscience; he should not without real necessity admit mutual visits or epistolary correspondence with them, nor long conversations, either in the sacristy, halls, parlors, or anywhere else, not even under pretext of giving spiritual direction.

The confessor must use all possible vigilance to prevent merely human affections from gradually insinuating themselves and being encouraged either in himself or in his penitents; but he must constantly bend all his efforts to the end that "whatever

---

[3] I John 5:19.
[4] Pius X, Exhortation to the Catholic Clergy, *Haerent animo,* 4 Aug., 1908.

he does for the sacred ministry be according to God and be done under the impulse and guidance of faith."[5]

IV. In order that confessors may be able the more readily and securely to perform this office, they must in good time be instructed and trained in it by their teachers, and not in the principles merely but also by trial and practice, so that they will know exactly how penitents should be questioned about the sixth commandment, whether they be children, young people or adults, especially women; what questions are necessary or useful, and what ones on the contrary are to be omitted; and what words are to be used in the language of the country.

Given at Rome, from the Holy Office, 16 May, 1943.

(Private); Holy Office, 16 May, 1943; *Periodica,* 33–130.

Copula Dimidiata: Prudence required of confessor. See c. 1081; private reply of Holy Office, 30 Nov., 1921.

Saint Alphonsus de Liguori. Patron of confessors and professors of Moral Theology. Pius XII, Ap. Letter, 26 April, 1950 (AAS 42–595).

CANON 900

Cases Formerly Reserved to the Vicar of Rome Are No Longer Reserved: Faculties of Confessors Approved in Rome: Irregularity for Abortion (Vicar of Rome, 4 March, 1920) Private.

The following *Monitum* was issued by the Vicar of Rome:

The Holy Father has deigned to grant to all confessors approved in Rome the faculty to absolve, in that city and its territory, from censures which are reserved to Ordinaries in the Code of Canon Law. The confessors are to enjoin upon the penitents the obligations which should rightly be imposed upon them in each case according to the rules given by approved authors, and, in the case of the irregularity arising from the procuring of abortion, they must apply for the dispensation to the Sacred Penitentiary. Moreover the cases which hitherto were reserved to the Cardinal Vicar are no longer reserved.

(Private); Vicar of Rome, 4 March, 1920. Reported by Roberti, *De Delictis et Poenis,* Vol. I, p. 337, note 1.

---

[5] Pius X, Exhortation to the Catholic Clergy, *Haerent animo,* 4 Aug., 1908.

CANON 912

Faculties to Annex Indulgences to Religious Objects: Interpretation (S. Paen., 2 March, 1942) **Private.**

The Sacred Penitentiary was asked:

Whether the clause: "provided he be approved for hearing sacramental confessions," which is found in certain faculties for applying indulgences to religious objects, is to be understood only of priests who are approved for hearing the confessions of the faithful of both sexes, or also of those who are approved for hearing the confessions of only the faithful of one sex.

Reply. In the negative to the first part; in the affirmative to the second.

(Private); S. Paen., 2 March, 1942; *Il Monitore Ecclesiastico*, Vol. 54, p. 80.

Faculties to Erect Stations of the Way of the Cross, given by the Minister General of the Friars Minor before 1 April, 1933, remain in effect. See c. 925; private reply of S. Paen., 14 July, 1951.

CANON 914

Papal Blessing: Rite and Formula When Given by Cardinals (S. C. Rit., 23 June, 1944) **AAS 36-221.**

A declaration of the Sacred Congregation of Rites, entitled: *Romana: Declaratio: De Benedictione Apostolica,* is as follows:

Since the *Roman Pontifical* prescribes the rite and formula for giving the Apostolic blessing, with a plenary indulgence, to the people after a solemn Mass, by Patriarchs, Primates, Archbishops and Bishops, the question has arisen whether the Most Eminent Cardinals themselves are to use the aforesaid rite and formula when they give this blessing, either in Rome or outside of Rome. And the Sacred Congregation of Rites decided to reply to the question:

Reply. Outside Rome, in the affirmative. In Rome, the case cannot occur, since, because of the presence of the Supreme Pontiff, the faculty of giving the Apostolic blessing is not granted to any one.

A report of the above having been given to His Holiness Pius XII by the undersigned Cardinal Prefect of the Sacred Congregation, His Holiness approved the declaration of this Sacred Congregation.

All things to the contrary notwithstanding. June 23, 1944.

AAS 36–221; S. C. Rit., Declaration, 23 June, 1944.

CANON 917

Privileged Altar; Jubilee Privilege (mentioned in Digest, Vol. 2, p. 223) extended to June 29, 1943. See S. Paen., 8 May, 1943 (AAS 35–158).

CANON 925

Toties Quoties **Crucifix: Interpretation Repeated** (S. Paen., 22 Sept., 1942) **AAS 34–303**.

For some time now, to the great astonishment of the faithful, crucifixes are being shown, to which it is said a plenary indulgence is attached, to be gained by the faithful every time they kiss one of these crucifixes with a contrite heart and making an act of love and contrition; and it is said that these crucifixes were blessed by a certain Prelate in virtue of a special faculty received from the Supreme Pontiff.

Especially recently some have even applied to this sacred Tribunal asking whether such a favor was actually granted as is claimed; and they indicate that so extraordinary a thing has caused no little astonishment.

Accordingly this sacred Tribunal, which decides questions about the grant and use of indulgences, in order to forestall a false interpretation of the bounty of Holy Mother Church in this matter, deems it not only appropriate but necessary to call the attention of all to the two declarations which have already been issued on this subject; namely, the one of the Supreme S. C. of the Holy Office, of 10 June, 1914 (AAS 6–347), and the other of this Sacred Penitentiary, of 23 June, 1929.[1] And we declare once more that the crucifixes which are being distributed even in the present time enriched with this favor, are to be considered as blessed in accordance with these declarations; so that only at the moment of death a plenary indulgence can be gained if the necessary conditions are fulfilled.

---

[1] AAS 21–510; Canon Law Digest, Vol. 1, p. 434.

When all this was reported to the Supreme Pontiff by the undersigned Cardinal Major Penitentiary in the audience of 4 July, 1942, His Holiness approved and confirmed the declaration of the Sacred Penitentiary and ordered that it be published.

Given at Rome, from the Sacred Penitentiary, 22 Sept., 1942.

AAS 34–303; S. Paen., 22 Sept., 1942. *Periodica,* 32–101 (Restrepo).

Hail Mary as Said by Orientals Good for Indulgences, Even for Rosary and for Members of Latin Rite (S. C. Eccl. Or., 22 Apr., 1944) AAS 36–245.

A Notification by the Sacred Congregation for the Oriental Church, 22 April, 1944, is as follows:

On the third of June, 1888, the Sacred Congregation of Indulgences and Relics issued the following rescript: "The S. C. of Indulgences and Sacred Relics, using faculties specially granted to it by His Holiness Leo XIII, graciously declares, and in as far as it may be necessary grants an indult, that the Angelic Salutation, as it has hitherto been customarily recited among the Ruthenians and other faithful of the Oriental rite, whenever it is prescribed as a necessary condition for gaining indulgences, is of equal value for this effect as is the Angelic Salutation which is recited by the faithful of the Latin Church. All things to the contrary, etc."

Since, however, certain discussions have arisen as to the meaning of this rescript, the Sacred Congregation for the Oriental Church proposed the following questions for solution to the Sacred Penitentiary:

1. Whether this rescript is still in effect.

2. Whether the rescript is good only for the faithful of the 'Oriental rites, or also for the faithful of the Latin rite, who recite the Angelic Salutation according to the text which is in use in the Oriental rites.

3. Whether the indulgences attached to the recitation of the Rosary of the Blessed Virgin Mary can be gained by all who recite the Angelic Salutation according to the text which is in use in the Oriental rites.

Reply. The Sacred Penitentiary, on 21 March, 1944, decided to reply to the proposed questions as follows:

1. In the affirmative.

2. In the negative to the first part; in the affirmative to the second.

3. In the affirmative; but let no change be made in the public recitation.

Given at Rome, from the S. C. for the Oriental Church, April 22, 1944.

AAS 36–245; S. C. Eccl. Or., 22 Apr., 1944.

Indulgences of the Way of the Cross: Some Interpretations (S. Paen., 20 March, 1946) AAS 38–160.

The Sacred Penitentiary was asked:

I. Whether the rule given in the decree of 6 Aug., 1757[1] — namely, that, for the pious exercise of the Way of the Cross, whenever it might cause confusion (for the whole crowd to attempt to pass from station to station), each one may remain in his own place while the priest with two clerics or choristers makes the round, pauses at each station and recites the usual prayers there, the others responding alternately — is valid only for the public exercise of the Way of the Cross performed in a church, or whether it also holds good when the exercise is performed by religious in their oratories.

Reply. In the affirmative to the first part, in the negative to the second.

II. Whether, under the circumstances mentioned in the decrees of 27 Feb., 1901, and 7 May, 1902 — namely, where, in the oratories of religious, on account of the lack of space all the religious cannot move together from station to station without creating a disturbance — they can gain the indulgences attached to the pious exercise of the Way of the Cross, if one religious man or woman as the case may be makes the round and recites the usual prayers at each station, while the others remain in their places and there rise and genuflect for each station.

Reply. In the affirmative.

III. Whether, under the same circumstances as those described above for religious and in the way there described, the faithful living in common as mentioned in canon 929 can gain the indulgences attached to the pious exercise of the Way of the Cross,

---

[1] S. C. Indulg., *Decr. Auth.*, n. 210.

if one man or woman as the case may be makes the round of the stations and recites the usual prayers.

Reply. In the affirmative.

The resolution containing these replies was adopted by the Sacred Penitentiary on January 25, 1946.

The above being reported to His Holiness Pius XII by the undersigned Cardinal Major Penitentiary in the audience of March 18, His Holiness approved and confirmed the resolution of the Sacred Penitentiary and ordered that it be published.

Given at Rome, from the Sacred Penitentiary, March 20, 1946.
AAS 38-160; S. Paen., 20 March, 1946.

Commentarium pro Religiosis, 26–85 (Gutiérrez).

Jubilee of 1950: Gaining the Jubilee Several Times (S. Paen., 22 Jan., 1950) Private.

In *L'Osservatore Romano* for 22 January, 1950, the Sacred Penitentiary caused to be published a document of which the dispositive part is as follows:

1. The works prescribed for gaining the Holy Jubilee are four: *Confession, Communion,* one *visit* to each of the four Patriarchal Basilicas (even on different days), *prayers.* The prayers to be recited at each visit are: three *Paters, Aves,* and *Glorias,* plus one *Pater, Ave,* and *Gloria* according to the intentions of the Supreme Pontiff, and once the *Credo.* The works can be performed in any order.

2. The Jubilee Indulgence during the Holy Year can be gained more than once, either for oneself or for the souls in Purgatory. But each time that one wishes to gain the Jubilee Indulgence it is necessary to perform the works prescribed as above in n. 1.

3. The works for gaining a second Jubilee cannot be begun until one has finished the works for gaining the preceding Jubilee.

(**Private**) ; S. Paen., 22 Jan., 1950.

Erections of Stations of the Cross in Virtue of Faculties Received From the Minister General of the Franciscan Order Before the Publication of the Decree of 20 March, 1933, Are Valid (S. Paen., 14 July, 1951) Private.

A certain Bishop presented this petition to the Sacred Penitentiary:

The Bishop ——, prostrate at the feet of Your Holiness, states: On the 15th day of September, 1930, the faculty to erect the Stations of the Way of the Cross in the churches of the diocese was obtained from the Minister General of the Friars Minor.

Although this faculty was revoked by the Decree of the Sacred Penitentiary of 20 March, 1933,[1] many Stations were nevertheless erected, in good faith, after the Decree. Wherefore, the petitioner humbly asks for a sanation of these erections which were performed in the said Diocese after the said Decree.

Reply. The Sacred Penitentiary replies to the above petition: Sanation is not necessary; and let His Excellency the Bishop continue even in the future to use his right according to the grant of 15 Sept., 1930, made by the Minister General of the Friars Minor, which remains in effect.

From the Sacred Penitentiary, 14 July, 1951.

(**Private**); S. Paen., 14 July, 1951. Petition and rescript kindly sent to us by the Committee on Research of the Canon Law Society of America.

NOTE: A careful reading of the Decree of 20 March, 1933, will show that it does not revoke faculties to erect the Way of the Cross, which were granted previously. It provides that *in future* (from the date of the publication of the Decree, 1 April, 1933), religious Orders which were formerly privileged to grant this faculty can no longer do so outside their own Order.

The Formula by which the faculty in this case was granted is as follows:

FR. BONAVENTURA MARRANI
TOTIUS ORDINIS FRATRUM MINORUM MINISTER GENERALIS ET HUMILIS IN DOMINO SERVUS

Potestate a Summis Pontificibus benigne Nobis facta, vigore praesentium Litterarum Ill.mo ac Rev.mo Domino Episcopo facultatem indulgemus, quatenus, intra limites suae Dioeceseos, si idonei Fratres Ordinis Nostri desint aut commode advocari non possint, etiam per alios Sacerdotes sive saeculares sive regulares, ad praedicandum Dei verbum vel ad confessiones audiendas approbatos, ab Ipso singulis vicibus in scriptis deputandos, sacras Viae Crucis Stationes benedicere ac erigere valeat in Ecclesiis, aut publicis Oratoriis, aut Coemeteriis, aut aliis locis publicis, ubi Ipsi visum fuerit expedire ut erigantur, cum adnexis Indulgentiis, lucrandis ab omnibus quidem fidelibus eas devote visitantibus: vel praeterea in Oratoriis privatis, Apostolico

---

[1] AAS 25–170; CANON LAW DIGEST, 1, p. 417.

tamen Brevi erectis, cum iisdem Indulgentiis, acquirendis a con-
sanguineis et affinibus postulantium ac eorum familiaribus cohabitantibus tantum; vel demum in Monasteriis, Conservatoriis, et aliis locis
piis, quamvis indulto celebrandi Missam non munitis, cum iisdem
pariter Indulgentiis, lucrandis ab omnibus cohabitantibus, vel eo,
scholae aut religionis causa, adventantibus. Servatis omnibus de iure
servandis, et relicto peractae erectionis testimonio propria erigentis
manu subscripto.

Fr. Antonius Yopsisius, O.F.M.
De mandato Paternitatis Suae Rev.mae

Rosary on the Air: Indulgences (S. Paen., 9 May, 1952) Private.

The Procurator General of the Order of Friars Preachers,
prostrate at the feet of Your Holiness, humbly presents the
following questions:

1. Whether the faithful can gain the Indulgences attached to
the Rosary of the Blessed Virgin Mary if they recite it with a
companion who is present only radiophonically; and if so,

2. Whether the faithful can gain the aforesaid indulgences if
they recite the Rosary of the Blessed Virgin Mary alternately
while part of the prayers are transmitted radiophonically and
are not being recited here and now by any person but were
previously recorded on a disc or transmitting wire or other
instrument.

Reply. The Sacred Penitentiary, in virtue of faculties granted
to it by His Holiness Pius XII, replies to the proposed questions:

1. In the affirmative.

2. In the negative.

Sacred Penitentiary, 9 May, 1952.

(**Private**); S. Paen., 9 May, 1952. *Analecta Sacri Ordinis Fratrum
Praedicatorum,* 1952, p. 290. Copy kindly supplied by the Very Reverend
Timothy M. Sparks, O.P.

Consecration to Immaculate Heart of Mary: Prayer of Pius XII in-
dulgenced. Pius XII, 17 Nov., 1942 (AAS 34–345).

Jubilee 1950: *Indictio Universalis Iubilaei.* Pius XII, 26 May, 1949 (AAS
41–257).

The Jubilee Prayer. Pius XII, 23 March, 1949 (AAS 41–187).

Suspension of faculties outside Rome. Pius XII, Const. *Fore confidimus,*
10 July, 1949 (AAS 41–337).

Extraordinary faculties for penitentiaries and extraordinary confessors in Rome. Pius XII, Const. *Decessorum Nostrorum,* 10 July, 1949 (AAS 41–340)

Monita on use of special faculties. S. Paen., 17 Sept., 1949 (AAS 41–513).

Indulgences of the Holy Year made available to nuns and others permanently unable to come to Rome. Pius XII, Const. *Iam promulgato,* 10 July, 1949 (AAS 41–345).

Pilgrim confessors in Rome during Holy Year: special faculties; broader faculties for ten chosen confessors; *Monita* as to the use of these faculties. S. Paen., 17 Sept., 1949 (AAS 41–518, 519, 520).

Extension of Jubilee to world outside Rome. Pius XII, Ap. Const., 25 Dec., 1950 (AAS 42–853).

Instruction of S. Paen. on the extension, 26 Dec., 1950 (AAS 42–900).

Midnight Mass specially permitted between years 1949 and 1950 with two hours of prayer (including time of Mass). S. C. Sacr., 15 Dec., 1949 (AAS 41–616).

Radio Address of Pius XII, 23 Dec., 1949, to the Cardinals, Bishops, and Prelates of the Roman Curia on the Holy Year (AAS 42–120).

Latin America: Gaining Jubilees without confession. See **c. 66**; private; S. C. Prop. Fid., 15 Sept., 1950.

Lord, save us; we perish: Indulgences. S. Paen., 18 Aug., 1943 (AAS 35–292).

Lord, teach us to pray: Indulgences, S. Paen., 30 Apr., 1952 (AAS 44–389).

Medal Instead of Scapular for Third Order. See **c. 692**; AAS 14–353.

My Jesus, mercy: Plenary indulgence during air attacks, for duration of World War II. See S. Paen., 23 Dec., 1942 (AAS 34–382).

New Edition of *Enchiridion Indulgentiarum* supplants the one of 1950. S. Paen., 3 March, 1952 (AAS 44–235).

War Dead, Indulgence for: To be gained only during Paschal season of 1948. See S. Paen., Decree, 23 Feb., 1948 (AAS 40–94).

CANON 929

Way of the Cross: Indulgences when made together by persons living in common according to this canon. See **c. 925**; AAS 38–160, III.

CANON 931

Portiuncula Indulgence: Confession and Communion Need Not Precede Visits (S. Paen., 1928) Private.

The Sacred Penitentiary was asked:

Whether, in order to gain the indulgence of the Portiuncula, it is required that the confession and Communion precede the visits; or whether the visits may be made on the day designated, and the confession and Communion within eight days following it, according to this canon.

Reply. In the negative to the first part; in the affirmative to the second.

(Private); S. Paen., 1928; reported in *Acta Ordinis Fratrum Minorum*, 1928, p. 117.

CANON 954

Co-consecrators in Consecration of Bishop: Change in Rubrics of *Roman Pontifical* (Pius XII, Apostolic Constitution, 30 Nov., 1944) AAS 37–131.

It is beyond all doubt and is proved by long observance that the minister of episcopal consecration is a Bishop, and that for the validity of this consecration one Bishop, who with the required intention performs the essential rites, is sufficient. Yet from the early ages of the Church several Bishops have assisted at such consecration, and in our own time it is prescribed by the *Roman Pontifical* that two other Bishops assist, although in special circumstances a dispensation from the ancient rite is granted if Assisting Bishops cannot be had. But, whether the Bishops who are thus present are cooperators and co-consecrators or merely witnesses of the consecration, is not sufficiently clear, especially as the rubrics of the *Roman Pontifical,* where they treat of the prayers to be recited, in several places by using the singular number suggest that there is only one Consecrator, and as it is not perfectly clear that the prescription of the rubric which is given in the beginning before the examination of the Bishop-elect — namely, that the Assisting Bishops are to say in a low voice whatever the Consecrator says — applies to the entire rite of consecration.

The consequence has been that in some places the Assisting Bishops, adhering to the words of the *Roman Pontifical,* after pronouncing the words *"Accipe Spiritum Sanctum"* while they touch the head of the Bishop-elect together with the Consecrator, do not pronounce the words which follow; in other places, as in Rome, the Bishops say not only the aforesaid words but also in a low voice the prayer *"Propitiare,"* with the Preface which follows it, without however saying all the words which the Consecrator recites or sings from the beginning of the rite to the end.

After carefully examining all this, with the intention of determining the office and ministry of the Bishops who assist at the consecration of a Bishop-elect, and to the end that henceforth one and the same rite be observed in this matter both in Rome and in other parts of the world, We, in the fulness of Our Apostolic authority, declare, decree, and establish the following:

Although for the validity of episcopal consecration only one Bishop is required and sufficient, provided he perform the essential rites, nevertheless the two Bishops who, according to ancient practice and the prescription of the *Roman Pontifical*, assist at the consecration, must, together with the Consecrator, being themselves Consecrators and therefore henceforth to be called Co-consecrators, not only touch the head of the Bishop-elect with both hands while they say *"Accipe Spiritum Sanctum,"* but, having beforehand formed the intention of conferring episcopal consecration together with the Bishop who is Consecrator, must also recite the prayer *"Propitiare"* with the entire Preface which follows it, and likewise, throughout the entire rite, read in a low voice everything which the Consecrator reads or sings, except the prayers prescribed for the blessing of the pontifical vestments which are to be imposed in the rite of consecration.

And We order by Our authority that what We have by these letters declared, decreed and established shall remain valid and firm, all things to the contrary, even such as are worthy of special mention, notwithstanding; and accordingly We will and decree that the *Roman Pontifical* be duly revised to conform to these prescriptions.

No one may infringe, etc.

Given at Rome, from Saint Peter's, the thirtieth day of November, the Feast of Saint Andrew the Apostle, in the year of Our Lord nineteen hundred and forty-four, the sixth year of Our Pontificate.

AAS 37–131; Pius XII, Apostolic Letter, 30 Nov., 1944.

CANON 955

Ordination With False Dimissorial Letters (Holy Office, 14 June, 1950) **AAS 42–489.**

A Notification from the Holy Office:
Since the priest Stanislaus Bojan, born at Nowy-Targ in Poland on the 27th of July, 1919, was promoted to the sacred

order of the priesthood by presenting false dimissorial letters, the Supreme Sacred Congregation of the Holy Office, in the plenary session held on Wednesday, 29 March, 1950, decreed that the said priest Stanislaus Bojan is to be regarded as a layman as to all legal effects, and is freed from all the obligations contracted through sacred ordination.

Given at Rome, from the Holy Office, 14 June, 1950.

AAS 42–489; Holy Office, Notification, 14 June, 1950.

CANON 974

Priestly Virtue: Apostolic Exhortation of Pius XII, *Mentis Nostrae,* 23 Sept., 1950 (AAS 42–657). For annotations, see c. 124, ref.
Vocation to Priesthood in Religion. See c. 487; AAS 43–26.

CANON 985

Irregularity From Abortion: Confessors approved in Rome are to apply to Sacred Penitentiary for power to dispense. See c. 900; *Monitum* of Vicar of Rome, 4 March, 1920.

CANON 1002

Ordination to Diaconate: Holding Right Hand Extended Is Not Essential for Validity (Three Replies of S. C. Sacr.: 7 Nov., 1912; 9 March, 1923; 4 March, 1932; and one of Holy Office, 27 April, 1923) **Private.**

I. The Vicar Apostolic of Mendez and Galaquiza (Ecuador) promoted six subdeacons to the diaconate, and afterward on reading the Rubrics of the *Pontifical,* thought that he had, after imposing his right hand, recited the words which follow, *"Emitte in eos . . .* etc.," with his hands extended as in the Preface, but not holding his right hand extended as the *Pontifical* prescribes.

From the *congressus* of the Sacred Congregation of the Sacraments, 7 Nov., 1912, Prot. N. 3204/12, the reply was: *Acquiescat et communicetur Vicario Apostolico.*

II. Edward Homar, titular Bishop Auxiliary to the Bishop of Tarnow (Poland), in conferring the diaconate at Tuchon on two subdeacons of the Congregation of the Holy Redeemer, at the formula, *"Accipe Spiritum Sanctum . . .* etc.," imposed both hands separately on their heads, but then proceeding with the Preface he did not extend his right hand over them, but held both hands extended before his breast as at the orations. Now he asks whether the ordination is valid or must he repeat it.

From the *congressus* of the Sacred Congregation of the Sacraments, 9 March, 1923, the reply was: *Episcopum non esse inquietandum.*

And the Holy Office confirmed the resolution of the S. C. of the Sacraments which was forwarded to it, replying to the aforesaid Bishop Homar, 27 April, 1923, Prot. N. 161/1923: *Episcopus Orator acquiescat.*

III. Sacred Congregation of the Sacraments, 4 March, 1932, *Pinsken., N.* 5663/31:

This S. C. of the Sacraments has received the petition of Your Excellency, in which is related the manner in which several deacons were ordained; namely, that at the words *"Emitte in eos . . ."* in the second part of the Preface, the right hand was not extended over them, but the words were recited "with hands joined before the breast." The doubt having arisen as to whether the said ordination should be repeated conditionally, the same Sacred Congregation considered the entire matter carefully and asked the opinion of two Consultors. Having received their opinion and having in mind certain resolutions given at other times by this same Sacred Congregation, and also the resolution of the Holy Office in *Tarnovien.*, 27 Apr., 1923, decided to reply: *Episcopus adquiescat.*

(Private); S. C. Sacr., 7 Nov., 1912; 9 March, 1923; 4 March, 1932; Holy Office, 27 April, 1923. Annotations, *Periodica*, 40–269 (Hecht).

Changes in the *Roman Pontifical* for the Rite of Ordination (S. C. Rit., 20 Feb., 1950) AAS 42–448.

A Decree, *Urbis et Orbis,* of the S. C. of Rites:

After the issuance by our Holy Father Pope Pius XII of the Apostolic Constitution, *Sacramentum Ordinis,* of 30 Nov., 1947,[1] in which is determined the sacramental form of the Orders of the Diaconate, the Priesthood, and the Episcopacy, the Sacred Congregation of Rites, in obedience to a pontifical mandate, has prepared the variations and additions to be made in the rubrics of the *Roman Pontifical,* and also indicated the manner in which the sacramental forms are to be printed, so that they may be

---

[1] AAS 40–5; reported above in this volume under this same canon 1002.

the more evident; and it now orders that these changes be inserted in the new editions of the *Roman Pontifical;* and in the meantime let them be published separately for the convenience of the Bishops, as indicated in the accompanying pages. All things to the contrary notwithstanding.

Given at Rome, 20 Feb., 1950.

AAS 42-448; S. C. Rit., Decree, 20 Feb., 1950.

Note: The approved changes are printed in AAS, Vol. 42 (1950), pp. 449-455.

Essential Rites of Ordination: Diaconate, Priesthood, Episcopacy (Pius XII, Apostolic Constitution, 30 Nov., 1947) AAS 40-5.

1. The Catholic Faith professes that the Sacrament of Order instituted by Christ, by which are conferred spiritual power and grace to perform properly ecclesiastical functions, is one and the same for the universal Church; for, just as Our Lord Jesus Christ gave to the Church but one and the same government under the Prince of the Apostles, one and the same faith, one and the same sacrifice, so too He gave her but one and the same treasury of efficacious signs of grace, that is, Sacraments. For these Sacraments instituted by Christ Our Lord, the Church in the course of the centuries never substituted other Sacraments, nor could she do so, since, as the Council of Trent teaches (Conc. Trid., Sess. VII, can. 1, *De Sacram. in genere*), the seven Sacraments of the New Law were all instituted by Jesus Christ Our Lord, and the Church has no power over "the substance of the Sacraments," that is, over those things which, as is proved from the sources of divine revelation, Christ the Lord Himself established to be kept as sacramental signs.

2. As regards the Sacrament of Order, of which We are now speaking, it is a fact that, notwithstanding its unity and identity, which no Catholic has ever dared to question, in the course of time, according to varying local and temporal conditions, various rites have been added in its conferring; this was surely the reason why theologians began to inquire which of the rites used in conferring the Sacrament of Order belong to its essence, and which do not; it also gave rise to doubts and anxieties in particular cases; and as a consequence the humble petition has

again and again been addressed to the Holy See that the supreme
Authority of the Church might at last decide what is required
for validity in the conferring of Sacred Orders.

3. All agree that the Sacraments of the New Law, as sensible
signs which produce invisible grace, must both signify the grace
which they produce and produce the grace which they signify.
Now the effects which must be produced and hence also signified
by Sacred Ordination to the Diaconate, the Priesthood, and the
Episcopacy, namely power and grace, in all the rites of various
times and places in the universal Church, are found to be sufficiently signified by the imposition of hands and the words which
determine it. Besides, every one knows that the Roman Church
has always held as valid Ordinations conferred according to
the Greek rite without the *traditio instrumentorum;* so that in
the very Council of Florence, in which was effected the union
of the Greeks with the Roman Church, the Greeks were not required to change their rite of Ordination or to add to it the
traditio instrumentorum: and it was the will of the Church that
in Rome itself the Greeks should be ordained according to their
own rite. It follows that, even according to the mind of the
Council of Florence itself, the *traditio instrumentorum* is not
required for the substance and validity of this Sacrament by the
will of Our Lord Jesus Christ Himself. If it was at one time
necessary even for validity by the will and command of the
Church, every one knows that the Church has the power to
change and abrogate what she herself has established.

4. Wherefore, after invoking the divine light, We of Our
Apostolic Authority and from certain knowledge declare, and as
far as may be necessary decree and provide: that the matter, and
the only matter, of the Sacred Orders of the Diaconate, the
Priesthood, and the Episcopacy is the imposition of hands; and
that the form, and the only form, is the words which determine
the application of this matter, which univocally signify the
sacramental effects — namely the power of Order and the grace
of the Holy Spirit — and which are accepted and used by the
Church in that sense. It follows as a consequence that We should
declare, and in order to remove all controversy and to preclude
doubts of conscience, We do by Our Apostolic Authority declare,
and if there was ever a lawful disposition to the contrary We

now decree that at least in the future the *traditio instrumentorum* is not necessary for the validity of the Sacred Orders of the Diaconate, the Priesthood, and the Episcopacy.

5. As to the matter and form in the conferring of each Order, We of Our same supreme Apostolic Authority decree and provide as follows: In the Ordination to the Diaconate, the matter is the one imposition of the hand of the Bishop which occurs in the rite of that Ordination. The form consists of the words of the "Preface," of which the following are essential and therefore required for validity: *"Emitte in eum, quaesumus, Domine, Spiritum Sanctum, quo in opus ministerii tui fideliter exsequendi septiformis gratiae tuae munere roboretur."* In the Ordination to the Priesthood, the matter is the first imposition of hands of the Bishop which is done in silence, but not the continuation of the same imposition through the extension of the right hand, nor the last imposition to which are attached the words: "Accipe Spiritum Sanctum: quorum remiseris peccata, etc." And the form consists of the words of the "Preface," of which the following are essential and therefore required for validity: *"Da, quaesumus, omnipotens Pater, in hunc famulum tuum Presbyterii dignitatem; innova in visceribus eius spiritum sanctitatis, ut acceptum a Te, Deus, secundi meriti munus obtineat censuramque morum exemplo suae conversationis insinuet."* Finally in the Episcopal Ordination or Consecration, the matter is the imposition of hands which is done by the Bishop consecrator. The form consists of the words of the "Preface," of which the following are essential and therefore required for validity: *"Comple in Sacerdote tuo ministerii tui summam, et ornamentis totius glorificationis instructum coelestis unguenti rore sanctifica."* All these things are to be done as was determined by Our Apostolic Constitution *"Episcopalis Consecrationis"* of 30 November, 1944.

6. In order that there may be no occasion for doubt, We command that in conferring each Order the imposition of hands be done by physically touching the head of the person to be ordained, although a moral contact also is sufficient for the valid conferring of the Sacrament.

Finally, what We have above declared and provided is by no means to be understood in the sense that it be permitted even in the slightest detail to neglect or omit the other rites which are prescribed in the *Roman Pontifical;* on the contrary We order that all the prescriptions laid down in the said *Roman Pontifical* be religiously observed and performed.

The provisions of this Our Constitution have not retroactive force; in case any doubt arises, it is to be submitted to this Apostolic See.

These things We proclaim, declare, and decree, all things to the contrary notwithstanding, even those worthy of special mention, and accordingly We will and order that in the *Roman Pontifical* they be clearly indicated. Let no man therefore infringe this Constitution which We have enacted, nor dare to contravene the same.

Given at Rome, from Saint Peter's, on the thirtieth of November, Feast of Saint Andrew the Apostle, in the year nineteen hundred and forty-seven, the ninth of Our Pontificate.

AAS 40–5; Pius XII, Apostolic Constitution, 30 Nov., 1947.

Cf. *Periodica*, 37–9 (Hürth); *Commentarium pro Religiosis*, 1948, p. 4 (Pujolras).

NOTE: Of special value by way of commentary is an article by Hürth in *Periodica*, Vol. 37 (1948), pp. 9–58 in which light is thrown on this epoch-making Constitution from the *Acta Praeparatoria*, special permission having been obtained both to consult them and to publish some of their contents. As to the moment when the dispositive provisions of the Constitution become effective, Hürth, applying canons 9; 34, § 3, nn. 1 and 2; and 32, § 1, holds that it is at midnight between the 27th and 28th of April, 1948. The date of the issue of the *Acta Apostolicae Sedis* in which it appeared is January 28.

CANON 1012

New Marriage Code for the Oriental Church (Pius XII, *Motu proprio*, 22 Feb., 1949) AAS 41–89.

Motu proprio on the discipline of the Sacrament of Matrimony for the Oriental Church:

Numerous petitions have come to Us, especially during these later years, from Our Legates and from the Bishops of the Oriental Church, beseeching Us to yield to their earnest entreaties and, now that the codification of the laws of the Oriental Church is almost finished, to promulgate without further delay certain chapters of those same laws, which are of special importance, so as to obviate in an effective way the serious and harmful circumstances which affect some portions of Christ's flock using the Oriental rite.

Accordingly, after having attentively and thoughtfully considered everything in the Lord, We of Our own motion, with certain knowledge and in the fullness of Apostolic power, have decided and determined to publish at once those canons which concern the discipline of the Sacrament of Matrimony.

Already at the beginning, when the work of making the Code was being organized, Cardinal Peter Gasparri, President of the Commission for the canonical Code of the Oriental Church, considering the facility and frequency of the relationships which arise between the peoples and nations of the world because of the highly developed means of communication of our age, consulted the sacred Pastors of the Oriental Church by a letter of 15 September, 1930, asking them whether, in carrying out the wishes which had been expressed to the Holy See from many quarters, it seemed desirable that ecclesiastical discipline regarding matrimonial impediments and the form for entering the nuptial union, be made uniform. He asked this question because, owing to the facility of travel, mixed marriages between persons of different rites were becoming more frequent, and also for the purpose of entirely removing uncertainties regarding the validity of marriages, a thing which is harmful to the sanctity of the married state.

Accordingly, after having duly weighed the replies of the said sacred Pastors, nearly all of which were in the affirmative, and after having reported them to the Supreme Pontiff Our immediate Predecessor of happy memory, the Commission for the canonical Code of the Oriental Church presented to Us for Our approbation these canons, which We now by Our Apostolic authority do approve:

CONCERNING THE SACRAMENT OF MATRIMONY
Can. 1 to Can. 131

Now, by this Apostolic Letter given of Our own motion, We promulgate the above canons and give them the force of law for the faithful of the Oriental Church, wherever in the world they may be, and though they be subject to a Prelate of a different rite. As soon as these canons go into effect in virtue of the present Apostolic Letter, every statute, whether general or particular or special, even though it be enacted by Synods which were especially approved, and every prescription and custom still exstant, whether general or particular, shall lose all force and effect, so that the discipline of the Sacrament of Matrimony shall be governed exclusively by these same canons, and any particular law which is contrary to them shall no longer have any force except when and in so far as it is admitted by them.

But in order that timely notice of this Our will may reach all the persons concerned, We will and decree that this *Motu proprio* Letter shall begin to take effect from the second day of May, 1949, feast of Saint Athanasius, Pontiff and Doctor, all things, even those worthy of special mention, to the contrary notwithstanding.

Given at Rome from Saint Peter's, the 22nd day of February, feast of the Chair of Saint Peter at Antioch, in the year 1949, the tenth of Our Pontificate.

AAS 41–89 to 41–117; Pius XII, *Motu proprio*, 22 Feb., 1949. Cf. *The Jurist*, 10–334 (Gulovitch); *Periodica*, 38–93 (Herman).

Family Life: Statement of the American Hierarchy, 21 Nov., 1949 (*The Catholic Mind*, 1950, p. 121).

CANON 1013

Decree of the Holy Office on the Ends of Marriage (Holy Office, 1 Apr., 1944) AAS 36–103.

A decree of the Holy Office, entitled *On the Ends of Marriage,* is as follows:

In the last few years a number of published writings concerning the ends of marriage and their relation and order have appeared, which assert either that the primary end of marriage is not the generation of children, or that the secondary ends are not subordinate to, but are independent of the primary end.

In these discussions the primary end of marriage is variously designated; for example, it is said that it consists in the complement and personal perfection of the spouses by a complete communion of life and action; in their mutual love and union, to be advanced and perfected through the psychical and corporal surrender of their persons; and various other things of this sort.

Sometimes in these writings a meaning is attached to words which occur in the teachings of the Church (for example, *end, primary, secondary*), which is not appropriate to these words according to their common use among theologians.

This new departure in thought and speech is liable to occasion errors and uncertainties; and in order to avert such consequences the Eminent and Most Reverend Fathers of this Supreme Sacred Congregation, which is in charge of safeguarding matters of faith and morals, in the plenary session of Wednesday the 29th of March, 1944, considered the question proposed to it as follows:

Question. Whether the opinion of certain modern writers can be admitted, who either deny that the primary end of marriage is the generation and education of children, or teach that the secondary ends are not essentially subordinate to the primary end, but are equally principal and independent.

Reply. In the negative.

And in the audience granted to His Excellency, the Most Reverend Assessor of the Holy Office, on Thursday, the 30th of the same month and year, His Holiness Pius XII, after receiving a report of the entire matter, deigned to approve the present decree, and ordered that it be published.

Given at Rome, from the Palace of the Holy Office, 1 April, 1944.

AAS 36–103; Holy Office, Decree, 1 Apr., 1944
Cf. annotations in *Periodica,* 33–219.

Primary End of Marriage: Exaltation of Personal Values Above the Procreation and Education of Children, Condemned (Pius XII, Allocution, 29 Oct., 1951) **AAS 43–835.**

In an Allocution to Italian Catholic Midwives, after referring to a mass of current literature which exalts "the personal values" of marriage and relegates the procreation and education of the child to a secondary place, His Holiness Pius XII continued as follows:

There is question here of a serious inversion of the order of values and ends established by the Creator Himself. We are confronted with a propaganda consisting of a mass of ideas and affections which are directly opposed to the clearness, depth, and seriousness of Christian truth. . . .

The truth is that marriage as a natural institution in virtue of the will of the Creator has not as its primary and central purpose the personal perfection of the parties, but the procreation and education of the new living being. The other ends, though also intended by nature, are not on the same level with the first, and much less are they superior to it, but are essentially subordinate to it. This is true of every marriage, even if it be unproductive; just as it can be said of every eye that it is destined and made for sight, even though in an abnormal case by reason of special internal and external conditions, it may never be able to produce visual perception.

Precisely to put a stop to all the uncertainties and vagaries which were threatening to propagate errors regarding the relative importance of the ends of marriage and their relation to one another, We Ourselves some years ago (on March 10, 1941)[1] drew up a declaration on the order of these ends, pointing out that which the very internal structure of the natural order reveals, which the heritage of Christian tradition embodies, which the Supreme Pontiffs have repeatedly taught, and which finally is crystallized into legal form by the Code of Canon Law (c. 1013, § 1). In fact, shortly afterward, in order to correct the contrary opinions, the Holy See declared by a public Decree: that one cannot admit the opinion of certain modern writers, who either deny that the primary end of marriage is the generation and education of children, or teach that the secondary ends are not essentially subordinate to the primary end, but are equally principal and independent.[2]

Does this mean that we must deny or depreciate what is good and right in the personal values which result from marriage and its use? Certainly not, because for the generation of the new life the Creator has destined in marriage human beings of flesh and blood, endowed with mind and heart, and they are called as men, not as irrational animals, to be the authors of their

---

[1] In the annotations in *Periodica* (Vol. 40, pp. 424–425), Hürth points out that, while the text of this declaration of Pius XII has not been published, it is evident that it was substantially the same as that which was later embodied in the Decree of the Holy Office of 1 April, 1944, AAS 36–103, which is reported above under this same canon 1013.

[2] Holy Office, 1 April, 1944; AAS 36–103; reported above under this same canon 1013.

progeny. It is to this end that God wills the union of the married couple. For Holy Scripture says of God that He created man according to His image; that He created them male and female (Gen. 1:27), and He wished, as is repeatedly stated in the Sacred Books, that a man should leave father and mother and cling to his wife, and that they should be two in one flesh (Gen. 2:24; Matt. 19:5; Eph. 5:31).

All this, therefore, is true and it is the will of God; but it must not be separated from the primary function of marriage, which is to provide for the generation of new life. Not only the cooperation of the parties in their exterior life, but also all the enrichment of their personality even in the intellectual and spiritual sphere, and even all that is most spiritual and profound in conjugal love as such, is by ordinance of nature and of the Creator placed at the service of the progeny. By its very nature, perfect conjugal life means also the complete dedication of the parents to the welfare of their children, and conjugal love with all its strength and tenderness supposes the most sincere care of the children that may be born and is a guarantee that that care will be provided (cf. S. Thos., 3ª, q. 29, a. 2 in c.; *Suppl.*, q. 49, a. 2 ad 1).

AAS 43-835; Pius XII, Allocution, 29 Oct., 1951. Annotations, *Periodica,* 40-402 (Hürth). Other moral pronouncements of the same Address are reported under canons 1081, 1086, 1111, 2350. Full English text, *The Catholic Mind,* 1952, p. 49.

CANON 1014

Favor of the Law for Validity of First Marriage Resulting in Invalidity of a Second (Code Com., 26 June, 1947) AAS 39-374.

The Code Commission was asked:

Whether, when there is a positive and insoluble doubt of the validity of a first marriage, a second marriage should, in virtue of canon 1014, be declared invalid.

Reply. In the affirmative, provided the case is handled according to the ordinary course of law.

AAS 39-374; Code Com., 26 June, 1947.
Cf. *Periodica,* 36-349 (Cappello).

Validity of Baptism in Certain Sects: Presumption, See c. 1070; AAS 41–650.

CANON 1015

To Be Putative, a Marriage Must Be Celebrated Before the Church (Code Com., 26 Jan., 1949) AAS 41–158.

The Code Commission was asked:

Whether the word *celebratum* of canon 1015, § 4, is to be understood only of a marriage celebrated before the Church.

Reply. In the affirmative.

AAS 41–158; Code Commission, 26 Jan., 1949. Annotations, *Monitor Ecclesiasticus,* 1949, p. 143 (Larraona).

CANON 1040

Dispensation From Impediment and Validation of Marriage by Special Authority of Holy See Through Sacred Penitentiary (S. Paen., 1927) Private.

The occasion of this very notable reply of the Sacred Penitentiary is thus described in the *Theologische-Praktische Quartalschrift,* Linz, 1927, p. 775:

Case. Titius and Caia, although not entirely ignorant of the fact, had kept silent about an impediment which is diriment according to both ecclesiastical and civil law and from which it is very difficult to obtain a dispensation. They are considered as lawfully married. Stung by an uneasy conscience, the putative husband and wife appeal to their pastor for help. The pastor describes the case accurately to the Sacred Penitentiary, and receives the following rescript.

Rescript. The Sacred Penitentiary, by special and express authority of the Holy See through the gracious consent of His Holiness the Pope, grants to you, beloved son, proper pastor of the aforesaid putative spouses, or to an assistant pastor acting in your place, the necessary and appropriate faculties, so that you may and can dispense these parties from the impediment of ——, and assist at a marriage to be celebrated secretly between them, omitting the publications of the banns and other formalities which are usually observed, and without witnesses, imposing moreover on the parties an oath that they will not abusively resort to the civil law against the indissolubility of their marriage, and on condition that all scandal be removed; also declaring and announcing as legitimate the children that have been born or may be born of this union. For the forum of conscience; yet so that this favor may benefit the parties also in the external forum. To this end the present Rescript, with an attestation of its execution and so of the contracting of the marriage, the marriage being also recorded in the register of secret marriages, is to be cautiously preserved in the parish archives, so that in any future contingency the validity of the marriage and the legitimacy of the children may be legitimately proved.

(Private); S. Paen., no date. Reported in *Theologische-Praktische Quartalschrift*, 1927, p. 775, and annotated in *Periodica*, 16–136.

NOTE: The anonymous annotator in *Periodica* (probably Vermeersch) points out especially that in difficult cases the Sacred Penitentiary can sometimes bring relief even beyond its ordinary competency, by asking special authority of the Supreme Pontiff, as was done here. Notable also is the special provision of this Rescript that it is to be kept in the archives of the parish, instead of the diocesan archives mentioned in canons 1047 and 379.

CANON 1052

Dispensation: When Valid for Impediment Not Mentioned (Code Com., 8 July, 1948) AAS 40–386.

The Code Commission was asked:

Whether canon 1052 is to be understood in the sense that a dispensation which has been obtained for a certain and determinate impediment is valid also for another impediment of the same species in an equal or lower degree, which in good or bad faith was omitted from the petition; or rather *only* in the sense that the dispensation from the impediment which was mentioned is not vitiated by the omission of another impediment of the same species in an equal or lower degree.

Reply. In the affirmative to the first part, in the negative to the second.

AAS 40–386; Code Com., 8 July, 1948.
Periodica, 37–292 (Cappello).

Orientals: Application of canon 1052. See c. 66; private, S. C. Eccl. Or., 24 July, 1948.

CANON 1053

Presumed Death of Former Spouse: Permission for New Marriage, Even by Ordinary, Carries Implicit Dispensation (Code Com., 26 March, 1952) AAS 44-496.

The Code Commission was asked:

Whether the words of canon 1053, "permission granted to contract another marriage," are to be understood only of a permission granted by the Holy See or also of a permission granted by the Ordinary of the place.

Reply. In the negative to the first part, in the affirmative to the second.

Given at Rome, from Vatican City, 26 March, 1952.

AAS 44-496; Code Com., 26 March, 1952. Annotations, *Monitor Ecclesiasticus*, 1952, p. 405 (Bidagor).

CANON 1061

Marriages of Communists. See c. 1065; AAS 41-428.
Sincerity of Promises: Made Condition of Matrimonial Consent. See c. 1092; private, Rota, 19 Feb., 1952.
Sincerity of Promises in Itself a Condition for the Validity of the Dispensation. See c. 1071, ref. and full discussion in *The Jurist*, 13-33 (Kelly).

CANON 1065

Marriages of Communists (Holy Office, Declaration, 11 Aug., 1949) AAS 41-427.

A Declaration of the Holy Office regarding the celebration of the marriage of Communists:

It has been asked whether the exclusion of Communists from the use of the Sacraments, prescribed by the Decree of the Holy Office of 1 July, 1949,[1] implies also exclusion from the celebration of marriage; and if not, whether the marriages of Communists are governed by the provisions of canons 1060-1061.

Reply. On this matter the Holy Office declares: In view of the peculiar nature of the Sacrament of matrimony, whose ministers are the contracting parties themselves and in which

---

[1] AAS 41-334; reported in this volume under canon 2314.

the priest acts as a witness *ex officio,* the priest can assist at the marriages of Communists according to canons 1065 and 1066.

But in the marriages of the persons referred to in n. 4 of the aforesaid Decree, the provisions of canons 1061, 1102, and 1109, § 3, are to be observed.

Given from the Holy Office, 11 Aug., 1949.

AAS 41–427; Holy Office, 11 Aug., 1949. *Periodica,* 38–305 (Fábregas).

CANON 1066

Marriages of Communists. See c. 1065; AAS 41–428.

CANON 1067

Matrimonial Impediments and Form of Marriage in China Under Communist Rule: *Equivalent Cautiones* **Further Defined** (Holy Office, 27 Jan., 1949, and 21 Feb., 1949) **Private.**

A Letter of the Papal Internuncio to China, addressed to all Ordinaries of China, is as follows:

Your Excellency: 19 Feb., 1949

The Most Reverend Leopold Brellinger, Bishop of Kinghsien, in July, 1948, proposed the following questions to the Holy Office:

1. Whether the faithful in the territories of China which are occupied by the Communists are bound by the impediments established by the Church, especially nonage and disparity of cult, if they can either not at all or only with the gravest difficulty ask for a dispensation, and cannot abstain from contracting marriage, nor postpone it.

2. Whether they are bound by the impediment of disparity of cult in a case where, through ignorance, forgetfulness, or some other inculpable cause, the required *cautiones* are not given, or where they are refused by the non-Catholic party.

The Supreme Sacred Congregation on 27 Jan., 1949, deigned to reply as follows: After attentively considering the circumstances, this Supreme Sacred Congregation, in the plenary session of Wednesday, January 26th, decided to reply to the proposed questions as follows:

Reply. 1. In the circumstances mentioned, marriages contracted without the canonical form or with an impediment of ecclesiastical law from which the Church usually dispenses, are to be considered as valid.

2. Marriages which are subject to the impediment of disparity of cult should be dealt with according to the provisions of the Holy Office regarding equivalent cautiones (cf. *Sylloge,* S. C. Prop. Fid., pp. 561–566).[1]

Which decision, His Holiness in the Audience of January 27th benignly deigned to approve.

All these matters should be brought to the attention of the faithful so that they may provide for the validity of marriages and be freed from anxieties of conscience. If, however, in regard to some marriages contracted in this way, special questions arise in the future owing to the peculiar circumstances of the particular case, the Ordinary may refer the matter to this Supreme Congregation.

The Reverend Francis Hürth, Consultor to the Sacred Congregation of the Holy Office, by order of His Eminence the Cardinal Secretary and of His Excellency the Assessor of the same Supreme Sacred Congregation, explained the above reply as follows:

I. The words "in the circumstances mentioned" (*in expositis circumstantiis*) mean "while these circumstances continue" or "while this state of affairs continues."

II. "Equivalent *cautiones,*" according to a Reply of the Holy Office given for Japan, are had, when the Catholic party sincerely manifests a firm resolve to do what he can to see that all the children are baptized and educated in the Catholic faith. If the non-Catholic party refuses to formulate and manifest the same resolve, the "equivalent *cautiones,*" according to the Reply cited, are not thereby destroyed.

III. The faithful are freed not only from the impediments of nonage and disparity of cult, but from all impediments of ecclesiastical law and from all canonical form (both ordinary and extraordinary). But the impediment of the sacred order of the priesthood and the impediment of affinity in the direct line when the marriage was consummated, are not suspended but remain in full force even under the circumstances mentioned.

The same Supreme Congregation requests me to inform the

---

[1] See CANON LAW DIGEST, 2, pp. 281–285.

Ordinaries of China of all this, and to authorize them to make use of these faculties in the same circumstances.

In complying with that request by the present letter, I present to Your Excellency my sentiments of profound esteem, and remain,

Devotedly yours,

Ant. Riberi

Internuncio Apostolic to China

(Private); Holy Office, 27 Jan., 1949. This document appeared in *China Missionary* for 4 April, 1949, p. 417, and in *Periodica,* 38–187, with further annotations by Hürth. In these annotations a further explanation of the term "equivalent *cautiones,*" as used in this particular document, is given *with official sanction,* as follows:

On 21 Feb., 1949, by order of His Excellency the Assessor of the Holy Office, the following Supplement regarding the *cautiones* was sent: "Equivalent *cautiones* are to be considered sufficient for contracting marriage with a pagan party or with a baptized non-Catholic party, only if, on consideration of the circumstances of the individual cases, it is morally certain that the sincere manifested will of the Catholic party to have all the children baptized and educated as Catholics, will also *have effect."*

Nonage: Non-Catholic Admitted as Plaintiff under canon 1990. See c. 1990; private reply of Holy Office, 24 May, 1952.

CANON 1068

Sterilization Imposed by Iniquitous Law in Form of Double Vasectomy Does Not Constitute Certain Impotence (Holy Office, 16 Feb., 1935) **Private.**

The following question was proposed to the Holy Office, 17 Dec., 1934, by the Bishop of Aachen in Germany:

Whether a man who has undergone bilateral vasectomy which is total and irreparable, or any other surgical operation having the same effect, that is, which irreparably closes off all communication with the testicles, so that no sperm can pass or be transferred from them by natural means, may nevertheless be safely allowed to contract marriage according to the rule laid down in canon 1068, § 2.

Reply. In the case of so-called sterilization imposed by iniquitous law, marriage, in accordance with paragraph 2 of canon 1068, is not to be impeded.

(Private); Holy Office, 16 Feb., 1935. *Periodica,* 36–14 (Aguirre).

NOTE: This reply, given in 1935, was not to be published at that time. It has, however, now been cited in several judicial decisions including at least one by the Rota, and is published and discussed in the article from *Periodica* cited above. As the author of that article points out, the Holy Office did not directly answer the question proposed. There is need of great caution in drawing conclusions from this reply. See the decision of the Rota, 25 Oct., 1945, reported below under this same canon 1068.

"True Semen" Is Whatever Is Secreted in the Testicles, Even Without *Spermatozoa* (Rota, 25 April, 1941) Private.

Facts. In this case the woman, after eight years of married life during which no conception occurred although she desired children, learned that her husband had before the marriage contracted a venereal disease and undergone an operation which made it impossible for him to generate children. Separation followed, and the woman brought suit in the Vicariate of Rome for nullity on the ground of impotence on the part of the man. The decision was: *non constare de nullitate.* On appeal to the Rota, the issue was extended by special permission of the Holy See, as follows:

I. *An constet de matrimonii nullitate in casu, et quatenus negative;*

II. *An consilium praestandum sit SS.mo pro dispensatione super matrimonio rato et non consummato.*

The case (*coram* Wynen) presents a rather thorough study of the physiology of the testicular function of the male, and a clear statement of the law as accepted in the jurisprudence of the Rota, as to what is and what is not required in this respect for potency, or capacity for acts which are *de se* suitable for the generation of children. In the following condensed summary we confine our attention to this point of law as applied to impotence and to nonconsummation.

The Law. The attorneys for the plaintiff contended, on the strength of certain medical authorities, that the testicles themselves produce nothing whatever besides the *nemaspermata, spermatozoa* or sperm cells; hence, that whatever liquid may be ejaculated in the act of copula is not the product of the testicles, but of other organs (the prostate, Cowper's glands, and the seminal vesicles). If this were certain, it would follow that a man who is incapable of contributing *nemaspermata* in the act of copula is *ipso facto* incapable of contributing anything from the testicles, or anything that can be called "true semen" in the accepted formula for defining the act of copula. Such a man would therefore be impotent.

The court, after weighing the medical authorities offered by the plaintiff's attorneys, considers and cites also a number of others, and concludes that this contention is not certain; and consequently that no certain conclusion in favor of impotence can be drawn from the sole fact that the man is incapable of producing *nemaspermata*.

During the latest centuries, authors were unanimous in teaching that "true semen" means "semen elaborated in the testicles"; during the last two decades, some authors have held that the term "true semen" means simply the liquid which is ejaculated in the act of copula, whatever be the glands from which it originates. Accordingly these same authors have denied that perfect copula requires that at least some part of the liquid ejaculated come from the testicles. But the Rota has not considered this new doctrine as probable, and has refused to accept it.

In the jurisprudence of the Rota, "true semen" means "semen elaborated in the testicles"; that is, in the didymus and epididymus considered as a unit. In order to be capable of perfect copula, the man must be capable of contributing to that act all that is required on his part to make the act *de se* suitable for the procreation of a new life. And the act is to be considered as *de se* suitable for the procreation of a new life, provided the substance naturally injected into the vagina is "true semen" in this sense, even though it be lacking in *nemaspermata*.

The following two paragraphs are translated *verbatim* from the decision:

I. As to *Impotence:* "Impotence on the part of the man for want of true semen can arise from two sources: either the testicles cannot produce semen, or the semen produced in the testicles cannot pass to the exterior. The first case is verified if the testicles either are from birth so insufficiently developed that they cannot produce semen, or after their normal development become so atrophied as a result of venereal disease that they are totally incapable of producing semen. The second case is realized when the little ducts of the epididymus or the other *canales deferentes* are so clogged by *epididymitis* or some other disease that the semen formed in the testicles cannot get out. *A fortiori* true semen is wanting in the liquid ejaculated, if the man suffers from both these defects, a condition which is often caused by the disease of *orchiepididymitis*. Such impotence renders marriage null and void only if it was certainly antecedent to the marriage and moreover certainly permanent or incurable."

II. As to *Nonconsummation*. "If in a particular case the diriment impediment of impotence is not proved with certainty, sometimes the dispensation from nonconsummated marriage can be asked of the Supreme Pontiff, provided both the fact of nonconsummation and a just cause for the dispensation be established (c. 1119). Since in the present case the man was able to penetrate the vagina of the wife, and in fact often did so, and since the alleged impotence of the man is ascribed exclusively to the lack of true semen elaborated in the testicles, it is clear that the fact of nonconsummation must be proved by showing that, at least from the first day of conjugal life until the definite separation of the parties, the man lacked this true semen; in other words it is sufficient to prove that this defect in the man was antecedent to the marriage and lasted during the entire time that the parties lived together, and it would make no difference if the man was cured or could have been cured of it, after the separation. If therefore the alleged defect is found to be doubtful, either at the beginning or *a fortiori* during the course of the conjugal relationship, the recommendation cannot be made to His Holiness for the dispensation from nonconsummated marriage."

The Decision: *Non constare de matrimonii nullitate in casu, neque consilium praestandum esse SS.mo pro dispensatione super matrimonio rato et non consummato in casu; seu ad bina dubia proposita respondemus negative ad utrumque.*

(Private); Rota, 25 April, 1941. *Periodica,* 33–200. Cf. also the discussion in *Periodica,* 36–5 (Aguirre).

NOTE: On the second issue (nonconsummation) this decision was reversed on appeal. An interesting procedural point also is involved. Permission of the Supreme Pontiff was obtained for an appeal to another *Turnus* of the Rota (*coram* Grazioli) on this issue only. The decision of this appellate tribunal (30 Nov., 1943) was: *Sententiam*

*Rotalem diei 25 Aprilis 1941 esse quoad alterum dubium infirmandam,
ideoque consilium praestandum esse SS.mo pro gratia dispensationis
super matrimonio rato et non consummato in casu, vetito viro transitu
ad alias nuptias inconsulta S. Sede.*

Although this latest decision was contrary to the earlier one on the
question of fact, it confirmed the view of the law held by the first
Rota decision as outlined above. The dispensation, as recommended by
the Rota's later decision, was granted by His Holiness, 10 Dec., 1943.

A further discussion of these same principles will be found in a
decision by the regional tribunal of Piceno, which is reported in
Monitor Ecclesiasticus, 1950, pp. 77–84.

Man Incapable of Ejaculating True Semen Within Vagina Is Impotent (Rota, 25 Oct., 1945) Private.

In this case the woman brought suit in a diocesan court for
the nullity of the marriage on the ground of impotence on the
part of the man. The court of first instance decided *non constare
de nullitate.* On appeal, the first *Turnus* of the Rota (*coram*
Canestri) reversed that decision and declared the marriage null
on the ground of impotence. The case is here on appeal brought
by the Defender of the Bond to another *Turnus* of the Rota
(*coram* Wynen).

Facts. All three tribunals accepted as fully proved the fact
that the man, as a result of a gonococcic infection contracted
long before the marriage, had both *caniculi deferentes* completely
occluded so that the secretion of the testicles could not pass
through them. All the experts also agreed, and it was regarded
as fully proved, that this condition existed before and at the
time of the marriage and that it was irremediable by any means
known to medical science. On this state of facts, a single question
of law is presented and very thoroughly discussed in this decision,
namely, whether such a condition constitutes impotence. We
shall attempt a very condensed summary of the views of this
tribunal on that question.

The Law. A man is impotent if he is incapable of perfect or
conjugal copula (*impotentia coeundi*). This is commonly defined
as *"copula de se apta ad generandam prolem, licet per accidens
generatio non sequatur."* Cappello (*De Matrimonio,* ed. 3, n. 342)
does not like this definition because the end or purpose (generation) should not be expressed in the definition of copula. Hence
he gives another definition: perfect copula is the act by which

true semen is infused by natural means into the vagina. In substance, there is no opposition between the two definitions. The question here presented is precisely whether a man is to be regarded as impotent when he is incapable of injecting true semen into the vagina, either because his testicles are atrophied and entirely inactive or because both ducts leading from them are entirely occluded and impervious to the passage of the semen secreted within them.

In the jurisprudence of the Rota, true semen is required for perfect copula. But this does not necessarily mean semen which contains live *spermatozoa*. This latter requirement was demanded for perfect copula by Alberti, who is cited by the court of first instance; and some modern writers have followed him; but all approved authors are to the contrary. The court of first instance also cites a decision of the Rota (8 Jan., 1913) as making that requirement. That decision, however, was reversed by the Rota itself the same year, and has never since been followed. In fact it has been so consistently contradicted that the contrary doctrine may be called the *settled jurisprudence* of this Tribunal.

Although the *spermatozoa* are the most important element in the secretion of the testicles, they do not constitute its entire content; there is in addition a small quantity of liquid without sperm cells. The requirement of *true semen* for the act of conjugal copula is therefore the same as that which is expressed by the formula *"semen in testiculis elaboratum";* and it is satisfied provided the product of the testicles, with or without sperm, is injected into the vagina by the natural process. A man who has at least one testicle functioning, and the corresponding *vas deferens* open so as to allow the passage of the secretion, is capable of copula so far as this element is concerned. He is, in this respect, capable of "acts which are *per se* suitable for the generation of children," in the words of canon 1081, § 2.

The court of first instance, while misunderstanding the jurisprudence of the Rota on the above point, erred in going to the other extreme and holding that true semen is not required at all for perfect or conjugal copula. In their view, copula is perfect if the sexual appetite is completely satisfied by it, even though no part of the semen, or secretion of the testicles, enters the vagina.

This view cannot be sustained. The judges of first instance attempt to sustain it by the argument that the Church permits the marriage of old men, who (as they suppose) ordinarily, because of atrophied testicles, are incapable of ejaculating true semen. But this supposition is false. It is true that the vigor of the functioning of the testicular secretion diminishes with old age. But there is no age at which a man is presumed to be deprived of this function and hence incapable of valid marriage. On the contrary, even old men are presumed capable until the contrary is proved; and there is no need of attempting to attain certainty on the fact by an examination in individual cases. The right to marry, founded as it is in the law of nature, prevails in the case of the old just as in other men, until it is proved with certainty that the individual in question is afflicted with some form of antecedent and perpetual impotence.

The court of first instance also cites a decision of the Holy Office which was reported in a letter of the Bishop of Aachen to other Ordinaries of Germany in 1935,[1] to the effect that "in the case of so-called sterilization imposed by iniquitous law, marriage, in accordance with canon 1068, § 2, is not to be impeded." The sterilization referred to in that decision consisted in the operation of double vasectomy. Of this operation, Cappello (*De Matrimonio*, nn. 375–379) holds that it constitutes impotence, according to the more common opinion, precisely because it makes it impossible for *true semen,* that is the product of the testicles, to be ejaculated. But this will be the diriment impediment of impotence mentioned in canon 1068, only if it is antecedent to the marriage, and perpetual or irremediable without danger to life. On the question of fact, whether such a condition is remediable or not, there is actual difference of opinion among medical experts. Therefore, according to Cappello, *in practice,* after such an operation, if it is doubtful whether the condition of impotence is permanent or not, a marriage already contracted is to be considered valid, and a marriage to be contracted is not to be prevented.

Now the decision of the Holy Office does not contradict this doctrine. The decision could well be explained on the assumption that the sterilization practiced in Germany at that time left room for some *doubt of fact* in individual cases, as to whether the closure of the ducts so produced might be remediable. If in

---

[1] Reported in this volume under this same canon 1068.

a given case the condition could be cured by remedial surgery, then obviously the impotence would not be permanent; and if this fact were doubtful, the impediment of impotence would not be certain, and consequently the marriage should not be prevented.

A further point not mentioned in the decision of the court of first instance is this. The Supreme Pontiffs have considered marriages as nonconsummated and have granted the dispensation, whenever this Tribunal has presented to them a case in which the man, though he had penetrated the vagina, had not ejaculated true semen within it, either because his testicles were atrophied or the ducts completely occluded.

Hence, upon mature consideration of the law and the facts, the judgment is: *Constare de nullitate matrimonii in casu.* The judgment of the first *Turnus* of the Rota is confirmed.

(**Private**); Rota, 25 Oct., 1945; *Periodica, 35–5.*

NOTE: A critical study of this decision and of the jurisprudence of the Rota on this question, is presented by Aguirre in *Periodica, 36–5.* A number of earlier Rota cases on the same question are briefly summarized in CANON LAW DIGEST, Vol. 2, p. 287.

Double Vasectomy Held to Constitute Certain, Perpetual Impotence (Metropolitan Tribunal of New York, 23 May, 1947) Private.

A remarkably clear and well-reasoned decision of the Metropolitan Tribunal of New York (*in Causa Nullitatis Matrimonii ex capite impotentiae viri,* 23 May, 1947, *coram* McCormick) is reported in *Monitor Ecclesiasticus,* 1950, pp. 207–223. The following is a very condensed summary.

Facts. It was a mixed marriage, contracted before the Church in 1941, the girl being a Catholic and the man a baptized Methodist. The marriage was consummated but no conception resulted therefrom. After a few years the man obtained a divorce and about the same time revealed the fact that, fourteen days before the marriage, he had undergone double vasectomy for the express purpose of avoiding children. At the trial this fact was confirmed by the surgeon who had performed the operation and by two experts called by the Court, who made a physical examination of the man.

The suit for nullity was brought by the woman in 1944, was abandoned for a time during a futile attempt at reconciliation, then resumed and brought to final judgment. Two grounds of nullity were alleged: (1) impotence on the part of the man; (2) an intention on his part *contra bonum prolis.* This report considers only the first ground.

Decision: On the cardinal point of the case, namely, whether the man was capable of *"effusio veri seminis elaborati in testiculis,"* the Court first considered three different opinions as to the requisites of "true semen."

1. The first opinion, first proposed by Vermeersch, recently defended strongly in a doctoral thesis by Nowlan, regarded by Cappello as intrinsically probable, holds that even after permanent and irremediable double vasectomy the man can produce true semen, and is therefore not impotent. The endocrine glands remain active in the testicles, and the gonadal hormones taken into the blood regulate the secretion of other glands, the prostate, the seminal vesicles, and Cowper's glands. Consequently (in this view) the testicles themselves can be considered to contribute something (indirectly) to the liquid ejaculated, which can therefore be held to satisfy the requirement of "semen formed in the testicles" (Sixtus V). This Court, however, holds that this opinion is neither intrinsically nor extrinsically probable; and shows moreover that it is rejected in the recent jurisprudence of the Rota, citing especially the decision of 25 April, 1941 (*coram* Wynen), which is reported above in this same volume under this same canon 1068.

2. The second opinion holds that, to satisfy the requirement of "true semen," the liquid ejected must contain *spermatozoa.* The Court holds that this opinion also is wanting in probability; and that, at least for the past thirty years, it has been consistently rejected in the jurisprudence of the Rota, citing especially the decision of 25 Oct., 1945 (*coram* Wynen), which is reported above under this same canon 1068.

3. The third opinion is that "true semen" includes whatever is produced in the testicles, that is, in the didymus and epididymus together considered as a unit; therefore, even though *spermatozoa,* which are produced in the didymus, be wanting, if the liquid produced in the epididymus be present, the matter ejaculated is to be considered "true semen formed in the testicles." This opinion, accepted in the recent jurisprudence of the Rota, is regarded by this Court as correct.

But, the Court goes on to say, *"effusio veri seminis"* is impossible if both the *vasa deferentia* are completely occluded and impervious. There can be no doubt that in this case the *vasa deferentia* are in that condition as a result of the operation of double vasectomy, which is proved to have been "successfully" performed; and this condition existed before the marriage.

Two further questions of fact remain to be decided: (1) whether in this particular case the restoration of the open passage through the *vasa deferentia* by a new operation not dangerous to life is possible (if this is true, the impotence is not permanent and hence does not annul the marriage); and (2) whether, even after the operation, some true semen might have remained in the seminal vesicles and been ejaculated at the consummation of the marriage, so that impotence would have to be denied on that ground.

On the first question, whether the vasectomy was remediable by a new operation, there was some conflict of opinion among the experts. All agreed that neither of the two forms of the operation designed to restore the connection is dangerous to life. As to the success of the new operation, the surgeon who had performed the vasectomy claimed that he could also restore the continuity of the ducts by a new operation. The two experts called by the Court, basing their judgment on long medical experience, testified that the probability of the success of such a reparative operation was extremely slight; and all the more so in this case in view of the thorough manner in which the first operation was done. The Court accepted this view, citing with approval the conclusion announced by Clifford in a very thorough study of the same general question in medical literature (*Theological Studies*, 1946, p. 263).

The bare possibility that there might have remained some true semen in the seminal vesicles after the operation and before the consummation of the marriage, cannot be admitted to prevent a decision in favor of impotence. On the contrary, after the operation of double vasectomy, the man is to be considered impotent *until the contrary is proved*. This presumption is strengthened by the fact that the operation in this case was performed for the very purpose of avoiding children.

The final decision was: *constare de nullitate matrimonii ob impotentiam viri.*

(**Private**); Metropolitan Tribunal of New York, 23 May, 1947. Reported in *Monitor Ecclesiasticus*, 1950, pp. 207–223.

Artificial Insemination: The possibility of resorting to artificial insemination does not make a marriage valid between persons who are unfit to contract it by reason of the impediment of impotence. See c. 1081; AAS 41–557.

CANON 1069

Presumed Death of Former Spouse: Implicit dispensation from crime. See c. 1053; AAS 44–496.

CANON 1070

Disparity of Cult: Dispensation for Marriage With a Jew; Meaning of Jew in Restriction of Quinquennial Faculties (Holy Office, 7 July, 1943) Private.

The Holy Office was asked:

Does the exception in regard to a Jewish party, which is mentioned in the Quinquennial Faculties in n. 3 of the faculties from the Holy Office, refer to all Jews indiscriminately, by the simple fact of their Jewish origin, even though they have abandoned or never followed the observance of their religion; or does it rather include only those who, whatever their origin, profess the Jewish religion?

Reply. In the affirmative to the first part; in the negative to the second.

(**Private**); Holy Office, 7 July, 1943. Reply kindly furnished by the Most Reverend Robert E. Lucey, Archbishop of San Antonio.

Restriction of Quinquennial Faculties Not Applicable to Person of Jewish Origin Whose Ancestors Were Converted to the Faith, Though They Afterward Fell Away, and Who Himself Has No Religion (Holy Office, 11 Apr., 1945) Private.

The Holy Office was asked:

Whether, according to the reply of the Holy Office of 7 July, 1943,[1] a person is still to be regarded as of Jewish origin if he

---

[1] Reported above in this volume, under this same canon 1070.

is descended from ancestors who were once Jewish but later were converted to the Catholic faith for one or more generations and afterward fell away, and if he himself never received baptism and professes no religion.

Reply. In the negative; that is, the person mentioned in the question is not to be regarded as a Jew.

(Private); Holy Office, 11 Apr., 1945. Reply kindly supplied by the Most Reverend Robert E. Lucey, Archbishop of San Antonio. It should be noted that in this particular case rather full genealogical tables were sent to the Holy Office to supply information on which to base the reply.

Documentum Libertatis Given by Holy Office Where Dispensation From Disparity of Cult (Under Earlier Formula of Quinquennial Faculties) Was for Marriage With a Jew (Holy Office, 26 March, 1947) Private.

The Tribunal of the Archdiocese of New York submitted the following questions to the Holy Office on December 29, 1945:

1. Whether the aforesaid exception for Jews, which is contained in the Quinquennial Faculties granted by the Holy Office, n. 3[1] concerns persons who are born of one Jewish parent, the other parent being a baptized non-Catholic.

2. Whether in the present case the woman A. S. is to be considered a Jew, so that a dispensation cannot be given her in virtue of the Quinquennial Faculties granted by the Holy Office, to enable her to marry a Catholic man.

Reply. The reply of the Holy Office, entitled *"Nullitatis Matrimonii vel Dissolutionis eiusdem,"* Prot. N. 230m/46, was as follows: This Supreme Sacred Congregation has examined the record in the case of the nullity of a marriage in the year 1945, with a dispensation from disparity of cult (whose validity, however, is in doubt), contracted between N. C., a Catholic man, and A. S., an unbaptized woman.

In the plenary session of Wednesday 26 March, 1947, the Eminent and Most Reverend Fathers of this Supreme Sacred Congregation, to the question:

"Whether a recommendation is to be made to His Holiness that — if the absence of baptism in the woman A. S. is proved with certainty — a *documentum libertatis* be granted to the

[1] Cf. Canon Law Digest, 2, p. 31. This exception was later revoked, but it remained in effect until July 1, 1946.

petitioner N. C., so that he can validly and licitly contract a new marriage before the Church," decided to reply:

In the affirmative.

On Thursday 27 March, 1947, His Holiness by divine Providence Pope Pius XII, in the audience granted to His Excellency the Most Reverend Assessor of the Holy Office, after receiving a report of the entire matter, graciously deigned to grant the favor according to the above Decree, *servatis de iure servandis,* all things to the contrary notwithstanding.

(**Private**); Holy Office, 26 March, 1947. Translation made from Latin text kindly sent to us by the Committee on Research of the Canon Law Society of America.

Marriage Between Oriental Schismatic Woman and Unbaptized Man Invalid for Disparity of Cult (Holy Office, 18 May, 1949) **Private.**

The following document came from the Holy Office to an Ordinary of the United States under date of 18 May, 1949:

Prot. N. 84m/49

In a letter received here on 26 April, 1949, your Most Reverend Curia presented the following case:

An Oriental Schismatical woman, Millie, contracted a civil marriage in 1935 with James, an unbaptized man, from whom she has now been parted by divorce. She now wishes to contract a new marriage before the Church with J. E., a Catholic man. Whereupon the Most Reverend Curia asked whether the marriage could be declared null on the ground of disparity of cult.

This Sacred Congregation, after having carefully considered all the circumstances of the case, ordered that the following reply be made:

Provided there is juridical proof of the absence of baptism in the man, and of the baptism of the woman and of her belonging to an Oriental Schismatical sect, the marriage can be declared null on the ground of disparity of cult; so that the petitioner, duly observing all the requirements of law, may contract marriage with a Catholic man.

(**Private**); Holy Office, 18 May, 1949. Translation made from the Latin text kindly sent to us by the Committee on Research of the Canon Law Society of America.

Validity of Baptism in Certain Sects: General Presumption (Holy Office, 28 Dec., 1949) AAS 41–650.

A reply of the Holy Office "regarding the validity of baptism conferred in certain sects":

Some Ordinaries of places in the United States of North America have proposed to this Supreme Sacred Congregation the following question:

Whether, in adjudicating matrimonial cases, baptism conferred in the sects of the Disciples of Christ, the Presbyterians, the Congregationalists, the Baptists, the Methodists, when the necessary matter and form were used, is to be presumed invalid because of the lack of the requisite intention on the part of the minister to do what the Church does or what Christ instituted, or whether such baptism is to be considered valid, unless the contrary is proved in the particular case.

Reply. Wednesday, Dec. 21, 1949: the Most Eminent and Most Reverend Cardinals who are placed in charge of the protection of faith and morals, having heard in advance the opinion of the Reverend Consultors, ordered that the question be answered as follows: In the negative to the first part; in the affirmative to the second part.

On the following Thursday the 22nd of the same month and year, His Holiness by divine Providence Pope Pius XII, in the customary audience granted to the Most Excellent Assessor of the Holy Office, approved the resolution of the Eminent Fathers when it was referred to him, confirmed it and ordered it to be published.

Given at Rome, from the Holy Office, 28 Dec., 1949.

AAS 41–650; Holy Office, 28 Dec., 1949. *Periodica,* 39–107 (Hürth).

Marriage Between Oriental Schismatic and Jew Invalid for Disparity of Cult: Ordinary May So Declare (Holy Office, 17 April, 1950) Private.

The following document came from the Holy Office to an Ordinary of the United States:

Your Most Reverend Curia presented the following case by letter of February 21, 1950: An Oriental Schismatic, Victor, celebrated a marriage by a civil act in 1940 with Gertrude, a Jewish woman. Whereupon your Most Reverend Curia asked whether the marriage of Victor with Gertrude might be declared null for disparity of cult.

This Sacred Congregation, having carefully considered all the circumstances of the case, ordered that the following reply be made:

Provided there is juridical proof of the absence of baptism in the woman, and of the baptism of the man and of his belonging to an Oriental Schismatical sect, the marriage can be declared null on the ground of disparity of cult; so that the petitioner, duly observing all the requirements of law, may contract marriage with a Catholic woman.

In similar cases, Your Excellency may proceed on your own authority, without recourse to the Holy Office.

(Private); Holy Office, 17 April, 1950. Translation made from Latin text kindly sent to us by the Committee on Research of the Canon Law Society of America.

Dispensation for Marriage of Catholic With Jew: Restrictive Clause in Former Quinquennial Faculties Held Certainly to Apply to Nonpracticing Jew, Even Before Reply of 7 July, 1943: Doubt of Law Not Admitted (Holy Office, 4 July, 1952) Private.

Summary of the Case. The plaintiff in this action was a baptized Roman Catholic. She contracted marriage on 16 January, 1943, with a Jew, who at the time of the marriage was described as a "nonorthodox, nonpracticing Jew." A dispensation was granted by the Chancellor of a certain diocese in virtue of the Quinquennial Faculties given to the Ordinaries by the Supreme Sacred Congregation of the Holy Office. It was alleged in the petition of the plaintiff that the dispensation was invalid because the Chancellor had exceeded his authority in granting a dispensation from the impediment of disparity of worship in the case of marriage between a Catholic and a Jew. This was based upon the private Reply of the Holy Office, of 7 July, 1943, to the Archbishop of San Antonio, Texas: "Does the exception in regard to a Jewish party, which is mentioned in the Quinquennial Faculties in n. 3 of the faculties from the Holy Office, refer to all Jews indiscriminately, by the simple fact of their Jewish origin, even though they have abandoned or never followed the observance of their religion; or does it rather include only those who, whatever their origin, profess the Jewish religion?" The answer given was: "In the affirmative to the first part, in the negative to the second."[1]

The Chancellor in question indicated that he had granted the dispensation on the basis that "the Ordinary could dispense from the impediment of disparity of worship in cases involving a person who was a Jew by race only and not by religion, and that the Ordinary could and did authorize the Chancellor and his Assistant to use this faculty." He further stated that there was no special mandate to use canon 81, nor did he invoke canon 209.

The Tribunal of first instance declared the marriage in question null on the ground that the Chancellor had exceeded his authority; it based its judgment chiefly on the Reply of the Holy Office to the Archbishop of San Antonio. This Reply was considered to be of general obligation even though it was directed to an individual Archbishop, and it was further considered by the Court of first instance to be a declarative interpretation not requiring any promulgation and being therefore retroactive.

The Reverend Defender of the Bond appealed the decision to the Archdiocesan Court of second instance. After due deliberation this Metropolitan Tribunal reversed the findings of the Court of first instance and held for the validity of the marriage in question.

In its decision the Court of second instance agreed that the Reply of 7 July, 1943, was a declarative interpretation and as such retroactive. Further, it agreed that in view of the fact that the respondent was Jewish, it logically followed that the Chancellor had no power under faculty n. 3 of the Quinquennials to grant a dispensation from the impediment of disparity of worship in the present case, and "if he did not have this power from some other source, the dispensation was invalid." However, the Court continued and declared: "It is our judgment, however, that at the time this dispensation was granted there was doubt as to the precise meaning of the phrase 'Jewish party' and therefore that, because of this *doubt of law*, the Church, through canon 209, supplied to the Chancellor the power to grant this dispensation validly."

To prove that there existed a doubt of law, the Court of second

_____

[1] Reported above in this volume, under this same canon 1070.

instance presented a series of arguments, one of which was expressed as follows: "The Curial practice in the United States was not uniform in regard to the interpretation of faculty n. 3 of the Quinquennial Faculties of 1939. It is a well-known fact that many Ordinaries and their delegates accepted professed adherence to Orthodox Judaism as the determining factor and granted dispensations in virtue of faculty n. 3 in cases which involved professing Reformed Jews and nonpracticing Jews. It would seem that these Ordinaries felt justified in such cases on the ground that their Quinquennial Faculties are habitual faculties, which are to be considered as privileges beyond the law (c. 66, § 1) and in cases of doubt are to be given a broad interpretation (c. 50). Some other Ordinaries indeed acted more cautiously and referred such cases to the Apostolic Delegate, but it cannot be stated that such was the general rule because no general instruction was given on this matter by the Holy See or the Apostolic Delegate."

Finally, the Court of second instance summarized its position on the issue as follows: "In view of the dubious and at times seemingly conflicting responses of the Holy Office prior to the Code, which still remained as the basis for interpretation until 7 July, 1943, and the controversy of the authors as to the proper interpretation of the phrase 'Jewish party,' and finally the varying Curial practice in America in granting dispensations involving Jews, it is our judgment that *there was an objective and a truly positive and probable doubt of law* present at the time the Chancellor granted the dispensation, and therefore that canon 209 supplied to him the power to grant a valid dispensation in this case."

After the decision of the Court of second instance, the plaintiff appealed to the Sacred Congregation of the Holy Office. The attached rescript settled the matter and declared that the decision of the first Court was to be sustained and that the marriage was null because of the invalid dispensation from the impediment of disparity of worship.

Reply. Your Excellency by letter of 1950 to the Holy Office presented the case of the marriage, N.N. After duly considering everything, this Supreme Sacred Congregation decreed: The judgment of the Court of first instance is to be sustained, that is, the marriage in question is null because of the invalid dispensation from disparity of cult.

From the Holy Office, 4 July, 1952.

(Private); Holy Office, 4 July, 1952. Summary of case and Latin text of rescript were kindly sent to us by the Committee on Research of the Canon Law Society of America.

Disparity of Cult in Oriental Churches. See c. 1; reply of Ap. Del. U. S., 19 April, 1945.

Jew: Restriction Against Dispensation for Marriage With, suppressed. See c. 66; Letters of Apostolic Delegate and new formula of faculties from Holy Office.

Russian Dissident woman, in marriage with man whose religion was unknown: disparity of cult. See c. 1099; private reply of S. C. Eccl. Or., 12 Apr., 1945.

Russian Schismatic, in marriage with unbaptized Methodist: disparity of cult. See c. 1099; private reply of S. C. Eccl. Or., 12 Apr., 1945.

Serbian Dissidents: Bound by impediment of disparity of cult. See c. 1099; private reply of S. C. Eccl. Or., 12 Apr., 1945.

CANON 1071

Cautiones Given Equivalently May Be Sufficient: Special Provision for China (Holy Office, 5 Apr., 1919) Private.

The Holy Office issued the following Decree to all Ordinaries of China:

If the guarantees cannot be obtained from the infidel woman in writing, let them be obtained at least orally. If even this cannot be obtained, it is left to the prudent and conscientious judgment of the respective Vicars Apostolic to decide in each case whether the guarantees are contained equivalently, either in the serious promise of the woman to embrace the Catholic Faith, or in her enrollment among the catechumens, or finally in the laws and customs of the people, according to which the woman has no power over the religious education of the children, which depends exclusively on the will of the husband; in all these cases, however, the obligation remains to demand the guarantees of the Catholic party, and not to grant the dispensation unless there is moral certainty of their fulfillment.

(**Private**); Holy Office, 5 Apr., 1918; reported by Sartori, *Enchiridion Canonicum*, c. 1061, and by Winslow, *A Commentary on the Apostolic Faculties*, pp. 119–120, from *Primum Concilium Sinense*, n. 404.

Insincere Promises Held to Invalidate Dispensation From Disparity of Cult: The Rota in a case decided 4 April, 1951 (*coram* Felici), held *constare de nullitate matrimonii on this ground*. The decision gives some reasons for this opinion, but the facts of the case are not given in the report, which is published in *Monitor Ecclesiasticus*, 1951, p. 271. A full discussion of this and other cases involving the same question, appeared in *The Jurist*, 13–33 (Kelly).

CANON 1076

Maronites: Impediment of consanguinity. See Rota, 1936 and 1934 (R. D., Vol. 28, decision 2, and Vol. 26, decision 27); also Marbach, *Marriage Legislation for the Catholics of the Oriental Rites in the United States and Canada*, p. 151, note 17, and p. 153, note 21.

CANON 1077

Maronites: Impediment of affinity. See Rota, 1934 (R. D., Vol. 26, decision 64); also Marbach, *Marriage Legislation*, p. 154, note 22.

CANON 1078

Maronites: Impediment of public propriety. See Rota, 1934 (R. D., Vol. 26, decision 15); also Marbach, *Marriage Legislation*, p. 152, note 18.

CANON 1081

Copula Dimidiata: **Not to Be Suggested by Confessor, Nor Declared Simply Licit** (Holy Office, 30 Nov., 1921) **Private.**

The Bishops of the Netherlands presented the following questions to the Holy Office:

I. Whether it can be tolerated that confessors of their own motion inculcate the practice of *copula dimidiata*, or recommend it promiscuously to all penitents who are worried lest they be burdened with too many children?

II. Whether a confessor is to be blamed who, after trying in vain all the remedies to avert a penitent who is abusing marriage from continuing to do so, tells him to practice *copula dimidiata* in order to avoid mortal sins?

III. Whether a confessor is to be blamed who, in the circumstances mentioned in n. II, urges the practice of *copula dimidiata* upon a penitent who already knows about it from other sources; or who, upon being asked by a penitent if this way of acting is licit, replies "that it is licit," without any restriction or explanation?

Reply: to I, in the negative; to II and III, in the affirmative.

(Private); Holy Office, 30 Nov., 1921. Regatillo, *Interpretatio et Iurisprudentia Codicis Iuris Canonici*, n. 435. More complete text, with annotations by Vermeersch, in *Periodica*, Vol. 12, pp. 33–37.

"Constitutional Immorality" or "Moral Insanity" Discussed as Affecting Matrimonial Consent (Rota, 25 Feb., 1941) Private.

In a case in which a declaration of nullity of a marriage was asked by the woman on the ground of want of consent on the part of the man, who was it appears a habitual criminal, seven medical and psychiatric experts, including one appointed by the court, gave it as their opinion that the man was incapable of true matrimonial consent. In stating their reasons for this opinion, all of them had recourse to the theory of so-called "constitutional immorality" or "moral insanity," developed in the nineteenth century, according to which some persons are to be considered as not responsible for actions which otherwise would be voluntary and imputable. In examining this theory, the court mentions Treccani, Pinel, Esquirol, Marcel, Falret, Prichard, Morel, Maudsley, Lombroso, Krafft-Ebing, and Tanzi-Lugaro, and proceeds to evaluate the theory with reference to the teachings of scholastic psychology.

It is true that an action cannot be the object of a choice by the will unless it is previously known in some way by the mind as a good. But two grades or degrees of cognition of the same object may be distinguished: the knowledge of what it is (*cognitio conceptualis*), and the knowledge of its value (*cognitio aestimativa*). These two represent the same object, but under different aspects. Normally, on reaching what is called the age of reason, a human person becomes capable of both, at least in some degree. Nor is it to be denied that, besides the mere concept of what a thing is (such as can be had by a small child or an adult in a dream), in order to have a sufficient cognitional foundation for free choice, there must exist also at least some degree of *cognitio aestimativa,* the knowledge of the object's value, its appetibility. According to scholastic psychology and ecclesiastical jurisprudence, the bare "use of reason" is by no means sufficient for true matrimonial consent; there is required moreover a certain discretion and maturity of judgment which is proportionate to the object, that is, to the marriage contract which must be entered into freely (cc. 1081, 1082). This does not mean that, in order to be capable of true matrimonial consent, a man must have a thorough knowledge of the institution of marriage and of its social, ethical, and juridical values.

The theory of "constitutional immorality" or "moral insanity" is of dubious value. Moreover, according to its exponents themselves it allows for varying degrees; the individuals supposed to be subject to this abnormality diverge from the normal state by almost infinite gradations. It is, therefore, very difficult to prove with certainty that a given individual who is otherwise sane, is so affected by it as to be incapable of a human act, or of any specific act such as matrimonial consent.

For these reasons, which in accordance with canon 1804, § 2 are stated at some length in the decision, the court, notwithstanding the unanimous opinion of the experts, considered that the absence of matrimonial consent was not sufficiently proved. The decision was: *non constare de nullitate.*

(**Private**); Rota, 25 Feb., 1941. *Periodica,* 30–5.

Matrimonial Consent. Intention on Part of Woman to Use Contraceptive Devices May Vitiate Consent and Nullify Marriage (Rota, 27 Feb., 1947) Private.

The point of law involved in this important decision was this: the woman before the marriage firmly and definitely resolved always to frustrate the effect of the marital relations by using contraceptive devices (pessary or poison capsules). No obstacle was placed to the perfect performance of the marital act on the part of the husband. The legal question presented was: whether the aforesaid antecedent, definite, and universal intention on the part of the woman vitiated the matrimonial consent and rendered the marriage null. The decision of the Rota was in the affirmative: *constare de nullitate matrimonii.* Some excerpts from the decision.

"If the question is considered in the abstract and superficially, it might seem that this evil intention to frustrate the effect of copula could be consistent with the transfer of the right in her own body for acts which are of themselves suitable for the generation of children. For the woman in such case has no will to prevent the man from effecting a copula which is in itself perfect; her evil intention concerns only the fruit or effect of the copula, not the act itself. But if the question is considered in the concrete and weighed attentively, the woman must be said to have substantially vitiated her matrimonial consent, if she elicited it together with the described evil intention.

"For, in explicitly conceiving and virtually preserving until the marriage the intention perpetually to impede all the efficacy of natural copula, she is proved to have at least implicitly refused to give to the man a right over her body for acts which of their nature subject the woman's body to the burden of pregnancy, gestation, parturition. The will of the woman in such case, therefore, is proved to be contrary, not only to these natural *effects,* but also, and indeed more immediately, to the *acts* themselves from which these effects proceed by natural necessity, and moreover, in a way which is prior and more fundamental, to the very *right* in virtue of which the man is entitled to require these acts. It must consequently be held that a woman who contracted marriage with the depraved intention which has been described, was unwilling to transfer and in fact did not transfer the right which is here concerned. For the validity of matrimonial consent, it is not sufficient to give over one's body to sexual life for the purpose of satiating lust, but it is altogether necessary that the woman give to the man a right to acts which are truly conjugal, and that she herself assume the obligation to perform those acts and to bear their natural consequences.

"Therefore, although the *consummation* of marriage is not prevented by the above-mentioned use of a pessary or of poison tablets, yet the prenuptial intention to have recourse perpetually to these depraved contraceptive measures substantially vitiates matrimonial consent; for this consent is not valid if the matrimonial right to perfect copula is either explicitly or implicitly excluded or restricted by a positive act of the will. We have here not merely an abuse of marriage but consent which is essentially vitiated: the essential defect is derived and proved from the total and radical exclusion of the primary end of marriage.

"The woman in this case seems to have conceded to the man *the right over her body,* but to have limited it to *the act of copula itself,* that is, to the placing of the essential elements of natural copula as these are determined and circumscribed by nature, including of course the right to imperfect acts."

Decision: *Constare de nullitate matrimonii in casu.*

(Private) ; Rota, 27 Feb., 1947.

NOTE: This decision was published in *Ephemerides Iuris Canonici,* Vol. 4 (1948), pp. 138–147 and 155–158, in which a writer criticized the decision as unsound. The decision and the adverse criticism were taken up in a further study in *Periodica,* 38–207, where Father Hürth defends the decision with rather convincing reasons.

Artificial Insemination (Pius XII, Allocution, 29 Sept., 1949) AAS 41–557.

On this subject, in the course of an Allocution given in Rome on 29 Sept., 1949, to the Fourth International Congress of Catholic Doctors, His Holiness Pius XII said:[1]

We cannot allow this occasion to pass without indicating briefly, in its broad lines, the moral judgment which must be given in this matter.

1. The practice of artificial insemination, where human beings are concerned, cannot be considered exclusively or chiefly from the biological and medical standpoint, leaving aside the claims of morality and right.

2. Artificial fecundation outside of marriage is to be condemned purely and simply as immoral.

This is the natural and the positive divine law, that the procreation of a new life can be only the fruit of marriage. Marriage alone safeguards the dignity of the parties (in this case principally of the woman), their personal welfare. It alone by its nature provides for the well-being and education of the child.

Consequently, as to the condemnation of artificial fecundation outside the conjugal union, no difference of opinion is possible

---

[1] We have translated this principal part of the address literally from the original French.

among Catholics. The child conceived under these conditions would be, by that very fact, illegitimate.

3. Artificial fecundation in marriage, but produced with the active element taken from a third party, is equally immoral and as such is to be condemned without recourse.

It is the spouses alone who have a mutual right over their bodies for generating a new life, and this right is exclusive, nontransferable, inalienable. And from the consideration of the child also, the same is necessarily true. Whoever gives life to a little human being, receives from nature herself, in virtue of that very relationship, the responsibility for his conservation and education. But between the lawful husband and a child who is the fruit of an active element derived from a third party (even should the husband consent), there is no link of origin, no moral and juridical bond of conjugal procreation.

4. As to the licitness of artificial fecundation in marriage, let it suffice for the moment to recall these principles of the natural law: the simple fact that the desired result is attained by this means does not justify the use of the means itself; nor is the desire of the parties to have a child, perfectly lawful as that is for married persons, sufficient to prove the lawfulness of resorting to artificial fecundation to attain this end.

It would be false to think that the possibility of resorting to this means might render valid a marriage between persons who are unfit to contract it by reason of the impediment of impotence.

It is needless to observe that the active element can never be procured licitly through acts that are contrary to nature.

Although one cannot *a priori* exclude new methods because they are new, yet, as far as artificial fecundation is concerned, not only does it call for an extreme reserve, but it is absolutely to be rejected. To say this is not necessarily to proscribe the use of certain artificial means designed only to facilitate the natural act or to enable that act, done in the normal way, to attain its end.

We must never forget this: it is only the procreation of a new life according to the will and plan of the Creator which imports — and it does this with astonishing perfection — the realization of the desired ends. This is in harmony with the bodily and spiritual nature of the parties, with their dignity and with the normal and happy development of the child.

AAS 41–557; Pius XII, Allocution, 29 Sept., 1949. *Periodica,* 38–282 (Hürth).

Artificial Insemination Condemned (Pius XII, Allocution, 29 Oct., 1951) AAS 43–835.

In an Allocution to Italian Catholic Midwives, His Holiness said on this subject:

To reduce the cohabitation of married persons and the conjugal act to a mere organic function for the transmission of the germ of life would be to convert the domestic hearth, sanctuary of the family, into nothing more than a biological laboratory. Hence in Our Allocution of 29 September, 1949, to the International Congress of Catholic Doctors,[1] We formally excluded artificial fecundation from marriage. The conjugal act in its natural structure is a personal action, a simultaneous and immediate cooperation of the parties which, by the very nature of the actors and the peculiar character of the act, is the expression of that mutual self-giving which, in the words of Holy Scripture, effects the union "in one flesh."

This is much more than the mere union of two life-germs, which can be effected also artificially, that is, without the natural action of the spouses. The conjugal act, as it is ordained and willed by nature, is a personal cooperation, the right to which the parties have mutually conferred upon each other in contracting marriage.

Hence, when the performance of this function in its natural form is, from the beginning, permanently impossible, the object of the matrimonial contract is affected by an essential defect. That is what We said on the occasion already referred to: "We must never forget this: it is only the procreation of a new life according to the will and plan of the Creator which imports — and it does this with astonishing perfection — the realization of the desired ends. This is in harmony with the bodily and spiritual nature of the parties, with their dignity and with the normal and happy development of the child."[2]

AAS 43–835; Pius XII, Allocution, 29 Oct., 1951. Annotations, *Periodica,* 40–402 (Hürth). Other pronouncements of this same Allocution are reported under canons 1013, 1086, 1111, and 2350. Full English text in *The Catholic Mind,* 1952, p. 49.

[1] AAS 41–557; reported above in this volume under this same canon 1081.
[2] *Ibid.,* p. 560.

Amplexus Reservatus: **Warning of the Holy Office** (Holy
Office, 30 June, 1952) **AAS 44–546.**

A *Monitum* of the Holy Office:

The Holy See has noticed with grave concern that recently
not a few writers treating of conjugal life frequently descend
without reserve to describing openly and minutely all its details:
and moreover that some of them describe, praise, and recommend
a certain act which is called the *amplexus reservatus.*

Lest it fail in its duty in regard to so grave a matter, which
concerns the sanctity of marriage and the salvation of souls,
the Supreme Congregation of the Holy Office, by express mandate
of His Holiness by divine Providence Pope Pius XII, issues a
serious warning to all the aforesaid writers that they desist from
acting in this way. It also earnestly exhorts the sacred Pastors
to maintain a strict vigilance over these matters and to apply
solicitously the appropriate remedies.

And priests in exercising the care of souls and the direction of
consciences should never, either spontaneously or upon being
asked, presume to speak as though there were no objection to the
amplexus reservatus from the standpoint of Christian morals.

Given at Rome, from the Holy Office, 30 June, 1952.

AAS 44–546; Holy Office, *Monitum,* 30 June, 1952. Annotations, *Periodica,*
41–251 (Hürth) ; *Monitor Ecclesiasticus,* 1952, p. 568 (Hering).

Hedonism in Use of Marriage Condemned. See c. 1111; AAS 43–835.

CANON 1082

**Nullity Declared on Ground of Insanity Although This
Was Discovered Only After the Marriage** (Rota, 26 Feb.,
1952) **Private.**

Facts. These parties had been engaged for some time before
the marriage, but had not seen each other as frequently as might
be expected, the girl being a domestic servant, free only on
Sundays, and the man often absent on military service. Strange
conduct on the part of the girl had been observed even by the
man himself, and several others had cautioned him against the
marriage for the same reason. But no one suspected that she was

in an incipient stage of insanity; her behavior was attributed merely to unusual traits of character. The marriage was celebrated normally in the parish church and conjugal life was begun. After fifteen days, the man had to leave on military service again; upon his return seven months later, he learned that his wife had been treated for a week in a mental clinic and pronounced a victim of *schizophrenia* or *dementia praecox*. Released from the hospital as not dangerous, she returned home, but within the year had to be sent again to a mental hospital. When the man finally finished his military service, she had again been released from the hospital and was living with her parents. Conjugal life could not be resumed. Shortly afterward she was definitely committed to an asylum as hopelessly insane. Suit was brought for nullity by the man, and the judgment of the Court of first instance was favorable. The case is now before the Rota on appeal by the Defender of the Bond.

Schizophrenia or Dementia Praecox: The decision contains quite a study of this form of mental derangement, taken from the testimony of the experts and from medical authorities, whose terminology is not uniform. From these sources the Court derived some general conclusions as to the nature and effects of the disease.

It is a progressive deterioration of the mental powers affecting principally the sphere of the affections and the will, while leaving the memory and the perceptive faculties often unimpaired. The subject withdraws into an inner world of his own, which some call "automatism" and others describe as a sort of dream.

The origin and course of the disorder are very varied, so that diagnosis is sometimes impossible until the later stages are reached.

It is capable of mitigation and of partial improvement, scarcely ever of a complete cure. Periods of improvement after treatment may be mistaken for a cure. Hence, so-called "lucid intervals" are very difficult to evaluate and can scarcely be relied on as indicating mental capacity sufficient for true matrimonial consent.

In view of the nature of the disease, after a careful weighing of all the circumstances of this particular case and of the testimony of the experts (which was unanimous against the existence of sufficient mental capacity at the time of the marriage) the Court held:

Decision. *Constare de nullitate matrimonii in casu.*

(Rrivate); Rota, 26 Feb., 1952 (*coram* Felici). *Monitor Ecclesiasticus,* 1952, p. 431.

CANON 1086

Exclusion of Actual Cohabitation, Not Necessarily an Exclusion of the Right to the Conjugal Act (Rota, 22 Jan., 1944) AAS 36–179.

The fact that this case, by way of exception, was reported in full in the *Acta Apostolicae Sedis,* in itself indicates some peculiar importance. After summarizing the facts, we shall attempt to indicate under distinct headings the salient points of the decision.

Facts. After becoming engaged this man seduced the girl and had illicit relations with her for some time. Learning that she was affected with tuberculosis, he was advised by a physician to cease from these relations; he failed to do so however, and the girl became pregnant. Both his mother and the girl's relatives now insisted that he marry her. Unwilling to do so, he took refuge in flight, but was persuaded to return, and eventually went through the form of marriage with her, after declaring that he did not intend to live with her, a condition which she accepted. There was evidence of threats, both from his mother and from the girl's relatives. Three issues are presented: 1. Was the marriage invalid because of grave fear (c. 1087)? 2. Was the man's consent merely simulated (c. 1086)? 3. Should a dispensation from non-consummated marriage be asked (c. 1119)?

1. *Grave fear.* Upon a review of the evidence, the court held that neither *metus gravis communis* nor *metus reverentialis qualificatus* was established. Threats to kill the man, made by female relatives of the girl, were not seriously meant nor seriously feared. The threat of his own mother to disown him unless he did his duty was not proved to have been the controlling motive in determining his consent.

2. *Simulation of consent.* Under this head (*In iure,* paragraphs 9–30) the decision goes into a careful study and explanation of the primary and secondary ends of marriage; but we shall not attempt a summary of that discussion. As to the exclusion of the right of cohabitation, the court held:

Cohabitation is included under one of the secondary ends of

marriage, namely, *mutuum adiutorium*. Normally, therefore, the right to cohabitation is included in the marriage contract. Yet the parties may renounce this right without invalidating the marriage, provided the right to the conjugal act, which is the essential object of the contract, is not excluded.

This holds true also where the parties agree not to use the conjugal right. It is true that if the non-use of the conjugal right were made a *conditio sine qua non* to the contract, some authors hold that matrimonial consent would be nullified. But even this is a disputed question and is not certain, since others contend that in such a case the essential right is transferred on condition that it is not to be actually used. The definite and firm determination of will *not to fulfill* an obligation can be distinguished from the will *not to assume* it. Now, if the determination not to use the conjugal right cannot with certainty be shown to be necessarily inconsistent with the transfer of the radical right itself and the assumption of the obligation, still less can it be maintained that the determination not to enter into cohabitation necessarily implies an exclusion of the radical right to the conjugal act, which is the substance of the marriage contract.

The evidence in this case shows that the parties agreed not to cohabit after their marriage; such was the expressed determination of the man, and the girl explicitly accepted it prior to the marriage. But the evidence fails to show that the man excluded from his consent the transfer of the radical right to the conjugal act. Rather, it tends to show that, though his consent was reluctant, it was genuine consent to a true marriage. The marriage is not proved to have been invalid on the ground of simulation of consent.

3. *Non-consummation.* The fact of non-consummation of the marriage was regarded as fully proved by the concordant testimony of the parties and of other witnesses, although the "physical argument" (namely, from the physical inspection of the woman) was lacking. An objection to the granting of the dispensation, which the court considered, was the danger that the dissolution of the marriage might seem to deprive the girl and her child of their right to support from the father. The court took care to point out that this right does not arise from the marriage, but from the fact of fatherhood. Hence the Holy See has occasionally granted the dispensation from non-consummated marriage in such cases,

with the explicit admonition to the father that, despite the dissolution of the marriage, he remains bound to assist the mother and child according to their need and his resources. The Holy See has even at times refused the petition for dissolution when the man showed himself unwilling to fulfill this duty.

Since the marriage is proved never to have been consummated, and there are sufficient reasons for the dispensation, the decision on this point was that the Holy Father be petitioned for dispensation *super matrimonio rato et non consummato,* with a warning to the man that he must provide for the material and spiritual welfare of the child begotten before the marriage.

His Holiness granted the dispensation on the above terms.

AAS 36–179; Rota, 22 Jan., 1944.

Exclusion of Obligation of Fidelity (Rota, 10 June, 1947) Private.

In this case the woman, before the marriage, had begun relations with another man. It was clear that she intended to continue them after the wedding, which she did. Two grounds of nullity were claimed in this suit brought by the husband: (1) complete simulation; that is, that the woman excluded matrimonial consent itself; (2) partial simulation, or a condition contrary to the unity of marriage. The usual rule of evidence was again stated: that simulation must be proved by circumstances before, at the time of, and after the marriage.

In spite of the woman's intention, even at the time of the marriage, to be unfaithful to her husband, the court held upon all the evidence that total simulation was not proved. She intended to contract marriage.

In discussing the second ground, the usual distinction was made between the exclusion of the obligation of fidelity itself, and the exclusion of its fulfillment. From all the evidence the court decided that the woman at the time of the marriage, while willing to marry, was not willing to oblige herself to fidelity to her husband. By a positive act of the will she excluded, not merely the fulfillment on her part of the obligation of fidelity which marriage implies, but the radical obligation itself.

Hence the marriage was declared null for partial simulation or the exclusion of the *bonum fidei*.

(Private); Rota, 10 June, 1947. *Periodica,* 37–119.

Distinction Between Right and Use of Right Upheld (Rota, 23 Feb., 1951) **AAS 43–872.**

In a marriage case *coram* Staffa, of which only excerpts from the decision are reported in the *Acta Apostolicae Sedis,* the Rota severely criticized some language quoted from the lower Court's decision, which seemed to question the validity of the distinction between the marriage right itself and the use of it.

The present decision takes pains to prove that the distinction between the right and its use is perfectly sound from the standpoint of natural reason and is upheld by the common and constant teaching of theologians and canonists as well as by the jurisprudence of the Rota and the Supreme Signatura.

The Rota in this decision does, however, reject as useless the distinction made by some writers and judges between the *ius radicale* and the *ius utile seu expeditum.*

Both the facts of the case and the substance of the decision are omitted from the report.

AAS 43–872; Rota, 23 Feb., 1951.

Marriage Invalid If Radical Right to Intercourse Is Limited to Sterile Periods: Use of "Rhythm" in Marriage (Pius XII, Allocution, 29 Oct., 1951) **AAS 43–835.**

In an Allocution to a Convention of Italian Catholic Midwives, His Holiness Pius XII, among other important pronouncements on moral questions, said:

To-day the grave problem arises whether and how far the duty of being ready to accept with alacrity the burdens of motherhood can be reconciled with the increasingly current practice of having recourse to the periods of natural sterility (the so-called period of agenesis in the woman), which seems to be a clear expression of the will contrary to such readiness.

It is reasonable to expect that you be well informed from the medical standpoint on this well-known theory and on the progress in it which may still be forthcoming; and also, that your counsel and services be not based merely on popular writings but on scientific truth and on the authoritative judgments of conscientious specialists in medicine and biology. It is not the part of the priest, but yours, to instruct the parties, either in private consultations or through serious publications, on the biological and technical aspects of this theory, without however allowing yourselves to be drawn into a propaganda which would be neither right nor appropriate. But also in this field your apostolate requires of you as women and as Christians, that you know and defend the moral norms which govern the application of this theory. These are within the competency of the Church.

First of all, there are two hypotheses to be considered. If the use of that theory be taken merely in the sense that the married couple may use the marriage right also on the days of natural sterility, there is no objection to it; for by so doing they do not impede or prejudice in any way the consummation of the natural act nor its ulterior natural consequences. It is precisely in this point that the theory under discussion is essentially distinguished from the abuse referred to above,[1] which consists in the perversion of the act itself. If on the other hand the parties go further and permit the conjugal act exclusively on those days, then their conduct must be more carefully examined.

And here again we are faced with two hypotheses. If already at the contracting of the marriage one at least of the parties had the intention of limiting to the sterile periods the marriage *right* itself, and not merely its *use,* so that outside those periods the other party should not have even the right to demand the act, that would imply an essential defect of matrimonial consent, which would entail the invalidity of the marriage itself, because the right which arises from the matrimonial contract is a right of each party in regard to the other, which is permanent, uninterrupted, not intermittent.

If on the other hand the limitation of the act to the days of natural sterility refers not to the right itself but merely to the use of the right, the validity of the marriage remains above suspicion; but as regards moral licitness, such conduct on the part of the married couple would be licit or not, according as their intention to observe constantly those periods were or were not based on moral reasons which are sufficient and certain. The mere fact that the parties do not pervert the nature of the act and that they are ready to accept and to educate a child which might be born in spite of their precautions, is not alone sufficient

---

[1] That is, in a part of the same Allocution which is not included in the present report.

to assure the rectitude of their intention and the perfect morality of their motives.

The reason is that marriage obliges the parties to a state of life, which, just as it confers certain rights, imposes also the accomplishment of certain positive duties with reference to that state of life. There is room here for the application of the general principle that a positive service can licitly be omitted if grave reasons, independently of the good will of the persons who are obliged to perform that service, show that its performance is inopportune, or prove that it cannot justly be exacted by the one to whom it is due — in this case, the human race itself.

The matrimonial contract, which gives the parties the right to satisfy the inclination of nature, establishes them in a state of life, the matrimonial state. Now nature and the Creator impose on spouses who make use of their state by the practice of its specific act, the duty to provide for the conservation of the human race. This is the characteristic service which constitutes the peculiar value of their state of life — *bonum prolis*. Both the individual and society, the nation and the State, and the Church herself, depend for their existence on the order established by God, that is, fertile marriage. Hence, to embrace the married state and to use constantly the right which is peculiar to it and licit only within it, and on the other hand, always and deliberately, without a grave reason, to evade its primary duty, would be to sin against the very nature of the conjugal state.

From this positive duty, grave reasons such as those which not infrequently are found in the so-called "indication" from the medical, eugenic, economic, and social standpoints, may excuse even for a long time or for the entire duration of the marriage. It follows that the observance of the sterile periods may be morally licit, and under the conditions mentioned it really is so. But if, according to prudent and right judgment, such grave reasons, either of a personal nature or deriving from exterior circumstances, do not exist, the will to avoid habitually the fertility of their union, while at the same time continuing to give full satisfaction to their sensual enjoyment, can proceed only from a false appreciation of life and from motives which are foreign to the right norms of morality.

AAS 43–835; Pius XII, Allocution, 29 Oct., 1951.

NOTE: Some other important pronouncements from this same Allocution will be found reported under canons 1013, 1081, 1111, and 2350. This entire address, and another which was delivered by His Holiness to members of an Association called the "Family Front" and of various other Associations of large families, on 26 Nov., 1951 (AAS 43–855), are carefully annotated in *Periodica*, 40–402 (Hürth). The full text of both Allocutions in English will be found in *The Catholic Mind*, 1952, at pages 49 and 307 respectively.

CANON 1087

Oriental Dissidents: "Impediment" of *Vis et Metus* Declared Effective in Marriage of Orthodox Rumanians (Rota, 10 June, 1948)[1] **Private.**

Facts. These parties, both belonging to the Orthodox Rumanian Church, were married on 28 June, 1914. Civil divorce followed within three years. In 1933 the woman, wishing to marry a Catholic, applied to the Catholic ecclesiastical tribunal of Bucharest for a declaration of nullity on the ground that she had been coerced to marry by threats from her mother and brother. The Bucharest tribunal declared she had no right to sue in a Catholic court, and referred the matter to the Holy Office, which decided that the suit could be entertained after the woman should become a Catholic. She embraced the Catholic faith in 1935 and filed a new petition. The decision of the Bucharest tribunal, rendered in 1940, was: *non constare de nullitate*. The appellate court of Jassi reversed this decision in 1945. Whereupon the Defender of the Bond brought the case on appeal to the Holy Office, which sent it to the Rota.

The Law. The single point of law discussed was whether the "impediment" of *vis et metus* applied to these parties at the time of their marriage. On this point the decision offers a juridical and historical study which we shall attempt to summarize very briefly.

I. As to *Oriental Catholics*, the court held that they were at that time clearly subject to this impediment.

1. That the impediment is *founded in the natural law* is beyond doubt; the question whether it is *in substance strictly of the natural law*, has been disputed. For the affirmative, the court

---

[1] This date is not exact. The court convened on this day to render the decision, and then postponed the actual judgment for a short time. The date of the judgment is not given.

cites St. Thomas (*Summa Theol. Suppl.*, 47, art. 3); Wernz (*Ius Decretalium*, IV, n. 266); Cappello (*De Matrimonio*, ed. 3, n. 609).

Moreover, the Holy Office, in an Instruction to the Bishops of Albania of 15 Feb., 1901 (*Fontes*, n. 1250, Vol. IV, p. 530), showed that a dispensation from *vis et metus* (as distinguished from the ecclesiastical impediment of abduction defined by the Council of Trent) was not even to be thought of.

It is true that the Church has not authoritatively defined that the impediment of *vis et metus* is of the natural law, but it is more probable that it is; and it is certain that no dispensation from it is ever granted. Hence, according to the principle that Orientals are bound by laws that are even probably of divine origin, Oriental Catholics are certainly bound by this law (Cicognani-Staffa, *Commentarium ad Librum I Codicis I.C.*, ed. 2, Vol. I, p. 28). And this is clearly stated by the Holy Office in the Instruction to the Bishops of the Oriental Rites in 1883.[2]

2. So much for the natural law. It is also clear that the *Councils or Synods for the various Oriental Catholic rites* have always recognized this impediment, and not one of them has ever dreamed of changing it.

The Rumanian Church, after it was freed from its long spiritual slavery, recognized it in the Provincial Councils of Fagaras held in 1872, 1882, and 1900, using in 1882 substantially the same formula which was in use in both the Latin and Oriental Church (LeClercq, *Les Eglises Unies d'Orient*, Bloud, 1935; *Cod. Can. Orient. Fonti*, fasc. X, p. 873). When the hierarchy was re-organized in Rumania by Leo XIII, this legislation was extended to the whole territory (Coussa, *Epit. Praelect. de Iure Eccl. Orient.*, ed. 2, Rome, 1948, p. 16).

II. As to Oriental *schismatics*, the above arguments hold for both the natural and ecclesiastical law. For schismatics also must be regarded as bound by a law which is even probably of *divine* origin; and they are equally bound by *purely ecclesiastical* laws of the Catholic Church, except in so far as the Church chooses to exempt them from the same. The fact that the Church has not exempted schismatics from this law nor from the law of ecclesiastical impediments in general, is clear from a number of sources.

---

[2] Cf. *Fontes*, n. 1076, Vol. IV, p. 395. Art. 3, nn. 36–40, treats of the impediment of *vis et metus*.

First, a discussion by a group of theologians at the S. C. for the Propagation of the Faith in 1631 (Mansi, *Collect. Concil.*, Vol. 50, col. 36, 37), which was afterward further clarified by Benedict XIV in the Encyclical *Allatae*, 26 July, 1755 (*Fontes*, n. 434, Vol. II, p. 456, esp. § 44, p. 473) leads to this conclusion.[3]

Secondly, the same conclusion is supported by the fact that in the preparatory sessions before the Vatican Council, it was very seriously discussed how to formulate a proposal which should exempt Oriental schismatics from certain new matrimonial impediments. For various reasons no such measure was approved by the Council; but the very fact that it was proposed shows that as to *future* laws an exempting clause was regarded as necessary, and as to laws *already in effect* it was assumed that they applied also to Oriental schismatics.

Thirdly, the Consultors who helped in the preparation of the Code of Canon Law, prepared a *schema* containing an exemption of baptized non-Catholics from merely ecclesiastical laws regarding marriage, and a number of Bishops forwarded another similar proposal. Neither of these proposals was adopted, but the Code on the contrary (canons 12 and 87) clearly binds baptized non-Catholics in general, exempting them explicitly only from the impediment of disparity of cult (c. 1070) and from the form of marriage (c. 1099). It is clear that there has never been any exemption as regards *vis et metus*.

While it is true that the Latin Code applies in general "only to the Latin Church" (c. 1), still the above historical arguments taken together show that the Church has never abandoned the general principle that her laws are binding on all baptized persons, even heretics and schismatics.

Moreover, this impediment is clearly contained in the laws of the *Uniate Rumanian Church,* and as such it is binding also on Orthodox Rumanians. (Cf. Herman, in *Periodica*, 27–10, *Regunturne Orientales Dissidentes Legibus Matrimonialibus Ecclesiae Latinae?*)

Another argument: this impediment was in effect in the universal Church before the schism. Cf. Wernz, *Ius Decretalium*, IV, n. 262.[4]

---

[3] We omit the argument for the sake of brevity.

[4] This argument is developed at some length with citations of historical sources which we are forced to omit.

As a matter of fact it is also contained in the laws of the Rumanian Orthodox Church; this, however, gives it no validity. It is the laws of the Catholic Church which matter.

Conclusion. These parties at the time of their marriage were subject to the impediment of *vis et metus;* and since the coercion is fully proved, the marriage must be declared null. *Constat de nullitate matrimonii in casu.*

(Private); Rota, 1948. *Periodica,* 37–313.

Armenians: Force and fear invalidate marriage. See Rota, 25 May, 1935 (R. D., Vol. 27, decision 39) and 23 Jan., 1936 (R. D., Vol. 28, decision 4), quoting the decrees of the Synod of 1911. See Marbach, *Marriage Legislation,* p. 143, note 6.

Maronites: Force and fear invalidate marriage. See Rota, 1934 (Vol. 26, decisions 15, 38, 78) and 1936 (R. D., Vol. 28, decision 74) ; Marbach, *Marriage Legislation,* pp. 152, notes 18 and 19; 154, note 23.

One Witness *de Scientia* Held Sufficient under special circumstances. See c. 1791; Rota, 17 July, 1952.

Threats Not Serious. See c. 1086; AAS 36–179.

CANON 1088

Marriage of Baptized Non-Catholics: Presence in Person or by Proxy Required for Validity (Holy Office, 30 June, 1949) AAS 41–427.

The Holy Office was asked:

Whether the prescription of canon 1088, § 1, applies also to the marriages of baptized non-Catholics.

Reply. In the affirmative.

Approved by His Holiness Pius XII in the audience of 26 June, 1949, and ordered to be published.

Given at Rome, from the Holy Office, the 30th of June, 1949.

AAS 41–427; Holy Office, 30 June, 1949. See *Periodica,* 39–156, where Hürth holds that this is not an interpretation of a doubtful law; hence that it should apply also to marriages contracted before this reply was given. The contrary view was proposed in *Münchener Theologische Zeitschrift,* Vol. I, p. 91. Cf. also *Periodica,* 38–228 (Hürth).

Marriage Without Presence in Person or by Proxy Invalid (Holy Office, 15 July, 1949) Private.

In regard to a particular marriage contracted by absent parties, the Holy Office on 15 July, 1949, sent the following reply to the Vicar Capitular of the Diocese of Limburg:

Upon careful consideration of the matter, this Supreme Sacred Congregation decided to reply: If it is certain that at least one of the parties was baptized, and the marriage was celebrated between parties who were absent, contrary to the prescription of canon 1088, § 1, the marriage can be declared invalid, following the ordinary legal procedure.

(**Private**); Holy Office, 15 July, 1949. *Münchener Theologische Zeitschrift*, Vol. I (1950), p. 92.

Marriage of Baptized Non-Catholics Contracted in Absence and Without Proxy Can Be Declared Invalid by Simple Investigation (Holy Office, 16 Nov., 1949) Private.

Prot. N. 2438/49   From the Holy Office, 16 Nov., 1949

Your Excellency:

By letter of 6 October, 1949, Your Excellency presented the case of the alleged nullity of a marriage celebrated between the non-Catholics, N. and N.

This Sacred Congregation decides in the case that, as the formalities of law were omitted, the marriage can be declared invalid, proceeding by way of simple investigation.

(**Private**); Holy Office, 16 Nov., 1949. *Periodica,* 41–59 (Hecht).

NOTE: The facts of the case, unfortunately not sufficiently indicated in the document itself, have to be gleaned from the brief article in which Father Hecht presents it in *Periodica.* It will be useful also to report briefly Father Hecht's exposition of the state of the question.

The marriage was between baptized non-Catholics, and was celebrated by parties not present and not represented by proxy, contrary to canon 1088.

That such a marriage is *invalid* is clear from the reply of the Holy Office of 30 June, 1949 (AAS 41–427, reported above in this volume under this same canon 1088). But what procedure, if any, is required for a declaration of nullity? This is the question which the rescript answers.

Formal procedure would seem entirely out of place in such a case, where the nullity is so clear and so easily proved.

Summary procedure under canon 1990 is not applicable, since the enumeration of exceptional cases in that canon is exclusive (Code Com., 6 Dec., 1943; AAS 36–94, reported in this volume under canon 1990), and this class of cases is not among those mentioned.

Simple investigation was declared sufficient in cases of evident lack of the canonical form, of which the Code Commission declared: "The cases above mentioned require neither judicial process of any kind nor the intervention of the defender of the bond, but are to be settled by the Ordinary himself, or by the pastor after having consulted the Ordinary, in the preliminary investigation prior to the celebration of the marriage, mentioned in canon 1019 and the following canons" (Code Com., 16 Oct., 1919; AAS 11–479; DIGEST, 1, pp. 810–811).

This same *simple investigation* is now declared by the Holy Office to be sufficient in the case in question.

CANON 1089

Marriage by Proxy: Principal Must Personally Designate Proxy (Code Com., 31 May, 1948) AAS 40–302.

The Code Commission was asked:

Whether the principal himself must designate the proxy mentioned in canon 1089, § 1; or whether he can entrust his designation to another.

Reply. In the affirmative to the first part, in the negative to the second.

AAS 40–302; Code Com., 31 May, 1948.

Marriage by Proxy: Transmission of Ceremony by Radio to Absent Principal. The conditions under which this is permitted, for the Italian soldiers, are described in a Circular Letter of the S. C. of the Sacraments, 10 Sept., 1941; reported in *Il Monitore Ecclesiastico*, 1941, pp. 269–271. There is also an earlier Letter of the S. C. Sacr., 1 May, 1932, to the Ordinaries of Italy. See *Il Monitore Ecclesiastico*, 1932, pp. 227–229.

CANON 1092

Sincerity of Promises Made a Condition of Matrimonial Consent (Rota, 19 Feb., 1952) Private.

Facts. In this case the girl, an ardent Catholic, had an aversion to mixed marriages, which was shared by her parents. When the man, an Episcopalian, proposed marriage, she made it perfectly clear that she would not marry him unless he consented to take ten instructions in the Catholic faith and showed by his conduct that he was favorably disposed. She did not demand actual conversion to the faith, but merely a favorable attitude which would show that the promises he would be required to make (which she explained to him) were sincerely made. She introduced him to a priest for the instructions. Thereafter the man began gradually to appear more and more favorably disposed. He went to the Catholic church with her, took holy water, made the sign of the cross, wore a medal. The parents, won over by these external signs, withdrew their opposition, but the girl herself, before entering into a formal engagement, again strongly represented to him that "she would not marry him unless she was to be free to have her children baptized and educated as Catholics, and unless he himself were a sincere believer in the doctrine of the Catholic Church and would permit her freely to practice her religion."

Similar clear expressions were repeated frequently before the marriage. The words "condition" or "conditional consent" were not used, but in explaining her state of mind to the Court in her testimony, she made it clear (and this was quite well understood also by the man) that she would not be content with a mere perfunctory signing of the promises, but wanted to be assured that they were sincerely entered into and would be kept. When asked why she expressed herself so frequently on the subject, she said it was because of her fear that the man might deceive her in this matter which to her was of paramount importance. She admitted, however, that at the time of the marriage her fears had vanished; she was confident that all was well.

The man's flagrant insincerity became apparent even during the honeymoon. He began to object to his wife's making the sign of the cross visibly, to her going to church or saying her prayers. It was proved that he had deliberately deceived her, had taken only one instead of the ten instructions he had promised, that all his external signs of a favorable attitude were feigned.

A definite break came only three months after the wedding. The girl then left him definitely, declaring that she had been deceived, and she never returned to him. The case for nullity brought by her, *ob conditionem de praesenti non verificatam,* is before the Rota (*coram* Fidecicchi) on appeal from the matrimonial Tribunal of Detroit.

Decision. After a very careful scrutiny of the evidence the Court decided that a genuine condition *de facto praesenti* had been placed and that the condition was not verified at the time of the marriage. But the serious question remained, whether the admitted fact that the girl at the time of the marriage had overcome her previous anxiety and was now satisfied of the man's sincerity, amounted to a withdrawal of the condition previously made. The Court held that it did not, and quoted from the decision rendered by a Commission of Cardinals in *Versaliensi*, 12 Aug., 1918 (Vol. XXVI, Dec. LXIX, p. 582, n. 4), the following principle: "The condition does not cease by the fact that the woman, because of the man's false assurances had become certain that he would keep his promise; for she placed the condition before receiving his assurances and therefore before acquiring certainty; her later certainty does not destroy the condition previously placed, but the consent remains subordinated to the condition notwithstanding the later certitude, which can coexist with the virtually conditioned will."

The condition was therefore made before the marriage, never withdrawn, and remained actually unfulfilled at the time of the marriage.

Constare de nullitate matrimonii in casu.

(Private); Rota, 19 Feb., 1952. *Monitor Ecclesiasticus*, 1952, p. 589.

CANON 1094

Armenian Catholics Outside Patriarchal Territory: Form of Marriage.
See c. 1; Holy Office, 14 July, 1950.

Maronites Outside Patriarchal Territory: Form of Marriage. See c. 1; private reply of Ap. Delegate, U. S., 19 April, 1945.

Marriage of Latin Catholic With Oriental Dissident: Delegation from Latin pastor necessary for validity. See c. 1097; two private replies of S. C. Eccl. Orient., 11 July, 1952.

Marriage of Two Oriental Catholics. See c. 1097; another private reply of S. C. Eccl. Orient., 11 July, 1952.

Oriental Code: Interpretation of Canon 86. See c. 1; AAS 44–552.

CANON 1095

Canon 209 Applies in Case of Priest Lacking Delegation. See c. 209; AAS 44–497.

Oriental Code: Canon 86 on valid assistance at marriage. See c. 1; AAS 44–552.

CANON 1096

General Delegation Given to Military Chaplains Before the Code for Assistance at Marriage of Soldiers Held Insufficient for Validity (S. C. Sacr., 21 July, 1919) **Private.**

The question proposed to the Sacred Congregation of the Sacraments concerned marriages contracted during World War I, in France, by Belgian soldiers, before military chaplains or chaplains of refugees, who had received from the respective Ordinaries of France general delegation to exercise parochial functions, and in particular to assist at marriages, for the Belgians.

Reply. As regards marriages which Belgian soldiers contracted up to the present day, in France, with Belgian or French women, before the Belgian military chaplains, on the strength only of a previous general delegation, this Sacred Congregation, in view of the peculiar circumstances, provided the consent of the parties continues and there exists no impediment from which the Holy See does not dispense, *heals the aforesaid marriages in radice and validates them,* and announces and declares that the children already born of them are legitimate.

The present rescript is to be carefully preserved in the archives of the military Vicariate, so that at any time and in any event the validity of the marriages and the legitimacy of the children can be proved. In future, however, the conditions required for valid delegation by canon 1096, § 1, are to be observed.

(**Private**) ; S. C. Sacr., 21 July, 1919. Reported by De Smet, *De Sponsalibus et Matrimonio,* ed. 1927, n. 116, p. 95, note 3. In his discussion of the document, De Smet intimates that the general delegation mentioned was given before the promulgation of the Code.

Even Episcopal Delegate *"ad universitatem negotiorum"* Does Not and Cannot Receive General Delegation for Marriages (Code Com., 25 Jan., 1943) **AAS 35–58.**

The Code Commission was asked:

Whether an episcopal Delegate, to whom is given the delegated faculty *ad universitatem negotiorum* according to canon 199, § 1, is understood to have thereby received, or whether he at least can receive, general delegation to assist at marriages, in view of canon 1096, § 1.

Reply. In the negative.

AAS 35–58; Code Com., 25 Jan., 1943.
Periodica, 32–292 (Aguirre).

CANON 1097

Latin Form of Marriage May Be Required for Validity Even Though the Marriage Is Contracted Before Oriental Pastor (Code Com., 8 July, 1948) AAS 40–386.

The Code Commission was asked:

Whether the provision of canon 1097, § 2, *at the end,* derogates from canon 1099, § 1, n. 3.

Reply. In the negative.

AAS 40–386; Code Com., 8 July, 1948.
Periodica, 37–291 (Cappello).

Right of Latin Pastor to Assist at Marriage of Latin Catholic to Oriental Dissident (S. C. Eccl. Or., 11 July, 1952) Private.

The Sacred Congregation for the Oriental Church was asked:
Titius, an Oriental dissident, wishes to marry Anna, a Latin Catholic; and he earnestly asks that the marriage be celebrated in an Oriental church, either dissident or Catholic; he refuses to appear before the Latin pastor of the woman. The questions are:

1. Has the Latin pastor the right to celebrate this marriage, so that the Oriental Catholic pastor ought to obtain permission of the Latin pastor if he wishes licitly to assist at the marriage?

2. Does the Oriental pastor in such a case have jurisdiction by law because of the status of the man, who is an Oriental but a dissident; or rather is jurisdiction and permission to be granted by the Latin Ordinary to the said Oriental pastor?

Reply. The pastor of the Latin Rite should grant to a priest of the Oriental rite the faculty to assist at the marriage in question in a Latin church or in a place under his jurisdiction. This faculty is necessary for validity and for licitness.

(Private); S. C. Eccl. Or., 11 July, 1952. *The Jurist,* Vol. 12, pp. 475, 476.

Marriage of Oriental Dissident and Latin Catholic: Latin Pastor to Assist: Children Belong to Latin Rite (S. C. Eccl. Or., 11 July, 1952) Private.

The Sacred Congregation for the Oriental Church was asked:

Titius, an Oriental dissident, attempted a civil marriage in 1941 with Anna, a Latin Catholic, and afterward had three children. Anna, now penitent, asks for the validation of that marriage, and Titius sincerely signs the promises. The questions are:

1. Whether the convalidation of the marriage is to be performed before the Oriental pastor (because of canon 1097, § 2) even though the man remains dissident, or rather before the Latin pastor of the woman, who alone professes the Catholic faith and communion?

2. When the marriage has been validated, are the children, who were illegitimate and are now legitimated, to be considered as belonging to the Oriental rite or rather to the Roman rite of the mother?

Reply. The validation of the marriage is to be performed before the pastor of the Latin rite. The children previously born belong to the Latin rite (c. 756, § 3).

(**Private**); S. C. Eccl. Or., 11 July, 1952. *The Jurist,* Vol. 12, pp. 475, 476.

Oriental Catholics Married by Latin Pastor: What Delegation Required (S. C. Eccl. Or., 11 July, 1952) Private.

The Sacred Congregation for the Oriental Church was asked:

Titius and Anna, both Oriental Catholics, grew up from infancy among people of the Latin rite and always went to the Latin church because they were entirely unfamiliar with the Oriental language and ways. Wishing to contract marriage, they refuse absolutely to appear before the Oriental pastor; wherefore the Oriental pastor kindly grants the Latin pastor permission to assist at the marriage in the Latin church and according to the Latin rite. The question asked is, whether such a marriage of two Orientals before the Latin pastor is to be regarded as valid by reason of the action of the Oriental pastor.

Reply. If there is in the place a canonically erected parish of the rite to which the contracting parties belong, and they are subjects of the local Ordinary of the Latin rite, the pastor of the Latin rite cannot validly assist at the marriage without the faculty from the same local Ordinary. If there is in the same territory a local Hierarch of the rite of the parties, the faculty to celebrate the marriage before the Latin pastor and in the Latin church is to be granted by the Holy See.

(Private); S. C. Eccl. Or., 11 July, 1952. *The Jurist,* Vol. 12, pp. 475–477.

Communists' Marriages: Assistance of priest. See c. 1065; AAS 41–427.

CANON 1098

Mixed Marriage Before Protestant Minister Valid If Conditions of Canon 1098 for Marriage Before Witnesses Only Are Verified (S. C. Sacr., 4 March, 1925) Private.

The following rescript was received by the Bishop of Pinsk in reply to a question concerning mixed marriages.

Reply. If all the conditions which are required by canon 1098 for the validity of marriages before witnesses only are verified, the circumstance that such marriages were blessed in a non-Catholic church is an argument, not against validity, but against licitness.

(Private); S. C. Sacr., 4 March, 1925. Reported by Dalpiaz in *Apollinaris,* Vol. 10, 1937, p. 277. See also Nevin in *The Australasian Catholic Record,* Vol. 19, 1942, p. 96.

Grave Inconvenience to Parties Themselves, Sufficient (Code Com., 3 May, 1945) AAS 37–149.

The Code Commission was asked:

Whether the grave inconvenience mentioned in canon 1098 is only one which threatens the pastor or Ordinary or delegated priest who assists at the marriage, or also one which threatens both parties or either party to the marriage.

Reply. In the negative to the first part; in the affirmative to the second.

AAS 37–149; Code Com., 3 May, 1945.
Periodica, 34–281 (Aguirre).

CANON 1099

Form of Marriage for Maronites Residing Outside Their Patriarchates and in Regions Where They Have No Diocese of Their Own Rite (S. C. Eccl. Or., 1935) Private.

An Instruction of the Sacred Congregation for the Oriental Church, not officially published, is as follows:

I. In a letter of March 31, 1935, followed by another letter dated April 18, His Excellency Monsignor Cicognani made inquiries at this Sacred Congregation whether the faithful of the Maronite rite residing in the United States are bound to contract marriage in the presence of the proper pastor *ad validitatem*. It was requested that a response be given independently of the Oriental Code, and that it be given exclusively in regard to Maronites residing outside of their Patriarchate and in regions where they have no diocese of their own rite.

II. Now, the received doctrine holds that the aforesaid marriages are undoubtedly valid even when not contracted in the presence of the *proper* pastor. Let us summarize the doctrine concerning *clandestinity* in marriages of the Maronites.

1. At the Lebanon Synod, held in 1736, the Maronites adopted the Tridentine discipline in these precise words: *"Nullum est matrimonium clandestinum, id est, quod aliter (contrahitur) quam praesente parocho vel sacerdote de ipsius parochi vel Ordinarii licentia et duobus vel tribus testibus"* (II, XI, 8, XII).

2. This discipline is obligatory for the validity of marriages in the following cases: (1) if two Maronites contract marriage in the territory of their own Patriarchate; (2) if two Maronites contract marriage outside of their Patriarchate, but in a place where they have not obtained a domicile or quasi-domicile, but retain it (*i.e.*, domicile or quasi-domicile) in the place of their origin.

3. This discipline is not obligatory for validity: (1) if the Maronites contract marriage in or outside of their Patriarchate with faithful of other Oriental rites (the exemption is communicated); (2) if, leaving their domicile which they had in their proper territory, two Maronites contract marriage outside of their territory, regardless whether they did or did not obtain a new domicile or quasi-domicile; (3) if, after having obtained a legitimate dispensation the Maronites contract marriage in or outside of their Patriarchate with non-baptized or baptized non-Catholics, who were not baptized and were not reared in the Catholic Church.

4. Furthermore, like all other Orientals, the Maronites are bound by the form prescribed by the Latin Code (c. 1094) if they contract marriage with Latins (c. 1099, § 1, 3) or Latin non-Catholics, heretics or schismatics who were baptized and reared in the Catholic Church or were converted to the Church but abandoned her later (c. 1099, § 1, 1).

III. The case proposed by Monsignor Cicognani contemplates Maronites who do not have a domicile or quasi-domicile in the Patriarchate and contract marriage outside of it (cf. *supra*, II, 2), but rather have a domicile or quasi-domicile in the place where they contract marriage. A marriage contracted in the presence of the local pastor and not in the presence of the Maronite pastor, or his delegate, etc., is valid.

IV. There is no difficulty in declaring that the Maronites, as all the Orientals for that matter, in places where they have no diocese of their own can contract marriage in accordance with the prescriptions of c. 1094, that is, for validity it is sufficient to celebrate the marriage *coram parocho, vel loci Ordinario, vel sacerdote ab alterutro delegato et duobus saltem testibus.*

(Private); S. C. Eccl. Or., 1935. This translation is taken from Marbach, *Marriage Legislation for the Catholics of the Oriental Rites in the United States and Canada,* pp. 158–159. The permission of the author is gratefully acknowledged. See also Gulovich, "Matrimonial Laws of the Catholic Eastern Churches," in *The Jurist,* Vol. 4, pp. 235–236.

Melchites: Not Bound to Form of Marriage (S. C. Eccl. Or., 22 Jan., 1941) Private.

A case submitted to the Sacred Congregation for the Oriental Church by the Bishop of Brooklyn concerned the validity of a marriage contracted civilly in Cuba by two Melchites. The pertinent part of the reply was as follows:

Reply. This Sacred Congregation has made a thorough study of the question presented by the above marriage case, namely, whether a marriage contracted by two of the faithful of the Greek-Melchite rite (which is the same as the Byzantine), without the blessing or *"incoronatio"* of the priest, is valid or not; and since upon this question there are opposite conclusions among learned men, the Sacred Congregation, after having submitted the question also to a plenary session of the Most Eminent Cardinals, concluded that, the law being uncertain, the principle *"standum esse pro validitate matrimonii"* should prevail, and consequently, in the case of N-N the invalidity of their marriage for want of form is not proved.

(Private); S. C. for the Oriental Church, 22 Jan., 1941. See Marbach, *Marriage Legislation for the Catholics of the Oriental Rites in the United States and Canada,* p. 263. Permission of the author to reproduce in the CANON LAW DIGEST is gratefully acknowledged.

Maronites in the United States, Not Held to Form of Marriage (S. C. Eccl. Or., 20 Apr., 1943) **Private.**

A reply of the Sacred Congregation for the Oriental Church to the Archbishop of Chicago (Prot. N. 178/43), concerning a marriage contracted by two Maronites before a civil magistrate, is as follows:

Reply. The prescription of the Lebanon Synod of 1736 introducing the diriment impediment of clandestinity, is not considered to extend to Maronites who have lost their domicile and quasi-domicile in their Patriarchal territory. Consequently, the nullity of the marriage contracted by N.N. with N.N. before a civil magistrate is not proved, at least according to the account of it which you have given. If the parties are in good faith, it is left to your prudent discretion, after carefully considering all the circumstances, especially the danger of scandal if the case is or becomes known, whether it be advisable to communicate this reply of the Sacred Congregation either to the aforesaid spouses or to the man with whom N.N. is now living.

(**Private**); S. C. Eccl. Or., 20 Apr., 1943. Cf. Marbach, *Marriage Legislation for the Catholics of the Oriental Rites in the United States and Canada*, p. 264.

Melchites: Form of Marriage (S. C. Eccl. Or., 30 July, 1943) **Private.**

The following case was presented to the Sacred Congregation for the Oriental Church by the Archbishop of Los Angeles.

N.N. was born in Wellington, New Zealand, on March 2, 1895, of N.N. and N.N., and was baptized in the church of the Sacred Heart in Wellington, by a Roman Catholic priest, Thomas G. Dawson, on May 5, 1895. He attended a Catholic school (Marist Brothers) in Auckland, N. Z., where he received the Sacraments of the Eucharist and Confirmation. Finally in July, 1919, he came to the United States with his parents.

His parents were born in Zahle, Lebanon, both were baptized in the Greek-Melchite rite, and were over thirty years of age when they came to New Zealand in 1892.

N. never ceased to attend the church of the Latin rite, but on November 22, 1921, he contracted marriage in Oklahoma City, in the State of Oklahoma, U.S.A., before a civil judge, with a certain

N.N. who was baptized in the Presbyterian sect. They had neither children nor happiness from this marriage, and many years ago, on the 30th of July, 1926, they were separated by a civil divorce, and there is now no possibility of restoring the conjugal life.

Question. Whether the aforesaid marriage is to be considered invalid for want of the juridical form.

Reply. The Sacred Congregation decided to reply: *non constare de nullitate matrimonii in casu.*

(Private); S. C. Eccl. Or., 30 July, 1943. See Marbach, *Marriage Legislation for the Catholics of the Oriental Rites in the United States and Canada,* pp. 262–263.

Maronites and Melchites in United States and Canada: Form of Marriage (S. C. Eccl. Or., 12 Apr., 1945) Private.

The following questions were proposed to the Sacred Congregation for the Oriental Church by the Archbishop of Montreal:

I. Whether Peter, a Maronite, who keeps his domicile in the diocese of Montreal, and Mary, baptized in a heretical sect and having a domicile in the diocese of Philadelphia in the United States of North America, validly contract marriage before a civil official in the city of New York in the presence of two witnesses.

II. Whether Peter, a Maronite, who keeps his domicile in the diocese of Montreal, and Catherine, a Greek schismatic, having a domicile in the diocese of Brooklyn (U.S.A.), validly contract marriage, when the marriage is witnessed and blessed by an Oriental schismatical Bishop in the city of Brooklyn:

1. In the presence of only one witness;
2. In the presence of at least two witnesses.

III. Whether Tita, a Greek-Melchite Catholic, and Titus, a Greek schismatic, both having a domicile in the diocese of Montreal, validly contract marriage before a heretical minister in the city of Montreal in the presence of two witnesses.

Reply. This Sacred Congregation has considered the three matrimonial questions proposed in your letter of March 6.

In this connection it is well to remember that the Tridentine form of marriage is in effect among the Maronites, not as a law of the Council of Trent applicable also to the Maronites and to the Maronite Church, but in the sense that the Tridentine law was received and adopted by them with the consent of the Holy See, so that their marriages must be celebrated, under pain of nullity, *"coram parocho et saltem duobus testibus."*

This form for the celebration of marriage, however, is binding only on the Maronites who are within the confines of their own Patriarchate, and not on those who are outside that territory.

The Melchites and the Greeks, on their part, are not held to this form either within the confines of their respective Patriarchates or outside those limits.

Consequently, this Sacred Congregation replies to the three questions proposed by Your Excellency, in the affirmative, that is, in favor of the validity of the marriage in each case, provided the Protestant party was validly baptized but not in the Catholic Church (cf. c. 1099).

(**Private**); S. C. for the Oriental Church, 12 Apr., 1945. See Marbach, *Marriage Legislation for the Catholics of the Oriental Rites in the United States and Canada*, pp. 261–262. This document was also sent to us directly by the Right Reverend Robert E. McCormick of the Archdiocesan Tribunal of New York.

Form and Disparity of Cult in Marriage of Russian Schismatic With Unbaptized Methodist (S. C. Eccl. Or., 12 Apr., 1945) Private.

The following questions were proposed to the Sacred Congregation for the Oriental Church by Bishop Basil Takach, Ordinary of the Pittsburgh Ordinariate of the Byzantine-Slavic rite in the United States:

On August 22, 1937, a certain Helen, a Catholic of the Byzantine-Slavic rite, attempted marriage before a non-Catholic minister with a certain Robert, an unbaptized Methodist. The said Helen, now repentant, asks for a dispensation in order to validate this marriage. Upon investigation, however, it appeared that the aforesaid Robert previously contracted marriage with a certain Patricia. Patricia had been baptized and educated in the schismatical Russian church, and, as far as is known, both her parents were of Russian nationality and were members of the Russian schismatical church. Hence it is asked:

1. Whether Patricia, baptized and educated in the Russian schismatical church, contracted a valid marriage with Robert, an unbaptized Methodist, when she contracted the marriage before the civil authority only, against the prescription of the ancient Byzantine discipline.

Reply. It is not proved that the marriage is invalid on this ground.

2. Whether Patricia, baptized and educated in the Russian schismatical church, wishing to enter into marriage with Robert, an unbaptized Methodist, is bound under pain of nullity to ask and obtain a dispensation from the impediment of disparity of cult, or from the impediment of mixed religion and from disparity of cult *ad cautelam*.

Reply. The marriage of Patricia with Robert is invalid because of the impediment of disparity of cult.

3. In case of an affirmative reply to the second question, who can validly give the dispensation?

Reply. In order to dispense from the impediment of disparity of cult, the faculty must be obtained from the Holy Office, unless the Apostolic Delegate can grant it.

(**Private**); S. C. Eccl. Or., 12 Apr., 1945; Marbach, *Marriage Legislation*, etc., pp. 264–265; also Gulovich, "The Principle Underlying the Validity of Oriental Marriage," in *The Jurist*, Vol. 6, p. 40.

Form and Disparity of Cult in Marriage of Russian Dissident Woman With Man Whose Religion Was Unknown, Before a Protestant Minister (S. C. Eccl. Or., 12 Apr., 1945) Private.

The following reply was given by the Sacred Congregation for the Oriental Church to the Apostolic Delegate in a case presented by him on behalf of Bishop Takach, Ordinary of the Pittsburgh Ordinariate of the Byzantine-Slavic rite in the United States:

Referring to Your Excellency's letter of 2 February (n. 375/45), I beg to inform Your Excellency that this Sacred Congregation has examined the question presented by His Excellency Bishop Takach concerning the marriage contracted by Mary, baptized and educated in the Russian dissident church, with a certain William, whose religion is unknown, before a Protestant minister.

Since it does not appear that the Russian dissidents are bound to any religious form whatever in the celebration of marriage, it follows that the marriage contracted by Mary with William is to be considered valid. It would be well, however, to investigate further the circumstance of the unknown religion of William, because if it should appear with certainty that he was not validly baptized, in that case his marriage with Mary would be null by reason of disparity of cult, because this impediment is in effect also for the dissident Russians, having been sanctioned in canon 14 of the Council of Chalcedon; likewise, if it should appear with certainty that William is a Latin Catholic, his marriage with Mary would be null for want of form.

(Private); S. C. Eccl. Or., 12 Apr., 1945. Marbach, *Marriage Legislation for the Catholics of the Oriental Rites in the United States and Canada,* p. 266; Gulovich, "The Principle Underlying the Validity of Oriental Marriage," in *The Jurist,* Vol. 6, p. 41.

NOTE: Gulovich points out that this reply, in as far as it declares the impediment of disparity of cult binding on Russian dissidents, is based on a general principle which contradicts the private reply of the Code Commission of 3 Dec., 1919 (CANON LAW DIGEST, Vol. 2, p. 336). As to a possible reconciliation of the two apparently contradictory propositions, see Marbach, *op. cit.,* p. 242.

Form of Marriage and Disparity of Cult as Affecting Serbian Dissidents (S. C. Eccl. Or., 12 Apr., 1945) Private.

Reply of the Sacred Congregation for the Oriental Church to the Apostolic Delegate, for Bishop Takach (Pittsburgh, Byzantine-Slavic rite):

Referring to the letter of 2 February (n. 375/45) concerning the matrimonial case B-V, in which the man, baptized and educated in the Serbian dissident church, and the woman, baptized and educated in a Protestant sect, contracted marriage before a Protestant minister, I beg to inform Your Excellency that, for the Serbians who do not belong to the Latin rite, it is not certain that the presence of the priest is required for the validity of the matrimonial contract, and therefore it is not proved that the marriage contracted by the aforesaid parties is invalid.

Since one of the parties in this case is a Protestant, the circumstance of her baptism might be further investigated, because if it appears with certainty that she was not validly baptized, her marriage with the Serbian dissident would be null by reason of the impediment of disparity of cult, which is binding also on the Serbian dissidents.

(Private); S. C. Eccl. Or., 12 Apr., 1945. See Marbach, *Marriage Legislation for the Catholics of the Oriental Rites in the United States and Canada,* p. 267; Gulovich, "The Principle Underlying the Validity of Oriental Marriage," in *The Jurist,* Vol. 6, p. 41.

Former Exemption for Children of Non-Catholics, Not Applied to Children of Nonpracticing Catholics (Holy Office, 7 Jan., 1947) Private.

The Case. The marriage in question here was contracted civilly by two baptized Catholics in 1929. The petition recited the following circumstances regarding the two contracting parties.

Rachel, born of two Catholic parents who were merely civilly married and were not receiving the Sacraments, was baptized in the Catholic Church but never received any Catholic instruction nor any other Sacraments.

George, born of a Catholic mother and of a father who was "probably an apostate" at the time of George's birth, was baptized in the Catholic Church but never received any instruction in the faith nor any other Sacraments.

The question was asked: whether Rachel was bound to observe the canonical form, so that the marriage in question is to be considered null and void; and whether the Ordinary can permit Rachel to contract a new marriage with a Catholic.

Reply. Your Excellency by letter of 18 Nov., 1946, asked this Supreme Sacred Congregation whether Rachel, who attempted marriage with George before a civil magistrate in 1929, was bound to observe the canonical form according to canon 1099, § 2, of the Code of Canon Law.

Rachel, who was born of Catholic parents who did not frequent the Sacraments and were only civilly married, was baptized a Catholic but never received any education or instruction in the Catholic Church and never received any other Sacrament.

Since Rachel was born of Catholic parents who were not formally apostates, she is not to be counted among the *"ab acatholicis nati"* mentioned in canon 1099, § 2, and therefore if she was truly baptized in the Catholic Church, she was bound to observe the canonical form in celebrating marriage. Consequently, if the truth of the representations is proved, Your Excellency can declare the marriage null for want of form.

(Private); Holy Office, 7 Jan., 1947. Translation made from Latin text kindly sent to us by the Committee on Research of the Canon Law Society of America.

Pre-Code Civil Marriage Held Null Under *Ne Temere:* Both Parties Born of Mixed Marriage, Baptized in

Catholic Church, Received No Catholic Training (Holy Office, 14 Feb., 1947) **Private.**

The Case. Civil marriage between Henry and Mary, 22 Oct., 1912. Mary was born of a Catholic mother and a non-Catholic father, was baptized in the Catholic Church, occasionally went to Catholic churches but received no Sacraments, grew up without any religion. Henry was born of a Catholic mother fallen into indifference and a non-Catholic father hostile to the Church, was baptized in the Catholic Church but grew up without any religion. The marriage proved unhappy and was terminated by divorce. Mary now wishes to marry a Catholic. The question asked was:

Question. According to the Decree of the Holy Office of 31 March, 1911, can the Ordinary pass judgment on the validity of this union; is the marriage valid or not?

Reply. Your Excellency by letter of 14 Feb., 1947, presented a doubt regarding the validity of a marriage between Henry and Mary. Everything considered, this Supreme Sacred Congregation declares: If it is proved that both parties or either of them received Baptism in the Catholic Church, the Ordinary can, according to the Decree *Ne Temere,* Chapter XI, declare the nullity of this marriage celebrated in 1912.

(**Private**); Holy Office, date not given. Translation made from Latin text kindly sent to us by the Committee on Research of the Canon Law Society of America.

NOTE: There was no provision in the *Ne Temere* (Decree of S. C. Conc., 2 Aug., 1907; Gasparri, *Fontes,* n. 4340, Vol. VI, p. 867) exempting the children of non-Catholics, even though they were educated from infancy outside the Church. The Decree of the Holy Office of 31 March, 1911 (AAS 3–163) declared that, as to the marriages of such persons, recourse should be had in each case.

Exemption of "ab Acatholicis Nati" Abrogated (Pius XII, *Motu proprio,* 1 Aug., 1948) AAS 40–305.

This *Motu proprio,* entitled *"Abrogatur Alterum Comma Paragraphi Secundae Canonis 1099,"* is as follows:

The Decree, *Ne temere,* issued by order of Our Predecessor of happy memory, Pius X, had provided (art. XI) that all persons baptized in the Catholic Church, even if they had afterward fallen away from it, were bound to observe the form of marriage prescribed in the Council of Trent.

However, as regards persons born of non-Catholics and baptized in the Catholic Church, who from infancy had grown up in heresy or schism or infidelity or without any religion, lest their marriages should be null, it was provided in the Code of Canon Law that baptized persons of this class are not bound to observe the canonical form of marriage.

But the experience of thirty years has sufficiently shown that the exemption from observing the canonical form of marriage, which was given to this class of persons baptized in the Catholic Church, has not conduced to the good of souls, and has moreover very frequently multiplied difficulties in the solution of cases; wherefore We have deemed it expedient that this exemption be revoked.

Accordingly, after hearing from the Eminent Fathers of the Supreme Sacred Congregation of the Holy Office, We of Our own motion and out of the fullness of Apostolic power, decree and provide that all persons baptized in the Catholic Church are bound to observe the canonical form of marriage; and We therefore abrogate the second clause of paragraph 2 of canon 1099, and order that the words, *"item ab acatholicis nati, etsi in Ecclesia catholica baptizati, qui ab infantili aetate in haeresi vel schismate aut infidelitate aut sine ulla religione adoleverunt, quoties cum parte acatholica contraxerint,"* be expunged from canon 1099.

And We take this occasion to admonish missionaries and priests to observe most carefully the provisions of canons 750–751.

We therefore order that this Apostolic Letter given of Our own motion be reported in the *Acta Apostolicae Sedis,* and We decree that its provisions shall go into effect from the first day of January, 1949.

All things to the contrary, even such as are worthy of special mention, notwithstanding.

Given from Castel Gandolfo near Rome, the first day of August, Feast of Saint Peter in Chains, in the year nineteen hundred and forty-eight, the tenth of Our Pontificate.

AAS 40–305; Pius XII, *Motu proprio,* 1 Aug., 1948. *Periodica,* 37–334 (Creusen).

Former Exemption Interpreted: Question Whether Person Grew Up Without Any Catholic Training (Holy Office, 29 March, 1949) Private.

The Case. Mary was born on 1 May, 1918, of John, a Catholic, and Jennie, a non-Catholic, and was baptized 18 May,

1918, at the Church of the Holy Name. Her parents separated when she was five years of age. The mother remarried with a divorced Catholic, William. Mary received no instruction nor any other Sacraments. In her early years she attended the Protestant church with her step-brothers and sisters. In the course of her deposition the mother said: "She was raised an Episcopalian." He brother also under oath states that she was raised "as a Methodist." On the other hand, however, Mary all her life felt a persuasion that she was a Catholic, and she attended the Catholic church, irregularly at least, from her fourteenth year. It was only after her civil marriage that she began to take a deeper interest in the Catholic faith. She contracted marriage with Merritt in 1936.

Reply. Your Very Reverend Episcopal Curia, by letter of 2 May, 1948, presented the case of a marriage contracted in a non-Catholic rite in 1936 between a non-Catholic, Merritt, and Mary, regarding whose obligation to observe the canonical form in the celebration of marriage a doubt arises owing to the prescription of canon 1099, § 2.

Having carefully considered the circumstances of the case, this Supreme Sacred Congregation decided to reply: "The nullity of the marriage in this case is established, for want of the canonical form."

(**Private**) ; Holy Office, 29 March, 1949. The case and solution were kindly sent to us by the Committee on Research of the Canon Law Society of America.

Former Exemption Not Admitted: Child of Catholic Parents Baptized in Danger of Death in Catholic Hospital by Episcopalian Minister (Holy Office, 3 Jan., 1950) Private.

The Petition. The undersigned Ordinary, prostrate at the feet of Your Holiness, presents the following question: whether the Catholic party mentioned below is bound according to canon 1099, § 2, to observe the canonical form, so that the marriage in question is null and void:

Vernon was born of Catholic parents 7 Sept., 1920. At the time of his birth in a Catholic hospital, being in danger of death, he was baptized by an Episcopalian minister. The certificate of Baptism says: "This Baptism was administered with valid matter and form by a threefold infusion in the name of the Holy Trinity according to the rite of the Book of Common Prayer, in order to regenerate and confer the Sacrament of the Universal Church of Christ."

On 12 May, 1933, Vernon received the Sacrament of the Eucharist in the church of Saint Luke; on 10 June, 1934, he received the Sacrament of Confirmation in the church of Saint Thomas.

On 10 June, 1944, Vernon contracted marriage with Blanche (who was born of a mixed marriage and was probably baptized a Catholic). The marriage turned out unhappily. Now Vernon, wishing to contract a new marriage with a Catholic, presents to the Curia the question as to the validity of his former marriage with Blanche.

The Question. What is to be said of Vernon's Baptism; and can the Ordinary permit Vernon to contract a new marriage with a Catholic?

The Reply. Your Excellency, by letter of 14 Sept., 1949, presented the case of a marriage celebrated in 1944 between a baptized non-Catholic, Blanche, and Vernon, regarding whose obligation to observe the canonical form according to canon 1099, § 2, Your Excellency presented the question.

After having carefully considered the circumstances of the case, especially as regards the Catholic education of the man in question, this Supreme Sacred Congregation decreed: "The nullity of the marriage for want of form is established."

(**Private**); Holy Office, 3 Jan., 1950. The petition and reply were kindly sent to us by the Committee on Research of the Canon Law Society of America.

Documentum Libertatis Given After Civil Marriage Where Baptism of Catholic Party Was in Doubt (Holy Office, 10 April, 1952) **Private.**

Case Stated. James contracted a civil marriage with Eunice, a baptized Protestant. They cohabited less than two years. One daughter was born, who was baptized in the Catholic Church. After a civil divorce obtained by Eunice, James petitioned for a declaration of free state because of the lack of canonical form.

James was born of a Catholic mother and a non-Catholic father. The mother at the present time is well over seventy years of age. Yet she had a clear and precise recollection of the circumstances on the day that her son James was taken shortly after birth from the home by the father and godparents to be baptized in the local Catholic Church. She related that the party left the house shortly before 4:00 in the afternoon to go to the church. The father and child and the godparents did not return until midnight. She stated it was quite evident that they had celebrated the baby's baptism. They told her that, after having the baby baptized, they went to a tavern in the vicinity. There is no record of the Baptism in the register of the parish where the family resided. A search was made in all the surrounding parishes and no record was discovered. No record could be found of the petitioner's first Communion or Confirmation, which he allegedly received.

About four years before a decision was rendered by the Holy Office, the petitioner had himself re-baptized conditionally because of the doubt surrounding his alleged baptism. The Holy Office was asked to allow James to marry a Catholic woman.

Reply. In the Curia of N., the process was drawn up to obtain a dispensation from a marriage contracted in 1933 between James, a baptized Catholic (?), and Eunice, a baptized non-Catholic.

After a careful examination of the record and the fulfillment of all due procedures in the case, the question was proposed on 7 Apr., 1952, to this Supreme Sacred Congregation, which, to the question: Whether recommendation should be made to His Holiness that a declaration of free state be granted to the petitioner James, so that he may validly and licitly contract a new marriage before the Church with a Catholic woman, decided to reply, after having discussed the case according to certain established rules:

In the affirmative.

His Holiness by divine Providence Pope Pius XII, in the audience granted on Thursday, 10 Apr., 1952, to the Most Excellent and Most Reverend Assessor of the Holy Office, after having received a report of the whole case, graciously deigned to grant the favor according to the above Decree.

Included in the present grant also, as far as it may be needed, is the dispensation from the impediment of crime mentioned in canon 1075, 1°.

Observing the provisions of law. All things to the contrary notwithstanding,

Given at Rome, from the Holy Office, 10 Apr., 1952.

(**Private**); Holy Office, 10 April, 1952. This document was kindly sent to us by the Committee on Research of the Canon Law Society of America.

Maronites: Form of Marriage: Case of insufficient delegation to assist under the Tridentine form, which was imposed on the Maronites by their Synod of 1911. See Rota, 4 Apr., 1933 (R. D., Vol. 25, decision 22); also Marbach, *Marriage Legislation for the Catholics of the Oriental Rites in the United States and Canada,* p. 155, note 25.

Orientals: May be bound to form of marriage even when contracting before Oriental pastor. See **c. 1097**; AAS 40–386.

CANON 1102

Illicitness of Assisting at Mixed Marriage Where Guarantees Are Not Given (Holy Office, 26 Nov., 1919) Private.

The Archbishop of Prague asked the Holy Office:

How should a priest conduct himself in receiving the consent of the parties when he assists at the celebration of a marriage between a Catholic and a non-Catholic, who do not give the guarantees.

Reply. In all respects the provisions of the Code of Canon Law are to be observed. Hence a priest may not assist at such marriages unless, after the guarantees have been given, a dispensation has been obtained from the impediment of mixed religion or disparity of worship, according to canons 1060 and 1061; the consent is to be asked according to canons 1102 and 1095. The contrary prescriptions of the Holy See and contrary indults are abrogated by the Code of Canon Law itself.

(**Private**); Holy Office, 26 Nov., 1919; reported by Sartori, *Enchiridion Canonicum,* c. 1102, from *Archiv. für Kathol. Kirchenrecht,* Vol. 100, p. 28.

Even in Hungary, Priest May Not Assist at Mixed Marriage Without Dispensation From the Impediment (Holy Office, 6 July, 1928) Private.

The Archbishop of Zagreb asked the Holy Office:

Whether in the territory mentioned in the Brief of Gregory XVI, *Quas vestro,* of 30 Apr., 1841,[1] a pastor, in the celebration

---

[1] *Fontes,* n. 497, Vol. II, p. 788. The Brief was addressed to the Bishops of Hungary.

of a mixed marriage for which no dispensation has been obtained, may ask and receive the consent of the contracting parties, omitting all sacred rites; or whether any assistance at such a marriage is forbidden.

Reply. In the negative to the first part; in the affirmative to the second; that is, the decision of the Holy Office of 26 Nov., 1919, is to be followed.

(Private); Holy Office, 6 July, 1928; reported by Sartori, *Enchiridion Canonicum,* c. 1102, citing Sipos, *Enchiridion Iuris Canonici,* ed. 1933, *Addenda,* p. 9, and *Linz Quartalschrift,* 1931, p. 376.

***

Marriages of Communists. See c. **1065**; AAS 41–428.

CANON 1109

Only Contracting Parties and Witnesses to Be Admitted to Sanctuary (S. C. Rit., 20 Nov., 1940) **Private.**

The Sacred Congregation of Rites was asked by the Bishop of Acireale:

Whether only the contracting parties and the witnesses are to be admitted to the sanctuary, and these latter only during the performance of the marriage itself, the expression of consent, etc., excluding the Mass; or whether, together with the parties and the witnesses, also the *parents and relatives* mentioned in the Ritual (cf. Tit. VII, cap. 2) are to be admitted, and that for the entire time of the ceremony including the nuptial Mass, even though the sanctuary be thus filled with lay persons.

Reply. The witnesses, because of their function, are reasonably present at the marriage; not, however, other persons, parents or relatives.

(Private); S. C. Rit., 20 Nov., 1940; reported in *Il Monitore Ecclesiastico,* Vol. 53, 1941, p. 168.

***

Marriages of Communists. See c. **1065**; AAS 41–428.

CANON 1111

Sexual Hedonism in Marriage Condemned (Pius XII, Allocution, 29 Oct., 1951) **AAS 43–835.**

On this subject, His Holiness Pius XII said in an Allocution to Italian Catholic Midwives:

The same Creator who in His goodness and wisdom wished to provide for the conservation and propagation of the human race through the cooperation of man and woman by uniting them in marriage, has also disposed that in performing that function they should experience pleasure and felicity of body and soul. Married persons, therefore, in seeking and in enjoying that pleasure, do no wrong. They accept what the Creator has disposed for them.

Nevertheless here also the parties must contain themselves within the bounds of just moderation. Just as in the enjoyment of food and drink, so in their sexual pleasure, they must not abandon themselves without restraint to the impulse of the senses. The right norm is therefore as follows: The use of the natural generative faculty is morally licit only in marriage, in subordination to and according to the order of the ends of marriage itself. From this it follows that likewise only in marriage and on condition that this rule be observed, the desire and enjoyment of that pleasure and satisfaction are licit. For the pleasure is subject to the law which governs the action from which it springs, and not vice versa, that is, the law is not subordinate to the pleasure. And this law so conformed to reason applies not only to the substance of the action but also to its circumstances, so that, even though the substance of the act be not perverted, there can be sin in the manner in which it is performed.

The transgression of this norm is as old as original sin. But to-day there is danger of losing sight of the fundamental principle itself. For at the present time it is a common thing (even on the part of some Catholics) to maintain in speech and writing the necessary autonomy, the proper end and proper value of sexuality and its use, independently of the purpose of generating a new life. Those who hold such views would subject the order established by God to a re-examination and to a new norm. They would admit no other restraint in the manner of satisfying the sexual instinct than that imposed by the observance of the essence of the instinctive act. The moral obligation of dominating one's passions would thus give place to the license to follow blindly and without restraint the caprices and impulses of nature; and this would sooner or later result in harm to human morality, conscience, and dignity.

If nature had intended exclusively, or at least primarily, the mutual giving of the spouses one to another and their mutual possession of one another in joy and pleasure, and if it had destined that act only for the purpose of enriching their personal experience with the highest possible felicity, and not in order to stimulate them to the service of life, the Creator would have adopted a different design in the formation and constitution of the natural act. Actually, however, this act is entirely subordinated and subject to that one great law of the "generation and education of children," that is, to the fulfillment of the primary end of marriage as the origin and source of life.

Unfortunately a flood of hedonism is pouring over the world, threatening to engulf every aspect of married life in a rising tide of hedonistic thoughts, desires, and acts, not without serious danger and grave harm to the primary duty of married persons.

This anti-Christian hedonism is often unblushingly erected into a doctrine, inculcating the eager desire to intensify without limit the pleasure experienced in the preparation and performance of the conjugal act; as though in marital relations the whole moral law consisted in the regular performance of the act itself, and all the rest, no matter how it were done, were justified by the outpouring of mutual affection, sanctified by the sacrament of marriage, meriting praise and reward before God and in conscience. The dignity of man, the dignity of the Christian, which impose some restraint on the excesses of sensuality — these count for nothing.

Well, really, no! The gravity and sanctity of the Christian moral law do not permit an unbridled satisfaction of the sexual instinct and the exclusive quest of pleasure and enjoyment; nor that man, endowed with reason, should permit himself to be dominated by passion to that extent, either as regards the substance of the act or its circumstances.

Some would argue that the happiness of marriage is in direct proportion to the mutual pleasure experienced in matrimonial relations. No; the happiness of marriage is in direct proportion to the mutual respect the parties show for each other, even in their most intimate relations. Not that they judge to be immoral and consequently refuse what nature offers and what the Creator has given them, but because this respect and the mutual esteem which it fosters is one of the soundest elements of a love that is pure, and for that very reason all the more tender.

AAS 43–835; Pius XII, Allocution, 29 Oct., 1951. Annotations, *Periodica,* 40–402 (Hürth). Other pronouncements of this same address are reported under canons 1013, 1081, 1086, and 2350. Full English text, *The Catholic Mind,* 1952, p. 49.

Copula Dimidiata. See c. 1081; private reply of Holy Office, 30 Nov., 1921.

CANON 1113

Education of the Conscience: Radio Address, Pius XII, 23 March, 1952 (AAS 44–270). Annotations, *Periodica,* 41–223 (Hürth). See also c. 1324, ref., "The New Morality."

CANON 1114

Artificial Insemination: Child conceived by such insemination outside of marriage would be illegitimate. See c. 1081; AAS 41–557.

CANON 1118

Indissolubility of Marriage: A strong document on the evil of divorce is the Joint Pastoral Letter of all the Archbishops and Bishops of England and Wales, 29 June, 1952. Text in *The Catholic Mind,* 1952, p. 637.

CANON 1119

Documentum Libertatis Given by Holy See Where, in the Instruction of the Process to Prove Non-consummation, the Evidence Proved Not Only Non-consummation but Indicated That Invalidity of the Marriage Would More Than Likely Be Declared If the Case Were Submitted to Formal Trial (Holy Office, 27 Nov., 1943) Private.

Facts. Two baptized non-Catholics married in 1920. The plaintiff asked the matrimonial tribunal of Cleveland for a declaration of nullity on the grounds of (*a*) force and fear exerted upon himself; (*b*) absence of true matrimonial consent on the part of both parties (intention *contra bonum sacramenti,* that is, agreement to obtain a divorce). The tribunal of judges rejected the petition on the ground that the plaintiff as a non-Catholic had no right to act as plaintiff without first obtaining the permission of the Holy See; but recommended that permission be asked of the Holy See to institute proceedings to establish non-consummation of the marriage. This permission was obtained and the investigation was instituted to establish non-consummation. The evidence not only proved that the marriage was not consummated, but the combined testimony of the witnesses clearly indicated that there was a vicious intention *contra bonum sacramenti.* The latter evidence was so strong that had the case been remanded there would undoubtedly have been an affirmative sentence of nullity. The defender of the bond in his *animadversions* objected against a petition for dissolution of a non-consummated marriage on the ground that such a dissolution supposes a valid marriage, whereas the present marriage was evidently invalid for want of consent. At the same time he contended that the plaintiff, having been the cause of the nullity of the marriage, was deprived of his standing in court by reason of canon 1971, § 1. The case was nevertheless forwarded to the Holy See asking for a dispensation of a marriage that was never consummated. The following rescript was received from the Holy Office:

Question. Whether the Holy Father should be asked for a dispensation of the marriage N.N.

Reply. The Holy Office, after having thoroughly discussed the matter according to certain established rules, decided to reply: *Facto verbo cum Sanctissimo,* let the petitioner have a *documentum libertatis. Et ad mentem:* let the Most Reverend Ordinary, before allowing the man to contract a new marriage, strive to bring him prudently to the true faith.

(**Private**); Holy Office, 27 Nov., 1943 (#14 m/40). This document, and a summary of the case, are taken from an article, *"Aut-Aut Causae,"* by the Reverend Louis A. Wolf, in *The Jurist,* Vol. 6, 1946, pp. 368–370. The permission of the author is gratefully acknowledged.

Consummation of Marriage (Holy Office, 2 Feb., 1949) Private.

It became known through the Advocates of the Rota that at the beginning of the year 1949 a Decree of the Holy Office was communicated to the Rota and to the Sacred Congregation of the Sacraments, of the following tenor:

To the proposed question: Whether a marriage is to be regarded as nonconsummated, if the essential elements of copula were placed by the husband, who arrived at sexual union only by the use of aphrodisiacs which actually deprived him for the time being of the use of reason,

The Most Eminent Fathers, on Wednesday the 2nd of February, decided to reply: *In the negative.*

(**Private**); Holy Office, 2 Feb., 1949. *Periodica,* 38–220 (Hürth). Father Hürth also discusses the question, left undecided by the above reply, whether a man who could arrive at sexual union only through such use of aphrodisiacs as actually deprived him of the use of reason, should be regarded as capable of a valid marriage or incapable by reason of impotence.

Non-consummation: Sufficiently proved without "physical argument." See c. 1086; AAS 36–179.

CANON 1120

Wrong Use of Pauline Privilege: Sanation. See c. 1127; Holy Office, 19 June, 1947.

CANON 1121

Delegated Faculty of Ordinaries to Dispense From Interpellations (Holy Office, 15 Nov., 1934) Private.

The following faculty was received by the Bishop of Denver:

To dispense, for ten cases, the Catholic spouse from interpellating the spouse who remains in infidelity, provided that, after all diligence has been used (including published notices in the papers where that is possible), it is proved with certainty, at least from a summary and extra-judicial inquiry, that the infidel spouse absolutely could not be found. The Bishop cannot delegate this faculty to anyone, but must exercise it in person.

In each case express mention must be made of the delegation from the Holy See (c. 1057).

After these cases are exhausted, the Ordinary must report to the Holy Office the circumstances in which he used the faculty each time.

(**Private**); rescript of Holy Office to Bishop of Denver, 15 Nov., 1934, Protoc. Num. 2619/34; reported by Woeber, *The Interpellations,* p. 133, note 126.

Dispensation From Interpellations: Apostolic Delegate to U. S. Given Power in Certain Conditions (Holy Office 1935, and Letter of Apostolic Delegate, 17 July, 1935) Private.

A Letter of the Apostolic Delegate to the Ordinaries of the United States:

Since the Ordinaries of this country are obliged from time to time to seek dispensation from the interpellations which are required for the lawful use of the Pauline privilege, the Supreme Sacred Congregation of the Holy Office has thought it opportune to grant the faculty to dispense from the interpellations to the Apostolic Delegate.

When, therefore, in an individual case, *there is danger in delay and no time for recourse to the Holy See,* Your Excellency may direct requests for this dispensation to the Apostolic Delegation. The petition, moreover, must state that the following conditions, by which the faculty is circumscribed, are verified in the case: "Provided that, after all diligence has been used (including published notices in the papers where that is possible), it is proved with certainty, at least from a summary and extra-judicial inquiry, that the infidel spouse absolutely could not be found, or that the interpellation could not be made without evident danger of grave harm either to the spouse who is already converted to the faith or to Christians."

(**Private**); Letter of Apostolic Delegate to Ordinaries of the United States, 17 July, 1935, No. 116/35, reporting faculty received from the Holy Office. Cf. Woeber, *The Interpellations,* p. 131.

Dispensation From Interpellations (Holy Office, 22 May, 1947) **Private.**

The Ordinary of Detroit, humbly prostrate at the feet of Your Holiness, represents the following:

Titius, unbaptized, contracted marriage with an unbaptized woman, Bertha, who became insane.

Titius, having been converted to the Faith and baptized, desires to enter a new marriage with a Catholic woman.

And now, since he has been received into the Catholic Church by baptism and desires to use the Pauline Privilege, he asks a dispensation from the interpellations to be made of the woman, in as much as they are useless.

The text of the rescript is as follows:

Supreme S. C. of the   22 May, 1947
    Holy Office
Prot. N. 1026/47

His Holiness, by Divine Providence Pope Pius XII, in the audience granted to His Excellency the Most Reverend Assessor of the Holy Office, graciously granted the favor of a dispensation from the interpellations to be made of the woman (provided it is morally certain, at least from a summary and extrajudicial process, that they would be useless).

Accordingly, after due preparation and the removal of any scandal by opportune measures, the petitioner Titius, without any interpellations, can validly and licitly contract marriage before the Church with a Catholic woman.

Servatis de iure servandis; contrariis quibuscumque non obstantibus.

(**Private**); Holy Office, 22 May, 1947. Received from the Reverend S. E. Fedewa, *Vice-Officialis* of the Archdiocese of Detroit.

Questionnaire for Application to Apostolic Delegate for Dispensation From Interpellations (Apostolic Delegation, U. S.) Private.

The Apostolic Delegation issued the following formula:

Questionary to Be Answered (in Duplicate) for Obtaining a Dispensation From the Interpellations Required in Cases of the Pauline Privilege.

(N.B. The answered questionary should bear the seal and signature of the Ordinary, as well as the date and place.)

1. Full name of the convert from infidelity
2. Full name of the so-called infidel spouse

About Non-Baptism

3. *a*) Has the convert's non-baptism been proved?
   b) The infidel spouse's?
4. *a*) What was the convert's religion at the time of their marriage?
   b) The infidel spouse's?
5. *a*) Before their marriage, did the convert belong to any other religion?
   b) Did the infidel spouse?
6. *a*) During their marriage or after separation, did the convert pass to another religion?
   b) Did the infidel spouse?

*If They, or Either of Them, Belonged at Any Time
to a Christian Sect, Answer the Following Questions: nn. 7–16:*

7. *a)* What are the proofs of the convert's non-baptism?
   b) Of the infidel spouse's non-baptism?
8. *a)* What witnesses were questioned about the convert's non-baptism?
   b) About the infidel spouse's?
9. *a)* Was the convert's father baptized? Was the convert's mother baptized?
   b) Was the infidel spouse's father baptized? Was the infidel spouse's mother baptized?
10. *a)* Why did not the convert's parents have him (her) baptized?
    b) The infidel spouse's?
11. *a)* Did the convert's parents have their other children baptized?
    b) Did the infidel spouse's?
12. *a)* Did the convert attend any church or religious school during infancy or at any other age?
    b) Did the infidel spouse?
13. Was baptism administered in those churches or schools?
14. *a)* Did the convert receive baptism there?
    b) Did the infidel spouse?
15. *a)* If the convert did not receive baptism there, why not?
    b) If the infidel spouse did not receive baptism there, why not?
16. *a)* Were the baptismal registers of those churches and schools searched for the record of the convert's baptism?
    b) Of the infidel spouse's baptism?

If the Infidel Spouse Cannot Be Found Please Answer the Following:

17. Has the impossibility of finding the infidel been proved at least by a *summary and extra-judicial process?*
18. Has all *diligence* been used in order to find that person?
19. Was that person *advertised for in the public press?*
20. To what *extent* was the advertising done?

If the Infidel's Residence Is Known Please Answer the Following:

17. Can the interpellations be made without *evident danger of grave harm?*
18. Has the *existence of such danger* been proved at least by a summary and extra-judicial process?

19. *a*) Does this danger threaten the convert?
    b) Other Christians?
20. What is the nature of this danger?

The Following Questions Must Be Answered in All Cases:

21. Is there such *danger in delay* that there is not time enough to await a dispensation from Rome?
22. What is the *nature of that danger?*
23. Full name of the Catholic whom the convert intends to marry.
24. Remarks.

(**Private**); Questionnaire kindly supplied by the Reverend S. E. Fedewa, *Vice-Officialis* of the Archdiocese of Detroit, 24 July, 1947.

CANON 1125

Interpellations: When Not Required: Interpretation of Constitution of Saint Pius V (S. C. Prop. Fid., 1924) Private.

The following question was proposed to the Sacred Congregation for the Propagation of the Faith by the First Council of China:

The Ordinaries of China have the faculty "to dispense pagans and infidels who have more than one wife, so that, after conversion and baptism, they may retain any of them whom they wish, provided she also embraces the faith, unless the first wife wishes to be converted."[1]

From which it seems to follow that, in every case of polygamy, even successive, the polygamous man cannot retain as his proper wife the woman who is baptized with him, unless the interpellations are previously made in order to learn whether the first wife wishes to be converted.

On the other hand, in the Constitution, *Romani Pontificis,* of Saint Pius V (c. 1125), it seems to be stated absolutely that in case of successive polygamy the convert can retain as his wife the woman who is baptized with him, without any question being raised about previous interpellation.

---

[1] Cf. *Formula Tertia Maior,* n. 24; Vermeersch-Creusen, *Epitome,* Vol. I, ed. 1937, p. 643.

The First Council of China, seeing that among us catechumens are frequently found who, with a second or successively later wife who consents to baptism, ask to be baptized, and for whom it is most difficult and almost impossible to dissolve such a marriage, most humbly asks the Apostolic See whether, according to the mind of the above cited Constitution of Saint Pius V, Vicars and Prefects Apostolic may baptize such catechumens together with such a wife who consents to baptism with them, with the further understanding that they may remain in such a marriage, absolutely and without any interpellation of the first wife, or not.

Reply. In the affirmative.

(**Private**); S. C. Prop. Fid., 1924; *Primum Concilium Sinense, Vota et Postulata,* n. 12, p. 273. Reported by de Léry, *Le Privilège de la Foi,* p. 108; Cappello, *De Matrimonio,* ed. 1939, Vol. II, p. 291; Payen, *De Matrimonio,* Vol. III, n. 2407 bis; Burton, *A Commentary on Canon 1125,* pp. 156–157, note 14. Several of these authors very reasonably contend that this reply is but an interpretation of the Constitution of Pius V, and hence of the common law.

Dissolution of Natural Bond (Holy Office, 25 May, 1933) Private.

The following case was presented to the Holy Office:

Facts. Helen, 24 years of age, who was baptized by an Episcopalian (Anglican) minister in the city of S in the United States, contracted marriage on Sept. 5, 1923, before a heretical minister, with Richard, who was never baptized.

In 1927 Helen obtained a divorce from Richard on the ground of non-support. Now she has been converted to the Catholic religion and baptized in the cathedral church of W on July 8, 1932.

Helen wishes to contract marriage with a good Catholic man, a widower, Francis, and she humbly asks for the Pauline Privilege to dissolve the first marriage with Richard so that she may be able to marry Francis.

Richard, Helen's husband, has signed a written declaration that he will never return to his wife Helen if she ever embraces the Catholic religion. This declaration, and a certificate signed by two witnesses to the fact that Richard was never baptized, are enclosed with this petition.

The diocesan tribunal held two sessions on this case. The judge interrogated Helen and the Reverend O. J. M. who baptized Helen; and the tribunal proposed that before any further sessions be held, the judge should write asking for the application of the Pauline Privilege in favor of Helen.

It is to be noted that Helen said she desired to be a Catholic even if she could not obtain the Pauline Privilege.

Reply. The Holy Father is to be petitioned for the favor of the dissolution of the natural bond of the marriage, so that the Catholic Helen, *servatis de iure servandis,* and all scandal being removed by appropriate measures, may licitly and validly contract marriage before the Church with the Catholic man. On Thursday, May 25, 1933, in the usual audience, His Holiness, having received a report of the case, graciously deigned to grant the favor in accordance with the above decree.

(**Private**); Holy Office, 25 May, 1933. Reported by de Léry, *Le Privilège de la Foi,* pp. 31–32.

Interpretations of Constitutions: Dispensation: Renovation of Consent (Holy Office, 30 June, 1937) **Private.**

The First Council of Indochina asked the Holy Office:

I. According to the Constitution of Paul III, *Altitudo,* of 1 June, 1537, when a newly baptized convert, who before his conversion had several wives and does not remember which one he married first, takes one of them who is not converted, is it required for the validity of this marriage that a dispensation from disparity of cult be obtained and that the *cautiones* prescribed by canons 1061 and 1071 be given?

Reply. In the negative, that is, a dispensation is not required, it being implicitly granted by the Constitution *Altitudo,* saving however the obligation, to be imposed before baptism, as to the requirements of divine law which are referred to in the *cautiones* mentioned in canons 1061 and 1071.

II. According to the Constitution of Saint Pius V, *Romani Pontificis,* of 2 Aug., 1571, when a newly baptized convert, who before his conversion had several wives, wishes to remain with the wife who is baptized with him: (*a*) Is it required for the validity of this marriage that both parties renew matrimonial consent in the form prescribed by law? (*b*) Could such a marriage stand even if there were no grave difficulty in finding the first or lawful wife?

Reply. (*a*) In the affirmative; (*b*) This is provided for in the faculties contained in the formula of faculties: and where the case is not included in the faculties which have been received to dispense from the interpellations, recourse must be had to the Holy See in particular cases.

(**Private**); Holy Office, 30 June, 1937. Cf. *Acta Primi Concilii Indosinensis*, Hanoi, 1938, pp. 176, 177.

CANON 1127

Documentum Libertatis **Given by the Holy See in an** *Aut-Aut* **Case** (Holy Office, 16 June, 1945) **Private.**

Facts. In this case the plaintiff married the respondent in 1916 before a minister. They lived together two years and were divorced. Nothing could be established about the baptism or non-baptism of the respondent, who has long since disappeared. The plaintiff's baptism is also in insoluble doubt owing to the following circumstances: his father, a non-Catholic, died when plaintiff was a baby; on his deathbed he became a Catholic and requested his non-Catholic wife to have the child brought up as a Catholic. The wife promised this, though she never became a Catholic herself. When the plaintiff was six years old, his mother was compelled to break up the home and go out to seek work for a living. She left the plaintiff with a Catholic woman, and at the same time arranged to have him attend a Catholic school. While at school, the plaintiff attended the Catholic catechism instructions. He made his first Communion, was confirmed, and always considered himself a Catholic. He presumed he must have been baptized a Catholic; but he has no memory of ever receiving baptism; neither his mother nor anyone else ever told him that he had been baptized; and after diligent search no record of his baptism can be found. His mother died many years ago.

Legal Aspect. The case presented the following dilemma: If the plaintiff was baptized as a baby — either in the Catholic Church or heretically — the marriage was invalid for want of canonical form. If the plaintiff was never baptized and (1) the respondent was baptized before the marriage, or (2) the respondent was not baptized at all either before or since the marriage up to the present time, or (3) the respondent was baptized only after the marriage, the following are possibilities involved: In the first of these three suppositions (respondent baptized before the marriage), the marriage would be invalid because of pre-Code disparity of worship; in the second supposition (respondent never baptized up to the present), the Pauline Privilege would be applicable to the plaintiff after his conditional baptism and a dispensation from interpellations; in the third supposition (respondent baptized since the marriage), a papal dispensation of the marriage *in favorem fidei* would be possible. The case was presented to the Holy See by the Curia of Cleveland.

Rescript. The rescript of the Holy Office (n. 89 m/45) was as follows: In the Episcopal Curia of Cleveland the process was drawn up in the case of the marriage which N.N. (a man brought up in the Catholic religion, but whose baptism was not proven) contracted in 1916 before a minister, with a non-Catholic woman, N.N.

After the record had been examined in this Supreme Sacred Congregation and after all due procedures had been taken in the case, the question was proposed in the plenary session of the Eminent Fathers on Wednesday the 13th of June, 1945.

Question. Whether the recommendation is to be made to the Holy Father to grant the petitioner N.N. a *documentum libertatis*, so that, after he shall have received baptism conditionally, he can validate before the Church the union which he contracted only civilly with a Catholic woman with whom he is living.

Reply. The Eminent Fathers, after thoroughly discussing the matter according to certain established rules, decreed to reply: in the affirmative.

His Holiness, by Divine Providence Pope Pius XII, in the audience granted to the Most Reverend Assessor of the Holy Office on Thursday the 14th of June, 1945, after receiving a report of everything, graciously deigned to grant the favor according to the aforesaid decree. In the present grant of the favor is included, as far as it may be necessary, a dispensation from the impediment of crime mentioned in canon 1075, § 1.

(**Private**); Holy Office, 16 June, 1945 (89 m/45). The rescript and the summary of the facts are taken from an article, *"Aut-Aut Causae,"* by the Reverend Louis A. Wolf, in *The Jurist*, Vol. 6, 1946, pp. 371–373. The permission of the author is gratefully acknowledged.

Pauline Privilege Wrongly Granted by Ordinary in Case of Doubtful Baptism of One Party: Sanation Later Granted by Holy Office (Holy Office, Reply to Petition of 19 June, 1947) Private.

The Petition. The Ordinary, humbly prostrate at the feet of Your Holiness, presents the following facts:

William, unbaptized, contracted marriage before a civil magistrate on 22 March, 1930, with Hattye, who had been baptized in the Methodist sect about the year 1914. This marriage was terminated by divorce on 10 July, 1931.

Later, William, after being duly instructed in the Catholic faith, was baptized as a Catholic in the Cathedral church, 20 March, 1937. William, now a Catholic, desiring to marry a Catholic, Elizabeth, applies for the Pauline privilege.

The following facts emerged in the course of the investigation:

1. William (Seymour) had never previously been baptized.

2. Hattye had been baptized in the Methodist sect about the year 1914.

3. Hattye's father, John, who acted as a sort of minister in the Methodist sect, testified that his daughter had really been baptized as alleged; he also stated that he understood baptism to be a mere external rite having no relation to the remission of sins or the infusion of grace.

4. He further testified that this was the meaning of the baptism which was intended by the minister who had baptized Hattye.

Whereupon, the interpellations having been made and refused by Hattye, the Vicar General on 12 Apr., 1937, declared that the Pauline privilege could be applied in the case of William, unbaptized, and Hattye, doubtfully baptized. The marriage between William and Elizabeth, a Catholic, was accordingly celebrated in the Cathedral church on 20 May, 1937.

Afterward in the year 1943 Hattye wishes to marry a Catholic, invoking the Pauline privilege which had already been granted in the case of her former husband, William.

The judgment of this Tribunal on the petition of Hattye was as follows: that Hattye is not free to marry, even though William, her former husband, has already married again in virtue of the Pauline privilege; because (as we warned) the Ordinary of the place, according to the Decree of the Holy Office of 10 June, 1937,[1] is not allowed to pass judgment on the validity of a doubtful baptism.

---

[1] AAS 29–305; CANON LAW DIGEST, II, p. 343.

Hence it is asked:

1. Whether the application of the Pauline privilege in the above case was valid?

2. If not, what about the validity of the marriage contracted between William and Elizabeth?

First Reply. The Holy Office replied on 30 Oct., 1946:

Your Excellency, by letter of 13 Sept., 1946, to the Holy Office, presented the case of the application of the Pauline privilege, granted by the Ordinary in the year 1937 to the newly baptized neophyte, William, affecting a marriage which he had contracted in 1930, at a time when he (as they say) was not yet baptized, with Hattye, who had been baptized in a non-Catholic sect, but concerning the validity of whose baptism some doubts had arisen based on the false or uncertain intention of the baptizing minister.

Since, however, the facts alleged are not sufficient to prove the invalidity of the baptism, this Supreme Sacred Congregation decided that the Pauline privilege was not properly, and perhaps was even invalidly, applied in the case.

Hence, in order that the matter may be decided with certainty and propriety, will Your Excellency please see to it that proofs are sent, both as to the absence of baptism and as to the non-consummation of the marriage after the baptism of the petitioner.

(In pursuance of this request, copies of affidavits submitted in the original consideration and testimony of the petitioner concerning his non-baptism, as also testimony concerning the non-consummation of the marriage after the Catholic baptism of the petitioner, were sent to the Holy See.)

Second Reply. The Holy Office replied (no date):

Your Excellency, by letter of 19 June, 1947, forwarded new documents in the marriage case of William and Hattye.

After full consideration, the Holy Office by these presents grants the dissolution of the marriage of William and Hattye and a *sanatio in radice* (without the knowledge of the parties) of the marriage contracted between William and Elizabeth. And let a document of free state be given to Hattye so that she may validly and licitly contract a new marriage with a Catholic.

(Private); Holy Office, Reply to letter of 19 June, 1947. Copies of petition and replies were kindly sent to us by the Committee on Research of the Canon Law Society of America.

The Fresno Case: Marriage Contracted With Dispensation From Disparity of Cult Dissolved in Favor of the Faith (Holy Office, 18 July, 1947) Private.

The Bishop of Monterey-Fresno received the following rescript from the Holy Office (Protoc. Num. 706/42–3172/46):

In October of last year, the Holy Office received from Your Excellency's Episcopal Curia the *acta suppletoria* in the case of the dispensation of the marriage (Bertha-Titius),[1] as a non-consummated marriage.

After having carefully compared the aforesaid records with those that had preceded them in the same case, and having carefully examined them, this Supreme Congregation decided that all doubt had not been removed regarding the alleged non-consummation of the marriage; but nevertheless it decided that the favor of dissolution which was asked for could be granted on another ground, namely *in favorem fidei,* because the woman petitioner was unbaptized during the entire time of her cohabitation with her spouse (Titius). Consequently, even though the marriage was contracted with a dispensation from the impediment of disparity of cult, yet in view of the peculiar circumstances of the case, and especially the probable non-consummation of the marriage, His Holiness by Divine Providence Pope Pius XII, in the audience granted to the Most Excellent Assessor of the Holy Office on July 17, 1947, graciously deigned to grant the favor of dissolution of the aforesaid marriage; so that the petitioner, after having been converted and received baptism, can contract a new marriage with a Catholic man. She must, however, be warned that the granting of the favor is based also on her alleged lack of baptism, and that therefore she cannot use this favor if she has any prudent reason to believe that she had already been baptized before.

The present concession contains also a dispensation from the impediment of crime mentioned in canon 1075, n. 1.

(**Private**); Holy Office, 18 July, 1947. Translated from the original rescript which was kindly sent to us by the Right Reverend John Galvin, *Officialis* of the diocese of Monterey-Fresno.

---

[1] Fictitious names have been substituted for the real names of the parties.

Privilege of the Faith: Dissolution of Former Marriage Contracted Before the Church (Holy Office, 30 Jan., 1950) **Private.**

Facts. B. Mary C., unbaptized and born of non-Catholic parents, contracted a civil marriage in 1947 with G. John C., a Catholic. Two months later this marriage was validated before the Church, a dispensation having been obtained from mixed religion and *ad cautelam* from disparity of cult. The union was not a happy one, and very soon the wife obtained a civil divorce on grounds of cruelty and drunkenness. The man later contracted another civil marriage.

Two years later B. Mary C. began keeping company with another Catholic man, and took instructions in the Catholic faith. At this time she applied to the Chancery of the Diocese of Monterey-Fresno for a dissolution of the natural bond of her former marriage, in favor of the faith.

The Petition. The petition presented to the Holy Office by the Bishop of Monterey-Fresno on 2 June, 1949, recites that the process has been drawn up under the direction of the Right Reverend John Galvin, *Officialis* of the Diocese, in accordance with the Instruction of the Holy Office of 1 May, 1934. It then recites the facts as we have summarized them above, and concludes *verbatim* as follows:

"The existence of the two-fold condition *sine qua non* for the granting of this dispensation, namely the lack of baptism in both parties during the entire time of their conjugal life and the non-use of the marriage after the baptism of the petitioner, is evident from the annexed proofs which have been gathered from the family of the petitioner, and from the fact that the petitioner has never been baptized up to the present time.

"As to the other conditions which are required, first the moral impossibility of restoring conjugal life is beyond doubt, because the man respondent is living in civil marriage with another woman. The existence of the other condition, absence of scandal, is not so evident. As the pastor states, the danger of wonder on the part of the faithful at the eventual concession of the dispensation is not excluded, because the granting of such a favor is rare when the former marriage was contracted before a priest.

"Having duly considered all these circumstances, and the facts above stated being proved in the annexed documents, I humbly lay the petitioner's prayer at the feet of Your Holiness, so that, if it be possible, the natural bond of the marriage between B. Mary C. and G. John C. be dissolved in favor of the faith and thus B. Mary C. may contract a marriage before the Church with E. N., a Catholic.

"Persuasive reasons for granting the dispensation are: the good of souls, the danger of incontinence in both parties owing to their youth, and the danger of civil marriage."

Reply. The Holy Office replied as follows (N. 1289/49):

In the Curia of Monterey-Fresno a process was drawn up to obtain the dissolution in favor of the faith, of the marriage contracted in 1947 between B. Mary C., unbaptized, and G. John C., a baptized Catholic.

The record having been examined in this Supreme Sacred Congregation, and everything that is required having been done, the question was proposed on Wednesday the 18th of January, 1950, in the Plenary Session of the Eminent Fathers:

Whether recommendation is to be made to His Holiness in favor of the dissolution of the above marriage in favor of the faith, so that the petitioner B. Mary C., after having received baptism, may validly and licitly contract a new marriage before the Church with a Catholic man.

The Eminent Fathers, having thoroughly discussed the case according to certain established rules, decided to reply: *In the affirmative.*

His Holiness by divine Providence Pope Pius XII, in the audience granted on Wednesday 27 January, 1950, to His Excellency the Most Reverend Assessor of the Holy Office, having received a report of the entire matter, graciously deigned to grant the petition according to the above Decree.

Included in the present concession also, as far as it may be needed, is the dispensation from the impediment of crime mentioned in canon 1075, 1°.

Servatis de iure servandis; all things to the contrary notwithstanding.

Given at Rome, from the Holy Office, 30 January, 1950.

(**Private**); Holy Office, 30 Jan., 1950. This case was kindly sent to us for publication in the CANON LAW DIGEST, by the Right Reverend John Galvin, *Officialis* of the Diocese of Monterey-Fresno.

NOTE: We also received from Monsignor Galvin, with permission to publish it, the following Rescript sent by the Holy Office to the Bishop of Monterey-Fresno as a sequel to the same case (N. 1289/49):

By letter of 10 April, 1950, Your Excellency asked whether the Catholic man, G. John C., who was the respondent in the case of the dissolution in favor of the faith of the marriage B. Mary C.–G. John C., can, in virtue of the granting of the favor of the dissolution itself, contract a new marriage before the Church with a non-Catholic woman (even one who is unbaptized).

The Holy Office replied: Mr. G. John C. will be able, *servatis de iure servandis,* to enter upon a new marriage even with a non-Catholic woman.

(**Private**) ; Holy Office, 4 May, 1950.

CANON 1133

Maronites: Form required in renewal of consent of marriage which was invalid for consanguinity. See Rota, 1934 (R. D., Vol. 26, decision 57) ; also Marbach, *Marriage Legislation,* p. 153, note 20.

CANON 1139

General Sanation of Marriages Contracted Invalidly for Want of Form. See c. 1096; S. C. Sacr., 21 July, 1919.

CANON 1141

Wrongful Application of Pauline Privilege: Cured by sanation. See c. 1127; private reply of Holy Office to letter of 19 June, 1947.

CANON 1147

Banners of Political Parties Not to Be Blessed (Holy Office, 20 March, 1947) AAS 39–130.

The Holy Office was asked:

Whether it is allowed to bless the banners of any political party.

Reply. The Eminent Cardinals in charge of safeguarding faith and morals, in view of the decree of this Supreme Sacred Congregation of 31 Aug., 1887, at the general session held on Wednesday the 5th of March, 1947, decided to reply: In the negative.

And on the following Thursday, the 6th of the same month and year, His Holiness, by divine Providence Pope Pius XII, in the audience granted to the Most Excellent Assessor of the Holy

Office, confirmed this resolution of the Eminent Fathers when it was reported to him.

Given at Rome, from the Holy Office, March 20, 1947.

AAS 39–130; Holy Office, 20 March, 1947.
Commentarium pro Religiosis, 26–45 (Gutiérrez).

Faculty to Consecrate Chalices and Patens Denied (S. C. Rit., 14 April, 1950) Private.

The Superior General of a certain Congregation of priests asked for himself and his successors the faculty to consecrate chalices and patens for the churches of his Institute, whenever the Bishop was absent, either because of a notable distance separating the place from the Episcopal See, or for some other reason.

Reply. *Non expedire.*

(**Private**); S. C. Rit., 14 April, 1950; Prot. N. C. 53/50. *Monitor Ecclesiasticus,* 1952, p. 453.

CANON 1156

Right to Bless Ship's Oratory. See c. 248; AAS 44–649, n. 30.

CANON 1161

Sacred Art: Instruction on. See c. 1261; AAS 44–542.

CANON 1162

Sacred Art: Instruction on. See c. 1261; AAS 44–542.

CANON 1164

Sacred Art: Instruction on. See c. 1261; AAS 44–542.

CANON 1165

Meaning of "Ecclesia" in Apostolic Faculties, nn. 9–11, to Be Understood in Strict Canonical Sense (S. C. Prop. Fid., 30 Jan., 1930) Private.

In reply to a question proposed by the Superior General of the Scheut Fathers, the Sacred Congregation for the Propagation of the Faith declared that the term *"ecclesia"* in faculties 9, 10, and 11 is to be understood in the strict canonical sense of canons 1161 and 1165, § 1.

(**Private**); S. C. Prop. Fid., 30 Jan., 1930. See Winslow, *A Commentary on the Apostolic Faculties,* p. 49, note 61.

NOTE: These three paragraphs of the Faculties refer respectively to permitting three Masses on Christmas night; to permitting the simpler rite of Benedict XIII for the functions of Holy Week; and to permitting private Masses *de requie.*

CANON 1169

Radio Instrument Instead of Bells (S. C. Rit., 27 Nov., 1941) Private.

The Sacred Congregation of Rites was asked by the Bishop of Papantia:

Whether what are commonly called radiophonic instruments (*instrumenta vulgo dicta radiophonica*) can be placed in bell towers or the tops of churches instead of bells made of metal.

Reply. It is not expedient.

(**Private**); S. C. Rit., 27 Nov., 1941. *Il Monitore Ecclesiastico,* 1942, p. 42.

CANON 1178

Sacred Art: Instruction on. See c. 1261; AAS 44–542.

CANON 1188

Indult of Private Oratory. See c. 813; AAS 41–493.

CANON 1195

Indult of Private Oratory: Entire matter regulated. See c. 813; AAS 41–493.

CANON 1197

Altar Liturgically Classed as Portable Although Materially Fixed to Its Base (S. C. Rit., 21 Aug., 1950) Private.

The Sacred Congregation of Rites was asked:

Whether the short formula can be used in the consecration of altars which are attached in a fixed manner to their supports, but which are consecrated separately from their supports.

Reply. Nothing prevents a portable altar from being set up as though it were a fixed altar. In the case proposed the altar, although materially fixed, is liturgically portable or movable, and hence it can be moved and separated from its supports without losing its consecration.

(Private); S. C. Rit., 21 Aug., 1950; Prot. N. T. 53/51. *Monitor Ecclesiasticus,* 1952, p. 451.

CANON 1216

Possession of Family Vault Does Not Imply Choice of Church for Funeral (Code Com., 4 Jan., 1946) AAS 38–162.

The Code Commission was asked:

Whether, according to canon 1216, § 1, compared with canon 1226, § 1, a family vault established in a certain church is to be regarded, since the Code, as a legal choice of the church for the funeral.

Reply. In the negative.

AAS 38–162; Code Com., 4 Jan., 1946.
Periodica, 35–191 (Schönegger).

CANON 1226

Choice of Church for Funeral, not necessarily implied by possession of family vault in that church. See c. 1216; AAS 38–162.

CANON 1229

Family Vault, established in certain church does not imply choice of that church for funeral. See c. 1216; AAS 38–162.

CANON 1233

Case on Priority of Right to Be Invited for Funeral Services (S. C. Conc., 13 July, 1941) AAS 34–101.

Facts. In the town of Arco, Archdiocese of Trent, there is one parish, St. Mary's, which is also a collegiate church. The care of souls is exercised, especially in the city, by the archpriest pastor, assisted by the Chapter and two secular assistants without benefice. The parish also includes ten suburbs or hamlets outside the city. Of these, the five nearest to the city are immediately under the pastor, being cared for by chaplains called *missarii* who work under his direction, receiving faculties *per modum actus* as they need them. The five more remote suburbs are mediately subject to the pastor, being cared for by *curates* who receive parochial faculties from him once for all at their appointment. In two of these remote suburbs there are also two convents: one of the Friars Minor and one of the Capuchins. The controversy arose between these regulars on the one hand and the pastor and Chapter on the other as to the priority of right to be invited to funerals, especially in the city and in the five remote suburbs. There is no dispute as to the so-called "general" funerals, as in their case the Statutes of the Chapter give an equal right to the parish priests and to the said religious. But as to so-called "partial" funerals, the same Statutes provide (chap. 13) that "in case other priests besides those of the hamlet in question are to be invited, the preference shall be given to the chaplains and canons over the regular clergy." The validity of this regulation was the issue in the case.

Remarks. 1. Canon 1233, § 1, gives the preference in this matter to "the clerics who are assigned to the church itself"; and this certainly means the parish church in which the funeral is to be held according to canons 1216 and 1217. Now it is clear that the religious in question are in no sense assigned to this church; they have no care of souls in the parish.

2. As to the members of the Chapter, the Code Commission has held that they are not, *as such,* that is, as capitulars, included in the words of canon 1233;[1] but in the present case they are certainly included as having the care of souls, because, as their Statutes clearly provide, they are obliged to assist the pastor in the care of souls.

3. The chaplains of both classes who work in the suburbs, the *missarii* and the *curati,* are also obviously "assigned to the church"; they are all to be regarded as *vicarii cooperatores,* since it is clear from canon 476, § 2, that assistants can be appointed not only for an entire parish but also for a determined part of it.

4. The objection that the Statutes do not amount to a diocesan law is irrelevant. They are in fact approved by the Bishop and hence binding in all relationships with the Chapter. Besides, they are quite in accord with the common law.

5. The claim of the religious that, as "praying clergy," they are entitled to preference over the "officiating clergy," is without merit.

Question. Is chapter 13 of the Statutes of the collegiate church, as regards funerals, to be sustained?

---

[1] Code Com., 8 Apr., 1941; AAS 33–173; CANON LAW DIGEST, Vol. 2, p. 354.

Reply. In the affirmative.

His Holiness Pius XII, in the audience of 13 July, 1941, approved and confirmed the above reply.

AAS 34–101; S. C. Conc., 13 July, 1941.

CANON 1240

Schismatics: Norms concerning sacraments and ecclesiastical burial. See c. 731; private reply of Holy Office, 15 Nov., 1941.

CANON 1248

Proper Observance of Days of Obligation: Urged on Ordinaries of Italy. S. C. Conc., 25 March, 1952 (AAS 44–232). Annotations, *Monitor Ecclesiasticus*, 1952, p. 206 (Cardini).

CANON 1249

Precept Fulfilled by Hearing Mass in Places Mentioned in Canon 822, § 4 (Code Com., 26 March, 1952) **AAS 44–497.**

The Code Commission was asked:

Whether, notwithstanding the prescription of canon 1249, the law on hearing Mass is satisfied by one who assists at Mass in a place mentioned in canon 822, § 4.

Reply. In the affirmative.

Given at Rome, from Vatican City, 26 March, 1952.

AAS 44–497; Code Com., 26 March, 1952. Annotations, *Monitor Ecclesiasticus*, 1952, p. 410 (Bidagor).

———

Hearing Mass in Private Chapel: When sufficient to fulfill precept. See c. 813; AAS 41–493.

CANON 1252

Fast and Abstinence: Indult Extended Indefinitely (S. C. Conc., 22 Jan., 1946) **AAS 38–27.**

In view of the difficult conditions following the recent war, His Holiness by Divine Providence Pope Pius XII has graciously deigned to extend on the same terms, until other provision is made, the Apostolic Indult of 19 Dec., 1941, regarding the law of ecclesiastical abstinence and fasting.[1]

———

[1] CANON LAW DIGEST, Vol. 2, p. 363; AAS 33–516.

Accordingly all Ordinaries of places of whatever rite can grant, according to their prudent judgment, in the territory of their respective jurisdictions, a general dispensation from the law of ecclesiastical abstinence and fast, in favor also of religious men and women, even those who enjoy the privilege of exemption.

But the law of ecclesiastical abstinence and fast remains in effect, for the faithful of the Latin rite, on Ash Wednesday and Good Friday; for the faithful of other rites, on two days to be determined by their respective Ordinaries.

Local Ordinaries who grant the above dispensation shall take care to exhort the faithful, especially the secular clergy and religious men and women, to try to compensate for this favor by voluntary practices of Christian perfection and expiation and by good works, especially of charity toward the poor and the sick; and let them not fail to offer pious prayers to God according to the intention of the same Holy Father.

Rome, the 22nd of January, 1946.

AAS 38-27; S. C. Conc., 22 Jan., 1946.

Fast and Abstinence: Indult Modified for Latin Church
(S. C. Conc., 28 Jan., 1949) AAS 41-32.

A Decree of the S. C. of the Council on the observance of the law of abstinence and fast, is as follows:

Since the adverse circumstances which counseled the relaxation, in December, 1941,[1] of the law of abstinence and fast, have nearly everywhere somewhat improved, it has been decided, at the approach of the propitious time of the Holy Year and at the request of a number of Most Excellent Ordinaries, to restore the law at least in part.

Accordingly His Holiness Pius XII by divine Providence Pope has deigned to decree for all the faithful of the Latin rite, including those who belong to religious orders and congregations, to limit the faculty granted to Ordinaries to dispense from the aforesaid law, so that, from the first day of the coming Lent and until some different provision is made, the law of abstinence is to be observed on all Fridays; and the law of abstinence and fast together is to be observed on Ash Wednesday, Good Friday, and the vigils of the Assumption of Our Lady and of the Nativity

---

[1] S. C. Neg. Eccl. Extr., 19 Dec., 1941; AAS 33-516; DIGEST, 2, p. 363.

of Our Lord; graciously providing, however, that it is allowed everywhere to take eggs and milk products even in the morning and evening on days of abstinence and fast together.

Local Ordinaries who make use of this new faculty to dispense from the law of abstinence and fast shall not fail to exhort the faithful, especially clerics and religious men and women, in view of the critical circumstances of the present time, to be generous in performing additional voluntary works of Christian perfection and of charity especially toward the poor and the sick, and also to pray for the intentions of the Holy Father.

Given at Rome, the 28th of January, 1949.

AAS 41-32; S. C. Conc., 28 Jan., 1949. *Periodica*, 38-73 (Abellán).

Fast and Abstinence: Indult Modified for Orientals (S. C. Eccl. Or., 28 Jan., 1949) AAS 41-31.

A Decree of the S. C. for the Oriental Church on the observance of the law of abstinence and fast, is as follows:

Since the adverse circumstances which counseled the relaxation, in December, 1941,[1] of the law of abstinence and fast, have nearly everywhere somewhat improved, it has been decided, at the approach of the propitious time of the Holy Year and at the request of a number of Most Excellent Ordinaries, to restore the law at least in part.

Accordingly His Holiness Pius XII by divine Providence Pope has deigned to decree for all the faithful of the Oriental rite, including those who belong to religious orders and congregations, to limit the faculty granted to Ordinaries to dispense from the aforesaid law, so that, from the first day of the coming *Great Lent* and until some different provision is made, the law of abstinence and fast is to be observed *"if and as it is in effect in the respective rites,"* on the following days:

I. *Abstinence:* on all Fridays;

II. *Abstinence and fast:*

1) On the first day of the Great Lent;

2) On Friday of Holy Week;

3) On the vigil of the Nativity of Our Lord; or, for the faithful of the Byzantine rite, on the vigil of the Epiphany;

---

[1] S. C. Neg. Eccl. Extr., 19 Dec., 1941; AAS 33-516; DIGEST, 2, p. 363.

4) On the vigil of the Assumption of Our Lady.

Graciously allowing, however, that, on days of abstinence and fast together, the Most Excellent Ordinaries can permit eggs and milk products even in the morning and evening.

Local Ordinaries who make use of this new faculty to dispense from the law of abstinence and fast shall not fail to exhort the faithful, especially clerics and religious men and women, in view of the critical circumstances of the present time, to be generous in performing additional voluntary works of Christian perfection and of charity especially toward the poor and the sick, and also to pray for the intentions of the Holy Father.

Given at Rome, from the Sacred Congregation for the Oriental Church, the 28th of January, 1949.

AAS 41–31; S. C. Eccl. Or., 28 Jan., 1949.

Uniform Norm for Fast and Abstinence in the United States (Report of Episcopal Committee, 14 Nov., 1951) Private.

I. ORIGIN AND MANDATE OF THE COMMITTEE

At the thirty-second annual meeting of the Hierarchy (November, 1950), the Episcopal Chairman appointed an Episcopal Committee to study existing laws on Fast and Abstinence in the United States and to draft a uniform set of regulations. This Committee included His Excellency, the Most Reverend Leo Binz, S.T.D., Coadjutor to the Archbishop of Dubuque, Chairman; His Excellency, the Most Reverend John P. Cody, S.T.D., Auxiliary to the Archbishop of Saint Louis, and His Excellency, the Most Reverend William A. O'Connor, S.T.D., Bishop of Springfield-in-Illinois.

It was the understanding of the members of the Committee that the Bishops generally have desired to clarify, simplify, and unify fast and abstinence practices in the United States, and that they had given this assignment to the Committee.

After having studied and discussed the problem at several preliminary meetings, the members of the Committee sought counsel and advice from various Theological and Canon Law Societies, as well as from a large number of individual Theologians and Canonists. Finally, on Sept. 18, 1951, a tentative formula entitled "Regulations on Fast and Abstinence," was sent to all the Archbishops and Bishops in the United States with a request for comments on the formula submitted. The answers received were given careful study, and the formula was revised to conform with certain suggestions made. The revised formula was submitted to the Hierarchy at their annual meeting on November 14, 1951, and, with one slight modification, was adopted by them as the uniform norm for the United States.

II. TEXT OF FORMULA SUBMITTED FOR UNIFIED REGULATIONS ON FAST AND ABSTINENCE

To foster the spirit of penance and of reparation for sin, to encourage self-denial and mortification, and to guide her children in the footsteps of Our Divine Saviour, Holy Mother Church imposes by law the observance of fast and abstinence.

In accordance with the provisions of Canon Law, as modified through the use of special faculties granted by the Holy See, we herewith publish the following regulations:

On Abstinence

Everyone over 7 years of age is bound to observe the law of abstinence.

Complete abstinence is to be observed on Fridays, Ash Wednesday, the Vigils of the Assumption and Christmas, and on Holy Saturday morning. On days of complete abstinence meat and soup or gravy made from meat may not be used at all.

Partial abstinence is to be observed on Ember Wednesdays and Saturdays and on the Vigils of Pentecost and All Saints. On days of partial abstinence meat and soup or gravy made from meat may be taken only once a day, at the principal meal.

On Fast

Everyone over 21 and under 59 years of age is also bound to observe the law of fast.

The days of fast are the weekdays of Lent, Ember Days, the Vigils of Pentecost, the Assumption, All Saints, and Christmas.

On days of fast only one full meal is allowed. Two other meatless meals, sufficient to maintain strength, may be taken according to each one's needs; but together they should not equal another full meal.

Meat may be taken at the principal meal on a day of fast

except on Fridays, Ash Wednesday, and the Vigils of the Assumption and Christmas.

Eating between meals is not permitted; but liquids, including milk and fruit juices, are allowed.

When health or ability to work would be seriously affected, the law does not oblige. In doubt concerning fast or abstinence, a parish priest or confessor should be consulted.

We earnestly exhort the faithful during the periods of fast and abstinence to attend daily Mass; to receive Holy Communion often; to take part more frequently in exercises of piety; to give generously to works of religion and charity; to perform acts of kindness toward the sick, the aged, and the poor; to practice voluntary self-denial especially regarding alcoholic drink and worldly amusements; and to pray more fervently, particularly for the intentions of the Holy Father.

III. COMMENTARY ON THE FORMULA[1]

1. "In accordance with the provisions of Canon Law . . ."

A. The Code of Canon Law prescribes the following:

I. *Abstinence only:* All Fridays of the year.

II. *Fast and Abstinence:*

1. Ash Wednesday;
2. Fridays of Lent;
3. Saturdays of Lent;
4. Holy Saturday morning;
5. Ember Days (four sets);
6. Four Vigils — Pentecost, Assumption, All Saints, and Christmas.

III. *Fast only:* All weekdays of Lent not mentioned in II.

B. The new formula differs from the Code of Canon Law on two points only:

I. The Saturdays of Lent are *omitted entirely* as days of abstinence; hence they are not transferred to Wednesdays.

II. Meat is allowed to all *once at the principal meal* on Ember Wednesdays and Saturdays, and on the Vigils of Pentecost and All Saints.

---

[1] This Commentary is by the Episcopal Committee itself; it forms an integral part of the Report. We have supplied merely some footnote references.

2. ". . . as modified through the use of special faculties granted by the Holy See, we herewith publish the following regulations."

For a clearer understanding of the faculties made use of, it will help to recall the special faculties granted by the Holy See to the Most Reverend Ordinaries:

I. December 19th, 1941:[2] Pope Pius XII, through the Sacred Congregation of Extraordinary Ecclesiastical Affairs, *for the duration of the war,* granted to all local Ordinaries of the world the faculty to dispense all their subjects, including religious (even exempt), from all the laws of the Church regarding fast and abstinence with the exception of two days only: Ash Wednesday and Good Friday.

II. January 22nd, 1946:[3] Pope Pius XII, through the Sacred Congregation of the Council, extended indefinitely ("until further notice") the above faculties, which had ceased with the termination of the war.

III. January 28th, 1949:[4] Pope Pius XII, through a Decree of the Sacred Congregation of the Council, restricted somewhat the faculties which had been extended "until further notice" in 1946, as follows:

1. *Abstinence must be observed on all Fridays;*
2. *The law of fast and abstinence* must be observed:
    a) on Ash Wednesday;
    b) on Good Friday;
    c) on the Vigils of the Assumption and Christmas.

3. *It is benignly permitted everywhere on days of fast and abstinence to eat eggs and milk products in the morning and in the evening also.*

This Decree of January 28th, 1949, is of the utmost importance:

1. Because it has been laid down as a minimum requirement for the whole world, no matter what indults were enjoyed previously (this was made clear through the Apostolic Nuncios and Delegates, to all of Latin America, South and Central America,

---

[2] AAS 33–516; CANON LAW DIGEST, 2, p. 363.

[3] AAS 38–27; CANON LAW DIGEST, 3, under canon 1252.

[4] AAS 41–32; CANON LAW DIGEST, 3, under canon 1252.

Cuba, and Mexico): similarly the privilege of the *Bulla Cruciata* was withdrawn from certain dioceses in the Southwest.

2. This Decree of January 28th, 1949, restricts the wide faculties given to the local Ordinaries in 1946, and these two are now the only source of faculties enjoyed by the Bishops of the United States to dispense from fast and abstinence. The indults for transferring the abstinence from Saturday to Wednesday during Lent, as well as the so-called "workingmen's privilege" will not be renewed. The Apostolic Delegate to the United States, writing to His Eminence, Cardinal Bruno, Prefect of the Sacred Congregation of the Council, informed him that the faculties mentioned above had lapsed, and received the reply that it would not be necessary to renew these Indults (transfer of abstinence from Saturday to Wednesday in Lent and the "workingmen's indult") since "the Ordinaries could make ample provision for such needs in virtue of the decree of Jan. 28, 1949."

It is to be noted that the faculties granted in the Decree of 1949 apply equally to all religious, even exempt, as well as to *all* the laity, irrespective of the type of work they do: *"pro omnibus fidelibus ritus latini, etiam pertinentibus ad Ordines et Congregationes religiosas . . ."*

The faculties which the local Ordinaries enjoy, to dispense on civil holidays, continue in force.[5]

3. "Everyone over seven years of age . . ."

According to the common teaching of canonists, a child completes its seventh year at midnight of his seventh birthday, and his obligation to abstain begins the day after. The Code of Canon Law, can. 1254, § 1, expressly states: *"Abstinentiae lege tenentur omnes qui septimum aetatis annum expleverint."*

4. ". . . is bound to observe the law of abstinence."

The law of abstinence forbids the eating of meat and of meat juices (can. 1250); however, lard, suet, drippings, etc., may be used in the preparation and seasoning of foods.

5. "Complete abstinence is to be observed . . ." (See below.)

6. "Partial abstinence is to be observed . . ."

The distinction between "complete" and "partial" abstinence

---

[5] Cf. CANON LAW DIGEST, 1, p. 584.

may seem to be new in theory, but it was widely used in interpreting the Workingmen's Indult in the past. The earliest form of the Workingmen's Indult of 1895, allowed *partial abstinence* to workingmen and their families on all abstinence days, with the exception of the Fridays of the year, Ash Wednesday, during Holy Week, and on the vigil of Christmas; on these latter days *complete abstinence* was required. The benefits formerly granted working people are now extended, by reason of the Decree of 1949, to all who are obliged to abstain. At the same time, it is to be noted that all, whether fasting or not, must abstain from meat on Ember Days and the two Vigils (Pentecost and All Saints), except at the principal meal, thus observing the law of abstinence (partial) at the two lesser repasts. There can be no doubt that sufficient authority for such a provision is included in the Indult of 1946 and the Decree of 1949.

The distinction between complete and partial abstinence should be readily grasped by the faithful and become commonly understood in a short time.

There will no longer be any question about the interpretation of "workingmen" since this new formula makes no distinction between manual laborers, stenographers, white collar workers, students, seminarians, religious, etc. — all may make use of the same privileges.

The *Ember Days* have been retained as days of partial abstinence. While some suggested that the Ember Days be dropped as days of abstinence, many others insisted that these days have traditionally a very important place in the Sacred Liturgy, and fear was emphatically expressed that a complete dispensation would diminish their traditional importance.

The distinction of the Vigils in the formula is due solely to the limitation embodied in the Decree of 1949, which does not grant to the local Ordinaries the faculty to dispense from fast or abstinence *on the Vigils of the Assumption or Christmas*. The other Vigils, Pentecost and All Saints, have been accorded the same status as the Ember Days because of their traditional importance in the life of the Church.

The Vigil of Christmas constituted a special problem, as many of the Bishops proposed the *"ieiunium gaudiosum,"* as known in certain parts of Europe, while others were in favor of having the fast and abstinence end at noon, or at least by sundown, on

Christmas Eve. Careful inquiry indicated that only in one nation had any concession been allowed for Christmas Eve, and then probably only because of war conditions. The Decree of 1949 expressly limited any use of the faculties for dispensing on Christmas Eve. Hence the Committee feels that, if desired, such a privilege should be the subject of a special petition to the Holy See.

The Wednesdays of Lent also presented a special problem:

1. It was evident from the letters of the Bishops that no one favors the observance of the Saturdays of Lent as days of abstinence, as prescribed by the Code of Canon Law.

2. The transfer of the Saturday abstinence to Wednesday, as has been our custom since 1887, has been the chief point of disagreement in the counsels given the Committee from so many sources. It was finally decided that it would be preferable to *dispense directly* from the Saturday abstinence prescribed during Lent by the Code of Canon Law. This may certainly be done in virtue of the faculties granted by the Indult of 1946 and the Decree of 1949. The Holy See seems to indicate these two grants as a practical norm to be followed in formulating regulations on fast and abstinence. The dropping of the Wednesday abstinence during Lent also does away with the confusion resulting from the four different kinds of Wednesdays during Lent (Ash Wednesday, Wednesday in Ember Week in Lent, the Wednesday in Holy Week, and the other Wednesdays are subject to different rules). Finally it is important to point out that since the Wednesdays of Lent remain days of fast, the vast majority of persons (who will now use the relative norm under the formula which has been adopted) will be entitled to the use of meat only once on those Wednesdays of Lent, as was the case under the Workingmen's Indult for those who fasted.

7. "Everyone over 21 and under 59 years of age is also bound to observe the law of fast."

The duty to fast begins on the day after one's 21st birthday and continues until midnight of one's 59th birthday.

8. "The days of fast are the weekdays of Lent, Ember Days, the Vigils of Pentecost, the Assumption, All Saints, and Christmas."

The days of fast mentioned in this formula are the same as those prescribed in the Code of Canon Law, can. 1252.

9. "On days of fast only one full meal is allowed. . . ."

The law of fast prescribes that only one meal (*unica comestio*) may be taken on a given day (can. 1251, § 1).

10. "Two other meatless meals, sufficient to maintain strength, may be taken according to each one's needs; but together they should not equal another full meal."

Here the *relative norm* has been incorporated in the adopted formula because experience shows that this norm makes it possible for most persons to fast, whereas, as a matter of fact, most persons cannot fast according to the *absolute norm* of two and eight ounces respectively. The relative norm has been approved by the Bishops for common use in Belgium, England, Ireland, the Netherlands, as well as in some dioceses in Canada. In the United States it was found that the relative norm was being used in at least fifty-seven Archdioceses and Dioceses, and had been partially adopted in twenty others. The relative norm is not contrary to the Code of Canon Law, and was in use in many places in Europe before Saint Alphonsus Liguori introduced the absolute norm of two and eight ounces respectively, to help scrupulous persons to make up their minds as to how much food they might take on a fast day.

According to the relative norm, the person who is fasting is allowed to take that amount of food on the lesser meals which will be sufficient for him to do his daily work properly without undue inconvenience. This amount will differ for each person.

11. "Meat may be taken at the principal meal on a day of fast . . ."

Meat may be eaten at the principal meal on a fast day which is not at the same time a day of abstinence. But, given the historical development of the collation and the morning crust of bread, it has always been essential to the law of fast that meat may not be taken except once a day at the principal meal. This common opinion of Moral Theologians was upheld by the answer of the President of the Commission for the Interpretation of the Code of Canon Law, given on October 29th, 1919, to the effect that one could not follow with a good conscience the doctrine proposed by certain authors that after (or since) the publication of the Code of Canon Law it is permitted to eat meat more than once on days of fast only.[6]

The idea, therefore, of a fast day does not exclude meat from the *one full meal* which constitutes the essence of the law of fast. Obviously, persons not bound by the law of fast, may eat meat as often as they wish on a fast day, which is not also a day of complete or partial abstinence.

12. ". . . except on Fridays, Ash Wednesday, and the Vigils of the Assumption and Christmas."

Per se meat is not allowed at the principal meal on any abstinence day. But here in the adopted formula the power to dispense, granted in the Indult of 1946 and the Decree of 1949, is made use of to allow meat at the principal meal on the Wednesdays and Saturdays of Ember Week, and on the Vigils of Pentecost and All Saints as explained above in n. 6.

13. "Eating between meals is not permitted: but liquids, including milk and fruit juices, are allowed."

Since the *relative norm* of fast is followed in the formula, it seems reasonable that eating between meals should not be allowed. Moral Theologians have generally adopted the so-called *"frustulum ne potus noceat"* once or twice a day on the supposition that the absolute norm is followed.

There seems no need to explain what is meant by "liquids"; suffice it to say that the usual amount of cream in tea or coffee, according to each one's taste, may be permitted.

During recent years some Moral Theologians have allowed the use of fruit juices between meals on a fast day for the same reason that wine and beer are permitted in European countries: they are considered *a beverage and not a food.*

In the United States milk is served as a drink and not as a food; it has been deemed permissible to follow this generally accepted practice, as in keeping with the Code of Canon Law (*"servata tamen circa ciborum quantitatem et qualitatem probata locorum consuetudine"* — can. 1251, § 1).

Only ordinary or homogenized milk is allowed. Such com-

---

[6] AAS 11–480; Canon Law Digest, 1, p. 586.

binations as malted milk, milk shakes, and the like are not included in the term "milk." On the other hand, combinations based on skim milk and a coloring or special flavoring such as the so-called "chocolate milk" are considered a drink rather than a food and are allowed.

14. **"When health or ability to work would be seriously affected, the law does not oblige. In doubt concerning fast or abstinence, a parish priest or confessor should be consulted."**

Moral Theologians list categories of persons who are exempt from the laws of fast and abstinence because of ill health or because of the nature of their employment. Pastors and confessors should be familiar with these exceptions, as well as with their powers to *dispense* from the law of fast and abstinence.

15. **"We earnestly exhort the faithful during the periods of fast and abstinence to attend daily Mass; to receive Holy Communion often; to take part more frequently in exercises of piety; to give generously to works of religion and charity; to perform acts of kindness toward the sick, the aged, and the poor; to practice voluntary self-denial especially regarding alcoholic drink and worldly amusements; and to pray more fervently, particularly for the intentions of the Holy Father."**

The Committee regards this exhortation as an *integral part* of the formula, since it is based on the concluding paragraph of the Decree of 1949,[7] and incorporates the suggestions received from many members of the Hierarchy.

(**Private**); Episcopal Committee, Report, 14 Nov., 1951.

Note: An official copy of the Report was graciously sent to us by His Excellency, the Most Reverend John P. Cody, S.T.D., Auxiliary

---

[7] "Local Ordinaries who make use of this new faculty to dispense from the law of abstinence and fast, shall not fail to exhort the faithful, especially clerics and religious men and women, in view of the critical circumstances of the present time, to be generous in performing additional voluntary works of Christian perfection and of charity especially toward the poor and the sick, and also to pray for the intentions of the Holy Father." Decree of S. C. Conc., 28 Jan., 1949; AAS 41–32; Canon Law Digest, 3, under canon 1252.

to the Archbishop of Saint Louis and a member of the Episcopal Committee. We have reproduced only the first three Chapters. Other valuable Chapters of the full Report are: on unification efforts in other countries and the history of the legislation and documents.

Latin America: Fast and Abstinence. See c. 66; private, S. C. Prop. Fid., 15 Sept., 1950.

CANON 1253

Fast Days of Religious Rule Not Affected by Code (S. C. Rel., 22 March, 1921) **Private.**

The Sacred Congregation of Religious was asked:

Whether the law of fast contained in the Rule of the Friars Minor ceases on feast days of obligation outside of Lent.

Reply. In the negative.

(**Private**); S. C. Rel., 22 March, 1921. Cf. Sartori, *Enchiridion Canonicum*, p. 328.

CANON 1258

Discussions With Non-Catholics. See c. 1325; AAS 40–257.

Schismatics: Norms concerning sacraments and ecclesiastical burial. See c. 731; private reply of Holy Office, 15 Nov., 1941.

The "Ecumenical Movement." See c. 1325; AAS 42–142.

CANON 1259

Devotion to "Merciful Love," Not to Be Propagated (Holy Office, 5 April, 1941) **Private.**

A Reply of the Holy Office to the Vicar Capitular of the Archdiocese of Havana is as follows (Prot. N. 78/41):

In a letter addressed to the S. C. of Rites, Your Reverence asked permission to propagate the devotion to "Merciful Love" in the form therein described. The documents having been forwarded to this Sacred Congregation, which has the competency in such questions, the Eminent and Most Reverend Fathers, after having thoroughly examined the matter, in the plenary session of Wednesday the second of April, decided to reply:

The practice established by the decision of Wednesday, May 5th, 1937, is to be observed; that is, the reply is in the negative, according to the Decree which was published in the *Acta Apostolicae Sedis* for July, 1937, Vol. 29, p. 304,[1] which forbids the introduction of new devotions and orders that existing abuses be eradicated.

(**Private**); Holy Office, 5 April, 1941. *Periodica,* 31–189.

NOTE: *Periodica* quotes this document from *Sal Terrae* for January, 1942, p. 54. The devotion is explained in a footnote as follows: The new form in which the devotion to the Most Holy Redeemer is proposed consists in a crucifix with a very large host under it. The Heart is shown on the breast. Beneath is the inscription: Merciful Love.

CANON 1261

Alleged Apparitions of the Blessed Virgin at Heroldsbach, Not Supernatural (Holy Office, 25 July, 1951) AAS 43–561.

Decree of the Holy Office:

In the general session of the Supreme Sacred Congregation of the Holy Office, the Most Eminent and Most Reverend Cardinals in charge of protecting faith and morals, after having examined the records and documents which concern alleged visions of the Blessed Virgin Mary in the village of Heroldsbach in the Archdiocese of Bamberg, and after hearing the opinion of the Reverend Consultors, decreed:

"It is proved that the aforesaid visions are not supernatural; hence the worship connected with them at that place or elsewhere is prohibited; priests who in future take part in this illicit worship incur *ipso facto* suspension *a divinis.*"

On the following Thursday, 19 July, 1951, His Holiness by divine Providence Pope Pius XII, in the usual audience granted to His Excellency the Assessor of the Holy Office, approved and confirmed the decree of the Eminent Fathers when it was reported to him, and ordered that it be published.

Given at Rome, from the Holy Office, 25 July, 1951.

AAS 43–561; Holy Office, 25 July, 1951.

Instruction on Sacred Art (Holy Office, 30 June, 1952) AAS 44–542.

An instruction of the Holy Office addressed to the Ordinaries of places is as follows:

---

[1] AAS 29–304; CANON LAW DIGEST, 2, p. 372.

The function and duty of sacred art, as its very name implies, is to enhance the beauty of the house of God and to foster the faith and piety of those who gather in the church to assist at divine services and implore heavenly favors. Hence sacred art has always been cultivated by the Church with assiduous care and vigilant interest, in order that it may be thoroughly true to its own proper laws, which stem from supernatural doctrine and true asceticism, and so give it a perfect right to call itself "sacred."

Hence the words which the Supreme Pontiff Blessed Pius X spoke when promulgating the wise norms concerning sacred music, are quite appropriate here: "Nothing therefore should have place in the church which disturbs or even merely diminishes the piety and devotion of the faithful, nothing which could be a reasonable ground for offense or scandal, nothing above all which . . . is unworthy of the house of prayer and the majesty of God."[1]

Already therefore in the earliest times of the Church, the Second Council of Nicea, by condemning the heresy of the Iconoclasts, confirmed the cult of sacred images and threatened with severe penalties those who dared "wickedly to invent anything contrary to ecclesiastical institution."[2]

The Council of Trent in its 25th session issued prudent laws on Christian iconography, and concluded its grave exhortation to Bishops with these words: "Finally, let Bishops exercise such diligence and care in these matters that nothing which is out of place may meet the eye, nothing which is distorted and confused in execution, nothing profane or unbecoming, since holiness befits the house of God."[3]

In order that the prescription of the Council of Trent concerning sacred images should be faithfully observed, Urban VIII enacted special norms, decreeing: "Let those objects which fall under the eyes of the faithful, not appear out of place or unusual, but *let them engender devotion and piety*."[4]

Finally, the Code of Canon Law gathers all the legislation of the Church on Sacred Art under summary headings (cc. 485,

---

[1] *Motu proprio, Tra le sollecitudini*, 22 Nov., 1903; *Acta Pii* X, Vol. I, p. 75.
[2] *Actio 7ª et ultima definitio Synodi 2ᵃᵉ*, Mansi, *Sacr. Conc.*, XIII, col. 730.
[3] Sess. XXV, *De invocatione, vener. et Reliquiis Sanct. et sacris Imaginibus.*
[4] *Sacrosancta Tridentina*, § 1, die XV mensis Martii, anno MDCXLII, *Bullarium Romanum,* Taurinen. editio, XV, 171.

1161, 1162, 1164, 1178, 1261, 1268, 1269, § 1, 1279, 1280, 1385, 1399).

Especially noteworthy are the provisions of canon 1261, according to which Ordinaries are bound to see to it that "nothing be admitted which is foreign to the faith or out of harmony with ecclesiastical tradition"; and of canon 1399, 12°, which declares to be *"ipso iure* forbidden . . . pictures, no matter how printed . . . which are foreign to the mind and decrees of the Church."

Recently also the Holy See reprobated corrupt and errant forms of sacred art. The objection raised by some, that sacred art must be adapted to the needs and circumstances of changing times, is of no weight. For sacred art, which originated with Christian society, has its own ends from which it can never diverge, and its proper function which it can never abandon. Accordingly Pius XI of venerable memory, when he inaugurated the new Vatican Gallery with a discourse on sacred art, after mentioning a so-called *new art,* added these momentous words: "In union with masters of art and with the Holy Pontiffs, We have already many times stated that Our hope, Our ardent desire, Our will can only be that the law of the Church, so clearly formulated and sanctioned in the Code of Canon Law, be obeyed: that is, that such art be not admitted into our churches, and especially that it be not called upon to construct, to remodel, or to decorate them. Rather, open wide the portals and give the most cordial welcome to every good and progressive development of the approved and venerable traditions, which in so many centuries of Christian life, in such diversity of circumstances and of social and ethnic conditions, have given such proof of their inexhaustible capacity to inspire new and beautiful forms, whenever they have been called upon or studied and cultivated by the twofold light of genius and of faith."[5]

Recently Pius XII, now happily reigning, in the Encyclical Letter "On the Sacred Liturgy," of 20 Nov., 1947, concisely and clearly formulated the duties of Christian art: "It is eminently fitting that the art of our times have a free opportunity *to serve the sacred edifices and sacred rites with due reverence and with due honor;* so that it too may add its voice to the

---

[5] Address of 27 Oct., 1932; AAS 24–356; CANON LAW DIGEST, 1, p. 559.

magnificent hymn of glory which men of high talent have sung throughout the passing centuries of the Catholic faith. Nevertheless in consciousness of Our office We cannot but deplore and reprove those images and forms recently introduced by some, which seem to be deformations and debasements of sane art, and which at times are even in open contradiction to Christian grace, modesty, and piety, and miserably offend true religious sentiment; these indeed are to be totally excluded and expelled from our churches, as 'in general whatever is out of harmony with the holiness of the place' (c. 1178)."[6]

After carefully considering all these matters, this Supreme Sacred Congregation, earnestly solicitous for the preservation of the faith and piety of the Christian people through sacred art, has decided to recall to the mind of all the Ordinaries of the world the following norms, to the end that the forms and methods of sacred art may fully correspond to the beauty and holiness of the house of God:

Concerning Architecture. Sacred architecture, although it may adopt new styles, can by no means be similar to that of profane buildings, but must always perform its own function, which properly concerns the house of God and the house of prayer. In building churches, it is right that care be taken also for the convenience of the faithful, so that they may be able to take part in the divine services with a better view and better attention; let the new church be notable also for the beautiful simplicity of its lines, rejecting all false ornamentation; but everything which betrays a neglect of art or carelessness of workmanship should be avoided.

In canon 1162, § 1, it is provided that: "No church shall be built without the express consent in writing of the Ordinary of the place, which cannot be given by the Vicar General without a special mandate."

In canon 1164, § 1: "Ordinaries shall see to it, taking counsel of experts if need be, that in the construction and remodeling of churches traditional Christian styles of architecture and true standards of sacred art be observed."

This Supreme Sacred Congregation strictly enjoins that the prescriptions of canons 1268, § 2, and 1269, § 1, be religiously

---

[6]AAS, Vol. 39 (1947), p. 590 seq.

observed: "The Most Blessed Sacrament shall be kept in the most distinguished and honorable place in the church, and hence as a rule at the main altar, unless some other be considered more convenient and suitable for the veneration and worship due to so great a Sacrament. — The Most Blessed Sacrament must be kept in an immovable tabernacle set in the middle of the altar."

Concerning Descriptive Art. 1. According to the prescription of canon 1279: "No one may place or cause to be placed in churches, even though they be exempt, or in other sacred places, any unusual image, unless it has been approved by the Ordinary of the place" (§ 1).

2. "The Ordinary shall not approve of images to be exposed publicly for the veneration of the faithful, if they are not in conformity with the approved usage of the Church" (§ 2).

3. "The Ordinary shall never permit to be shown in churches or other sacred places, images which represent a false dogma, or which are not sufficiently decent and moral, or which would be an occasion of dangerous error to the unlearned" (§ 3).

4. If experts are lacking on the Diocesan Commissions, or if doubts or controversies arise, let the local Ordinaries consult the metropolitan Commissions or the Roman Commission on Sacred art.

5. In accordance with canons 485 and 1178 the Ordinaries should see to it that whatever is in any way contrary to the holiness of the place and the reverence due to the house of God be removed from sacred buildings; and they should strictly forbid that a hoard of statues and images of little worth, mostly of a stereotyped form, be inanely and awkwardly presented for the veneration of the faithful on the altars themselves or against the adjoining walls of the chapels.

6. Bishops and religious Superiors should refuse their permission for the publication of books, papers, or periodicals, in which are printed pictures which are foreign to the mind and decrees of the Church.[7]

In order that local Ordinaries may more safely ask and receive of the diocesan Commission for Sacred Art advice which is in perfect accord with the demands of the Holy See and of sacred art itself, let them see to it that the aforesaid Commission be

---

[7] Cf. cc. 1385 and 1399, 12°.

provided with members who are not only competent in the field of art but also firm in their allegiance to the Christian faith, brought up in piety and ready to follow the definite norms which are prescribed by ecclesiastical authority.

And works of painting, sculpture, and architecture should be entrusted only to men who are outstanding for their artistic taste and skill and who can express in their work that sincere faith and piety which is the purpose of all sacred art.

Finally, care must be taken that the aspirants to sacred orders in schools of philosophy and theology receive some instruction in sacred art and be trained to appreciate it, in a way suited to each one's capacity and age, by teachers who revere the ways and traditions of our ancestors and obey the prescriptions of the Holy See.

Given at Rome, from the Holy Office, 30 June, 1952.

AAS 44-542; Holy Office, 30 June, 1952. Our translation makes free use of the one which appeared in *The Catholic Mind,* Vol. 50, p. 699. For a very authoritative commentary, see *Monitor Ecclesiasticus,* 1952, p. 379 (Costantini).

Function of Art: Address of Pius XII, 8 April, 1952, to a group of Italian artists *(The Catholic Mind,* Vol. 50, p. 697).

CANON 1264

Electric Organ May Be Permitted by Ordinaries (S. C. Rit., 13 July, 1949) **AAS 41-617.**

A Communication from the Sacred Congregation of Rites:

The war with its lamentable disasters and ruins did not spare even the churches, many of which were destroyed, very many damaged, so that not only important works of art but also not a few musical organs were destroyed or rendered useless.

It is needless to observe that in the sacred liturgy the organ is called upon to play a part, and that in its manufacture, even though it be of small size, considerable expense is involved. For this reason in these later times, companies engaged in the manufacture of musical instruments have devised electric organs, which, though decidedly inferior to the pipe organs, yet offer some notable advantages in their manufacture and use.

In consideration of all this, the Sacred Congregation of Rites, while reaffirming that the old pipe organ is altogether preferable as being more suited to liturgical needs, yet does not forbid the use of electric organs. Hence this Sacred Congregation, although it acknowledges that this instrument, in order to be a worthy substitute for the pipe organ, needs to be perfected and improved — and it earnestly exhorts the manufacturers to undertake this task — yet leaves it to the discretion of the Bishops and other Ordinaries, in individual cases where it is not easy to buy a pipe organ, after hearing the opinion of the Diocesan Council of Music, to permit the use of the electric organ in the churches, making such changes as the Diocesan Council of Music may suggest.

Given at Rome, the 13th of July, 1949.

AAS 41–617; S. C. Rit., 13 July, 1949.

Pontifical Institute of Sacred Music: General Superiors of Religious Institutes Urged to Send Select Students (S. C. Rel., Letter, 11 April, 1951) Private.

The following Letter of Father Larraona, Secretary of the Sacred Congregation of Religious, was sent to the Superiors General of Religious Institutes:

Prot. N. 2545/51

Everyone knows what great services Orders and Congregations of Religious rendered in past centuries to the cultivation of sacred music, as well as to that of the other departments of culture in the arts.

This is not to be wondered at, for from the time when monasteries throughout the Catholic world seemed to be almost the only beam of light in the darkness, until now, when Congregations of men and women founded in earlier times or in our own, as well as secular Institutes, by new forms of apostolate, are bringing to an evil world, or rather injecting into it, the divine ferment of the religious spirit and the religious life, religious, dedicated to the common good of the Church, have stood as effective witnesses to the value of truly sacred music for advancing divine worship and raising the minds of the faithful to God.

However, not all religious families have in this matter followed faithfully and constantly the example of their fathers; some have even, by a sort of levity, been gradually drawn to depart here and there from the right road and from their earlier traditions.

Hence this Sacred Congregation, as a watchful guardian also

of this treasure, feels obliged to recall to Major Superiors the documents of the Holy See in this regard, among which are especially noteworthy the prescriptions of the Apostolic Constitution, *Divini cultus sanctitatem,* of the Supreme Pontiff Pius XI of happy memory, of 20 Dec., 1928.[1]

The Sacred Congregation, moreover, feels bound to mention to the General Superiors of religious the exhortation of the same Supreme Pontiff in this regard and to urge compliance with it; that is, that they should send to the Pontifical Institute of Sacred Music in Rome at least some select persons among their subjects, endowed with a truly liturgical spirit and a talent for music, who, after finishing the usual course of training, can exercise an "apostolate of liturgy and music" among the members of their Institute.

There is no doubt that such action will, as far as may be necessary, give to religious Institutes of men and women a growing knowledge of and participation in the genuine spirit of the Church, and rid them of new and strange notions and practices.

May God grant, through the prayers of His Servant Pope Pius X, that all religious Institutes may so comply with the exhortations of the Holy See that sacred music will retain its place of due honor among them and be the resonant voice and herald of the fervent charity which they all have toward Almighty God.

From Rome, 11 April, 1951.

(**Private**); S. C. Rel., Letter of Secretary, 11 April, 1951. Annotations, *Monitor Ecclesiasticus,* 1951, p. 244 (Romita).

Unofficial "Code of Sacred Music": An interesting study of the various ecclesiastical documents on sacred music is presented in the form of a "Code" of 70 canons by Romita, in *Monitor Ecclesiasticus,* 1952, p. 457. It is entirely unofficial.

CANON 1265

Indult for Keeping the Most Blessed Sacrament in Private Oratory. See c. 813; AAS 41–493.

CANON 1268

Sacred Art: Instruction on. See c. 1261; AAS 44–542.

---

[1] AAS 21–33; summarily reported in Canon Law Digest, 1, p. 598.

CANON 1269

Protection of the Most Blessed Sacrament From Incursions of War (S. C. Sacr., 15 Sept., 1943) AAS 35–282.

As everyone knows, the unleashed fury of war, raging over almost the entire earth, is attacking everything with engines of war of every sort, on land and sea and in the air.

This cruel destruction, alas, does not spare even the sacred temples of God which cherish the sacred Body of Christ hidden under the Eucharistic Species.

In order to protect the Most Blessed Eucharist as far as possible from all irreverence, this Sacred Congregation desires to direct the attention of Ordinaries (canon 198, § 1) toward seeking more appropriate means to this end: although it is aware that some of the Most Excellent Bishops have already commendably given to their pastors and rectors of churches suitable directions in this matter.

Accordingly it has been decided to present in this letter certain measures which may be of service to the Ordinaries and priests who have the custody of the Most Blessed Eucharist in fulfilling the grave duty with which they are charged.

1. In the first place, if priests should be startled by the warning of an attack while celebrating Mass, let them bear in mind the rubric of the Missal, *De defectibus in celebratione Missarum occurentibus*, X, n. 2, which among other things prescribes: "If, while a priest is celebrating . . . there is imminent danger of an enemy attack, or a flood, or the destruction of the place where the Mass is being said, if it is before the consecration, he should stop the Mass, if after the consecration, he may hasten the reception of the Sacrament, omitting everything else."

2. In view of the danger of enemy attacks, the Ordinary is given the power, to be used according to his prudent judgment, to suspend for a time, that is while the danger lasts, the right of keeping the Most Blessed Eucharist in churches, provided they be not parish churches or others among the most distinguished of the place; and in semipublic oratories, that is, chapels of communities, seminaries, hospitals, etc., where there is no priest or deacon to put the sacred Species in a place of safety during attacks; and especially in domestic oratories.

3. But in communities which are governed by priests or nuns,

and which have, as is customary, a semipublic oratory, if there is a special place designated as a *refuge* exclusively for the community in case of war attacks, and the place is fit and suitable, the Most Blessed Eucharist may be kept there, even habitually, instead of in the oratory, an altar being arranged and suitably equipped, with a ciborium covered with a veil, and an electric lamp kept lighted day and night; and there the members of the community may perform their usual exercises of piety. And whenever Mass is celebrated in the oratory in order to afford a convenient opportunity to receive Holy Communion, let only the number of particles which is necessary be consecrated.

4. So too, in the cities which are most exposed to the aforesaid attacks, if the church has a crypt or underground chapel, or if a place can easily be prepared there, which will afford security against damage from the enemy, the Most Blessed Eucharist may be continually kept there, in an altar with a tabernacle hidden in a rather safe place, observing what was said in n. 3; and, if there is easy access to the place and enough space there, the faithful may assist at sacred functions.

5. Canon 1269, § 3, provides for a case where "if there is a grave reason approved by the Ordinary, it is not forbidden to keep the Most Blessed Eucharist at night outside the altar . . . in a secure and suitable place. . . ." We have already explained this provision of law in the Instruction, *De Sanctissima Eucharistia sedulo custodienda,* of 26 May, 1938, n. 5,[1] where it was stated that this way of keeping the Most Blessed Eucharist provides greater security especially against thieves; but obviously the same holds good for the attacks of war, and even in the daytime if necessary.

The "secure place" here referred to may also be some special recess under the church or sacristy or in the parish rectory, especially if the sacred Species be enclosed in some sort of iron box constructed by skillful craftsmen so as to protect them from fire, dampness, and any other unwelcome environment — the box to be inserted in the lower walls of the church or inside the marble base of a pillar, observing as far as possible the liturgical laws and the above cited Instruction.

6. Sometimes, as we have already suggested above in n. 3, it

---

[1] Canon Law Digest, Vol. 2, p. 377; AAS 30–198.

will be well to consecrate each day only as many hosts as will be sufficient for the Communion of the faithful, consuming those which may be left over, except some which may be kept for giving Viaticum or Communion to the sick; and these it would be advisable to put, not in an ordinary ciborium, but in some sort of box made of solid metal and entirely enclosed, suited to the purpose, which can easily be put away and moved from place to place.

And a priest who lives near the church shall, in case of an attack, quickly take possession of this box with the sacred Particles so reserved, and carry it to a safe place.

7. It is very strongly recommended that the pastor instruct some of the faithful who are notable for their prudence and piety — preferably members of the Confraternity of the Blessed Sacrament, which has as its special purpose to care for and to promote the worship of the Most Blessed Eucharist — so that, in extreme necessity, that is, if there is no pastor or priest in the place and an imminent danger of profanation to the Most Blessed Eucharist arises, they may know how to put the sacred Species in a safe place, or, if the Species have been scattered, how to search for them and collect them as carefully as possible.

8. These directions which we have given are only some of the measures which may be taken to attain the end in view; nothing prevents others also from being employed, which may be found more suitable in peculiar local circumstances; in fact we earnestly exhort Ordinaries to make use of any other means which they may find more effective.

This Sacred Congregation would indeed be happy to be informed, in due course, of all the measures which the Ordinaries may have taken to protect the Most Holy Eucharist from the dangers of war.

His Holiness by divine Providence Pope Pius XII, in the audience granted to His Excellency the Secretary of this Sacred Congregation on the 14th of September, 1943, deigned to approve this letter, which had already been thoroughly and carefully examined by the Eminent Fathers in their plenary session, and ordered that it be published in the Official Commentary, *Acta Apostolicae Sedis,* and immediately put into practice; with the necessary and appropriate derogations.

Given at Rome, from the Sacred Congregation of the Sacraments, the 15th of September, 1943.

AAS 35–282; S. C. Sacr., 15 Sept., 1943.

Sacred Art: Instruction on. See c. 1261; AAS 44–542.

CANON 1271

Indult Allowing Use of Electric Lights for Tabernacle Lamp and Altar Candles Modified (S. C. Rit., 18 Aug., 1949) **AAS 41–476.**

A Decree of the S. C. Rit., *Urbis et Orbis*, on the tabernacle lamp and on lights to be used in sacred functions, is as follows:

This Sacred Congregation, by a Decree of 13 March, 1942,[1] acceding to the requests of many Ordinaries, renewed an indult which had been granted provisionally in 1916 during the European war, by committing to their prudent judgment, in view of the peculiar circumstances of the new war, "wherever olive oil or beeswax are either entirely lacking or cannot be obtained without grave inconvenience and expense," the faculty to permit that the lamp before the Blessed Sacrament be maintained with other oils, vegetable if possible, and in the last resort to permit that even electric lights be used. The Sacred Congregation also permitted that in default of beeswax the number of candles which is duly prescribed for the various sacred functions be reduced, and that this deficiency of candles be supplied for by providing, up to the required number of candles, other lights, even electric lights.

Now, although neither beeswax nor oil is entirely lacking, yet in view of their high cost, this Sacred Congregation intends to modify the indult so that, whereas the indult remains in effect as regards the lamp before the Blessed Sacrament, for the celebration of private Mass, two wax candles are to be used, at least four for a solemn Mass or *Missa cantata*, and four for the solemn exposition of the Most Blessed Sacrament, supplying with other lights for any larger number which may be required.

Moreover the S. C. exhorts the Most Reverend Ordinaries to

---

[1] AAS 34–112; CANON LAW DIGEST, 2, p. 389.

restore the venerable century-old tradition as soon as possible.

All things to the contrary notwithstanding. The 18th of August, 1949.

AAS 41–476; S. C. Rit., Decree, *Urbis et Orbis,* 18 Aug., 1949.

CANON 1274

Mass at the Altar of Exposition, Not Permitted (S. C. Rit., 26 June, 1950) **Private.**

A certain pious Association asked for the faculty whereby, in a much frequented sanctuary in a large city, Mass might be celebrated at the altar where the Most Blessed Sacrament was exposed, "lest there occur some irreverence toward the Most Blessed Sacrament if the Mass were celebrated at another altar."

Reply. *Non solere concedi;* 26 June, 1950, Prot. N. P. 50/50.

(Private); S. C. Rit., 26 June, 1950. *Monitor Ecclesiasticus,* 1952, p. 455.

CANON 1275

Forty Hours Not Permitted on Holy Thursday and Good Friday (S. C. Rit., 15 March, 1950) **Private.**

The Archconfraternity of the Immaculate Conception in a certain diocese asked the Sacred Congregation of Rites to confirm a custom, said to be immemorial, whereby the Forty Hours were celebrated on Holy Thursday and Good Friday.

Reply. *Negative.*

(Private); S. C. Rit., 15 March, 1950; Prot. N. N. 13/50. *Monitor Ecclesiasticus,* 1952, p. 456.

CANON 1276

Rosary of Our Lady: Crusade in England. Pius XII, Letter to Cardinal Griffin, 14 July, 1952 (AAS 44–624).

Encyclical of Pius XII, 15 Sept., 1951 (AAS 43–577). Text in *The Catholic Mind,* 1951, p. 826.

On the air. See **c. 925**; private reply of S. Paen., 9 May, 1952.

CANON 1278

Philippines: Blessed Virgin Mary, under title of Immaculate Conception, primary Patroness: secondary, the holy virgins SS. Pudentiana and Rose of Lima. See Pius XII, Apostolic Letter, 12 Sept., 1942 (AAS 34–336).

U. S. Military Vicariate: Immaculate Blessed Virgin Mary, Patroness. See Pius XII, Apostolic Letter, 8 May, 1942 (AAS 34–221).

CANON 1279

Sacred Art: Instruction on. See c. 1261; AAS 44–542.

CANON 1280

Sacred Art: Instruction on. See c. 1261; AAS 44–542.

CANON 1295

Sacred Processions: Participation by Women (S. C. Rit., 24 Aug., 1933) **Private.**

The Sacred Congregation of Rites sent the following reply to a letter of inquiry from the Bishop of Acireale:

Reply. There is no objection to women members of pious associations and Catholic Action taking part with lighted candles in Catholic liturgical processions, provided they march after the celebrant and the proper order be observed so that the more worthy associations march nearer to the celebrant, as was decided in the Decree of the Sacred Apostolic Visitation of Rome, published in the *Bolletino del Clero Romano* 1903, pp. 40–42, and also in the Decree of the S. C. Rit., 11 Dec., 1903, n. 4127.

(Private); S. C. Rit., 24 Aug., 1933. *Perfice Munus,* 1938, p. 581.

Altar Boys in Cassocks: Place in Processions (S. C. Rit., 25 Aug., 1938) **Private.**

The Sacred Congregation of Rites replied to an inquiry from the Bishop of Acireale:

Reply. As regards the proper place of the "little clergy" in processions, seeing that they are dressed like the seminarians of the diocesan seminary, Your Excellency is informed that these boys clothed in the clerical dress should march first under the cross of the secular clergy, or that of the cathedral chapter, before the students of the seminary.

(Private); S. C. Rit., 25 Aug., 1938. *Il Monitore Ecclesiastico,* 1938, p. 285.

CANON 1308

Canon 81: Gives no power to dispense from vows reserved to Holy See. See c. 81; AAS 41–158.

CANON 1322

Scope of the Church's *Magisterium* and Ministry (Pius XII, Letter to Hierarchy of Hungary, 2 Jan., 1949) **AAS 41–29.**

In this touching Letter to the Archbishops and Bishops of Hungary, Pius XII has this paragraph referring to Cardinal Mindszenty:

The fact that he vigorously resisted when he saw the liberty of the Church being daily impaired and restricted in a variety of ways, and when he perceived that, to the great injury of the faithful, her *magisterium* and ministry were being impeded — a *magisterium* and ministry which must be exercised not only in the churches, but also publicly in the open profession of the faith, in elementary and higher schools, in published writings, in pious pilgrimages to holy places and in the reunions of Catholic Action — this surely is not to his discredit, but entirely to his honor, for it was inspired by the vigilance which was part of his pastoral office.

AAS 41–29; Pius XII, Letter, 2 Jan., 1949.

Catholic Teaching: Its Purpose and Ideals. See c. 1372; AAS 42–395.

Dogma of the Assumption of Our Lady: Dogmatic Bull of Pius XII, *Munificentissimus Deus,* 1 Nov., 1950, defining the dogma (AAS 42–753). English text, *The Catholic Mind,* 1951, p. 65.

Homily of Pius XII, 30 Oct., 1950, in the Consistory prior to the definition of the dogma (AAS 42–774). *The Catholic Mind,* 1951, p. 78.

CANON 1323

Assumption of the Blessed Virgin Mary: Definition of the dogma; Pius XII, Ap. Const., *Munificentissimus Deus,* 1 Nov., 1950 (AAS 42–753).

Ceremonies of the definition, 1 Nov., 1950 (AAS 42–778).

Sacred Consistory of 30 Oct., 1950 (AAS 42–774).

Encyclical Letter to all Patriarchs, Primates, Archbishops, and other Ordinaries consulting them about the definition. Pius XII, 1 May, 1946 (AAS 42–782).

Oration to the assembled Cardinals, Archbishops, Bishops, and other Ordinaries gathered in Rome for the definition, 2 Nov., 1950 (AAS 42–784).

New Mass of the Assumption. S. C. Rit., 31 Oct., 1950 (AAS 42–793).

Council of Chalcedon: Encyclical of Pius XII, 8 Sept., 1951 (AAS 43–625).

CANON 1324

Mitigated Millenarianism, Unsafe Doctrine (Holy Office, 21 July, 1944) AAS 36–212.

A decree of the Holy Office is as follows :

In these latter years this Supreme Sacred Congregation of the Holy Office has more than once been asked what is to be thought of the system of *Mitigated Millenarianism,* which teaches that before the last judgment, either after many of the just have risen from the dead, or before this, Christ Our Lord is to come upon earth to reign in visible form.

Accordingly, after examining the matter in the plenary session of Wednesday, the 19th of July, 1944, and after having heard the opinions of the Reverend Consultors, the Eminent and Most Reverend Cardinals who are in charge of safeguarding matters of faith and morals decided to reply:

Reply. That *the system of Mitigated Millenarianism cannot safely be taught.*

And on the following Thursday, the 20th of the same month and year, His Holiness Pius XII, in the usual audience granted to the Most Reverend Assessor of the Holy Office, approved and confirmed this reply, and ordered that it be published.

Given at Rome, from the Palace of the Holy Office, 21 July, 1944.

AAS 36–212; Holy Office, 21 July, 1944. *Periodica,* 31–168 (Rosadini).

Date of Sources of Pentateuch: Literary Forms of First Eleven Chapters of Genesis (Bibl. Com., Letter, 16 Jan., 1948) AAS 40–45.

Letter addressed in French to Cardinal Suhard, Archbishop of Paris, by the Reverend Jacques M. Vosté, O.P., Secretary of the Biblical Commission:

Your Eminence:

The Holy Father has deigned to refer to the Pontifical Commission for Biblical Studies two questions which were recently submitted to him regarding the sources of the Pentateuch and the historicity of the first eleven chapters of Genesis. These two questions, with their respective considerations and hoped-for solutions, have been studied most attentively by the Very Reverend

Consultors and by the Eminent Cardinals who are members of the Commission. Pursuant to their deliberations, His Holiness, in the audience granted to the undersigned on the 16th of January, 1948, deigned to approve the following reply:

The Pontifical Biblical Commission is happy to acknowledge the filial confidence which inspired the proposal of the questions to it, and desires to respond by a sincere effort to promote biblical studies by securing for them, within the bounds of the traditional teaching of the Church, the most complete freedom. This freedom has been affirmed explicitly in the Encyclical of the present gloriously reigning Pontiff, *"Divino afflante Spiritu,"* in these words: "The Catholic exegete, urged by an active and courageous attachment to his specialty, and sincerely devoted to our Holy Mother the Church, must by no means hesitate to approach, even repeatedly, the difficult questions which have not yet been solved, not only in order to refute the objections of adversaries but also to try to find a solid explanation for them which will be in perfect accord with the teaching of the Church, particularly regarding the inerrancy of the Scriptures, and at the same time capable of fully meeting the certain conclusions of the profane sciences. The efforts of these valiant workers in the Lord's vineyard deserve to be judged not only with equity and justice but also with perfect charity; and this must be borne in mind by all the other children of the Church. The latter must be on their guard against that zeal, anything but prudent, which imagines it must attack or hold in suspicion whatever is new" (AAS 35–319).

If one will understand and interpret in the light of this recommendation of the Sovereign Pontiff the three official replies given by the Biblical Commission some years ago regarding the abovementioned questions, namely, the reply of 23 June 1905, about narratives in the historical books of Scripture which would have only the appearance of history (*Enchiridion Biblicum,* 154), that of 27 June, 1906 on the Mosaic authorship of the Pentateuch (*ibid.,* 174–177), and that of 30 June, 1909 on the historical character of the first three chapters of Genesis (*ibid.,* 332–339), one will agree that these replies constitute no objection against a further truly scientific examination of these problems in the light of the results achieved during the last forty years. Consequently the Biblical Commission does not believe that there is any need, at least for the present, to promulgate any new decrees on these questions.

As regards the authorship of the Pentateuch, already in the above-mentioned decree of 27 June, 1906 the Biblical Commission acknowledged it as permissible to affirm that Moses "in composing his work used written documents or oral traditions," and also to admit modifications and additions later than the time of Moses (*Ench. Bibl.*, 176–177). Today there is no one who doubts the existence of such sources or who refuses to admit a progressive growth of the Mosaic laws due to the social and religious conditions of later times, a progression which appears also in the historical narratives. However, even among non-Catholic exegetes, there are today very divergent opinions about the nature and number of these documents and about their denomination and date. There are even in various countries authors who for purely critical and historical reasons, without any apologetic motive, resolutely reject the theories which have hitherto been most in vogue, and who seek the explanation of some of the peculiarities of composition of the Pentateuch, not so much in the diversity of the supposed documentary sources, as in the peculiar psychology and particular methods of thought and expression among the ancient Orientals — of which we have more knowledge now than formerly — or in the variation of literary forms to fit diversities of subject-matter. Hence we invite Catholic scholars to study these problems impartially in the light of sound critical standards and the findings of other sciences which are related to the subject; such a study will establish beyond doubt the great part played by Moses and his profound influence as author and lawgiver.

The question of the literary forms of the first eleven chapters of Genesis is much more obscure and complex. These literary forms do not correspond to any of our classic categories, and cannot be judged in the light of either graeco-roman or modern literary types. It is therefore impossible either to deny or to affirm their historicity as a whole without unjustifiably applying to them the norms of a literary type to which they do not belong. Though it be agreed that these chapters are not history in the classical and modern sense, it must also be admitted that the presently available scientific data do not permit a *positive* solution to all the problems which they present. In this connection the primary task of scientific exegesis consists first of all in the careful study of all the literary, scientific, historical, cultural, and religious problems which are connected with these chapters; next, a close study should be made of the literary procedures of the ancient Oriental peoples, their psychology, their way of expressing themselves, and their very concept of historical truth; in a word all the data of paleontological and historical as well as of epigraphic and literary science should be assembled without prejudice. It is only thus that one may hope to get a clearer vision of the true nature of certain narratives of the early chapters of Genesis. To declare *a priori* that their narratives do not contain history in the modern sense would give the impression that they do not contain it in any sense, whereas the truth is that they relate in simple and figurative language, adapted to the minds of men not highly cultured, the fundamental truths prerequisite to the economy of salvation, and at the same time give a popular description of the origins of the human race and of the chosen people. In the meantime patience, the prudence and wisdom of life, must be practiced. And this also the Holy Father inculcates in the Encyclical already cited. "No one," says he, "should be astonished that all the difficulties have not yet been cleared away and settled. . . . This is no reason to lose courage; we must remember that in human sciences progress is like that which we observe in nature; growth begins little by little, and it is only after many labors that the fruit can be gathered. . . . One may therefore hope that these difficulties which today seem the most complicated and perplexing will, thanks to constant effort, one day be fully solved" (AAS 35–318).

AAS 40–45; Bibl. Com., Letter of Secretary, 16 Jan., 1948. Annotations, *Periodica,* 38–80 (Asensio).

True Sense of Catholic Doctrine That There Is No Salvation Outside the Church. A Catholic School Cannot Remain in Rebellion Against Ecclesiastical Authority (Holy Office, 8 Aug., 1949) Private.

This important Letter of the Holy Office is introduced by a letter of the Most Reverend Archbishop of Boston. We report first the introductory letter of the Archbishop and then the Letter of the Holy Office.

Letter of Archbishop Cushing

The Supreme Sacred Congregation of the Holy Office has

examined again the problem of Father Leonard Feeney and St. Benedict Center. Having studied carefully the publications issued by the Center, and having considered all the circumstances of this case, the Sacred Congregation has ordered me to publish, in its entirety, the letter which the same Congregation sent me on the 8th of August, 1949. The Supreme Pontiff, His Holiness, Pope Pius XII, has given full approval to this decision. In due obedience, therefore, we publish, in its entirety, the Latin text of the letter as received from the Holy Office with an English translation of the same approved by the Holy See.

Given at Boston, Mass., the 4th day of September, 1952.

Walter J. Furlong, Chancellor

☩ Richard J. Cushing, Archbishop of Boston.

Letter of the Holy Office

Prot. N. 122/49

From the Headquarters of the Holy Office,
Aug. 8, 1949.

Your Excellency:

This Supreme Sacred Congregation has followed very attentively the rise and the course of the grave controversy stirred up by certain associates of "St. Benedict Center" and "Boston College" in regard to the interpretation of that axiom: "Outside the Church there is no salvation."

After having examined all the documents that are necessary or useful in this matter, among them information from your Chancery, as well as appeals and reports in which the associates of "St. Benedict Center" explain their opinions and complaints, and also many other documents pertinent to the controversy, officially collected, the same Sacred Congregation is convinced that the unfortunate controversy arose from the fact that the axiom, "outside the Church there is no salvation," was not correctly understood and weighed, and that the same controversy was rendered more bitter by serious disturbance of discipline arising from the fact that some of the associates of the institutions mentioned above refused reverence and obedience to legitimate authorities.

Accordingly, the Most Eminent and Most Reverend Cardinals of this Supreme Congregation, in a plenary session held on

Wednesday, July 27, 1949, decreed, and the august Pontiff in an audience on the following Thursday, July 28, 1949, deigned to give his approval, that the following explanations pertinent to the doctrine, and also that invitations and exhortations relevant to discipline be given:

We are bound by divine and Catholic faith to believe all those things which are contained in the word of God, whether it be Scripture or Tradition, and are proposed by the Church to be believed as divinely revealed, not only through solemn judgment but also through the ordinary and universal teaching office (*Denzinger,* n. 1792).

Now, among those things which the Church has always preached and will never cease to preach is contained also that infallible statement by which we are taught that there is no salvation outside the Church.

However, this dogma must be understood in that sense in which the Church herself understands it. For, it was not to private judgments that Our Saviour gave for explanation those things that are contained in the deposit of faith, but to the teaching authority of the Church.

Now, in the first place, the Church teaches that in this matter there is question of a most strict command of Jesus Christ. For He explicitly enjoined on His apostles to teach all nations to observe all things whatsoever He Himself had commanded (Matt. 28:19–20).

Now, among the commandments of Christ, that one holds not the least place by which we are commanded to be incorporated by baptism into the Mystical Body of Christ, which is the Church, and to remain united to Christ and to His Vicar, through whom He Himself in a visible manner governs the Church on earth.

Therefore, no one will be saved who, knowing the Church to have been divinely established by Christ, nevertheless refuses to submit to the Church or withholds obedience from the Roman Pontiff, the Vicar of Christ on earth.

Not only did the Saviour command that all nations should enter the Church, but He also decreed the Church to be a means of salvation without which no one can enter the kingdom of eternal glory.

In His infinite mercy God has willed that the effects, necessary for one to be saved, of those helps to salvation which are directed toward man's final end, not by intrinsic necessity, but only by divine institution, can also be obtained in certain circumstances when those helps are used only in desire and longing. This we see clearly stated in the Sacred Council of Trent, both in reference to the sacrament of regeneration and in reference to the sacrament of penance (*Denzinger,* nn. 797, 807).

The same in its own degree must be asserted of the Church, in as far as she is the general help to salvation. Therefore, that one may obtain eternal salvation, it is not always required that he be incorporated into the Church actually as a member, but it is necessary that at least he be united to her by desire and longing.

However, this desire need not always be explicit, as it is in catechumens; but when a person is involved in invincible ignorance God accepts also an implicit desire, so called because it is included in that good disposition of soul whereby a person wishes his will to be conformed to the will of God.

These things are clearly taught in that dogmatic letter which was issued by the Sovereign Pontiff, Pope Pius XII, on June 29, 1943, *On the Mystical Body of Jesus Christ* (AAS, Vol. 35, an. 1943, p. 193 ff.). For in this letter the Sovereign Pontiff clearly distinguishes between those who are actually incorporated into the Church as members, and those who are united to the Church only by desire.

Discussing the members of which the Mystical Body is composed here on earth, the same august Pontiff says: "Actually only those are to be included as members of the Church who have been baptized and profess the true faith, and who have not been so unfortunate as to separate themselves from the unity of the Body, or been excluded by legitimate authority for grave faults committed."

Toward the end of this same encyclical letter, when most affectionately inviting to unity those who do not belong to the body of the Catholic Church, he mentions those who "are related to the Mystical Body of the Redeemer by a certain unconscious yearning and desire," and these he by no means excludes from eternal salvation, but on the other hand states that they are in a condition "in which they cannot be sure of their salvation" since "they still remain deprived of those many heavenly gifts and helps which can only be enjoyed in the Catholic Church" (AAS, l. c., p. 243).

With these wise words he reproves both those who exclude from eternal salvation all united to the Church only by implicit desire, and those who falsely assert that men can be saved equally well in every religion (cf. Pope Pius IX, Allocution, *Singulari quadam,* in *Denzinger,* n. 1641 ff.; also Pope Pius IX in the encyclical letter, *Quanto conficiamur moerore,* in *Denzinger,* n. 1677).

But it must not be thought that any kind of desire of entering the Church suffices that one may be saved. It is necessary that the desire by which one is related to the Church be animated by perfect charity. Nor can an implicit desire produce its effect, unless a person has supernatural faith: "For he who comes to God must believe that God exists and is a rewarder of those who seek Him" (Heb. 11:6). The Council of Trent declares (Session VI, chap. 8): "Faith is the beginning of man's salvation, the foundation and root of all justification, without which it is impossible to please God and attain to the fellowship of His children" (*Denzinger,* n. 801).

From what has been said it is evident that those things which are proposed in the periodical *From the Housetops,* fascicle 3, as the genuine teaching of the Catholic Church are far from being such and are very harmful both to those within the Church and those without.

From these declarations which pertain to doctrine, certain conclusions follow which regard discipline and conduct, and which cannot be unknown to those who vigorously defend the necessity by which all are bound of belonging to the true Church and of submitting to the authority of the Roman Pontiff and of the Bishops "whom the Holy Ghost has placed . . . to rule the Church" (Acts 20:28).

Hence, one cannot understand how the St. Benedict Center can consistently claim to be a Catholic school and wish to be accounted such, and yet not conform to the prescriptions of canons 1381 and 1382 of the Code of Canon Law, and continue to exist as a source of discord and rebellion against ecclesiastical authority and as a source of the disturbance of many consciences.

Furthermore, it is beyond understanding how a member of a religious Institute, namely Father Feeney, presents himself as a "Defender of the Faith," and at the same time does not hesitate to attack the catechetical instruction proposed by lawful authorities, and has not even feared to incur grave sanctions threatened by the sacred canons because of his serious violations of his duties as a religious, a priest, and an ordinary member of the Church.

Finally, it is in no wise to be tolerated that certain Catholics shall claim for themselves the right to publish a periodical, for the purpose of spreading theological doctrines, without the permission of competent Church authority, called the *"imprimatur,"* which is prescribed by the sacred canons.

Therefore, let them who in grave peril are ranged against the Church seriously bear in mind that after "Rome has spoken" they cannot be excused even by reasons of good faith. Certainly, their bond and duty of obedience toward the Church is much graver than that of those who as yet are related to the Church "only by an unconscious desire." Let them realize that they are children of the Church, lovingly nourished by her with the milk of doctrine and the sacraments, and hence, having heard the clear voice of their Mother, they cannot be excused from culpable ignorance, and therefore to them apply without any restriction that principle: submission to the Catholic Church and to the Sovereign Pontiff is required as necessary for salvation.

In sending this letter, I declare my profound esteem, and remain,

Your Excellency's most devoted,

✝ F. Cardinal Marchetti-Selvaggiani.

A. Ottaviani, *Assessor.*

(**Private**); Holy Office, 8 Aug., 1949. *The Catholic Mind,* 50, p. 749.

Encyclical, *Humani Generis:* On some false opinions which threaten to undermine the foundations of Catholic doctrine. Pius XII, 12 Aug., 1950 (AAS 42–561). English text, *The Catholic Mind,* 1950, p. 688.

The "New Morality" Condemned: Pius XII dealt with this important subject in two separate documents:

1) Radio Address "on the formation of a right conscience in the young," 23 March, 1952 (AAS 44–270).

2) Allocution to the "Fédération Mondiale des Jeunesses Féminines Catholiques," 18 April, 1952 (AAS 44–413).

Both documents are annotated in *Periodica,* 41–223 and 231 by Hürth. An appendix to these annotations discusses the binding force of papal pronouncements in addresses of this sort.

CANON 1325

Discussions With Non-Catholics (Holy Office, *Monitum*, 5 June, 1948) **AAS 40-257.**

Since it has been learned that in various places, contrary to the prescriptions of the sacred canons and without previous permission from the Holy See, mixed congresses of Catholics with non-Catholics have been held, in which matters of faith were discussed, all are reminded that according to canon 1325, § 3, lay people as well as clerics whether secular or religious are forbidden to attend such meetings without the above-mentioned permission. And much less is it allowed that Catholics should convoke or institute such congresses. Accordingly Ordinaries are to insist that these prescriptions be exactly observed by all.

Of still greater importance is the observance of these provisions when there is question of so called "ecumenical" congresses, which Catholics, whether lay or clerical, are in no wise permitted to attend without the previous consent of the Holy See.

Since moreover, both in the aforesaid meetings and out of them, acts of mixed worship have not infrequently been done, all are again warned that all communication in sacred things is entirely forbidden, according to canons 1258 and 731, § 2.

Given at Rome, from the Holy Office, 5 June, 1948.

AAS 40-257; Holy Office, *Monitum*, 5 June, 1948.
Periodica, 37-174 (Hürth).

Ecumenical Congress at Amsterdam (Pastoral Letter of Netherlands Bishops, 31 July, 1948) **Private.**

Beloved Faithful:

In the near future, from the 22nd of August to the 5th of September, the "Ecumenical Council of Churches" will hold a Congress to deal with the subject "The Plan of God and the Disorder of the World." This Congress on so vital a subject will be held in our own country, in Amsterdam, and will undoubtedly attract the attention of many of our Catholic people. For this reason alone We deemed it Our duty to address a Pastoral Letter to you on the subject.

Many non-Catholic Christians have for a long time been distressed by the division which exists among Christians in religious matters. They see that this division is contrary to the precept of Our Lord Jesus Christ and that it necessarily leads to consequences which are harmful to the salvation of men. This anxiety has given rise to the so-called Ecumenical Movement, which seeks to bring about a new religious unity among all who are willing to acknowledge Jesus Christ as their God and Saviour. Shortly before the latest world war, this Movement achieved a more permanent organization by forming what is called the Ecumenical Council of Churches; and the Congress soon to be held in Amsterdam will be the first complete Congress of this Ecumenical Council of Churches.

Beloved Faithful, the Catholic Church too — and no one more than she — is grieved by the division among Christians in religious matters. She too understands how harmful are its consequences. Moreover she freely grants that these efforts toward a new religious unity are motivated in many cases by a right intention. But notwithstanding all this she knows that she cannot take part; and consequently the Holy Catholic Church can in no way participate in the Amsterdam Congress.

The reason why she holds aloof is not the fear of loss of authority, nor any merely tactical consideration; but it is this alone: the Catholic Church knows that she must absolutely stand firm in the faithful performance of the commission entrusted to her by Jesus Christ.

For she is the one, holy, catholic, and apostolic Church, which Jesus Christ established, in order, through her, to make His work perennial; she is the Mystical Body of Christ, the Spouse of Christ. In her the unity which Christ willed exists forever, because of His promise that the gates of hell would not prevail against her (Matt. 16:18). For this reason the division among Christians can be ended in one way only, by return to the Church, by return to that unity which in her has remained intact. If the Church were to take part in the efforts to create a new religious unity, and were to do so on a par with others, she would by that very fact concede that the unity which Christ willed has not endured in her, and hence that strictly speaking the Church of Christ does not exist. Never can she make such a concession: for she is the one holy Church of Christ, the one Mystical Body of Christ, the one Spouse of Christ. She must precisely by her abstention constantly proclaim that in her the unity which

Christ willed has been preserved and that in her this unity is ever accessible to all.

There is also another reason which shows that this abstention is imperative. True unity cannot exist without unity of faith; and this is being daily more fully realized also by many members of the Ecumenical Movement. But how can this unity of faith be secured? Our Lord Jesus Christ commanded Peter and the other Apostles, and their successors, to preach the Gospel in His name and by His authority: "He that heareth you, heareth me; and he that despiseth you, despiseth me" (Luke 16:10). To this end He promised them the assistance of His Holy Spirit. By the power of this Holy Spirit the Supreme Pontiffs and the Bishops, as the successors of Saint Peter and of the other Apostles, have preserved the revealed truth inviolate and proclaimed it with infallible authority; and they will not cease to do so until the second coming of the Lord. He who accepts their word accepts the word of Christ, and by that very fact enters into the unity of the faith. How, then, could the Supreme Pontiff and the Bishops enter into a discussion with others to consider whether they might not perhaps have misunderstood the word of divine revelation and taught human doctrine instead of divine truth? This would amount to defection from the faith, rejection of the promise of Christ, doubting the power of the Holy Spirit. Never could they do such a thing. They have but one course, to preach constantly the doctrine of Christ with infallible authority, and so preserve the unity of the faith.

For these reasons the question of participation by Catholics in the Amsterdam Congress cannot even be considered. Nevertheless we will follow its proceedings with interest. For it springs from the deep and sincere desire of many persons who wish to acknowledge Christ as their God and Saviour, to attain to the unity which Christ willed. How indeed could We, who are placed by the Holy Spirit, under a Successor of Saint Peter, to keep the Church united and to extend it, remain indifferent or cold toward a sincere effort for unity? It cannot be a matter of indifference to Us whether this Congress is to be an advance or a retrogression; it will be an advance if it nourishes a desire for the Mother Church and for the unity which is hers; it would be a retrogression if it should result in the wide acceptance of a sort of unity very different from that which Christ gave.

A return to the Mother Church — that, Beloved Faithful, is
the one way to true unity. Yet, as we all know, there is an
inveterate prejudice against taking this course. Because of the
divergencies which existed at the time the division began, now
that the breach has gone on widening for centuries, the dissidents
are so far away from and so foreign to the Church that they no
longer understand her language. In many cases a return to the
Church is impossible without a grave interior struggle and great
personal sacrifices. There can be no sincere return unless the
human mind be enlightened and the human will be moved by the
grace of God. And we know that God wants us to pray to Him
for the outpouring of His grace.

Wherefore We earnestly invite you all, priests and faithful
people, to pray fervently. Pray during these days for those who
are taking part in the Congress and for the countless other non-
Catholic Christians who eagerly look for unity, who really
adhere to Christ and live in His love, who although separated
from the flock of Christ, yet look to the Church, sometimes
without fully realizing it, as the one door of salvation. Pray first
for those who are in a position of leadership among non-Catholic
Christians; they have a great personal responsibility for the
simple faithful depend on their guidance, having often not
sufficient talents to arrive at a true understanding of the matter
through their own efforts. Pray to our heavenly Father, who
"will have all men to be saved and to come to the knowledge
of the truth" (1 Tim. 2:4). Pray to Him through Jesus Christ,
who is "always living to make intercession for us" (Heb. 7:25).
Pray to Him in the one Holy Spirit, who gives life to the one
Mystical Body of Christ. Pray that all may attain to that true
unity which is not man-made but was given to this world by
Christ Our Lord.

But remember, Beloved Faithful, that your example is needed
no less than your prayers. In other days defection from the
Church was occasioned by the unworthy lives of many Catholics.
The Church herself put an end to that by the salutary reform
which was effected (in the head and in the members) by the
Council of Trent. And so now the greatest encouragement toward
a return to the Church will be our manifestation of the holiness
of our faith by the holiness of our lives and works.

If in other times, in their defense of Catholic unity, Catholics were not always guided by a spirit of charity, and were therefore not mindful of the words of the Apostle "doing the truth in charity" (Eph. 4:15), and consequently were not entirely free from blame for the alienation which took place between ourselves and non-Catholic Christians, such certainly was not the spirit of our Holy Mother the Church. For she is and ever remains the holy Church: holy in her worship, in her Sacraments, in her Sacrifice, and in the communication of the supernatural life which she imparts through these means. She remains holy in her doctrine, which comes from God and leads to God; holy in her laws, which aim only at the glory of God and the salvation of men; holy as the mother of great Saints in every age. And this holiness is a constant proof of her divine origin. The members of the Church, however, are and remain men: in whom what is human — sometimes indeed too human (*Mit brennender Sorge*) — may break out; and these human and at times too human elements can be a source of scandal and prevent many persons from seeing the true holiness of the Church.

And therefore also in these times we have a grave obligation in conscience. Now that a strong and manifest desire for unity has arisen among many persons who acknowledge Christ, it is imperative that our whole lives should be imbued with the spirit of Christ; and that in all our activities, in every walk of life, we should seek only Christ and the spread of His Kingdom. Now if ever we must especially observe that precept of Christ, "So let your light shine before men, that they may see your good works, and glorify your Father who is in heaven" (Matt. 5:16). Now if ever we must manifest in our own lives the holiness of the Church. God grant that all may recognize this duty; and in its fulfillment, may the Holy Spirit, who is the Spirit of Christ, "help our infirmity" (Rom. 8:26).

Finally, Beloved Faithful, We order that in all churches which belong to the ecclesiastical Province of the Netherlands, and in all chapels of which a rector is in charge, a solemn Mass or at least a *Missa cantata* be offered, to obtain from God that all may share in the unity of the Church. The Mass will be the one indicated in the Roman Missal as the votive Mass for the removal of schism. We trust that you will be united as closely as possible in this Holy Sacrifice.

And let this Our Pastoral Letter be read in the usual way

from the pulpit during all the Masses which are publicly announced, in all the churches of Our Ecclesiastical Province and in all chapels of which a rector is in charge, on Sunday the 22nd of August.

Given at Utrecht, 31 July, 1948.

Signed by the Archbishop of Utrecht and the Bishops of Breda, Roermond, Haarlem, and Bois-le-Duc.

(**Private**); Bishops of the Netherlands, Pastoral Letter, 31 July, 1948. *Periodica,* 37–390 (Tromp). *The Catholic Mind,* 1948, p. 718.

The "Ecumenical Movement": Instruction (Holy Office, 20 Dec., 1949) **AAS 42–142.**

An Instruction of the Holy Office, addressed to the Ordinaries of places, on the "Ecumenical Movement" is as follows:

The Catholic Church, although she does not take part in congresses and other conventions called "ecumenical," yet has never ceased, as is clear from many Pontifical documents, nor will she in future ever cease, to follow with the most intense interest and to promote by earnest prayers to God, all efforts toward the attainment of what is so dear to the Heart of Christ Our Lord, namely, that all who believe in Him "may be made perfect in one."[1]

For she embraces with truly maternal affection all who return to her as the true Church of Christ; and hence, worthy of all praise and encouragement are all those plans and projects which, with the consent of Ecclesiastical Authority, have been undertaken and are being carried forward, either for the proper Catholic instruction of future converts or for the more thorough training of persons already converted to the faith.

Now in many parts of the world, as a result of various external events and changes of views on the part of people, but especially in consequence of the common prayers of the faithful through the grace of the Holy Spirit, there has grown constantly in the minds of many persons separated from the Catholic Church the desire for a return to unity on the part of all who believe in the Lord Christ. To the children of the Church this is surely a cause of true and holy joy in the Lord, and at the same time an invitation to help all those who sincerely seek the truth, by

---

[1] John 17:23.

earnest prayer to God imploring for them the grace of light and strength.

However, some of the initiatives that have hitherto been taken by various individuals or groups, with the aim of reconciling dissident Christians to the Catholic Church, although inspired by the best of intentions, are not always based on right principles, or if they are, yet they are not free from special dangers, as experience too has already shown. Hence this Supreme Sacred Congregation, which has the responsibility of conserving in its entirety and protecting the deposit of the faith, has seen fit to recall to mind and to prescribe the following:

I. Since the above-mentioned "union" is a matter which pertains primarily to the authority and office of the Church, it should be attended to with special care by the Bishops, whom "the Holy Ghost hath placed to rule the Church of God."[2] They should, therefore, not only diligently and effectively watch over this entire activity, but also prudently promote and direct it, for the purpose of both helping those who seek the truth and the true Church, and protecting the faithful against the dangers which may easily flow from the activity of this "Movement."

Hence they must in the first place be fully aware of everything that has been and is being done through this "Movement" in their dioceses. For this purpose they shall designate well-qualified priests who, according to the doctrine and norms prescribed by the Holy See, for example by the Encyclicals *"Satis cognitum,"*[3] *"Mortalium animos,"*[4] and *"Mystici Corporis Christi,"*[5] shall pay close attention to everything which concerns the "Movement" and report thereon to the Bishops in the manner and at the time which they shall prescribe.

They shall watch with special care over publications which may be issued in any form by Catholics on this matter, and shall see that the canons "on the previous censure and prohibition of books" (canons 1384 seq.) are observed. And they shall not fail to do the same with regard to publications of non-Catholics on the same subject, in as far as these are published, or read, or sold by Catholics.

---

[2] Acts 20:28.
[3] *Acta Leonis XIII,* Vol. 16 (1897), p. 157.
[4] AAS, Vol. 20 (1928), p. 5.
[5] *Ibid.,* Vol. 35 (1943), p. 193.

They shall also diligently provide whatever may be of service to non-Catholics who desire to know the Catholic faith; they shall designate persons and Offices to which these non-Catholics may go for consultation; and *a fortiori* they shall see to it that those who are already converted to the faith shall easily find means of more exact and deeper instruction in the Catholic faith, and of leading a more positively religious life, especially through appropriate meetings and group assemblies, through Spiritual Exercises and other works of piety.

II. As regards *the manner and method of proceeding in this work,* the Bishops themselves will make regulations as to what is to be done and what is to be avoided, and shall see that these are observed by all. They shall also be on guard lest, on the false pretext that more attention should be paid to the points on which we agree than to those on which we differ, a dangerous indifferentism be encouraged, especially among persons whose training in theology is not deep and whose practice of their faith is not very strong. For care must be taken lest, in the so-called "irenic" spirit of to-day, through comparative study and the vain desire for a progressively closer mutual approach among the various professions of faith, Catholic doctrine — either in its dogmas or in the truths which are connected with them — be so conformed or in a way adapted to the doctrines of dissident sects, that the purity of Catholic doctrine be impaired, or its genuine and certain meaning be obscured.

Also they must restrain that dangerous manner of speaking which generates false opinions and fallacious hopes incapable of realization; for example, to the effect that the teachings of the Encyclicals of the Roman Pontiffs on the return of dissidents to the Church, on the constitution of the Church, on the Mystical Body of Christ, should not be given too much importance seeing that they are not all matters of faith, or, what is worse, that in matters of dogma even the Catholic Church has not yet attained the fullness of Christ, but can still be perfected from outside. They shall take particular care and shall firmly insist that, in going over the history of the Reformation and the Reformers, the defects of Catholics be not so exaggerated and the faults of the Reformers be so dissimulated, or that things which are rather accidental be not so emphasized, that what is most essential, namely the defection from the Catholic faith, be scarcely any longer seen or felt. Finally, they shall take precautions lest, through an excessive and false external activity, or through imprudence and an excited manner of proceeding, the end in view be rather harmed than served.

Therefore the *whole* and *entire* Catholic doctrine is to be presented and explained: by no means is it permitted to pass over in silence or to veil in ambiguous terms the Catholic truth regarding the nature and way of justification, the constitution of the Church, the primacy of jurisdiction of the Roman Pontiff, and the only true union by the return of the dissidents to the one true Church of Christ. It should be made clear to them that, in returning to the Church, they will lose nothing of that good which by the grace of God has hitherto been implanted in them, but that it will rather be supplemented and completed by their return. However, one should not speak of this in such a way that they will imagine that in returning to the Church they are bringing to it something substantial which it has hitherto lacked. It will be necessary to say these things clearly and openly, first because it is the truth that they themselves are seeking, and moreover because outside the truth no true union can ever be attained.

III. With regard especially to *mixed assemblies and conferences of Catholics with non-Catholics*, which in recent times have begun to be held in many places to promote "union" in the faith, there is need of quite peculiar vigilance and control on the part of Ordinaries. For if on the one hand these meetings afford the desired opportunity to spread among non-Catholics the knowledge of Catholic doctrine, which is generally not sufficiently known to them, yet on the other hand they easily involve no slight danger of indifferentism for Catholics. In cases where there seems to be some hope of good results, the Ordinary shall see that the thing is properly managed, designating for these meetings priests who are as well qualified as possible to explain and defend Catholic doctrine properly and appropriately. The faithful, however, should not attend these meetings unless they have obtained special permission from Ecclesiastical Authority, and this shall be given only to those who are known to be well instructed and strong in their faith. Where there is no apparent hope of good results, or where the affair involves special dangers on other grounds, the faithful are to be prudently kept away from the meetings, and the meetings themselves are soon to be ended or gradually suppressed. As experience teaches that larger meetings of this sort usually bear little fruit and involve greater danger, these should be permitted only after very careful consideration.

To *colloquies between Catholic and non-Catholic theologians,* none should be sent but priests who have shown themselves truly fit for such work by their knowledge of theology and their firm adherence to the principles and norms which the Church has laid down in this matter.

IV. All the aforesaid conferences and meetings, public and non-public, large and small, which are called for the purpose of affording an opportunity for the Catholic and the non-Catholic party for the sake of discussion to treat of matters of faith and morals, each presenting on even terms the doctrine of his own faith, are subject to the prescriptions of the Church which were recalled to mind in the *Monitum, "Cum compertum,"* of this Congregation under date of 5 June, 1948.[6] Hence mixed congresses are not absolutely forbidden; but they are not to be held without the previous permission of the competent Ecclesiastical Authority. The *Monitum,* however, does not apply to catechetical instructions, even when given to many together, nor to conferences in which Catholic doctrine is explained to non-Catholics who are prospective converts: even though the opportunity is afforded for the non-Catholics to explain also the doctrine of their church so that they may understand clearly and thoroughly in what respect it agrees with the Catholic doctrine and in what it differs therefrom.

Neither does the said *Monitum* apply to those mixed meetings of Catholics and non-Catholics in which the discussion does not turn upon faith and morals but upon ways and means of defending the fundamental principles of the natural law or of the Christian religion against the enemies of God who are now leagued together, or where the question is how to restore social order, or other topics of that nature. Even in these meetings, as is evident, Catholics may not approve or concede anything which is in conflict with divine revelation or with the doctrine of the Church even on social questions.

---

[6] AAS 40–257; reported above in this same volume, under canon 1325.

As to *local* conferences and conventions which are within the scope of the *Monitum* as above explained, the Ordinaries of places are given, for three years from the publication of this Instruction,[7] the faculty of granting the required previous permission of the Holy See, on the following conditions:

1. That *communicatio in sacris* be entirely avoided;

2. that the presentations of the matter be duly inspected and directed;

3. that at the close of each year a report be made to this Supreme Sacred Congregation, stating where such meetings were held and what experience was gathered from them.

As regards the *colloquies of theologians* above mentioned, the same faculty for the same length of time is granted to the Ordinary of the place where such colloquies are held, or to the Ordinary delegated for this work by the common consent of the other Ordinaries, under the same conditions as above, but with the further requirement that the report to this Sacred Congregation state also what questions were treated, who were present, and who the speakers were for either side.

As for the *interdiocesan conferences and congresses, either national or international,* the previous permission of the Holy See, special for each case, is always required; and in the petition asking for it, it must also be stated what are the questions to be treated and who the speakers are to be. And it is not allowed, before this permission has been obtained, to begin the external preparation of such meetings or to collaborate with non-Catholics who begin such preparation.

V. Although in all these meetings and conferences any communication whatsoever in worship must be avoided, yet the recitation in common of the Lord's Prayer or of some prayer approved by the Catholic Church, is not forbidden for opening or closing the said meetings.

VI. Although each Ordinary has the right and duty to conduct, promote, and preside over this work in his own diocese, yet the cooperation of several Bishops will be appropriate or even necessary in establishing offices and works to observe, study, and control this work *as a whole*. Accordingly it will rest with

---

[7] The date of *publication* is 31 January, 1950.

the Ordinaries themselves to confer together and consider how a proper uniformity of action and coordination can be obtained.

VII. Religious Superiors are bound to watch and to see to it that their subjects adhere strictly and faithfully to the prescriptions laid down by the Holy See or by the local Ordinaries in this matter.

In order that so noble a work as the "union" of all Christians in one true faith and Church may daily grow into a more conspicuous part of the entire care of souls, and that the whole Catholic people may more earnestly implore this "union" from Almighty God, it will certainly be of assistance that in some appropriate way, for example through Pastoral Letters, the faithful be instructed regarding these questions and projects, the prescriptions of the Church in the matter, and the reasons on which they are based. All, especially priests and religious, should be exhorted and warmly encouraged to be zealous by their prayers and sacrifices to ripen and promote this work, and all should be reminded that nothing more effectively paves the way for the erring to find the truth and to embrace the Church than the faith of Catholics, when it is confirmed by the example of upright living.

Given at Rome, from the Holy Office, 20 Dec., 1949.

AAS 42–142; Holy Office, Instruction, 20 Dec., 1949. *Periodica,* 39–204 (Hürth) ; *Monitor Ecclesiasticus,* 1950, p. 21 (Boyer) ; *The Jurist,* 10 (1950), p. 206.

Communists: Those who profess, defend, or propagate their materialistic and anti-Christian doctrine incur excommunication as apostates from the Catholic faith. See **c. 2314;** AAS 41–334.

CANON 1329

Catechetical Instruction: Letter of Pius XII to Cardinal Stritch, presiding over the Ninth National Catechetical Congress, 14 Sept., 1951 (AAS 43–778).

CANON 1341

Preaching for Mission Collections. See **c. 622;** AAS 44–549.

CANON 1350

Excessive Nationalism to Be Avoided: Instruction to Missionaries in China (S. C. Prop. Fid., Epiphany, 1920) **Private.**

To put into effect the prescriptions of the Letter of Benedict XV, *Maximum illud,* the Sacred Congregation for the Propagation of the Faith, on the Feast of Epiphany, 1920, issued an Instruction of which the following is a brief summary:

Missionaries are to avoid efforts to propagate their own national language among the peoples to whom they are sent; they are not to introduce the laws or customs of their own land, especially in the matter of feasts, fast and abstinence; they are not to promote the subordination of the lands where they are working as missionaries to the preponderant power of their own nation; let them abstain from promoting political designs or temporal business of any kind either with their own country or other countries; let them encourage the people to obey the civil authorities; let them carefully observe the provisions of canon 1386 regarding the publication etc. of books, papers, and periodicals, especially on political matters. The mission papers and magazines should reflect zeal for the Kingdom of God, not for the prestige of their own country.

(**Private**); S. C. Prop. Fid., Epiphany, 1920. This summary is taken from the text of the Instruction in *Primum Concilium Sinense,* pp. 372–375.

Collecting Money for Missions: Instruction on. See **c.** *622*; AAS 44–549.

Contribution of European and American Dioceses to Foreign Mission Clergy: Replying to a letter suggesting that European dioceses be invited to send missionaries to Japan, the Cardinal Prefect of the Sacred Congregation for the Propagation of the Faith recalls the practice by which the S. C. has for many years encouraged the formation of such institutions as the Paris Seminary for Foreign Missions and of various Missionary Institutes. It is, he says, by encouraging vocations to such institutions, rather than by direct sending of diocesan priests to the mission field, that the dioceses can best contribute to the foreign mission work. Text of Letter (20 Feb., 1951) in *Monitor Ecclesiasticus,* 1951, p. 449. Annotations, *ibid.* (Paventi).

Missions: Address of Pius XII, 28 April, 1952, to the national directors and other officials of the Pontifical Society for the Propagation of the Faith (AAS 44–425). English text, *The Catholic Mind,* 1952, p. 445.

Encyclical of Pius XII on Foreign Missions, 2 June, 1951 (AAS 43–497). English text, *The Catholic Mind,* 1951, p. 574. Annotations, *Monitor Ecclesiasticus,* 1951, p. 406 (Paventi).

Letter of Pius XII on the occasion of the Foreign Mission Congress in Rome, 9 Aug., 1950 (AAS 42–725).

Ordinaries of Italy Urged to Lend Priests to Other Dioceses (in Italy and elsewhere) where they are insufficient. S. C. Consist., 24 Oct., 1951 (AAS 44–231).

Schismatics: Norms concerning sacraments and ecclesiastical burial. See c. 731; private reply of Holy Office, 15 Nov., 1941.

CANON 1352

Education of the Clergy in Brazil: Prefect of S. C. Sem., Letter, 7 March, 1950 (AAS 42–836).

CANON 1363

Practice of the S. C. of Seminaries Regarding Admission of Ex-Postulants and Students From Apostolic Schools (S. C. Sem. et Univ., 12 Jan., 1950) Private.

A Letter from the S. C. of Seminaries and Universities in reply to some questions presented by the Vicar General of Cologne, is as follows:

N. 2748/40/20   12 January, 1950

We are replying to your inquiries of January 4, and are herewith giving the clarifications which are desired by the Most Reverend Vicar General of Cologne in regard to the Decree of 25 July, 1941.[1]

1. We quite understand the attitude of the Sacred Congregation of Religious,[2] since the case of clerics passing to a more austere life is very different as a rule from that of religious who leave their community to enter the diocesan clergy. In fact, the Code of Canon Law provides sanctions for this latter case, but not for the former.

2. This Sacred Congregation insists on the application of the aforesaid Decree as to that which concerns it, namely, the admission of ex-religious to a Seminary. But, to expedite and facilitate the practice (which in many cases can be a mere formality, implying nothing unfavorable to the candidate), it is better that the Most Excellent Ordinaries and the Most Reverend Curiae send us, together with the petition, a clear documentation

---

[1] Cf. AAS 33–371; CANON LAW DIGEST, 2, p. 426.

[2] Cf. private reply of 11 May, 1942; CANON LAW DIGEST, 2, p. 166.

of the earlier record of the aspirant to the priesthood, with testimonials (in the original or certified copy) from the religious
Superiors and if possible also from other ecclesiastical persons.

3. Among those who have belonged "by any title" to a religious family, we continue to include also students of religious
schools which are destined to form religious vocations ("apostolic
schools") and these only. Of course the manner of handling the
case of a youthful candidate for the religious life who has contracted no canonical bond, is quite different from that to be used
in the case of a religious in the strict sense.

We ask Your Reverence to inform any of the Most Reverend
Ordinaries who may ask you about the matter that there is a
very grave reason for these dispositions. Sometimes religious
Superiors, in order to get rid of subjects whose vocations are
deficient, make it easier for them to get into the ranks of the
secular clergy. So it happens that there may be among the clergy
some ex-religious who are not very edifying. If religious Superiors
are bound in conscience to present sincerely the true condition
of affairs, they will conceal nothing in giving their testimonials,
and thus it will be less easy for persons with deficient vocations
to penetrate the ranks of the secular clergy.

(**Private**); S. C. Sem. et Univ., Letter of Cardinal Pizzardo, 12 Jan.,
1950. *Periodica,* 41–360; annotations, *ibid.,* p. 363 (Hecht). Hecht respectfully points out that the *extensive* provisions of the above practice cannot
be urged as a matter of law. For some of these declarations, in as much as
they clearly go beyond the existing law, require promulgation according to
canon 17, § 2; and they are not promulgated by a private document such
as the above.

CANON 1365

The Study of Pedagogy in Seminaries (S. C. Sem. et Stud., 21 Dec., 1944) AAS 37–173.

An Instruction of the Sacred Congregation of Seminaries and
Universities to the Most Excellent Ordinaries on the Importance
of the Study of Pedagogy in Seminaries, is as follows:

Your Excellency:

The training of seminarians in pedagogy, didactics, and catechetics has always been the object of many cares and grave solicitude on the part of this Sacred Congregation.

It is clear from the pages of the Gospel, from the letters of the
Apostles and from the whole history of the Church, that the priest

of Christ is not only a minister of worship and an official of the liturgy, but also an educator, an instructor, charged with the training of minds and consciences. In fact, in the commission of Christ to the Apostles, the *magisterium* or teaching office precedes the sacramental and liturgical *ministry: Going, therefore, teach ye all nations, baptizing them in the name of the Father, and of the Son, and of the Holy Ghost* (Matt. 28, 19).

In obedience to this divine command the Apostles actually placed the *magisterium* before all other activities; so that Saint Paul could say: *Christ sent me not to baptize, but to preach the Gospel* (I Cor., 1:17).

The reason for this precedence of the teaching office is evident: a soul cannot be endowed with grace until it has been enlightened with truth.

It follows that, for priests, *pedagogy,* dealing with education in general, *didactics,* which is concerned in general with teaching and method, and *catechetics,* that is, didactics applied to the teaching of religion, are of primary importance.

It might be objected that the basic laws of education are easily learned by experience, and that in the field of pedagogy good natural dispositions joined to the Christian virtues and aided by grace have always borne abundant fruits. But it is also true that art perfects nature, and religious education may truly be called the *art of arts.*

The importance of this preparation has greatly increased in recent times. Priests are often called upon to serve as Assistants in Catholic Action and as Directors of religious associations, offices which are primarily educational. "The ecclesiastical Assistants," said His Holiness Pius XII (in his discourse to the Directors of Italian Catholic Action, September 4th, 1940), "have the special task of forming and instructing the members of Catholic Action, nourishing and building them up in the pastures of a safe, sound and deep spirituality."

Still more recently a new field has been opened to the clergy in the government schools, in which they have to teach religion. Now this environment, which receives the greater number of the young people who are studying, presents, as has often been noted, special needs and difficulties. These demand of the teacher more than ordinary pedagogical qualities, the lack of which is largely responsible for the scarcity of results thus far achieved.

It is clear, therefore, that today more urgently than in the past, there is need of giving to candidates for the priesthood proper training also in the matter of pedagogy and didactics.

Hence the following provisions are made.

I. *The Course in Philosophy.*

A theoretical-practical course in pedagogy and didactics shall be established (two years, one hour a week); this may be entrusted to the professor of philosophy, in as much as these subjects are closely connected with psychology and ethics.

It will not be possible in this course to give an exhaustive treatment of the various aspects of the matter; but the general principles and directives should be given clearly and precisely:

The concept of education;

Its purpose, principles, means;

The nature of the person to be educated in his educational development through successive age-periods;

The educator: his duties, qualifications;

The right to educate: the Church, the family, the State;

Educational milieu: the family, the school, the college, educational institutions: chapel exercises, associations, sports;

Didactics: general notions, systems, methods suited to various kinds of teaching.

All these matters must be exemplified from time to time from the actual practice of the principles on the part of the great Saints and educators who have adorned the ancient and modern history of the Church.

To these should be added by way of complement outlines of the history of pedagogy, for the purpose of giving the students the proper norm for distinguishing what is true and good from what is false and dangerous in the various theories and methods.

Thus future priests will at least not be inferior to the teachers in elementary schools, who in their normal training have had courses in pedagogy and the history of education, and they will also be better able to make their way in the various departments of the sacred ministry, especially in the teaching of religion. (A footnote at this point calls attention to various books on pedagogy: first of all the Encyclical of Pius XI on Education, then a number of Italian works by Ausonio Franchi, Father Valle, S.J., Professor G. Milanese, Father Amado, S.J., and Fathers Borla and Testore, S.J.)

It will be very useful to have the seminarians explain in the form of lectures — to high school students, educated persons, and members of study clubs — some of the theses which are studied in the course of philosophy and which confute the errors of the present day (for example, the theses on the spirituality and immortality of the soul, the freedom of the will, the end of man, the moral law and its sanctions, etc.). Likewise the seminarians should be made to discuss among themselves under the direction of the professor the best methods of presenting and effectively proving these truths, so that they will become accustomed to put their theoretical knowledge into practice.

II. *The Course in Theology*

A practical course in catechetics is to be established, with special reference to the teaching of religion in schools. It is less a question of establishing such a course, since it is already included in pastoral theology, than of increasing its effectiveness and making it more specific. Accordingly, two of the four hours assigned to pastoral theology shall be given to catechetics.

The students of theology shall develop in writing and orally the theological subjects which have a connection with catechetics, not only in the form of homilies and explanations of the Gospel, but also by way of lectures to students of various schools, under the direction of the professor; and they shall discuss the best method of giving such lectures.

Moreover practical exercises in catechetical teaching are to be introduced where they are not already in use (cf. c. 1365, § 3), not only in a parish but also in a public or private school or in the seminary itself. For example the students of the fourth year of theology could give some lectures to the college or high school students, always however under the direction of the professor of catechetics, who shall, at the end of the course in theology, give his considered judgment on the fitness and general aptitude of each of the seminarians as regards the teaching of religion in schools.

It must be observed that in these exercises, whether oral or in writing, and in both the courses of philosophy and theology, attention is to be directed to the positive side, that is, to establishing the truth clearly and thoroughly, avoiding useless controversies and above all any invective in the refutation of erroneous doctrines.

Let the candidates for the priesthood be persuaded that the teaching of religion is not only the teaching of the most noble of the sciences but is also the bestowal of the *word of life,* which the Lord will bring to fruition in the hearts of the listeners. It is therefore not merely a task of teaching, for which scientific preparation would be sufficient, but it is above all an apostolate in which the grace of God and the co-operation of good example on the part of the teacher are indispensable.

We are confident that these norms will be put into practice beginning with the coming month of January; still, we should be pleased to receive some assurance in this regard.

Rome, December 21, Feast of Saint Thomas the Apostle, 1944.

AAS 37–173; Instructions, S. C. Sem. et Stud., 21 Dec., 1944.

Course in Sacred Music Prescribed for Seminaries (S. C. Sem. et Univ., 15 Aug., 1949) AAS 41–618.

A Letter of the Sacred Congregation of Seminaries and Universities addressed to all the Ordinaries of places:

Everyone surely knows how much the Holy See has always favored Sacred Music for the promotion of divine worship. There are many proofs of this solicitude; notable among them are the wise and vigorous prescriptions which Pius XI of happy memory handed down by his Apostolic Constitution, *Divini cultus sanctitatem,* of 20 December, 1928.[1]

This Sacred Congregation too has been tirelessly working to the end that young men on the way to the priesthood should be properly trained both theoretically and practically in Sacred Music. But, although in most seminaries many praiseworthy measures have been taken to secure this training, in others the happy results which were expected have by no means been attained, and this for various reasons, but especially because properly trained teachers were not available. This deficiency is becoming more apparent now that the study of liturgy and music is daily becoming more widespread, both among the followers of Catholic Action and among the faithful in general, especially at the approach of the Holy Year.

Wherefore, in order to provide a new and stronger impulse to secure the careful training of seminary students in the theory and practice of Sacred Music according to the didactic and

---

[1] AAS 21–33; see Canon Law Digest, 1, p. 598.

disciplinary principles laid down by the Holy See, we have decided to prescribe as follows:

I. Sacred Music is one of the necessary courses; hence it must absolutely be given to all sacred students from the first year of humanities to the end of the course of theology.

II. The annual programs proposed by the teachers of Sacred Music are to be approved by the Most Excellent Ordinary.

III. The assignment of hours in the week to Sacred Music shall be governed by the Apostolic Constitution, *Divini cultus sanctitatem* (nn. 1–2): the hours of the lectures shall be inserted in the general schedule of studies.

In the fall term more time shall be assigned to practice, both for each student and for many or all together, and, for the students of philosophy and theology, study weeks shall be assigned for the thorough treatment of the principal questions of Sacred Music.

IV. The students shall be obliged to take an annual examination in Sacred Music just as in all other courses.

V. Every seminary shall have a well-qualified master in Sacred Music, who shall for all purposes be classed among the professors.

In this matter we call the attention of the Most Excellent local Ordinaries to the very earnest recommendation of Pius XI of happy memory, to the effect that from every part of the world there be sent to Rome, to the Roman Pontifical Institute of Sacred Music, select young priests who are sincerely imbued with the liturgical spirit, who have some special talent for music and sufficient preparation, so that after finishing the prescribed course, they may exercise a fruitful apostolate in liturgy and music in the diocese and especially in the seminary.

VI. These prescriptions shall become effective at the beginning of the next scholastic year.

It will rest with Your Excellency, therefore, to attend with all solicitude to these provisions. For we are convinced that, now as in the past ages of the Church, Sacred Music plays no small part in winning the Christian people to Christ Our Lord: drawn by the suavity and melody of sacred singing, the faithful will more willingly frequent the House of God when it is resounding with "hymns and spiritual canticles"; they will more eagerly approach the Sacraments of the Lord and draw from them more abundant life.

With all good wishes in the Lord, I am,
Very sincerely yours,

Joseph Cardinal Pizzardo, Prefect

AAS 41–618; S. C. Sem. et Univ., 15 Aug., 1949.

Teaching of Sacred Scripture (Biblical Commission, Instruction, 13 May, 1950) AAS 42–495.

An Instruction of the Pontifical Biblical Commission "to the Most Excellent Ordinaries of places and the highest Superiors of religious Institutes, the Very Reverend Rectors of Seminaries and professors of Sacred Scripture: on the proper teaching of Sacred Scripture in Seminaries of clerics and Colleges of religious":

His Holiness Pope Pius XII now happily reigning, in order to commemorate worthily the fiftieth year after the publication of the Encyclical, *Providentissimus Deus,* issued another Encyclical, *Divino afflante Spiritu,* on the 30th of September, 1943. After lucidly demonstrating what his Predecessors had zealously done for the advancement of biblical studies during those fifty years, the Supreme Pontiff earnestly reminded both Bishops and people how important these studies are in the Church, and what measures should be taken to promote them and to make them an effective aid in the spreading of the Kingdom of God among men; and he also laid down some wise provisions and precepts as to the way and method of cultivating these studies ever more perfectly.

In order that the recommendations and ordinances of the Supreme Pontiff may be put into practice with the greatest care and fidelity, the Pontifical Biblical Commission decided to apply them in a special way to the biblical courses which are given in clerical Seminaries and religious Colleges, where they cannot be given with the same thoroughness as is done in theological Faculties and special Institutes. For in these latter, teachers are being trained, whose task it will be both to instruct future priests in sacred science and to conduct research in those same branches; and this thorough special training is for the few. But in Seminaries of clerics and Colleges of religious, men are being trained who will one day be priests and pastors of Christ's flock, charged with the duty of teaching the truths of faith to the people and defending divine revelation against the attacks of unbelievers.

Not infrequently during these past decades the Supreme Pontiffs have explicitly pointed out with what care local Ordinaries and

General Superiors of religious Institutes are bound to see to it both by exhortation and authority that in clerical Seminaries and the Colleges of religious, scriptural studies "be held in high regard and flourish accordingly,"[1] as Leo XIII of happy memory wrote, and that the divine Books be so taught "as the importance of the subject itself and the needs of the times require."[2]

But recently, His Holiness Pope Pius XII now happily reigning, accepting the ordinances of his Predecessors and confirming them by his authority, earnestly declared that priests who have the care of souls are by no means qualified to present and explain the Sacred Books properly and with profit, "unless they themselves, when they were in the seminary, imbibed an active and enduring love for Sacred Scripture. Therefore Bishops, who are charged with a paternal responsibility for their seminaries, must diligently see to it that in this matter also nothing be left undone which may help to attain this end."[3]

At that time, however, when so many nations lay under the burden of calamity and ruin, local Ordinaries and Rectors of Seminaries, preoccupied too with daily anxieties for life and safety, were perhaps unable to attend to this matter as effectively as its gravity and importance require. But now that the turmoil has subsided, it seems appropriate to recall to mind and to inculcate anew these admonitions and instructions of the Supreme Pontiffs, so that, through the solicitous attention of Superiors and the diligent industry of professors, the training of future priests in Sacred Scripture may be undertaken and advanced with enthusiasm, to the end that the faithful may more effectively be led to the salutary fountainheads of Christian living, and that the world so sadly afflicted may be imbued and refreshed with the doctrine of Christ, the one source of liberty, love, and peace.

I. THE TEACHER OF SACRED SCRIPTURE

In order properly to establish and promote biblical studies in clerical Seminaries and Colleges of religious, the greatest need

---

[1] Encyclical, *Providentissimus Deus; Ench. Bibl.*, n. 118: *"iusto in honore consistant vigeantque."*

[2] *Ibid.*, n. 88: *"quemadmodum et ipsius gravitas disciplinae et temporum necessitas admonet."* See also n. 99, and the Apostolic Letter of Pius X, *Quoniam in re biblica*, 27 March, 1906, *Ench. Bibl.*, n. 155.

[3] Encyclical, *Divino afflante Spiritu; AAS*, Vol. 35 (1943), p. 321.

is professors who are in all respects qualified to teach properly this subject, which is holy and sublime above all others.

1. It is scarcely necessary to observe that the professor of Sacred Scripture should be outstanding among the rest and even surpass them in priestly virtue, since he enjoys a daily familiar contact with the word of God.

2. But moreover he should be equipped with the requisite knowledge of biblical matters, which is acquired by serious study and must be conserved and augmented by constant work.[4]

a) As a guarantee of the extent and quality of this learning, the requirement wisely made by Pius XI of holy memory, is effective and valid also to-day, namely, that no one should be a professor of Sacred Scripture in Seminaries "unless he shall have completed the special course of studies in that subject and shall have duly received a degree from either the Biblical Commission or the Biblical Institute."[5]

b) But as the scope of this subject is so vast that within the space of a few years only a general view of it, the method of study and of teaching, and a knowledge of certain important questions can be attained, whereas the rest must be left to the further study and industry of the teacher himself, unflagging personal work is necessary on the part of the professor, to increase, perfect, and consolidate what he has already learned, to examine and discuss with discernment the new questions which may arise, and to study more deeply and thoroughly the various branches of the subject which have to be taught to clerics. To do this, he has to read carefully the new books that are published on biblical matters and the commentaries in biblical reviews, to consult libraries, attend the conventions that are held for the advancement of biblical studies, and, if circumstances permit, also find occasion to go to the Holy Land in order to see with his own eyes and visit the towns and countries that are connected with the Sacred Story. For so wide is the sweep of biblical science, so many and such important advances are being made in the explanation of the Sacred Books, so many other sciences have to be called on for collateral help (such as the study of languages,

---

[4] Cf. Leo XIII, *Providentissimus Deus; Ench. Bibl.,* n. 88.

[5] *Motu proprio, Bibliorum scientiam,* 27 April, 1924; *Ench. Bibl.,* n. 522; AAS 16–180; Canon Law Digest, 1, p. 670.

history, geography, archaeology, and others), that unless the teacher applies himself daily to serious study, he will soon become unfit for his arduous task and unable to give the priests who are engaged in the ministry, or even to the faithful themselves, what they may reasonably expect of him.

c) These conditions make it clear how essential it is that the professor of Sacred Scripture *be able to give himself wholly to his work*, "so that he may, by daily renewing his resources, continue with all zeal and diligence the work he has happily undertaken."[6] Hence he should not be required, in addition to Sacred Scripture, to teach at the same time any other of the more important subjects in the Seminary. For the Code of Canon Law explicitly provides that care should be taken "that there be distinct professors at least for *Sacred Scripture,* dogmatic theology, moral theology, and church history."[7] Moreover he should not be burdened with other serious duties or ministries even outside the Seminary, for fear that those duties, however holy and praiseworthy in themselves, may interfere with this scriptural work, for which, if it is to be done properly, he needs time, mental energy, and peace of mind.

II. THE MANNER OF TEACHING
SACRED SCRIPTURE

Now as to the manner of teaching Sacred Scripture in Seminaries of clerics and Colleges of religious, the following points should be kept in mind.

1. It is the part of the professor of Scripture to arouse and promote in the students, together with a sufficient knowledge of the Sacred Books, "an active and enduring love for them."[8] For this teaching should nourish and daily augment in the future priests such veneration for the word of God that they will find in it during their whole lives the principal object of their mental culture and occupation and the solace and delight of their souls.

a) To do this properly the greatest help even today is the *daily reading of Sacred Scripture,* which formerly was for all clerics and secular and religious priests, a daily exercise no less

---

[6] Encyclical, *Divino afflante Spiritu,* AAS, Vol. 35 (1943), p. 324.
[7] Canon 1366, § 3.
[8] Encyclical, *Divino afflante Spiritu.*

sacred than the daily meditation, nay this reading itself was their meditation.[9] The professor should therefore teach the students to have a high esteem for the daily reading of the Scriptures and to do it with faith and religious devotion.[10] He should urge them to continue this useful exercise so constantly during the entire time of their studies that they may during that time read the entire Scriptures either in the Vulgate or in some more recent translation approved by ecclesiastical Superiors, from the earliest text into the vernacular, unless they find the original text itself more helpful. This reading of the Bible will be done more profitably if the students, from the very beginning of their course, are capably instructed and directed how to read the Sacred Books, and are given a brief conspectus or analysis of the different books, as is usually done in the "special introduction."[11] This daily reading, if done in an orderly and intelligent manner, and continued, will be for candidates to the priesthood an excellent preparation, not only for understanding properly and performing worthily the sacred liturgy, but also for drawing profit from their theological studies. And this daily reading of the Sacred Scriptures should not be omitted even during the time of vacation, whether it is done by all in common or separately by the individual students at home; in fact it should be done all the more faithfully during this time of greater leisure. The fidelity with which they strive to acquire a more and more intimate knowledge of and taste for the Sacred Scriptures, will be a measure of the sincerity with which they love the word of God and the earnestness with which they intend to fulfill the duties of their priestly vocation.

2. In conducting the classes themselves, the professor of Sacred Scripture must be solicitous to give his students all that they will need in their future priestly life, both for personal sanctity and for winning souls to God. Hence:

a) Sacred Scripture in clerical Seminaries and Colleges of religious should be taught so scientifically, soundly, and thoroughly that the students will know it in its entirety and in all

---

[9] Cf. Josue, I, 8; St. Jerome, *In Titum,* III, 9; *PL,* XXVI, col. 594; *Ep.* 52, 7, 8; *PL,* XXII, col. 533 sq. (*CSEL,* Vol. LIV, pp. 426, 428).

[10] Cf. *Imitation of Christ,* I, cap. 5.

[11] Cf. Pius X, Ap. Letter, *Quoniam in re biblica; Ench. Bibl.,* n. 169; Pius XI, *L'Osservatore Romano,* 1 Oct., 1930; cf. *Ench. Clericorum,* n. 1476.

its parts, and will know what are the more important questions which are being discussed in these days regarding the various books of the Bible, what are the objections and difficulties commonly raised against their history and doctrine, and finally, that they may have a sound scientific foundation for their explanation of biblical passages to the people.

b) As the time available for teaching Scripture is generally not sufficient for giving in its entirety the immense amount of matter concerning biblical subjects, the professor will have to make a prudent selection of the more important questions, not with a view to satisfying his own tastes and inclinations, but rather keeping carefully in mind what is required for the benefit of the students who are to be preachers of the word of God. The professor will fully meet these needs of the students only when he has clearly and perspicuously shown what are the principal *doctrines* which are presented by the Holy Spirit either in the Old or the New Testament, what progress of revelation can be discerned from the first beginnings up to the time of Christ Our Lord and the Apostles, what is the relation and connection between the Old and the New Testaments; and he should not fail to show clearly how great is the spiritual importance of the Old Testament, even in our own times. He should therefore strive earnestly to present these matters wherever he can find opportunity to do so, in the general or special introduction or in the class of exegesis. It will be useful also to show by appropriate examples from sacred or profane history, how much God has done to give salvation to all men and to bring them to the knowledge of the truth,[12] and how He has wisely disposed and directed all things by His paternal Providence, to make them "work together unto good, to such as, according to His purpose, are called to be saints."[13]

Beyond a doubt the proper explanation and demonstration of these high religious considerations will produce in the minds of the students a deeper love and higher esteem for the Sacred Books, which will render easier and more acceptable even the drier studies such as Hebrew and Greek; for these, even in Seminaries and Colleges, cannot be entirely omitted without giving

---

[12] Cf. 1 Tim. 2:4.
[13] Cf. Rom. 8:28.

rise to the danger that the clerics by their ignorance of the languages will be cut off from the original inspired texts and will be unable to understand properly and to have a discriminating appreciation of even the more recent translations.[14] This study of languages and also of the science of criticism, although in Seminaries and Colleges it has to be restricted to the highest essentials, will become more profitable and agreeable and will develop an ever growing capacity to understand the Sacred Books, when it is thus suffused with light from above.

In giving the *general introduction*, without entirely neglecting other questions, most of the time should be spent on the doctrine of the inspiration and veracity of the Sacred Scriptures and on the rules of interpretation (hermeneutics); whereas in the *special introduction*, both in the Old and especially in the New Testament, the teacher should carefully treat of the Sacred Books, showing clearly what is the content of each, its purpose, by whom it was written, and at what date.[15] In this matter he should avoid all vain erudition regarding the opinions of the critics, which is a source of disturbance rather than of culture for the minds of the students, and should instead present and vigorously prove things that may be of spiritual service to the people of our times and that may help them in solving questions and difficulties. In order to be able to treat sufficiently of all the Sacred Books, the teacher must make a careful use of the time assigned to him, and not delay on matters that are useless or of lesser importance.

In teaching *exegesis*, the professor must never forget that Sacred Scripture has been delivered by God *to the Church*, not only to be conserved but also to be interpreted, and that it is not to be explained otherwise than in the name and according to the mind of the Church, which is "the pillar and the ground of truth."[16] Hence "let him make it a sacred duty never to deflect a hair's breadth from the common teaching and tradition of the Church: let him make use of any real scientific advances which the industry of modern scholars has produced, but let him neglect the rash commentaries of innovators."[17]

---

[14] Cf. Pius X, Ap. Letter, *Quoniam in re biblica; Ench. Bibl.*, n. 165.

[15] *Ibid.*, n. 159.

[16] 1 Tim. 3:15.

[17] Cf. Pius X, Ap. Letter, *Quoniam in re biblica; Ench. Bibl.*, n. 168.

In selecting the parts of the matter for fuller explanation, he should not consider mere erudition, but present the matters that outline and define the *doctrine* of both Testaments, lest, as Saint Gregory says, he spend his time gnawing at the shell without reaching the kernel.[18] Accordingly, in the Old Testament, he should *chiefly* explain the doctrine of the origin of the human race, the messianic prophesies, the Psalms; in the New, he should give an orderly conspectus of the whole life of Our Lord, and explain rather fully at least those parts of the Gospels and Epistles which are publicly read in church on Sundays and feast days; moreover he should give the history of the passion and resurrection of Christ and should explain thoroughly at least one of the principal letters of Saint Paul, without omitting those parts of the other Epistles which have reference to doctrine.

In interpreting the Scriptures the professor should first clearly and perspicuously explain what is called the *literal sense,* using also the original text where that is of service. But in determining the literal sense of the text let him not follow the example given by not a few, alas, of the modern exegetes, who take account only of the words and the immediate context, but rather let him carefully bear in mind those ancient norms which the Supreme Pontiff Pius XII now gloriously reigning inculcated once more in his Encyclical, *Divino afflante Spiritu;* that is, let the exegete look up what the Sacred Scripture teaches in other comparable passages, what is the explanation of the text in question in the holy Fathers and in the tradition of the Church, what the "analogy of the faith" requires, and finally what if anything the living authority of the Church has declared about that text.[19] To do all this properly, he has to be well versed also in sacred theology and deeply and sincerely devoted to sound doctrine, and he must never, in reliance on mere critical and literary principles, let his exegesis become divorced from his general theological training.

He should take due care to explain the *spiritual sense* of the words, provided it be duly established according to the wise norms repeatedly laid down by the Supreme Pontiffs, that it was

---

[18] Cf. *Moralia,* XX, 9; *PL,* LXXVI, 149.
[19] Cf. Pius XII, *Divino afflante Spiritu;* AAS, Vol. 35, p. 310.

intended by God.[20] That spiritual sense which is explained with such care and affection by the Fathers and great interpreters of Scripture will be the more easily grasped by the teacher and the more reverently given to his students, the more he himself is endowed with purity of heart, high qualities of soul, the spirit of humility, and reverence and love for God the giver of revelation.

As to the difficulties and obscurities which the interpreter not infrequently encounters in the Books of Sacred Scripture, the professor should neither make little of them nor gloss them over, but should present the question fairly and honestly and do his best to solve it with the help of the various branches of knowledge which are at his disposal. But let him remember that "God has purposely scattered difficulties through the Sacred Books which He Himself inspired, in order that we might be more keenly stimulated to read and study them, and by learning through wholesome experience the limitations of our minds, we might make due progress in humility."[21]

Let the professor present all this as far as possible in the so-called *synthetic* manner, that is, treating rather fully of the matters that are of greater importance and assigning to the others the time and place which they seem to deserve. In this art of exposition he should train himself earnestly from the start, and strive to become ever more proficient, being persuaded that the fruit and effectiveness of his teaching are in large part dependent upon it.

As to the *purpose and character* of the lectures in Sacred Scripture which are given to the students of Seminaries and Colleges, it must be said that these are not intended to form specialists but to train future priests and apostles. Now the formation of priests, although it depends upon all the conditions of the life and order of the Seminary or College, is certainly advanced in a special way by the study and knowledge of Sacred Scripture. For it is through these classes that the future priests will understand and be convinced that the Sacred Books are of great benefit both for advancing their own priestly life and for fulfilling

---

[20] Encyclical, *Providentissimus; Ench. Bibl.,* n. 97; Encyclical, *Spiritus Paraclitus; Ench. Bibl.,* n. 498 sq.; Encyclical, *Divino afflante Spiritu,* AAS, Vol. 35, p. 311.

[21] Pius XII, Encyclical, *Divino afflante Spiritu, l. c.,* p. 318.

fruitfully the obligations of their priestly office. Wherefore the professor, far from being content with giving his students useful and necessary information and knowledge of biblical matters, should also find occasion to show them earnestly how a sound understanding, assiduous reading, and pious meditation of the Sacred Scriptures can nourish, confirm, and promote the sanctity of their own priestly lives,[22] and render fruitful their apostolic ministry, especially of preaching and catechetical instruction.[23]

III. COUNSELS AND NORMS

Accordingly, no one surely can fail to see that biblical studies, being of such value for the personal piety and apostolic work of the priest, should be pursued and advanced with the greatest diligence; and it is therefore very deplorable that they are not always appreciated as they should be, but are often unworthily made to yield to the study of other subjects, or sometimes are even entirely neglected. Wherefore this Pontifical Biblical Commission, stirred to action by various informations and requests from various parts of the world, decided to make the following earnest recommendations to the Most Excellent Ordinaries of places and Supreme Superiors of religious Institutes and to the Most Reverend Rectors of Seminaries and professors of Sacred Scripture.

1. In the *biblical library*[24] of Seminaries and Colleges, besides the commentaries of the Fathers and of the great Catholic interpreters, there should be the better works on biblical theology, archaeology, and sacred history, as well as biblical encyclopedias or lexicons and reviews on biblical subjects; for the individual teachers, much to their own loss and that of their students, cannot easily acquire these books personally.

2. With the same care and diligence the heads of Seminaries and Colleges should see to it that *clerics* also, besides the sacred Book of the Bible and the biblical manual with which the individuals are provided, should in their own special library have

---

[22] Cf. St. Jerome, *Ep.* 130 at the end; *PL,* XXII, col. 1224 (*CSEL,* LVI, p. 201).

[23] Cf. Leo XIII, Encyclical, *Providentissimus; Ench. Bibl.,* n. 72; Benedict XV, Encyclical, *Spiritus Paraclitus; ibid.,* n. 496 sq.; Pius XII, Encyclical, *Divino afflante Spiritu, l. c.,* p. 320 sq.

[24] Cf. Pius X, Ap. Letter, *Quoniam in re biblica; Ench. Bibl.,* n. 173.

access to the works which are most suitable to help them to review and supplement the lectures which they have heard in class.

3. The professor of Scripture, if he is to do his work in a praiseworthy manner, *must be left entirely free for his work* and not be charged with other important duties, and he should be so taken care of by Superiors, even through pecuniary subsidies and other appropriate aids, that he will gladly persevere in his teaching office even for his entire life.

For the first condition for promoting biblical studies in Seminaries and Colleges is that the professor of Scripture be supplied with all the helps in the way of books or money which will enable him to advance in the knowledge of his subject and to keep up with the progress that is being made in it, to attend the conventions which may be held for purposes of study, to visit the Holy Land in case an opportunity to do so should present itself, and to publish the fruits of his scholarly labors.

It is recommended that, where the number of students is large (and even elsewhere by way of farsighted provision for the future), there be two professors of Scripture, one for the Old and one for the New Testament.

4. The professor of Scripture who is solicitous for the progress of his students is earnestly encouraged to give to a select group of more talented students an optional special course, in either the biblical or other languages which are necessary or useful for biblical studies,[25] or in biblical theology, history, archaeology, or some other auxiliary subject. In such a course he could also deal with the special questions which are being most discussed in connection with the various Books of the Bible and which he could study more thoroughly either by his own research or by reading up on them.

5. It is also recommended to the professor of Scripture that, prudently and with moderation, following the advice of Superiors, and without allowing the students to neglect their other studies, he prepare the more promising students who show a special love for Sacred Scripture, to pursue special studies in it.[26] To these students he should give an opportunity to learn even those

---

[25] Cf. Pius X, Ap. Letter, *Quoniam in re biblica; Ench. Bibl.*, n. 165.

[26] Cf. Pius X, Ap. Letter, *Quoniam in re biblica; Ench. Bibl.*, nn. 165, 167; Pius XI, *Motu proprio, Bibliorum scientiam; Ench. Bibl.*, n. 518 sq.

modern languages which are most necessary for Scripture study, and he should prepare them to know and read works "on the history of both Testaments, the life of Christ Our Lord and the Apostles, and travels and pilgrimages to the Holy Land."[27] For he must remember that these students suffer great harm when they are sent on for special studies without adequate preparation, especially in languages; and he must be persuaded that one of his chief duties is to make use of his own experience in order to prepare for his Seminary excellent future professors who will contribute by their work to the progressive growth and vigor of biblical studies.

6. Since, within the short time that is usually assigned to Scripture classes, it is scarcely possible to do all that is required for the theological and ascetical instruction of the clerical students and for teaching them the right use of the Sacred Books in the liturgy and in preaching, it is very praiseworthy and is strongly recommended that the practice which we know to exist in the Colleges of some religious orders be followed; that is, that from the very beginning of the course of higher studies, the students be given *a sort of summary introduction,* which may serve as a stimulus and guide to all the Scripture reading which they will do in the course of their studies. If this is done properly the professor will be able, during the four-year course of theology, to spend more time in explaining biblical doctrine.

7. The students of theology shall be obliged once or twice a year to write a *homily* on some biblical passage, and this work is to be directed and carefully graded by the professor. Thus the students will, from the beginning of their theology, learn how to prepare by proper study and pious meditation and how to write well the homilies that are given on Sundays and feast days, and also how to present and explain the true and genuine sense of the word of God properly, appropriately, and reverently from the pulpit.

8. Finally, in order that the study of Sacred Scripture may be properly cultivated and perfected even after the completion of the theological course and may be faithfully continued for life, in the examinations in various sacred branches which according to canon law secular priests are required to take for at least

---

[27] Cf. Pius X, Ap. Letter, *Quoniam in re biblica; Ench. Bibl.,* n. 172.

three years and religious for at least five years after their studies,[28] the assignment shall include every year the preparation of some of the graver questions from the general and special introduction and from exegesis. Moreover in the *conferences* on moral and liturgical subjects which according to canon law are to be held at stated times for both secular and regular clergy,[29] there shall also be proposed for explanation — as is very commendably done in certain places — some biblical passage of the Old or New Testament which shall be chosen by the professor of Scripture in the Seminary and shall afterward be explained by him in the light of biblical science and published in the diocesan paper or elsewhere.

We earnestly entreat the Most Excellent Ordinaries and Most Reverend Superiors of religious Institutes, in their care and solicitude for the common good, to accept and follow these recommendations, so that the education of our future priests may daily become more perfect and that they may be imbued with the solid sacred doctrine which they must use already during their studies and thereafter during their whole life. And they must use it, not lightly or thoughtlessly or according to their own whim and taste, but according to the norms of sacred science, according to the laws and precepts of the Church and the rules of genuine Catholic tradition, so that the Sacred Books shall be to them as their daily bread, light and strength for the nourishment and growth of their own spiritual life, and in their apostolic ministry an effective aid by which they may lead many to the truth, to the fear and love of God, to virtue and holiness. We are well aware how many and how great are the difficulties which oppose the perfect realization of these recommendations within a short time; but we are sure that the Bishops and religious Superiors, without losing courage, will leave nothing undone to make the study and love of Sacred Scripture flourish with renewed vigor in all their clerics and priests and bear rich fruits of life and grace in their souls and in their work.

In the audience graciously granted to the undersigned Consultor and Secretary on the 13th of May, 1950, His Holiness Pius XII, approved this Instruction and ordered that it be published.

---

[28] Canons 130, 590.
[29] Canons 131, 591.

AAS 42–495; Biblical Commission, Instruction, 13 May, 1950. *Periodica,* 40–136 (Asensio).

Post-Seminary Training for Priests: Pontifical Institute of St. Eugene. See c. 129; AAS 41–165.

Study of the Psalms: Special course to be established in regional seminaries of Italy. S. C. Sem., N. 855/41/7 (undated). See *Periodica,* 30–385, with annotations by Galdos.

CANON 1366

Order of Examinations for Scriptural Degrees (Bibl. Com., 6 July, 1942) **AAS 34–232.**

Question. Whether, in examinations for the *Prolytatus* or Licentiate to be held before the Pontifical Biblical Commission, the various examinations whether oral or written which according to the statutes are usually given at the same session, may be so divided that there is even a fairly long interval between them.

Reply. In the affirmative; it being understood, however, that the examinations in the Hebrew and Greek languages should come first, together with the entire special introduction, and orally (*Ench. Bibl.,* nn. 355, 356, 358). When these have been successfully passed, the candidate is entitled to be named *Bachelor.*

When the other examinations of the program have been passed (*ibid.,* nn. 352, 353, 354, 357, 359), the degree of *Prolytatus* will be conferred.

His Holiness Pius XII, in the audience granted to the undersigned Most Reverend *Consultor ab Actis* on July 6, 1942, confirmed this reply and ordered that it be published.

Rome, 6 July, 1942.

AAS 34–332; Bibl. Com., 6 July, 1942.

Training of Professors in Ecclesiastical History (Pius XII, Letter, 10 Feb., 1944) **AAS 36–101.**

A Letter of Pius XII to Father Peter Leturia, S.J., Dean of the Faculty of Ecclesiastical History in the Pontifical Gregorian University, is as follows:

Beloved Son: Health and Apostolic Benediction:

Among the many tokens of regard and filial devotion with which the Pontifical Gregorian University has marked the twenty-fifth anniversary of Our episcopal consecration, We were particularly pleased by the work entitled *"Xenia Piana,"* which was reverently dedicated to Us by the Professors of Ecclesiastical History.

For at the very beginning of Our Pontificate, on the 24th of June, 1939, in the speech which We addressed to the students of institutions of the secular and religious clergy in Rome,[1] We clearly stated how highly We esteem those studies, what norms should be followed in teaching them, and finally what a wealth of material is to be found for a fuller and better understanding of the history of the Church, in the monuments, libraries, and records of the Holy City. "Historical studies," We then declared,[2] "in so far as they are pursued in schools, should not be limited to critical and merely apologetic questions, though these too have their value, but should rather be always directed to setting forth the active life of the Church." And that life, We now wish to say once more, when presented as it were in one view through the centuries, is a powerful help in forming a ripe judgment on the condition of the Church and in cultivating a sincere love for her.

It is clear that professors will not have this knowledge of ecclesiastical history unless they constantly improve themselves by special studies and training. This is the more necessary as ecclesiastical history, in itself a rather difficult study, is subject to the dangers of undigested erudition, of criticism which is either deficient through ignorance or rashly exuberant, and finally of that attitude toward the affairs of the Church, easily picked up through imitation of non-Catholic writers, which boldly attempts to judge and measure by the standards of our little minds, events which often transcend the scope of unaided human powers.

Accordingly, after Our Predecessor of happy memory, Pius XI, by the Apostolic Constitution, *Deus scientiarum Dominus,* raised ecclesiastical history to the grade of a primary subject in the Faculty of Theology, and decreed that the professors of the various subjects should each have their own doctoral degree, it was very appropriate that, as there had long existed in Rome Institutes and Faculties for training professors in the other sacred

---

[1] Cf. Canon Law Digest, 2, p. 427; AAS 31–245.
[2] Canon Law Digest, 2, p. 430.

subjects mentioned in that Constitution, a complete Faculty also in Ecclesiastical History should be established in Our Gregorian University.

As a proof of the energetic attention which for ten years now has been given to the special task of preparing the best teachers and providing them with all facilities for their work, you have presented to Us nineteen dissertations industriously composed by students of that Faculty, from various nations and in various languages.

We also express Our well-merited praise for the series entitled *"Miscellanea Historiae Pontificiae,"* which was begun by that same Faculty in the first year of Our Pontificate, of which the *"Xenia Piana"* make up the seventh volume; and We hope that it will be a prelude to a still more extensive work in which you will apply your attention and industry to the continuance and completion of the History of the Popes, which already has been the object of distinguished labors on the part of scholars. And certainly nowhere more fittingly than in this Holy City where everything invites to it, can the history of the Roman Pontiffs be studied and perfected, a work for which there formerly was no continuing series of publications.

So that your work and that of your collaborators may be the more fruitful, as an augury of heavenly blessings and in token of Our affection, We lovingly impart the Apostolic Benediction to you, Beloved Son, to the companions of your labors and to all the students of your Faculty.

Given at Saint Peter's in Rome, the 10th of February, 1944, the fifth year of Our Pontificate.

AAS 36–101; Pius XII, Letter, 10 Feb., 1944. *Periodica,* 33–231 (Leturia).

NOTE: The Decree of the S. C. of Seminaries and Universities, 6 Aug., 1932, establishing the Faculty of Ecclesiastical History at the Gregorian University, is given verbatim in the annotations in *Periodica,* as follows:

For the purpose of better preparing scholars and teachers of historical studies and also for the fuller training of those who treat of missionary matters and of preachers of the word who are sent to foreign missions, the directors of the Pontifical Gregorian University have petitioned that there be established in the said University a Faculty of Ecclesiastical History and a Faculty of Missionology.

His Holiness Pius XI, upon the matter being referred to him by the undersigned Cardinal Prefect of this Sacred Congregation in the audience of 26 July, 1932, after duly considering all aspects of the question, graciously deigned to grant the petition.

Accordingly this Sacred Congregation, by the mandate and authority of His Holiness the Pope, does by the present Decree erect and declare to be erected in the Pontifical Gregorian University a Faculty of Ecclesiastical History and a Faculty of Missionology, with power to confer academic degrees according to the Statutes approved by this Sacred Congregation. All things to the contrary notwithstanding.

Given at Rome, from the Palace of Saint Callistus, the 6th of August, 1932.

(Private) ; S. C. Sem. et Univ., Decree, 6 Aug., 1932. *Periodica*, 33–232.

The Appropriate Doctoral Degree for Teaching in a Theological Faculty (S. C. Sem. et Univ., 28 Aug., 1945) AAS 37-272.

The Sacred Congregation of Seminaries and Universities was asked:

Whether, for teaching any course in a Theological Faculty, besides a Doctor of Sacred Theology, one also may be considered as having the appropriate doctoral degree according to the provision of art. 21 of the Apostolic Constitution, *Deus scientiarum Dominus*, who has acquired the Doctorate — in a Faculty of ecclesiastical studies — either in Sacred Scripture or in Canon Law, Oriental Studies, Ecclesiastical History, Missiology, Christian Archaeology, or Philosophy.

Reply. In the affirmative, provided the candidate has also the licentiate in Sacred Theology, or the licentiate in the matter which he is to teach.

From the Palace of Saint Callistus, August 28, 1945, Feast of Saint Augustine, Doctor of the Church.

AAS 37-272; S. C. Sem. et Univ., 28 Aug., 1954. Annotations, *Periodica*, 35–181 (Dezza).

Licentiate: Juridical Effects (S. C. Sem. et Univ., *Declaratio*, 23 May, 1948) AAS 40-260.

Since in virtue of the Apostolic Constitution *Deus scientiarum Dominus*, of 24 May, 1931, all the requirements which were formerly demanded for the attainment of the Doctorate are now required for the academic degree of the Licentiate, the Sacred Congregation of Seminaries and Universities, by special mandate of the Supreme Pontiff, declares and decrees that the *Licentiate* attained by observing the norms of the said Constitution has the same juridical effects as the *Doctorate* obtained before the said Constitution, unless the Holy See in particular cases decides otherwise, without prejudice especially to the provisions of canon 1598, § 2, and Article 21, 2°, of the aforesaid Constitution.

From the Audience of 23 May, 1948.

AAS 40–260; S. C. Sem. et Univ., *Declaratio*, 23 May, 1948.
Periodica, 37–279 (Dezza).

Biblical Studies: Encyclical of Pius XII, *Divino afflante Spiritu*, 30 Sept., 1943 (AAS 35–297). Annotations, *Periodica*, 33–119 (Vaccari).

Examination in Scripture before the Biblical Commission: Subjects defined (effective 1953) for the Baccalaureate, the Licentiate, and the Doctorate. Bibl. Com., 20 June, 1951 (AAS 43–747). Annotations by Bea in *Monitor Ecclesiasticus*, 1951, p. 615.

CANON 1372

Purposes of Catholic Teaching: Ideal of the Catholic Teacher (Pius XII, Allocution, 10 April, 1950) AAS 42–395.

Excerpts from an Allocution of Pius XII, 10 April, 1950, to an audience composed of various groups representing all classes and grades of Catholic teachers and students, from France:

To open, expand, enlighten, and equip progressively the mind of the child and the youth just awakening to life; to guide youth in its curiosity, its ardor, its high ambition to discover the truth, its eagerness to pluck the fruit from all branches of the tree of knowledge! Is there a calling more beautiful, of wider scope, more varied in its marvelous unity, than this? For after all, at every age, in every field of study there is but one thing in view: the acquisition and possession of light ever purer, in order to love and enjoy it, to defend and propagate it, to give it to everyone according to each one's capacity, to multiply and spread its blessings everywhere.

We congratulate you, therefore, members of the Catholic teaching profession, with your truly heavy burden and your task which might seem an ungrateful one, were you not sustained in it by your ideal. For without an ideal, without the highest ideal, who would have the courage, or even the right, to sacrifice — apparently — the researches and creations of an intellectual life which he feels to be rich and exuberant, the brilliant conquests of an apostolic life which is throbbing within him eager to spend itself in the service of the Church and of souls, the joys of family life during the short hours of leisure in a home that is often quite modest, though secure? Who would have the courage, or the right, to sacrifice all this in order to dedicate himself without respite and without reserve to teaching other people's children, at that wild age when profit and progress are scarcely apparent at all or begin to be faintly discernible only at the moment of passing to the next grade? Concerning every child, one may well ask himself: "What a one, think ye, shall this child be?"[1] Disillusionments are so frequent, disappointments so many and so bitter! But, thanks be to God, even while you wear yourselves out in talking, and tire your eyes in deciphering and correcting papers, your hearts are lifted to God, to Christ, to Whom you wish to give these children whom He has entrusted to you. Many of them, even though they forget you, will owe to you the vigor and charity of their Christian lives, and most of those who fall away will at their last hour feel an awakening within them of the convictions and sentiments of their earlier years.

In the hope and confidence that, through the grace of the Holy Spirit, under the protection of the Immaculate Queen who is the Throne of Wisdom, you will transform yourselves daily more and more into "burning and shining lights,"[2] We impart to all of you, to your families, your colleagues, and your pupils, Our Apostolic Benediction.

AAS 42–395; Pius XII, Allocution, 10 April, 1950.

Catholic Universities and Schools: Their purpose, a synthesis of all branches in an atmosphere of Catholic culture. Allocution of Pius XII to the Roman pilgrimage of the professors and students of the "Instituts Catholiques" of France, 21 Sept., 1950 (AAS 42–735).

Catholic University of Rio de Janeiro. See decree, S. C. Sem. et Univ., 20 Jan., 1947 (AAS 40–43).

Education of the Child: Statement issued by the Catholic Bishops of the United States at the close of their annual meeting, 15–17 Nov., 1950 (*The Catholic Mind*, 1951, p. 137).

Laval University: Congratulatory Letter of Pius XII to Archbishop Roy of Quebec on occasion of centenary, 28 Aug., 1952 (AAS 44–768).

---

[1] Luke 1:66.
[2] Cf. John 5:35.

Notre Dame University: Letter of congratulation on centenary. Pius XII, 2 Apr., 1943 (AAS 35–394).

Parents Entrusting Children to Communist Associations. See c. 2316; AAS 42–553.

Saint John Baptist de la Salle, Patron of Teachers. Pius XII, Ap. Letter, 15 May, 1950 (AAS 42–631). English text in *The Catholic Mind,* 1950, p. 511.

Sex Initiation: Literature on this subject emanating from Catholic sources was most severely condemned by Pius XII in an Allocution of 18 Sept., 1951 (AAS 43–730).

Subjection of Catholic School to Authority of the Church. See c. 1324; Holy Office, 8 Aug., 1949.

CANON 1375

Religious Schools Ought Not to Be Placed in a Worse Condition Than State Schools (Pius XII, Apostolic Exhortation, 13 Sept., 1951) **AAS 43–738.**

In the course of an Apostolic Exhortation to the first International Congress of Teaching Nuns, 13 Sept., 1951, His Holiness Pius XII said:

It may be added, not for Italy alone, but in general: Those who have a part in the framing of school legislation must have a sufficient intent of justice and a sufficient — so to speak — democratic sense, to meet the will of the parents in such a way that schools founded and directed by religious Institutes be not placed in a worse condition than State schools and that they be given the liberty necessary for their development.

AAS 43–738; Pius XII, Exhortation, 13 Sept., 1951.

Catholic Education in Hungary: Joint Pastoral of the Hungarian Hierarchy, 1 Sept., 1948. English text, *The Catholic Mind,* 1949, p. 122.

Vocation of Teaching: Freedom of the Church in Teaching. Pius XII, Allocution, 4 Sept., 1949. English text, *The Catholic Mind,* 1950, p. 569.

CANON 1376

Catholic University of Porto Alegro, Brazil: Decree establishing. S. C. Sem., 1 Nov., 1950 (AAS 43–495).

Federation of Catholic Universities: Established, Pius XII, Ap. Letter, 27 July, 1949 (AAS 42–385).

CANON 1381

A School Cannot Be Catholic and yet remain in rebellion against legitimate ecclesiastical authority: Saint Benedict's Center. See c. 1324; Holy Office, 8 Aug., 1949.

CANON 1382

Catholic Schools Subject to Legitimate Ecclesiastical Authority. See c. 1324; Holy Office, 8 Aug., 1949.

CANON 1385

Sacred Art: Instruction on. See c. 1261; AAS 44–542.

CANON 1386

Books: Laws on publication, etc., recalled to missionaries. See c. 1350; private, S. C. Prop. Fid., Pentecost, 1920.

CANON 1390

Decree on the Permission to Publish Liturgical Books
(S. C. Rit., 10 Aug., 1946) AAS 38–371.

The sedulous care with which the Sacred Congregation of Rites has always watched over the publication of liturgical books, is clearly evident both from the decrees which it has issued from time to time on this subject and from the reverence which it has desired to be shown by all toward the sacred volumes. Hence the reservation of the title "Printers to the Holy See," which it has granted in the course of time to but few and select publishers; hence also the revision of the sacred books, which the Congregation itself regularly attends to most carefully.

Nevertheless for various reasons the practice has for some time been growing, for any publisher, with the consent and approval of the proper Ordinary, to publish liturgical books, and especially the Roman Missal and Breviary, not always with the form and purity of text which they require. In order to obviate this difficulty and to secure that elegance which should characterize things pertaining to divine worship, so that a most carefully revised reading of the sacred text may be provided, His Holiness Pope Pius XII has decreed as follows, removing any contrary concession or abuse which may exist:

1. The right to print liturgical books shall belong only to the Vatican Press, excluding all others.

2. Any printer or publisher, whether he has a pontifical certificate or not, must obtain permission from the Sacred Congregation of Rites as often as he desires to publish these books.

3. It pertains to the Administration of the Property of the Holy See to specify each time the conditions for the publication of these books.

4. The certification that the book agrees with the Vatican edition, which according to canon 1390 is to be given by the Ordinary, is to be signed by Ordinaries only after a careful and accurate revision has been made by a man who is learned in liturgy.

5. For the purpose of this decree, the following are considered liturgical books: the Roman Breviary, the Roman Missal, the Roman Ritual, the Roman Pontifical, the Roman Martyrology, the Bishops' Ceremonial, the *Memoriale Rituum*, the *Octavarium Romanum*, the Collection of the Decrees of the Sacred Congregation of Rites.

All things to the contrary, even those worthy of special mention, notwithstanding.

Rome, the 10th of August, 1946.

AAS 38–371; S. C. Rit., 10 Aug., 1946.

CANON 1391

Versions of Scripture for Private and Public Reading. See c. 818; AAS 35–270.

CANON 1395

Summary of Common Law on Prohibition of Books (Holy Office, 17 Apr., 1943) AAS 35–144.

This document, which we translate *verbatim*, is entitled simply: *De Prohibitione Librorum:*

Seeing that delays and omissions in denouncing bad books frequently occur, and that many of the faithful are in a state of deplorable ignorance regarding the denunciation and prohibition of harmful books, the Supreme Sacred Congregation of the Holy Office deems it appropriate to call to mind the principal provisions of the sacred canons on this subject; for it is beyond doubt that bad or harmful writings expose purity of faith, integrity of morals, and the very salvation of souls to the greatest dangers.

Certainly the Holy See cannot by itself, with adequate care and in due time, prohibit the numberless writings against faith and morals which, especially in our time, are being published almost daily in various languages all over the world. Hence it is necessary that the Ordinaries of places, whose business it is to preserve sound and orthodox doctrine and to protect good morals (c. 343, § 1), should, either personally or through suitable priests, be watchful as to the books which are published or sold in their territory (c. 1397, § 4), and forbid to their subjects those which they judge should be condemned (c. 1395, § 1). The right and duty to forbid books for just cause belongs also to an Abbot of an independent monastery and to the Superior General of a clerical exempt Institute acting with his Chapter or Council; nay, in case of urgency, it belongs also to the other Major Superiors with their proper Council, it being understood, however, that these must as soon as possible report the matter to the Superior General (c. 1395, § 3). Nevertheless, books which require a more expert scrutiny, or in regard to which, for salutary results, the judgment of the supreme authority seems to be required, should be referred by the Ordinaries to the judgment of the Holy See (c. 1397, § 5).

It is of course the duty of all the faithful, and especially of clerics, to denounce pernicious books to the proper authority; but this duty is especially incumbent on clerics who have some ecclesiastical dignity, such as the Legates of the Holy See and the Ordinaries of places, and on those who are eminent in doctrine, as for example the Rectors and Professors of Catholic Universities.

The denunciation is to be made either to this Congregation of the Holy Office or to the Ordinary of the place, giving by all means the reason why it is thought the book should be forbidden. The persons to whom such a report is made have a strict duty to keep secret the names of those who make it (c. 1397, §§ 1, 2, 3).

Finally, Ordinaries of places and others who have the care of souls should duly inform the faithful of the following:

a) The prohibition of books has the effect that, unless due permission is obtained, the forbidden book may not be published, nor republished (without making the corrections and obtaining due approbation), nor read, nor retained, nor sold, nor translated into another language, nor in any way communicated to other persons (c. 1398, §§ 1, 2);

b) Books condemned by the Holy See are considered as forbidden everywhere and in whatever language they may be translated (c. 1396);

c) The positive ecclesiastical law forbids not only those books which are individually condemned by a special decree of the Holy See and placed on the *Index of Forbidden Books,* or which are proscribed by particular Councils or Ordinaries for their subjects, but also the books which are forbidden *by the common law itself,* that is, in virtue of the rules contained in canon 1399, which forbids in a general manner nearly all books which are bad and harmful in themselves;

d) The natural law forbids the reading of any book which occasions proximate spiritual danger, since it forbids anyone to place himself in danger of losing the true faith or good morals; accordingly, permission to use forbidden books, from whomsoever it be obtained, in no way exempts from this prohibition of the natural law (c. 1405, § 1).

Given at Rome, from the Palace of the Holy Office, 17 April, 1943.

AAS 35-144; Holy Office, 17 Apr., 1943.
Periodica, 32-290 (Creusen).

Warning Against Lascivious and Obscene Books (Holy Office, 20 May, 1952) **AAS 44-432.**

On the occasion of condemning and placing on the Index all the works of one Albert Pincherle (or Moravia), the Holy Office proceeded to say:

On this occasion the Most Eminent and Most Reverend Fathers, deploring the immense harm that is done to souls, first by the unrestrained license to publish and diffuse books, booklets, and periodicals which of set purpose narrate, describe, and teach things that are lascivious and obscene, and also by the fatal eagerness to read such matter indiscriminately, decided to issue the following *warnings:*

To all the faithful: that they remember their very grave obligation to abstain entirely from the reading of such books and periodicals;

To those who have charge of the instruction and education of youth: that, conscious of their grave responsibility, they keep their charges away from such writings entirely, as from an insidious poison;

Finally, to those who in virtue of their office have the responsibility of regulating the morality of citizens: that they do not permit such writings, which strive to subvert the very principles and foundations of natural morality, to be published and distributed.

On the 3rd day of April, 1952, in the audience granted as usual to His Excellency the Most Reverend Assessor of the Holy Office, His Holiness Pius XII approved the resolution of the Eminent Fathers when it was reported to him, confirmed it and ordered that it be published.

Given at Rome, from the Holy Office, 20 May, 1952.

AAS 44–432; Holy Office, *Decretum: Proscriptio Librorum — Monitum,* 20 May, 1952. Annotations: on the specific works condemned, *Monitor Ecclesiasticus,* 1952, p. 388; on the *Monita, ibid.,* p. 561 (Spiazzi).

CANON 1397

Ordinaries: Duty Regarding Books. Ordinaries are to be watchful as regards books and periodicals; to forbid those which they judge harmful, and to report to the Holy See those which seem to require a higher sanction. See S. C. Consist., 14 June, 1938; *Il Monitore Ecclesiastico,* 1938, p. 242.

CANON 1399

Orientals: Prohibition of Books by the Code Itself (S. C. Eccl. Or., 1944) AAS 36–25.

A Declaration of the Sacred Congregation for the Oriental Church, undated but published in the AAS for 20 Jan., 1944, is as follows:

The question having been asked whether the faithful of the Oriental rite are bound not only by canon 1396, but also by canon 1399, the S. C. decided to reply: In the affirmative.

AAS 36–25; S. C. Eccl. Or., 1944.

Good Friday: Translation of Liturgical Prayers Regarding Jews (S. C. Rit., 10 June, 1948) AAS 40–342.

A Declaration of the Sacred Congregation of Rites:

In the two-fold prayer in which Holy Mother Church, in the solemn prayers of Good Friday, implores the mercy of God for the Jewish people,[1] these words occur: *"perfidi Judaei"* and *"judaica perfidia."* Inquiry has been made as to what is the true meaning of this Latin expression, especially as in various translations which have been made into the vernacular for the use of the faithful, the words have been expressed in terms which would seem to give offense to the people of that race.

The Sacred Congregation, when asked about this matter, decided to make only the following declaration: "That in translations into the vernacular there is no objection to the use of expressions whose meaning is *infidelitas, infideles in credendo."*

Rome, 10 June, 1948.

AAS 40–342; S. C. Rit., Declaration, 10 June, 1948.

Sacred Art: Instruction on. See c. 1261; AAS 44–542.

Sacred Congregation of the Council declared a magazine forbidden *ipso iure.* S. C. Conc., 12 April, 1949 (AAS 41–221).

Use of New Translation of the Psalms. See c. 135; AAS 37–65; 39–508.

Writings of Communists: *Ipso iure* forbidden. See c. 2314; AAS 41–334.

CANON 1432

Intentio in Iure Fundata: Not upheld against express provision of law. See c. 1435; AAS 35–399.

CANON 1435

Reservation of Benefices "to Which the Roman Pontiff Has Put His Hand" (S. C. Conc., 20 Dec., 1942) AAS 35–148.

This important and general resolution of the Sacred Congregation of the Council was occasioned by the following communication which that Sacred Congregation received from the Apostolic Datary:

"In some diocesan Curiae it usually happens that, when someone is proposed for a benefice which is to be conferred by the Holy See, if he already has another benefice he is first invited

---

[1] In the Mass of the Presanctified on Good Friday, of the nine double prayers between the singing of the Passion and the *"Ecce lignum Crucis,"* the eighth is for the conversion of the Jews.

to resign the one which he has; and thus, disengaged of the benefice which he formerly possessed, he is proposed to the Holy See (for the new benefice). These diocesan Curiae, relying on the literal sense of canon 1435, imagine that in this way they succeed in evading the apostolic reservation mentioned in canon 1435, § 1, 4°: *Si Romanus Pontifex beneficiarium promoverit vel transtulerit,* etc."

The Apostolic Datary believes that in these circumstances there is an *appositio manuum Romani Pontificis,* and that consequently the benefice (which was resigned) is reserved to the Holy See; because the resignation was made in evasion of the apostolic reservation, and so is to be considered as not made.

Accordingly, the Apostolic Datary referred the matter to the Supreme Pontiff, who directed the Sacred Congregation of the Council to study the question carefully and to communicate its decision to the diocesan Curiae as the rule to be observed by them in such cases.

Summary of the Discussion. 1. In plain language, the point is this. If the person who is appointed to a benefice by the Holy See, has another (incompatible) benefice at the time of his appointment, the words cited above from canon 1435, § 1, 4°, are literally verified; he has been promoted or transferred by the Roman Pontiff; and so the benefice (which is vacated by his promotion or transfer to the new benefice) is reserved to the Holy See. If, on the other hand, before being appointed to the new benefice, he has already resigned the former one, it is evident that the words of the canon are not *literally* verified; and on this ground the diocesan Curiae considered that the benefice (which was vacated) was not reserved.

2. While admitting that the words of the canon do not literally cover the case, the Sacred Congregation of the Council had no difficulty in showing that *under the pre-Code law,* such a case was certainly considered to be one in which "the Supreme Pontiff had put his hand" to the vacated benefice. This had been explicitly provided by the Constitution, *Iam dudum,* of Paul V, 25 Feb., 1609, and was held by a line of old authorities (Riganti, Lotterius, Pitonius, Barbosa).

3. In the old law the procedure in question here was said to be *"in fraudem reservationis apostolicae,"* and for this reason the resignation of the former benefice was regarded as null, and

the apostolic reservation attached to it despite the resignation. Moreover, it was not necessary that there be any fraud in the ordinary sense, nor even any intention on the part of anyone to evade the apostolic reservation. For the application of this rule it was sufficient that the benefice to be filled by papal appointment was already vacant at the time when the appointee resigned the other benefice which he was holding.

4. All this was under the old law. Now the question is: does it still hold, despite the words of canon 1435 above cited? The Sacred Congregation held that it does. The canon is to be interpreted in the sense of the old law, for two reasons: first, by reason of canon 6, 2°–4° (a canon which integrally re-enacts the old law is to be interpreted in the light of the old law; and in doubt the old law is to be retained); secondly, the constant practice of the Apostolic Datary has been in accordance with this rule, and hence, according to canon 20, this *praxis Curiae* furnishes a norm of law.

Question. Whether, according to the meaning of canon 1435, § 1, 4°, compared with canons 6, 2°–4°, and 20, of the Code of Canon Law, a benefice which has been resigned in view of another benefice which is reserved, is itself reserved to the Holy See.

Reply. In the affirmative.

In the audience of 20 Dec., 1942, His Holiness Pius XII deigned to approve and confirm this resolution.

AAS 35–148; S. C. Conc., 20 Dec., 1942. *Periodica,* 33–146 (Aguirre).

Appointment to Vacant Canonries in Titular and Diaconal Churches of Rome (S. C. Conc., 18 June, 1943) AAS 35–399.

State of the Question. A doubt having arisen as to who has the right to appoint to vacant canonries in the titular and diaconal churches of Rome, while their titular Cardinal priests or deacons are absent from Rome, that is, whether the right pertains even then to the respective Cardinals titular or to the Apostolic Datary, the question was, by special mandate of His Holiness, referred for solution to this Sacred Congregation.

Remarks. 1. Canon 1435, § 3, expressly provides: "As to the conferring of benefices which are founded in Rome, the special laws which are in force in their regard are to be observed." These laws are to be found in the *Regulae Cancelleriae Apostolicae,* of which Rule VIII is especially in point. This Rule, as explained by Riganti (*Comment. in Re. VIII,* § 1, n. 27–29), while it recognizes the quasi-episcopal power of the Cardinals titular over their titular or diaconal churches, does not permit them to exercise the right of appointment to benefices in them, except on condition of their own presence in Rome. Moreover, this presence must be actual; constructive or fictional presence is not sufficient. *Regula Iuris 68, in VI°,* which reads: *"Potest quis per alium quod potest facere per se ipsum,"* does not apply where, as in this case, the matter in question demands personal presence. Other noted authorities on the *Regulae Cancelleriae* (Lotterius, Fagnanus et Gonzalez, Cardinal De Luca) hold the same opinion.

2. It is true that the *Regulae Cancelleriae* as such have not the force of law since the Code; but the Code itself has re-enacted some of their provisions, and this one is among them. For this Rule is precisely what is meant here by the words of canon 1435, § 3, *"leges peculiares de eisdem vigentes."* According to canon 6, 2°, where a provision of the old law is incorporated without change into the Code, it is to receive the same interpretation as under the old law.

3. The practice of the Apostolic Datary, even since the Code, has been in accord with this view; and this amounts to a norm of law under canon 20.

4. Nor can an argument to the contrary be drawn from canon 1432, § 1. That canon provides that a Cardinal titular has an *"intentionem in iure fundatam"* for conferring benefices in his own titular or diaconal church. But the general priority of right which is signified by the expression quoted, does not hold where, as in this case, there exists an express provision of law to the contrary.

Question. Whether, according to canon 1435, § 3, of the Code of Canon Law, the conferring of vacant benefices in titular or diaconal churches is reserved to the Holy See, when the respective Cardinals titular are absent from Rome.

Reply. In the affirmative.

His Holiness Pius XII, in the audience of June 18, 1943, deigned to approve and confirm this resolution.

AAS 35–399; S. C. Conc., 18 June, 1943. *Periodica,* 33–144 (Aguirre).

CANON 1470

Lay Right of Patronage Extinguished. See c. 396; AAS 37–118.

CANON 1495

Oriental Code: Canons on Ecclesiastical Property. See c. 487; AAS 44–65.

CANON 1503

Collecting Money for the Missions. See c. 622; AAS 44–549.

CANON 1517

Faculties to Reduce Masses: Revoked. See c. 828; AAS 41–374.
Revoked also in Oriental Church. See c. 828; AAS 41–373.

CANON 1520

In the Missions, these consultors or counsellors may be the same as those chosen for the Mission Council. Prefect of S. C. Prop. Fid., 13 June, 1921; *Primum Concilium Sinense*, n. 82.

CANON 1531

Proceeds of Alienation May Be Used for Extraordinary Repairs of Parish House or for Purchasing Necessary Equipment (Praes. Code Com., 17 Feb., 1920) Private.

The Bishop of Orense (Spain) asked the question to which the President of the Commission for the Interpretation of the Code replied as follows:

To the question presented by Your Excellency, namely:

Question. Whether according to canon 1531, § 3 the money received from the alienation of ecclesiastical property is all to be invested in securities or other productive property, or whether it can also be used for extraordinary repairs to the parish house or for buying something else, for example, sacred furnishings which are necessary or very convenient.

Reply. The Eminent President of the Commission replies: In the negative to the first part, in the affirmative to the second, observing, however, canon 1530, § 1, 2°, and canon 1477, § 2.

(**Private**); President, Code Com., 17 Feb., 1920. Reported by Beste, *Introductio in Codicem, ad can.* 1531.

Proceeds of Alienation to Be Invested Exclusively in Immovable Property (S. C. Conc., 17 Dec., 1951) AAS 44-44.

A Declaration of the Sacred Congregation of the Council:

Since it has been provided by the Decree of the Sacred Consistorial Congregation of 13 July, 1951,[1] that "in applying the prescriptions of canons 534, § 1, and 1532, § 1, n. 2, of the Code of Canon Law . . . while the present conditions continue . . . recourse is to be had to the Holy See whenever the sum of money involved exceeds ten thousand gold francs or lire," the question has been asked of this Sacred Congregation of the Council, whose business it is, according to canon 250, § 2 of the Code of Canon Law, also "to regulate matters which concern ecclesiastical property, movable and immovable."

Question. Whether the amount of money which is realized from these alienations of ecclesiastical property is to be invested only in acquiring immovable property for the benefit of the Church or of the corporation concerned.

Reply. Now this S. C. of the Council, after having carefully considered all aspects of the matter, and with the approval of His Holiness Pius XII, replied: In the affirmative, all things to the contrary notwithstanding.

Given at Rome, 17 Dec., 1951.

AAS 44-44; S. C. Conc., 17 Dec., 1951.

NOTE: Where there is question of alienations by religious Institutes, which are exclusively under the jurisdiction of the Sacred Congregation of Religious, the above norm has not been adopted. The practice of the S. C. of Religious still follows canon 1531, § 3, as explained by standard authors, and in particular by Larraona in *Commentarium pro Religiosis,* Vol. 13, pp. 359-362.

CANON 1532

Alienation: When Permission of Holy See Required. See c. 534; AAS 43-602.

In the Oriental Churches: Amount for which papal permission is required in alienations and debts. See c. 1; AAS 44-632.

---

[1] AAS 43-602; reported in this volume under canon 534.

CANON 1544

Pious Foundations Administered by Holy See. See c. 250; AAS 34–217.

CANON 1551

Faculties to Reduce Masses: Revoked. See c. 828; AAS 41–374.
Revoked also in Oriental Church. See c. 828; AAS 41–373.

BOOK IV

PROCEDURE

Canons 1552–2194

BOOK IV

PROCEDURE

Canons 1552–2194

CANON 1552

New Code of Procedure for the Oriental Church (Pius XII, *Motu proprio*, 6 Jan., 1950) **AAS 42–5.**

The *Motu proprio* of Pius XII, *De Iudiciis pro Ecclesia Orientali,* is as follows:

Turning Our solicitous attention to the welfare and progress of the Oriental Church, We promulgated on February 22, 1949, an Apostolic Letter regarding the discipline of marriage to be observed among the faithful of that Church,[1] and We rejoice that its results and consequences have not fallen short of Our expectations. For it has been no slight consolation to Us to receive from Our Legates in the territories of the Oriental Church and from the Bishops in those same territories, expressions of thanks and communications which openly attest that Our undertaking is commonly regarded as being of very great service. And these same persons, while they repeatedly begged that the entire Code of laws for the Oriental Church be published as soon as possible, also stated that it was quite urgent that at least the canons concerning ecclesiastical tribunals be published at once: for if this necessity were not met, great inconvenience and harm to the souls of the faithful would occur.

A further consideration is that some of the procedural laws

---

[1] AAS 41–89, reported in this volume under canon 1012.

which are in effect in the Oriental Church, suited to ancient times, had with the change of circumstances become either difficult to put into operation or not very conducive to the good of souls.

Not a few of them were of no use whatever, and often constituted an obstacle to the study of canon law, either because they constantly repeated the same things or because they were in conflict with other laws more recently enacted.

Moreover, it is necessary to protect and keep intact the sacred rights of the Church in the exercise of her judicial power, rights which are hers by divine commission, and thus to curb the attempts which notably flare up here and there in those territories, to arrogate trials of this kind to the civil magistrates.

In order to provide a remedy for these inconveniences and dangers, and to protect and restore rights concerning the due conduct of judicial trials, which involve in no small measure the peace and welfare of human society, having attentively and thoughtfully considered everything in the Lord, of Our own motion, with certain knowledge and in the fulness of Apostolic power, We have decided and decreed to publish now those canons concerning the aforesaid trials, which had been prepared by the Commission appointed to prepare a Code of laws for the Oriental Church.

The canons which We approve by Our Apostolic authority are the following:

(Here follows the text of canons 1–576. The matter covered corresponds to canons 1552–1998 of the Latin Code, that is, all of Book IV, *De Processibus*, except Part II, *De Causis Beatificationis*, etc., canons 1999–2141, and Part III, *De Modo Procedendi in Nonnullis Negotiis*, etc., canons 2142–2194.)

By this Apostolic Letter given of Our own motion, We promulgate the above canons and give them the force of law for the faithful of the Oriental Church, wherever in the world these may be. As soon as these canons go into effect in virtue of this Apostolic Letter, every statute, whether general or particular or special, even though enacted by Synods which were especially approved, and every prescription and custom still extant, whether general or particular, shall lose all force and effect, so that the discipline *de iudiciis* shall be governed solely by these canons, and particular law which is contrary to them shall no longer have any force except when and in so far as it is admitted in them.

But in order that timely notice of this Our Will may reach

all the persons concerned, We will and decree that this *motu proprio* Letter shall begin to take effect from the sixth day of January, the Epiphany of Our Lord, 1951, all things, even those worthy of most special mention, to the contrary notwithstanding.

Given at Rome, on the 6th of January, the Epiphany of Our Lord, in the year 1950, the eleventh of Our Pontificate.

AAS 42–5; Pius XII, *Motu proprio,* 6 Jan., 1950.

CANON 1553

Judicial Jurisdiction of the Church: Its Origin and Nature
(Pius XII, Allocution, 2 Oct., 1945) **AAS 37–256.**

An Allocution of His Holiness Pius XII, delivered to the Most Reverend Auditors and to the other Officials and Ministers of the Tribunal of the Sacred Roman Rota, and to the Advocates and Procurators, on October 2, 1945, is as follows:

Since that time when it pleased the Lord, Supreme Judge of all justice among men, to constitute Us His Representative and Vicar here below, to-day, after listening to the complete and learned annual report of the work of this Sacred Tribunal which has been presented to Us by your worthy Dean, We have for the first time the opportunity, beloved sons, to express Our gratitude and to set forth Our thoughts, without Our voice being drowned by the sinister rumblings of armed strife. Dare we say that we have peace? Not yet, alas! God grant that it be at least the dawn of peace! Once the violence of battle subsides, there rings the hour of justice, whose work consists in restoring by its judgments the order which has been upset or disturbed. Awful indeed are the dignity and power of the judge, which, whether in deciding controversies or repressing crimes, must rise above all passions and prejudices and reflect the justice of God Himself.

Such is in fact the object of all judgment, the purpose of all judicial power, ecclesiastical or civil. A rapid and superficial survey of judicial laws and practice might give the impression that ecclesiastical and civil procedure present only secondary differences, about the same as those which are to be observed in the administration of justice in two States which belong to the same juridical family. They seem to coincide in their immediate purpose: the enforcement or protection, either through a judicial sentence or through an authoritative decree rendered according to law, of a right which is established by law but which is contested or violated in a particular case. In both systems too, we find various stages of judicial procedure; in both, the procedure consists in about the same principal elements: a petition for the introduction of the case, a summons, the examination of witnesses, the communication of documents, the questioning of the parties, the termination of the trial, the judgment, the right of appeal.

Yet this broad similarity, both external and internal, must not obscure the profound difference which exists between the two systems: (1) in their origin and nature; (2) in their object; (3) in their purpose. Today We shall confine ourselves to speaking of the first of these three points, reserving the treatment of the other two to future years, if so it please the Divine Majesty.

I

The judicial power is an essential part and a necessary function of the two perfect societies, the Church and the State. Hence the question of the origin of judicial power in each is the same as that of the origin of their authority in general.

And precisely for this reason, some have thought to find in the two systems further similarities more fundamental than those which have already been noted. It is interesting to observe how some of the exponents of the various modern theories regarding civil authority have adduced, in confirmation or in support of their opinions, the supposed analogies of civil with ecclesiastical authority. This is true of so-called "totalitarianism" and "authoritarianism" as well as of their opposite pole, modern democracy. In truth, however, those more fundamental similarities do not exist in any of the three cases, as a brief survey will easily demonstrate.

It is undeniable that one of the vital exigencies of every human community, hence also of the Church and the State, consists in the permanent assurance of unity in the diversity of their members.

Now "totalitarianism" is utterly incapable of providing for this need, because it extends the civil power beyond due limits; it determines and fixes, both in substance and form, every field of activity, and thus compresses all legitimate manifestation of life

— personal, local, and professional — into a mechanical unity or collectivity under the stamp of nation, race, or class.

We have already, in Our Christmas Radio Message of 1942, pointed out the deplorable consequences for the judiciary power of this attitude in theory and in practice, which destroys the equality of all persons before the law, and leaves judicial decisions to the whim of changeable collective instinct.

For that matter, who could ever dream that interpretations of law so false and so flagrantly in violation of human rights, could have determined the origin or influenced the action of ecclesiastical tribunals? This is not the case, and it never will be, because it is contrary to the very nature of the social authority of the Church, as we shall presently see.

The fundamental exigency which has been mentioned is also far from being satisfied by that other concept of civil authority, which may be called "authoritarianism," because it excludes the citizens from all effective participation in or influence upon the formation of the will of the society. Consequently, it splits the nation into two categories, the rulers and the ruled, and the relations between the two are either purely mechanical as the result of force or have no more than a biological basis.

Who can fail to see that this is a complete perversion of the true nature of the power of the State? For this power, both in itself and through the exercise of its functions, must tend to make of the State a true community, intimately united in a final purpose which is the common good. But in this system the concept of the common good is so unsubstantial and is so obviously but a mask for the unilateral interests of the ruler, that an unrestrained "dynamism" on the part of the law-making power excludes all juridical security and so destroys a basic element of every true judicial order.

Such a false dynamism could not fail to submerge and destroy the essential rights which are acknowledged as belonging to physical and moral persons in the Church. The nature of ecclesiastical authority has nothing in common with this "authoritarianism"; the latter can claim no point of resemblance to the hierarchical constitution of the Church.

It remains to examine the democratic form of government, in which some would find a closer similarity to the power of the Church. Beyond a doubt, where there is true democracy in theory and in practice, this form of government satisfies the vital exigency of every sound community to which We have referred. But the same is to be said, or may under the same conditions be said, also of the other legitimate forms of government.

Certainly the Christian Middle Ages, especially inspired as they were with the spirit of the Church, demonstrated by the abundance of their flourishing democratic communities that the Christian faith can produce a genuine and true democracy, nay, that it is the only durable foundation for democracy. For a democracy without an accord of spirits, at least as to the fundamental maxims of life, especially as to the rights of God and the dignity of the human person, and as to the respect which is due to the honest activity and liberty of the person — such a democracy would be defective and unsound even from a political standpoint. And therefore, when the people fall away from the Christian faith or fail to hold it resolutely as the principle of civil life, then even democracy is easily altered and deformed, and in the course of time is liable to fall into "totalitarianism" or the "authoritarianism" of a one-party government.

If, on the other hand, we bear in mind the favorite thesis of democracy — a doctrine which great Christian thinkers have proclaimed in all ages — namely, that the original subject of civil power derived from God is the people (not the "masses"), the distinction between the Church and even the democratic State becomes increasingly clear.

II

The fact is that the authority of the Church, and hence also its judicial power, are essentially different from those of the State.

The origin of the Church, in contrast to that of the State, is not from the natural law. The most complete and accurate analysis of the human person offers no ground for the conclusion that the Church, like civil society, was naturally bound to come into existence and to develop. The Church is the product of a positive act of God, and is therefore on a plane above the social nature of man, though in perfect accord with it; and hence the authority of the Church — and consequently also her corresponding judicial power — are born of the will and act by which Christ founded His Church. It remains true, however, that, once the

Church was established as a perfect society by the act of the Redeemer, there sprang from her very nature not a few elements of resemblance to the structure of civil society.

However, this fundamental difference between the two is particularly manifest in one point. The establishment of the Church as a society was effected, not from below, as in the case of the origin of the State, but on the contrary from above; that is to say, Christ, who in His Church established on earth the Kingdom of God which He announced and destined for all men and for all times, did not entrust to the community of the faithful the mission of Master, Priest, and Pastor which He had received from His Father for the salvation of the human race, but He transmitted and communicated it to a college of Apostles or messengers chosen by Himself, so that they, by their preaching, by their priestly ministry, and by the social power of their office, should bring the multitude of the faithful into the Church, in order to sanctify them, enlighten them, and bring them to the full maturity of followers of Christ.

Look at the words in which He communicated to them their powers: the power to offer sacrifice in remembrance of Him (Luke, 22:19), the power to forgive sins (John, 20:21–23), the promise and the gift of the supreme power of the keys to Peter and to his Successors in person (Matt., 16:19; John, 21:15–17), the communication to all the Apostles of the power to bind and to loose (Matt., 18:18). Finally, ponder the words with which Christ, before His Ascension, transmitted to these same Apostles the universal commission which He received from the Father (Matt., 28:18–20; John, 20:21). Is there anything in all this which can leave room for doubt or equivocation? The whole history of the Church, from its beginning to our own day, does not cease to echo those words and to give the same testimony with a clearness and precision which no subtlety can disturb or conceal. Now, all these words, all these testimonies proclaim with one accord that in the authority of the Church the essence, the central point according to the express will of Christ, and hence by divine law, is the commission which He gave to the ministers of the work of salvation in the community of the faithful and in the whole human race.

Canon 109 of the Code of Canon Law has put this marvelous edifice in a clear light and in monumental relief: "Those who are admitted to the ecclesiastical hierarchy are chosen, not by the consent or at the call of the people or of the secular power; but they are established in the various grades of the power of order by sacred ordination; in the supreme pontificate, by the divine law itself upon fulfillment of the condition of legitimate election and the acceptance thereof; in the other grades of jurisdiction, by canonical mission."

"Not by the consent or at the call of the people or of the secular power": The faithful or the secular power may in the course of the centuries have participated often in the designation of those upon whom ecclesiastical offices were to be conferred; and to all of these, including the supreme pontificate, the son of the most humble workingman's family is as eligible as the scion of a noble stock. Yet in reality the members of the ecclesiastical Hierarchy have received and always do receive their authority from above, and are responsible for the exercise of their mandate only immediately to God, to whom alone the Roman Pontiff is subject, or, in the case of the other grades, to their hierarchical Superiors; they have no account to render either to the people or to the civil power, without prejudice, of course, to the right of any of the faithful to present in due form to the competent ecclesiastical authority, or even directly to the supreme power in the Church, their petitions and recourses, especially when the petitioner or the institutor of the recourse is actuated by motives which concern his personal responsibility for his own or other persons' spiritual welfare.

From what we have said there follow two principal conclusions:

1. In the Church, otherwise than in the State, the primordial subject of power, the supreme judge, the highest court of appeal, is never the community of the faithful. There is not, therefore, and there cannot be in the Church, as it is founded by Christ, a popular tribunal or a judicial power deriving from the people.

2. The question of the extent and scope of ecclesiastical authority also presents itself in a way totally different from that of the State. For the Church the primary source of authority is the express will of Christ, who could give her, according to His wisdom and goodness, means and powers of greater or lesser extent, saving always the minimum which is necessarily required by her nature and purpose. The power of the Church embraces man in his entirety, his internal and external relations, for the

attainment of his supernatural destiny, so that he is completely subject to the law of Christ, of which the Church has been constituted by her divine Founder the custodian and executrix, in the external as well as in the internal forum or forum of conscience. It is therefore a full and perfect power, though far removed from that "totalitarianism" which does not admit or recognize proper regard for the clear and inalienable dictates of conscience, and which does violence to the laws of individual and social life which are written in the hearts of men (Rom., 2:15). In fact the Church in the use of her power does not aim to enslave the human person, but to assure its liberty and perfection, redeeming it from the weaknesses, errors, and aberrations of the spirit and of the affections, which sooner or later always end in dishonor and servitude.

The sacred character which belongs to ecclesiastical jurisdiction by reason of its divine origin and of the fact that it is part of the hierarchical power of the Church, must inspire you, beloved sons, with a high esteem of your office, and spur you on to fulfill its austere duties with a lively faith, unswerving rectitude and ever vigilant zeal. But, behind the veil of this austerity, what splendor reveals itself to one who sees in the judicial power the majesty of justice, which in all its action tends to make the Church, the Spouse of Christ, appear "holy and without blemish" (Eph., 5:27) before her divine Spouse and before the world of men!

On this day, which marks the opening of your new juridical year, We invoke upon you, beloved sons, the favor and the aid of the Father of light, of Christ, to whom He hath given all judgment (John, 5:22), of the Spirit of wisdom, counsel, and fortitude, of the Blessed Virgin Mary, mirror of justice and seat of wisdom, while with cordial affection We impart to all of you here present, to your families and all persons who are dear to you, Our paternal Apostolic Blessing.

AAS 37–256; Pius XII, Allocution, 2 Oct., 1945. Annotations, *Periodica*, 34–256 (Aguirre).

Judicial Power of the Church Compared With That of the State in Regard to the Ends of the Two Societies
(Pius XII, 29 Oct., 1947) **AAS 39–493.**

An allocution of His Holiness Pius XII, of 29 October, 1947, to the Auditors and other Officials and Ministers of the Tribunal of the Sacred Roman Rota, and to its Advocates and Procurators, is as follows:

It is particularly pleasing to Us, beloved sons, to have you gathered before Us once more, and to extend to you Our thankful greetings, after having heard from the lips of your venerated Dean the account of the ever increasing and arduous work which has been done by your Sacred Tribunal in the course of the past year. For the Church it has been a year of consolations and also of trials, of conquests and of struggles, in the ever changing and contradictory, yet persistent, opposition to her on the part of the world, according to those words of the Redeemer: "If the world hate you, know ye that it hath hated me before you."[1]

Thus, what yesterday was by many regarded as a duty on the part of the Church and was demanded of her even in unseemly ways, namely, that she should resist the unjust impositions of totalitarian governments in their oppression of consciences, and should denounce and condemn them before the world (a thing which she never failed to do, but of her own free choice and in the proper manner), has become in the eyes of those same men, now that they have risen to power, a crime and an unlawful interference by the Church in the field of civil authority. And the same arguments which were adduced by the tyrannical governments of yesterday against the Church in her fight for the defense of the rights of God and the true dignity and liberty of man, are today being used by new dictators to oppose the continuing action of the Church in defense of truth and justice. But the Church goes straight along her way, ever tending toward the end set for her by her divine Founder, that is, to lead men by the supernatural paths of virtue and welldoing, to the eternal happiness of heaven; and in doing this she is at the same time promoting peace and prosperity in the common life of men upon earth.

This thought brings Us naturally to the third point of the subject which We proposed for your consideration in the past two years.[2] And so, as We have already spoken of the differences between the judicial systems of the Church and of the State in

---

[1] John 15:18.

[2] The Allocution of 2 Oct., 1945, is reported above, in this volume, under this same canon 1553; that of 6 Oct., 1946, is in this volume under canon 2314.

their respective origins and natures and in their respective objects, We shall speak today of the essentially different ends of the two societies.

This last difference based on the end undoubtedly excludes that forced subjection of the Church to the State, and as it were her absorption in it, contrary to the very nature of both, which every totalitarian government tries, at least in the beginning, to bring about. It certainly does not, however, deny all union between the two societies, and much less does it interpose between them a cold and unfriendly atmosphere of agnosticism and indifference. One who would thus misunderstand the true doctrine that the Church and the State are two distinct perfect societies, would be mistaken. He could not explain the many forms of union between the two powers which, both in the past and in the present, have been fruitful though in varying degrees; he would above all be losing sight of the fact that the Church and the State arise from the same source, that is, from God, and that both are concerned with the same object, man, his personal dignity, natural or supernatural. All this, Our glorious Predecessor Leo XIII could not have overlooked, nor did he intend to, when in his Encyclical, *Immortale Dei*, of 1 Nov., 1885, he clearly outlined, on the basis of their different ends, the limits of the two societies, and observed that the State is concerned proximately and chiefly with caring for the earthly interests, and the Church with the quest of the heavenly and eternal interests of men, that is, in as much as men need protection and support both from the State in earthly matters and from the Church in those that are eternal.

Do we not find here, in some respects, a certain analogy with the relation between body and soul? Both act conjointly in such a way that the psychological character of a man is influenced at every moment by his temperament and his physiological conditions, while conversely, moral impressions, affections, and passions are so strongly reflected in the physical sensibility that the soul models the very outlines of the face, tracing upon it as it were her own image.

There is, therefore, that difference as regards the end, which has a profound and different influence on the Church and the State, especially on the supreme power of the two societies, and hence also on the judicial power, which is but one of their parts and functions. Whether individual ecclesiastical judges are conscious of it or not, all their judicial activity is and remains within the scope of the full life of the Church, with her exalted end: *to secure the heavenly and eternal values*. This *finis operis* of the ecclesiastical judicial power impresses upon it an objective character and makes of it an institution of the Church as a supernatural society. And because this character derives from the supernatural end of the Church, the ecclesiastical judicial power will never fall into that rigidity and immobility to which merely earthly institutions are easily subject through fear of responsibility, or through indolence, or even through a mistaken anxiety to protect the security of law, though this last is certainly a highly estimable good.

This does not mean, however, that in the ecclesiastical judicial order there is a field left free to the mere whim of the judge in dealing with particular cases. Such mistaken ideas of a pretended "vitality" of the law, in reality deplorable, are the sad fruits of our time in activities foreign to the Church. Untouched by an anti-intellectualism which is rather widespread today, the Church holds fast to the principle: the judge decides each case according to law; a principle which, without favoring an excessive "juridical formalism" of which We spoke on another occasion,[3] nevertheless rejects that "subjective caprice" which would end by placing the judge no longer under but above the law. To have a right understanding of the law as expressed by the legislator, and to make a correct estimate of the particular case with a view to the application of the law — this intellectual labor is an esential part of the activity of the judge in concrete cases. Without it, the sentence of the judge would be a mere command, and not what is expressed by the term *"positive* law," that is, in the particular and hence concrete case, a *placing* of order in the world, which as a whole has been created by the wisdom of God in order and for order.

Is not this field of judicial activity rich with life? Nay, more: ecclesiastical law is applied to the common good of the ecclesiastical society, and is therefore inseparably bound to the end of the Church. Hence the judge, when he applies the law to a par-

---

[3] See this volume, under canon 1869; Allocution to Rota, 1 Oct., 1942; AAS 34–338.

ticular case, is cooperating to bring to its full fruition the end which lives in the Church. On the other hand, when he finds himself confronted with doubtful cases, or when the law leaves him free, the bond which unites the ecclesiastical judicial system to the end of the Church herself will help him even then to find and to motivate the right decision and to keep his office free from the taint of mere arbitrary action.

Hence, from whatever point of view the relation of ecclesiastical judicial power to the end be considered, it reveals itself as the surest guarantee of the vitality of judicial decisions, and at the same time it puts the ecclesiastical judge in an office which is willed by God, and inspires him with that high sense of responsibility which, also in the Church, is the indispensable safeguard, superior to any legal ordinance, of the security of law.

In saying this We do not wish in any way to overlook the practical difficulties which, in spite of all, modern life creates for the ecclesiastical judicial power, even more notably in some respects than it does in the civil field. Think only of certain spiritual goods in regard to which the judicial power of the State feels itself less strictly bound, or even remains consciously indifferent. Typical cases of this sort are those of the crimes against the faith, or apostasy, those which concern "freedom of conscience" and "religious tolerance," as well as matrimonial trials. In these cases the Church, and hence too the ecclesiastical judge, cannot adopt the neutral attitude of States of mixed religious faith, and still less that of a world fallen into incredulity and religious indifferentism, but she must be guided solely by her essential end as given her by God.

Thus we are ever encountering anew the profound difference which the diversity of ends makes between the ecclesiastical and the civil judicial powers. Nothing of course prevents one of them from taking advantage of results obtained by the other, whether in the way of theoretical knowledge or practical experience; but it would be a mistake to seek to transfer mechanically the elements and norms of one system to the other, or, worse still, to regard them as directly equal. The judicial power of the Church and the ecclesiastical judge have not to seek their ideal elsewhere; they must carry it within themselves; they must keep ever before their eyes the fact that the Church is a supernatural organism, quick with a vital principle which is divine and which must move and direct also the judicial power and the office of the ecclesiastical judge.

In virtue of their office and by the will of God, the Bishops, of whom the Apostle says that they are "placed by the Holy Ghost to rule the Church of God,"[4] are judges in the Church. "To rule" includes "to judge" as a necessary function. Hence according to the Apostle the Holy Spirit calls Bishops to the office of judge no less than to the government of the Church. The sacred character of that office, therefore, comes from the Holy Spirit. The faithful of God's Church, whom He has "purchased with His own blood," are those upon whom the judicial activity is exercised. The law according to which judgments are pronounced in the Church is fundamentally the law of Christ. It is the divine vital principle in the Church which moves every one and everything in her — hence also the judicial power and the judge — toward her end: *to secure the heavenly and eternal values.*

You who have the office of judges in this ordinary Tribunal of the Apostolic See must be conscious of your peculiar dignity; not in any spirit of pretension or of pride, but in the simple and humble sense of fulfilling a sacred duty. Then will the ideal of your office be renewed in you, not so much as a result of your own efforts, but rather as a grace of the Holy Spirit.

But We intend on this occasion above all to express Our gratitude for the work which you have done, and especially for the spirit of religious devotedness which it clearly manifests. Bitter criticisms, of opposite content and proceeding from contrary principles, such as those which are directed against you, are already of themselves usually a sign that those at whom they are aimed are in the right; and since in your case this presumption is confirmed by the eloquent statistical data which have been presented by your Dean, all honest men must be convinced that conscientious respect for the law of God, together with a firm determination to protect truth and justice and that "goodness and kindness"[5] which the divine Saviour brought into the world and which is characteristic of those who have at heart the salvation of souls, are truly the guiding star which directs all your activity as judges.

On that star keep your outlook ever fixed, without allowing

---

[4] Acts 20:28.   [5] Tit. 3:4.

yourselves to be disturbed by the tempestuous waves of human passions and hostile attacks, contented and happy in the con- sciousness that you are contributing by your work to "the edifying of the body of Christ."[6]

Imploring on your behalf an abundance of divine grace to make your labors fruitful, We cordially impart to you, beloved sons, Our paternal Apostolic Blessing.

AAS 39–493; Pius XII, 29 Oct., 1947.

CANON 1594

One Appellate Tribunal for the Vicariates Apostolic of Egypt. See S. C. Eccl. Or., 12 July, 1943 (AAS 36–307).

CANON 1598

Organization of Studies in the Sacred Roman Rota (Rota, 8 June, 1945) AAS 37–193.

A Decree regarding the organization of the course of studies in the Rota:

The Sacred Roman Rota has nothing more at heart than the progress of its Course of Studies, which has brought it no little credit and prestige in the history of jurisprudence.

It is not surprising that, as soon as it was restored to its ancient practice, the Sacred Rota took energetic measures to establish its new Course of Studies by the ordinance issued on December 21, 1911.

The Sacred Congregation of the Sacraments too, which is especially interested in the sacrament of marriage, when it issued its new Instruction of August 15, 1936, declared: "It is therefore the wish of the Holy See, as the Most Reverend Ordinaries of places well know, that select young priests who have received at least the doctorate in Canon Law in this Holy City, should be trained, especially in the School of the Sacred Roman Rota, to conduct trials properly and to decide cases rightly according to justice and truth."[1]

Hence, in order to respond more closely to the mind of the Holy See and to provide for the dignity of ecclesiastical tribunals

---

[6] Eph. 4:12.
[1] CANON LAW DIGEST, Vol. 2, p. 472.

and the good of souls, the Sacred Rota has decided to supplant the earlier ordinance, which in some respects had already grown obsolete, with the present one, which is better suited to the needs of the times.

I. The Sacred Roman Rota conducts a Course of Studies, which must be attended for three years by all who aspire to the title of Procurator and Advocate of the Rota.

II. The School is under the authority and supervision of the Dean of the Sacred Roman Rota.

III. Upon presentation by the Dean, the College of Auditors elects the Director of the School from among the Auditors, and it may elect also an Assistant Director from among the Officials of the Sacred Tribunal.

IV. The instructors in the School shall be Auditors or Officials of the Rota, or other persons selected each year by the Dean after consulting the Director.

V. The following courses are given in the School:

1. Judicial Deontology, that is, moral theology applied to the work of the tribunal;

2. Jurisprudence of various departments of canon law, especially the law of marriage, the penal law, and the law of procedure;

3. Practice in the offices of the tribunal.

The method in use in the School consists chiefly of exercises and discussions.

VI. It is the duty of the Director to organize and arrange the prescribed courses, to make provisions for the proper conduct of the School, to report to the Dean on the condition of the School, and to make suggestions for its improvement.

VII. The Assistant Director shall assist the Director in conducting the School, keep the documents which pertain to it, and in general see that the orders of the Director are perfectly carried out.

VIII. Those who may be enrolled in the School are clerics, secular or religious, and laymen, who have at least the licentiate in canon law and are properly recommended by their Ordinary; clerics must moreover present a *"nihil obstat"* from the Vicariate of Rome. But no one shall be admitted to the examination for Procurator or Advocate, unless he has acquired at least the doctorate in canon law in a University or Faculty recognized by the Holy See.

One who has received the baccalaureate in canon law, and who wishes to attend the School, without aspiring to the title of Procurator or Advocate of the Rota, may apply to the Dean to be admitted as a special student (*auditor extraordinarius*).

IX. Enrollment in the School is reserved to the decision of the Dean.

Enrolled students are bound to take an oath each year according to the usual formula; and the fact that it has been taken by each one shall be inscribed by a notary in the records.

X. The students must be present at the exercises, must study the cases assigned to them, give their decisions upon them, explain the questions submitted to them, make the assigned researches in the library, and perform other tasks of the same sort; they may also assist at oral discussions unless the Dean or the *Ponens* forbids it.

XI. The students may, in accordance with the rules of the tribunal, look over the statement of cases which are assigned to them, and also, on designated days and hours, frequent the library of the tribunal; but they may not take away with them either the statements of cases or books from the library. On the completion of each task, they must return to the tribunal the summaries and whatever other records they may have.

XII. The Instructors are to pass judgment on the trials of the students and enter them in the record; and these written judgments together with the grade attained in the examinations are to be preserved in the archives of the School.

XIII. At the completion of each year, after a special examination, the Instructors shall give their judgment in writing on the diligence, industry, work and merit of each student, and declare whether they deem them worthy of being advanced to the next year; this advancement is decided by the Dean.

XIV. Upon the completion of the three years' course, if he has passed all the annual examinations, the candidate may apply to the Dean to take the written examination before the College of the Rota, to receive the title of Advocate of the Rota.

If he passes this examination successfully, the candidate, upon taking the oath before the College of the Rota, is admitted to practice as a Procurator and Advocate and receives a diploma as Advocate of the Rota.

His Holiness, in the audience of 8 June, 1945, confirmed and approved this Decree and ordered that it be observed.

Rome, 8 June, 1945.

AAS 37-193; Rota, Decree, 8 June, 1945.

Rota: Some Notes Concerning Relations With Diocesan Curias (Ap. Del., U. S., 3 Dec., 1946) Private.

Your Excellency:

The Most Reverend Monsignor Jullien, Dean of the Sacred Roman Rota, advised me to call the following points to the attention of the Most Reverend Ordinaries:

1. When the diocesan Curias have occasion to send copies of the authentic text of a process, they are respectfully asked to send at the same time an authentic translation of the same into Latin, Italian, or French. In that way considerable expense will be saved the parties to the suit and also the Holy See in causes which are of gratuitous advocacy.

2. The Tribunal of the Sacred Roman Rota desires to be spared, as much as possible, the necessity of intervening between the parties and their advocates for the transmission of honoraria and other sums which the clients may owe to their advocates.

3. It will help a great deal toward the formation of future officials of the diocesan tribunals, if the Most Reverend Ordinaries, especially those of the courts of appeal, will please to send some priests who have at least the licentiate in canon law, to the *Studium Rotale* (cfr. *Acta Apostolicae Sedis*, Vol. 37, p. 193).[1]

A course of practical exercises, such as can be had at the *Studium Rotale*, will prove to be of great service to the Curias and Tribunals.

(**Private**); Apostolic Delegate, U. S., 3 Dec., 1946. The Most Reverend Apostolic Delegate kindly sent us the letter.

Allocutions of Pius XII to Roman Rota:
   1942: see c. 1869; AAS 34-338;
   1944: see c. 1960; AAS 36-281;
   1945: see c. 1553; AAS 37-256;
   1946: see c. 2314; AAS 38-391;
   1947: see c. 1553; AAS 39-493.

---

[1] See document reported above in this volume under this same canon 1598.

Spanish Rota: Suppressed. By letter of 1 Aug., 1933, to the Ordinaries of Spain, the Nuncio announced that the Holy See suppressed the Spanish Rota as to ecclesiastical cases, in view of the violations of the Concordat and the secularization of marriage. See *Periodica*, 22–207; *Sal Terrae*, 1933, p. 1007.

Spanish Rota Re-established. See Pius XII, *Motu proprio*, 7 Apr., 1947 (AAS 39–155). Cf. *Nouvelle Revue Théologique*, Vol. 69, p. 868. For an outline of the history of the Spanish Rota, see *Annuario Pontificio*, 1937, p. 656.

CANON 1651

Decree of Ordinary Sufficient for Appointment of Guardian (Code Com., 25 Jan., 1943) AAS 35–58.

The Code Commission was asked:

I. Whether, in virtue of canon 1651, § 1, in order to appoint a guardian for persons who are deprived of the use of reason or who are weak-minded, a regular judgment is necessary, or whether a decree of the Ordinary, given after he has prudently investigated the matter, is sufficient.

Reply. In the negative to the first part, in the affirmative to the second.

AAS 35–58; Code Com., 25 Jan., 1943.
Periodica, 32–294 (Aguirre).

NOTE: A second reply given at the same time is reported under canon 1712.

CANON 1709

Recourse From Decree Rejecting Bill of Complaint. See c. 1971; Rota, 6 Aug., 1952.

CANON 1712

Notice of Summons and Publication of Sentence to Be Made to Guardian (Code Com., 25 Jan., 1943) AAS 35–58.

The Code Commission was asked:

II. Whether the notice of the summons and the communication of the sentence, which are mentioned in canons 1712 and 1877, should be made to the person himself who is deprived of the use of reason or weak-minded, or to the lawfully appointed guardian of the same.

Reply. In the negative to the first part, in the affirmative to the second.

AAS 35–58; Code Com., 25 Jan., 1943.
Periodica, 32–294 (Aguirre).

NOTE: Another reply given at the same time is reported under canon 1651.

CANON 1789

Moral Certainty Possible Even With Only One Witness *de Scientia*. See c. 1791; Rota, 17 July, 1952.

CANON 1791

Moral Certainty of Nullity of Marriage Attained Although Only One Witness *de Scientia* Was Produced (Rota, 17 July, 1952) **Private.**

In a very incomplete report of a case for the nullity of marriage on the ground of force and fear, which was definitely decided by the Rota, 17 July, 1952 (*coram* Felici), only that part of the decision is given which discusses the sufficiency of proof.

In order to pronounce judgment the judge must have moral certainty (c. 1869, § 1). In attaining this certainty, much depends on the prudent discretion of the judge himself. Yet he is not left beyond control from certain definite procedural laws. He is subject to exception if reasonably suspected of prejudice (c. 1896); he is given certain general norms by which to evaluate testimony (c. 1789); he is cautioned that the testimony of a single witness, unless he is a *testis qualificatus* testifying to matters within the scope of his office, does not amount to full proof (c. 1791, § 1).

The Court discusses these principles in the light of the authorities. Against too formalistic an interpretation of procedural norms, the Court quotes the words of Pius XII on the attainment of moral certainty, from the Allocution of 1 October, 1942.[1]

Finally, on this question of the sufficiency of the evidence, the Court says:

"Therefore, although there is but one witness *de scientia,* never-

---

[1] AAS 34–338, reported in full in this volume under canon 1869.

theless in view of the facts that: 1) this one witness is of the highest credibility and is strongly and unequivocally corroborated by hearsay witnesses who, because the time at which they heard the story gives no ground for suspicion and because of their trustworthiness both by reason of their character and the circumstances, serve as an excellent support for the witness *de scientia* mentioned in canon 1791; 2) that the plaintiff is of the highest character and is regarded as exemplary by men high in ecclesiastical dignity; 3) that the defendant, who coerced the plaintiff to consent, did not dare openly to deny the charge though it would have been much to his advantage to do so; 4) that many circumstances following the marriage tend to support the plaintiff's case; there is moral certainty that the coercion alleged by the plaintiff, that is, grave and unjust, and such as to nullify the marriage, of a truth really existed."

(**Private**); Rota, 17 July, 1952 (*coram* Felici). *Monitor Ecclesiasticus,* 1952, p. 599.

CANON 1804

Unanimous Opinion of Experts: Disregarded by the Rota, and reasons for rejection given in a case for declaration of nullity of marriage. See c. 1081; Rota, 25 Feb., 1941.

Weight of Expert Testimony. See c. 1960; S. C. Sacr., 15 Aug., 1949, n. 5.

CANON 1869

Moral Certitude Especially in Marriage Cases (Pius XII, Allocution to Rota, 1 Oct., 1942) AAS 34–338.

An Allocution of His Holiness Pius XII to the Prelates, Auditors, and other Officials and Ministers of the Sacred Roman Rota, and to its Advocates and Procurators:

To see you, beloved sons, assembled in Our presence for the inauguration of the new juridical year of the Sacred Roman Rota, is a refreshment and comfort to Us, not only for what the well ordered speech of your most worthy Dean has reported to Us about your work and the many cases you have disposed of, but still more because this reunion of filial homage was preceded by the devout ritual invocation of the gifts of the Holy Spirit, that Spirit sent by the Father[1] and by Christ[2] to renew the face of

---

[1] John 14:26.   [2] John 16:7.

the earth.[3] Oh, that under the impulse of that life-giving Spirit, which hovered over the primordial darkness of the abyss, the face of the earth were again to-day to be renewed! Oh, that the world of men, embroiled by the calamitous clashes between peoples and nations, might blossom forth once more in a springtime of justice and peace! Surely the Spirit of God, who gives Us once more the joy of speaking to you, gives you afresh the life and vigorous strength which you need for the mental labors that await you in the guardianship of right and justice amid the Christian people; whilst Our words confirm, and as it were renew, the dignity and authority which Our Predecessors wished to see attributed and entrusted to the Sacred Roman Rota.

The Spirit of Christ, Redeemer of the human race, who through His Gospel raised to a higher perfection the faith and worship of the true God, also renewed the morals of mankind and of human marriage, restoring marriage to that unity and indissolubility which, as experience shows, constitute the greater part of the matter of your judicial sentences. The conditions requisite for the validity of marriage, the impediments and the effects of the conjugal bond (without prejudice to the competency of the State regarding the merely civil effects) have their guardian and defender in the Church, through the authority which she has received from her divine Founder and which is supremely personified in the Roman Pontiff.

1. In cases which involve psychic or physical incapacity to contract marriage, as well as in those which have for their object a declaration of nullity of marriage or, in certain determinate cases, the dissolution of the bond of a marriage validly contracted, We spoke, in Our discourse to you last year, of the need of *moral certainty*. The importance of the subject induces Us to examine this concept more thoroughly; because, according to canon 1869, § 1, in order that the judge may be able to pronounce his decision, there is required moral certainty regarding the facts of the case which is to be decided. Now this certainty, based on the constancy of the laws and practices which govern human life, admits of various degrees.

There is an absolute certainty, in which all possible doubt

---

[3] Ps. 103:30.

as to the truth of the fact and the unreality of the contrary is entirely excluded. Such absolute certainty, however, is not necessary in order to pronounce the judgment. In many cases it is humanly unattainable; to require it would be to demand of the judge and of the parties something which is unreasonable; it would put an intolerable burden on the administration of justice and would very seriously obstruct it.

In contrast to this supreme degree of certitude, common speech often designates as certain a cognition which strictly speaking does not merit to be so called, but should rather be classed as a greater or lesser probability, because it does not exclude all reasonable doubt, but leaves a foundation for the fear of error. This probability, or quasi-certainty, does not afford a sufficient basis for a judicial sentence regarding the objective truth of the fact.

In such a case, that is, when the lack of certainty regarding the fact at issue forbids pronouncing a positive judgment on the merits of the case, the law, and especially the rules of procedure, supply the judge with obligatory norms of action, in which *presumptions of law* and rules regarding *the favor of the law* have a decisive importance. The judge cannot afford to ignore these rules of law and of procedure. Yet it would be an exaggerated and wrong application of these norms, and as it were a false interpretation of the mind of the legislator, were the judge to seek recourse to them, when there is not only a quasi-certainty, but certitude in the proper and true sense. There are no presumptions nor favor of law as against the truth and a sure knowledge thereof.

Between the two extremes of absolute certainty and quasi-certainty or probability, is that *moral certainty* which is usually involved in the cases submitted to your court, and of which We principally wish to speak. It is characterized on the positive side by the exclusion of well-founded or reasonable doubt, and in this respect it is essentially distinguished from the quasi-certainty which has been mentioned; on the negative side, it does admit the absolute possibility of the contrary, and in this it differs from absolute certainty. The certainty of which We are now speaking is necessary and sufficient for the rendering of a judgment, even though in the particular case it would be possible either directly or indirectly to reach absolute certainty. Only thus is it possible to have a regular and orderly administration of justice, going forward without useless delays and without laying excessive burdens on the tribunal as well as on the parties.

2. Sometimes moral certainty is derived only from an aggregate of indications and proofs which; taken singly, do not provide the foundation for true certitude, but which, when taken together, no longer leave room for any reasonable doubt on the part of a man of sound judgment. This is in no sense a passage from probability to certainty through a simple cumulation of probabilities, which would amount to an illegitimate transit from one species to another essentially different one: εἰς ἄλλο γένος μετάβασις;[4] it is rather to recognize that the simultaneous presence of all these separate indications and proofs can have a sufficient basis only in the existence of a common origin or foundation from which they spring, that is, in objective truth and reality. In this case, therefore, certainty arises from the wise application of a principle which is absolutely secure and universally valid, namely the principle of a sufficient reason. Consequently, if in giving the reasons for his decision, the judge states that the proofs which have been adduced, considered separately, cannot be judged sufficient, but that, taken together and embraced in a survey of the whole situation, they provide the necessary elements for arriving at a safe definitive judgment, it must be acknowledged that such reasoning is in general sound and legitimate.

3. In any event, this certainty is understood to be objective, that is, based on objective motives; it is not a purely subjective certitude, founded on sentiment or on this or that merely subjective opinion, perhaps even on personal credulity, lack of consideration, or inexperience. This moral certainty with an objective foundation does not exist if there are on the other side, that is, in favor of the reality of the contrary, motives which a sound, serious, and competent judgment pronounces to be at least in some way worthy of attention, and which consequently make it necessary to admit the contrary as not only absolutely possible but also in a certain sense probable.

To make sure of the objective nature of this certainty, procedural law establishes well defined rules of inquiry and proof.

---

[4] Aristotle, *De coelo,* I, 1.

Determinate proofs or corroborating evidences are required; others on the other hand are declared to be insufficient;[5] there are special offices and persons charged with the duty of keeping certain rights or facts in mind throughout the trial.[6] What is this but a well balanced juridical formalism, which lays emphasis at one time on the material, at another on the formal side of the process or juridical action?

The conscientious observance of these norms is a matter of duty for the judge; but on the other hand in their application he must remember that they are not ends in themselves, but means to an end, that is, to attain and guarantee a moral certainty with an objective foundation as to the reality of the fact. It should not come about that what the will of the legislator intended as a help and security for discovering the truth, become instead an obstacle to its discovery. If ever the observance of formal rules of law results in injustice or is contrary to equity, there is always a right of recourse to the legislator.

4. Hence you see why, in modern, even ecclesiastical, procedure, the first place is given, not to the principle of juridical formalism, but to the maxim of the free weighing of the evidence. The judge must — without prejudice to the aforesaid procedural rules — decide according to his own knowledge and conscience whether the proofs adduced and the investigations undertaken are or are not adequate,[7] that is, sufficient for the required moral certainty regarding the truth and reality of the matter to be decided.

No doubt there may at times be conflicts between "juridical formalism" and "the free weighing of the evidence," but they will usually be only apparent and hence not difficult to resolve. Now, as the objective truth is one, so too moral certainty objectively determined can be but one. Hence it is not admissible that a judge declare that personally, from the record of the case, he has moral certainty regarding the truth of the fact at issue, while at the same time, in his capacity as judge, he denies the same objective certainty on the basis of procedural law. Such contradictions should rather induce him to undertake a

---

[5] Cf. canons 1747–1836, as well as various particular provisions of the penal and matrimonial law.

[6] Cf. canons 1585–1590.

[7] Cf. canon 1869, § 3.

further and more accurate examination of the case. Not in-frequently such conflicts are due to the fact that certain aspects of the case, which attain their full importance and value only when viewed as a whole, have not been properly weighed, or that the juridical-formal rules have been incorrectly understood or have been applied in a manner contrary to the mind and purpose of the legislator. In any event, the confidence of the people, which the tribunals should possess, demands that, if it is at all possible, such conflicts between the official opinion of judges and the reasonable public opinion of well educated people should be avoided and reconciled.

5. But since moral certainty, as We have said, admits of various degrees, what degree can or should the judge demand in order to be able to proceed to judgment? In the first place, he must always make sure that there is in reality an objective moral certainty, that is, that all reasonable doubt of the truth is excluded. Once this is assured, he should as a rule, not require a higher degree of certainty, except where the law prescribes it especially in view of the importance of the case.[8] At times, it is true, even though there be no such express provision of law, it may be prudent for the judge not to be satisfied with a low degree of certitude, in cases of great importance. Yet, if after serious consideration and study, a grade of certitude is attained which corresponds to the requirements of law and the importance of the case, there should not be insistence, to the serious incon-venience of the parties, that new proofs be adduced so as to attain a still higher degree of certitude. To require the highest possible certainty, notwithstanding that a sufficient certainty already exists, is without justification and should be discouraged.

In thus expressing Our mind on so delicate a subject as that of the judge's office, Our purpose has been, in you, to extend Our greetings, Our commendation and Our thanks to the sagacious members of this distinguished College and Tribunal of Christian jurisprudence — in you, who not only understand but are putting in practice the words of the Angelic Doctor: *unusquisque debet niti ad hoc quod de rebus iudicet, secundum quod sunt.*[9] Because the truth is coextensive with being and reality, hence it is that our mind, which acquires a knowledge of things, grasps also

---

[8] Cf. canons 1869, § 3, and 1791, § 2.

[9] *Summa,* 2^a–2^{ae}, q. 60, a. 4, ad 2.

their rule and measure according to which they are or are not; so that truth is the law of justice.[10] The world has need of that truth which is justice, and of that justice which is truth; because, as was said already by the great Stagirite Philosopher, justice is, *et in bello et in pace utilis: καὶ ἐν πολέμῳ καὶ ἐν εἰρήνῃ χρήσιμος.*[11] May the eternal Sun of Justice enlighten the earth and its rulers; and may He, for the glory of God and of the Church and of the Christian people, accompany you at every step in the quest of that reality and truth which sets the face of justice at rest in the tranquil repose of moral certitude.

Now therefore, with this sacred wish, We invoke upon all and each of you the most luminous favors of the divine Wisdom, as with paternal affection We impart to you Our Apostolic Blessing.

AAS 34–338; Pius XII, Allocution, 1 Oct., 1942. Annotations, *Periodica,* 31–358.

One Witness *de Scientia* **Held Sufficient** in special circumstances. See c. 1791; Rota, 17 July, 1952.

CANON 1877

Communication of Sentence to Guardian. See c. 1712; AAS 35–58.

CANON 1892

Incurable Nullity of Judgment: Does not necessarily follow from incapacity of one of contracting parties to attack the marriage. See c. 1971; AAS 38–162.

Incurable Nullity of Judgment: The three cases of incurable nullity of judgment mentioned in canon 1892 are discussed at some length in excerpts from a Rota decision of 12 Nov., 1949 (*coram* Wynen), in *Monitor Ecclesiasticus,* 1950, pp. 71–76.

CANON 1894

Curable Nullity of Judgment: Briefly discussed in excerpts from a Rota decision of 12 Nov., 1949 (*coram* Wynen), in *Monitor Ecclesiasticus,* 1950, pp. 71–76.

CANON 1903

Marriage Case, appealed to court of third instance after two concordant decisions of nullity; defender of bond in third instance may abandon the appeal. See c. 1987; AAS 39–373.

---

[10] *Ibid.,* 1ᵃ, q. 21, a. 2.   [11] Aristotle, *Rhetoric,* I, 9.

CANON 1933

Vindictive Suspension *a divinis,* imposed by Holy Office extrajudicially, for contumacy. See Holy Office, 26 Nov., 1943 (AAS 35–398).

CANON 1960

Matrimonial Trials in Relation to the Ends of the Church
(Pius XII, Allocution, 2 Oct., 1944) **AAS 36–281.**

An Allocution delivered by His Holiness Pius XII on October 2, 1944, to the Auditors, Officials and Ministers of the Sacred Roman Rota and to its Advocates and Procurators, is as follows:

The Single Purpose of the Handling of Matrimonial Cases

The inauguration of the new juridical year of the Sacred Roman Rota has given Us in past years an opportunity to call attention to certain particular points in the treatment of matrimonial cases, and to show how the Church, in accordance with her mission and character, looks upon these points, and how in consequence she wishes them to be regarded and dealt with also by ecclesiastical judges and officials.

We spoke in the first place of the natural right to marriage and of psychic and physical incapacity for contracting marriage. Likewise We discussed certain fundamental principles governing the declaration of nullity of marriage and the dissolution of a bond which has been validly contracted. Later We made some reflections on the certitude which is requisite in order that the judge can proceed to pronounce judgment, and We pointed out that moral certainty is sufficient, that is, certainty which excludes all reasonable doubt as to the truth of the fact, recalling also that it must have an objective character and not be founded only on the opinion or merely subjective feeling of the judge.

With the same purpose of expressing the spirit and mind of the Church, which attaches the highest importance to marriage for the welfare of the faithful and the sanctity of the family, We propose to-day — after having heard the thorough and accurate annual report of your worthy and deserving Dean — to say a few words on the unity of purpose which must inform the work and collaboration of all persons who take part in the handling of matrimonial cases in ecclesiastical courts of whatever kind and degree, and which must inspire and unite them in one and the same unity of intention and action.

Three Elements of Unity of Action

1. In general it is to be observed that unity in human action results and proceeds from the following elements: a single purpose, a common direction of all participants to this single purpose, a juridical and moral obligation to take this direction and preserve it. You readily understand that the single purpose constitutes the principle and the formal term of these elements, both on the objective and the subjective side. This is true because, as every motion receives its determination from the end toward which it tends, so too all conscious human activity is specified by the end which it has in view.[1]

Now, in a matrimonial trial, the *single end* is a judgment in accordance with truth and law; which, in a suit for the declaration of nullity, is concerned with the alleged nonexistence of the matrimonial bond, and in the informative process *de vinculo solvendo,* with the existence or nonexistence of the necessary prerequisites for the dissolution of the bond. In other words, the end is the authoritative determination and enforcement of the truth and the law which corresponds to it, in regard to the existence or the continuance of a matrimonial bond.

The *personal direction* is obtained through the will of the persons who have a part in the handling of the case, in as much as they direct and subordinate all their thought, will, and action, in matters which concern the trial, to the attainment of that end. If, therefore, all those engaged in the trial constantly follow this direction, it will naturally result in their unity of action and cooperation.

Finally, the third element, that is, the *juridical-moral obligation* of preserving this direction, comes, in matrimonial trials, from the divine law. In fact, the nuptial contract is by its very nature, and in the case of two baptized persons by its elevation to the dignity of a Sacrament, ordained and determined, not by the will of man, but of God. It is enough to recall the words of Christ: "What God hath joined together, let no man put asunder" (Matt., 19:6), and the teaching of Saint Paul: "This is a great sacrament; but I speak in Christ and in the Church" (Eph., 5:32). The profound gravity of this obligation in the service of truth in matrimonial trials, springing as it does from

[1] Cf. St. Thomas, 1^a–2^{ae}, q. 1, a. 2.

the supreme and imperishable source of the law of God, must always be strongly asserted and inculcated. In matrimonial cases before ecclesiastical tribunals there is never room for trickery, perjury, subornation, or fraud of any kind! Hence all persons who have any part in these trials must keep an alert conscience, and at need must awaken and revive their conscience to remember that basically these trials are conducted not before the tribunal of men but before that of the omniscient God, and that consequently the judgments rendered, if they are falsified by any fraud affecting the substance of the case, are without value before God and in the realm of conscience.

The Unity of Purpose and Action in the Various Persons Who Take Part in Matrimonial Cases

2. Unity and collaboration in matrimonial cases, therefore, are effected through the unity of the end, the direction toward the end, the obligation of subordination to the end. This three-fold element imposes upon the particular action of all participants certain essential exigencies and marks it with a particular imprint.

a) The Judge. First of all as regards the judge, who is as it were the personification of justice, his work reaches its climax in the pronouncement of the sentence; which certifies and juridically determines the truth and gives it legal effect, both as regards the fact to be determined and the law to be applied. But the entire process is ordained as to its proper end, to this clarification and service of the truth. Hence, in this objective orientation toward the end, the judge finds also a reliable directive norm for every personal inquiry, judgment, prescription, or prohibition which may occur in the course of the trial. It is therefore apparent that the juridical-moral obligation of the judge is none other than that which has already been mentioned as deriving from the divine law, namely, to inquire and decide according to truth whether a bond which, as far as external appearances go, seems to have been effected, exists in reality, or (if it has in reality been effected) whether the prerequisite conditions for its dissolution are verified; and, having established the truth, to pronounce judgment accordingly. Here lies the profound importance of the personal responsibility of the judge in the direction and termination of the trial.

b) The Defender of the Bond. The function of the defender

of the bond is to sustain the existence or the continuance of the matrimonial bond, not however absolutely, but in subordination to the purpose of the trial, which is the quest and presentation of the objective truth.

The defender of the bond must work toward the common end, in as much as he seeks out, exposes, and clarifies everything which can weigh in favor of the bond. In order that he, who is considered as *"pars necessaria ad iudicii validitatem et integritatem."*[2] may effectively perform his duty, the procedural order gives him particular rights and assigns him definite duties (cf. cc. 1967–1969). And as it would be inconsistent with the importance of his office and the careful and conscientious fulfillment of his duty were he to content himself with a prefunctory review of the record and a few superficial remarks, so too it is not proper that this office be entrusted to persons who are still wanting in experience of life and maturity of judgment (cf. Norms for the Sacred Roman Rota, 29 June, 1934, art. 4, § 2; AAS 26–449). The fact that the observations of the defender of the bond are subject to scrutiny by the judges does not exempt from this rule, for the judges should find in the careful work of the defender of the bond an aid and complement to their own activity, and it is not to be supposed that they must do all his work and conduct all his investigation over again in order to be able to rely on his representations.

On the other hand, it is not to be expected that the defender of the bond shall elaborate and make up at all cost an artificial defense, without concern as to whether his statements have or have not a serious foundation. Such a requirement would be contrary to sound reason; it would burden him with a useless and meaningless task; it would not clarify but rather confuse the question; it would do harm by dragging out the trial to interminable lengths. In the interest of truth itself and for the dignity of his office, therefore, it should be acknowledged as a maxim for the defender of the bond that, in a proper case, he has the right to declare that after a careful, thorough, and conscientious examination of the record, he has found no reasonable objection to propose against the petition of the plaintiff or petitioner.

---

[2] Benedict XIV, Const., *Dei miseratione,* 3 Nov., 1741, § 7; *Fontes,* n. 318, Vol. I, p. 697.

This fact and this consciousness that he is not bound to contend unconditionally for a predetermined thesis, but is working in the interest of truth as it is, will save the defender of the bond from proposing questions which are unilaterally suggestive or tricky; from exaggerating and changing possibilities into probabilities and finally into accomplished facts; from claiming or feigning contradictions where a sound judgment sees none or easily explains them; from impugning the veracity of testimony because of discrepancies or inaccuracies in matters which are not essential or are without importance to the object of the trial, discrepancies, and inaccuracies which, according to the well-known psychology of testimony, are within the limits of normal causes of error and do not substantially impair the value of the testimony itself. Finally, the consciousness of being bound to serve the truth will deter the defender of the bond from demanding new proofs when those already adduced are fully sufficient to establish the truth — a practice which We have on another occasion designated as not to be approved.

Let it not be objected that the defender of the bond is required to write his observations, not *"pro rei veritate,"* but *"pro validitate matrimonii."* If by this is meant that his part is to bring out everything that is in favor of, and not what is contrary to, the existence or continuance of the bond, it is quite correct. But if it were meant to assert that the defender of the bond is not obliged as much as any one else to make his activity serve as its ultimate purpose the ascertainment of objective truth, but that he must sustain the imposed thesis of the existence or necessary continuance of the bond, unconditionally or without regard to the proofs and to the truth brought out in the trial, this assertion must be held false. In this sense all those who have part in the trial, without exception, must make their action converge to the one end: *pro rei veritate!*

c) *The Promoter of Justice.* We would not omit some brief remarks also in regard to the promoter of justice. It may happen that the public good requires the declaration of nullity of a marriage, and that the promoter of justice should present a regular petition for this to the competent tribunal. In no other point might one be so inclined to cast doubt upon the singleness of the end and of the collaboration of all in the matrimonial trial, as here, where two public officials seem to take positions directly contrary one to the other before the court: one, the defender of the bond, must in virtue of his office deny what the other, also in virtue of his office, is bound to present. On the contrary, it is precisely here that the singleness of the end and the single direction of all participants toward this end are clearly manifest; because, notwithstanding their apparent opposition, both are presenting to the judge fundamentally the same request: to pronounce judgment according to truth and the reality of the objective fact. There would be a rupture of the unity of the end and of the collaboration, only if the defender of the bond and the promoter of justice considered their proximate and opposite ends as absolute, and if they detached them from their connection and subordination to the common and ultimate end.

d) The Advocate. But the unity of the end, the direction toward it, and the obligation of subordination to it in the matrimonial trial, must be considered and pondered with particular attention in their relation to the legal counsellor or *advocate,* who represents the plaintiff or the defendant or the petitioner, because no one is more exposed than he is to the danger of losing sight of them.

The advocate assists his client in drawing up the introductory *libellus* of the case, in rightly determining the issue and the basis of the controversy, in bringing out the decisive points of the fact which is in issue; he indicates to him what proofs to adduce, what documents to present; he suggests to him what testimony to bring out at the trial, what points are essential in the depositions of the witnesses; in the course of the trial he helps him to evaluate rightly the exceptions and adverse arguments and to refute them: in a word, he gathers and gives effect to everything that can be alleged in favor of the contention of his client.

In this multiple activity the advocate may well exert every effort to win the case for his client; but in all his action he must not withdraw himself from the one common final end: the discovery, ascertainment, and legal assertion of the truth, the objective fact. You who are here present, distinguished jurists and upright defenders of the ecclesiastical forum, well know how the consciousness of this subordination must guide the advocate in his calculations, in his counsels, in his contentions and his proofs, and how it not only protects him from artificially building up and sponsoring cases which are devoid of serious foundation, from employing any fraud or deceit, from inducing parties or witnesses to give false testimony, from resorting to any other dishonest device, but how it also impels him positively to act according to the dictates of conscience throughout every stage of the trial. Toward the supreme goal of making the truth shine forth, both the work of the advocate and that of the defender of the bond must converge, because both, though actuated from opposite sides by different proximate ends, must tend to the same final end.

Hence it is clear what must be thought of that principle which, unfortunately, is not infrequently asserted and even followed. "The advocate," it is said, "has the right and duty to bring out everything which helps his contention, no less than the defender of the bond has the same right and duty in regard to the contrary contention; the rule *pro rei veritate* applies neither to the one nor to the other! The evaluation of the truth is exclusively the business of the judge; to saddle that responsibility on the advocate would be to impede and even paralyze all his activity." Such a statement is based on a theoretical and practical error: it ignores the inner nature and the essential final purpose of a juridical controversy. A matrimonial case cannot be compared to a contest or a joust, where the two contenders have not a common final purpose, but each pursues his own particular and absolute goal, without regard for or even in opposition to that of his adversary, namely, to defeat his opponent and carry off the victory. In such a case the winner, by his very success in the contest, creates the objective fact which is the deciding motive for the judge of the engagement or contest in conferring the prize; for he only follows the law, "to the winner belongs the prize." But it is altogether different in the juridical trial of a matrimonial case. Here there is no question of creating a fact by means of eloquence or argument, but of making evident and juridically effective a fact which already exists. The above mentioned principle seeks to sunder the work of the advocate from its attachment to the service of objective truth; it pretends, in a sense, to attribute to skillful argumentation the power to create a right, as in the case of the winning side in a contest.

This same thought of the unconditional obligation toward the truth, holds good also in the case of the simple informative process pursuant to a petition for the dissolution of the bond. The conduct of the case in the ecclesiastical forum makes no provision for the intervention of a legal representative of the petitioner; but the latter has a natural right to make use, on his own account, of the counsel and assistance of a jurist in the drawing up and substantiation of the petition, in the choice and presentation of evidence, in meeting such difficulties as may arise. The legal counsellor or the advocate may also in this case bring into play all his knowledge and energy in favor of his client; but also in this extrajudicial activity he must remember the obligation which binds him to the service of truth, his subordination to the common end of the whole proceeding, and the part he has to play in the common concerted action toward the attainment of that end.

From what We have said it is evident that, in the treatment of matrimonial cases in the ecclesiastical forum, the judge, the defender of the bond, the promoter of justice, and the advocate must, so to speak, make common cause and collaborate together, each one, without confusing his own proper office, acting in conscious and deliberate union and subordination to the same end.

e) The Parties, Witnesses, and Experts. It is needless to add that the same fundamental law — to investigate, bring to light, give legal effect to the truth — is equally obligatory on the other persons who participate in the trial. To secure the attainment of this end, they are required to take an oath. In this subordination to the end they have a clear norm to govern their internal attitude and their external action; it gives them security of judgment and peace of conscience. Neither the *parties,* the *witnesses,* nor the *experts* may make up facts which do not exist, nor give to those which do exist a baseless interpretation, nor deny, confuse or befog them. Any such action would conflict with the service which is due to the truth and which is obligatory by the divine law and the oath which they have taken.

The Matrimonial Trial Considered in Its Ordination and Subordination to the Universal End of the Church, the Good of Souls

3. Considering now what has been said, we see clearly how the matrimonial trial represents a unity of purpose and action, in which the individual participants must fulfill their particular function in mutual co-ordination and in a common orientation toward the same end; like the members of a body, in which, though each member has its proper function and activity, yet

all are mutually co-ordinated and directed to the attainment of the same final object, that is, the good of the whole organism.

This consideration of the inner nature of the matrimonial trial would, however, be incomplete without a glance also at its external aspects.

The matrimonial trial in the ecclesiastical forum is a function of the juridical life of the Church. In Our Encyclical on the Mystical Body of Christ, We explained how the so-called "juridical Church," though it is truly of divine origin, is not the whole Church; in a certain sense it represents only the body, which must be vivified by the spirit, that is, by the Holy Spirit and the grace of God. In the same Encyclical We also explained how the whole Church, body and spirit, as regards the participation in its blessings and the benefit which comes from them, is established exclusively for "the salvation of souls," according to the word of the Apostle, "All things are yours" (1 Cor. 3:22). This indicates the higher unity and the higher purpose to which the juridical life and all juridical functions in the Church are directed. It follows that every thought, will, and personal operation in the exercise of such activity must tend to the proper end of the Church, the salvation of souls. In other words, the higher end, the higher principle, the higher unity is simply this: the care of souls, just as all the work of Christ on earth was the care of souls, and as that was and is the whole work of the Church.

But the jurist as such looks to mere law and rigid justice; he shows an instinctive aloofness from the ideas and preoccupations of the care of souls, and champions a clear separation between the two fora, the forum of conscience and that of external juridical-social intercourse. This inclination toward a definite line of demarcation between the two is, to a certain extent, legitimate, in as much as the judge and his collaborators in the judiciary process have not the pastoral responsibility directly as their proper office. But it would be a fatal error to deny that they too, in the last and definitive instance, are in the service of souls. For thus they would, in the ecclesiastical trial, exclude themselves from the end and unity of action which belong to the Church by divine institution; they would be like members of a body which no longer cohere with the whole and are no longer ready to subordinate and direct their activity to the end of the whole organism.

The Influence of This Direction and Subordination on Juridical Activity

Juridical, and especially judiciary, activity has nothing to fear from this direction and subordination; but on the contrary draws life and advancement from it. It is this which assures the necessary breadth of view and of decision, because, whereas a one-sided juridical activity is always attended by the danger of an exaggerated formalism and attachment to the letter of the law, the care of souls furnishes a counterpoise, by keeping in the forefront of the conscience the maxim: "Laws are for men, and not men for laws." For this reason, We have on another occasion pointed out that, where the letter of the law is an obstacle to the attainment of truth and justice, there must always be opportunity for recourse to the lawmaker.

The thought of being in the service of the end of the Church gives, moreover, to all those who take part in her juridical activity, the necessary independence and autonomy in regard to the civil judiciary power. Between the Church and the State, as We pointed out in the above mentioned Encyclical on the Mystical Body of Christ, though both are in the full sense of the word perfect societies, there is nevertheless a profound difference. The Church has a proper particular character which is of divine origin and imprint. And from this source there comes also into her juridical life a quality which is peculiar to her, an orientation even to the last consequences toward thoughts and blessings which are of a higher order, otherworldly, eternal. Hence, for various reasons, the dictum of certain persons that the ideal of ecclesiastical juridical practice consists in its greatest possible resemblance and conformity to the civil judiciary system, should be regarded, not as a matter of opinion, but as a simply erroneous judgment; which, however, does not mean that the Church cannot appropriately take advantage of true juridical science also in this field.

Finally, the thought of belonging to the higher unity of the Church and of being subordinated to her universal end, the *welfare of souls,* gives to juridical activity the strength to proceed securely in the way of truth and law, and preserves it alike from a weak condescension to the disordered cravings of the passions and from a hard and unjustifiable inflexibility. The welfare of souls has as its guide a supreme and absolutely safe rule: the law and will of God. To this law and will of God a juridical activity which recognizes and is conscious of having no other end than that of the Church, will direct itself firmly in the handling of particular cases which are submitted to it, and will thus see the confirmation in a higher order of that which was already a fundamental maxim in its own proper sphere: the service and assertion of the truth by the ascertainment of the true facts and the application to them of the law and will of God.

Hence it brings Us a peculiar satisfaction to know that this Sacred Tribunal is unswervingly faithful to so exalted a rule and can therefore be held up as an example to diocesan tribunals, which look to it as to their model and norm.

May God grant that the new juridical year of the Sacred Roman Rota, which is inaugurated to-day under the invocation of the Holy Spirit, may be also a presage of the inauguration of a new year of peace and justice in the world!

With this wish, We invoke upon you and your work the light of the divine Wisdom, while with all Our heart We impart to each and all Our paternal Apostolic Blessing.

AAS 36–281; Pius XII, Allocution, 2 Oct., 1944. Annotations, *Periodica,* 34–101 (Aguirre).

Canada: Organization of Ecclesiastical Tribunals for Cases of Nullity of Marriage (S. C. Sacr., 13 May, 1946) AAS 38–281.

The Most Excellent Ordinaries of Canada, having observed the wise and helpful provisions which were established for ecclesiastical tribunals in Italy by the *Motu proprio* of Pius XI, 8 Dec., 1938,[1] and for the reduction of the tribunals in the Philippine Islands by the decree of the Sacred Congregation of the Sacraments, of 20 Dec., 1940,[2] in view of the rarity of matrimonial cases of nullity in their tribunals, and especially of the difficulty which they commonly have in establishing proper tribunals, in their general meeting held in January, 1945, decided to present humbly to the Holy See the following petition:

Namely, that, in the same way as was done for Italy by the above mentioned *Motu proprio* and for the Philippines by the aforesaid decree, there be established also for Canada provincial

[1] AAS 30–410.
[2] Canon Law Digest, Vol. 2, p. 534; AAS 33–363.

tribunals for handling cases of nullity of marriage, and that similarly among these tribunals certain courts of appeal be organized.

After this Sacred Congregation of the Sacraments had duly considered this petition, and also the opinion of the Most Excellent Apostolic Delegate of Canada, it referred it, through the undersigned Cardinal Prefect, to His Holiness by Divine Providence Pope Pius XII in the audience of 28 January, 1946.

His Holiness deigned to make all the provisions which follow, and decreed that they were to be put into execution, all things to the contrary, even such as are worthy of special mention, notwithstanding.

I. In the district of Canada, for the handling of cases of nullity of marriage in the first instance, the following shall be the tribunals and their jurisdictional boundaries:

1. The tribunal of *Quebec*, for the two ecclesiastical Provinces of Quebec and Rimouski, that is, for the territory of the following dioceses: Quebec, Amos, Chicoutimi, Nicolet, Trois Rivières, Rimouski, Gaspé, Gulf of Saint Lawrence, the Vicariate Apostolic of Labrador and the Magdalen Islands;

2. The tribunal of *Montreal*, for that entire ecclesiastical Province, that is, for the territory of the following dioceses: Montreal, Joliette, Saint Hyacinth, Saint Jean-de-Quebec, Sherbrooke, Valleyfield;

3. The tribunal of *Halifax*, for the two ecclesiastical Provinces of Halifax and Moncton, that is, for the territory of the following dioceses: Halifax, Antigonish, Charleston, Moncton, Bathurst, Edmonton, Saint John;

4. The tribunal of *Ottawa*, for that entire ecclesiastical Province, that is, for the territory of the following dioceses: Ottawa, Hearst, Mont-Laurier, Pembroke, Timmins, the Vicariate Apostolic of James Bay;

5. The tribunal of *Toronto*, for the two ecclesiastical Provinces of Toronto and Kingston, that is, for the territory of the following dioceses: Toronto, Hamilton, London, Kingston, Alexandria, Peterborough, Sault Sainte Marie;

6. The tribunal of *Regina*, for the two ecclesiastical Provinces of Regina and Saint Boniface and for the Archdiocese (immediately subject to the Holy See) of Winnipeg, that is, for the territory of the following dioceses: Regina, Gravelbourg, Prince

Albert, Saskatoon, the Abbacy *nullius* of Saint Peter (Muenster), Saint Boniface, the Vicariate Apostolic of Hudson Bay, the Vicariate Apostolic of Keewatin, the Archdiocese of Winnipeg;

7. The tribunal of *Vancouver,* for the two ecclesiastical Provinces of Vancouver and Edmonton, namely, for the territory of the following dioceses: Vancouver, Nelson, Victoria in Vancouver Island, Kamloops, the Vicariate Apostolic of Prince Rupert, the Vicariate Apostolic of Whitehorse, Edmonton, Calgary, the Vicariate Apostolic of Grouard, the Vicariate Apostolic of Mackenzie.

II. For handling the above cases on appeal, always without prejudice to the right to appeal directly to the Sacred Roman Rota according to canon 1599, § 1, of the Code of Canon Law, let the following be observed:

Cases which were tried in the first instance in the tribunals of Quebec and Toronto shall be brought on appeal to the tribunal of Montreal; those tried in the first instance at Montreal shall be appealed to Ottawa; those tried at Ottawa and Halifax shall be appealed to Quebec; those tried at Regina and Vancouver shall be appealed to Toronto.

III. The *Officiales,* judges, promoters of justice, defenders of the bond, and other officers of the provincial tribunals above mentioned shall be chosen and appointed for a definite time by the Most Excellent Ordinaries of the dioceses belonging to the respective tribunals, at the provincial meetings.

IV. As to the rights and duties of the aforesaid provincial tribunals, and their procedure, the Sacred Congregation of the Sacraments will establish regulations, and will also determine the time for putting the above provisions into effect, and will issue temporary norms.

V. The Sacred Congregation of the Sacraments, in the fulfillment of its proper office, will exercise a watchful care that the *Officiales,* the judges, and especially the promoters of justice and defenders of the bond perform their functions properly and with diligence according to the norms issued or to be issued by the said Sacred Congregation.

Given at Rome, from the office of the Sacred Congregation of the Sacraments, 28 January, 1946.

NORMS

For Executing the Decree of 28 Jan., 1946, Regarding
the Organization of Ecclesiastical Tribunals
in Canada

In order to put into effect the provisions of the Decree of
28 Jan., 1946, this Sacred Congregation makes the following
regulations:

Chapter I. The Moderator, Judges, and Officers
of the Provincial Tribunal

Art. 1. The provincial tribunal is under the authority of the
Archbishop of the place where it has its seat; and he shall therefore govern and direct it in the name of all the Bishops of the
territory assigned to it, and shall have all the rights and duties
which belong to local Ordinaries as regards their own tribunals,
according to the sacred canons and the *Instruction* of this Sacred
Congregation of the Sacraments, of 15 Aug., 1936,[3] unless some
different provision is hereinafter made or the matter shall so
require.

Art. 2. The judges and officers of the provincial tribunal shall
be appointed by a majority vote in the meeting of the Most
Excellent Ordinaries of the territory assigned to the tribunal.

Art. 3. Those so chosen should not only be of the highest
moral integrity, and be doctors or at least licentiates in canon
law, or at least have *genuine* legal learning and juridical experience, but must also be in a position to give a sufficient amount
of time to the duties entrusted to them to fulfill them properly.

Art. 4. The names of those who are appointed *Officialis* (or
vice-Officialis or *vice-Officiales* if there are such), judge, promoter
of justice, defender of the bond (and their substitutes if any),
shall be communicated as soon as possible by the Most Excellent
President of the Bishops' meeting to the Most Excellent Apostolic
Delegate of Canada, together with a statement of their age,
studies, career, and a testimonial as to their priestly virtues; this
notification will moreover give the Apostolic Delegate the opportunity to make known whether there is any objection to any of
the appointees.

---

[3] Canon Law Digest, Vol. 2, pp. 471–530; AAS 28–313.

Art. 5. The above appointments shall usually be made for five years, and may be confirmed for successive terms of five years.

Art. 6. All persons who belong to or work for the provincial tribunal shall take an oath duly and faithfully to fulfill their office, before the Archbishop of the See where the provincial tribunal is, in the case of the *Officialis,* and in the case of the others before the Ordinary of the same See, or before the judge by whom they were appointed, or before some ecclesiastic delegated by either of them. This must be done at the beginning of their term of office if the appointment is a stable one, or before the case is begun if they are appointed for a particular case, or before they begin their official work if they are appointed while a case is pending, according to article 19 of the above mentioned *Instruction.*

Art. 7. The *Officiales,* judges, promoters of justice, and defenders of the bond (and their substitutes if any, unless these are deputed merely for a single instance) cannot be removed during their term of office by the Archbishop of the See of the provincial tribunal, except for grave cause and after consulting the Bishops of the entire territory assigned to the tribunal.

Art. 8. No one may act as judge in a case if he is actually engaged as an advocate or procurator in matrimonial cases, either directly or through another person, even though it be before other tribunals or even those of the Holy See: the same holds for the promoter of justice and the defender of the bond. These same officers of the court are also strictly forbidden to take any part whatever in any marriage cases outside the scope of their office.

Art. 9. The Archbishop of the See of the provincial tribunal, taking counsel with the other Bishops of the territory of the tribunal, shall have a roster of the procurators and advocates for the tribunal prepared according to articles 47–53 of the said *Instruction.*

Chapter II. Manner of Proceeding in the Handling of Matrimonial Cases

Art. 10. That the procedure in handling matrimonial cases before the provincial tribunals may be duly safeguarded, let the above mentioned *Instruction* be exactly observed, with only the following additions and amendments.

Art. 11. As to the competence of the provincial tribunal, the norms of articles 1–12 of the said *Instruction* are to be observed, bearing in mind that, for marriage cases, the provincial tribunal is both a common one for the dioceses of its territory and the proper one for each diocese of the territory.

Art. 12. The cases shall be entitled as follows: first the name of the provincial tribunal, then the diocese of the place of marriage or of the defendant's domicile, finally the title of the case; for example: *"Tribunal of Quebec-Nicolet. Nullity of Marriage* (Names of parties)": however, when the case is being tried on appeal, it should be entitled: *"Appellate Tribunal of Montreal-Nicolet. Nullity of Marriage* (Names of parties)."

Art. 13. It pertains to the Bishop of the domicile of the parties to pass judgment as to the existence of the circumstances mentioned in articles 38, § 2, and 39, *b*, of the *Instruction;* but before passing such judgment it will be appropriate to consult the Archbishop of the See of the provincial tribunal.

Art. 14. It is the part of the Archbishop of the See of the provincial tribunal to admit a guardian or curator or to appoint one according to article 78 of the *Instruction*, after consulting with the Ordinary of the defendant for whom a guardian or curator is to be appointed.

Art. 15. In the exceptional cases mentioned in canons 1990–1992, every petition shall be sent to the Archbishop of the See of the provincial tribunal, who, after he has heard the opinion of the Bishop of the parties' domicile, shall decide upon it as provided in Title XV of the said *Instruction*. The *Officialis* referred to in article 228 of the *Instruction* is the *Officialis* of the provincial tribunal.

Art. 16. The defender of the bond must not be too ready to omit the appeal to the court of second instance, which is provided for in article 229 of the *Instruction*, especially when the case is one involving impediments from which a dispensation is usually obtained.

Chapter III. Salaries to Be Assigned to the Judges and Officers of the Tribunals

Art. 17. The salaries or remunerations and honoraria of the judges and officers of the tribunal shall be determined by the Most Excellent Ordinaries in the meetings of the Bishops of the territory assigned to the tribunal, bearing in mind the circumstances of the dioceses and especially the number of cases to be handled: so that they may receive a suitable compensation proportionate to the work which they have actually done for the court.

Art. 18. These emoluments should generally be moderate, taking into consideration also the fact that the judges and officers of the tribunal for the most part already have some ecclesiastical benefice: yet they should at the same time be sufficient lest these officers be prevented from giving diligent service to the court by the necessity of earning their living from other sources.

Art. 19. The Most Excellent Ordinaries shall (if they deem it necessary), at their meetings for the territory of the tribunal, determine the amount of the contributions to be made by each diocese for the expenses of the provincial tribunal, in proportion to the number of Catholics, and also, if this seems advisable, in proportion to the number of cases from each diocese.

Chapter IV. The Judicial Taxes and Expenses and the Fees of Procurators and Advocates

Art. 20. The Most Excellent Ordinaries, at the Bishops' meetings for the territory of the provincial tribunal, upon due consideration of the circumstances of places and times, shall approve a schedule of taxes and judicial expenses, and of fees due to procurators and advocates for handling cases in the provincial tribunal; which fees, as is only right, shall be appreciably less than those which are in effect for procurators and advocates in the tribunal of the Sacred Roman Rota.[4]

Art. 21. The schedule of expenses and fees mentioned in the preceding article shall be made known to all litigants; and the Most Excellent Ordinaries and the tribunals shall carefully bear in mind the provisions of article 54 of the *Instruction*.

TEMPORARY OR TRANSITORY NORMS

The above provisions shall be put into effect at a date to be fixed by the Most Excellent Apostolic Delegate of Canada.

As to cases which on that date may be pending in the first instance in the diocesan tribunals, the procedure shall be as follows:

1. If the petition has already been presented but the case has

---

[4] CANON LAW DIGEST, Vol. 2, p. 453; AAS 31-622.

not progressed to the joinder of issue or concordance of questions (canon 1727, and *Instruction,* article 88), the petition itself shall be transmitted to the competent provincial tribunal, and the diocesan tribunal shall proceed no farther with the case.

2. If the trial has only begun, and if the parties and the defender of the bond, and, in the event that he has intervened in the case, also the promoter of justice, do not object, the trial can be transferred to the provincial tribunal.

3. If the case is closed (article 177 of the *Instruction*), the diocesan tribunal must of necessity give the final judgment.

4. The above provisions are also to be applied, *mutatis mutandis,* in cases which are pending on appeal.

5. From a judgment by a diocesan tribunal, if that was the first trial, the appeal shall be taken to that appellate court which would have been competent if the judgment had been rendered by a provincial tribunal of first instance.

If the judgment to be appealed from be that of the second trial, the common provisions of articles 212–222 of the *Instruction* are to be applied.

His Holiness by Divine Providence Pope Pius XII, in the audience granted to the undersigned Prefect of this Sacred Congregation on May 13, 1946, graciously deigned to confirm and ratify these regulations.

Given at Rome, from the Office of the Sacred Congregation of the Sacraments, the 13th of May, 1946.

AAS 38–281; S. C. Sacr., 13 May, 1946.

The Handling of Marriage Cases (S. C. Sacr., 15 Aug., 1949) Private.

This document, captioned "The Commission of Vigilance over Tribunals for Matrimonial Cases," addressed to "All Ordinaries of Places and Judges of Matrimonial Courts," and signed by the Cardinal Pro-Prefect and by the Secretary of the Sacred Congregation of the Sacraments, is as follows:

As usual, along with the statistical forms regarding the marriage cases dealt with during the preceding year by the various tribunals of the Catholic world, some examples of the decisions rendered and of the remarks of the defenders of the bond were also sent to this Sacred Congregation.

These examples having been subjected to a careful examination on the part of the Consultors of the special Commission of Vigilance over ecclesiastical tribunals for marriage cases, the said Commission thought it well to make the following general remarks for the consideration of Ordinaries and ecclesiastical judges, so that they may be able to perform ever more perfectly their arduous judicial duties.

1. The decision of formal cases on the nullity of marriage, as everyone knows, is fraught with peculiar difficulty. Speaking of these decisions, the Instruction of this Sacred Congregation of 15 August, 1936, Art. 21, declared: "In view of the importance and difficulty of these cases, both as regards the observance of the procedural laws and the intrinsic merits of the case, it is a *grave obligation in conscience* on the part of the Bishops to choose carefully and diligently priests whose prudence and probity are beyond exception, and who have the doctorate or at least the licentiate in canon law, or if not, are *really* possessed of juridical learning and experience."[1]

2. Cases which are to be tried according to formal procedure do not admit of arguments which are evident and incontrovertible, for in such cases either the procedure for exceptional cases is used (cf. cc. 1990–1992 and the reply of the Code Commission of 6 Dec., 1943),[2] or the case is referred for decision to this Sacred Congregation according to canon 249, § 3. Hence great prudence and acumen are required in the judges, lest on the one hand "the sacredness of so great a Sacrament" be needlessly endangered, or on the other hand the demands justly presented by the faithful for the declaration of nullity of their marriage be wrongly rejected.

3. Judging from the text of the decisions, the following are the principal observations to be made:

a) In the preparatory stage of the trial, the judge and defender of the bond sometimes remain almost inert, examining only the witnesses called by the plaintiff (and often by the attorneys of the parties), and would that these witnesses were free from all suggestion or instruction as to the answers to be given!

It is useful on the contrary, and often quite necessary, that the judge (at the instance as occasion demands of the defender

---

[1] AAS 28–318; Canon Law Digest, 2, p. 478.
[2] AAS 36–94; Canon Law Digest, 3, under canon 1990.

of the bond) call witnesses *ex officio,* who are above all suspicion, after the defender, either personally or through others, has made careful inquiries, in the place where the parties are well known, of persons who are capable of establishing the truth of the facts without passion or prejudice.

For if the defender of the bond assumes a passive attitude, it can happen that the judge is easily deceived by parties who are carried away by "the desire to dissolve their marriages whenever married life has not brought them that happiness and peace which sensual indulgence had taught them to hope for."[3]

In this way "the door is opened to fraud and dishonesty both on the part of the parties themselves, who may conspire against the sanctity and unity of Christian marriage, and also on the part of persons eager for gain, who instruct the parties as to how they must draw up their case, and then, more interested in the outcome of the trial than in the truth, procure and instruct the witnesses to make and adhere to such statements as will produce the desired result."[4]

b) Concerning the decisive stage of the trial, the following observations are to be made:

Since matrimonial cases are daily growing in number and in some of them the facts are very similar, the decisions unconsciously tend toward a certain uniformity and automatic repetitions, both as regards the law, and what is more deplorable, in the application of the law to the facts, where the greatest industry on the part of the judge is required.

Thus in writing their decisions, judges sometimes can easily fall into a kind of mere formalism; and it not infrequently happens that under the appearance of solemn and lengthy procedure the substance of the whole trial is reduced to schematic formulae, which are either prepared by the attorney of the party and presented to the judges, or, what is worse, are drawn up by the judge almost automatically from the evidence that has been offered.

4. We need not here dwell at length on the conduct of attorneys, blameable as it is, when unfortunately without regard to the truth they coach the witnesses and the parties, propose leading questions or demand supplementary proofs, which are admitted

---

[3] AAS 22–168; Canon Law Digest, 1, p. 797.
[4] AAS 22–168; Canon Law Digest, 1, p. 798.

almost inadvertently and without suspicion by the defender of the bond and the judge. Rather we call attention to the conduct of some judges, who in weighing the evidence do not act as real judges but rather as simple compilers. They attend to the form of words without weighing them critically; without consideration or reasoning, they put together excerpts from the testimony of witnesses or experts, and draw the facile conclusion that the case presents credible and concordant testimony establishing the nullity of the marriage.

5. Regarding the testimony of experts, Article 154 of the Instruction, *Provida,* should be kept in mind: "§ 1. The court is not bound to follow the judgment of the experts, even if their conclusions agree, but must attentively consider also the other elements of the case (cf. can. 1804, § 1). § 2. The court in giving the reasons for its decision must state by what considerations it was moved either to accept or to reject the conclusions of the experts (cf. can. 1804, § 2)."[5]

6. Then there are judges who regularly and without choice or exception, without any definite consideration, admit offhand any and all witnesses as though upon an *a priori* presumption that they are trustworthy; they are satisfied with replies given to leading questions; they do not notice whether the witness, even in good faith, may be building something out of nothing, or exaggerating at least certain words or certain reasons; whether the witness does not seem to know more than the parties themselves, or does not transfer to the time before the marriage things which on the contrary he saw or heard or thought, only after the marriage had turned out unhappily.

7. Thus, for example, sometimes a declaration of the nullity of a marriage is easily obtained on the ground that one of the *bona matrimonii* was excluded, whereas, in view of the growing laxity of morals and the currency of the idea of free unions, it should become more difficult to prove a *positive act of the will* (contrary to the blessings of marriage), since it is to be presumed that the more usual case is simple error on the part of the contracting party, who was not too much concerned about the rights and duties of marriage; and this is especially true if on the eve of the wedding, in reply to the questioning by the

---

[5] AAS 28–343; CANON LAW DIGEST, 2, p. 508.

pastor, he stated under oath that he did not wish to exclude the blessings of marriage (cf. the Instruction, *Sacrosanctum,* 29 June, 1941, Exhibit I).[6]

8. The attention of Ordinaries is called to the following three points:

a) Ordinaries have the gravest obligation to admit none but persons who are entirely unexceptionable to practice before their tribunal, for whose action they are responsible to God. They have the right (and sometimes the obligation) to revoke the permission given to an attorney to practice in their tribunal; and they can do this by an administrative decree, without being obliged to give the reasons for such action except to this Sacred Congregation.

To avoid disputes it is well to mention expressly this power of revoking the permission to practice at the time when it is first given.

b) The selection of proper judges is a fundamental element in the right administration of justice (as shown by Art. 21 of the aforesaid Instruction, *Provida*). For an experienced and active judge, one who is moved only by the desire for truth and justice, will not easily be deceived by the ruses and pretenses of the parties; he will find out the truth by properly weighing the evidence, by calling witnesses *ex officio,* and so on.

Judges of this stamp and defenders of the bond who are qualified for their arduous duties, have to be trained with special care and solicitude.

On this matter His Holiness Pius XII in his Allocution to the Tribunal of the Sacred Roman Rota, deigned to declare:

"The judge . . . is as it were the personification of justice. His work reaches its climax in the pronouncement of the sentence, which certifies and juridically determines the truth and gives it legal effect, both as regards the fact to be determined and the law to be applied. But the entire process is ordained as to its proper end, to this clarification and service of the truth. Hence, in this objective orientation toward the end, the judge finds also a reliable directive norm for every personal inquiry, judgment, prescription or prohibition which may occur in the course of the trial. It is therefore apparent that the juridical-moral obliga-

---

[6] CANON LAW DIGEST, 2, p. 265.

tion of the judge is none other than that which has already been mentioned as deriving from the divine law, namely, to inquire and decide according to truth whether a bond which, as far as external appearances go, seems to have been effected, exists in reality, or (if it has in reality been effected) whether the pre-requisite conditions for its dissolution are verified; and, having established the truth, to pronounce judgment accordingly. Here lies the profound importance of the personal responsibility of the judge in the direction and termination of the trial."[7]

c) When the conditions of the diocese require it, Ordinaries should not hesitate to act as directed in the Letter of this Sacred Congregation of 1 July, 1932, n. III:

"If in view of the smallness of his diocese and especially its scarcity of priests, any of the Most Excellent Bishops or Ordinaries of places is unable to constitute an ecclesiastical tri-bunal which can perform its function in the manner called for by the special importance of matrimonial cases and the respect due to so great a sacrament, let him not hesitate, after having well considered the importance of the matter, to ease his con-science by informing this Sacred Congregation of the aforesaid circumstances, so that it may at least temporarily relieve the situation by transferring the jurisdiction of the tribunal to the Curia of some other ecclesiastical province or district, which may be better fitted, by reason of its more learned officials and other officers, to bear the burden."[8]

9. For marriages which were contracted after the issuance of the Instruction, *Sacrosanctum,* of this Sacred Congregation, the judge should obtain through the diocesan Curia, from the pastor of the place where the marriage was celebrated, the *"processicu-lum depositionum coniugum ante nuptias"* (that is, the dossier of the sworn replies of the parties given in the prenuptial investiga-tion); and he should take due account of those sworn statements, especially if the party or parties are trying to prove that they *freely and knowingly* excluded the blessings of marriage, whereas in that preliminary inquiry they stated under oath that they were being married without any such exclusion. It follows that the judge cannot, unless forced to do so by the most convincing

---

[7] AAS 36, pp. 281–294; CANON LAW DIGEST, 3, under canon 1960.

[8] AAS 24–272; CANON LAW DIGEST, 1, p. 802.

arguments, admit that the parties, in making these sworn statements, either did not know what they were doing or perjured themselves.

10. The following recommendations are made especially to the defenders of the bond:

It sometimes happens, as we stated above, that defenders of the bond remain merely inert during the preliminary stage of the trial. They do nothing; call no witnesses *ex officio;* make no inquiries regarding the truth of the facts from trustworthy persons who have no interest in the case; they approve as a matter of course the questions proposed by the attorneys for the examination of the parties, even if these questions are leading. Then in the decisive stage of the case, they write only superficial observations, giving no assistance or practically none to the judge in ferreting out the truth of the facts.

11. On this point the Allocution of the Holy Father already cited admonishes defenders of the bond in these words:

"As it would be inconsistent with the importance of his office and the careful and conscientious fulfillment of his duty were he to content himself with a perfunctory review of the record and a few superficial remarks, so too it is not right that this office be entrusted to persons who are still wanting in experience of life and maturity of judgment. The fact that the observations of the defender of the bond are subject to scrutiny by the judges, does not exempt them from this rule, for the judges should find in the careful work of the defender of the bond an aid and complement to their own activity, and it is not to be supposed that they must do all his work and conduct all his investigation over again in order to be able to rely on his representations."[9]

On the other hand if the defender performs properly his task of protecting the marriage bond, not only will "the sacredness of so great a Sacrament" be kept inviolate, but out of the reasonable interchange of views between the plaintiff and the defender of the bond, the genuine truth of the facts, which is the ultimate and principal end result of all judicial trials, will more easily emerge.

12. Finally it is recommended to all tribunals that they do their work earnestly and without excessive delays, never as far as in them lies allowing the cases to drag on beyond the terms

---

[9] AAS 36–281; CANON LAW DIGEST, 3, under canon 1960.

fixed in canon 1620; deciding incidental questions quickly; rejecting requests for further testimony which are made for the purpose of delaying the case; fixing peremptory terms for action, and so forth.

13. Since the judges and officers of the tribunal cannot proceed apace with their judicial work unless they are provided with adequate maintenance, Ordinaries should see to it that the tribunal do not lack the necessary temporal subsidies, which should be provided through the payment of appropriate taxes by the litigants and through other suitable means according to circumstances.

14. In making these recommendations to the zeal of the Ordinaries, this Sacred Congregation cherishes the hope that their marriage tribunals will prove equal to their task, "in view of the importance of the matter and the consequences thereof."[10]

Canada: Newfoundland: Organization of Matrimonial Tribunals (S. C. Sacr., 7 Aug., 1950) AAS 44–280.

After the entrance of Newfoundland into the Canadian Confederacy, 1 Apr., 1949, the Sacred Congregation of the Sacraments, at the request of the Bishops and of the Apostolic Delegate, issued a Decree, the dispositive part of which is as follows:

His Holiness has deigned to make the following provisions, decreeing that they are to be observed, all things, even though worthy of special mention, to the contrary notwithstanding:

1. From the 15th day of August, 1950, causes for the nullity of marriage in the Archdiocese of Saint John's and in the Dioceses of Harbor Grace and Saint George's, Newfoundland, shall be tried in the first instance before the Provincial Tribunal of Halifax, which from that date shall include, not only the two Provinces of Halifax and Moncton, but also the entire Island of Newfoundland.

2. Consequently, cases for the nullity of marriage in the Island of Newfoundland, which have been tried in the first instance

---

[10] Quoted from the formula by which His Holiness approved and confirmed the Letter of the S. C. Sacr. on the Handling of Marriage Cases, 1 July, 1932; AAS 24–274; CANON LAW DIGEST, 1, p. 803.

(Private); S. C. Sacr., 15 Aug., 1949. *Periodica,* 39–95. Annotations, *Monitor Ecclesiasticus,* 1950, p. 41 (Bartoccetti).

before the Provincial Tribunal of Halifax, shall be brought for trial in the second instance to the appellate Tribunal of Quebec, always without prejudice to the right of going directly to the Sacred Roman Rota according to canon 1559, § 1.

3. For the rest, as regards the three dioceses above mentioned, let the provisions of the above mentioned Decree and of the executive Norms which accompanied it, of 14 May, 1946,[1] be fully observed.

AAS 44–280; S. C. Sacr., Decree, 7 Aug., 1950.

Canada: Sherbrooke: Organization of Matrimonial Tribunals (S. C. Sacr., 25 March, 1952) AAS 44–281.

After the establishment of the new ecclesiastical Province of Sherbrooke, with the Dioceses of Saint Hyacinth and Nicolet as suffragans (2 March, 1951; AAS, 43–449), the Sacred Congregation of the Sacraments, at the request of the Bishops and of the Apostolic Delegate, issued a Decree of which the dispositive part is as follows:

His Holiness has deigned to make the following provisions, decreeing that they are to be observed, all things, even though worthy of special mention, to the contrary notwithstanding:

1. From the first day of June, 1952, the matrimonial Tribunal of Montreal will serve for the two Provinces of Montreal and Sherbrooke, and hence also for causes for the nullity of marriage in the Diocese of Nicolet, which hereafter shall no longer send those cases to the Tribunal of Quebec to be tried in the first instance.

2. For the rest, let the provisions of the above mentioned Decree and of the executive Norms which accompanied it, of 14 May, 1946,[1] be fully observed.

3. Let this Decree and the preceding one of 7 Aug., 1950, regarding cases from the Island of Newfoundland be published in the *Acta Apostolicae Sedis*.

AAS 44–281; S. C. Sacr., 25 March, 1952.

---

[1] The Decree referred to is that of 28 Jan., 1946, with Norms of 13 May, 1946, AAS 38–281; reported above in this volume under this same canon 1960.

[1] The Decree referred to is that of 28 Jan., 1946, with Norms of 13 May, 1946; AAS 38–281; reported above in this volume under this same canon 1960.

CANON 1963

Opinion of Bishop in Nonconsummation Cases (S. C. Sacr., 31 July, 1941) **Private.**

The Sacred Congregation of the Sacraments was asked by the Archbishop of Trent:

Whether the provision of n. 98, paragraphs 1 and 2, of the Rules of Procedure for Cases on Nonconsummation, which were issued on May 7th, 1923,[1] is to be understood in the sense that the Bishop, or the one who takes his place in this matter, in drawing up his opinion, may take into account, besides all the records of the case, also the observations of the Defender of the Bond; or rather in the sense that the Bishop is bound to give his opinion without taking into account the aforesaid observations drawn up by the Defender of the Bond.

Reply. In the affirmative to the first part; in the negative to the second.

(**Private**); S. C. Sacr., 31 July, 1941. *Il Monitore Ecclesiastico*, 1942, p. 5.

China: Instruction for Matrimonial Procedure, S. C. Prop. Fid., 18 Feb., 1929, to supplant earlier Instruction of 1883. See *Primum Concilium Sinense*, Appendix.

CANON 1971

Competent Ordinary for Receiving Notice of Invalidity of Marriage When Parties Are Incapable of Attacking It (Code Com., 6 Dec., 1943) **AAS 36–94.**

The Code Commission was asked:

Whether the parties to a marriage, who are incapable of attacking it, but who wish to exercise their right to denounce the nullity of the marriage according to canon 1971, § 2, and the interpretation of 17 February, 1930,[1] are bound to apply to the Ordinary or to the promoter of justice of the tribunal which is competent to decide the case of the nullity of their marriage according to canon 1964, or whether they can also apply to another Ordinary or to another promoter of justice.

---

[1] See CANON LAW DIGEST, Vol. 1, p. 790.
[1] Code Com., 17 Feb., 1930; AAS 22–196; CANON LAW DIGEST, Vol. 1, p. 808.

Reply. In the affirmative to the first part, in the negative to the second.

AAS 36–94; Code Com., 6 Dec., 1943.
Periodica, 33–286 (Aguirre).

Appeal or Recourse by Party Incapable of Attacking Marriage (Code Com., 3 May, 1945) AAS 37–149.

The Code Commission was asked:

Whether a party to the marriage, who is incapable of attacking the marriage according to canon 1971, § 1, 1°, has the right to appeal or to take a recourse against a judgment in favor of the marriage.

Reply. In the negative, except as to extrajudicial recourses.

AAS 37–149; Code Com., 3 May, 1945.
Periodica, 34–285 (Aguirre).

Incapacity of Party to Attack Marriage Does Not Entail Incurable Nullity of Judgment (Code Com., 4 Jan., 1946) AAS 38–162.

The Code Commission was asked:

Whether the incapacity of one of the contracting parties to attack the marriage, established by canon 1971, § 1, 1°, involves incapacity of standing in court, so that the sentence is incurably null according to canon 1892, 2°.

Reply. In the negative.

AAS 38–162; Code Com., 4 Jan., 1946.
Periodica, 35–195 (Cappello).

What Is Meant by a Direct and Guilty Cause of Nullity (Rota, 30 May, 1949) Private.

The following is a condensed outline of part of a decision by the Rota on this subject, handed down in the Harrington-Nick case, from New York (Rota, 30 May, 1949, *coram* Jullien).

Before 1942 there was considerable discussion as to when a party to a marriage should be considered "the cause of the impediment" (c. 1971, § 1, 1°), or "the culpable cause of the impediment or of the nullity of the marriage" (Code Com., 17

July, 1933; AAS 25–345; CANON LAW DIGEST, I, p. 808). Now, in view of the Reply of the Code Commission of 27 July, 1942 (AAS 34–241; CANON LAW DIGEST, II, p. 548), we know that a party is not incapable of attacking a marriage unless he was both the *direct* and the *guilty* (*dolosa*) cause of the impediment or of the nullity of the marriage.

A person is the *direct* cause of the impediment or nullity if he procures it by a directly voluntary act (*voluntarium directum*). This is defined by St. Thomas (1ª 2ᵃᵉ, q. 77, a. 7) as *"id in quod voluntas fertur,"* and is opposed to what "is from the will as not acting" or "what the will could prevent but did not."

This will be better understood by considering four relations of the will toward a certain object: intention, choice or election, passive permission, active permission. It is clear that the first two, intention and choice, are direct acts of the will; and it is equally clear that passive permission is not. What is to be said of active permission? This means that the will permits another cause to be inserted in its own action. When this happens, one and the same act of the will has two effects, but only one of them really proceeds from the will directly; the other proceeds from an independent cause which is engrafted upon or inserted in the act of the will, with the will's permission. This latter effect is therefore not a *voluntarium directum* according to St. Thomas' definition; and this remains true even though the effect was foreseen.

Applying this to the matter in hand, we see that one is only an indirect cause of an impediment or nullity if, in as far as he himself is concerned, or to the best of his ability (*suo pro marte*), he duly contracts marriage with a partner who, to his knowledge, is placing an obstacle to the validity of the marriage: in this case he foresees and permits the invalidity, but does not directly will it. The qualification "in as far as he himself is concerned" or "to the best of his ability" (*suo pro marte*) is important. For, if he had the means of bringing his reluctant partner to contract validly and failed to use them, he would have to be considered as directly procuring the nullity and not merely permitting it. On the other hand it cannot be maintained that, since marriage is a contract between two persons, one must necessarily be directly responsible for the evil will of the other, even though he do all in his power to correct it.

To be excluded from attacking the marriage, the party must also be the *guilty* cause of the impediment or nullity. This is not the same as the direct cause already discussed. One may be a direct cause without being a guilty cause (cf. Code Com., 17 July, 1933, ad 3; CANON LAW DIGEST, 1, p. 808).

Dolus in canon law supposes "a deliberate will to violate the law" (c. 2200, § 1), that is, a theological fault, and a grave one if there is question of a grave law, as in the present matter. This deliberate will is indeed presumed from the fact of the violation of the law (c. 2200, § 2); but the presumption yields to contrary proof. In a case of a directly voluntary act, guilt (*dolus*) is absent when on the part of the intellect there is lacking the degree of knowledge, or on the part of the will there is lacking the degree of liberty, which are required for a grave theological fault (cc. 2200; 2229, § 3). In an act which is only indirectly voluntary there is no guilt if one, for a good end and for a pro-portionately grave reason, places an act which is good or indif-ferent, from which the evil effect is not more immediate than the good. These are the well-known principles of the double effect.

Accordingly, in the following cases the party *is not the guilty cause* of the impediment or nullity:

a) One who does not know the malice of his act or does not know that it is against the law. However, one does not cease to be a guilty cause and hence incapable of attacking the marriage, if he knowingly violates the law without knowing its invalidating character, and still less if he knowingly violates it merely in ignorance that its violation renders him incapable of suing for nullity (cf. cc. 16, § 1, and 2229, § 3, 1°).

b) One who is forced to contract marriage in that way by grave extrinsic fear (cf. c. 2205, § 2, and Reply of Code Commission of 17 July, 1933; CANON LAW DIGEST, 1, p. 808).

c) One who for a proportionately grave reason, for example through ardent love for the other party, or to legitimate the children, or to escape the shame arising from an illicit union, allows the other party to give an invalid consent, provided of course that he himself consents properly and has previously done all that he could to prevent the nullity of the marriage. In this last case there is no ground on which the act can be shown to be malicious: the action itself is good; the end intended is good; the evil effect is not directly intended, nor is it the cause of the good effect which is directly intended; finally, the cause for permitting the evil effect is proportionately grave.

Finally, it must be remembered that in these preliminary investigations the word of the parties must be accepted with caution. For it often happens that they exaggerate their own culpability in the belief that this will make it easier to obtain a declaration of nullity. Hence, whenever, all things considered, it is not proved with certainty that the party was the direct and guilty cause of the nullity, we cannot and ought not to decide that he is incapable of attacking the marriage.

(**Private**); Rota, 30 May, 1949. This outline is made from the Latin text of this part of the decision, which was kindly sent to us by the Committee on Research of the Canon Law Society of America.

In Doubt as to the Capacity of the Plaintiff to Attack the Marriage, the Bill of Complaint Should Not Be Rejected (Rota, 6 Aug., 1952) Private.

The woman plaintiff in this case, upon rejection by the lower Court of her bill of complaint (*libellus*) on the ground that, being herself the cause of the nullity, she was incapable of attacking the marriage, took a recourse to the Rota on that question in accordance with canon 1709, § 3, and the Instruction on Matrimonial Procedure, Art. 66.[1]

The Rota begins by laying down the following principles: A party is not incapable:

a) who was only the indirect cause, that is, was the cause of the impediment or nullity by an indirect voluntary act, in as much as he did not directly place the impediment but only permitted it or failed to prevent it;

b) who was coerced into contracting marriage by fear at least relatively grave, unjust, and external (Reply of Code Commission, 17 July, 1933; CANON LAW DIGEST, I, p. 808).

c) who was under invincible ignorance of law or fact, or under *simply vincible* ignorance (not affected, crass, or supine), provided it was not ignorance merely of the penalty or of the invalidating force of the law (c. 16, § 1);

d) who is or was so weak or so disturbed in mind that his action was not gravely culpable;

e) in doubt, that is, when it is not certain that the party was

---

[1] Cf. CANON LAW DIGEST, 2, p. 488.

the direct and culpable cause of the impediment or of the nullity.

It was clear that in this case the woman was the *direct* cause of the nullity (her consent was simulated); but the question is whether she was also the *guilty* cause.

Her attorney in the lower Court had contended that her simulation of consent was simply justified as a measure of self-defense. The Rota holds that the lower Court rightly rejected this contention.

However, though not entirely justified, the simulation of consent, in the position in which the woman was placed, is mitigated by many extenuating circumstances which reduce its guilt. A widow at twenty-four, and bereaved also of her little son, psychologically depressed and suffering from tuberculosis, she had yielded to the ardent courtship of the man and entered into illicit relations with him. These she succeeded for a time in breaking off, but a new combination of circumstances (separation from her mother, economic hardship due to the war, absence of anyone to whom she could turn for guidance and support) threw her again into the power of her lover, and she became pregnant. Not wishing to marry him, unwilling to procure abortion, wishing in some way to provide for her child, she had finally gone through the ceremony of marriage, simulating a consent which she did not intend.

In view of all this, the Rota decided that she should not be excluded from attacking the marriage.

"It cannot reasonably be denied that the guilt of a crime is at least doubtful in this case; it is not certain. Now in doubt no one can be prevented from attacking the marriage, especially not this plaintiff who, as is proved by the testimony of the Pastor, gave many signs of sincere reform and is now living a good and pious life.

"In consideration of all this, the undersigned Fathers, Auditors of this *turnus* lawfully convened in the Tribunal of the Sacred Roman Rota, after reading the statements of the Advocate and hearing from the Defender of the Bond and the Promoter of Justice, decreed:

"*Non constare de inhabilitate mulieris in casu, ideoque libellum esse admittendum.*"

(**Private**); Rota, 6 Aug., 1952 (*coram* Pinna). *Monitor Ecclesiasticus,* 1952, p. 611.

CANON 1987

Abandonment of Appeal by Defender of Bond, in Third Instance, After Two Judgments Declaring Nullity of Marriage (Code Com., 29 May, 1947) **AAS 39–373.**

The Code Commission was asked:

Whether, when the defender of the bond has appealed according to canon 1987 against a second judgment confirming the nullity of a marriage, in the third instance, although there is question of an Apostolic tribunal, the defender of the bond of this instance can, according to his conscience, abandon the appeal, so that the tribunal cannot compel him to prosecute the appeal.

Reply. In the affirmative.

AAS 39–373; Code Com., 29 May, 1947.
Cf. *Periodica,* 36–341 (Aguirre).

CANON 1990

Declaration of Nullity for Want of Form: Previous Divorce Not an Absolute Requisite for Summary Procedure (S. C. Sacr., 20 Dec., 1923) **Private.**

The Sacred Congregation of the Sacraments was asked by the Cardinal Archbishop of Berlin:

I. Whether the clause "having obtained a civil divorce," which occurs in the preceding declaration[1] is a condition *sine qua non* for this procedure?

II. Whether those cases mentioned in the preceding declaration can be decided in this summary manner, even when a civil divorce not only has not yet been obtained but has not even been asked for?

Reply. In the negative to the first part, in the affirmative to the second, *et ad mentem.* The mind is that there should really be proof of the state of liberty in the case, and an oath should be taken that freedom will also be obtained according to the civil law.

(**Private**); S. C. Sacr., 20 Dec., 1923. Reported by Sartori, *Enchiridion Canonicum,* p. 431, from the official commentary of the Archdiocese of Berlin, *Verordnungen des Fuerstbisch. Ordinariat zu Breslau,* n. 745, 15 Jan., 1924.

---

[1] See CANON LAW DIGEST, Vol. 1, p. 810; AAS 11–479, Code Com., 16 Oct., 1919.

Exceptional Cases of Canon 1990 Are Exclusive: Process, Judicial: Ordinary Does Not Include Vicar General: Appellate Judge Includes *Officialis* (Code Com., 6 Dec., 1943) **AAS 36–94.**

The Code Commission was asked:

I. Whether the *exceptional cases* of canon 1990 are enumerated exclusively or by way of illustration.

Reply. In the affirmative to the first part, in the negative to the second.

II. Whether the process of canon 1990 is judicial or administrative.

Reply. In the affirmative to the first part, in the negative to the second.

III. Whether the *Ordinary,* mentioned in canon 1990, includes the Vicar General, at least with a special mandate from the Bishop.

Reply. In the negative.

IV. Whether the words *judge of the second instance,* in canons 1991 and 1992, include only the Bishop, or also the *Officialis.*

Reply. In the negative to the first part, in the affirmative to the second.

AAS 36–94; Code Com., 6 Dec., 1943.
Periodica, 33–289 (Aguirre).

Non-Catholic Allowed to Stand as Plaintiff in Case of Nonage Under Canon 1990 (Holy Office, 24 May, 1952) Private.

Summary of the Case. Records were offered by the petitioner, a non-Catholic, of her birth and baptism, both of which attested to her date of birth less than fourteen years before the date of her marriage (a non-Catholic marriage). According to the marriage record, the petitioner had given herself as sixteen years of age at the time of her marriage. A brief deposition was on hand from the mother of the petitioner, stating that the age shown by the marriage record was false and that the records of birth and baptism were accurate. Copies of the above documents and depositions were presented to the Holy Office when permission was sought to instruct the case according to the procedure of canon 1990.

Reply. In a recent letter to the Holy Office, Your Excellency recommended the petition of the non-Catholic VIOLA, praying that she be granted the right to attack her marriage contracted in 1927 with the non-Catholic STUART.

After considering everything, this Supreme Sacred Congregation granted the petition, so that the petitioner, although a non-Catholic, may stand as plaintiff in the trial of the case before your Tribunal, according to canon 1990.

From the Holy Office, 24 May, 1952.

(**Private**); Holy Office, 24 May, 1952. Matter kindly sent to us by the Committee on Research of the Canon Law Society of America.

Declaration of Nullity of Marriage of Baptized Non-Catholic contracted in absence and without proxy. See c. 1088; private reply of Holy Office, 16 Nov., 1949.

CANON 2141

Solemn Canonization of Blessed Grignion de Montfort: Historical Question Decided (S. C. Rit., 25 Apr., 1947) AAS 39–240.

In connection with a decision regarding the right to assist at the solemn canonization of the Blessed Grignion de Montfort, the Sacred Congregation of Rites had to decide this question:

Whether the Blessed Louis Marie Grignion de Montfort can be considered as the founder, not only of the Priests of the Society of Mary, and of the Daughters of Wisdom, but also of the Brothers of Christian Instruction of Saint Gabriel.

Reply. The Eminent Fathers in charge of sacred rites, after maturely considering the question, and in view of the unanimous opinion of the Consultors of the Historical Section, replied: In the negative. Rather it is established that the founder of the Brothers of Christian Instruction of Saint Gabriel was Father Gabriel Deshayes.

Afterward, the matter having been referred by the undersigned Cardinal Prefect of the Sacred Congregation of Rites to His Holiness Pius XII, His Holiness graciously deigned to confirm the **reply of the Cardinals.**

AAS 39–240; S. C. Rit., 25 Apr., 1947.

BOOK V

CRIMES AND PENALTIES

Canons 2195–2414

BOOK V

CRIMES AND PENALTIES

Canons 2195–2414

CANON 2209

Cardinal Mindszenty: Necessary cooperators in his arrest incur excommunication. See c. 2343; AAS 41–80.

Rumania: Penalties declared for crimes against the Church. See c. 2334; AAS 43–603.

CANON 2229

Grave Fear Does Not Excuse From New Excommunication. See c. 2245; AAS 43–217.

CANON 2245

New Excommunication Most Specially Reserved to Holy See: Consecrating Bishop Not Nominated or Expressly Confirmed by the Holy See (Holy Office, 9 April, 1951) **AAS 43–217.**

A Decree of the Holy Office "concerning the consecration of a Bishop without canonical provision" is as follows:

A Bishop, of whatsoever rite or dignity, who consecrates to the Episcopacy anyone who is neither appointed nor expressly confirmed by the Holy See, and the person who receives the consecration, even though they were coerced by grave fear (c. 2229, § 3, 3°), incur *ipso facto* an excommunication *most specially reserved* to the Holy See.

This Decree is effective from the very day of its promulgation.

Given from the Palace of the Holy Office, 9 April, 1951.

AAS 43–217; Holy Office, Decree, 9 April, 1951. Annotations, *Monitor Ecclesiasticus,* 1951, p. 221 (Crovini).

Faculties of Confessors Approved in Rome: As to censures reserved to Ordinaries by the Code. See **c. 900**; *Monitum* of Vicar of Rome, 4 March, 1920.

CANON 2258

Excommunicatus Vitandus: Priest so declared by Holy Office for pertinacity in spreading heresy. See Holy Office, 4 June, 1946 (AAS 38–280).

CANON 2261

Excommunication as *Vitandus* **Inflicted** for accepting office from lay authority. See **c. 2394**; AAS 42–195.

CANON 2314

Objects of Judicial Jurisdiction: the Church Has the Right to Protect the Faith: True Principle of Freedom of Conscience (Pius XII, 6 Oct., 1946) AAS 38–391.

An Allocution of His Holiness Pius XII to the Auditors and other Officials and Ministers of the Sacred Roman Rota and to its Advocates and Procurators, delivered on October 6, 1946, is as follows:

A year has passed, beloved sons, since the last time you were assembled in Our presence, a year of the most intense labor for you, especially in the field of marriage cases. Continuing the consideration which We began in Our last discourse, We take occasion to-day to return once more to this subject which constitutes the greater part of your activity, and of which your respected Dean also has treated in his customary address.

Last year[1] We began to speak of the difference between the ecclesiastical and the civil judicial systems. After examining, in their origin and nature, the fundamental distinction between the two supreme authorities, both of which have the judicial power as one of their important and necessary functions, We found likewise

---

[1] The Allocution of 1945 is reported above in this same volume under canon 1553.

in the two respective judicial systems an essential diversity, not-withstanding the many similarities which are to be found in both.

The same conclusion is reached if one considers the proper *object* of each system. Here again we find common elements and characteristic traits. In both of the perfect societies, certainly, the protection of the *common good* demands that the rights and the goods of their members be capable of being realized, guaranteed, restored through judicial action. Moreover these rights and goods are partly the same in both the Church and the State, since the Church too is a visible society, whose life is necessarily bound up with a physical mode of existence and with the conditions of space and time in which man's life is cast. But on the other hand there are rights and goods which belong so peculiarly and properly to ecclesiastical jurisdiction that by their very nature they are not and cannot be the object of the judicial power of the State.

I

Among the goods in whose defense the ecclesiastical tribunals (those of local Ordinaries as well as those of the Holy See) have, in the course of history, intervened — sometimes severely — is the faith itself, the foundation of all supernatural life. The Tribunal for the defense of the faith is therefore a legitimate organ of the judicial power in the Church, in as much as she is a perfect religious society. It is her duty to react juridically against every attack directed at one of her most important and vital goods. The crimes of heresy and apostasy never could, nor can they now, leave the Church indifferent or inert. No doubt in the course of the centuries the tribunal for the defense of the faith may have assumed forms and adopted methods which were not required in the very nature of things, but which find their explanation in the light of particular historical circumstances; nevertheless it would be false to draw from them an argument against the legitimacy of the tribunal itself.

We are aware that the very name of this tribunal shocks the sentiments of not a few men of our time. They are those whose thoughts and feelings are under the spell of a doctrine which, ex-cluding all idea of the supernatural and of revelation, attributes to human reason the power to understand the world completely and to dominate the whole of life, and which consequently de-mands that in this respect man must be entirely independent of any bond of authority whatsoever. We know the origins, the advocates, the development of this doctrine; We know the influence it has exercised on intellectual, moral and social life, as well as on economics and politics; but We also know its contradictions in the history of the last centuries and especially of the last hundred years. Its adherents appeal to the principles of "liberty of conscience" and "tolerance" in matters which concern the spiritual and especially the religious life. But too often they themselves, as soon as they have attained to power, have found nothing more urgent to be done than to violate consciences and to impose on the Catholic part of the population a yoke of oppression, especially in regard to the rights of parents in the education of their children.

If in past centuries the reaction against crimes which injure the faith may seem to the modern conscience to have at times overstepped legitimate bounds, in our own time on the contrary, human society generally shows an extreme indifference and want of sensibility in this regard. The ever increasing frequency of contacts and the promiscuity of the various religious confessions within the same country have led the civil tribunals to follow the principle of "tolerance" and "freedom of conscience." And indeed there is a tolerance, political, civil, and social, toward the adherents of other faiths, which is, under these circumstances, a moral obligation also for Catholics.

The Church herself, in canon 1351 of the Code of Canon Law, has given the force of law to the maxim: *No one is to be forced to embrace the Catholic faith against his will.* This canon, which reproduces the very words of Our great Predecessor Leo XIII in the Encyclical, *Immortale Dei,* of 1 November, 1885, is the faithful echo of the doctrine taught by the Church from the first centuries of Christianity. Let it suffice to cite the testimony of Lactantius, written about the years 305–310: "There is no need of force or injury, for religion cannot be forced; to move the will, words rather than blows are to be used. . . . And so we keep no one against his will — for he who lacks devotion and faith is useless to God. . . . There is nothing so voluntary as religion; for if the heart of the one who offers sacrifice is turned away, religion is gone, it is nothing. . . . "[2]

If then a few days ago, according to the news given out by the press, in the course of a deplorable trial, the statement was made

---

[2] *Divinae institutiones,* 1. 5, c. 19; *Corpus Script. Eccles. Lat.,* Vol. XIX, pp. 463–465.

by the Public Minister that the Pope himself had approved of
so-called "forced conversions," and, what would be even worse,
that he had done so through motives of nationalistic imperialism,
We have the right and the duty to reject so false an accusation.
And, in order that Our statement may not lack due documentation, We deem it appropriate to read to you a *Pro-Memoria* of
Our Secretariate of State, of 25 January, 1942, in reply to an
inquiry from the Legation of Jugoslavia to the Holy See about
the conversion movement, in which, for that matter, the Legation
itself admitted that neither the Holy See nor the Catholic Bishops
of Croatia had had any part. Here is the text of the *Pro-Memoria:*[3]

"Referring to the Note of the Royal Legation of Jugoslavia to
the Holy See, no. 1/42, of 9 January of the present year, the
Secretariate of State of His Holiness has the honor to inform the
said Legation of the following:

"According to the principles of Catholic doctrine, conversion
must be the result, not of external constraint, but of an interior
adherence of the soul to the truths taught by the Catholic Church.

"It is for this reason that the Catholic Church does not admit
to her communion adult persons who apply either for the first time
or for readmission, except on condition that they be fully aware
of the meaning and consequences of the step which they wish to
take.

"Therefore, the fact that suddenly a great number of Croatian
dissidents asked to be received into the Catholic Church, could
not fail to cause a lively concern to the Croatian Bishops, to whom
naturally belong the defense and protection of Catholic interests
in Croatia.

"Far from taking advantage of this fact, either officially or
unofficially, they made it a point of duty formally to call to the
attention of the proper authorities the necessity that the return
of the dissidents be accomplished in entire liberty, and at the
same time to vindicate for the ecclesiastical Authority exclusive
competence in giving orders and directions in the matter of
conversions.

"If an episcopal Committee was at once established with the
charge of considering and deciding all questions concerning this
matter, that was done precisely for the purpose of guaranteeing

---

[3] We translate it from the original French in which it is quoted by
His Holiness.

that the conversions should be, in conformity to the principles of Catholic doctrine, the fruit of persuasion and not of constraint.

"The Holy See, for its own part, did not fail to recommend and inculcate the exact observance of the canonical prescriptions and of the directives which have been given in this matter."

Taking up again the thread of Our argument, We must add that the ecclesiastical tribunal in the exercise of its jurisdiction, cannot adopt the same norm which is followed by civil tribunals. The Catholic Church, as We have already said, is a perfect society which has for its foundation the truth of the faith infallibly revealed by God. Whatever is opposed to this truth is necessarily error; and error cannot be objectively entitled to the same rights as the truth. And so freedom of thought and freedom of conscience have their essential limitations in the veracity of God the author of revelation. We say, their essential limitations, if in reality truth is not the same as error and if the right conscience of man is in reality the voice of God. It follows that a member of the Church cannot without fault deny or repudiate Catholic truth which he has once known and acknowledged; and if the Church, after having made certain of the fact of heresy or apostasy, punishes it, for example by excluding the guilty person from the communion of the faithful, she remains strictly within the bonds of her competency, and acts in defense, so to speak, of her domestic right.

II

Another object which brings out clearly the difference between the ecclesiastical and civil judicial systems, is matrimony. Marriage is, by the will of the Creator, a *sacred thing*. Hence, if there is question of a union between baptized persons, it remains by its nature outside the competency of the civil authority. But even between non-baptized persons, marriages legitimately contracted are in the order of nature a sacred thing, so that civil tribunals have not the power to dissolve them, and the Church in such cases has never recognized the validity of decrees of divorce. Nevertheless, simple declarations of nullity of these same marriages — relatively rare in comparison with decrees of divorce — can in certain circumstances be justly pronounced by civil tribunals, and hence can be recognized by the Church.

As regards the merely civil effects of marriage even between baptized persons, the civil authority is undoubtedly competent to pass judgment, as every one knows.[4] But the competence of the Church in matrimonial questions is far broader and deeper, because upon her depends by divine institution what concerns the protection of the conjugal bond and the holiness of marriage.

In this competency, you too, beloved sons, have your share, being called upon to pronounce your judgments in matrimonial cases.

If at the opening of Our address we expressed Our paternal gratitude to you for your assiduous labors especially in this field, We cannot now conceal from you Our anxiety over the growing number of such cases, an anxiety which We know is also your own, as is clearly shown by the remarks made a moment ago by your worthy speaker.

For are not the matrimonial cases pending before your Tribunal an index, and do they not perhaps give the measure of the progressive disintegration of conjugal life, a disintegration which threatens to poison and corrupt also the morals of the Catholic people? A large contribution to the development of this lamentable disorder was made by both world wars, but an incomparably greater one by the second than by the first. No one can remain coldly insensible in the face of this tragedy, which is still dragging along its train of disastrous consequences, at the thought of the millions of young married people whom a forced separation has held apart for long months and years. What a degree of courage, of self-denial, of patience, what a treasure of loving mutual trust, what a spirit of Christian faith were required in order to keep intact their plighted faith, in order to resist! Many, beyond a doubt, with the help of grace obtained through prayer, were able to hold firm. But along with these, how many others there were who proved less strong! What masses of ruined homes, what injuries to souls wounded in their human dignity, in their conjugal delicacy, what mortal blows to the happiness of the family!

Now it is a question of repairing these losses, healing these wounds, curing these disorders. The motherly heart of the Church bleeds at the sight of the unspeakable anguish of so many of her children; to come to their aid, she spares no effort, and carries her condescension to its extreme limit. This extreme limit is solemnly

---

[4] Cf. canon 1016.

formulated in canon 1118 of the Code of Canon Law: *Marriage which is sacramental and consummated cannot be dissolved by any human power, nor by any cause save death.*

There can be no doubt that at the present time one of the principal cares of the Church must be that of checking by every means the progressive decadence of marriage and the family; and of this she herself is fully conscious, while at the same time she is well aware that her efforts can attain effective results only in the measure in which the general conditions, economic, social, and above all moral, make it in practice less difficult to live a conjugal life that is acceptable to God. In this respect very great responsibilities rest upon the public authorities.

Meanwhile, until this amelioration of public morality can be had, it will be your task, beloved sons, with "labor and patience"[5] to suffer and to control the incessant flow of matrimonial trials. Because, action looking to the improvement of conjugal and family life is one thing, and judicial procedure regarding marriage is another. The latter has the duty of judging and deciding the cases which are presented to it, objectively, according to the state of facts and the rules of canon law. Continue to bring to the discharge of your official duties, together with the unalterable impartiality of the conscientious judge, also the consciousness that in doing so you are making a high contribution to the edification of the Church. The wise equity with which your Tribunal considers also the financial side of these same cases in the difficult economic conditions of the present time — an equity which is matched by the generous cooperation of the Advocates of the Rota — is already a clear proof that you conceive your work to be what it really is: a service to the true welfare of the faithful and to the salvation of souls.

III

Among the objects of ecclesiastical judicial power, We must include also the matters which (in addition to the guardianship of the faith) are proper to the tribunal of the Supreme Sacred Congregation of the Holy Office. The severity of its procedure is required by the sanctity of the goods which it has the mission to defend, and by the gravity of the crimes which it is called upon to judge. There would be no point in making particular mention

---

[5] Cf. Apoc. 2:2.

of this, were it not that its method of procedure has been represented as being in conflict with the principle, now generally admitted, of publicity in judicial trials, regarded as a necessary
guarantee against abuses to the detriment of justice.

The activity of that Supreme tribunal even in criminal cases is
in fact exercised with the obligation of secrecy. But first of all it is
well to remember that the criminal procedure of civil States also
provides in certain cases that the discussion take place, either in
whole or in part, "behind closed doors," that is, whenever such a
provision is required by the common good: and it is precisely
this same principle which the Church applies in the penal trials of
the Holy Office. Nevertheless it is indispensable that in these cases
all the essential guarantees for a just and fair trial be assured:
the communication of the charges to the accused, with the opportunity to refute them or to bring out whatever he judges useful
to excuse or diminish his guilt; the right of defense, to be exercised either personally or through counsel appointed by the court
or chosen by the accused; the quality of perfect objectivity and
conscientiousness in the judges. Now all these requisites are realized in the tribunal of the Holy Office.

Your office is a weighty one, beloved sons, not only in its extent
but also because of the responsibility which it implies and the
intensity of austere labor which it imposes. A holy and beneficent
office, it is nonetheless ignored by many, misunderstood by others.
But the Lord looks upon it with complacency, and seeing with
what spirit you are laboring for His honor, for the service of the
Church, for the good of souls, for the salvation of society, He
sends down upon you the abundance of His graces; and as a
presage of those heavenly blessings We cordially impart to all of
you here present, Our paternal Apostolic Benediction.

AAS 38–391; Pius XII, Allocution, 6 Oct., 1946

Schismatical "Catholic Action" in Czechoslovakia Condemned (Holy Office, 20 June, 1949) AAS 41–333.

Decree of the Holy Office:

Very recently the enemies of the Catholic Church in Czechoslovakia have fraudulently set up a spurious "Catholic Action"
in Czechoslovakia, through which they are trying to induce the
Catholics of that country to fall away from the Catholic Church

and to withdraw from due obedience to the legitimate Pastors of the Church.

This "action" is the more damnable as its promoters have not hesitated to compel many persons by force or fraud to become members; they have even gone so far as brazenly to number and announce as members many priests and lay Catholics who not only never adhered to it but showed themselves opposed to it.

Wherefore this Supreme Sacred Congregation of the Holy Office, in the fulfillment of its charge to protect the integrity of faith and morals, in the name and by the authority of His Holiness by divine Providence Pope Pius XII, reprobates and condemns as schismatical the aforesaid action fraudulently called "Catholic Action," and at the same time declares that all persons, clerical or lay, who knowingly and of their own accord have adhered to it, or who shall do so in future, and in particular its authors and promoters, have incurred or shall incur *ipso facto* as schismatics and apostates from the Catholic Church, the excommunication specially reserved to the Holy See, which is mentioned in canon 2314, without prejudice to the other sanctions of Canon Law, with which they are thereafter to be punished if (which God forbid) they remain contumaciously in the censure.

Given at Rome, from the Holy Office, 20 June, 1949.

AAS 41–333; Holy Office, Decree, 20 June, 1949.

Materialistic and Anti-Christian Communist Doctrine: Penalty for Professing, Defending, or Propagating (Holy Office, Decree, 1 July, 1949) AAS 41–334.

The following questions were asked of the Holy Office:

1. Whether it is licit to join the Communist party or to favor it.

2. Whether it is licit to publish, propagate, or read books, periodicals, daily papers, or sheets which promote the doctrine or action of Communists, or to write in them.

3. Whether the faithful who knowingly and freely do the acts mentioned in 1 and 2 can be admitted to the sacraments.

4. Whether the faithful who profess the materialistic and anti-Christian doctrine of Communists, and especially those who defend or propagate it, incur *ipso facto* as apostates from the Catholic faith the excommunication specially reserved to the Holy See.

The Eminent and Most Reverend Fathers who are in charge of the safeguarding of faith and morals, after hearing the opinions of the Reverend Consultors, in the plenary session of Tuesday (instead of Wednesday) the 28th of June, 1949, decided to reply:

Replies: 1. In the *negative;* for Communism is materialistic and anti-Christian; and the leaders of the Communists, even though they sometimes verbally profess that they are not attacking religion, in fact nevertheless by doctrine and action show themselves to be enemies of God and of the true religion and the Church of Christ.

2. In the *negative:* for they are forbidden *ipso iure* (cf. c. 1399 of the Code of Canon Law).

3. In the *negative,* according to the ordinary principles governing the refusal of the sacraments to those who are not properly disposed.

4. In the *affirmative.*

On the following Thursday, the 30th of the same month and year, His Holiness by divine Providence Pope Pius XII, in the customary audience granted to the Most Excellent and Most Reverend Assessor of the Holy Office, approved the resolution referred to him by the Eminent Fathers and ordered that it be promulgated in the official Commentary, *Acta Apostolicae Sedis.* Given at Rome, the 1st of July, 1949.

AAS 41–334; Holy Office, Decree, 1 July, 1949. *Periodica,* 38–126 and 38–301 (Fábregas). For an earlier study of the question, cf. *Periodica,* 37–103 (Ganzi).

Leader of Schism in Rumania Declared *Excommunicatus Vitandus:* Other Priests Favoring Schism Subject to Same Penalty (Holy Office, Decree, 2 May, 1950) Private.

A Decree of the Holy Office:

Certain Catholic priests of the Latin rite in Rumania, urged on by the Communists, are striving privately and publicly to alienate the Catholic clergy and people from due allegiance to their lawful Pastors and especially to the Roman Pontiff.

The leader of this group is the priest Andreas Agotha, who, although he has already received warning from the Holy See, contumaciously persists in his course.

Wherefore the Most Eminent and Most Reverend Fathers who are in charge of the safeguarding of faith and morals have decreed:

1) The priest Andreas Agotha is declared *excommunicatus vi-*

tandus, with all the legal effects referred to in canon 2258 and the following canons.

2) The aforesaid priests are warned that they too will be declared *excommunicati vitandi,* unless they immediately desist from giving favor to the said schismatical movement.

3) Let other priests and all faithful Catholics beware of adhering to the schismatical sect, which is *ipso facto* struck by the excommunication mentioned in canon 2314.

Given at Rome, from the Holy Office, 2 May, 1950.

(**Private**); Holy Office, Decree, 2 May, 1950. *L'Osservatore Romano,* 4 May, 1950.

————

Communism: Pastoral Letter by the four Cardinals of France, 8 Sept., 1949, defining for French Catholics the meaning and scope of the Decree of the Holy Office of 1 July, 1949. *The Catholic Mind,* 1949, p. 752.

Persistence in Spreading Heresy: Priest declared *excommunicatus vitandus.* See Holy Office, 4 June, 1946 (AAS 38–280).

CANON 2316

Communist Associations: Persons Who Teach Children Contrary to Christian Faith and Morals Incur Excommunication Specially Reserved (Holy Office, 28 July, 1950) AAS 42–553.

A *Monitum* of the Holy Office:

Some associations have been set up, under the pressure and leadership, as everyone knows, of the Communist party, which have for their purpose to imbue boys and girls with principles and training which are materialistic and contrary to Christian morality and faith.

The faithful are therefore warned that such associations, whatever be the name under which they disguise themselves, are subject to the sanctions mentioned in the Decree of the Holy Office issued on the 1st of July, 1949.[1]

1. Hence parents or those who stand in their place, who contrary to canon 1372, § 2 and the above mentioned Decree of the Holy Office, turn children over to the aforesaid associations to be trained, cannot be admitted to the reception of the sacraments.

————

[1] AAS 41–334; reported in this volume under canon 2314.

2. Those who teach boys and girls what is contrary to the faith and to Christian morals incur an excommunication specially reserved to the Holy See.

3. The boys and girls themselves, as long as they have part in these associations, cannot be admitted to the sacraments.

Given at Rome, from the Holy Office, 28 July, 1950.

AAS 42–553; Holy Office, 28 July, 1950. *Periodica,* 39–310 (Fábregas).

CANON 2331

Contriving Against Ecclesiastical Authority: New Excommunication.
See c. 147; AAS 42–601.

CANON 2334

Rumania: Penalties Declared for Impeding Ecclesiastical Jurisdiction (S. C. Consist., 17 Sept., 1951) AAS 43–603.

A Declaration of the Sacred Consistorial Congregation:

In the Republic of Rumania in these very recent times the Catholic Church has been attacked and her sacred rights have been violated in many and unheard-of ways. Moreover all the Bishops have not only been impeded from the fulfillment of their office but with sacrilegious effrontery have been thrown into prison; many clerics and religious have also been deprived of their liberty.

Very recently His Excellency Augustine Pacha, Bishop of Timisoara, after a long captivity, has most iniquitously been summoned before a lay judge and unjustly condemned.

Wherefore this Sacred Consistorial Congregation declares that all the persons who have perpetrated these crimes, whether they were principals of whatever kind or degree, or accomplices which these crimes by their nature require, or persons who induced to the consummation of the crimes or in any way cooperated therein, provided however that without their help the crime would not have been committed, have contracted the excommunication *latae sententiae* specially reserved to the Holy See — according to canons 2343, § 3; 2334, n. 2; 2341; and 2209, §§ 1–3 — and have incurred the other penalties proportionate to the quality of the delinquents, according to the Sacred Canons of the Code of Canon Law.

Given at Rome, from the Sacred Consistorial Congregation, 17 Sept., 1951.

AAS 43–603; S. C. Consist., 17 Sept., 1951.

Cardinal Mindszenty: Persons guilty of impeding his exercise of ecclesiastical jurisdiction declared excommunicated. See **c. 2343;** AAS 41–31. Also cooperators in those same crimes. See **c. 2343;** AAS 41–80.

Documentation on Recent Persecution of the Church: Bulgaria: Text of the Bulgarian law of 17 Feb., 1949 on religion (*The Catholic Mind,* 1949, p. 371).

China: Apostolic Letter of Pius XII, 18 Jan., 1952 (AAS 44–158).

Czechoslovakia: 1) Text of Pastoral Letter of Archbishop Josef Beran, 15 June, 1949, directed to be read in all churches on Sunday, June 19, on the persecution of the Church in Czechoslovakia (*The Catholic Mind,* 1949, p. 510).

2) Pastoral Letter of entire Hierarchy of Czechoslovakia, 15 June, 1949 (*The Catholic Mind,* 1949, p. 690).

3) Statement of the clergy of Czechoslovakia released to the foreign press, 8 Sept., 1949, rejecting the proposed law subjecting the Church to the State (*The Catholic Mind,* 1949, p. 698).

4) Outrages against Archbishop Beran and the authorities of the Church denounced. See **c. 2341;** AAS 43–173.

Hungary: Persecution of Cardinal Mindszenty: various documents: 1) Pius XII, Letter to Hungarian Bishops, 2 Jan., 1949; 2) Pius XII, Exhortation to the Bishops of the world, 12 Feb., 1949; 3) Pius XII, Allocution at Secret Consistory, 14 Feb., 1949; 4) Pius XII, Address to Catholics of Rome, 20 Feb., 1949 (all in *The Catholic Mind,* 1949, p. 247); 5) A statement by Cardinal Mindszenty, 16 Nov., 1948, issued for publication in Hungary and seized there by the police (*London Tablet,* Dec. 18, 1948; *The Catholic Mind,* 1949, p. 187).

Outrages against Archbishop Grösz. See **c. 2343;** AAS 43–481.

Poland: 1) Letter of Pius XII to the Polish Hierarchy on the condition of the Church, 1 Sept., 1949 (AAS 41–450). English text, *The Catholic Mind,* 1950, p. 253.

2) Polish Church-State Agreement, 14 April, 1950 (*The Catholic Mind,* 1950, p. 438).

3) Statement of the Polish Bishops, 22 April, 1950 (*The Catholic Mind,* 1950, p. 440).

Rumania: Pius XII, Ap. Letter, 27 March, 1952 (AAS 44–249). English text, *The Catholic Mind,* 1952, p. 509.

Russia: Pius XII, Ap. Letter, 7 July, 1952 (AAS 44–505).

CANON 2341

Declaration of Excommunications Incurred *Ipso Facto* by Persecutors of Archbishop Stepinac (S. C. Conc., 14 Oct., 1946) **AAS 38–401.**

The judicial action by which His Excellency Aloysius Stepinac, Archbishop of Zagreb, was arbitrarily thrown into prison and unjustly condemned by a civil magistrate of Jugoslavia, has deeply shocked the whole Catholic world and civil society itself.

The Church protects her sacred Pastors and safeguards their dignity and liberty, chiefly by three canons of the Code of Canon Law, threatening with excommunication to be incurred *ipso facto,* those persons:

1. Who summon a Bishop, especially their own, before a lay tribunal (canon 2341);

2. Who lay violent hands upon the person of an Archbishop or Bishop (canon 2343, § 3);

3. Who directly or indirectly impede the exercise of ecclesiastical jurisdiction or power, and for this purpose have recourse to any lay authority (canon 2334, 2°).

All these excommunications are reserved to the Holy See, simply or specially according to the case.

Therefore, the Sacred Congregation of the Council, which is in charge of the discipline of the Christian clergy and people, since it is known that the aforesaid crimes had no attending circumstances which diminish their imputability (canons 2205, § 3; 2229, § 3, 3°), but that they were attended by circumstances which increase it, especially the singular dignity of the Most Excellent Archbishop whom they injured (canon 2207, 1°), does by these presents declare that all persons who participated physically or morally in the perpetration of the aforesaid crimes, or who were necessary cooperators in them (canon 2209, §§ 1–3), incurred the above mentioned excommunications, and will remain affected by them until they obtain absolution from the Holy See.

Given at Rome, the 14th of October, 1946.

AAS 38–401; S. C. Conc., 14 Oct., 1946.

Summoning Before Lay Tribunal: Requisites of Crime and Penalty for Future (Code Com., 26 Apr., 1948) AAS 40–301.

The Code Commission was asked:

I. Whether to incur the excommunication or suspension mentioned in canon 2341, it is sufficient that one temerariously summon before a lay judge any of the persons mentioned in the said canon; or is it required that the person summoned be actually called by the judge.

Reply. In the affirmative to the first part, in the negative to the second.

II. Whether the interpretation given in reply to question I, above, is retroactive.

Reply. In the negative; it becomes effective from the day of its publication in the Official Commentary, *Acta Apostolicae Sedis.*

AAS 40–301; Code Com., 26 Apr., 1948.
Periodica, 37–288 (Cappello).
NOTE: Day of publication, 10 July, 1948.

Outrages Against Archbishop Beran and the Authority of the Church in Czechoslovakia Denounced: Penalties Declared (S. C. Consist., 17 March, 1951) AAS 43–173.

A Declaration of the Sacred Consistorial Congregation:

Several months ago in the Republic of Czechoslovakia, in many ways hitherto unheard of, the rights of the Church have been violated and ecclesiastical persons themselves unjustly attacked: Ordinaries of places are prevented from performing their official duties; their pastoral rights are usurped; the very offices of the Curiae or Ordinariates as well as ecclesiastical benefices are conferred upon intruders at the whim of lay persons who presume to interfere in the government of the dioceses.

Many clerics and religious have moreover been deprived of their liberty; some Bishops have been summoned with impious effrontery before lay tribunals and thrown into prison.

Very recently His Excellency Joseph Beran, Metropolitan of Prague, who had already for a long time been held a prisoner in the episcopal palace and entirely prevented from exercising his jurisdiction, has been outrageously deported from his See and Archdiocese.

Against those who commit crimes of this sort there are a number of Sacred Canons punishing them with excommunication incurred *ipso facto* and reserved, according to the case, either simply or specially to the Holy See:

a) Those who summon a Bishop before a lay judge (c. 2341);

b) Those who lay violent hands upon the person of an Archbishop or Bishop (c. 2343, § 3);

c) Those who directly or indirectly impede the exercise of ecclesiastical jurisdiction and for this purpose have recourse to any lay authority (c. 2334, 2°);

d) Those who contrive against legitimate ecclesiastical authorities or who attempt in any way to subvert their authority (Decree of the S. C. of the Council, 29 June, 1950; AAS, 42–601);[1]

e) Those who, without a canonical investiture or provision made according to the Sacred Canons, occupy an ecclesiastical office, benefice, or dignity, or allow anyone to be unlawfully intruded into the same, or who retain the same (*ibid.*).

Therefore the Sacred Consistorial Congregation declares that all persons who have cooperated morally or physically in the aforesaid crimes, or who have participated in the same in the ways mentioned in canon 2209, §§ 1–3, have incurred the excommunications above mentioned and shall remain subject to them until they obtain absolution from the Holy See.

Given at Rome, from the Sacred Consistorial Congregation, 17 March, 1951.

AAS 43–173; S. C. Consist., 17 March, 1951.

Cardinal Mindszenty: Principals and necessary cooperators in his arrest incur excommunication. See c. 2343; AAS 41–80.

Czechoslovakia: Ap. Letter of Pius XII to the Bishops, 28 Oct., 1951 (AAS 43–768).

Rumania: Penalties declared for crimes against the Church. See c. 2334; AAS 43–603.

CANON 2343

Special Excommunication Declared (S. C. Consist., 24 June, 1947) **AAS 39–273.**

The Sacred Consistorial Congregation issued the following Declaration:

Since certain persons recently dared sacrilegiously to lay violent hands on His Excellency Anthony Santin, Bishop of Trieste, the Sacred Consistorial Congregation declares that all those who perpetrated the said crimes have incurred, according to canon 2343, § 3, an excommunication *specially* reserved to the Holy See.

Given at Rome, the 24th of June, 1947.

AAS 39–273; S. C. Consist., 24 June, 1947.

---

[1] Reported in this volume under canon 147.

Excommunication Declared by Sacred Congregation of the Council (S. C. Conc., 8 Sept., 1947) AAS 39–420.

A Declaration of the Sacred Congregation of the Council is as follows:

Whereas, on the 24th of August, 1947, certain wicked men laid violent hands on the Very Reverend James Ukmar, a priest who had gone to the village of Lanischie with faculties for conferring the sacrament of Confirmation; and whereas the same ruffians killed the priest Mirus Bulesic, who tried to defend the aforesaid Father Ukmar from injury; the Sacred Congregation of the Council hereby declares that all persons who concurred physically or morally in committing these crimes, or who were necessary cooperators in the same (c. 2209, §§ 1–3), incurred excommunication *latae sententiae* according to canon 2343, § 4.

Given at Rome, the 8th of September, 1947.

AAS 39–420; S. C. Conc., 8 Sept., 1947.

Excommunication Specially Reserved to the Holy See and Infamy of Law Declared Against the Persecutors of Cardinal Mindszenty (S. C. Consist., 28 Dec., 1948) AAS 41–31.

Declaration of the Sacred Consistorial Congregation:

Seeing that certain persons have recently had the effrontery to lay sacrilegiously violent hands upon His Eminence Cardinal Mindszenty, Archbishop of Strigonia, and to interfere with his exercise of ecclesiastical jurisdiction, the Sacred Consistorial Congregation declares that, in accordance with canons 2343, § 2, and 2334, 2°, all those who perpetrated the aforesaid crimes have incurred excommunication specially reserved to the Holy See and are *ipso iure* infamous.

Given at Rome, the 28th of December, 1948.

AAS 41–31; S. C. Consist., 28 Dec., 1948.

Necessary Cooperators in Crimes Against Cardinal Mindszenty Incur Penalties (S. C. Consist., 12 Feb., 1949) AAS 41–80.

A Declaration of the Sacred Consistorial Congregation:

Since certain persons have dared not only sacrilegiously to lay violent hands upon His Eminence Cardinal Joseph Mindszenty, Archbishop of Strigonia, but moreover to summon him before a lay judge and through a most iniquitous judgment to prevent him from exercising his archiepiscopal jurisdiction, this Sacred Consistorial Congregation again declares and gives warning that all persons who have committed such crimes or who shall do so in the future, whether they be *mandantes* of any kind or degree, or accomplices whom the said crimes of their nature required or shall require, or persons who induced or shall induce the consummation of the crimes, or who in any way concurred or shall in future concur in such consummation, provided however that without their help the crime was not[1] or would not in future be committed, have contracted or shall contract an excommunication *latae sententiae* specially reserved to the Holy See, according to canons 2343, § 2, 1°; 2341; 2334, 2°; 2209, §§ 1, 2, 3; and that they are or shall be *ipso iure* infamous according to canon 2343, § 2, 2°, and have incurred or shall incur the other penalties according to the quality of the delinquents, as provided by the sacred canons of the Code of Canon Law.

Given at Rome, from the Sacred Consistorial Congregation, the 12th of February, 1949.

AAS 41–80; S. Consistorial Congregation, Declaration, 12 Feb., 1949.

Outrages Against Archbishop Grösz of Colocza in Hungary: Penalties Declared (S. C. Consist., 29 June, 1951) AAS 43–481.

A Declaration of the Sacred Consistorial Congregation:

Since certain persons have dared not only sacrilegiously to lay violent hands on His Excellency Joseph Grösz, Archbishop of Colocza, but also to summon him before a lay judge, subject him to an unjust sentence, and impede him from exercising his archiepiscopal jurisdiction, this Sacred Consistorial Congregation declares that all those who have perpetrated these crimes, whether they be principals of whatever kind or degree, or accomplices

---

[1] We translate the text as it stands: *"si tamen sine eorum auxilio delictum non fuerit vel foret commissum."* It seems certain, however, that the sense intended is the same as that expressed in canon 2209, § 3: *"si delictum sine eorum opera commissum non fuisset"* — provided that without their help the crime *would not have been* committed.

such as these crimes by their nature require, or those who induced to or in any way concurred in the consummation of the crimes, provided that without their help the crime would not have been committed, have incurred an excommunication specially reserved to the Holy See — according to canons 2343, § 3; 2341; 2334, 2°; 2209, §§ 1-3 — and also the penalties proportioned to the quality of the delinquents according to the Sacred Canons of the Code of Canon Law.

Given at Rome, from the Sacred Consistorial Congregation, 29 June, 1951.

AAS 43-481; S. C. Consist., 29 June, 1951. Annotations, *Monitor Ecclesiasticus,* 1951, p. 437 (***).

———

Rumania: Penalties declared for crimes against the Church. See **c. 2334**; AAS 43-603.

CANON 2346

Excommunication Incurred by Renter of Usurped Property (S. Paen., 14 Jan., 1920) Private.

The Sacred Penitentiary was asked:

Whether Titius, who rented a piece of property which had been usurped by the civil Government, incurred the censure mentioned in canon 2346.

Reply. In the affirmative.

(Private); S. Paen., 14 Jan., 1920. Reported by Sartori, *Enchiridion Canonicum,* ed. 1945, p. 447.

Excommunication Incurred by Buyers of Usurped Property (S. Paen., 13 Dec., 1923) Private.

The Sacred Penitentiary was asked:

Whether those who buy ecclesiastical property which has been usurped by the Government incur the excommunication simply reserved to the Holy See, which is mentioned in canon 2346.

Reply. In the affirmative.

(Private); S. Paen., 13 Dec., 1923. Reported by Sartori, *Enchiridion Canonicum,* ed. 1945, p. 447.

CANON 2350

Moral Doctrine on Abortion, Direct and Indirect, and the Principle of the Double Effect (Pius XII, Allocutions, 29 Oct., 1951, and 26 Nov., 1951) **AAS 43–835** and **AAS 43–855.**

In these two Allocutions His Holiness Pius XII summarized and repeated the common moral doctrine of the Church on abortion, distinguishing clearly between direct and indirect abortion, and explaining the principle of the double effect and its application.

AAS 43–835 and AAS 43–855 (Pius XII, Allocutions, 29 Oct., 1951 and 26 Nov., 1951). English text in *The Catholic Mind,* 1952, pp. 49 and 307. Annotations, *Periodica,* 40–402 (Hürth). Other pronouncements of the Holy Father in the first Allocution are reported under canons 1013, 1081, 1086, and 1111.

NOTE: In the annotations cited, Hürth refers to the more commonly cited extant pronouncements of the Holy See in recent times on the morality of direct and indirect abortion and killing. We reproduce them here for convenience of reference.

In addition to the Decree of the Holy Office of 2 Dec., 1940, AAS 32–553, condemning the direct killing of innocent persons by order of public authority (cf. CANON LAW DIGEST, II, p. 96), Hürth cites the following:

1. Sacred Penitentiary, 28 Nov., 1872, on the licitness of craniotomy: Let the petitioner consult approved authors and act prudently.

2. Holy Office, 28 May, 1884: the licitness of craniotomy cannot safely be taught (*Acta Sanctae Sedis,* 17–556).

3. Holy Office, 19 Aug., 1889: on the licitness of other surgical operations which are direct killing of the mother or of the fetus, see the Reply of 28 May, 1884 — it cannot safely be taught (*Acta Sanctae Sedis,* 22–748).

4. Holy Office, 24 July, 1895: operations for directly procuring abortion, when the mother and fetus would otherwise perish, cannot safely be performed (*Acta Sanctae Sedis,* 28–383).

5. Holy Office, 4 May, 1898: *a*) Acceleration of birth for just reasons, without harm to the life of the fetus, is licit; *b*) When the mother would otherwise perish, acceleration of birth is licit, procuring abortion is not; *c*) Provided the life of both be protected, laparotomy for the removal of ectopic fetuses is licit, provided the life of the fetus and of the mother be provided for as far as possible (*Acta Sanctae Sedis,* 30–703).

6. Holy Office, 5 March, 1902: The extraction of an immature ectopic fetus is not licit (*Acta Sanctae Sedis,* 35–162).

7. Pius XI, Encyclical, *Casti connubii*, 31 Dec., 1930: The direct procuring of abortion is never justified by any "indication" nor by any human law; nor is it shown to be licit by appealing to the argument of self-defense or of extreme necessity (AAS 22–562 and 563).

CANON 2351

Penalty for Challenging or Accepting Challenge to Duel
(Code Com., 26 June, 1947) **AAS 39–374.**

The Code Commission was asked:

Whether, in those places where the judgment as to whether a duel is to be had is reserved to a so-called tribunal "of honor," those who challenge to a duel and those who accept such a challenge, by the very fact of such challenge or acceptance, incur the penalties mentioned in canon 2351.

Reply. In the affirmative, unless it is certain that the challengers and accepters did not have the intention of dueling.

AAS 39–374; Code Com., 26 June, 1947.
Cf. *Periodica,* 36–347 (Cappello).

CANON 2370
New Excommunication Most Specially Reserved. See c. 2245; AAS 43–217.

CANON 2380
New Penalty for *Negotiatio.* See c. 142; AAS 42–330.

CANON 2394

Accepting Ecclesiastical Office From Lay Authority: Excommunication Inflicted (S. C. Consist., 18 Feb., 1950) AAS 42–195.

A Decree of the S. Consistorial Congregation:

Since the priest John Dechet has presumed to accept from lay authorities the office of "Administrator" of the vacant See of Neosolio,[1] and to enter upon the office thus accepted, the Sacred Consistorial Congregation inflicts upon the aforesaid priest the penalty of excommunication specially reserved to the Holy See and expressly orders that he be avoided.

---

[1] In Czechoslovakia; also called Bánská Bystrica, Neusohl, Beszterzebánya.

The Sacred Congregation, therefore, reminds clerics and the faithful that they must treat the aforesaid priest according to the norm of canon 2261, § 3 of the Code of Canon Law.

Given at Rome, from the Sacred Consistorial Congregation, 18 Feb., 1950.

AAS 42–195; S. C. Consist., 18 Feb., 1950.

NOTE: The Bishop of this diocese in Czechoslovakia, His Excellency Andrea Skrabik, died on January 8, 1950. The Cathedral Chapter took charge provisionally according to the Code. The Government claimed the right to exclude the duly elected Vicar Capitular unless he asked their consent to enter upon the office. This he refused to do; whereupon the government appointed the priest John Dechet, described as a "loyal servant of the State," as "Administrator." Cf. *L'Osservatore Romano,* 19 Feb., 1950.

New Penalty for Occupying or Retaining Office Without Canonical Provision. See c. 147; AAS 42–601.

CHRONOLOGICAL INDEX

In the column next to the last, the reference is to the volume and page of the *Acta Apostolicae Sedis,* or of the *Rota Decisions* (marked *RD*); in the last column, it is to the volume and page of this DIGEST where the document appears.

Year	Day	Mon.	Document and Source	AAS (or *RD*)	C. L. D.
1584	5	Dec.	Bull, Gregory XIII	......	III. 262
1587	5	Jan.	Bull, Xystus V	......	III. 262
1587	29	Sept.	Bull, Xystus V	......	III. 262
1602	30	Aug.	Brief, Clement VIII	......	III. 262
1621	15	Apr.	Bull, Gregory XV	......	III. 262
1630	23	Mar.	Decree, S. C. Rit.	......	I. 256
1637	3	Dec.	Reply, Holy Office	......	II. 243
1661	3	Dec.	Decree, S. C. Rit.	......	II. 246
1697	1	Aug.	Reply, Holy Office	......	II. 245
1707	19	Nov.	Reply, S. C. Conc.	......	II. 245
1740	15	July	Brief, Benedict XIV	......	III. 263
1747	14	Jan.	Letter, Benedict XIV	......	II. 247
1748	24	Apr.	Brief, Benedict XIV	......	III. 263
1748	27	Sept.	Bull, Benedict XIV	......	III. 263
1751	8	Sept.	Brief, Benedict XIV	......	III. 263
1758	15	Feb.	Brief, Benedict XIV	......	III. 263
1765	7	Jan.	Bull, Clement XIII	......	III. 263
1775	2	May	Decree, Pius VI	......	III. 263
1775	9	Dec.	Decree, Pius VI	......	III. 263
1776	20	Mar.	Decree, Pius VI	......	III. 263
1820	11	Mar.	Decree, S. C. Rit.	......	II. 245
1821	31	July	Decree, S. C. Rit.	......	II. 241
1824	17	May	Brief, Leo XII	......	III. 263
1825	7	Mar.	Decree, S. C. Indulg.	......	III. 270
1830	16	Oct.	Indult, S. C. Prop. Fid.	......	II. 216
1840	27	May	Reply, Holy Office	......	II. 243
1840	6	Aug.	Reply, S. C. Prop. Fid.	......	II. 241
1841	22	May	Decree, S. C. Rit.	......	II. 243
1843	18	Feb.	Decree, S. C. Rit.	......	II. 241
1848	8	July	Decree, Pius IX	......	III. 263
1851	19	Aug.	Reply, Holy Office	......	II. 241, 243
1859	8	Aug.	Decree, S. C. Ind. et Rel.	......	I. 437
1861	10	Apr.	Replies, Holy Office	......	III. 307
1863	21	Jan.	Decree, S. C. Rit.	......	II. 246
1863	10	Feb.	Brief, Pius IX	......	III. 263
1863	21	Aug.	Reply, S. C. Rit.	......	I. 375
1866	25	July	Reply, Holy Office	......	II. 246
1868	..	....	Instruction, Holy Office	......	I. 510
1870	27	Apr.	Reply, Holy Office	......	II. 242

Year	Day	Mon.	Document and Source	AAS (or RD)	C. L. D.
1871	22	Nov.	Reply, Holy Office	......	II. 246
1872	31	Aug.	Decree, S. C. Rit.	......	II. 241
1872	28	Nov.	Reply, S. Paen.	......	III. 669
1873	14	June	Decree, S. C. Rit.	......	II. 242
1874	23	Jan.	Reply, Holy Office	......	II. 245
1874	4	Mar.	Reply, Holy Office	......	II. 243
1874	22	July	Reply, Holy Office	......	II. 243
1875	9	June	Reply, Holy Office	......	II. 246
1877	12	Sept.	Reply, Holy Office	......	II. 242
1884	27	May	Brief, Leo XIII	......	III. 263
1884	28	May	Reply, Holy Office	......	III. 669
1885	23	June	Decree, S. C. Indulg.	......	III. 270
1885	31	Aug.	Statuta Gen. CC. MM.	......	III. 271
1886	8	Jan.	Brief, Leo XIII	......	III. 263
1886	20	Jan.	Reply, Holy Office	......	II. 244
1887	17	Sept.	Rescript, S. C. Indulg.	......	III. 270
1887	23	Nov.	Decree, S. C. Rit.	......	II. 195
1888	31	Mar.	Decree, S. Paen.	......	II. 242
1889	11	Aug.	S. C. Episc. et Reg.	......	III. 139
1889	19	Aug.	Reply, Holy Office	......	III. 669
1890	22	Jan.	Reply, Holy Office	......	II. 241
1892	22	June	Reply, Holy Office	......	II. 246
1892	7	Sept.	Reply, Holy Office	......	I. 493, II. 244
1895	15	Mar.	Indult, S. C. Prop. Fid.	......	I. 592
1895	8	May	Reply, Holy Office	......	II. 246
1895	24	July	Reply, Holy Office	......	III. 669
1895	18	Sept.	Letter, Leo XIII	......	I. 621
1896	2	Dec.	Reply, Holy Office	......	II. 242, 247
1897	17	Mar.	Reply, Holy Office	......	II. 242, 246
1897	12	May	Letter, Ap. Del. U. S.	......	II. 79
1897	7	Sept.	Reply, Holy Office	......	II. 246
1897	9	Dec.	Reply, Holy Office	......	II. 243
1898	20	Apr.	Reply, Holy Office	......	II. 245
1898	4	May	Replies, Holy Office	......	III. 669
1898	8	June	Reply, Holy Office	......	II. 243
1898	6	July	Reply, Holy Office	......	II. 242, 245
1898	30	Nov.	Reply, Holy Office	......	I. 494, II. 242
1898	14	Dec.	Reply, Holy Office	......	II. 242, 246, 247
1899	11	Jan.	Reply, Holy Office	......	II. 244
1899	3	May	Reply, Holy Office	......	II. 241, 245
1899	19	July	Reply, Holy Office	......	II. 242
1900	17	Jan.	Reply, Holy Office	......	II. 245, 246
1900	4	July	Reply, Holy Office	......	II. 241
1900	22	Aug.	Reply, Holy Office	......	II. 241, 245
1900	28	Nov.	Reply, Holy Office	......	II. 243
1901	16	Jan.	Reply, Holy Office	......	II. 245
1902	5	Mar.	Reply, Holy Office	......	III. 669
1903	11	Mar.	Reply, Holy Office	......	II. 245
1904	24	July	Decision, Rota	1–660	I. 533
1909	19	Feb.	Reply, S. C. Rit	1–288	II. 8
1910	19	Jan.	Decision, Rota	2–297	I. 530
1910	10	May	Decree, Pius X	......	III. 263
1910	21	July	Decree, Pius X	......	III. 263

				AAS	
Year	Day	Mon.	Document and Source	(or RD)	C. L. D.
1915	20	Nov.	Resolution, S. C. Conc.	11–9	I. 226
1915	19	Dec.	Allocution, Bened. XV	......	III. 265
1915	30	Dec.	Decision, Rota	8–324	I. 529
1916	25	Feb.	Brief, Benedict XV	9–61	I. 621
1916	25	Feb.	Reply, S. C. Sacr.	8–151	I. 511
1916	31	Mar.	Decree, S. C. Consist.	8–147	I. 138
1916	1	Apr.	Resolution, S. C. Conc.	11–9	I. 226
1916	17	Apr.	Decision, Rota	RD 8–103	II. 288
1916	26	Apr.	Decision, Rota	9–144	I. 530
1916	29	May	Decision, Rota	RD 8–147	II. 288, 340
1916	2	June	Decree, S. C. Rit.	......	II. 195
1916	27	June	Decision, Rota	9–242	I. 807
1916	25	July	Decree, S. C. Consist.	8–400	I. 194
1916	31	July	Reply, S. C. Conc.	......	I. 728
1916	1	Aug.	Decision, Rota	9–441	I. 529
1916	20	Oct.	Decision, Rota	9–356	I. 528
1916	11	Dec.	Decision, Rota	9–464	I. 529
1916	22	Dec.	Reply, Holy Office	9–13	I. 556
1917	3	Jan.	Decision, Rota	10–378	I. 528
1917	12	Jan.	Decree, S. C. Rit.	......	II. 243
1917	19	Jan.	Reply, S. C. Sacr.	9–120	I. 511
1917	10	Feb.	Decision, Rota	9–503	I. 529
1917	17	Feb.	Decision, Rota	RD 9–31	II. 288
1917	9	Mar.	Decision, Rota	10–108	I. 528
1917	9	Mar.	Reply, Holy Office	9–178	I. 460
1917	2	Apr.	Decision, Rota	10–70	I. 528
1917	23	Apr.	Resolution, S. C. Conc.	10–239	I. 203
1917	27	Apr.	Reply, Holy Office	9–268	I. 155
1917	30	Apr.	Decision, Rota	9–574	I. 529
1917	1	May	Motu proprio, Benedict XV	9–529	II. 114
1917	5	June	Decision, Rota	10–158	I. 528
1917	12	June	Resolution, S. C. Conc.	10–285	I. 253
1917	15	June	Encyclical, Benedict XV	9–305	I. 622
1917	16	June	Letter, S. C. Prop. Fid.	......	II. 237
1917	28	June	Norms, S. C. Consist.	9–328	I. 622
1917	7	July	Reply, S. Paen.	9–399	I. 42
1917	14	July	Resolution, S. C. Conc.	10–194	I. 697
1917	14	July	Decision, Rota	RD 9–150	II. 289
1917	25	July	Declaration, Holy Office	......	II. 333
1917	27	July	Decision, Rota	10–215	I. 526
1917	7	Aug.	Decree, S. C. Sem.	9–439	I. 662
1917	16	Aug.	Decision, Rota	10–291	I. 526
1917	20	Aug.	Notification, Sec. St.	9–475	I. 588
1917	20	Aug.	Resolution, S. C. Conc.	9–497	I. 719
1917	15	Sept.	Motu proprio, Benedict XV	9–483	I. 55
1917	22	Oct.	Reply, S. Paen.	9–539	I. 423
1917	10	Nov.	Resolution, S. C. Conc.	10–368	I. 400
1917	19	Nov.	Decision, Rota	RD 9–274	II. 288, 340
1917	9	Dec.	Reply, Code Com.	10–77	I. 57
1917	10	Dec.	Declaration, S. C. Consist.	10–17	I. 137
1917	21	Dec.	Decision, Rota	10–420	I. 527
1918	3	Jan.	Reply, Code Com.	......	I. 53
1918	7	Jan.	Decision, Rota	10–517	I. 518

Year	Day	Mon.	Document and Source	AAS (or RD)	C. L. D.
1918	13	Jan.	Reply, Code Com.	......	I. 593
1918	28	Jan.	Decision, Rota	11–22	I. 527
1918	9	Feb.	Resolution, S. C. Conc.	10–285	I. 253
1918	17	Feb.	Reply, Code Com.	10–170	I. 253, 585, 587
1918	22	Mar.	Decree, Holy Office	10–136	I. 50
1918	30	Mar.	Reply, Code Com.	......	I. 545
1918	5	Apr.	Resolution, S. C. Conc.	11–9	I. 226
1918	..	....	Sermon, Benedict XV	10–92	I. 636
1918	15	Apr.	Resolution, S. C. Conc.	11–236	I. 247
1918	25	Apr.	Decree, S. C. Consist.	10–190	I. 72
1918	30	Apr.	Decree, S. C. Consist.	10–237	I. 115, 245
1918	9	May	*Motu proprio,* Benedict XV	10–225	I. 201
1918	10	May	Decision, Rota	11–89	I. 526
1918	25	May	Decree, Vicariate of Rome	10–300	I. 54
1918	26	May	Decree, S. Paen.	10–255	I. 201
1918	3	June	Reply, Code Com.	10–344	I. 126, 275, 330, 344, 487, 495, 496, 499, 500, 513, 600
1918	6	June	Indult, S. C. Sem.	......	I. 483
1918	7	June	Letter, Benedict XV	10–440	I. 126
1918	14	June	Reply, S. C. Rit.	10–332	I. 547
1918	15	June	Resolution, S. C. Conc.	10–504	I. 211, 395
1918	26	June	Decree, S. C. Rel.	10–290	I. 270
1918	27	June	Decision, Signatura	10–391	I. 705
1918	29	June	Reply, Code Com.	......	III. 258
1918			Reply, Code Com.	......	III. 215
1918	1	July	Reply, S. C. Consist.	10–325	I. 75
1918	1	July	Reply, S. C. Sacr.	13–436	I. 405
1918	2	July	Decision, Rota	11–192	I. 527
1918	4	July	Decision, Rota	RD 10–71	II. 287
1918	10	July	Decree, S. C. Eccl. Or.	10–417	I. 84
1918	13	July	Decision, Rota	11–382	I. 749
1918	13	July	Resolution, S. C. Conc.	11–46	I. 254
1918	13	July	Resolution, S. C. Conc.	11–78	I. 705
1918	28	July	Reply, Code Com.	......	I. 298
1918	2	Aug.	Decree, S. C. Consist.	10–363	I. 75
1918	2	Aug.	Reply, S. C. Consist.	10–365	I. 188
1918	5	Aug.	Reply, Code Com.	......	III. 71
1918	3	Sept.	Decree, S. C. Consist.	10–415	I. 84
1918	25	Oct.	Decree, S. C. Consist.	10–481	I. 99
1918	31	Oct.	Decree, S. C. Sem.	11–19	I. 663
1918	4	Nov	Decree, S. C. Consist.	10–487	I. 202
1918	15	Nov.	Decision, Rota	11–290	I. 527
1918	18	Nov.	Decision, Rota	11–358	I. 519
1918	24	Nov.	Reply, Code Com.	......	I. 240
1918	7	Dec.	Reply, S. C. Sacr.	11–8	I. 352
1918	13	Dec.	Decision, Rota	12–338	I. 518
1918	14	Dec.	Resolution, S. C. Conc.	11–128	I. 97
1918	21	Dec.	Declaration, S. C. Consist.	11–6	I. 104
1918	23	Dec.	Reply, S. C. Rel.	10–18	I. 98
1918	30	Dec.	Decree, S. C. Consist.	11–39	I. 93, III. 86
1919	10	Jan.	Reply, S. C. Rit.	11–143	I. 368

Year	Day	Mon.	Document and Source	AAS (or RD)	C. L. D.
1919	16	Oct.	Replies, Code Com.	11–478	I. 85, 804, 323, 337, 384, 410, 487, 566, 569, 657, 810
1919	29	Oct.	Reply, Code Com.	11–480	I. 586
1919	31	Oct.	Decision, Rota	. . . . . .	I. 533
1919	4	Nov.	Replies, Code Com.	. . . . . .	III. 72, 73
1919	9	Nov.	Resolution, S. C. Conc.	11–462	I. 587
1919	11	Nov.	Decree, S. C. Conc.	11–463	I. 160
1919	14	Nov.	Decision, Rota	13–54	I. 518
1919	21	Nov.	Reply, S. C. Rel.	12–17	I. 299
1919	26	Nov.	Reply, S. C. Rit.	12–177	I. 204
1919	26	Nov.	Reply, Holy Office	. . . . . .	III. 468
1919	30	Nov.	Reply, S. C. Rel.	12–73	I. 109
1919	3	Dec.	Reply, Code Com.	. . . . . .	II. 336
1919	8	Dec.	Letter, S. C. Prop. Fid.	12–120	I. 144
1919	28	Dec.	Decree, S. C. Conc.	12–42	I. 254
1920	3	Jan.	Letter, Benedict XV	12–32	I. 120
1920	6	Jan.	Instruction, S. C. Prop. Fid.	. . . . . .	II. 74, 421; III. 543
1920	9	Jan.	Reply, S. C. Consist.	12–41	I. 211
1920	10	Jan.	Resolution, S. C. Conc.	12–43	I. 51, 123
1920	11	Jan.	Resolution, S. C. Conc.	12–70	I. 401
1920	14	Jan.	Reply, S. Paen.	. . . . . .	III. 668
1920	15	Jan.	Decree, Holy Office	12–37	I. 620
1920	26	Jan.	Reply, S. C. Rit.	12–122	I. 369
1920	28	Jan.	Instruction, S. C. Rit.	. . . . . .	III. 340
1920	28	Jan.	Instruction, S. C. Rit.	. . . . . .	III. 343
1920	11	Feb.	Benedict XV	. . . . . .	III. 71
1920	14	Feb.	Resolution, S. C. Conc.	12–163	I. 707
1920	15	Feb.	Resolution, S. C. Conc.	12–117	I. 51, 232
1920	17	Feb.	Reply, Code Com.	. . . . . .	III. 580
1920	28	Feb.	Reply, S. C. Rit.	12–128	I. 569
1920	4	Mar.	*Monitum,* Vicariate of Rome	. . . . . .	III. 383
1920	9	Mar.	Letter, S. C. Rel.	12–365	I. 276
1920	11	Mar.	Letter, Benedict XV	12–109	I. 258
1920	13	Mar.	Resolution, S. C. Conc.	13–438	I. 230, 235
1920	14	Mar.	Resolution, S. C. Conc.	12–444	I. 719
1920	25	Mar.	Decision, Rota	RD 12–71	II. 288
1920	6	Apr.	Decision, Signatura	12–252	I. 734, 761
1920	22	Apr.	Reply, Holy Office	12–158	I. 607
1920	25	Apr.	*Motu proprio,* Benedict XV	12–149	I. 203
1920	27	Apr.	Indult, S. C. Prop. Fid.	. . . . . .	II. 357
1920	9	May	Resolution, S. C. Conc.	12–536	I. 393, 402
1920	20	May	Letter, S. C. Prop. Fid.	. . . . . .	II. 276
1920	31	May	Letter, S. C. Conc.	12–299	I. 631
1920	4	June	Notification, S. C. Rel.	12–301	I. 294
1920	4	June	Reply, S. C. Rit.	. . . . . .	III. 346
1920	9	July	Reply, S. C. Rit.	12–372	I. 209
1920	10	July	Resolution, S. C. Conc.	12–357	I. 712
1920	10	July	Letter, S. C. Prop. Fid.	. . . . . .	II. 447
1920	25	July	Instruction, S. C. Prop. Fid.	12–331	I. 147
1920	27	July	Decision, Rota	RD 12–202	II. 299

Year	Day	Mon.	Document and Source	AAS (or RD)	C. L. D.
1920	29	July	Decision, Rota	RD 12–215	II. 287
1920	17	Aug.	Decision, Rota	RD 12–234	II. 340
1920	9	Sept.	Formula, S. C. Rit.	12–449	I. 563
1920	15	Sept.	Encyclical, Benedict XV	12–385	I. 116
1920	15	Oct.	Reply, S. C. Rit.	12–548	I. 452
1920	23	Oct.	S. C. Consist.	12–534	III. 90
1920	5	Nov.	Letter, Holy Office	12–595	I. 607
1920	6	Nov.	Reply, S. C. Consist.	13–259	I. 461
1920	14	Nov.	Resolution, S. C. Conc.	13–135	I. 714
1920	14	Nov.	Resolution, S. C. Conc.	13–43	I. 262
1920	18	Nov.	Reply, S. C. Sacr.	14–96	I. 508
1920	18	Nov.	Letter, Sec. St.	......	I. 116
1920	20	Nov.	Decree, S. C. Consist.	13–13	I. 198
1920	24	Nov.	Replies, Code Com.	12–574	I. 119, 218, 229, 240, 248, 279, 293, 295, 297, 327, 415, 417, 582, 588, 702, 729, 837
1920	2	Dec.	Reply, S. C. Rel.	......	III. 256
1920	9	Dec.	Decree, S. C. Prop. Fid.	13–17	I. 149
1920	11	Dec.	Resolution, S. C. Conc.	13–262	I. 740
1920	11	Dec.	Resolution, S. C. Conc.	14–42	I. 222
1920	11	Dec.	Resolution, S. C. Conc.	13–350	I. 720
1920	16	Dec.	Allocution, Benedict XV	12–585	I. 120
1921	12	Jan.	Reply, S. C. Rit.	13–154	I. 370
1921	13	Jan.	Decision, Rota	14–472	I. 504
1921	13	Jan.	Formula, S. Paen.	......	I. 174
1921	14	Jan.	Reply, S. C. Rit.	13–157	I. 373
1921	16	Jan.	Resolution, S. C. Conc.	13–198	I. 237
1921	10	Feb.	Letter, Benedict XV	13–127	I. 127, 630, 683
1921	18	Feb.	Reply, S. Paen.	13–164	I. 421
1921	18	Feb.	Reply, S. Paen.	13–165	I. 420
1921	18	Feb.	Rescript, S. C. Rit.	......	II. 198
1921	19	Feb.	Resolution, S. C. Conc.	14–551	I. 259
1921	19	Feb.	Resolution, S. C. Conc.	13–228	I. 399
1921	25	Feb.	Rescript, S. C. Rit.	......	II. 198
1921	28	Feb.	Letter, S. C. Prop. Fid.	......	II. 358
1921	1	Mar.	Replies, Code Com.	13–177	I. 306, 308, 331, 502
1921	6	Mar.	Norms, S. C. Rel.	13–312	I. 272
1921	7	Mar.	Declaration, S. C. Consist.	13–134	I. 76
1921	12	Mar.	Resolution, S. C. Conc.	13–438	I. 235
1921	15	Mar.	Recursus, Signatura	13–271	I. 743
1921	19	Mar.	Decree, S. C. Consist.	13–222	I. 198
1921	22	Mar.	Reply, S. C. Rel.	......	III. 506
1921	26	Mar.	Notification, S. C. Consist.	13–309	III. 97
1921	30	Mar.	Declaration, Holy Office	13–197	I. 686
1921	16	Apr.	Resolution, S. C. Conc.	13–532	I. 403
1921	17	Apr.	Reply, S. C. Conc.	13–477	I. 121
1921	21	Apr.	Reply, S. Paen.	13–239	I. 847
1921	27	Apr.	Rescript, S. C. Rit.	......	II. 199
1921	30	Apr.	Decree, S. C. Consist.	13–379	I. 198

Year Day Mon.	Document and Source	AAS (or RD)	C. L. D.
1921 10 May	Decision, Rota	......	II. 299
1921 19 May	Decision, Rota	13–546	I. 759
1921 28 May	Decision, Rota	RD 13–115	II. 288
1921 11 June	Resolution, S. C. Conc.	13–498	I. 125
1921 13 June	Reply, S. C. Prop. Fid.	......	III. 580
1921 19 June	Letter, Benedict XV	13–416	I. 321
1921 2 July	Reply, S. C. Rel.	13–481	I. 279
1921 4 July	Instruction, S. C. Sacr.	13–348	I. 497
1921 9 July	Resolution, S. C. Conc.	13–534	I. 573
1921 9 July	Resolution, S. C. Conc.	16–397	I. 238
1921 9 July	Resolution, S. C. Conc.	13–501	I. 396
1921 10 July	Reply, S. C. Conc.	13–477	I. 121
1921 16 July	Letter, Benedict XV	13–424	I. 127
1921 3 Aug.	Decision, Rota	......	II. 340
1921 11 Aug.	Decision, Rota	14–512	I. 538
1921 16 Aug.	Decision, Rota	14–239	I. 731
1921 20 Aug.	Decree, S. C. Consist.	13–430	I. 198
1921 15 Oct.	Letter, Benedict XV	14–7	I. 114
1921 21 Oct.	Decree, S. C. Prop. Fid.	13–541	I. 187
1921 21 Oct.	Decree, S. C. Prop. Fid.	13–542	I. 187
1921 26 Oct.	Declaration, S. C. Rel.	13–538	I. 271
1921 3 Nov.	Instruction, S. C. Rel.	13–539	I. 302
1921 10 Nov.	Reply, S. C. Rit.	13–566	I. 453
1921 12 Nov.	Resolution, S. C. Conc.	14–459	I. 87, 218, 223, 702, 705, 708, 711
1921 17 Nov.	Reply, Bibl. Com.	14–27	I. 684
1921 21 Nov.	Allocution, Benedict XV	13–521	I. 47
1921 30 Nov.	Letter, Benedict XV	13–554	I. 656, 663
1921 30 Nov.	Reply, Holy Office	......	III. 428
1921 1 Dec.	Letter, S. C. Rel.	......	I. 296
1921 3 Dec.	Letter, S. C. Prop. Fid.	13–561	I. 163
1921 6 Dec.	Decision, Rota	RD 13–278	II. 287
1921 23 Dec.	Letter, Benedict XV	14–37	I. 657
1922 9 Jan.	Decision, Rota	RD 14–1	II. 322
1922 14 Jan.	Reply, S. C. Conc.	14–160	I. 730
1922 14 Jan.	Resolution, S. C. Conc.	14–229	I. 699
1922 22 Jan.	Declaration, S. Paen.	13–163	I. 452
1922 3 Feb.	Decision, Rota	14–395	I. 603
1922 17 Feb.	Declaration, S. Paen.	14–143	I. 422
1922 1 Mar.	Motu proprio, Pius XI	14–145	I. 141
1922 6 Mar.	Reply, S. C. Rel.	14–163	I. 275
1922 8 Mar.	Decree, S. C. Rel.	14–161	I. 282; III. 159
1922 14 Mar.	Letter, S. C. Prop. Fid.	......	II. 445
1922 16 Mar.	Reply, S. C. Rel.	14–196	I. 311
1922 18 Mar.	Decision, Rota	14–652	I. 749
1922 20 Mar.	Reply, S. C. Rel.	14–352	I. 300
1922 25 Mar.	Instruction, S. C. Rel.	15–459	I. 284
1922 25 Mar.	Reply, S. C. Rel.	14–353	III. 291
1922 31 Mar.	Decision, Rota	RD 14–78	II. 322
1922 31 Mar.	Decision, Rota	RD 14–83	II. 310
1922 1 Apr.	Reply, S. C. Prop. Fid.	......	I. 511
1922 11 Apr.	Decision, Rota	RD 14–92	II. 322

Year	Day	Mon.	Document and Source	AAS (or RD)	C. L. D.
1922	16	Apr.	Letter, S. C. Prop. Fid.	14–287	I. 192
1922	25	Apr.	Reply, Code Com.	14–313	I. 127
1922	25	Apr.	Reply, S. Paen.	......	I. 419
1922	28	Apr.	Decision, Rota	RD 14–100	II. 328
1922	29	Apr.	Decision, Rota	RD 14–108	II. 288
1922	29	Apr.	Decision, Rota	RD 14–119	II. 311
1922	3	May	Motu proprio, Pius XI	14–321	I. 163; III. 254
1922	17	May	Decision, Rota	RD 14–147	II. 322
1922	18	May	Decision, Rota	RD 14–155	II. 325
1922	31	May	Reply, Holy Office	......	II. 334
1922	10	June	Decision, Rota	RD 14–179	II. 311
1922	10	June	Resolution, S. C. Conc.	14–459	I. 87, 140, 218, 702, 705, 708
1922	10	June	Resolution, S. C. Conc.	15–225	I. 60, 252, 346
1922	14	June	Decree, Holy Office	14–379	I. 853
1922	14	June	Reply, S. Paen.	14–394	I. 450
1922	20	June	Decision, Rota	14–600	I. 760
1922	23	June	Decree, S. C. Sem.	14–510	I. 681
1922	1	July	Replies, Code Com.	14–406	I. 142, 218
1922	1	July	Decision, Rota	RD 14–209	II. 299
1922	3	July	Decision, Rota	RD 14–222	II. 299
1922	8	July	Resolution, S. C. Conc.	15–115	I. 226
1922	14	July	Replies, Code Com.	14–526	I. 83, 119, 143, 250, 255, 325, 347, 487, 539, 602, 726, 741, 758, 791, 845
1922	1	Aug.	Ap. Letter, Pius XI	14–449	I. 643
1922	1	Aug.	Reply, S. C. Rel.	14–501	I. 326
1922	2	Aug.	Reply, Holy Office	......	I. 353
1922	4	Aug.	Rescript, S. C. Rit.	14–505	II. 199
1922	4	Aug.	Decision, Rota	RD 14–252	II. 311
1922	9	Aug.	Decision, Rota	RD 14–263	II. 556
1922	9	Aug.	Decree, S. C. Rit.	14–506	I. 460
1922	10	Aug.	Decision, Rota	RD 14–272	II. 287, 328
1922	16	Aug.	Decision, Rota	RD 14–308	II. 304
1922	17	Aug.	Decision, Rota	RD 14–312	II. 299
1922	11	Oct.	Reply, S. C. Rel.	14–554	I. 266
1922	20	Oct.	Reply, S. C. Rit.	14–556	I. 706
1922	30	Oct.	Reply, S. C. Rit.	14–598	I. 568
1922	9	Nov.	Reply, Holy Office	......	I. 449
1922	10	Nov.	Letter, Ap. Del. U. S.	......	I. 149
1922	11	Nov.	Resolution, S. C. Conc.	15–454	I. 838
1922	12	Nov.	Replies, Code Com.	14–661	I. 251, 301, 326, 345, 502, 707, 710, 846
1922	18	Nov.	Resolution, S. C. Conc.	......	I. 408
1922	22	Nov.	Motu proprio, Pius XI	14–623	I. 597
1922	22	Nov.	Monita, S. C. Prop. Fid.	14–647	I. 163
1922	23	Nov.	Reply, Holy Office	......	I. 155
1922	25	Nov.	Decision, Signatura	15–180	I. 747
1922	26	Nov.	Reply, Code Com.	15–128	I. 225
1922	30	Nov.	Decree, S. C. Rel.	14–644	I. 267

Year	Day	Mon.	*Document and Source*	*AAS* (or *RD*)	*C. L. D.*
1924	13	June	Decision, Rota	RD 16–223	II. 329
1924	21	June	Decision, Rota	RD 16–257	II. 287
1924	21	June	Decision, Rota	16–473	I. 722
1924	24	June	Letter, S. C. Conc.	16–332	I. 634
1924	25	June	Decision, Rota	RD 16–265	II. 340
1924	7	July	Decision, Rota	RD 16–284	II. 569
1924	10	July	Decree, S. Paen.	16–345	I. 453
1924	10	July	Reply, Holy Office	......	I. 552
1924	26	July	Letter, S. C. Sacr.	16–370	I. 385
1924	30	July	Decision, Signatura	......	II. 312
1924	31	July	Instruction, S. Paen.	16–337	I. 424
1924	4	Aug.	Decision, Rota	RD 16–303	II. 329
1924	13	Aug.	Decision, Rota	RD 16–365	II. 320
1924	29	Oct.	Decision, Rota	RD 16–371	II. 300
1924	5	Nov.	Reply, Holy Office	......	I. 553
1924	7	Nov.	Resolution, S. C. Prop. Fid.	......	II. 107
1924	12	Nov.	Decision, Rota	RD 16–391	II. 296
1924	25	Nov.	Decision, Rota	RD 16–404	II. 328
1924	28	Nov.	Reply, S. C. Rel.	......	I. 486
1924	2	Dec.	Decision, Rota	RD 16–415	II. 325
1925	..	....	Declaration, Holy Office	17–137	I. 687
1925	13	Jan.	Decision, Rota	RD 17–30	II. 322
1925	26	Jan.	Declaration, S. C. Eccl. Or.	......	III. 374
1925	4	Feb.	Decision, Rota	RD 17–39	II. 344
1925	5	Feb.	Reply, S. C. Rel.	17–107	I. 309
1925	7	Feb.	Decision, Rota	RD 17–47	II. 304
1925	11	Feb.	Decision, Rota	RD 17–61	II. 313
1925	11	Feb.	Decision, Rota	RD 17–67	II. 323
1925	13	Feb.	Decision, Rota	RD 17–74	II. 312
1925	14	Feb.	Resolution, S. C. Conc.	18–48	I. 91
1925	21	Feb.	Decision, Rota	RD 17–101	II. 339
1925	21	Feb.	Decision, Rota	RD 17–108	II. 302
1925	4	Mar.	Reply, S. C. Sacr.	......	III. 454
1925	5	Mar.	Reply, S. Paen.	......	I. 859
1925	6	Mar.	Decree, S. C. Consist.	18–42	I. 245
1925	7	Mar.	Letter, S. C. Consist.	......	II. 75
1925	9	Mar.	Reply, S. Paen.	17–327	II. 225
1925	10	Mar.	Decision, Rota	RD 17–124	II. 287
1925	23	Mar.	Decision, Rota	RD 17–129	II. 311
1925	24	Mar.	Decision, Rota	RD 17–141	II. 328
1925	30	Mar.	Reply, S. C. Rel.	......	III. 293
1925	1	Apr.	Decision, Rota	RD 17–149	II. 329
1925	4	Apr.	Resolution, S. C. Conc.	18–132	I. 856
1925	8	Apr.	Reply, Holy Office	......	I. 763
1925	25	Apr.	Decision, Rota	RD 17–155	II. 323
1925	28	Apr.	Decision, Rota	RD 17–165	II. 323
1925	28	Apr.	Decision, Rota	RD 17–173	II. 323
1925	1	May	Reply, Holy Office	......	I. 543
1925	2	May	Decision, Rota	RD 17–182	II. 323
1925	8	May	S. C. Rit.	......	II. 10
1925	16	May	Resolution, S. C. Conc.	18–10	I. 77
1925	25	May	Decision, Rota	RD 17–195	II. 277
1925	8	June	Reply, S. C. Rit.	......	II. 10

Year	Day	Mon.	Document and Source	*AAS* (or *RD*)	C. L. D.
1925	13	June	Resolution, S. C. Conc.	18–132	I. 856
1925	21	June	Reply, Holy Office	......	I. 493
1925	21	June	Reply, S. C. Sacr.	......	II. 244, 245
1925	26	June	Decision, Rota	*RD* 17–262	II. 318
1925	30	June	Decision, Rota	*RD* 17–268	II. 312
1925	4	July	Replies, S. C. Sacr.	17–452	I. 346
1925	5	July	Notification, Pius XI	18–89	I. 168
1925	10	July	Decree, S. C. Conc.	17–381	I. 217
1925	11	July	Resolution, S. C. Conc.	18–48	I. 91
1925	15	July	Reply, Holy Office	......	II. 193
1925	27	July	Decision, Rota	*RD* 17–293	II. 301
1925	4	Aug.	Decision, Rota	*RD* 17–329	II. 295
1925	5	Aug.	Brief, Pius XI	......	II. 409
1925	6	Nov.	Reply, S. C. Rit.	18–21	I. 374, 455, 545
1925	10	Nov.	Replies, Code Com.	17–582	I. 59, 88, 225, 244, 252, 298, 415, 542, 546, 583
1925	13	Nov.	Decision, Rota	*RD* 17–372	II. 314
1925	14	Nov.	Decision, Rota	*RD* 17–384	II. 329
1925	14	Nov.	Reply, S. C. Conc.	......	I. 234
1925	24	Nov.	Declaration, S. C. Rel.	18–14	I. 269
1925	25	Nov.	Instruction, S. C. Sacr.	18–43	I. 338
1925	30	Nov.	Decision, Rota	*RD* 17–390	II. 295
1925	5	Dec.	Decision, Rota	*RD* 17–396	II. 341
1925	9	Dec.	Reply, S. C. Rit.	18–58	I. 374
1925	12	Dec.	Decision, Rota	*RD* 17–400	II. 323
1925	14	Dec.	Allocution, Pius XI	17–641	II. 74
1925	14	Dec.	Allocution, Pius XI	17–633	I. 609
1925	18	Dec.	Decision, Rota	*RD* 17–418	II. 289
1925	21	Dec.	Reply, S. Paen.	18–24	I. 422
1925	22	Dec.	Decision, Rota	*RD* 17–423	II. 288, 289, 330
1925	25	Dec.	Bull, Pius XI	17–611	I. 411, 486, 555, 854, 858
1926	5	Jan.	Rescript, S. C. Conc.	......	I. 592
1926	20	Jan.	Decision, Rota	*RD* 18–4	II. 296
1926	30	Jan.	Decision, Rota	*RD* 18–17	II. 335
1926	2	Feb.	Letter, Pius XI	18–175	I. 127
1926	10	Feb.	Decision, Rota	*RD* 18–22	II. 312
1926	13	Feb.	Decision, Rota	*RD* 18–33	II. 305
1926	28	Feb.	Encyclical, Pius XI	18–65	I. 462, 656
1926	1	Mar.	Decision, Rota	*RD* 18–58	II. 287
1926	17	Mar.	Decision, Rota	*RD* 18–68	II. 297
1926	20	Mar.	Decision, Rota	*RD* 18–76	II. 289, 340
1926	24	Mar.	Decision, Rota	*RD* 18–93	II. 324
1926	29	Mar.	Indult, S. C. Sacr.	......	I. 409
1926	30	Mar.	Decision, Rota	*RD* 18–103	II. 312
1926	4	Apr.	*Statuta,* S. C. Prop. Fid.	18–231	II. 109
1926	7	Apr.	Decision, Rota	*RD* 18–108	II. 300
1926	9	Apr.	Decision, Rota	*RD* 18–116	II. 323
1926	14	Apr.	Rescript, S. C. Rit.	19–23	II. 234
1926	16	Apr.	Reply, Holy Office	......	II. 342
1926	17	Apr.	Decision, Rota	*RD* 18–133	II. 288, 339

Year	Day	Mon.	Document and Source	AAS (or RD)	C. L. D.
1926	19	Apr.	Decision, Rota	RD 18–140	II. 319
1926	3	May	Reply, S. C. Sacr.	18–388	I. 386
1926	27	May	Decision, Rota	RD 18–183	II. 300
1926	5	June	Decision, Rota	RD 18–190	II. 312
1926	19	June	Instruction, Holy Office	18–282	I. 564
1926	25	June	Decision, Rota	RD 18–213	II. 300
1926	1	July	Letter, S. C. Conc.	18–312	I. 138
1926	7	July	Decision, Rota	RD 18–221	II. 309
1926	13	July	Decision, Rota	RD 18–228	II. 330
1926	15	July	Letter, S. C. Rel.	......	III. 216
1926	16	July	Reply, S. C. Prop. Fid.	......	I. 552
1926	25	July	Replies, Code Com.	18–393	I. 236, 278, 693, 699, 854
1926	26	July	Decision, Rota	RD 18–252	II. 305
1926	26	July	Decision, Signatura	......	II. 311
1926	28	July	Decision, Rota	RD 18–262	II. 305
1926	29	July	Decision, Rota	RD 18–287	II. 335
1926	29	July	Decision, Rota	18–501	I. 523
1926	4	Aug.	Decision, Rota	RD 18–292	II. 324
1926	10	Aug.	Decision, Rota	RD 18–318	II. 43
1926	11	Aug.	Decision, Rota	RD 18–325	II. 330
1926	12	Aug.	Decision, Rota	RD 18–331	II. 312
1926	17	Aug.	Decision, Rota	RD 18–353	II. 313
1926	8	Sept.	Letter, S. C. Sem.	18–453	I. 664
1926	9	Nov.	Reply, S. C. Rel.	18–490	I. 324
1926	10	Nov.	Reply, S. Paen.	18–500	I. 209
1926	4	Dec.	Decision, Rota	RD 18–381	II. 330
1926	17	Dec.	Decision, Rota	RD 18–403	II. 324
1926	18	Dec.	Decision, Rota	RD 18–416	II. 319
1926	20	Dec.	Allocution, Pius XI	18–513	I. 610
1926	29	Dec.	Decree, Holy Office	18–529	I. 611
1927	..	....	Reply, S. Paen.	......	III. 405
1927	24	Jan.	Chirograph, Pius XI	19–41	I. 616
1927	24	Jan.	Letter, Pius XI	19–45	II. 74
1927	31	Jan.	Rescript, S. C. Conc.	......	II. 184
1927	5	Feb.	Decision, Rota	RD 19–20	II. 319
1927	7	Feb.	Decision, Rota	RD 19–25	II. 288, 339
1927	9	Feb.	Decision, Rota	RD 19–42	II. 307
1927	22	Feb.	Decision, Rota	RD 19–49	II. 316
1927	22	Feb.	Decree, S. C. Conc.	19–99	I. 116
1927	24	Feb.	Declaration, Pius XI	19–185	I. 692
1927	26	Feb.	Declaration, Bibl. Com.	19–160	I. 672
1927	6	Mar.	Replies, Code Com.	19–161	I. 334, 582, 602
1927	8	Mar.	Reply, S. Paen.	19–157	I. 612
1927	14	Mar.	Decision, Rota	RD 19–70	II. 278
1927	15	Mar.	Reply, S. C. Conc.	19–138	I. 128
1927	21	Mar.	Decision, Rota	RD 19–82	II. 289
1927	22	Mar.	Faculties, S. C. Sacr.	......	II. 28
1927	25	Mar.	Reply, S. C. Rel.	19–138	I. 266
1927	7	Apr.	Reply, S. C. Prop. Fid.	......	II. 452
1927	11	Apr.	Decision, Rota	19–217	I. 536
1927	22	Apr.	Indult, S. C. Sacr.	......	II. 189
1927	23	Apr.	Resolution, S. C. Conc.	19–415	I. 231

Year	Day	Mon.	Document and Source	AAS (or RD)	C. L. D.
1927	27	Apr.	Reply, S. C. Rit.	19–192	I. 375
1927	29	Apr.	Declaration, S. C. Sem.	19–194	I. 673
1927	3	May	Instruction, Holy Office	19–186	I. 687
1927	4	May	Decision, Rota	RD 19–161	II. 308
1927	10	May	Decision, Rota	RD 19–169	II. 306
1927	14	May	Decision, Rota	RD 19–177	II. 324
1927	21	May	Resolution, S. C. Conc.	21–116	I. 734
1927	1	June	Decision, Rota	RD 19–192	II. 301
1927	4	June	Decision, Rota	RD 19–199	II. 324
1927	7	June	Decision, Rota	RD 19–208	II. 308
1927	8	June	Decision, Rota	RD 19–214	II. 305
1927	28	June	Decision, Rota	RD 19–237	II. 288, 340
1927	8	July	Reply, Holy Office	19–278	I. 620
1927	9	July	Decision, Rota	RD 19–299	II. 309
1927	16	July	Decision, Rota	RD 19–304	II. 316
1927	16	July	Resolution, S. C. Conc.	20–389	I. 695
1927	23	July	Decision, Rota	RD 19–315	II. 324
1927	30	July	Decision, Rota	RD 19–351	II. 298
1927	2	Aug.	Letter, Pius XI	......	III. 265
1927	4	Aug.	Decision, Rota	RD 19–363	II. 287
1927	10	Aug.	Decision, Rota	RD 19–404	II. 324
1927	11	Aug.	Decision, Rota	RD 19–426	II. 321
1927	4	Sept.	Ap. Letter, Pius XI	20–376	I. 450
1927	24	Sept.	Motu proprio, Pius XI	19–329	I. 170
1927	27	Sept.	Concordat	19–432	II. 74
1927	18	Oct.	Faculties, S. C. Conc.	......	II. 28
1927	21	Oct.	Reply, S. C. Rit.	19–381	I. 561
1927	4	Nov.	Motu proprio, Pius XI	19–393	I. 170
1927	12	Nov.	Resolution, S. C. Conc.	20–84	I. 245, 255
1927	12	Nov.	Resolution, S. C. Conc.	20–142	I. 578
1927	22	Nov.	Decision, Rota	RD 19–453	II. 76
1927	24	Nov.	Reply, Code Com.	......	II. 215
1927	2	Dec.	Decision, Rota	RD 19–473	II. 331
1927	5	Dec.	Decision, Rota	RD 19–497	II. 309
1927	10	Dec.	Decision, Rota	RD 19–517	II. 331
1927	10	Dec.	Resolution, S. C. Conc.	20–261	I. 566
1927	21	Dec.	Decision, Rota	RD 19–535	II. 317
1927	22	Dec.	Faculties, S. C. Sacr.	......	II. 27
1927	23	Dec.	Faculties, S. C. Conc.	......	II. 26
1927	27	Dec.	Letter, Ap. Del. U. S.	......	II. 29
1927	28	Dec.	Replies, Code Com.	20–61	I. 296, 412, 503, 541
1927	30	Dec.	Decision, Rota	RD 19–540	II. 324
1927	30	Dec.	Decision, Rota	RD 19–548	II. 316
1928	2	Jan.	Faculties, S. Paen.	......	II. 29
1928	..	....	Reply, S. Paen.	......	III. 391
1928	5	Jan.	Reply, S. C. Sacr.	20–79	I. 391
1928	5	Jan.	Reply, S. C. Sacr.	20–81	I. 404
1928	6	Jan.	Encyclical, Pius XI	20–5	I. 621
1928	11	Jan.	Reply, S. C. Rit.	20–90	I. 377
1928	13	Jan.	Decision, Rota	RD 20–1	II. 554
1928	20	Jan.	Decision, Rota	RD 20–13	II. 465, 466
1928	25	Jan.	Decision, Rota	RD 20–27	II. 293

Year	Day	Mon.	Document and Source	AAS (or RD)	C. L. D.
1929	23	Dec.	Decree, S. C. Eccl. Or.	22–99	I. 17
1929	23	Dec.	Encyclical, Pius XI	21–707	I. 433
1929	23	Dec.	Instruction, S. C. Sacr.	22–169	I. 797
1929	24	Dec.	Allocution, Pius XI	21–766	II. 74
1929	31	Dec.	Encyclical, Pius XI	22–49	I. 337, 548, 677, 679, 680, 682
1930	7	Jan.	Decree, S. C. Eccl.Or.	22–106	I. 24
1930	7	Jan.	Decree, S. C. Eccl. Or.	22–108	I. 27
1930	12	Jan.	Instruction, S. C. Conc.	22–26	I. 212
1930	13	Jan.	Reply, S. Paen.	22–43	I. 456
1930	20	Jan.	Indult, Com. Russia	......	II. 207
1930	23	Jan.	Reply, S. Paen.	22–43	I. 535
1930	30	Jan.	Reply, S. C. Prop. Fid.	......	III. 489
1930	6	Feb.	*Motu proprio*, Pius XI	22–87	I. 166
1930	6	Feb.	*Motu proprio*, Pius XI	22–93	I. 171
1930	17	Feb.	Replies, Code Com.	22–195	I. 91, 220, 419, 544, 725, 808
1930	12	Mar.	Ap. Letter, Pius XI	22–343	I. 635
1930	15	Mar.	Resolution, S. C. Conc.	25–315	I. 709
1930	30	Mar.	Allocution, Pius XI	......	III. 265
1930	30	Mar.	Reply, Holy Office	......	II. 182
1930	6	Apr.	*Motu proprio*, Pius XI	22–153	I. 172
1930	29	Apr.	Reply, S. Paen.	22–292	I. 456
1930	24	May	Decree, S. C. Eccl. Or.	22–346	I. 29; III. 33
1930	25	May	Resolution, S. C. Conc.	25–155	I. 576
1930	11	June	Declaration, S. C. Eccl. Or.	22–354	I. 39
1930	21	June	Resolution, S. C. Conc.	25–38	I. 260
1930	21	June	Instruction, S. C. Conc.	22–395	I. 679
1930	28	June	Allocution, Pius XI	......	III. 268
1930	30	June	Allocution, Pius XI	22–296	I. 378
1930	5	July	Decree, S. Paen.	22–363	I. 457
1930	13	July	Replies, Code Com.	22–365	I. 301, 404, 661
1930	13	July	Reply, Holy Office	22–344	I. 685
1930	19	July	Resolution, S. C. Conc.	22–251	I. 256
1930	26	July	Reply, S. C. Eccl. Or.	22–394	I. 174
1930	5	Aug.	Decision, Rota	23–100	II. 321
1930	19	Sept.	Reply, S. C. Sacr.	......	II. 193
1930	23	Oct.	Decree, S. Paen.	22–493	I. 121
1930	10	Nov.	Decision, Rota	23–102	II. 296
1930	11	Nov.	Norms, Ap. Datary	22–525	I. 220
1930	15	Nov.	Resolution, S. C. Conc.	25–83	I. 234
1930	15	Nov.	Resolution, S. C. Conc.	25–155	I. 576
1930	20	Nov.	Resolution, S. C. Conc.	23–16	I. 714
1930	2	Dec.	Decree, S. C. Caer.	23–56	I. 167
1930	5	Dec.	Decree, S. Paen.	23–23	I. 122
1930	6	Dec.	Replies, Code Com.	23–25	I. 210, 550
1930	24	Dec.	Address, Pius XI	22–529	I. 506
1930	27	Dec.	Instruction, S. C. Sacr.	23–120	I. 463
1930	31	Dec.	Decree, S. C. Caer.	23–22	I. 210
1930	31	Dec.	Encyclical, Pius XI	22–539	I. 495, 504, 517, 554, 617
1930	31	Dec.	Encyclical, Pius XI	22–562	III. 670
1931	18	Jan.	*Motu proprio*, Pius XI	23–33	I. 175

Year	Day	Mon.	Document and Source	AAS (or *RD*)	C. L. D.
1932	4	Mar.	Reply, S. Paen.	......	II. 226
1932	5	Mar.	Resolution, S. C. Conc.	25–436	I. 151
1932	1	Apr.	Bull, Pius XI	24–105	II. 152, 439
1932	9	Apr.	Reply, S. C. Conc.	25–492	I. 236
1932	11	Apr.	Reply, Holy Office	......	I. 492; II. 245
1932	21	Apr.	Ap. Del. U. S.	......	II. 361, 364
1932	1	May	Letter, S. C. Sacr.	......	III. 448
1932	18	May	Reply, S. C. Prop. Fid.	......	III. 348
1932	18	May	Reply, S. C. Conc.	......	II. 361
1932	30	May	Encyclical, Pius XI	24–183	II. 74
1932	3	June	Ap. Letter, Pius XI	24–231	I. 109
1932	7	June	Decree, S. C. Conc.	24–240	I. 596
1932	7	June	Reply, S. Paen.	......	II. 226
1932	8	June	Reply, Holy Office	......	II. 291
1932	18	June	Resolution, S. C. Conc.	26–58	II. 132
1932	21	June	Disposition, S. C. Conc.	24–242	I. 189
1932	25	June	Replies, Code Com.	24–284	I. 250, 501, 554
1932	30	June	Reply, Holy Office	......	I. 513; II. 291
1932	30	June	Reply, S. C. Sacr.	24–271	I. 348
1932	..	July	Rescript, S. C. Sacr.	......	II. 194
1932	1	July	Letter, S. C. Sacr.	24–272	I. 801
1932	15	July	Letter, S. C. Prop. Fid.	......	II. 348
1932	16	July	Resolution, S. C. Conc.	25–470	I. 717
1932	18	July	Rescript, S. C. Prop. Fid.	......	II. 52
1932	25	July	S. C. Rel.	......	III. 101
1932	28	July	Replies, Code Com.	24–314	I. 742, 835
1932	4	Aug.	Reply, Holy Office	......	I. 506
1932	6	Aug.	Decree, S. C. Sem.	......	III. 566
1932	26	Aug.	Rescript, S. C. Eccl. Or.	......	II. 218
1932	26	Sept.	Instruction, S. C. Eccl. Or.	24–344	I. 39
1932	29	Sept.	Encyclical, Pius XI	24–331	II. 74
1932	8	Oct.	Reply, S. C. Consist.	......	II. 377
1932	27	Oct.	Address, Pius XI	24–355	I. 559
1932	7	Nov.	Decree, S. Paen.	24–411	I. 122
1932	7	Nov.	Decision, Signatura	......	I. 804
1932	7	Nov.	Reply, S. C. Prop. Fid.	......	III. 346
1932	25	Nov.	Decree, S. C. Rit.	......	II. 195
1932	2	Dec.	Rescript, S. C. Prop. Fid.	......	II. 218
1932	10	Dec.	Resolution, S. C. Conc.	26–23	II. 134
1932	23	Dec.	Reply, S. C. Rit.	......	II. 196
1933	6	Jan.	Bull, Pius XI	25–5	I. 438
1933	12	Jan.	Decree, S. Paen.	25–69	I. 443
1933	30	Jan.	Ap. Const., Pius XI	25–10	I. 443
1933	30	Jan.	Ap. Const., Pius XI	25–14	I. 443
1933	30	Jan.	Ap. Const., Pius XI	25–19	I. 443
1933	1	Feb.	Instruction, S. C. Eccl. Or.	26–181	II. 190
1933	4	Feb.	Resolution, S. C. Conc.	26–183	II. 132
1933	28	Feb.	*Monita*, S. Paen.	25–60	I. 443
1933	28	Feb.	Decrees, S. Paen.	25–65	I. 443
1933	2	Mar.	Chirograph, Pius XI	25–73	I. 443
1933	4	Mar.	Resolution, S. C. Conc.	27–341	II. 140, 442
1933	13	Mar.	Allocution, Pius XI	25–108	II. 74
1933	13	Mar.	Allocution, Pius XI	25–116	I. 853

Year	Day	Mon.	Document and Source	AAS (or RD)	C. L. D.
1933	20	Mar.	S. C. Prop. Fid.	......	II. 181
1933	20	Mar.	Decree, S. Paen.	25–170	I. 417
1933	21	Mar.	Decree, S. Paen.	25–171	I. 444
1933	30	Mar.	Decree, S. Paen.	25–173	I. 443
1933	4	Apr.	Decision, Rota	......	III. 468
1933	12	Apr.	Reply, S. C. Prop. Fid.	......	II. 332
1933	5	May	Letter, S. C. Prop. Fid.	......	II. 452, 540
1933	16	May	Letter, S. C. Prop. Fid.	......	II. 121
1933	18	May	Decree, S. Paen.	25–322	I. 122
1933	25	May	Reply, Holy Office	......	III. 479
1933	3	June	Encyclical, Pius XI	25–273	II. 74
1933	5	June	Concordat	26–249	II. 24, 74
1933	15	June	Ap. Const., Pius XI	26–85	II. 436
1933	24	June	Decree, S. C. Caer.	25–341	I. 168
1933	26	June	Decree, S. C. Eccl. Or.	25–340	I. 459
1933	1	July	Reply, Bibl. Com.	25–344	I. 618
1933	15	July	Resolution, S. C. Conc.	26–234	II. 173
1933	17	July	Replies, Code Com.	25–345	I. 603, 808
1933	24	July	Decree, S. Paen.	25–381	I. 445
1933	1	Aug.	Decree, S. Paen.	25–343	I. 444
1933	1	Aug.	Letter, Nuncio to Spain	......	III. 603
1933	10	Aug.	*Monitum,* S. C. Eccl. Or.	25–346	I. 173
1933	24	Aug.	Reply, S. C. Rit.	......	III. 520
1933	30	Aug.	Letter, Pius XI	25–462	II. 74
1933	13	Sept.	Reply, Code Com.	......	II. 333
1933	20	Sept.	Declaration, S. Paen.	25–446	I. 458
1933	25	Oct.	Reply, S. C. Rit.	......	II. 348
1933	9	Nov.	Decree, S. Paen.	25–502	I. 445
1933	10	Nov.	Ap. Letter, Pius XI	26–628	II. 75
1933	7	Dec.	Decree, S. Paen.	26–35	II. 233, 236
1933	29	Dec.	Decree, S. Paen.	26–35	II. 235
1934	20	Feb.	Decree, S. Paen.	26–109	II. 233
1934	27	Feb.	Decree, Bibl. Com.	26–130	II. 393
1934	6	Mar.	Letter, Pius XI	26–227	II. 74
1934	9	Mar.	Decree, Holy Office	26–180	II. 394
1934	10	Mar.	Decree, S. C. Eccl. Or.	26–302	II. 7
1934	17	Mar.	Decree, Holy Office	26–233	II. 394
1934	2	Apr.	Ap. Const., Pius XI	26–137	I. 863
1934	3	Apr.	*Monita,* S. Paen.	26–149	I. 874
1934	3	Apr.	Decree, S. C. Eccl. Or.	26–319	II. 8
1934	10	Apr.	Decree, S. Paen.	26–243	II. 233
1934	24	Apr.	Decree, S. C. Sem.	......	II. 109
1934	25	Apr.	Decree, S. C. Rit.	26–559	II. 10
1934	27	Apr.	Instruction, S. C. Prop. Fid.	......	II. 422
1934	30	Apr.	Decree, Bibl. Com.	26–315	II. 196
1934	1	May	Letter, Pius XI	27–47	II. 75
1934	20	May	Instruction, S. C. Sacr.	27–11	II. 185; III. 305
1934	25	May	Rescript, S. C. Rit.	......	II. 217
1934	29	May	Reply, Code Com.	26–493	II. 95
1934	30	May	Decree, S. Paen.	26–312	II. 201, 235
1934	31	May	Letter, Pius XI	26–547	II. 74
1934	4	June	Decree, S. Paen.	26–313	II. 232
1934	4	June	Rescript, S. C. Rit.	......	II. 197

Year	Day	Mon.	Document and Source	AAS (or RD)	C. L. D.
1939	15	June	Decree, S. Paen.	31–277	II. 231
1939	24	June	Address, Pius XII	31–245	II. 427
1939	5, 10	July	Decree, Holy Office	31–303	II. 397
1939	16	July	Reply, Bibl. Com.	31–320	II. 434
1939	18	July	Decree, S. C. Rit.	32–197	II. 10
1939	24	July	Reply, Code Com.	......	II. 547
1939	24	July	Replies, Code Com.	31–321	II. 52, 173, 178, 237
1939	24	July	Reply, S. Paen.	31–317	II. 399
1939	20	Oct.	Encyclical, Pius XII	31–415	III. 264
1939	9	Nov.	Ap. Letter, Pius XII	31–670	II. 233
1939	24	Nov.	Indult, S. Paen.	......	II. 571
1939	8	Dec.	Faculties, S. C. Consist.	31–710	II. 141, 586
1939	8	Dec.	Instruction, S. C. Prop. Fid.	32–24	II. 370
1939	8	Dec.	Exhortation, Pius XII	31–696	II. 53
1939	9, 16	Dec.	Resolution, S. C. Conc.	32–75	II. 350
1939	12	Dec.	Reply, Holy Office	32–24	II. 400
1939	21	Dec.	*Summarium,* S. Paen.	32–58	II. 178, 233, 419
1940	7	Jan.	Letter, Pius XII	32–43	II. 116
1940	15	Jan.	Decree, S. Paen.	32–60	II. 233
1940	15	Jan.	Reply, Holy Office	32–52	II. 534
1940	19	Jan.	Replies, Code Com.	32–62	II. 141, 237
1940	23	Jan.	Letter, S. C. Rel.	......	III. 214
1940	27	Jan.	Decree, S. C. Eccl. Or.	32–152	II. 8, 238
1940	24	Feb.	Reply, Holy Office	32–73	II. 96
1940	12	Mar.	Decree, S. C. Rit.	32–200	II. 222
1940	3	Apr.	Decree, S. C. Rit.	32–311	II. 10
1940	8	Apr.	Declaration, Ap. Datary	32–163	II. 137
1940	9	Apr.	Reply, S. C. Prop. Fid.	32–379	II. 9
1940	19	Apr.	Resolution, S. C. Conc.	32–374	II. 167
1940	29	Apr.	Replies, Code Com.	32–212	II. 49, 290, 451
1940	7	May	Concordat, etc.	32–217	II. 11
1940	18	May	Indult, S. C. Sacr.	......	II. 249
1940	11	June	Reply, S. C. Eccl. Or.	32–303	II. 6
1940	15	June	Resolution, S. C. Conc.	33–70	II. 440
1940	18	June	Resolution, S. C. Conc.	33–333	II. 139
1940	1	July	Faculties, S. C. Consist.	......	II. 588
1940	6	July	Ap. Letter, Pius XII	......	III. 265
1940	8	July	Reply, Code Com.	32–317	II. 105
1940	10	July	Decree, S. C. Sacr.	32–304	II. 540
1940	21	July	Resolution, S. C. Conc.	33–369	II. 150
1940	22	Aug.	Signatura	32–381	II. 24
1940	4	Sept.	Allocution, Pius XII	32–369	III. 265
1940	12	Sept.	Letter, S. C. Rel.	......	III. 101
1940	21	Sept.	Instruction, S. C. Sacr.	33–29	II. 252
1940	16	Oct.	Indult, S. C. Rit.	......	II. 200
1940	20	Nov.	Reply, S. C. Rit.	......	III. 469
1940	23	Nov.	S. C. Eccl. Or.	33–27	II. 6
1940	23	Nov.	S. C. Eccl. Or.	33–28	II. 50
1940	1	Dec.	*Motu proprio,* Pius XII	32–529	II. 202
1940	**2**	Dec.	Reply, Holy Office	32–553	II. 96

Year	Day	Mon.	Document and Source	AAS (or RD)	C. L. D.
1940	10	Dec.	Reply, S. Paen.	32–571	II. 146
1940	20	Dec.	Indult, S. C. Conc.	33–24	II. 363
1940	24	Dec.	Allocution, Pius XII	33–5	II. 95
1941	15	Jan.	S. C. Rit.	33–128	II. 10
1941	20	Jan.	Reply, S. C. Sacr.	......	II. 250
1941	22	Jan.	Reply, S. C. Eccl. Or.	......	III. 456
1941	2	Feb.	Letter, S. C. Rel. and Sem.	......	III. 215
1941	22	Feb.	Decree, S. Paen.	33–73	II. 217
1941	25	Feb.	Decision, Rota	......	III. 429
1941	27	Feb.	Indult, Holy Office	......	II. 593
1941	8	Mar.	Decree, Holy Office	33–69	II. 374; III. 82
1941	10	Mar.	Decree, S. Paen.	33–129	II. 232
1941	18	Mar.	Letter, S. C. Conc.	......	III. 292
1941	24	Mar.	Indult, S. C. Sacr.	......	II. 593
1941	29	Mar.	Decree, Holy Office	33–121	II. 436
1941	5	Apr.	Reply, Holy Office	......	III. 506
1941	8	Apr.	Replies, Code Com.	33–173	II. 354, 552
1941	9	Apr.	Reply, S. C. Sacr.	......	II. 590
1941	13	Apr.	Radio Message, Pius XII	33–112	II. 95
1941	20	Apr.	Letter, Pius XII	33–110	II. 95
1941	25	Apr.	Decision, Rota	......	III. 411
1941	28	Apr.	Instruction, S. C. Sacr.	33–363	II. 534
1941	10	May	Replies, Holy Office	33–294	II. 292
1941	1	June	Radio Address, Pius XII	33–216	II. 393
1941	7	June	Agreement, Pius XII	33–480	III. 38
1941	12	June	Letter, Ap. Del. U. S.	......	II. 147
1941	26	June	Pastoral, German Bishops	......	II. 123
1941	29	June	Instruction, S. C. Sacr.	33–297	II. 253
1941	4	July	Indult, S. C. Conc.	......	II. 356
1941	13	July	Resolution, S. C. Conc.	34–101	III. 491
1941	14	July	Instruction, S. C. Conc.	33–389	II. 358
1941	25	July	S. C. Rel. and Sem.	33–371	II. 426
1941	31	July	Reply, S. C. Sacr.	......	III. 638
1941	5	Aug.	Replies, Code Com.	33–378	II. 119, 132
1941	20	Aug.	Letter, Bibl. Com.	33–465	II. 400
1941	25	Aug.	Letter, Ap. Del. U. S.	......	II. 68
1941	8	Sept.	Letter, Ap. Del. U. S.	......	II. 356
1941	10	Sept.	Letter, S. C. Sacr.	......	III. 448
1941	3	Oct.	Allocution, Pius XII	33–421	II. 454
1941	4	Nov.	*Motu proprio,* Pius XII	33–479	II. 110
1941	15	Nov.	Replies, Holy Office	......	III. 299
1941	27	Nov.	Reply, S. C. Rit.	......	III. 490
1941	19	Dec.	Indult, S. C. Neg. Extr.	33–516	II. 363
1941	24	Dec.	Allocution, Pius XII	......	II. 80
1941	26	Dec.	Indult, S. C. Neg. Extr.	......	II. 357
1942	1	Jan.	Letter, Ap. Del. U. S.	......	II. 44
1942	1	Jan.	Instruction, Ap. Datary	34–113	II. 135
1942	2	Jan.	Letter, Ap. Del. U. S.	......	II. 215
1942	9	Jan.	S. C. Rit.	34–111	II. 9, 201; III. 37, 359
1942	16	Jan.	Reply, Holy Office	34–22	II. 286
1942	21	Jan.	Letter, Pius XII	......	III. 265
1942	31	Jan.	Replies, Code Com.	34–50	II. 332, 353, 469

Year	Day	Mon.	Document and Source	AAS (or RD)	C. L. D.
1949	30	May	Decision, Rota	......	III. 639
1949	15	June	Pastoral, Archbishop Beran	......	III. 662
1949	15	June	Pastoral, Hierarchy, Czechs	......	III. 662
1949	20	June	Decree, Holy Office	41–333	III. 657
1949	30	June	Decree, S. C. Eccl. Or.	41–373	III. 365
1949	30	June	Decree, S. C. Conc.	41–374	III. 365
1949	30	June	Reply, Holy Office	41–427	III. 446
1949	1	July	Replies, Holy Office	41–334	III. 658
1949	10	July	Ap. Const., Pius XII	41–345	III. 391
1949	10	July	Ap. Const., Pius XII	41–337	III. 390
1949	10	July	Ap. Const., Pius XII	41–340	III. 391
1949	11	July	Indult, S. C. Sacr.	......	III. 360
1949	13	July	Declar., S. C. Rit.	41–617	III. 512
1949	15	July	Reply, Holy Office	......	III. 446
1949	27	July	Ap. Letter, Pius XII	42–385	III. 290, 570
1949	8	Aug.	Letter, Holy Office	......	III. 525
1949	11	Aug.	Declar., Holy Office	41–427	III. 407
1949	15	Aug.	Letter, S. C. Sem.	41–618	III. 549
1949	15	Aug.	Instr., S. C. Sacr.	......	III. 629
1949	16	Aug.	Letter, Archb. New Orleans	......	III. 370
1949	18	Aug.	Decree, S. C. Rit.	41–476	III. 518
1949	1	Sept.	Letter, Pius XII	41–450	III. 662
1949	4	Sept.	Allocution, Pius XII	......	III. 570
1949	8	Sept.	Statement, Clergy, Czechs	......	III. 662
1949	8	Sept.	Pastoral, Cardinals of France	......	III. 660
1949	11	Sept.	Allocution, Pius XII	41–547	III. 290
1949	14	Sept.	Ap. Letter, Pius XII	43–722	III. 59
1949	17	Sept.	*Monita*, S. Paen.	41–513	III. 391
1949	17	Sept.	*Monita*, S. Paen.	41–518, 519, 520	III. 391
1949	20	Sept.	Allocution, Pius XII	41–551	III. 290
1949	29	Sept.	Allocution, Pius XII	41–557	III. 432
1949	1	Oct.	Instr., S. C. Sacr.	41–493	III. 318
1949	6	Nov.	Allocution, Pius XII	41–597	III. 3
1949	12	Nov.	Decision, Rota	......	III. 611
1949	13	Nov.	Allocution, Pius XII	41–604	III. 10
1949	16	Nov.	Reply, Holy Office	......	III. 447
1949	21	Nov.	Statement, U. S. Hierarchy	......	III. 401
1949	15	Dec.	Indult, S. C. Sacr.	41–616	III. 391
1949	20	Dec.	Instr., Holy Office	42–142	III. 536
1949	23	Dec.	Address, Pius XII	42–120	III. 391
1949	24	Dec.	Indult, S. C. Sacr.	......	III. 363
1949	28	Dec.	Reply, Holy Office	41–650	III. 423
1950	3	Jan.	Reply, Holy Office	......	III. 465
1950	6	Jan.	*Motu proprio*, Pius XII	42–5	III. 585
1950	12	Jan.	Letter, S. C. Sem.	......	III. 544
1950	22	Jan.	Declar., S. Paen.	......	III. 388
1950	25	Jan.	Exhort., Pius XII	42–247	III. 290
1950	26	Jan.	Reply, S. C. Rit.	......	III. 360
1950	30	Jan.	Reply, Holy Office	......	III. 486
1950	2	Feb.	Indult, S. C. Sacr.	......	III. 360
1950	9	Feb.	Letter, S. C. Rel.	......	III. 207
1950	17	Feb.	Allocution, Pius XII	42–251	III. 290

				AAS	
Year	*Day*	*Mon.*	*Document and Source*	*(or RD)*	*C. L. D.*
1950	18	Feb.	Decree, S. C. Consist.	42–195	III. 670
1950	18	Feb.	Reply, S. C. Rit.	. . . . . .	III. 360
1950	2	Mar.	Reply, S. C. Rit.	. . . . . .	III. 361
1950	7	Mar.	Letter, S. C. Sem.	42–836	III. 544
1950	8	Mar.	Indult, S. C. Prop. Fid.	. . . . . .	III. 361
1950	15	Mar.	Reply, S. C. Rit.	. . . . . .	III. 519
1950	22	Mar.	Decree, S. C. Conc.	42–330	III. 68
1950	29	Mar.	Reply, S. C. Rit.	. . . . . .	III. 111
1950	29	Mar.	Reply, S. C. Rit.	. . . . . .	III. 253
1950	29	Mar.	Reply, S. C. Rit.	. . . . . .	III. 360
1950	10	Apr.	Allocution, Pius XII	42–395	III. 568
1950	14	Apr.	Agreement, Polish Govt.	. . . . . .	III. 662
1950	14	Apr.	Reply, S. C. Rit.	. . . . . .	III. 489
1950	15	Apr.	Ap. Letter, Pius XII	42–437	III. 280
1950	17	Apr.	Reply, Holy Office	. . . . . .	III. 423
1950	22	Apr.	Statement, Polish Bishops	. . . . . .	III. 662
1950	26	Apr.	Ap. Letter, Pius XII	42–595	III. 37, 383
1950	2	May	Reply, S. C. Rit.	. . . . . .	III. 359
1950	2	May	Decree, Holy Office	. . . . . .	III. 659
1950	13	May	Instr., Bibl. Com.	42–495	III. 551
1950	15	May	Ap. Letter, Pius XII	42–631	III. 37, 570
1950	1	June	Reply, S. C. Rit.	. . . . . .	III. 360
1950	3	June	Allocution, Pius XII	42–485	III. 291
1950	7	June	Letter, Pius XII	42–552	III. 291
1950	12	June	Reply, S. C. Rit.	. . . . . .	III. 360
1950	14	June	Notification, Holy Office	42–489	III. 393
1950	26	June	Reply, S. C. Rit.	. . . . . .	III. 362
1950	26	June	Reply, S. C. Rit.	. . . . . .	III. 519
1950	29	June	Decree, S. C. Conc.	42–601	III. 69
1950	8	July	Reply, S. C. Rit.	. . . . . .	III. 215
1950	14	July	Reply, Holy Office	. . . . . .	III. 30
1950	15	July	Address, Pius XII	. . . . . .	III. 23
1950	18	July	Concordat	42–811	III. 38
1950	28	July	*Monitum*, Holy Office	42–553	III. 660
1950	29	July	Reply, S. C. Rit.	. . . . . .	III. 301
1950	6	Aug.	Letter, Pius XII	42–635	III. 290
1950	7	Aug.	Decree, S. C. Sacr.	44–280	III. 636
1950	9	Aug.	Letter, Pius XII	42–725	III. 544
1950	12	Aug.	Encyclical, Pius XII	42–561	III. 530
1950	21	Aug.	Reply, S. C. Rit.	. . . . . .	III. 490
1950	3	Sept.	Radio Address, Pius XII	42–639	III. 290
1950	12	Sept.	Reply, S. C. Rit.	. . . . . .	III. 67
1950	15	Sept.	Faculties, S. C. Prop. Fid.	. . . . . .	III. 54
1950	15	Sept.	Reply, S. C. Rit.	. . . . . .	III. 360
1950	17	Sept.	Allocution, Pius XII	42–734	III. 290
1950	21	Sept.	Allocution, Pius XII	42–735	III. 569
1950	23	Sept.	Exhort., Pius XII	42–657	III. 61
1950	14	Oct.	Allocution, Pius XII	42–816	III. 290
1950	30	Oct.	Homily, Pius XII	42–774	III. 521
1950	30	Oct.	Consistory	42–774	III. 521
1950	31	Oct.	Text, S. C. Rit.	42–793	III. 359, 521
1950	1	Nov.	Decree, S. C. Sem.	43–495	III. 570
1950	1	Nov.	Dogmatic Bull, Pius XII	42–753	III. 521

Year	Day	Mon.	Document and Source	AAS (or RD)	C. L. D.
1950	1	Nov.	Ceremonies of definition	42–778	III. 521
1950	2	Nov.	Oration, Pius XII	42–784	III. 521
1950	6	Nov.	Decree, S. C. Consist.	43–91	III. 117
1950	11	Nov.	Resolution, S. C. Conc.	43–177	III. 363
1950	13	Nov.	Concordat	43–80	III. 38
1950	15–17	Nov.	Statement, U. S. Hierarchy	. . . . . .	III. 569
1950	21	Nov.	Ap. Const., Pius XII	43–5	III. 221
1950	23	Nov.	Instr., S. C. Rel.	43–37	III. 240
1950	8	Dec.	Allocution, Pius XII	43–26	III. 119
1950	8	Dec.	Decree, S. C. Consist.	44–743	III. 118
1950	25	Dec.	Ap. Const., Pius XII	42–853	III. 391
1950	26	Dec.	Instr., S. Paen.	42–900	III. 391
1951	10	Jan.	Letter, S. C. Rel.	. . . . . .	III. 217
1951	11	Jan.	Decree, Holy Office	43–91	III. 284
1951	12	Jan.	Ap. Letter, Pius XII	44–216	III. 37
1951	9	Feb.	Decree, S. C. Rit.	43–128	III. 34
1951	12	Feb.	Reply, Holy Office	43–217	III. 358
1951	17	Feb.	Decree, S. C. Consist.	43–477	III. 117
1951	20	Feb.	Letter, S. C. Prop. Ed.	. . . . . .	III. 543
1951	23	Feb.	Decision, Rota	43–872	III. 440
1951	7	Mar.	Letter, S. C. Rel.	. . . . . .	III. 248
1951	17	Mar.	Declar., S. C. Consist.	43–173	III. 664
1951	21	Mar.	Letter, S. C. Prop. Fid.	. . . . . .	III. 256
1951	4	Apr.	Tribunal, Brooklyn	. . . . . .	III. 428
1951	9	Apr.	Decree, Holy Office	43–217	III. 649
1951	11	Apr.	Letter, S. C. Rel.	. . . . . .	III. 513
1951	12	Apr.	Reply, S. C. Rit.	. . . . . .	III. 361
1951	25	Apr.	Instr., S. C. Consist.	43–562	III. 113
1951	5	May	Allocution, Pius XII	. . . . . .	III. 291
1951	12	May	Decree, S. C. Consist.	43–480	III. 108
1951	20	May	Notification, Vic. Urb.	. . . . . .	III. 315
1951	30	May	Notification, Holy Office	43–477	III. 76
1951	2	June	Letter, S. C. Consist.	43–565	III. 117
1951	2	June	Encyclical, Pius XII	43–497	III. 543
1951	20	June	Decree, Bibl. Com.	43–747	III. 568
1951	29	June	Declar., S. C. Consist.	43–481	III. 667
1951	30	June	Letter, Pius XII	43–589	III. 290
1951	6	July	Letter, Pius XII	43–592	III. 290
1951	13	July	Decree, S. C. Consist.	43–602	III. 212
1951	14	July	Reply, S. Paen.	. . . . . .	III. 388
1951	25	July	Decree, Holy Office	43–561	III. 507
1951	8	Sept.	Encyclical, Pius XII	43–625	III. 521
1951	13	Sept.	Exhortation, Pius XII	43–738	III. 570
1951	14	Sept.	Letter, Pius XII	43–778	III. 542
1951	15	Sept.	Encyclical, Pius XII	43–577	III. 519
1951	17	Sept.	Declar., S. C. Consist.	43–603	III. 661
1951	18	Sept.	Allocution, Pius XII	43–730	III. 570
1951	14	Oct.	Allocution, Pius XII	43–784	III. 290
1951	23	Oct.	Decree, S. C. Rel.	43–806	III. 101
1951	24	Oct.	Letter, S. C. Consist.	44–231	III. 544
1951	28	Oct.	Ap. Letter, Pius XII	43–768	III. 665
1951	28	Oct.	Letter, Pius XII	44–365	III. 284

Year	Day	Mon.	Document and Source	*AAS* (or *RD*)	*C. L. D.*
1951	29	Oct.	Allocution, Pius XII	43–835	III. 402, 434, 440, 469, 669
1951	12	Nov.	Rescript, S. C. Rel.	......	III. 252
1951	14	Nov.	Decree, S. C. Eccl. Or.	44–382	III. 32
1951	14	Nov.	Report, Episc. Com. U. S.	......	III. 496
1951	26	Nov.	Allocution, Pius XII	43–855	III. 669
1951	4	Dec.	Ap. Letter, Pius XII	44–616	III. 37
1951	17	Dec.	Declaration, S. C. Conc.	44–44	III. 581
1952	11	Jan.	Decree, S. C. Rit.	44–48	III. 35
1952	18	Jan.	Ap. Letter, Pius XII	44–158	III. 662
1952	9	Feb.	*Motu proprio,* Pius XII	44–65	III. 131
1952	19	Feb.	Decision, Rota	......	III. 448
1952	26	Feb.	Decision, Rota	......	III. 435
1952	3	Mar.	Decree, S. Paen.	44–235	III. 391
1952	10	Mar.	Decree, S. C. Eccl. Or.	44–632	III. 31
1952	21	Mar.	Ap. Letter, Pius XII	44–520	III. 157
1952	23	Mar.	Radio Address, Pius XII	44–270	III. 530
1952	24	Mar.	Reply, S. C. Sacr.	......	III. 372
1952	25	Mar.	Decree, S. C. Sacr.	44–281	III. 637
1952	25	Mar.	Letter, S. C. Conc.	44–232	III. 493
1952	26	Mar.	Replies, Code Com.	44–496	III. 220, 314, 407
1952	26	Mar.	Replies, Code Com.	44–497	III. 73, 76, 493
1952	27	Mar.	Ap. Letter, Pius XII	44–249	III. 662
1952	8	Apr.	Address, Pius XII	......	III. 512
1952	10	Apr.	Allocution, Pius XII	44–411	III. 288
1952	10	Apr.	Reply, Holy Office	......	III. 466
1952	18	Apr.	Allocution, Pius XII	44–413	III. 530
1952	27	Apr.	Address, Pius XII	44–468	III. 291
1952	28	Apr.	Address, Pius XII	44–425	III. 543
1952	29	Apr.	Allocution, Pius XII	44–371	III. 15
1952	30	Apr.	Prayer, S. Paen.	44–389	III. 391
1952	5	May	Indult, S. C. Sacr.	......	III. 372
1952	9	May	Decree, S. C. Rit.	44–489	III. 37
1952	9	May	Reply, S. Paen.	......	III. 390
1952	20	May	Decree, Holy Office	44–432	III. 574
1952	24	May	Reply, Holy Office	......	III. 645
1952	6	June	Address, Pius XII	44–578	III. 290
1952	29	June	Pastoral, Hierarchy, England and Wales	......	III. 472
			Instr., S. C. Prop. Fid.	44–549	III. 254
1952	30	June	*Monitum,* Holy Office	44–546	III. 435
1952	30	June	Instr., Holy Office	44–542	III. 507
1952	4	July	Reply, Holy Office	......	III. 424
1952	7	July	Ap. Letter, Pius XII	44–505	III. 662
1952	8	July	Reply, Code Com. Eccl. Or.	44–552	III. 32
1952	11	July	Reply, S. C. Eccl. Or.	......	III. 302
1952	11	July	Reply, S. C. Eccl. Or.	......	III. 452
1952	11	July	Reply, S. C. Eccl. Or.	......	III. 452
1952	11	July	Reply, S. C. Eccl. Or.	......	III. 453
1952	14	July	Letter, Pius XII	44–624	III. 519
1952	17	July	Decision, Rota	......	III. 604
1952	25	July	Letter, Pius XII	44–811	III. 157
1952	26	July	Decree, S. C. Consist.	44–744	III. 117

GENERAL INDEX

(References are to volume and page of Canon Law Digest,
Vols. I, II, and III)

Ab Acatholicis Nati: Bound by disparity of cult, II. 290
    Case involving interpretation, I. 544
    Contracting marriage with Orientals, II. 338
    Exemption abrogated, III. 463
    Exemption interpreted, III. 462, 465
    Includes child of apostates, I. 544
    Includes child of mixed marriage, I. 543
    Interpretation of Code Commission was declarative, I. 544
    Under *Ne temere,* III. 462
Abbott: Benedictine, blessing of, I. 321
    Nullius: consecration of church outside his territory, I. 194
    Violet skull cap, I. 323
Abduction: II. 293
Abjuration: New formula, II. 182
Ablutions: At first Mass, priest binating, I. 352
Abortion: III. 383, 669
Absolutio Complicis: I. 858; II. 578
Absolution: By general formula, without confession, I. 416; II. 146;
    III. 377
    Of adherents of *L'Action Française,* I. 614; II. 399
    Of apostates and fugitives from religion, I. 327
    Of *falsa delatio,* I. 415
    Of priest excommunicated for attempting marriage, II. 579, 580
Absolutism, State: I. 609; III. 10
Academic Degrees: Canon Law, I. 663, 673
    Doctorate defined, I. 682
    Magister Aggregatus, I. 681
    Power to confer, I. 681
    Regulation of, I. 171
    Requirements for admission, I. 675
    Sacred Scripture, I. 674
Administrator of Diocese: I. 242, 243
Advocate: Contract for excessive fees, void, I. 751
    Fees, in Rota, II. 453
    Gratuitous service, II. 470
    In marriage cases, II. 461
    Qualifications, I. 199; II. 461
    Removal, II. 462
Age: For confirmation, I. 348; III. 314
    For marriage, not a vested right, I. 508
    For sacred orders; dispensation of religious, I. 162
    Impediment to marriage, II. 553
Air Travel: Confessions, III. 376